GW00866024

The 4Ps Framework

ADVANCED NEGOTIATION AND INFLUENCE STRATEGIES FOR GLOBAL EFFECTIVENESS

YADVINDER S. RANA

The 4Ps Framework:
Advanced Negotiation and Influence
Strategies for Global Effectiveness

Published by
CreateSpace Independent Publishing Platform,
North Charleston, SC, US

Library of Congress Control Number: 2014918983
ISBN 978-1502909237

Dedication

To my wife and children, who teach me new perspectives. And without whom this book would have been completed at least a year earlier.[1]

To my sister, who is still trying to find time to edit the first draft of the first chapter.

And to my mom and dad, who have always been there for me.

Acknowledgements

I owe a great intellectual debt to, among others:
Michael W. Morris, Deepak Malhotra, Jeswald Salacuse, Guy Olivier Faure, Jeanne Brett, Michele Gelfand, Wendi Adair, Max Bazerman, Jeffrey Rubin, William Zartman, James Sebenius, David Lax, Dean Pruitt, Shirli Kopelman, Richard Shell, Leigh Thompson, Howard Raiffa, Denis Leclerc, Karen Walch, Brian Gunia, Michael Benoliel, Rajesh Kumar, Stephen Weiss, Tetsushi Okumura, Devdutt Pattanaik, Peter Carnevale, Tony Fang, Catherine Thinsley, Moty Cristal, Roy Lewicki, Howard Raiffa, Larry Susskind, Jeffrey Rubin, Victor Kremenyuk, Stephen Weiss, Daniel Kahneman, Richard Nisbett, Pervez Ghauri, Jean-Claude Usunier, Richard Sorrentino, Elke Weber, Thomas Gilovich, Jeff Hawkins.

The Author

Yadvinder S. Rana is Professor of Cultural Management at the Catholic University in Milan, Italy, lecturer on Intercultural negotiation and influence in International MBA programs, and founder of Neglob, a management consultancy firm that assists companies in international negotiations and global teams performance improvement.

Yadvinder holds an MBA from the Manchester Business School, a Master's Degree in Mechanical Engineering and an Executive Certificate in Global Negotiation from the Thunderbird School of Global Management

Between 2004 and 2010 he was APMEA (Asia, Pacific, Middle East and Africa) Sales Director for a global company leader in the luxury goods sector, directly managing commercial and marketing organizations in China and India, and establishing the company presence in Japan, S. Korea, South East Asia (Singapore, Malaysia, Philippines), Middle East (UAE, Bahrain, Kuwait, Qatar, Saudi Arabia, Lebanon), Egypt, Tunisia, Morocco, Australia, New Zealand and South Africa.

Previously, between 1998 and 2003, he worked for Fiat Group in Pennsylvania, USA, London, UK and Lyon, France, leading cross functional teams implementing post M&A integration strategies (Case and New Holland, Iveco and Renault V.I., Fiat-GM JV).

Contents

Preface

In a world where change is occurring faster than ever before, where economies and societies are becoming more and more integrated and interdependent, and where distances are getting smaller and boundaries more permeable, it is crucial for managers to be able to negotiate with and influence others in a dynamic and discontinuous environment where trends and best practices become rapidly outdated.

The following statistics further highlight the accelerating and irregular pace of change occurring in the world today.

In 1990, the G7[2] share of the world gross domestic product (GDP) in purchasing power parity (PPP) was 62%.

In 2000, it was 49%.

Today, it is less than 37%.

Almost 60% of the global middle class resides in developing regions. In 2030, 80% of the global middle class will reside in emerging countries.

By 2025, annual consumption in emerging markets will reach $30 trillion, the biggest growth opportunity in the history of capitalism.

China's middle class will become the world's top consumers, while India and Indonesia will rank third and eighth, respectively.[3]

Of the 7,000 large companies expected to develop by 2025, 68% will be from emerging regions.[4]

A HISTORY OF WORLD GDP

Angus Maddison was a British economist and professor emeritus at the Faculty of Economics at the University of Groningen. He specialized in quantitative macroeconomic history and comparative analysis of long-run developments in the world economy throughout history.

He calculated the levels of GDP in PPP for emerging countries like China and India and developed countries all the way back to the year 1.

The results are summarized in Figure 1.

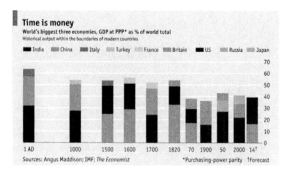

Figure 1. A history of world GDP from the year 1.[5]

As seen in Figure 1, starting in the year 1 through the late 18th century, India and China alone accounted for more than 50% of the world economy. However, the British colonization in India and the opium war in China started a rapid decline that lasted more than two centuries.

What we see today with the fast rise of China and India is perhaps only a repetitive economic pattern – nothing more than a historic recurrence.

THE RATIONALE BEHIND THE BOOK

The rationale behind this book is my dissatisfaction with the current literature on international negotiation and influence. Reading most of the present research in cross-cultural management, communication, negotiation, leadership, and influence, I often ask myself: How do these models and theories apply to the real world?

Often they don't. And this is for seven main reasons:

Reason 1: US bias in current research. More than 90% of research on negotiation and influence is based on less than 10% of humankind. Western, and above all US, ethnocentrism confines and biases our understanding of negotiation and influence elements and processes.

However, if we could shrink the Earth's population (7 billion) to a village of exactly 100 people, there would be only 5 North Americans and 11 Europeans; the rest of the village would comprise 14 Africans, 9 South Americans, and 61 Asians, including 19 Chinese and 18 Indians.

Because US models and theories cannot explain, or even detect, occurrences that are exclusively significant to other cultures, they cannot be applied universally.

Reason 2: Theories based on rational negotiators. Most negotiation and influence models are based on the expected utility theory, fabricated on negotiators acting as rational players, and game theory frameworks.

Limited research on social influence, emotions, judgmental heuristics, and behavioral decision making has been applied to the negotiation and influence field. Most negotiation models, with the purpose of providing universal and tidy results, discount the intricacy of multidimensional negotiation and influence processes, neglecting fundamental psychological factors and the complexity of decision-making processes that involve multiple actors.

Reason 3: The use of nations as units for studying cultures. Most cross-cultural negotiation and influence books still adopt the term culture as a synonym of nation. Nations are not the best entities for studying cultures. Geographic boundaries are often just artificial and unnatural divisions. Nationality and culture are connected, but any generalization must take into account within-nation variances and the great deal of diversity among people in any culture.

Cultural dimensions are not independent variables, and most cultural differences are relative rather than absolute. Factors that are dominant in one culture tend to be recessive in another, and vice versa. Individuals can embrace opposite poles according to the situation and context.

We should never forget that we communicate and negotiate with individuals, not nations.

Cultural boundaries are not national boundaries.[6]

Reason 4: Abuse of the notion of culture in explaining international negotiation failures and cross-cultural communication misunderstandings. Many scholars agree that culture is just an artificial, abstract, and purely analytic concept. The problem is that culture is often adopted as a justification whenever differences in behavior among people from different parts of the globe must be explained. However, we can't understand human behavior only through a cultural lens. Most current studies still focus on cultural influences on negotiation, without taking situational factors into account. Though important, culture is not the only contributor to an individual's negotiating and influencing behavior: We also need to consider two other key elements: the individual's *personality* and the *social context* in which the individual operates.

Without taking social context into consideration, we can't recognize the adjustment of specific cultural patterns under particular circumstances. Indeed, sometimes what we identify as cultural barriers in communication are just language obstacles.

When comparing management and organizations in different nations, it is easy to attribute too much to societal culture.[7]

In the first session of a new student class, I used to write in capital letters: CULTURE DOESN'T EXIST. In the same way values don't exist, dimensions don't exist. They are constructs that have to prove their usefulness by their ability to explain and predict behavior.[8]

The real question is not does culture matter? but when does culture matter?

An individual's motivation and context variables are key elements in determining the impact of culture and in understanding why the influence of culture is remarkable in some cases and insignificant in others.[9]

Reason 5: The concept of culture as a static framework. In most cross-cultural management literature, cultural elements are considered static and invariant across situations and generations. However, most of today's cultures differ from what they were just 5 or 10 years ago. Current models discount cultural change over time, even though change is occurring rapidly in many countries (e.g., the fast move from collectivism to individualism in the major cities of emerging economies). We need a dynamic framework to understand how cultures transform and modify.

Reason 6: Cross-cultural negotiation and influence theories based on questionable data. The use of data from simulations involving international managers enrolled in MBA programs in the United States raises an interesting question in cross-culture literature: Can these individuals be regarded as a relevant and illustrative sample of managerial behavior in different cultures? Does their decision to attend US MBA programs mean they are more Westernized and cosmopolitan than their average fellow countrymen?

Another problem that arises with class simulations is that, because they are built around conventional and simplifying assumptions, they often oversimplify the complex and multidimensional systems governing real-world negotiations.

Reason 7: Concepts such as power, interests, and, above all, best alternative to a negotiated agreement (BATNA) take on different implications in an international context. Understanding people's interests, other than money, is strategic because interests motivate individuals and affect their behavior. Interests differ from individual to individual, and they are strongly influenced by culture, context, and circumstances.

Negotiation power doesn't lie only in wealth, networks, authority, and status; the relative negotiation power of each party is primarily determined by the attractiveness of its option if no agreement is reached.

Most of the negotiation literature focuses on the concept of BATNA, the best alternative each side has if no agreement can be reached between the parties.

The BATNA is the reference against which the terms of the agreement should be assessed to determine if you should accept the deal or walk away and pursue alternatives.

However, the concept of BATNA doesn't apply straightforwardly to complex international negotiations. Committing to only one course of action if the negotiation ends without an agreement could present a risk in multiparty, multidimensional, and unpredictable international negotiations held in a volatile, uncertain, complex, and ambiguous (VUCA) world. A better strategy calls for identification of multiple feasible alternatives (MATNAs).

Therefore, a better approach to international negotiations requires the identification and simultaneous pursuit of MATNAs.

PURPOSE AND AUDIENCE OF THIS BOOK

It has always been my opinion that 'education' is something people do to you, whereas 'learning' is something you do for yourself.[10]

This book provides a practical and innovative framework for negotiating deals and leading organizations in a multicultural business environment.

The 4Ps Framework: Advanced Negotiation and Influence Strategies for Global Effectiveness is about becoming better negotiators and leaders in a global setting.

The book is intended for managers, graduates, and business students who are already, or expect to be, negotiating and influencing across cultures.

But why did we decide to bring together negotiation and influence in the same book?

First, because they are two sides of the same coin: The boundaries between influence and negotiation are feeble and the two concepts often overlap. According to some scholars, negotiation is a part of influence; according to others, influence is an element of negotiation.

This book will provide a simple and well-defined distinction: Influence is internal to the organization, while the focus on negotiation is external to the organization. Second, because the same framework can be applied successfully to both negotiation and influence in a global context.

Negotiation is a basic means of getting what you want from others. It is back-and-forth communication designed to reach agreement when you and the other side have some interests that are shared and others that are opposed.[11]

The reasons why negotiation skills are fundamental in the present global environment are obvious.

Managers regularly negotiate with domestic and international customers, suppliers, agents, and distributors. Organizations are repeatedly involved in international negotiations concerning joint ventures, strategic alliances, partnerships, licenses, franchising, and mergers and acquisitions.

However, no negotiator can be prepared to face the range of specific situations he or she may encounter during international negotiations. Simply too many variables come into play.

This is why we developed a framework based on four key elements – *preparation, process, power perception,* and *people* – that provides international leaders with a map by which to navigate dynamic and complex international negotiations.

The same model applies to influencing in a global context.

Influencing is the ability to affect others' attitudes, beliefs, and behaviors without using force or formal authority.

Modern leaders and managers increasingly recognize the importance of being able to influence people over whom they don't have formal authority. Because authority is becoming an ambiguous concept, contemporary leaders can no longer simply tell others what to do, particularly when facing common issues such as:

- Working across departments in a matrix and flat structure, where authority and responsibility are unclear.
- Working across cultures in multi-site or multinational organizations.
- Managing projects across national boundaries.
- Managing cross-functional and cross-cultural teams located in different countries.
- Trying to get ideas accepted upward and across organizations.

Let's make one thing perfectly clear up front: This book does not provide a list of do's and don'ts on a country-by-country basis. The reasons for this choice are threefold:

- As stated earlier, we negotiate with individuals, and we influence individuals. And there's a great deal of heterogeneity among people within any country.
- Societies are dynamic. As products of culture and economics, history and politics, geographically defined regions change over time.
- Our aim is to provide a generalizable negotiation and influence framework that works across dynamic and complex international contexts.

The focus is thus not only on how to behave in a specific country (the so-called etiquette), but mainly on understanding why certain behaviors occur and how specific behaviors affect negotiations and organizations across cultures.

CROSS- OR INTER-CULTURAL?

In this preface, it is also useful to provide definitions of *cross-cultural* and *intercultural*. Even if the two terms are often used interchangeably, they carry different implications.

Cross-cultural refers to a comparison between two different cultural groups. Intercultural describes what happens when two different cultural groups communicate, negotiate, and interact.[12]

In other words, cross-cultural communication is not the same as intercultural communication. While intercultural communication deals with interaction, communication, and the sharing of meaning between at least two people from different cultures, cross-cultural communication describes the comparison of occurrences between two different cultures.

Cross-cultural communication is a precondition for understanding intercultural communication.

Understanding cross-cultural communication involves understanding what each culture values in terms of interaction with others.[13]

Cultural dimensions (e.g., individualism vs. collectivism, power distance, high and low context communication) are cross-cultural notions because they allow for comparison between cultures.

Negotiation, leadership, and influence, regarded as interactions across cultures, are intercultural concepts.

MAJOR THEMES

The book has two main themes: negotiation and influence.

The map in Figure 2 describes the structure of the book.

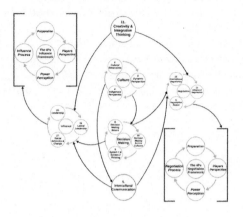

Figure 2 - Book structure.

Four sections of the book are common to both the main topics:

Culture (Chapters 2, 3, and 4), Decision Making (Chapters 8, 9, and 10), Communication (Chapter 5), and Creativity and Integrative Thinking (Chapter 11).

Chapters 6, 7, 12, and 13 are primarily relevant to the negotiation theme, whereas Chapters 14, 15, 16, and 17 mainly refer to the influence theme.

In Chapter 1, we introduce the 4Ps Framework, a model based on four interdependent and dynamic stages: preparation, process, power perception, and player perspective.

In Chapter 2, we present the concept of culture and the main static models of national culture.

Chapter 3 discusses the main dynamic cultural frameworks and two cultural competencies models that aim to overcome some limitations of the static and bipolar models of culture introduced in Chapter 2.

In Chapter 4, we explain the concept of indigenous perspectives on culture, applying an emic approach to the description of certain aspects of specific cultures.

In Chapter 5, we focus on how to communicate across cultures.

Chapter 6 presents the basic negotiation concepts.

In Chapter 7, we introduce the 4Ps Framework as applied to international negotiations.

Chapter 8 explains relevant decision-making theories.

In Chapter 9, we define the difference between system 1 and system 2 thinking and the consequences of the spontaneous search for intuitive solutions.

In Chapter 10, we introduce how decision-making is affected by Culture.

Chapter 11 discusses the concepts of integrative thinking and creativity and their application to negotiation and influence.

In Chapter 12 we present relevant advanced negotiation strategies.

In Chapter 13, we focus on how to negotiate across cultures. In Chapter 14, we discuss the 4Ps Framework as applied to leadership and influence across cultures.

In Chapter 15, we define the concept of leadership.

In Chapter 16, we present influence and persuasion strategies.

Chapter 17 we introduce social network theory as applied to organizations.

The last section presents a comprehensive bibliography designed primarily to assist readers who want to learn more about the field of intercultural negotiation and influence.

(ENDNOTES)

1   Suggested by Joseph J. Rotman in his book, An Introduction to Algebraic Topology.

2   Established in 1975, the G7 is an organization, consisting of what were at that time the seven most developed and wealthiest countries in the world: US, Canada, UK, France, Germany, Italy, and Japan.

3   KPMG: Future State 2030, retrieved from: http://www.kpmg.com/PH/en/PHConnect/ArticlesAnd-Publications/Investors-Guide/Documents/future-state-2030-v1.pdf

4   Atsmon, Y., Child, P., Dobbs, R., & Narasimhan, L. (2012). Winning the $30 trillion decathlon: Going for gold in emerging markets. McKinsey Quarterly, 4, 20-35.

5   Angus Maddison, University of Groningen: The Economist.

6   Medina Walker, D., Walker, T., & Schmitz, J. (2002). Doing business internationally (2nd ed.). New York, NY: McGraw-Hill.

7   Hickson, D. J., & Pugh, D. S. (2003). Management worldwide (2nd ed.). London: Penguin Business.

8   Hofstede, G. (2002). Dimensions do not exist: A reply to Brendan McSweeney. Human Relations, Vol. 55, N. 11, 1355-1361.

9   Ho-ying Fu, J., Morris, M. W., Lee, S., Chao, M., Chiu, C., & Hong, Y. (2007). Epistemic motives and cultural conformity: Need for closure, culture, and context as determinants of conflict judgments. Journal of Personality and Social Psychology, Vol. 92, N. 2, 191-207.

10   Joi Ito, Director of the MIT Media Lab.

11   Fisher, R., Ury, W. L., & Patton, B. (1991). Getting to yes: Negotiating agreement without giving in (2nd ed.). London: Penguin Books.

12   Lustig, M., & Koester, J. (2012). Intercultural competence (7th ed.). London: Pearson.

13   Gudykunst, W. B. (2003). Cross-cultural and intercultural communication. Thousand Oaks, CA: Sage Publications.

CHAPTER 1:

An Introduction to the 4Ps Framework

INTRODUCTION

Because negotiation and influence are nonlinear, non-rational, multi-step, complex social processes, it is challenging to condense them within one model. Nevertheless, frameworks provide an indispensable conceptual structure and frame of reference.[1]

Some negotiation books have attempted to formulate a model, with an emphasis on specific dimensions, stages, or skills.

For example, Richard Shell (2006)[2] provided a compendium of the six foundations of effective negotiation:

- Your bargaining style.
- Your goals and expectations.
- Authoritative standards and norms.
- Relationships.
- The other party's interests.
- Leverage.

In addition, Shell suggested four steps that constitute the negotiation process:

- Preparing your strategy.
- Exchanging information.
- Opening and making concessions.
- Closing and gaining commitment.

Roger Fisher and William Ury (1991)[3] based their model of principled negotiation on five propositions:

- Separate the people from the problem.
- Focus on interests, not positions.
- Invent options for mutual gain.
- Insist on using objective criteria.
- Develop your BATNA (Best Alternative to a Negotiated Agreement).

Lax and Sebenius (2003)[4] developed their model around three dimensions of negotiation:

- Tactics (people and processes).
- Deal design (value and substance).
- Setup (scope and sequence).

Malhotra and Bazerman (2008)[5] and Thompson (2011)[6] were among the first to provide a framework that integrates research on social psychology and behavioral decision making with negotiation elements.

Many books have also attempted to provide a framework and a structure for the influence process.

For example, Cialdini (1993)[7] organized his book around six basic categories of influence:

- Reciprocation.
- Commitment and consistency.
- Social proof.
- Liking.
- Authority.
- Scarcity.

Cohen and Bradford (2005)[8] provided a five-step influence model based on reciprocity and exchange:

- Clarify your goals.
- Diagnose the word of the other person.
- Identify relevant currencies.
- Deal with relationships.
- Influence through reciprocity.

Shell and Moussa (2007)[9] followed a four-step process for influencing:

- Survey your situation.
- Confront the five barriers (relationship, credibility, communication, belief system, and conflicting interests).
- Make your pitch.
- Secure commitment.

Diamond (2010)[10] suggested six tools for influence:

- Be dispassionate. Be calm.
- Prepare.
- Find the decision maker.
- Focus on your goals, not on who is right.
- Make human contact.
- Value the other party's position and power.

Negotiation and influence complexity and unpredictability are amplified when working across cultures, under conditions of ambiguity and uncertainty,[11] with often inadequate communication patterns.[12]

Cohen (1997)[13] investigated the effects of cultural differences in four phases of the negotiation process:

- Preparation.

- Beginning.
- Middle.
- End.

Brett (2001)[14] provided a framework for understanding how culture affects negotiation:

- Culture affects the players' interests and priorities and therefore the potential for integrative agreement.
- Culture affects the players' strategies and consequently their pattern of interaction.

Kremenyuk (2002)[15] organized his book into four main sections:

- Level of analysis: negotiation process, strategy, actors, and outcomes.
- Approaches and perspectives: legal perspective, game theory, psychological approach, cognitive theory.
- Issues: conflict resolution, business negotiations, arms control.
- Education and training in negotiating skills.

Salacuse (2003)[16] suggested a framework based on 10 elements that constantly affect the negotiator's behavior during intercultural negotiations:

- Negotiating goal: contract or relationship?
- Negotiating attitude: win-lose or win-win?
- Personal style: informal or formal?
- Communication: direct or indirect?
- Sensitivity to time: high or low?
- Emotionalism: high or low?
- Form of agreement: general or specific?
- Building an agreement: bottom up or top down?
- Team organization: one leader or group consensus?
- Risk taking: high or low?

Gelfand and Brett (2004)[17] organized their Handbook of Negotiation and Culture into three main sections:

- Psychological process.
- Social process.
- Negotiation context.

WHY THIS SPECIFIC MODEL

Given all the previously described models, why do we need a new one?

The reason is because we need a simple and at the same time comprehensive theoretical framework that can guide us through nonlinear and multi-stage negotiation and influence processes within a volatile, uncertain, complex, and ambiguous international context.

We have developed a systemic and dynamic framework[18] in which four linked and overlapping stages influence one another: A change in one element triggers changes in the others.

The four interrelating stages (the 4Ps) that we employ to describe and analyze negotiation and influence are: *preparation, process, power perception,* and *players' perspective* (see Figure 1).

Chapters 7 and 14 will provide a detailed breakdown of these four stages in negotiation and influence, respectively.

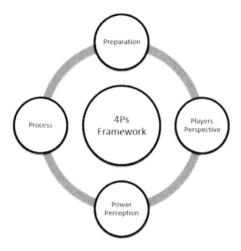

Figure 1. The 4Ps framework.

THE PREPARATION STAGE

Little details separate the mediocre from the excellent[19].

Most negotiators make their prime mistake before they even arrive at the bargaining table: They don't set aside time to prepare for the negotiation.

And the same goes for influence.

Preparation stage activities, which include behind-the-scenes research, planning, and organizing, are the basis for effective negotiation and influence.

It is fundamental to identify not only our goals, our MATNAs (Multiple Alternatives to a Negotiated Agreement, our alternatives if no agreement can be reached), and the zone of potential agreement, but also the interests, constraints, and MATNAs of the other party.

Furthermore, we must map the informal organization and identify options for integrative agreements, key players, and relevant exchange currencies.

The chapters partially or totally associated with the preparation stage are:

- Chapter 6: Negotiation Basics.
- Chapter 9: System 1 and System 2 Thinking.
- Chapter 10: Decision Making Across Cultures.
- Chapter 11: Creativity and Integrative Thinking.
- Chapter 12: Advanced Negotiation.

- Chapter 13: International Negotiation.
- Chapter 16: Lateral Leadership.
- Chapter 17: Social Networks and Change.

THE PROCESS STAGE

During the process phase, the two or more parties meet to find an agreement. We can arbitrarily identify seven indefinite, overlapping, and non-chronological steps in negotiation (which will be examined in depth in Chapter 7):

- Designing the game (off-the-table negotiation).
- Exchanging information.
- Opening moves.
- Competitive phase.
- Integrative phase.
- End game.
- Negotiation post-mortem analysis.

In addition, we see five barriers to the influence process[20] (which will be analyzed in Chapter 14):

- Negative relationships.
- Poor credibility.
- Communication gaps.
- Conflicting interests.
- Diverging belief systems.

The chapters to some extent or entirely related to the process stage are:

- Chapter 5: Intercultural Communication.
- Chapter 6: Negotiation Basics.
- Chapter 8: Decision-Making Basics.
- Chapter 9: System 1 and System 2 Thinking.
- Chapter 10: Decision Making Across Cultures.
- Chapter 11: Creativity and Integrative Thinking.
- Chapter 12: Advanced Negotiation.
- Chapter 13: International Negotiation.
- Chapter 15: Leadership.
- Chapter 16: Lateral Leadership.
- Chapter 17: Social Networks and Change.

THE POWER PERCEPTION STAGE

Power is a key factor in negotiation and influence.

Most people associate power with wealth, status, role, and network. These factors are important, but only partially explain power.

When influencing, people perceive that you have power when you have what others want or need. Position, relationship, expertise, charisma, and access to valuable information are all sources of power.

When negotiating, power lies with the party that needs the agreement less: The relative negotiation power of each party is primarily determined by the attractiveness of its option if no agreement is reached.

A strong correlation between time and power is apparent. Power is dynamic: Exchange currencies and alternatives change their value over time.

The chapters partially or entirely correlated to the power perception stage are:

- Chapter 6: Negotiation Basics.
- Chapter 12: Advanced Negotiation.
- Chapter 13: International Negotiation.
- Chapter 15: Leadership.
- Chapter 16: Lateral Leadership.
- Chapter 17: Social Networks and Change.

THE PLAYERS' PERSPECTIVE STAGE

Most negotiation and influence models are based on the expected utility theory, founded on game theory frameworks and on rational players.

In the players' perspective stage, we introduce studies on social influence, emotions, judgmental heuristics, and behavioral decision making.

Furthermore, we acknowledge psychological and cultural factors that arise in multidimensional and multiparty international negotiation and influence processes.

All the chapters of the book are to some extent related to the players' perspective phase, some more explicitly than others.

It is important to emphasize that, though important, culture is not the single contributor to an individual's negotiating and influencing behavior. Two other key elements must be taken into consideration: the individual's *personality* and the *social context* in which the individual operates (see Figure 2).

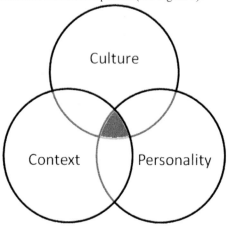

Figure 2. Individual = context + culture + personality.

I think people are as individual as snowflakes, they kinda look alike but no two are exactly the same.[21]

Another important element of the players' perspective phase is that negotiation and influence usually involve different players at different stages.

Both negotiation and influence are not only dynamic, complex, and multi-stage, but they are also multi-player processes involving various parties acting in specific contexts with often conflicting objectives, priorities, concerns, constraints, cultures, and personalities.

The ability to map the decision-making process and identify the key players and their relationships is a vital element of the preparation phase.

An in-depth analysis of the players' perspective stage in negotiation and influence will be provided in Chapters 7 and 14, respectively.

(ENDNOTES)

1   Merriam-Webster, retrieved from http://www.merriam-webster.com/dictionary/framework

2   Shell, G. R. (2006). Bargaining for advantage: Negotiation strategies for reasonable people (2nd ed.). London: Penguin Books.

3   Fisher, R., Ury, W. L., & Patton, B. (1991). Getting to yes: Negotiating agreement without giving in (2nd ed.). London: Penguin Books.

4   Lax, D. A., & Sebenius, J. K. (2003). 3-D Negotiation: playing the whole game. Harvard Business Review, Vol. 81, N. 11, 65-74.

5   Malhotra, D., & Bazerman, M. (2008). Negotiation genius. New York, NY: Bantam.

6   Thompson, L. (2011). The mind and heart of the negotiaton (5th ed.). Upper Sadler River, NJ: Pearson Prentice Hall.

7   Cialdini, R. B. (1993). Influence: The psychology of persuasion. New York, NY: HarperCollins Publishers.

8   Cohen, A. R., & Bradford, D. L. (2005). Influence without authority (2nd ed.). Hoboken, NJ: John Wiley & Sons.

9   Shell, G. R., & Moussa, M. (2007). The art of woo: Using strategic persuasion to sell your ideas. New York, NY: Penguin Group.

10 Diamond, S. (2010). Getting more: How to negotiate to achieve your goals in the real world. New York, NY: Crown Business.

11 Watkins, M. (1999). Negotiating in a Complex World. Negotiation Journal, Vol. 15, N. 3, 245-270.

12 Winham, G. R. (2002). Simulation for teaching and analysis. In V. A. Kremenyuk (Ed.), International Negotiation: analysis, approaches, issues (2nd ed.). San Francisco: Jossey-Bass.

13 Cohen, R. (1997). Negotiating across cultures: International communication in an interdependent world. Washington, DC: United States Institute of Peace.

14 Brett, J. M. (2001). Negotiating globally: How to negotiate deals, resolve disputes, and make decisions across cultural boundaries. San Francisco, CA: Jossey-Bass.

15 Kremenyuk, V. A. (Ed.) (2002). International negotiation: Analysis, approaches, issues (2nd ed.), San Francisco, CA: Jossey-Bass.

16 Salacuse, J. W. (2003). The global negotiator: Making, managing, and mending deals around the world in the twenty-first century. New York, NY: Palgrave Macmillan.

17 Gelfand, M. J. & Brett, J. M. (Eds.) (2004). Handbook of negotiation and culture. Palo Alto, CA: Stanford University Press.

18 Moty Cristal: The Negosystem™ Model.

19 Steve Jobs.

20 Shell, G. R., & Moussa, M. (2007). The art of woo: Using strategic persuasion to sell your ideas. New York, NY: Penguin Group.

21 Craig Ferguson.

CHAPTER 2:

Culture and Cultural Dimensions

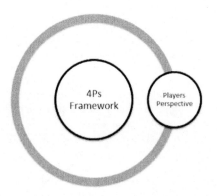

Stage 4: Players Perspective

Oh, Great Spirit, keep me from ever judging a man until I have walked in his moccasins.[1]

DEFINITIONS OF CULTURE

Following are definitions of culture from leading academics and scholars:

Culture: the ideas, customs, attitudes, and social behavior of a particular social group (Oxford Dictionary).

Culture . . . is that complex whole which includes knowledge, belief, art, morals, law, custom, and any other capabilities and habits acquired by man as a member of society (Tylor, 1871).

Culture means organization, regulation of our inner selves; it means taking possession of our own personality and conquering a superior consciousness that allows us to understand our historical role, our function in life, our rights, and our obligations (Gramsci, 1916).

Culture is what binds (people) together (Benedict, 1934).

Culture is roughly anything we do and the monkeys don't (Lord Raglan, 1939).

Culture is the unique social identity of a group (Kroeber, 1952).

One possible way to think about culture is that culture is to society what memory is to individuals (Kluckhohn, 1954).

Culture can therefore be seen as a kind of language, a silent language that the parties need in addition to the language they are speaking if they are to arrive at a genuine understanding (Hall, 1959).

Culture is a system for creating, sending, storing, and processing information (Hall, 1959).

Culture is what makes you a stranger when you're away from home (Brock, 1970).

Culture includes the plans and rules members of a group employ to interpret their world and to act purposefully within it (Spradley & McCurdy, 1971).

Culture is a socially shared knowledge structure, or schema, giving meaning to incoming stimuli and channeling outgoing reactions (Triandis, 1972).

A culture has two aspects: the known meanings and directions, which its members are trained to; the new observations and meanings, which are offered and tested; (…) that it is both the most ordinary common meanings and the finest individual meanings. We use the word culture in these two senses: to mean a whole way of life, the common meaning; to mean the arts and learning, the special processes of discovery and creative effort (Geertz, 1973).

Culture consists of interrelated patterns or dimensions which come together to form a unique social identity shared by a minimum of two or more people (Deutsch, 1973).

Culture is also that aspect of our existence which makes us similar to some people, yet different from the majority of the people in the world... it is the way of life common to a group of people, a collection of beliefs and attitudes, shared understandings and patterns of behavior that allow those people to live together in relative harmony, but set them apart from other peoples (Friedl & Pfeiffer, 1977).

Cultures are based on empirical knowledge gathered through trial and error involving the interrelationship between the natural environment, social organization, and technical knowledge (Mabogunje et al., 1978).

Culture encompasses all that human beings have and do to produce, relate to each other and adapt to the physical environment. It includes agreed-upon principles of human existence (values, norms, and sanctions) as well as techniques of survival (technology) (Rossi, 1980).

In its widest sense, culture may now be said to be the whole complex of distinctive spiritual, material, intellectual, and emotional features that characterize a society or social group. It includes not only the arts and letters, but also modes of life, the fundamental rights of the human being, value systems, traditions, and beliefs (World Conference on Cultural Policies, Mexico City, 1982).

Culture is a pattern of basic assumptions, invented, discovered, or developed by a given group as it learns to cope with its problems of external adaptation and internal integration, that has worked well enough to be considered valid and, therefore, to be taught to new members as the correct way to perceive, think, and feel in relation to those problems (Schein, 1985).

Culture provides a learned, shared, and interrelated set of symbols, codes, and values that direct and justify human behavior (Harris & Moran, 1987).

Culture is not a set of specific models, but it is rather a set of possibilities and conditions which define reality as a dynamic process, in which our culture gets in touch with other different cultures. Basically, the idea moves from the classic vision of culture as roots to a more modern vision of culture as routes (Clifford, 1988).

Culture is our social legacy as contrasted with our organic heredity. It regulates our lives at every turn (Peck, 1988).

The role of Culture is to answer questions even before they are raised (Akoun, 1989).

The study of culture is the study of communication (Carey, 1989; Denzin, 1992).

Culture provides a language for labeling experience (Markus & Kitayama, 1991; Triandis, 1994, 1995).

Culture: the systems of knowledge shared by a relatively large group of people (Gudykunst & Kim, 1992).

Culture is tautological, vague and epiphenomenal (Zartman, 1993).

Culture may be thought of as the set of shared and enduring meanings, values, and beliefs that characterizes a group and orients members' behavior (Faure & Sjostedt, 1993).

Culture is the unique character of a social group and the values and norms common to its members that set it apart from other social groups (Lytle, Brett, Barsness, Tinsley, & Janssens, 1995).

Culture is a little like dropping an Alka-Seltzer into a glass: you don't see it, but somehow it does something (Enzensberger, 1997).

Culture consists of patterns, explicit and implicit, of and for behavior acquired and transmitted by symbols, constituting the distinctive achievement of human groups, including their embodiments in artifacts; the essential core of culture consists of traditional ideas and especially their attached values; culture systems may, on the one hand, be considered as products of action, on the other hand, as conditioning influences upon further action (Hofstede, 1997).

Culture is the way in which a group of people solves problems (Trompenaars, 1998).

Culture is the collective programming of the mind which distinguishes the members of one group or category of people from another (Hofstede, 2001).

Cultures consist of psychological elements, the values and norms shared by members of a group, as well as social structural elements: the economic, social, political, and religious institutions that are the context for social interaction (Brett, 2001).

Culture is ubiquitous, multidimensional, complex, and pervasive. Because culture is so broad, there is no single definition or central theory of what it is. Definitions range from the all-encompassing ('it is everything') to the narrow ('it is opera, art, and ballet'). For our purposes we define culture as the cumulative deposit of knowledge, experience, beliefs, values, attitudes, meanings, hierarchies, religions, notions of time, roles, spatial relations, concepts of the universe, and material objects and possessions acquired by a group of people in the course of generations through individual and group striving (Samovar & Porter, 2003).

Culture refers to the socially transmitted values, beliefs, and symbols that are more or less shared by members of a social group, and by means of which members interpret and make meaningful their experience and behavior (including the behavior of 'others') (Avruch, 2003).

Culture is the unique characteristic of a social group; the values and norms shared by its members set it apart from other social groups. And culture is concerned with economic, political, social structure, religion, education, and language (Chang, 2003).

Culture serves as a type of social adhesive that binds a group of people together and gives them a distinct identity as a community. It may also give them a sense that they are a community different from other communities (Salacuse, 2003).

Individuals have personalities; groups have cultures (Adair & Brett, 2004)

Culture enables people to communicate, to organize thoughts, to be self-reflective, in other words culture makes it possible for people to understand the environment they are living in (Kim, Yang, & Hwang, 2006).

Culture is a pervasive influence which underlies all facets of social behavior and interaction and it is evident in the values and norms that govern society (Craig & Douglas, 2006).

Culture is the world and the values, moral norms, and actual behaviour – and the material, immaterial, and symbol results thereof – which people (in a given context and in a given period of time) take over from a preceding generation, which they – possibly in a modified form – seek to pass on to the next generation; and which in one way or another make them different from people belonging to other cultures (Gullestrup, 2006).

A unique meaning and information system, shared by a group and transmitted across generations, that allows the group to meet basic needs of survival, by coordinating social behavior to achieve a viable existence, to transmit successful social behaviors, to pursue happiness and well-being, and to derive meaning from life (Matsumoto, 2008).

Culture is a distinctly human capacity for adapting to circumstances and transmitting this coping skill and knowledge to subsequent generations. Culture gives people a sense of who they are, of belonging, of how they should behave, and what they should be doing (Harris & Moran, 2007).

Culture is not so much about what we as individuals do but more about what we tolerate in those around us (Trickey, 2012).

The biggest problem with the word culture is that nobody seems to know exactly what it means, or rather, that it means very different things to different people. Culture is a verb: culture is not something that you think or possess or live inside of. It is something that you do (Scollon, 2013).

Definitions from Hughes, R. (2010). CULT-URE. London, Fiell Publishing. include:

Culture is your local consensus reality; your clothing and cuisine, the music you listen to, the books you read, the films you see; your values, ideas, beliefs, and prejudices (Hughes, 2010).

Culture, unlike eye color or race, is not a compulsory genetic accident of birth, but an optional intellectual position. And unlike your race, your culture is in a vibrant daily state of flux. Your culture is not your parent's culture, nor will it be your children's (Hughes, 2010).

Culture evolves, particularly cultural ideas can spread rapidly, while others atrophy or are wiped out. Some aspects of culture are fleeting and transient, while other strains are carefully nurtured and survive unchanged for generations (Hughes, 2010).

A culture could be defined as the sum of the ideas a group, whether a nation, corporation, or social circle, have. In fact, sharing a common set of ideas can now easily become the defining aspect of group membership, trumping geographical location or nationality (Hughes, 2010).

Culture acts as an externalized memory, an off-brain backup (Hughes, 2010).

Culture is a map of who, as a whole, we think we are; our values, our art, our intellectual efforts, our gossip, our history. Culture is a map that makes experience intelligible. Like a physical map, it will offer a schematic representation, a codified and symbolic reproduction, with its simplifications, approximations, short cuts, errors, and unwanted detail (Hughes, 2010).

Culture, being a human creation, is as complex and varied as humans themselves. From simplicity, we move toward complexity (Hughes, 2010).

Culture thrives in the gap between chaos and order. Two much of either will kill it (Hughes, 2010).

Though born into a culture, our cultural identity is not who we are, it is who we are taught to be. Culture is learned, it is not genetic (Hughes, 2010).

Culture is our discussion with ourselves as to how we think we should be. It is a map that has the potential for redrawing the territory. It makes meaningful the set of assumptions, deductions, insights, and prejudices we have inherited. It has sometimes loose connections to facts, to faith, and to philosophy. It can be impassioned and rational, but also illogical and messy, and needs the sharpest tools in our intellectual toolbox to do it justice (Hughes, 2010).

Culture is what is left after we have forgotten everything else (Herriot, n. d.).

The following definitions are taken from ExchangesConnect (http://connect. state.gov), an international community managed by the U.S. Department of State:

I understand culture as a treasure that is part of our collective memory, of our perception of ourselves.

Culture is the acquired pair of glasses through which we see life.

It is a call for individuals to agree on some common values that bind them in harmony.

CULTURE AS AN ABSTRACT CONCEPT

The definitions introduced in the previous section and used in most academic work have two common descriptions of the word culture:

- Culture is what distinguishes one group from another.
- Culture is viewed as nation and to some degree as ethnicity.

However, because nations and ethnic groups are too large to be real communities (i.e., no group member will ever know all the other group members), a corollary of the previous definitions is that the word culture is not a real concept, but an abstract and theoretical notion.[2]

ANALOGIES OF CULTURE

Cultural values represent shared abstract ideas about what is good, right, and desirable in a society.[3]

These cultural values (e.g., freedom, prosperity, security) are the foundations for the distinctive norms that tell people what is appropriate in various situations.[4]

Therefore, values refer to what a society considers important, whereas norms refer to what is considered appropriate behavior.[5]

Beliefs are convictions about the veracity of a concept, statement, or assumption. Social beliefs are shared organizational structures and expectations around which the daily social life of a group is organized (e.g., marriage, family, kinship).

The *culture-iceberg* analogy graphically exemplifies the manifest and hidden elements of culture (Fig. 1).[6]

Because of the difference in density between pure ice and sea water, only 11% of the volume of an iceberg is visible. The peak of the iceberg represents behaviors, artifacts, traditions, and habits that characterize a culture. The submerged 89% can be divided into two elements: just below water level we can find deeper held values, beliefs, and norms that are driven by fundamental assumptions about the world, that are represented by the base of the iceberg.

Figure 1. The cultural iceberg.

Another often used analogy is the *culture as the onion* (Fig. 2),[7] with behavior, attitudes, norms, and values forming concentric circles like layers of an onion. We first perceive behaviors, then attitudes toward specific circumstances, followed by rules to be followed in specific situations (norms), and finally, the core values.

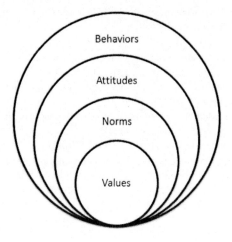

Behaviors

Attitudes

Norms

Values

Figure 2. Culture as an onion.

CULTURAL DIMENSIONS MODELS

At the moment, at least eight models of national culture are extensively used in academic and organizational contexts, including frameworks suggested by Kluck-hohn and Strodtbeck, Hofstede, Hall, Trompenaars, Schwartz, Lewis, Walker and Schmitz, and House and GLOBE.[8]

Each model offers a set of dimensions by which researchers and managers can assess and compare different cultures. The models attempt to provide a common language to understand cultural differences.

It is important to emphasize that most of the models are built around the following assumptions:

- A within nation (or even cluster) homogeneity.
- A bipolar either-or approach based on opposites (doesn't apply to Lewis's model).
- The view that cultural dimensions don't change over generations.

These assumptions will be questioned in chapter 3 (Dynamic Perspective of Culture) and chapter 4 (Indigenous Perspective on Culture).

In the next paragraphs, we introduce the eight above mentioned models.

VALUES ORIENTATION THEORY

One of the original frameworks of cultural dimensions was developed by Clyde Kluckhohn, an American anthropologist, and Fred Strodtbeck, an American social psychologist, in 1961.[9]
They identified five value orientations, which represent solutions to problems that are common to all human societies.[10]

The first value orientation is *relationship with nature*:

- *Mastery*: Members of mastery societies believe they should use their knowledge and skills to control the environment.
- *Harmony*: Members of harmony societies believe they should live in harmony and balance with the environment.
- *Subjugation*. Members of subjugation societies believe they should resign themselves to the external environment.

The second value orientation is *relationship with people*:

- *Individualistic*: Members of individualistic cultures believe that societies should be organized around individuals and that decisions should be made according to individual needs, independently from the group.
- *Collateral*: Members of collateral cultures believe that societies should be organized around extended groups of equals and decisions should be based on group consensus.
- *Lineal*: Members of lineal cultures believe that societies should be organized according to a clear and rigid hierarchy and decisions should be made by the higher authorities within the group.

The third value orientation is *motive for human behavior*:

- *Being*: Members of being cultures are motivated by inner values that are important for them, but not necessarily for others.
- *Becoming*: Members of becoming cultures are motivated by the desire to develop skills and abilities that are important for them, but not necessarily for others.
- *Doing*: Members of doing cultures are motivated by external goals and objectives that are important for them and at the same time approved by others.

The fourth value orientation is *relationship with time*, or the extent to which past, present, and future influence decisions.

- *Past*: Members of past cultures are influenced by history and past events in making decisions. The focus is on preserving traditions, beliefs, and customs.
- *Present*: Members of present cultures are influenced by current circumstances in making decisions. The focus is on the present and adapting traditions and beliefs to new situations.
- *Future*: Members of future cultures are influenced by future projections in making decisions. The focus is on planning ahead and preparing to adopt new beliefs and customs.

The fifth value orientation is *nature of human nature*:

- *Good*: Members of good societies believe that people are inherently good.
- *Neutral*: Members of neutral societies believe that people have both good and bad traits.

• *Evil*: Members of evil societies believe that people are inherently evil.

Each of these categories can be further expanded based on two variables:

• *Mutable*: Members of mutable societies believe that people can change over time. If they are born good, they can be subject to corruption, and if they are born evil, they can learn to be good.

• *Immutable*: Members of immutable societies believe that people don't change. If they are born good, they will stay good, and if they are born evil, they will stay evil.

HOFSTEDE'S CULTURAL DIMENSIONS

Between 1967 and 1973, Geert Hofstede, a Dutch mechanical engineer and social psychologist, conducted an extended survey study with the intention of identifying differences in national values across the worldwide subsidiaries of IBM. The study, which first focused on 40 countries, was extended to more than 70 national subsidiaries of IBM around the world, collecting responses to 117,000 questionnaires and building the largest cross-national database of the time.[11]

The statistical analysis of the answers to the questionnaires revealed four common anthropological problems with different solutions across countries:

• Relationship with authority and ways of coping with social inequality.
• Relationship between the individual and the group.
• Social and emotional implications of gender differences.
• Ways of coping with uncertainty and expressing emotions.

The four fundamental problems correspond to four dimensions of national cultures:

• *Power distance index (PDI)*: The degree to which the most vulnerable members of societies and organizations accept and expect power to be distributed unequally. The power distance index defines how people perceive power differences; it doesn't reveal actual differences in power distribution. Members of low power distance cultures expect and accept egalitarian and open relationships, regardless of formal rank. Subordinates are comfortable criticizing and participating in the decision-making process. Members of high power distance societies expect and accept autocratic and paternalistic power relationships. Subordinates recognize and assent to power and authority based on formal and inherited hierarchical positions.

• *Individualism vs. collectivism (IDV)*: The extent to which individuals are integrated into groups and the relative importance given to individual vs. group interests. Members of individualistic societies focus on individual accomplishment, independence, and rights. Individual and nuclear family interests take priority over collective interests because ties between individuals are loose. Identity is based on the individual and individual skills and achievements; communication tends to be low context, and tasks outweigh relationships. In contrast, members of collectivistic societies focus on group welfare and harmony. Collectivist interests take priority over individualistic interests. Extended families, composed of interdependent individuals connected by tight ties, protect and take care of their members in exchange for absolute loyalty. Identity is based on the social network to which one belongs, communication tends to be high context, and relationships outweigh tasks.

- *Uncertainty avoidance index (UAI)*: The degree to which members of a society feel threatened by uncertain and unknown situations and try to avoid such situations. Members of high uncertainty avoidance societies tend to minimize unpredictable or ambiguous situations with detailed planning and careful implementation. They have a need for predictability shaped by written rules, laws, and procedures. When facing new and ambiguous situations, they become highly emotional and anxious. What is different is dangerous. On the other hand, members of low uncertainty avoidance cultures display a high tolerance for uncertainty and ambiguity, embracing change and preferring unstructured situations with as few rules as possible. What is different is curious.

- *Masculinity vs. femininity (MAS)*: The degree to which the dominant values of a society are masculine with respect to the distribution of emotional roles between genders. Masculine cultures display a well-defined distinction of social gender roles that emphasizes assertiveness, competitiveness, materialism, ambition, and power for men and tenderness, generosity, and modesty for women. In feminine cultures, social gender roles are overlapping and both men and women are expected to be gentle, generous, modest, and concerned with relationships and quality of life.

In 1991, based on a survey developed with Chinese employees and managers, Hofstede added a fifth dimension to his model which describes societies' time horizon: *long-term vs. short-term orientation (LTO)*, initially called *Confucian dynamism*. Members of long-term-oriented societies stress the future, cultivating values such as persistence, thrift, capacity for adaptation, respect for status in relationships, and dialectical thinking. Members of short-term-oriented societies emphasize the past and the present, promoting values such as short-term results, personal steadiness, respect for tradition, face saving, reciprocation of gifts and favors, fulfilling social duties, and normative thinking.

Based on the World Values Survey data analysis, in 2010, the scores for the five dimensions were updated and extended to 72 countries and three additional regions (East and West Africa, Arab countries). [12]

Table 1, 2 and 3 show the available scores for the 5 dimensions (LTO scores are not accessible for all countries). [13]

Country	PDI	IDV	MAS	UAI	LTO
Africa East	64	27	41	52	32
Africa West	77	20	46	54	9
Arab countries	80	38	53	68	23
Argentina	49	46	56	86	20
Australia	36	90	61	51	21
Austria	11	55	79	70	60
Bangladesh	80	20	55	60	47
Belgium total	65	75	54	94	82
Belgium Dutch speakers	61	78	43	97	
Belgium French speakers	67	72	60	93	
Brazil	69	38	49	76	44
Bulgaria	70	30	40	85	69
Canada total	39	80	52	48	36
Canada French speakers	54	73	45	60	
Chile	63	23	28	86	31
China	80	20	66	30	87
Colombia	67	13	64	80	13
Costa Rica	35	15	21	86	
Croatia	73	33	40	80	58
Czech Rep	57	58	57	74	70
Denmark	18	74	16	23	35
Ecuador	78	8	63	67	
Egypt	70	25	45	80	
El Salvador	66	19	40	94	20
Estonia	40	60	30	60	82
Finland	33	63	26	59	38
France	68	71	43	86	63

Table 1. Scores for Hofstede dimensions - A

Country	PDI	IDV	MAS	UAI	LTO
Germany	35	67	66	65	83
Great Britain	35	89	66	35	51
Greece	60	35	57	112	45
Guatemala	95	6	37	101	
Hong Kong	68	25	57	29	61
Hungary	46	80	88	82	58
India	77	48	56	40	51
Indonesia	78	14	46	48	62
Iran	58	41	43	59	14
Ireland	28	70	68	35	24
Israel	13	54	47	81	38
Italy	50	76	70	75	61
Jamaica	45	39	68	13	
Japan	54	46	95	92	88
Korea South	60	18	39	85	100
Latvia	44	70	9	63	69
Lithuania	42	60	19	65	82
Luxembourg	40	60	50	70	64
Malaysia	104	26	50	36	41
Malta	56	59	47	96	47
Mexico	81	30	69	82	24
Morocco	70	46	53	68	14
Netherlands	38	80	14	53	67
New Zealand	22	79	58	49	33
Norway	31	69	8	50	35
Pakistan	55	14	50	70	50
Panama	95	11	44	86	

Table 2. Scores for Hofstede dimensions - B

Country	PDI	IDV	MAS	UAI	LTO
Peru	64	16	42	87	25
Philippines	94	32	64	44	27
Poland	68	60	64	93	38
Portugal	63	27	31	104	28
Romania	90	30	42	90	52
Russia	93	39	36	95	81
Salvador	66	19	40	94	
Serbia	86	25	43	92	52
Singapore	74	20	48	8	72
Slovak Rep	104	52	110	51	77
Slovenia	71	27	19	88	49
South Africa white	49	65	83	49	
Spain	57	51	42	86	48
Suriname	85	47	37	92	
Sweden	31	71	5	29	53
Switzerland	34	68	70	58	74
Switzerland French speakers	70	64	58	70	
Switzerland German speakers	26	69	72	56	
Taiwan	58	17	45	69	93
Thailand	64	20	34	64	32
Trinidad and Tobago	47	16	58	55	13
Turkey	66	37	45	85	46
Uruguay	61	36	38	100	26
U.S.A.	40	91	62	46	26
Venezuela	81	12	73	76	16
Vietnam	70	20	40	30	57

Table 3. Scores for Hofstede dimensions - C

To determine how to interpret the Hofstede cultural dimension scores, we focus on a number of countries, specifically nation members of the G20, the group that represents 20 major world economies (19 countries and the EU), and Spain, which is a permanent guest at all meetings of the group. Because we don't have the scores for Saudi Arabia (a G20 member) or the UK, we include the Arabic countries' region and Great Britain in the sample.

Argentina is an uncertainty-avoiding society with a short-term orientation. Argentina is also a relatively low power distance and individualistic society (particularly if compared to other Latin American countries).

Australia is an egalitarian and individualistic society with a short-term orientation.

Brazil is a high power distance and collectivistic society that doesn't welcome ambiguous situations.

Canada and the US are relatively low power distance and very individualistic societies that can cope with change and uncertainty.

China is a very high power distance and collectivistic society with a great propensity toward change and ambiguity and a very high long-term orientation.

France is a relatively high power distance society (particularly if compared with other Western societies) with a moderately feminine culture and a low inclination toward uncertainty and change.

Germany is a low power distance society with a relatively low tolerance for change and ambiguity and a high long-term orientation (particularly if compared to other Northern European countries).

Great Britain (we don't have scores for the UK) is a very egalitarian and individualistic society with a high inclination toward change and uncertainty.

India is a high power distance and relatively individualistic society (at least if compared to other Asian countries). Indians also show a propensity toward change and ambiguity.

Indonesia is a very high power distance and collectivistic culture with a relatively low score on masculinity.

Italy is an individualistic and masculine society that dislikes uncertain situations.

Japan is a very masculine, uncertainty-avoiding, and long-term-oriented society.

South Korea is a very collectivistic, uncertainty-avoiding, and long-term-oriented culture that also scores relatively low on masculinity.

Arab countries (we don't have scores for Saudi Arabia) are very high power distance, relatively collectivistic, and uncertainty-avoiding societies with a short-term orientation.

Mexico is a high power distance, uncertainty-avoiding, and relatively masculine society with a short-term orientation.

Russia is a high power distance, feminine, and uncertainty-avoiding society with a long-term orientation.

South Africa (white sample) is a very masculine and relatively low power distance and individualistic society.

Spain is a feminine, uncertainty-avoiding, and relatively collectivistic society (at least compared to other European countries).

Turkey is a relatively collectivistic and feminine society with a low propensity toward uncertain situations and change.

EDWARD T. HALL'S THEORIES

Edward T. Hall (1973), an American anthropologist, proposed a model of culture based on his ethnographic research on interpersonal communication, personal space, and time.

Hall's intercultural communication model is based on the relative importance of the context of the message over the message itself.[14]

In *low-context communication*, the message is more important than the context. The verbal factor is more important than the paraverbal and the nonverbal factors and great importance is attached to written communication. The contract is the foundation of any business agreement.

In *high-context communication*, the message is less important than the context. What is not said is as important as what is said, and the message is conveyed indirectly; paraverbal and nonverbal elements are essential to decode the meaning of the message. The relationship is the foundation of any business agreement.

Problems arise when high-context individuals try to communicate with low-context individuals.

Members of high-context cultures will perceive low-context individuals as arrogant and detached.

Members of low-context cultures will perceive high-context individuals as confusing and unreliable. (More information on high- and low-context communication appears in chapter 5).

The concept of *proxemics* (the study of cultural, behavioral, and sociological aspects of spatial distances between individuals) was introduced by Hall (1982) to describe the extent to which people from different cultures are comfortable sharing physical space with others.[15]

Hall was influenced by biologist Heini Heidiger's studies on interaction distances between animals.

Hall identified four zones of personal space (values in parentheses refer to Hall's estimates for an average American):

- *Intimate space* is reserved for family and very close friends (less than 46 cm / 18 in).
- *Personal space* is reserved for friends and informal connections (between 46 cm / 18 in and 1.2 m / 47 in).
- *Social space* extends to impersonal and formal interactions, such as business meetings (between 1.2 m / 47 in and 3.7 m / 145 in).
- *Public space* is the outermost zone, the one that is not secured and that extends to people we don't know (more than 3.7 m / 145 in).

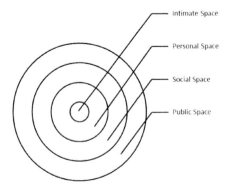

Figure 3. Personal space.

The theory of proxemics proposes that an individual's personal space, or comfort zone, is highly variable: People maintain different degrees of personal distance depending on social circumstances and cultural experiences. Figure 3 refers to the degree of personal space expected by individuals in various contexts. Values suggested for the US are quite similar to those suggested for Germany, Scandinavian countries, and the UK.

Personal distance will be smaller for individuals living in densely populated countries, such as India, Japan, Bangladesh, the Philippines, and South Korea.

Reactions to space violations are processed in the amygdala, which is also the location of our most negative emotions (details in chapter 8).

The third new concept proposed by Hall (1984) is the notion of *monochronic and polychronic time*.[16]

Members of monochronic cultures perceive time as rigid and divided into fixed elements. Time is tangible and recognized as a valuable commodity: Time is money. They prefer doing one thing at a time. Careful planning and scheduling is fundamental to define clear deadlines and priorities. Examples of monochromic societies are the US, Germany, Scandinavian countries, and Japan.

Members of polychronic cultures perceive time as open and flexible. They prefer doing several things at the same time. Relationship takes precedence over tasks, deadlines, and plans. Examples of polychronic societies are Italy, Spain, France, Mexico, Brazil, and Saudi Arabia.

As a general rule, monochronic cultures are also likely to be low context, while polychronic societies tend to be high context.

THE SEVEN DIMENSIONS OF CULTURE

As a result of more than 30,000 questionnaires sent to managers in Shell and other companies in 28 different countries, Fons Trompenars (1997), a Dutch economist and expert in organizational behavior, and Charles Hampden-Turner, a British professor of organizational behavior and management, identified seven cultural dimensions that they believed could explain differences among national cultures.[17]

According to their theory, culture has three layers.

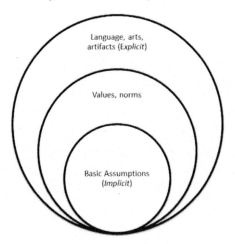

Figure 4. The three layers of culture.

The external layer is explicit culture, which can easily be observed in language, food, buildings, monuments, economy, fashions, and arts.

Values and norms, which define important and appropriate behavior, are situated in the central layer.

The innermost layer is the implicit culture, the core and embedded set of basic assumptions on which a culture is built.

Consistent with the seven dimensions framework, culture can be defined as the way a group of people solves seven basic problems in three specific spheres: human relationships, time, and nature (Fig. 5). The first five dimensions focus on relationships among people, while the last two focus on society's relationship with nature and time management and perception.

Figure 5. The seven dimensions framework.

The first dimension, *universalism vs. particularism*, answers the question: What is more important, rules or relationships? This factor differentiates societies according to the relative emphasis given to procedures and relations. This dimension does not appear in Hofstede's framework.

According to members of universalistic societies, rules, laws, policies, procedures, standards, and processes take precedence over the needs, demands, and requests of friends and relatives.

Business is based on inflexible and unalterable agreements and contracts.

Examples of universalistic nations include the US, Australia, Germany, Switzerland, Sweden, the UK, the Netherlands, the Czech Republic, Slovakia, Belgium, and France.

In particularistic societies, the emphasis is more on personal relationships than on formal rules and procedures. Laws, policies, and processes can be circumvented to accommodate a friend's request.

Exceptions are acceptable and rules are bendable according to the situation and the significance of the relationship.

Examples of particularistic nations include Brazil, Italy, Japan, Argentina, Mexico, Thailand, China, Venezuela, Indonesia, and Korea.

The second dimension, *individualism vs. collectivism*, answers the question: Do we operate as a group or as individuals? This factor differentiates societies according to the relative emphasis given to individual versus group interests. This dimension is equivalent to the individualism dimension of Hofstede's framework.

In individualistic societies, people are expected to take care of themselves, and individual needs, requirements, interests, and desires come before group necessities. The focus is on individual achievement and independence. Individual societies are exemplified by frequent use of the term I.

Examples of individualistic societies are Scandinavian countries, New Zealand, Australia, Switzerland, and the US.

On the other hand, collectivist societies place the group before the individual. The focus is on group realization and prosperity. The group takes care of the individual. Collectivistic societies are characterized by frequent use of the term we.

Example of collectivistic societies are China, Singapore, Thailand, Japan, and Brazil.

The third dimension, *achievement vs. ascription*, answers the question: Do we have to prove ourselves to receive status or is it given to us? This factor differentiates societies according to how status and authority are assigned. This dimension is comparable to Hofstede's power distance.

In achievement-oriented societies, status is based on skills, knowledge, achievements, experience, and track record. Rank is assigned on the basis of what you know and what you have accomplished.

Examples of achievement-oriented societies are the US, Canada, Switzerland, Australia, and Scandinavian countries.

In contrast, ascription-oriented societies attribute status based on age, seniority, religion, education, gender, family and social background, position, and wealth. Status is ascribed and inherited, and rank is assigned on the basis of who you are and where you come from.

Examples of ascription-oriented societies are Japan, Saudi Arabia, Malaysia, Indonesia, France, and Italy.

The fourth dimension, *neutral vs. affective*, answers the question: Do we display our emotions? This factor differentiates societies based on how their members express their emotions in public. This dimension does not appear in Hofstede's framework.

In neutral societies, individuals abstain from displaying emotions, control and conceal their feelings, restrain body language and facial expressions, and avoid physical contact.

Examples of neutral societies are Japan, Singapore, Finland, the UK, Netherlands, and Germany.

In affective societies, emotional displays are not only tolerated but sometimes even sought after. Members of these societies are exemplified by passionate and vibrant nonverbal, paraverbal, and verbal expressions of feelings and sentiments.

Examples of affective societies are the United Arab Emirates, Italy, Mexico, and Venezuela.

The fifth dimension, *specific vs. diffuse*, answers the question: How far do we get involved? The factor differentiates societies based on the degree to which members separate their personal and professional lives. This dimension is not present in Hofstede's framework, but it includes elements of the masculinity and individualism dimensions.

Members of specific societies maintain their private and professional lives as separate and do not feel the need to cultivate relationships to achieve work objectives. Social and work-related groups have different and not overlapping hierarchies. An individual's social roles (e.g., employee, father, son) are compartmentalized.

Examples of specific societies are Sweden, Germany, Canada, the UK, and the US.

In diffuse societies, there is no clear partition between personal and work life. Relationships must be continuously developed to achieve professional targets. Social and work hierarchies can correspond. An individual's social roles are integrated.

Examples of diffuse societies are China, Venezuela, Mexico, Japan, and Spain.

The sixth dimension, *internal vs. external*, answers the question: Do we control our environment or work with it? The factor differentiates societies according to the extent to which members believe they can exercise control over their environment as opposed to being controlled by it.

In internal societies, members believe that through the appropriate knowledge, skills, and expertise, the environment can be controlled, influenced, and shaped to achieve one's own goals.

Examples of internal societies are the US, the UK, Australia, Israel, and to a certain degree India and China.

In an external society, members believe in living in harmony with the environment and adapting to external circumstances.

Examples of external societies are Russia, Saudi Arabia, Sweden, Egypt, Korea, and to a certain degree India, China, and Italy.

The last dimension, *sequential vs. synchronic*, answers the question: Do we do things one at a time or several things at once? This factor differentiates societies based on whether members prefer to do one thing at a time or work on a number of things at the same time. This dimension is not present in Hofstede's framework and is analogous to Hall's monochromic and polychromic time concept.

Members of sequential societies follow one activity at a time, set clear deadlines and priorities, and follow plans and agendas. Time is rigid and concrete because it provides for deadlines and planning.

Examples of sequential societies are Japan, Canada, Germany, the US, and the UK.

In contrast, members of synchronic societies see time as flexible and intangible and are at ease doing several activities at the same time. Plans, deadlines, and priorities are flexible and can be changed.

Examples of synchronic societies are China, Saudi Arabia, Russia, Mexico, and Greece.

Another differentiation among societies relative to time orientation is the relative weight assigned to the past, present, and future.

Past-oriented societies interpret the future as a repetition of the past; tradition and history are highly valued and respect is shown for ancestors, predecessors, and elders (e.g., Italy, France).

Present-oriented societies emphasize the here and now; current activities and short-term results and execution are more valued than planning (e.g., Brazil, the US).

Future-oriented societies focus on planning, controlling, and organizing. The emphasis is on future opportunities and long-term results (e.g., China, Germany).

SEVEN VALUE TYPES

The value type theory was proposed by Shalom Schwartz (1999), a US-Israeli professor of social psychology,[18] to understand the implications of work-related variables for members of different cultures.

The theory, which has been validated across approximately 50 countries, suggests that seven cultural dimensions (types of values) address the three basic problems with which all societies must cope.

The first fundamental issue is the relationship between the individual and the group: To what extent are individuals autonomous vs. embedded in their groups?

- *Embeddedness (conservatism)*: Cultures that focus on a set of values that tend to preserve the status quo and limit actions and dispositions that can disrupt the social order. The emphasis is on values such as family, security, respect for traditions, and respect for elders. Individuals identify themselves with the group and find meaning through social relationships.
- *Autonomy*: Cultures that encourage their members to express their independence and to convey their preferences, feelings, and motivations. Individuals are viewed as autonomous and self-determining entities.

It is possible to differentiate between two types of autonomy:

- *Intellectual autonomy*: An emphasis on values such as curiosity, creativity, and open-mindedness. Individuals are encouraged to pursue new ideas and paths.
- *Affective autonomy*: An emphasis on values such as pleasure and a stimulating life. Individuals are encouraged to pursue quality of life and a work-leisure balance.

The second basic issue is preserving the social structure by assuring that individuals will behave responsibly: How can we ensure social order? By restrictions or by voluntary cooperation?

- *Hierarchy*: In hierarchal societies, individuals are bound to comply with the duties and rules attached to their ascribed roles. The social structure is based on an unequal distribution of power, roles, authority, and wealth within the group.
- *Egalitarianism*: In egalitarian societies, people voluntarily give precedence to group welfare over self-interest. The social structure is based on a uniform distribution of power, roles, wealth, and authority within the group. The emphasis is on values such as fairness, social justice, independence, responsibility, and rectitude.

The third fundamental issue is the relationship between people and the environment: To what extent can individuals control vs. adapt to the environment?

- *Mastery*: Members of mastery societies believe they can control and change the environment to fit their interests. There is an emphasis on action, success, ambition, competency, and conflict management.
- *Harmony*: Members of harmony societies believe they should adapt to the environment, accepting it as it is, rather than try to control it. There is an emphasis on unity with nature, conflict avoidance, and reflection.

Figure 6 shows the relationships of contradiction and compatibility among the seven cultural value types.

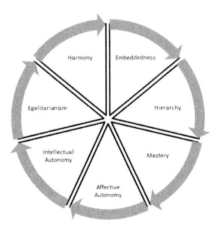

Figure 6. Schwartz's integrated value types system.

Value types that are close to each other are compatible (relate positively). Value types that are opposite to each other are in contradiction (relate negatively).

For example, hierarchy and embeddedness relate positively because they are both present in societies that value interdependent relationships, group welfare over self-interests, preservation of the status quo, and rigid social structure.

Egalitarianism and autonomy relate positively because they are both present in cultures that value independence, self-determination, and responsibility.

Harmony and embeddedness relate positively because both emphasize the status quo.

However, harmony also relates positively to egalitarianism because both focus on cooperative relationships.

28

Figure 7. Value type clusters.

Through a survey analysis of urban school teachers in more than 50 countries, Schwartz also identified eight cultural clusters (with some within-cluster variations), based on geographic proximity, common history, language affinity, religion, and economic development, as shown in Figure 7:[19]

- *West Europe*, typified by egalitarianism, intellectual autonomy, and harmony, with low hierarchy and embeddedness.
- *English-speaking*, characterized by affective autonomy and mastery, with low harmony and embeddedness.
- *Confucian region*, characterized by hierarchy and mastery, with low egalitarianism and harmony.
- *Africa and the Middle-East*, characterized by embeddedness and hierarchy with low affective and intellectual autonomy.
- *South Asia*, characterized by high hierarchy and embeddedness and low autonomy and egalitarianism.
- *East Europe*, typified by medium-high scores in embeddedness, hierarchy, and mastery and medium-low scores in harmony, egalitarianism, and autonomy.
- *East-Central, and Baltic Europe*, characterized by high scores in harmony and egalitarianism, and low scores in autonomy, mastery and hierarchy
- *Latin America*, with average and homogeneous scores in all value types.

Between 1988 and 2000, Schwartz also mapped 76 national cultures on his seven dimensions using samples of school teachers and college students from 67 nations.

In accordance with the theory, if a country emphasizes one polar value orientation, it typically deemphasizes the opposing polar orientation. In addition, adjacent cultural orientations display similar relative importance (Fig. 8).

It must be emphasized that mapping national cultures on the seven orientations in a two-dimensional space automatically leads to some inaccuracy and incoherence with the overall theory.

For example, Italian culture, compared to all the others, is very high in both egalitarianism and in the adjacent harmony orientation, but very low in the opposing hierarchy and adjacent mastery orientations. Chinese culture displays the opposite profile, high on hierarchy and mastery and relatively low on egalitarianism and harmony. China's relatively low score on harmony contrasts with its Confucian tradition, which underscores conflict avoidance (as we'll see in chapter 4), and is in opposition to Schwartz theory, where adjacent cultural values show similar relative scores. One simple explanation for this inconsistency is that harmony and mastery address the fundamental issue of the relationship between people and the environment. Chinese culture emphasizes control and changing the environment to fit people's interests, but deemphasizes conflict in a social context.

Other examples of opposite cultures are Sweden and Zimbabwe. Culture in Sweden (upper left of Figure 8) strongly emphasizes harmony, intellectual autonomy, and egalitarianism and moderately emphasizes affective autonomy. The cultural importance of embeddedness is low, and it is very low for mastery and hierarchy. In contrast, in Zimbabwe (lower right of Fig. 8), mastery, embeddedness, and hierarchy are highly accentuated, affective autonomy is moderately emphasized, and egalitarianism, intellectual autonomy, and harmony receive little cultural emphasis.[20]

Japan represents another exception to the theory. Japan displays an uncommon pattern of cultural elements. The culture strongly emphasizes hierarchy and harmony but not the adjacent embeddedness, and it strongly emphasizes intellectual autonomy but not the adjacent egalitarianism.

Incoherencies are also present among the eight cultural clusters: Because of its secular democracy and Eastern European influence, Turkey is higher on egalitarianism and autonomy and lower on hierarchy and embeddedness than other Middle Eastern Muslim countries.

Because Bolivia and Peru were least exposed to European culture, they display a much higher orientation in hierarchy and embeddedness than other Latin American countries.

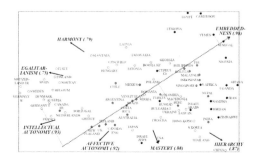

Figure 8. Co-Plot Map of 76 National Groups.

RICHARD LEWIS'S CULTURAL MODEL

According to Richard Lewis (2005), a British linguist, Einstein was wrong; there aren't four dimensions, but five: time, three space dimensions, and culture.

Lewis's cultural model breaks away from the traditional classification system of polar opposites, organizing cultures into three groups, which he called linear-active, multi-active, and reactive.[21]

Figure 9 illustrates different countries along a triangle whose vertexes represent the three cultural norms. Along the sides of the triangle are countries that can be represented as a combination of two different attributes (e.g., India is a combination of reactive and multi-active cultural norms).

Figure 9. Lewis's model of cultural types.

Members of *linear-active* cultures are task oriented, highly organized, and prefer planning, scheduling, and tackling activities based on priorities; they use a sequential approach, doing one thing at a time and favor confrontations based on facts and argumentation.

Germany, Switzerland, the US, Scandinavian countries, Austria, the UK, and South African are examples of linear-active cultures.

Members of *multi-active* cultures are extroverted, talkative, and people oriented. Priorities are not rigid and can change in line with the urgencies of the moment and not according to a fixed schedule. They prefer emotional confrontations based on subjective opinions and passionate argumentation.

Spain, Italy, Latin American countries, African countries, Portugal, and Arab countries are examples of multi-active cultures.

Members of *reactive cultures* are introverted, detached, and discreet. They value politeness and respect, tend to listen quietly before replying carefully, and tend to avoid explicit confrontations.

China, Japan, Vietnam, Korea, and Singapore are examples of linear-active cultures.

According to the cultural model, the world population is about 10% mostly linear-active, 29% mainly reactive, 56% primarily multi-active, and 5% a combination of multi-active and reactive.

THE GLOBE STUDY

In 1993, Robert House, an American professor of organizational studies at Wharton, founded the Global Leadership and Organizational Behavior Effectiveness Research Project (GLOBE), an international assessment of how cultural differences influence leadership behavior and effectiveness.[22]

Based on the results collected from more than 17,000 managers in 62 countries, the GLOBE researchers identified nine cultural dimensions:

Power distance: The extent to which people expect power to be distributed evenly. In high power distance cultures, power provides social order by dividing society into classes, social mobility is limited, and authority roles are circumscribed to only a few people. In low power societies, there is higher social mobility, power sources are temporary and accessible to many, and the social pyramid is flatter.

Uncertainty avoidance: The degree to which people depend on norms, rules, and procedures to reduce the unpredictability of the future. In high uncertainty avoidance societies, social interactions are formal, there is high reliance on rules, policies, and legal contracts, and people tend to keep records of meetings and interactions. In low uncertainty avoidance cultures, interactions are informal, agreements are based on relationships and not on legal bindings, people tend to rely on informal norms of behavior, and they do not feel the need to maintain records of meetings.

Humane orientation: The degree to which people reward fairness, altruism, and generosity. In high humane orientation societies, individuals display a need for belonging and membership, show interest in the needs of others, and value thoughtfulness and generosity. In low human orientation cultures, individuals display a need for power and possessions, value pleasure and leisure, and focus on self-interests.

Institutional collectivism: The degree to which society encourages collective distribution of resources and collective action. In high institutional collectivistic societies, individuals are interdependent with groups, and collective goals take precedence over individual goals. In low institutional collectivistic cultures, individuals are independent and individual goals take precedence over collective goals.

In-group collectivism: The degree to which members of a society convey pride, loyalty, and integration in their organizations and families. In high in-group collectivistic cultures, decisions are made by the group, and organizations take care of the welfare of their employees in exchange for their loyalty (a job for life mind-set). In low in-group collectivistic societies, organizations are mainly concerned about employee performance, and individuals are independent from the group.

Assertiveness: The extent to which people are assertive, argumentative, and aggressive in relationships with others. High assertiveness societies respect aggressive and authoritarian behavior, value direct and explicit communication, and tend to admire strong and competitive individuals. Low assertiveness cultures favor modesty and discretion and respect cooperative and reserved individuals.

Gender egalitarianism: The degree to which gender differences are minimized. In high gender egalitarian societies, women have equal opportunities, hold positions of authority and power, and are highly involved in the workforce at all levels. In low gender egalitarian societies, women have fewer opportunities, and fewer women participate in the workforce and hold positions of authority.

Future orientation: The degree to which people employ future-oriented behaviors such as planning and saving. High future-oriented societies give high priority to economic achievements and tend to delay gratification based on intrinsic motivation. Low future-oriented societies place less emphasis on economic accomplishments and have a predisposition for immediate gratification based on extrinsic motivation.

Performance orientation: The degree to which performance is promoted and compensated. High performance-oriented cultures emphasize tasks over relationships, admire assertive and competitive behavior, and believe that people can control the environment. Low performance-oriented societies emphasize relationships, seniority, and affiliation and believe that people must live in harmony with the environment.

Clusters provide an appropriate way to analyze intercultural differences and similarities and build significant generalizations to develop and test cross-cultural theories.

GLOBE researchers divided the 62 countries into 10 cultural clusters based on:

- Geographic proximity.
- Ethnicity.
- Religious and linguistic commonalities.
- Similarities in social and psychological variables such as values, beliefs, and attitudes.
- Degree of modernity and economic development.
- Degree of socio-political development.

The 10 clusters are:

- *Anglo cultures*: England, Australia, South Africa (white sample), Canada, New Zealand, Ireland, and the US. Anglo countries are high performance-oriented and low in-group collectivistic societies.
- *Latin Europe*: Israel, Italy, Portugal, Spain, France, and Switzerland (French-speaking). Latin European countries are high power distance and low human-oriented and institutional collectivistic societies.
- *Nordic Europe*: Finland, Sweden, and Denmark. Nordic countries are high future-oriented, institutional collectivistic, gender-egalitarian, and uncertainty-avoiding societies with low assertiveness, in-group collectivism, and power distance scores.
- *Germanic Europe*: Austria, Switzerland, the Netherlands, and Germany. Germanic countries are high performance-oriented, assertive, future-oriented, and uncertainty-avoiding societies with low human-orientation and institutional and in-group collectivism scores.

- *Eastern Europe*: Hungary, Russia, Kazakhstan, Albania, Poland, Greece, Slovenia, and Georgia. Eastern European countries are high assertive, in-group collectivistic, and gender-egalitarian societies with low performance- and future-orientation and uncertainty-avoiding scores.

- *Latin America*: Costa Rica, Venezuela, Ecuador, Mexico, El Salvador, Colombia, Guatemala, Bolivia, Brazil, and Argentina. Latin American countries are low-performance and future-oriented, institutional collectivistic, and uncertainty-avoiding societies with a high in-group collectivistic score.

- *Sub-Sahara Africa*: Namibia, Zambia, Zimbabwe, South Africa (black sample), and Nigeria. Sub-Saharan countries are high in-group collectivistic and human-oriented societies with low gender-egalitarianism and relatively low performance-orientation scores.

- *Arab cultures*: Qatar, Morocco, Turkey, Egypt, and Kuwait. Arab countries are high in-group collectivistic and human-oriented societies with low gender-egalitarianism, future-orientation, and uncertainty-avoidance scores.

- *Southern Asia*: India, Indonesia, the Philippines, Malaysia, Thailand, and Iran. Southern Asian countries are high in-group collectivistic and human-oriented societies with low assertiveness and gender-egalitarianism scores.

- *Confucian Asia*: Taiwan, Singapore, Hong Kong, South Korea, China, and Japan. Confucian countries are high performance-oriented, institutional and in-group collectivistic societies with low gender-egalitarianism scores.

On each GLOBE dimension, a society is positioned in terms of both its cultural practices (the current perception of each dimension by a society) and its cultural values (how a society should be, relating to a specific cultural dimension; how a culture should develop in the future, concerning each dimension). The potential range for each dimension is from 1 (lowest) to 7 (highest).[23] [24]

Countries	Assertiveness		Institutional Collectivism		In-Group Collectivism	
	Practices	Values	Practices	Values	Practices	Values
Albania	4,57	4,39	4,28	4,30	5,51	4,98
Argentina	4,18	3,18	3,66	5,29	5,51	6,07
Australia	4,29	3,83	4,31	4,47	4,14	5,82
Austria	4,59	2,85	4,34	4,78	4,89	5,32
Bolivia	3,78	3,68	3,96	5,03	5,44	5,91
Brazil	4,25	3,06	3,94	5,57	5,16	5,17
Canada English speakers	4,09	4,15	4,36	4,20	4,22	5,94
China	3,77	5,52	4,67	4,52	5,86	5,12
Colombia	4,16	3,45	3,84	5,77	5,59	5,99
Costa Rica	3,83	4,04	3,95	5,14	5,26	5,94
Denmark	4,04	3,59	4,93	4,41	3,63	5,71
Ecuador	3,98	3,57	3,82	5,19	5,55	5,81
Egypt	3,91	3,22	4,36	4,72	5,49	5,39
El Salvador	4,49	3,67	3,74	5,60	5,22	6,28
England	4,23	3,76	4,31	4,39	4,08	5,66
Finland	4,05	3,91	4,77	4,34	4,23	5,60
France	4,44	3,57	4,20	5,27	4,66	5,88
Georgia	4,15	4,29	4,03	3,79	6,18	5,58
Germany (former East)	4,77	3,24	3,67	4,86	4,59	5,38
Germany (former West)	4,66	3,21	3,97	5,07	4,16	5,46
Greece	4,55	3,05	3,41	5,41	5,28	5,47
Guatemala	3,96	3,65	3,78	5,16	5,54	5,95
Hong Kong	4,53	4,80	4,03	4,35	5,33	5,11
Hungary	4,71	3,42	3,63	4,57	5,31	5,58
India	3,70	4,65	4,25	4,59	5,81	5,22
Indonesia	3,70	4,50	4,27	4,96	5,50	5,46
Ireland	3,93	4,00	4,57	4,55	5,12	5,72
Israel	4,19	3,74	4,40	4,25	4,63	5,69
Italy	4,12	3,87	3,75	5,20	4,99	5,76
Japan	3,69	5,84	5,23	4,01	4,72	5,44

Table 4. Scores for GLOBE dimensions - A

Countries	Assertiveness		Institutional Collectivism		In-Group Collectivism	
	Practices	Values	Practices	Values	Practices	Values
Kazakhstan	4,51	3,88	4,38	4,16	5,50	5,62
Korea (South)	4,36	3,69	5,20	3,84	5,71	5,50
Kuwait	3,56	3,61	4,32	5,04	5,70	5,32
Malaysia	3,77	4,73	4,45	4,78	5,47	5,77
Mexico	4,31	3,67	3,95	4,77	5,62	5,78
Morocco	4,72	3,68	4,18	5,34	6,37	6,03
Namibia	3,81	3,76	4,02	4,26	4,39	6,13
Netherlands	4,46	3,13	4,62	4,76	3,79	5,39
New Zealand	3,47	3,52	4,96	4,31	3,58	6,54
Nigeria	4,53	3,14	4,00	4,86	5,34	5,31
Philippines	3,85	4,93	4,37	4,55	6,14	5,86
Poland	4,11	3,95	4,51	4,24	5,55	5,69
Portugal	3,75	3,61	4,02	5,40	5,64	5,97
Qatar	4,39	3,72	4,78	5,10	5,07	5,55
Russia	3,86	2,90	4,57	4,01	5,83	5,90
Singapore	4,06	4,28	4,77	4,42	5,66	5,46
Slovenia	4,01	4,61	4,09	4,36	5,49	5,71
South Africa (Black sample)	4,43	3,97	4,47	4,46	5,18	5,14
South Africa (White sample)	4,49	3,65	4,54	4,36	4,42	5,82
Spain	4,39	4,01	3,87	5,25	5,53	5,82
Sweden	3,41	3,49	5,26	3,91	3,46	6,25
Switzerland	4,58	3,31	4,20	4,87	4,04	5,16
Switzerland Freanch Speakers	3,61	3,83	4,31	4,42	3,82	5,54
Taiwan	3,70	2,91	4,30	4,95	5,45	5,30
Thailand	3,58	3,43	3,88	5,08	5,72	5,73
Turkey	4,42	2,68	4,02	5,18	5,79	5,63
United States	4,50	4,36	4,21	4,20	4,22	5,79
Venezuela	4,25	3,34	3,96	5,28	5,41	5,92
Zambia	4,00	4,24	4,41	4,55	5,72	5,64
Zimbabwe	4,04	4,60	4,08	4,84	5,53	5,74

Table 5. Scores for GLOBE dimensions - B

35

Countries	Future Orientation Practices	Values	Gender Egalitarianism Practices	Values	Humane Orientation Practices	Values
Albania	3,69	5,17	3,48	4,04	4,40	5,16
Argentina	3,10	5,73	3,44	4,89	3,94	5,50
Australia	4,09	5,21	3,41	5,02	4,32	5,60
Austria	4,47	5,15	3,18	4,83	3,77	5,68
Bolivia	3,55	5,56	3,45	4,65	3,99	5,11
Brazil	3,90	5,60	3,44	4,91	3,76	5,52
Canada English speakers	4,40	5,34	3,66	5,04	4,51	5,58
China	3,68	4,70	3,03	3,73	4,29	5,34
Colombia	3,35	5,52	3,64	4,85	3,72	5,43
Costa Rica	3,64	5,10	3,56	4,59	4,38	5,08
Denmark	4,59	4,49	4,02	5,20	4,67	5,59
Ecuador	3,66	5,62	3,09	4,42	4,45	5,13
Egypt	3,80	5,60	2,90	3,34	4,60	5,13
El Salvador	3,73	5,89	3,23	4,66	3,69	5,38
England	4,31	5,15	3,67	5,20	3,74	5,52
Finland	4,39	5,24	3,55	4,47	4,19	5,80
France	3,74	5,35	3,81	4,71	3,60	5,91
Georgia	3,45	5,45	3,52	3,83	4,17	5,48
Germany (former East)	4,04	5,36	3,17	4,97	3,45	5,56
Germany (former West)	4,41	5,06	3,25	5,06	3,30	5,63
Greece	3,53	5,17	3,53	4,84	3,44	5,28
Guatemala	3,35	5,78	3,14	4,49	3,91	5,24
Hong Kong	3,88	5,52	3,26	4,27	3,72	5,38
Hungary	3,31	5,74	4,02	4,65	3,39	5,48
India	4,04	5,43	2,89	4,40	4,45	5,20
Indonesia	3,61	5,48	3,04	3,71	4,47	5,06
Ireland	3,93	5,18	3,19	5,07	4,96	5,45
Israel	3,82	5,17	3,21	4,66	4,07	5,51
Italy	3,34	6,01	3,30	4,88	3,66	5,57
Japan	4,29	5,42	3,17	4,41	4,34	5,53

Table 6. Scores for GLOBE dimensions - C

Countries	Future Orientation Practices	Values	Gender Egalitarianism Practices	Values	Humane Orientation Practices	Values
Kazakhstan	3,72	5,22	3,87	4,85	4,44	5,66
Korea (South)	3,90	5,83	2,45	4,23	3,73	5,61
Kuwait	3,18	5,62	2,59	3,50	4,44	5,06
Malaysia	4,39	5,84	3,31	3,72	4,76	5,43
Mexico	3,75	5,74	3,50	4,57	3,84	5,10
Morocco	3,50	6,33	3,08	4,07	4,52	5,73
Namibia	3,32	6,30	3,69	4,20	3,83	5,47
Netherlands	4,72	5,24	3,62	5,10	4,02	5,41
New Zealand	3,46	5,90	3,18	4,32	4,43	4,85
Nigeria	3,95	5,80	3,04	4,16	3,96	5,71
Philippines	3,92	5,66	3,42	4,36	4,88	5,19
Poland	3,21	5,17	3,94	4,53	3,67	5,32
Portugal	3,77	5,50	3,69	5,12	3,96	5,40
Qatar	4,08	5,92	3,86	3,49	4,79	5,31
Russia	3,06	5,60	4,07	4,34	4,04	5,62
Singapore	4,88	5,46	3,52	4,43	3,29	5,66
Slovenia	3,56	5,43	3,84	4,78	3,75	5,31
South Africa (Black sample)	4,66	5,25	3,78	4,43	4,46	5,23
South Africa (White sample)	4,08	5,59	3,25	4,54	3,45	5,53
Spain	3,52	5,66	3,06	4,82	3,29	5,63
Sweden	4,37	4,96	3,72	5,19	4,09	5,72
Switzerland	4,80	4,93	3,12	5,01	3,73	5,63
Switzerland Freanch Speakers	4,36	4,89	3,46	4,77	3,98	5,68
Taiwan	3,65	4,94	2,92	3,88	3,82	5,15
Thailand	3,27	6,26	3,26	4,12	4,87	5,05
Turkey	3,74	5,71	3,02	4,46	3,92	5,40
United States	4,13	5,34	3,36	5,03	4,18	5,51
Venezuela	3,43	5,61	3,60	4,70	4,19	5,24
Zambia	3,55	5,76	2,88	4,27	5,12	5,37
Zimbabwe	3,76	6,01	3,09	4,40	4,38	5,20

Table 7. Scores for GLOBE dimensions - D

Countries	Performance Orientation		Power Distance		Uncertainty Avoidance	
	Practices	Values	Practices	Values	Practices	Values
Albania	4,57	5,47	4,44	3,47	4,45	5,17
Argentina	3,63	6,28	5,56	2,30	3,63	4,62
Australia	4,37	5,99	4,81	2,77	4,40	3,99
Austria	4,47	6,12	5,00	2,52	5,10	3,65
Bolivia	3,57	5,98	4,46	3,31	3,32	4,64
Brazil	4,11	5,98	5,24	2,59	3,74	5,00
Canada English speakers	4,46	6,13	4,85	2,73	4,54	3,73
China	4,37	5,72	5,02	3,01	4,81	5,34
Colombia	3,93	6,15	5,37	2,21	3,62	4,92
Costa Rica	4,10	5,78	4,70	2,66	3,84	4,58
Denmark	4,40	5,82	4,14	2,96	5,32	4,01
Ecuador	4,06	5,95	5,29	2,36	3,63	4,95
Egypt	4,15	5,71	4,76	3,20	3,97	5,24
El Salvador	3,72	6,37	5,56	2,76	3,69	5,27
England	4,16	6,03	5,26	2,82	4,70	4,17
Finland	4,02	6,23	5,08	2,46	5,11	4,04
France	4,43	6,10	5,68	2,96	4,66	4,65
Georgia	3,85	5,63	5,15	2,86	3,54	5,23
Germany (former East)	4,16	6,24	5,70	2,74	5,19	4,02
Germany (former West)	4,42	6,27	5,48	2,66	5,35	3,38
Greece	3,34	5,79	5,35	2,57	3,52	5,16
Guatemala	3,85	5,96	5,47	2,49	3,44	4,85
Hong Kong	4,69	5,71	4,94	3,00	4,17	4,52
Hungary	3,50	5,97	5,57	2,59	3,26	4,74
India	4,11	5,87	5,29	2,58	4,02	4,58
Indonesia	4,14	5,54	4,93	2,38	3,92	5,04
Ireland	4,30	5,99	5,13	2,66	4,25	3,94
Israel	4,03	5,71	4,71	2,72	3,97	4,34
Italy	3,66	6,11	5,45	2,51	3,85	4,52
Japan	4,22	5,37	5,23	2,76	4,07	4,40

Table 8. Scores for GLOBE dimensions - E

Countries	Performance Orientation		Power Distance		Uncertainty Avoidance	
	Practices	Values	Practices	Values	Practices	Values
Kazakhstan	3,72	5,57	5,40	3,19	3,76	4,52
Korea (South)	4,53	5,41	5,69	2,39	3,52	4,74
Kuwait	3,79	5,89	4,97	3,02	4,02	4,65
Malaysia	4,16	5,96	5,09	2,75	4,59	4,81
Mexico	3,97	6,00	5,07	2,75	4,06	5,18
Morocco	4,31	6,12	6,14	3,30	3,95	5,77
Namibia	3,52	6,52	5,29	2,59	4,09	5,19
Netherlands	4,46	5,71	4,32	2,61	4,81	3,34
New Zealand	4,86	6,24	5,12	3,56	4,86	4,17
Nigeria	3,79	5,99	5,32	2,66	4,14	5,45
Philippines	4,21	6,00	5,15	2,54	3,69	4,92
Poland	3,96	6,06	5,09	3,19	3,71	4,75
Portugal	3,65	6,41	5,50	2,45	3,96	4,50
Qatar	3,76	5,94	5,05	3,18	4,26	4,82
Russia	3,53	5,68	5,61	2,73	3,09	5,26
Singapore	4,81	5,70	4,92	2,84	5,16	4,08
Slovenia	3,62	6,41	5,32	2,50	3,76	5,03
South Africa (Black sample)	4,72	5,09	4,31	3,80	4,64	4,92
South Africa (White sample)	4,07	6,13	5,10	2,67	4,06	4,65
Spain	4,00	5,85	5,53	2,23	3,95	4,80
Sweden	3,67	6,01	4,94	2,49	5,36	3,45
Switzerland	5,04	6,00	5,05	2,54	5,42	3,20
Switzerland French Speakers	4,36	6,17	5,00	2,80	5,05	3,84
Taiwan	4,27	5,58	5,00	2,77	4,04	5,14
Thailand	3,84	5,76	5,62	2,74	3,79	5,71
Turkey	3,82	5,34	5,43	2,52	3,67	4,61
United States	4,45	6,14	4,92	2,88	4,15	3,99
Venezuela	3,41	6,11	5,22	2,43	3,55	5,19
Zambia	4,01	6,08	5,23	2,37	3,92	4,45
Zimbabwe	4,20	6,33	5,54	2,65	4,12	4,68

Table 9. Scores for GLOBE dimensions - F

Based on the GLOBE study scores and the main differences between values and practices, we can infer the expected cultural change in a society.

To understand how to decode the GLOBE scores, as we did previously with Hofstede, we'll focus on the 20 major world economies. Because we don't have GLOBE scores for Saudi Arabia (one of the G20 members) or the UK, we include Kuwait and England in the sample.

Argentina is a low institutional collectivistic, future-oriented, performance-oriented, and uncertainty-avoiding society with a high power distance score. The cultural change focus is toward a decrease in power distance and an increase in institutional collectivism and future and performance orientation.

Australia is a low in-group collectivistic and power distance society with a relatively high human-orientation score. The cultural change preference is given to an increase in in-group collectivism and gender egalitarianism.

Brazil is a low institutional collectivistic and uncertainty-avoiding culture. The cultural change focus is toward a decrease in assertiveness and an increase in institutional collectivism and uncertainty avoidance.

Canada is a low in-group collectivistic and power distance society. Canada is also a high future-, human-, and performance-oriented culture with a relatively high uncertainty-avoidance score. The cultural change preference is for an increase in in-group collectivism and a decrease in uncertainty avoidance.

China is a high in-group collectivistic and uncertainty-avoidance society with a low assertiveness score. The cultural change focus is toward a decrease in in-group collectivism and an increase in assertiveness.

England is a very low in-group collectivistic, a relatively low human-oriented, a high future-oriented, and a relatively high uncertainty-avoiding society. The cultural change preference is given to an increase in in-group collectivism.

France is a high gender-egalitarian and power distance society with a relatively high performance-orientation and low human-orientation score. The cultural change focus is toward an increase in in-group collectivism and human orientation.

Germany is a high assertive, future- and performance-oriented, power distance, and uncertainty-avoiding society with low in-group collectivism and human-orientation scores. The cultural change preference is given to a decrease in assertiveness, power distance, and uncertainty avoidance and to an increase in in-group collectivism, gender egalitarianism, and human orientation.

India is a low assertiveness and gender-egalitarian society with high in-group collectivism and human-orientation scores. The cultural change focus is toward an increase in assertiveness and gender egalitarianism and a decrease in in-group collectivism.

Indonesia is a low assertiveness and future-orientation society with a high human-orientation score. The cultural change preference is for an increase in assertiveness and future orientation.

Italy is a low institutional collectivistic, future-, human-, and performance-oriented society with high power distance. The cultural change focus is on an increase in institutional collectivism and future-, human-, and performance-orientation and a decrease in power distance.

Japan is a high institutional collectivistic, future- and human-oriented society with low assertiveness. The cultural change preference is for a decrease in institutional collectivism and an increase in assertiveness.

South Korea is a high institutional and in-group collectivistic, performance-oriented, power distance society with low gender-egalitarianism and uncertainty-avoidance scores. The cultural change focus is toward a decrease in institutional collectivism and power distance and an increase in gender egalitarianism and uncertainty avoidance.

Kuwait is a low assertive, future-oriented, gender-egalitarian, and performance-oriented society. The cultural change preference goes to an increase in future and performance orientation.

Mexico is a low institutional collectivistic and performance-oriented society high in in-group collectivism. The cultural change focus is toward an increase in performance orientation and uncertainty avoidance.

Russia is a high in-group collectivistic, gender-egalitarian, and power distance culture with low future- and performance-orientation and uncertainty-avoidance scores. The cultural change preference is given to an increase in future- and performance-orientation and uncertainty avoidance and a decrease in assertiveness.

South Africa (black sample) is a high future-, human-, and performance-oriented society with relatively high scores in gender egalitarianism and uncertainty avoidance. The GLOBE scores don't present a clear cultural change preference in any dimension.

On the other hand, the South African white sample displays a relatively low humane-orientation and high institutional collectivism score. The cultural change focus is toward an increase in human- and performance-orientation and in-group collectivism.

Spain is a relatively low institutional collectivistic and high in-group collectivistic society with a low human orientation. The cultural change preference is given to an increase in institutional collectivism, future and human orientation, gender egalitarianism, and, most of all, a decrease in power distance.

Turkey is a high in-group collectivist and power distance society. The cultural change focus is on an increase in institutional collectivism and future orientation and a decrease in power distance.

The US is a high assertiveness and performance-oriented and low in-group collectivistic society. The cultural change preference goes to an increase in in-group collectivism and gender egalitarianism and a decrease in power distance.

HOFSTEDE AND GLOBE SCORES

Looking at the numbers, we can see inconsistencies between Hofstede and GLOBE scores for different dimensions.

For example, Argentina is a medium power distance society according to Hofstede and a high power distance culture according to GLOBE. Argentina is also a very high uncertainty-avoiding country according to Hofstede, while according to GLOBE the score is low, and the cultural change focus is toward only a moderate increase in uncertainty avoidance.

Another example of contradictions between Hofstede and GLOBE is Germany, specifically in the power distance dimension: According to Hofstede, Germany is a low power distance country, while the GLOBE score in the power distance dimension is very high.

The following reasons can help explain some of the discrepancies:

- As in all cultural dimension models, neither theory takes into account cultural heterogeneity within the basic unit of analysis, the nation.
- The theories overlook cultural change over time.
- Hofstede's database of more than 117,000 questionnaires is based on a single company with a very strong organizational culture across the globe. GLOBE's research is based on different organizations in different countries.
- In some countries, the number of respondents was very small for both studies.
- The different meaning of the questions in different cultures and the respondents' foreknowledge of the purpose of the study could alter the authenticity of the answers.
- All theories tend to oversimplify a very complex phenomenon, that is, culture.

THE CULTURAL ORIENTATION MODEL

The Cultural Orientation Model™ is a framework that attempts to identify important social features and basic social orientations of different national cultures.[37]

The model endeavors to integrate and adapt the dimensions presented in the previous models, and the result is a 10-dimension framework.

The first dimension is *environment* (analogous to Trompenaars' sixth dimension): How do individuals relate to the context and the environment? They can employ the following three approaches:

- *Control*: Members of control-oriented societies believe that they can constraint and shape the environment to reach their own objectives. Planning is a fundamental skill.
- *Harmony*: Members of harmony-oriented societies believe that they need to adapt to the environment, finding a balance with it.
- *Constraint*: Members of constraint-oriented societies believe that the environment defines the boundaries of action. We cannot change what we cannot control. Because people learn to react quickly to external forces, planning is not a required skill.

The second dimension is *time* (analogous to Trompenaars's seventh dimension and Hall's time dimension): How do individuals perceive and manage time? The time dimension has three sub-dimensions:

Time management:

- *Single-focused*: Individuals of single-focused societies tackle one task at a time, assigning priorities to the different tasks and accurately planning their activities.
- *Multi-focused*: Individuals in multi-focused societies tackle multiple tasks simultaneously. Priorities and schedules are flexible.

Time perception:

- *Fixed*: Time is rigid and schedules cannot be amended. Deadlines and priorities are firm.
- *Fluid*: Time is flexible and personal relationships take precedence over tasks. Deadlines and priorities are elastic.

Time outlook:

- *Past*: Past-oriented societies place high value on history, as well as pre-established processes and procedures.
- *Present*: Present-oriented societies focus on short-term results. Implementation is more important than planning.
- *Future*: Future-oriented societies focus on long-term results. Preparation and organization are fundamental skills for members of these societies.

The third dimension is *action*: Where do individuals put more emphasis, actions or interactions?

- *Being* cultures emphasize relationships, reflection, and assessment.
- *Doing* cultures emphasize implementation and tasks.

The fourth dimension is *communication* (analogous to Hall's communication dimension): How do individuals express themselves? The communication dimension is composed of four sub-dimensions:

Communication context:

- *High context*: Members of high-context societies emphasize implicit communication based on shared assumptions, as well as verbal, nonverbal, and paraverbal hints.
- *Low context*: Members of low-context societies emphasize explicit communication with clear, frank, and unambiguous expressions.

Conflict handling:

- *Direct*: Members of direct societies see conflict as positive and tend to handle conflict in a straightforward and explicit manner.
- *Indirect*: Members of indirect societies try to preserve harmony, avoiding explicit divergences, and tend to handle conflict implicitly and indirectly or through third parties.

Emotional display (comparable to Trompenaars's fourth dimension, neutral vs. affective):

- *Expressive*: Expressive societies display emotions and feelings passionately.
- *Instrumental*: Instrumental societies refrain from displaying emotions, concealing body language and facial expressions.

Abiding protocol:

- *Formal*: In formal societies, there is a strong emphasis on protocol, etiquette, and conventions. Members of these societies follow a rigid code of behavior that usually includes deference to hierarchy and respect for elders.
- *Informal*: In informal societies, the emphasis on protocol is very low and there is no rigid code of behavior to follow. Deference to hierarchy and elders is limited.

The fifth dimension is *space* (analogous to Hall's space dimension): How do individuals define their physical and psychological space?

- *Public*: Members of public societies value loose boundaries and little distance between people. Access to people is free and open.
- *Private*: Members of private societies value clear demarcation and respect for boundaries. Access to people is controlled and restricted.

The sixth dimension is *power* (analogous to Hofstede's power distance and Trompenaars's achievement vs. ascription dimension): How do individuals perceive differential power relationships?

- *Hierarchy*: Members of hierarchical societies accept high levels of power relationship disparity and a high degree of social stratification.
- *Equality*: Members of equal societies show little acceptance for high degrees of power relationship disparity and a high level of social stratification.

The seventh dimension is *individualism* (a dimension present in all previous frameworks, except for Hall's): How do individuals define their identity? The individualism dimension is made of two sub-dimensions:

Balance between *individual and group interests*:

- *Individualistic*: Members of individualistic societies emphasize independence and individual accomplishments and interests over group necessities.
- *Collectivistic*: Members of collectivistic societies place group interests and requirements before individual interests and requirements. The focus is on group prosperity and welfare.

Balance between *rules and relationships*:

- *Universalistic*: Members of universalistic cultures give precedence to rules and laws over relationships.
- *Particularistic*: Members of particularistic cultures believe that laws and rules can be bypassed to benefit important relationships.

The eighth dimension is *competitiveness* (comparable to a certain extent to Hofstede's masculinity dimension): How are individuals motivated?

- *Competitive*: In competitive societies, the focus is on personal achievements and realizations.
- *Cooperative*: In cooperative societies, the focus is on relationships, family, quality of life, and work-leisure balance.

The ninth dimension is *structure* (comparable to a certain extent to Hofstede's uncertainty avoidance): How do individuals deal with change, risk, ambiguity, and uncertainty?

- *Order*: Order-oriented societies emphasize the observance of rules, processes, and procedures. There is a tendency toward risk aversion, planning, and monitoring. Out-of-the-box thinking is not valued. Decision-making processes tend to be slow, complex, and bureaucratic.
- *Flexibility*: Flexibility-oriented societies value creativity and improvisation. There is a tendency toward risk taking and the decision-making process is fast and straightforward.

The tenth dimension is *thinking* (a dimension that is not present in any previous framework; this dimension is the real innovation of the Cultural Orientation Model): How do individuals conceptualize? The thinking dimension is made of two sub-dimensions:

Approach to thinking (Fig. 10).

- *Deductive*: Members of deductive cultures use a top-down approach, placing emphasis on theory, that generates hypotheses and principles that are finally confirmed through observations. Deductive thinking is driven by abstract logic.

- *Inductive*: Members of inductive societies use a bottom-up approach, placing emphasis on data collection that leads to patterns. These patterns generate tentative hypotheses that if confirmed become theory. Inductive thinking is based on observation.

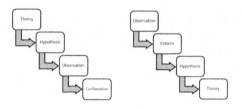

Figure 10. Deductive and inductive thinking.

Approach to Problem Solving.

- *Linear*: Members of linear cultures adopt an analytical approach to problem solving, emphasizing a sequential and methodical step-by-step progression through segmentation of issues and cause-and-effect relationships. The focus is on repeatability and efficiency.

- *Systemic*: Members of systemic cultures adopt a holistic approach to solving problems, emphasizing the relationship among parts and how each component affects the others and the system. The focus is on the big picture and on the connections and interactions among the different elements of the system.

The 20 major world economies according to the COI framework can be depicted as follows:

The 4 Ps Framework

		Country			
		China	France	Germany	India
	Environment	Harmony	Constraint	Control	Harmony
	Time	Multi-Focus	Single-Focus	Single-Focus	Multi-Focus
		Fluid	Fluid	Fixed	Fluid
		Past	Past	Future	Present
	Action	Being	Being	Doing	Being
	Communication	High Context	High Context	Low Context	High Context
		Indirect	Indirect	Direct	Indirect
		Instrumental	Expressive	Instrumental	Expressive
		Formal	Formal	Formal	Formal
	Space	Private	Private	Private	Public
	Power	Hierarchy	Hierarchy	Equality	Hierarchy
	Individualism	Collectivistic	Individualistic	Individualistic	Collectivistic
			Universalistic	Universalistic	Universalistic
	Competitiveness	Competitive	Competitive	Competitive	Cooperative
	Structure	Order	Order	Order	Order
	Thinking	Inductive	Deductive	Inductive	Inductive
		Systemic	Linear	Linear	Linear

(Left margin label: Cultural Dimensions)

		Country			
		China	France	Germany	India
	Environment	Harmony	Constraint	Control	Harmony
	Time	Multi-Focus	Single-Focus	Single-Focus	Multi-Focus
		Fluid	Fluid	Fixed	Fluid
		Past	Past	Future	Present
	Action	Being	Being	Doing	Being
	Communication	High Context	High Context	Low Context	High Context
		Indirect	Indirect	Direct	Indirect
		Instrumental	Expressive	Instrumental	Expressive
		Formal	Formal	Formal	Formal
	Space	Private	Private	Private	Public
	Power	Hierarchy	Hierarchy	Equality	Hierarchy
	Individualism	Collectivistic	Individualistic	Individualistic	Collectivistic
			Universalistic	Universalistic	Universalistic
	Competitiveness	Competitive	Competitive	Competitive	Cooperative
	Structure	Order	Order	Order	Order
	Thinking	Inductive	Deductive	Inductive	Inductive
		Systemic	Linear	Linear	Linear

(Left margin label: Cultural Dimensions)

Table 10, 11. Cultural Orientation Indicator – A, B

		Country		
	Indonesia	**Italy**	**Japan**	**Mexico**
Environment	Harmony	Control / Constraint	Harmony	Harmony
Time	Single-Focus	Multi-Focus	Single-Focus	Multi-Focus
	Fluid	Fluid	Fluid	Fluid
	Present	Past / Present	Present	Past
Action	Being	Being	Being	Being
Communication	High Context	High Context	High Context	High Context
	Indirect	Indirect	Indirect	Indirect
	Expressive	Expressive	Instrumental	Expressive
	Formal	Formal	Formal	Formal
Space	Public	Public	Public	Private
Power	Hierarchy	Hierarchy	Hierarchy	Hierarchy
Individualism	Collectivistic	Individ / Collect	Collectivistic	Individualistic
	Particularistic	Particularistic	Particularistic	Particularistic
Competitiveness	Cooperative	Compet. / Cooperat.	Cooperative	Cooperative
Structure	Order	Flexibility	Order	Flexibility
Thinking	Inductive	Deductive	Inductive	Deductive
	Linear	Systemic	Linear / Systemic	Systemic

		Country		
	Russia	**Saudi Arabia**	**South Africa**	**South Korea**
Environment	Constraint	Control / Constraint	Control / Constraint	Harmony / Const.
Time	Multi-Focus	Multi-Focus	Multi-Focus	Multi-Focus
	Fixed / Fluid	Fluid	Fixed / Fluid	Fluid
	Present	Past / Future	Past / Present	Present
Action	Being	Being	Being	Being
Communication	Low Context	High Context	High Context	High Context
	Direct	Indirect	Indirect	Indirect
	Instrumental	Expressive	Expressive	Expressive
	Formal	Formal	Instrument. / Formal	Formal
Space	Private	Private / Public	Public	Public
Power	Hierarchy	Hierarchy	Hierarchy	Hierarchy
Individualism	Individualistic	Collectivistic	Individualistic	Collectivistic
	Particularistic	Particularistic	Univers / Particul	Universalistic
Competitiveness	Competitive	Compet / Cooperat	Competitive	Cooperative
Structure	Order / Flexibility	Order	Order	Order
Thinking	Deductive	Deductive	Inductive	Deductive
	Systemic	Systemic	Linear	Linear / Systemic

Table 12, 13. Cultural Orientation Indicator – C, D

		Country			
		Spain	Turkey	UK	USA
	Environment	Harmony / Constraint	Harmony	Harmony	Control
	Time	Multi-Focus	Multi-Focus	Single-Focus	Single-Focus
		Fluid	Fluid	Fixed	Fixed
		Present	Present	Present	Present
	Action	Being	Being	Doing	Doing
	Communication	High Context	High Context	High Context	Low Context
		Indirect	Indirect	Indirect	Direct
		Expressive	Expressive	Instrumental	Instrumental
		Informal	Formal	Formal	Formal
	Space	Public	Public	Private	Private
	Power	Hierarchy	Hierarchy	Hierarchy	Equality
	Individualism	Individualistic	Individ / Collect	Individualistic	Individualistic
		Particularistic	Particularistic	Universalistic	Universalistic
	Competitiveness	Competitive	Compet / Cooperat.	Competitive	Competitive
	Structure	Order	Flexibility	Order	Flexibility
	Thinking	Deductive	Inductive	Inductive	Inductive
		Systemic	Systemic	Linear	Linear

Table 14. Cultural Orientation Indicator - E

THE ROLE OF RELIGION IN SHAPING CULTURE

Even if religion, culture, and human behavior are indissolubly intertwined, the relationship between religion and culture is not explicitly apparent in most of the cultural dimension models presented in the previous paragraphs.[38]

Because religion shapes values, and values are the foundation of culture, it is essential to understand the role of religion in shaping culture. Furthermore, and most relevant for us, religion influences relationships among individuals, families, societies, and organizations.

Human existential needs contribute to religious faith.

Religions provides people with meaningful framework to understand the world, existential comfort against the idea of death, motives to justify social differences, and provide an answer to human need for belonging and affiliation creating communities that share the same faith.[39]

The five largest religious groups that account for around 5 billion people are Christianity, Islam, Buddhism, Hinduism, and Chinese folk religion.

The main religions can be divided in three broad categories:

• *Abrahamic religions*, which include all the main monotheistic religions, Christianity, Judaism, and Islam, that trace their origin to the patriarch Abraham.

• *Indian religions*, which include religions that were founded in the Indian subcontinent, such as Hinduism, Buddhism, Sikhism, and Jainism.

• *Folk religions*, which include a broad category of traditional religions that are closely associated with a particular ethnic group or tribe. Among these religions are Confucianism and Taoism in China.

CHRISTIANITY

Christianity began as a Jewish faction in the mid-first century, becoming the official religion of the Roman Empire by the end of the fourth century. Christianity has played a leading role in shaping Western culture and society. Since the decline of the Roman Empire, Christianity has been the only integrating and consistent element in Europe. Christianity has had a substantial influence on philosophy, art, literature, education, politics, science, and medicine. The institution of universities has its origin in the medieval period, when the Church founded the first academies. Christianity also guided the introduction of social welfare and the establishment of hospitals and shaped the role of families in society.

The Roman Empire remains a unifying element of Western Europe, integrating through a common language and the common religion of Christianity all of Europe south of the Rhine River.

Christians are split into many groups, among which the largest are the Catholics, the Orthodox, and the Protestants.

Catholicism

The Roman Catholic Church has its origins in the Christian community started by Jesus Christ and is structured around the concept of papal supremacy: The Pope, successor of the Apostles, is the Church's highest authority in matters of faith and morality.

The Catholic doctrine has always been strongly opposed to the capitalist economic principles based on both moral and religious grounds. According to theologian Thomas Aquinas, profit making was irreconcilable with Christianity. Even a recent Pope, John-Paul II, strongly affirmed his objections to a market economy.

From the end of the fifteenth century, Spanish and Portuguese empires imposed their Romance languages (derived from Latin) and Catholicism in their colonies in Central and South America, Africa, and Asia.

Today, there are around 880 million Catholics in the world (57% of all Christians), living mainly in South America, Europe, and Africa.

Protestantism

During the Reformation of the sixteenth century, the churches in Northern Europe protested and broke away from the Roman Catholic Church.

The creeds of the more than 30,000 Protestant denominations differ in many ways, but conform to four main principles:

- Denial of the universal authority of the pope (separation between church and state).
- Justification by faith alone (sola fide).
- Priesthood of all believers.
- The primacy of the Bible as the supreme authority in matters of faith and morals (sola scriptura).

Protestantism strongly enhanced education at all levels, founding, for example, many of the main US universities during the eighteenth century, and furthered the development of the humanities and the sciences.

The Protestant moral code, based on hard work, thrift, discipline, and a strong sense of responsibility, was the pillar of the development of capitalism and the Industrial Revolution.

It must be emphasized that Protestantism started and spread first in countries that were not ruled by the Roman Empire (the Roman Empire at its maximum extent covered all of Western Europe, stopping at the Danube and the Rhine).

The British Empire, incorporating more than a quarter of the human race, was the means through which Protestantism in all its forms prevailed in the New World. India always remained an exception in the British Empire because of its populous and ancient civilization.

Today, there are more than 360 million Protestants (including Anglicans) in the world, representing 22% of all Christians and living mainly in North America and Europe.

Orthodoxy

A number of conflicts within the Roman Catholic Church led to the Great Schism in 1054, separating Orthodox Christianity from the Roman Catholic Church.

Orthodox Christianity, which originated in the old Byzantine Empire, is a collective term for the Eastern Orthodox Church and Oriental Orthodoxy. The two groups split over disagreements about the nature of Christ but they retained similar doctrines, similar Church structures, and similar worship practices. Unlike the Catholic Church, both the Eastern Orthodox Church and Oriental Orthodoxy are organized according to a federal structure, without central leadership. All bishops are considered to be sacramentally equal, with the same spiritual authority.

Also, Orthodox Christianity, like Catholicism, holds a negative standpoint toward a capital economy and wealth accumulation.

Today, there are more than 130 million Orthodox Christians, representing 8% of all Christians and living mainly in Russia, Romania, and Greece.

JUDAISM

Judaism is the oldest Abrahamic religion, originating in the people of ancient Israel and Judea. Judaism is based primarily on the Torah, a text that some Jews believe was handed down to the people of Israel through the prophet Moses. This along with the rest of the Hebrew Bible and the Talmud are the central texts of Judaism. The Jewish people were scattered after the destruction of the Temple in Jerusalem in 70 CE. Today, there are around 14 million Jews, 40% of them living in Israel and 40% in the United States.

It is not easy to categorize Judaism into conventional Western groups such as religion, ethnicity, and culture.[40] Judaism has its origins in the Levant and has been strongly influenced by ancient Egyptian, Babylonian, Persian, and Hellenic cultures.

Judaism believes that God is concerned with the actions of humanity and demands Jewish people to reciprocate God's concern for the world. According to the Hebrew Bible, God promised Abraham to give his descendants a great nation.

Today, many variations exist within Judaism, even if all are based on the principles of the Hebrew Bible.

In an era of strong anti-Semitism in many Arab and Muslim countries, it is worth emphasizing that the relationship between Judaism and Islam is distinctive and close. Muslims view Jews as people of the book, while Jews view Muslims as people observing the Seven Laws of Noah. In many elements, Islam's core principles are based on Judaism, and Jews view Muslims as virtuous people of God.

ISLAM

Islam is a monotheistic and Abrahamic religion based on the Qur'an (the book that contains the word of God) and, on the teachings of the Prophet Muhammad (Hadith). With approximately 1.57 billion followers, Islam is the second-largest and one of the fastest-growing religions in the world.

Islam believes that the purpose of every Muslim is to love and serve the only God. Muslims also believe that Islam is the complete and inclusive revelation of God, while previous teachings and revelations by prophets such as Abraham, Moses, and Jesus have been altered or misinterpreted over time.

The Pillars of Islam are five basic and mandatory practices for all Muslims. They form the basic creed of Islam:

• Recitation under oath (*shahadah*).
• Five ritual daily prayers (*salat*).
• Religious compulsory charity (*zakah*).
• Fasting during Ramadan (*sawm*).
• Pilgrimage to Mecca at least once in a lifetime (*hajj*).

Another important aspect of Islam is Islamic law, Shariah law, which affects all aspects of life and society from governance to banking and welfare, from inheritance and marriage to rules for fasting, charity, and prayer.

There are two major denominations in Islam: Sunni Islam, which encompasses around 75% to 90% of all Muslims and Shia Islam. Sunnis believe that Muhammad did not appoint a successor and therefore consider that any righteous and just person acting consistent with the Qur'an and the Hadith can be elected as Caliph. Shias believe that during Muhammad's final pilgrimage to Mecca, he appointed his son-in-law as his successor; therefore only members of Muhammad's family and their heirs can be appointed Caliphs.

Islam and the shared high-context language (Arabic) are the unifying elements of the Arab world.

It must be emphasized that while most Arabs are Muslims (although with some significant Christian minorities), not all Muslims are Arabs: Iran is predominantly Persian, 75% of the population in Turkey is ethnic Turk, until 1947 Pakistan was part of India (Indo-Aryan ethnicity), and Indonesians are mostly Pribumi.

HINDUISM

Hinduism has around 700 million followers, mainly living in India. A distinctive feature of Hinduism is that it allows for total freedom of belief and worship. A second distinguishing element of Hinduism is the complex concept of God, which depends on each individual and the tradition and philosophy abided by; the Rig Veda, the oldest scripture in Hinduism, retains a free view on the concept of God, allowing each individual to seek his or her own answers to the central questions of God and the universe.

Unlike other religions in the World, the Hindu religion does not claim any one Prophet, it does not worship any one God, it does not have a single holy book, it does not believe in any one philosophic concept, it does not follow any one act of religious rites or performances; in fact, it does not satisfy the traditional features of a religion or creed. *It is a way of life and nothing more.*[41]

The aim of all Hindus (*moksha*) is freedom from *samsara*, the continuing cycle of birth, life, death, and rebirth, and union with God.

Other central concepts of Hinduism are:

- *Dharma* defines those behaviors considered necessary for maintenance of the natural order of things, and therefore considered morally correct.
- *Karma* is the concept of action that produces the entire cycle of cause and effect (samsara).
- *Yogas* are the different paths to reach one's goals in life. Each individual can have different purposes, such as living an honest life, pursuing wealth, engaging in sensual pleasure, or aiming at freedom from samsara.

The Caste System

The caste system has its origins in the thousands of loose hereditary groups referred to family profession, called Jatis. An individual's *Jati* was her identity and her support system. The Brahminical texts grouped these Jatis into four caste groups: *Brahmins* (priests and scholars), *Kshatriyas* (kings and warriors), *Vaishyas* (agriculturists, artisans, and merchants), and *Shudras* (laborers and service providers). Certain people were left out and banished by all other castes (the *Untouchables*).

Caste is usually identified with Hinduism, but many scholars have claimed that the caste system as it exists today was created by the British regime as a way to organize and administer the complex Indian subcontinent made of 500,000 villages and a population of more than 200 million people.

According to these scholars, before colonialism, affiliation with groups was more open and less rigid, even if still based on virtue of birth. Only under the British was a strict hierarchy enforced, dividing the society into rigid castes.

Today, in the villages, caste still determines marriage, rituals regarding birth and death, and profession. In large cities, although the traditional caste conventions of the villages cannot be strictly followed at work, people still tend to respect traditional caste rituals and rules in their private time.[42]

BUDDHISM

Buddhism is an Indian indigenous religion based on teachings accredited to Siddhartha Gautama (the Buddha), who lived and taught in the eastern part of the Indian subcontinent around the fifth century BC. Today, there are between 350 million and 500 million Buddhists in the world.

The main Buddhist concepts are in some ways inherited from or similar to Hinduism:

- *Samsara*, the repetitive cycle of birth, death, and rebirth and the associated suffering and frustration (*dukkha*).

- *Karma*, the force that drives samsara; a person's actions determining his or her destiny.
- *Nirvana*, the ultimate goal of all Buddhists, the liberation from suffering and samsara, overcoming the human primary misperception of reality and ignorance.
- *Anicca*, the notion that all things and experiences are in constant fluctuation. Because things are transient, attachment to them leads to suffering. Existence is perceived as a chain of interconnected transitory events that occur in a series.
- *Karuna*, the concept that because people's actions are led by fear, they should not be condemned. Our role is to understand what are the reasons behind the fear underlying their actions.

Another important guiding principle of Buddhism is the *Middle Way*, the practice of non-extremism, the search for the middle ground and the reconciliation of opposites.

CONFUCIANISM

Confucianism is an ethical and philosophical system developed from the teachings of the Chinese philosopher Confucius, who lived around 500 BC.

At the core of Confucianism is the promotion of virtues. Among them, we can find:

- *Ren*: A responsibility for altruism, the ideal of how each individual should treat other people.
- *Li*: An abstract idea that can be translated as etiquette and rules of appropriate behavior.
- *Zhong*: Loyalty to one's social role, doing what one is supposed to do.
- *Xiao*: Obedience, care, and respect for parents, elder family members, and ancestors.

The ultimate purpose of Confucianism is social harmony: Every individual should know his or her place in the social order and play the appropriate role. Every individual is at the center of different relationships with different people: son, brother, husband. Specific duties are specified for each participant in the five bonds of Confucianism:

Ruler to ruled, father to son, husband to wife, elder to younger brother, and friend to friend.[43]

Confucius was one of the first advocates of meritocracy: Written government examinations provided the opportunity for anyone to become a government officer. According to some scholars, *Confucius replaced nobility of blood with nobility of integrity and knowledge.*

TAOISM

Taoism is a philosophical and religious tradition that emphasizes living in harmony with the Tao, which means the way, path, or principle, according to the teachings attributed to Chinese philosophers Laozi and Zhuangzi.

Taoist principles are based on the following ethical concepts:

- *Wu-wei*: Action through non-action. Each individual must exert his or her will in harmony with the natural universe.
- *Ziran*: The primordial state associated with spontaneity and simplicity, free from egocentricity.
- *The three treasures*: Compassion, moderation, and humility.

Yin and Yang

Yin and yang describe the dynamic system of opposite and complementary forces that constantly act against and with each other to form a whole greater than either separate part. The concept defines many natural dichotomies: light and dark, fire and water, life and death.

The Chinese view of paradox as independent opposites, compared with the conventional Western view of contradiction as exclusive opposites, is exemplified by the yin and yang symbol (Fig. 11): a circle divided into two equal halves by a curvy line, one side of which is black (yin) and the other white (yang). Yin represents female energy, such as the moon, night, weakness, darkness, softness, and femininity; yang stands for male energy, such as the sun, day, strength, brightness, hardness, and masculinity. The white dot in the black area and the black dot in the white area connote the coexistence and unity of the opposites in forming the whole. The curvy line signifies that there are no absolute separations between opposites. The yin yang principle embodies duality, paradox, unity in diversity, change, and harmony, offering a holistic approach to problem solving.

Figure 11 - Yin & Yang symbol

CONCLUSIONS

As we have seen, religion, culture, and human behavior are intimately interconnected. For example:

- Individualism in Northern Europe, North America, Australia, and New Zealand has been strongly influenced by the Protestant ethic that laid responsibility for conduct and after-life recompenses on the individual's self-restraint, hard work, and dedication.
- The hierarchical Hindu pantheon of Gods can help explain the Indian social structure and its high power distance score.
- The Confucian ethic, based on mutual dependability and duties in a stable social order, can clarify the importance of social networks and the family orientation of businesses in China.
- Christian cultures, particularly Protestant cultures, view life as the only chance for realization, while the concept of samsara shared by Indian religions, such as Hinduism and Buddhism, allows for a more casual view of time and personal success.
- The one life concept can also explain why in Protestant countries planning, scheduling, and controlling become fundamental skills for managing and organizing time. At the same time, Islam's respect for the will of Allah, and a sense of fatalism, can help clarify the relatively low interest in planning among some Arabs.
- The yin and yang concept can explain the Chinese attitude toward dialectic and integrative thinking.
- The complex and at the same time unrestricted concept of God in Hinduism can account for the Indian flexible approach toward uncertainty and time.

(ENDNOTES)

1   Sioux prayer, as quoted by Jane Elliott in A Class Divided, PBS Frontline, Retrieved from http://www.pbs.org/wgbh/pages/frontline/shows/divided/

2   Piller, I. (2007). Linguistics and Intercultural Communication. Language and Linguistic Compass, Vol. 1, N. 3, 208-226.

3   Williams Jr., R. M. (1970). American society: A sociological interpretation (3rd ed.). New York, NY: Knopf.

4   Schwartz, S. H. (1999). A theory of Cultural Values and Some Implications for Work. Applied Psychology: An International Review, Vol. 48, N. 1, 23-47.

5   Katz, D., & Kahn, R. (1978). The social psychology of organizations (2nd ed.). New York, NY: Wiley.

6   Schneider, S. C., & Barsoux, J. L. (1997). Managing across cultures. London, UK: Prentice Hall.

7   Salacuse, J. W. (2010). Teaching international business negotiation: Reflections on three decades of experience. International Negotiation, 15, 187-228.

8   Nardon, L., & Steers, R. M. (2009). The culture theory jungle: divergence and convergence in models of national culture. In R. S. Bhagat, & R. M., Steers (Eds.), Cambridge Handbook of Culture, Organizations, and Work. New York: Cambridge University Press.

9   Kluckhohn, F. R., & Strodtbeck, F. L. (1961). Variations in Value Orientations. Evanston, IL: Row, Peterson & Company.

10 Hills, M. D. (2002). Kluckhohn and Strodtbeck's Values Orientation Theory. Online Readings in Psychology and Culture, Unit 4. Retrieved from http://scholarworks.gvsu.edu/orpc/vol4/iss4/3

11 Hofstede, G. (2001). Culture's consequences: Comparing values, behaviors, institutions and organizations across nations (2nd ed.). Thousand Oaks, CA: Sage.

12 Hofstede, G., Hofstede, G. J., & Minkov, M. (2010). Culture and organizations: Software of the mind (3rd ed.). New York, NY: McGraw-Hill.

13 Source: Geert Hofstede. Retrieved from: http://www.geerthofstede.nl/dimension-data-matrix

14 Hall, E. (1973). The silent language. New York, NY: Anchor Books.

15 Hall, E. (1982). The hidden dimension. New York, NY: Anchor Books.

16 Hall, E. (1984). The dance of life: The other dimension of time. New York, NY: Anchor Books.

17 Hampden-Turner, C., & Trompenaars, F. (1997). Riding the Waves of Culture: Understanding Diversity in Global Business. (2nd ed.). New York: McGraw-Hill.

18 Schwartz, S. H. (1999). A theory of Cultural Values and Some Implications for Work. Applied Psychology: An International Review, Vol. 48, N. 1, 23-47.

19 Schwartz, S. (2004). Mapping and Interpreting Cultural Differences around the World. In H. Vinken, J. Soeters, & P. Ester (Eds.), Comparing Cultures, Dimensions of Culture in a Comparative Perspective. Leiden, the Netherlands: Brill.

20 Schwartz, S. H. (2006). A Theory of Cultural Value Orientations: Explication and Applications. Comparative Sociology, Vol.5, N. 2-3, 137-182.

21 Lewis, R. D. (2005). When cultures collide (3rd ed.). London, UK: Nicholas Brealey Publishing.

22 House, R. J., Hanges, P. J., Javidan, M., Dorfman, P. W., & Gupta, V. (Eds.). (2004). Culture, leadership, and organizations: The GLOBE Study of 62 Societies. Thousand Oaks, CA: Sage.

23 Javidan, M., Dorfman, P. W., Sully de Luque, M., & House, R. J. (2006). In the eye of the beholder: Cross Cultural lessons in leadership from project GLOBE. Academy of Management Perspectives, February, 67-90.

24 House, R. J., Hanges, P., Javidan, M., Dorfman, P., & Gupta, V. (2002). Leadership and Cultures Around the World: Findings from GLOBE. Journal of World Business, Vol. 37, N. 1, 3-10

25 Javidan, M., Dorfman, P. W., Sully de Luque, M., & House, R. J. (2006). In the eye of the beholder: Cross Cultural lessons in leadership from project GLOBE. Academy of Management Perspectives, February, 67-90.

26   House, R. J., Hanges, P., Javidan, M., Dorfman, P., & Gupta, V. (2002). Leadership and Cultures
      Around the World: Findings from GLOBE. Journal of World Business, Vol. 37, N. 1, 3-10.

27   Javidan, M., Dorfman, P. W., Sully de Luque, M., & House, R. J. (2006). In the eye of the beholder:
      Cross Cultural lessons in leadership from project GLOBE. Academy of Management Perspectives,
      February, 67-90.

28   House, R. J., Hanges, P., Javidan, M., Dorfman, P., & Gupta, V. (2002). Leadership and Cultures
      Around the World: Findings from GLOBE. Journal of World Business, Vol. 37, N. 1, 3-10.

29   Javidan, M., Dorfman, P. W., Sully de Luque, M., & House, R. J. (2006). In the eye of the beholder:
      Cross Cultural lessons in leadership from project GLOBE. Academy of Management Perspectives,
      February, 67-90.

30   House, R. J., Hanges, P., Javidan, M., Dorfman, P., & Gupta, V. (2002). Leadership and Cultures
      Around the World: Findings from GLOBE. Journal of World Business, Vol. 37, N. 1, 3-10.

31   Javidan, M., Dorfman, P. W., Sully de Luque, M., & House, R. J. (2006). In the eye of the beholder:
      Cross Cultural lessons in leadership from project GLOBE. Academy of Management Perspectives,
      February, 67-90.

32   House, R. J., Hanges, P., Javidan, M., Dorfman, P., & Gupta, V. (2002). Leadership and Cultures
      Around the World: Findings from GLOBE. Journal of World Business, Vol. 37, N. 1, 3-10.

33   Javidan, M., Dorfman, P. W., Sully de Luque, M., & House, R. J. (2006). In the eye of the beholder:
      Cross Cultural lessons in leadership from project GLOBE. Academy of Management Perspectives,
      February, 67-90.

34   House, R. J., Hanges, P., Javidan, M., Dorfman, P., & Gupta, V. (2002). Leadership and Cultures
      Around the World: Findings from GLOBE. Journal of World Business, Vol. 37, N. 1, 3-10.

35   Javidan, M., Dorfman, P. W., Sully de Luque, M., & House, R. J. (2006). In the eye of the beholder:
      Cross Cultural lessons in leadership from project GLOBE. Academy of Management Perspectives,
      February, 67-90.

36   House, R. J., Hanges, P., Javidan, M., Dorfman, P., & Gupta, V. (2002). Leadership and Cultures
      Around the World: Findings from GLOBE. Journal of World Business, Vol. 37, N. 1, 3-10.

37   Medina Walker, D., Walker, T., & Schmitz, J. (2002). Doing business internationally (2nd ed.). New
      York, NY: McGraw-Hill.

38   Tarakeshwar, N., Stanton, J., & Pargament, K. I. (2003). Religion: An overlooked dimension in
      cross-cultural psychology. Journal of Cross-Cultural Psychology, Vol. 34, N. 4, 377-394.

39   Uhlmann, E. L., Poehlman, A., & Bargh, J. A. (2008). Implicit Theism. In R. Sorrentino, & S.
      Yamaguchi (Eds.), Handbook of Motivation and Cognition Across Cultures. San Diego: Academic
      Press.

40   Boyarin, D., & Boyarin, J. (2002). Powers of Diaspora: Two Essays on the Relevance of Jewish
      Culture. Minneapolis, MN: University of Minnesota Press.

41   Klostermaier, K. K. (2007). A survey of Hinduism (3rd ed.). Albany, NY: Suny Press.

42   Jensen, A. F. (1991). India: its Culture and People. New York: Longman.

43   Zhu, Y., McKenna, B., & Sun, Z. (2007). Negotiating with Chinese: success of initial meetings is the
      key. Cross Cultural Management: An International Journal, Vol. 14, N. 4, 354-364.

CHAPTER 3:

Dynamic Perspective of Culture

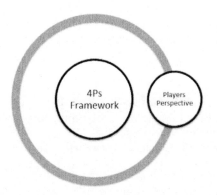

Stage 4: Players Perspective

Everything changes and nothing remains still ... and ... you cannot step twice into the same stream[1]

ETIC AND EMIC APPROACHES

There are two major approaches to cross-cultural studies, the etic and the emic. The etic methodology views phenomena from a metacultural perspective; the etic perspective is culturally neutral and can be applied across cultures through generalizations about universal human behavior. The emic approach views phenomena through the eyes of the culture's subjects; the emic perspective is culture specific because it investigates how local people think, how they perceive and categorize the world.[2]

57

CRITIQUE OF THE ETIC APPROACH

According to the etic approach, culture is a set of independent variables (cultural dimensions). As we saw in the previous chapter, because societies are not homogeneous and static, the primary criticism is that culture can only be represented by a systemic and dynamic framework. For example, China is considered a highly collectivistic society, but in specific urban areas, individualistic inclinations are offsetting collectivistic inclinations.

CRITIQUE OF THE EMIC APPROACH

The emic approach attempts to reconstruct phenomena through an individual's own accounts and descriptions. There are two risks related to this approach: *systematic bias* and *hindsight bias*.

Systematic bias occurs when individuals misrepresent or misinterpret their own behavior, describing behavioral norms instead of the behavior itself.

Hindsight bias occurs when the outcome of actions is reflected in the reconstruction instead of the process that led to the outcome. The awareness of unexpected consequences biases the retroactive view.

Despite the potential pitfalls, it remains essential to study human behavior and human cognitive processes in their natural context, taking into account local sociopolitical, historical, religious, and ecological factors.

We will develop our knowledge of the emic approach in the next chapter of the book.

DYNAMIC CULTURAL FRAMEWORKS

Cultural dimension theories have been criticized because of their static and bipolar perspective on national cultures.[3]

These models don't take into account within-nation heterogeneity, hypothesizing an either-or approach, and discount cultural change over time, which is occurring rapidly in many developing and developed countries (e.g., the rapid shift from collectivism to individualism occurring in the major cities of emerging economies and the slower, but steady, change from individualism to collectivism taking place in some developed countries facing strong financial and economic challenges).[4]

Moreover, the models overlook individuals' capacity to reconcile the opposites of any cultural dimension: Value orientations exist on a continuum and are all present, to a greater or lesser extent, in all societies. People can embrace opposite poles according to the situation and the context: An individual can be both individualistic and collectivistic according to the circumstances (e.g., very individualistic at work and more collectivistic in a family or social context). According to research conducted in China and Korea, individuals recognize their self-concept not as either I or we, but as I and we, both present at the same time.[5]

In the next paragraphs, we will introduce theories that attempt to overcome the limits of the static and bipolar (tripolar) frameworks, without moving into the emic approach to culture, which will be tackled in the next chapter.

GRID AND GROUP CULTURAL THEORY

The grid and group cultural theory, introduced by the British anthropologist Mary Douglas (2003), tries to find the answer to the two basic questions that any culture must confront:[6]

- Who am I?
- How should I behave?

The answer to the question Who am I? is provided by the relationship of the individual with a specific group and the boundaries between the group and the outside world (*group dimension*), while the answer to the question How should I behave is offered by the degree to which an individual is subject to specific social values, norms, and beliefs (*grid dimension*).

According to the cultural theory, group and grid influence reduces individual choices and represents the foundation of any culture.

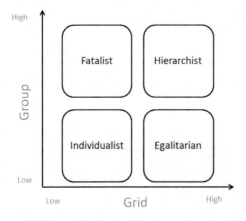

Figure 1. The grid and group dimensions.

The grid and group dimensions combine into four cultural models: individualist, hierarchist, egalitarian, and fatalist.

Individualist cultures mainly stress the freedom of individuals. They focus on results and competence, not on relationships. Independence, selfishness, pragmatism, social mobility, risk taking, and self-interest are regarded more highly than group values.

In *hierarchist cultures*, social order is more important than efficiency. Long-term goals require stability, and order is preserved through institutionalized sanctions, procedures, and rules. Inequalities are part of the system. Societies are highly prescribed and ranks are based on seniority.

In *egalitarian cultures*, equality and justice are fundamental values that must be respected even if they constrain individual freedom. Individuals are connected through cooperation in a common purpose, egalitarianism, self-imposed values, and an in-group vs. out-group perspective.

In *fatalist cultures*, individuals experience low autonomy and feel relatively isolated. They are connected by strong values, but seldom take risks and initiative. They tend to act as subordinates, depending on God, fate, government, or management.

According to cultural theory, and in contrast to Hofstede, individuals and groups often engage in cultural shifts;[7] depending on the circumstances and the context, people can belong to multiple cultures.

A German manager can be individualist when it comes to contending market share to a competitor, hierarchist when dealing with project delays, egalitarian when discussing environmental issues, and fatalist when her role is downsized.

At the same time, because cultures are pluralistic, a trader in Sao Paulo may be culturally closer to a trader in New York than to an assembly worker in Betim (an industrial town close to Belo Horizonte, in Brazil).

FROM CULTURAL TO INDIVIDUAL LEVEL

Some scholars have highlighted the difference between the cultural and psychological levels of individualism and collectivism.[8] At the cultural level, they have proposed employing the terms individualism and collectivism. At the psychological level, they have advocated use of the terms *allocentrism* and *idiocentrism*, corresponding to collectivism and individualism, respectively. All cultures are composed of different proportions of allocentrics and idiocentrics. Idiocentrics can be found in collectivistic societies, allocentrics in individualistic societies.

This flexibility allows for accounting for individual differences in bipolar cultural dimensions theories.

GULLESTRUP'S CULTURAL FRAMEWORK

Because of the dynamic nature of any given culture and its elusive boundaries, Hans Gullestrup (2006), a Danish professor of social and economic planning, proposed a three-dimensional cultural framework that includes the time dimension.[9]

Gullestrup's cultural framework is composed of three dimensions: the *horizontal dimension*, the *vertical dimension*, and the *time dimension*.

When encountering a new culture, observing the culture segments comprising the horizontal dimension will provide a first impression of that culture.

The eight culture segments are:
- *The processing segment*: How a culture procures and prepares food and gets clothing.
- *The distribution segment*: How the materials in a given culture are distributed (trade, import, export).
- *The social segment*: How relationships among people are established and developed. It defines social patterns and social structures.
- *The management and decision segment*: How power and authority distribution affects the decision-making process in a society.
- *The conveyance segment*: How thoughts and ideas are communicated.

- *The integration segment*: How culture is transmitted from one generation to the next.
- *The identity-creating segment*: How members of a culture perceive themselves and others.
- *The security-creating segment*: How people deal with ambiguity, insecurity, and change (traditions, religion).

However, no culture can be examined only through the horizontal dimension; otherwise, we would have only a superficial snapshot of a given society. Deeper cultural elements need to be analyzed, and this is where the vertical dimension comes into play.

The vertical dimension deals with shared basic assumptions, implicit rules, values, and norms that generate a common world conception among the members of a culture.

The third dimension, time, is fundamental because it introduces the concept of evolution into the framework. Without the time dimension, we would be left with only a moment-in-time image of a society. According to Gullestrup, cultures are dynamic and in constant progress: Change usually occurs first in the upper layers of a culture, the horizontal dimension, but sometimes transformation can move to the core layers (vertical dimension) of a society, changing the values and norms of a culture.

WORLD VALUES STUDY

The World Value Survey represents a global network of social scientists who have surveyed the basic values and beliefs of more than 100 societies.

According to the results of the survey, large numbers of basic values across societies are closely interrelated; therefore, they can be represented by just two main dimensions that, according to the scientists, summarize over 70% of the cross-cultural variance on scores of more specific values related to religion, politics, economics, and social life.[10]

The two dimensions are:

- *Traditional values vs. secular-rational values*: Members of traditional societies emphasize religion, marriage, family principles, respect for seniors, and deference to authority. Members of secular cultures understate traditional principles and emphasize rational values, accepting concepts such as divorce, egalitarianism, abortion, and suicide.
- *Survival values vs. self-expression values*: Members of survival societies focus on economic and physical security, showing an ethnocentric perspective and a relatively low degree of trust and tolerance toward out-group members and values. Members of self-expression cultures press for participation in economic decision making and political life, supporting gender equality and environmental protection and exhibiting a xenocentric perspective with a relatively high level of tolerance and trust toward out-group members and values.

The two value dimensions have different reference points; the first is focused on the community, the second on the individual.

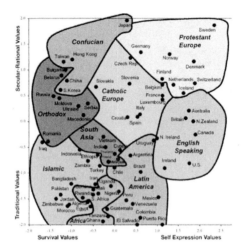

Figure 2. World Value Survey cultural map.

The cultural map in Figure 2 shows a distinct pattern: The strongest emphasis on traditional values and survival values is found in the Islamic societies of the Middle East. In contrast, the strongest emphasis on secular-rational values and self-expression values is located in the Protestant societies of Northern Europe.

The shift from an agricultural to an industrial society is accompanied by a transition from traditional to secular values.

The shift from industrial to knowledge societies is linked to a transition from survival to self-expression values.

In the last 20 years, on average, the cultural zones have been moving toward stronger self-expression values. At the same time, there has also been a less marked transition toward stronger secular-rational values in most of the cultural zones.

THE DYNAMIC CONSTRUCTIVIST THEORY

According to the dynamic constructivist hypothesis, too much attention is paid to general differences and similarities between cultures, without exploring the context in which these differences surface. A dynamic constructivist view suggests that culture influences individuals' behaviors through the activation of cultural knowledge in specific contexts.[11]

Thus, culture is specific, situational, and contextual.

Many studies have pointed out that collectivists tend to be more cooperative with in-group members than do individualists, but are as competitive or even more competitive than individualists when negotiating with out-group members.[12] Accountability reinforces the relationship-oriented approach for collectivistic negotiators when they negotiate with in-group members.

The dynamic constructivist theory is based on the notion of knowledge activation, which claims that a knowledge construct is activated only when it is relevant and applicable to the social context.

Without taking social contexts into consideration, we would not know under which circumstances specific cultural patterns and behaviors are triggered or halted.

THE ARROW OF TIME

Because we can see where we have been but not where we are going, certain Pacific tribes have traditionally believed that we face the past and have our backs to tomorrow.[13]

According to Einstein (1916), not only is time relative, but the separation between past, present, and future is only an illusion.[14]

According to Feynman (1959), if one could look at a particle in isolation, past and future would be hard to distinguish and time could be described just as a direction in space.[15]

However, the *time-reversal symmetry* implied by both Einstein and Feynman has been violated at the matter and antimatter levels. Also, recent experiments at the SLAC, the national accelerator laboratory close to Stanford University in California, have determined that going forward is not the same as going backward: A time arrow really exists.

CULTURAL COMPETENCIES

During cross-cultural interactions, our aim is to build a bridge between our differences and to leverage our similarities to achieve our goal.

In recent years, researchers have developed different approaches to cultural competency, the ability to move effectively across different cultures.

However, what are the differences between cultural dimensions and cultural competencies?

While cultural dimensions are static and polarized, cultural competencies are dynamic and evolving.

While cultural dimensions are specific to a particular culture, cultural competencies develop overall skills to manage differences and barriers across cultures.

Individuals with high cultural competencies develop a systemic view of the world that recognizes the value of both the similarities and the differences among people, fueled by a high level of curiosity and interest in individuals with different backgrounds.

In the next paragraphs, we will introduce two of the most accepted frameworks: *cultural intelligence* and *international profiler*.

CULTURAL INTELLIGENCE

Interacting with people from our own culture, we unconsciously use information and signals that help us relate effectively. When we experience new cultures, these cues and information are absent, and what works in different contexts becomes irrelevant and even misleading.[16]

Cultural intelligence refers to an individual's competence to function effectively across cultures (culture can be national, ethnic, or organizational).

Theory about cross-cultural interaction focuses mainly on how to recognize the values, the norms, the beliefs, the practices, and the behaviors of specific cultures.

Cultural intelligence, on the other hand, supports people in developing an overall attitude and a range of approaches and behaviors that allow them to move across different cultural contexts.[17]

Cultural intelligence (CQ) (as all forms of intelligence) is made up of four complementary factors: motivational CQ, cognitive CQ, metacognitive CQ, and behavioral CQ. Each is explained below.[18]

Motivational CQ (CQ drive) refers to your confidence, drive, motivation, level of interest, and curiosity to adapt in international contexts. It is the ability to persevere despite the challenges and divergences that arise during cross-cultural encounters. Most cross-cultural theories basically take for granted that people have the drive and the confidence to work across cultures.

Motivational CQ is composed of three sub-dimensions:

- *Intrinsic CQ drive*, the degree of inherent interest and motivation you have in exploring different cultures.
- *Extrinsic CQ drive*, the degree of tangible and personal benefits you perceive in interacting with different cultures (e.g., career development).
- *Self-efficacy*, the degree of confidence you have in being able to work effectively across cultures and to persevere despite the likely difficulties.

Cognitive CQ (CQ knowledge) refers to your knowledge of different cultural norms and values; it includes the level of understanding about cultural differences and consistencies and their influence on people's behavior and interactions.

The four sub-dimensions of cognitive CQ are:

- *Business*, the knowledge of how culture influences business practices in different contexts.
- *Interpersonal*, the knowledge of how values, norms, beliefs, and behaviors differ across cultures.
- *Socio-linguistics*, the knowledge of different languages and the rules of verbal and nonverbal communication.
- *Leadership*, the knowledge of how effective leadership styles differ across cultures.

Metacognitive CQ (CQ strategy) refers to the capability of using your cultural knowledge to plan an appropriate strategy, properly translate cross-cultural situations, and assess and improve your expectations.

The metacognitive CQ dimension is made of these sub-dimensions:

- *Awareness*: You are aware of the different dynamics influencing multicultural interactions and of how your culture affects your relationships with people from different cultures.
- *Planning*: The amount of time you set aside to prepare for a cross-cultural encounter.
- *Checking*: The degree of monitoring and adjustment of your behavior during a cross-cultural situation.

Behavioral CQ (CQ action) refers to the capability to be flexible when interacting in an international context by appropriately changing verbal and nonverbal behaviors. A fundamental feature of behavioral CQ is identifying when adapting to another culture will increase your effectiveness and when it would be better not to change your standard behavior.

The behavioral CQ is made of these three sub-dimensions:

- *Nonverbal*: The degree to which you can comfortably modify your nonverbal behavior in cross-cultural situations (e.g., gestures, facial expressions).
- *Paraverbal*: The degree to which you can comfortably adjust your paraverbal behavior in cross-cultural situations (e.g., pause, silence, accent, tone, pronunciation, volume, speed).
- *Verbal*: The degree to which you can comfortably change your verbal behavior in cross-cultural situations to achieve your goals and to fit the cultural setting (e.g., the way you provide feedback, the way you express appreciation, the way you disagree).

The four factors are correlated: A person who knows (cognition) how to relate in an international context, but has no desire (motivation) to do so will not be effective in a cross-cultural encounter. The same goes for an individual who can explore (meta-cognition) a situation but cannot in reality solve it (behavior).

STRATEGIES TO IMPROVE CULTURAL INTELLIGENCE

How Can Motivational CQ Be Improved?

The first strategy to improve intrinsic motivational CQ is to acknowledge the fact that implicit prejudices and biases are key elements of your brain functioning. You have to learn to continuously adjust your preconceptions according to revised information. Biases are inevitable. Acting on them is not (more on this in chapter 9).

Another strategy is to picture potential career repercussions of cultural unawareness: Job opportunities and career progressions could be unavailable to you if you do not improve your CQ drive.

A third strategy is to ask yourself to make a list of the potential tangible benefits you can obtain by improving your extrinsic CQ drive. The focus should be not on potential disappointments, but likely opportunities.

The fourth strategy involves rewarding yourself every time you achieve a goal, even a very small one, because modifying behavior can be extremely challenging.

A fifth strategy concerns finding time and ways to recharge your batteries (e.g., allowing time for a workout or meeting familiar faces) because cross-cultural interactions can be demanding and exhausting.

The sixth strategy allows you to start slowly, without being overwhelmed by a new culture. Keeping a perception of control is fundamental for efficient brain functioning. Immersing yourself gradually (e.g., going to a store on your own, taking the metro by yourself) can enhance your self-confidence.

The last strategy to develop your CQ drive is also the most obvious: Travel as much as you can.

How Can Cognitive CQ Be Improved?

When you are in a foreign city, potential strategies to improve cognitive CQ include:

- Sit in a public spot and watch people: observe their behavior, look for similarities and differences.

- Try to stop at small grocery stores and eat local food.
- Visit museums and ride public transportation.

You can increase your global perspective by:

- Watching the news on international TV channels such as BBC, CNN, Al Jazeera, France 24, NHK World, and NewsAsia.
- Reading different newspapers with an international focus, such as the International Herald Tribune, Financial Times, International Times, and Wall Street Journal Europe and Asia editions.
- Reading local newspapers while traveling.
- Learning about major historical and current events around the world (e.g., historical conflicts between countries, major sport events, political situations). Knowing that Iran and Turkey are not Arab countries and that the Czech Republic is not the equivalent of Chechnya[19] should be common knowledge for any international manager.
- Reading a novel or watching a movie about the specific culture.
- Seeking distinctive perspectives by meeting people with diverse backgrounds and looking for different information sources.
- Understanding the main cultural dimensions defining a society, taking into account the opinions in support and against such categorization.
- Studying a new language. Some say language is culture (more on that in chapter 5).

How Can Meta-Cognitive CQ Be Improved?

The first strategy to improve your CQ strategy is to remove yourself from the situation and notice what is happening in the cross-cultural interaction. The key is to suspend judgment. Without jumping to conclusions, just observe with detachment.

The second strategy is to think beyond categories. Don't put labels on behaviors and situations. Train your mind to think systemically, looking for the large picture. Learn to be comfortable during circumstances that don't fit a specific category. Few behaviors are absolutely right or wrong. Most behaviors during cross-cultural interactions should be evaluated according to the context.

Increase your category width. Narrow categorizers have a disposition to classify things according to a right or wrong dichotomy.

Broad categorizers allow for a larger width: Few things are absolutely right or wrong; most are just different.

Cross-cultural interactions are full of paradox and contradiction. Train yourself to hold things in tension, without jumping to conclusions (more on this in chapter 11).

The third strategy is to carry a journal with you while traveling abroad. Log your observations and, without jumping to conclusions, start testing your assumptions.

Most of us tend to gravitate toward people with similar opinions, interests, and beliefs. However, in doing so, we miss the perspective of people with different experiences and coming from different contexts. The fourth strategy is to surround yourself with people from different cultures. Consciously plan your cross-cultural encounters. Take part in international projects; attend social gatherings with people from different cultures. Travel and meet people with different backgrounds.

The fifth strategy is to shift your perspective. Don't blame the other person for something he or she did; reframe the situation from the other person's point of view.

The sixth strategy is to check your assumptions and interpretations. Always question your expectations and observations. Look for feedback to calibrate your strategy.

The seventh strategy involves asking yourself *why* when you experience a perplexing situation due to cultural differences. Try to understand what's behind a behavior you observe.

How Can Behavioral CQ Be Improved?

Because it is impossible to master all the dos and don'ts of every culture, the first strategy is to develop a set of social skills that can be employed effectively in different cross-cultural interactions.

The second strategy is to mirror the behavior of locals. Be careful not to fall into the trap of mockery; otherwise, this strategy could backfire.

The third strategy is to learn basic sentences in the foreign language. Learn some fundamental phrases.

The fourth strategy is to learn to speak more slowly and thoughtfully, particularly when communicating in English with people whose mother tongue is not English.

THE INTERNATIONAL PROFILER

The international profiler is a web-based psychometric questionnaire and personal feedback process that shows the relative emphasis, attention, and energy that individuals bring to a set of 10 international competencies, with 22 dimensions representing associated skills, attitudes, and areas of knowledge.[20]

The first competency is *openness*: Working in an international context, having an open mind is vital. Openness is composed of three dimensions:

- *New thinking*, the degree to which you welcome and embrace new and different ideas.
- *Welcoming strangers*, the degree to which you originate exchange with strangers who have different experiences and backgrounds.
- *Acceptance*, the degree to which you tolerate and accept different behaviors.

The openness competency includes elements that parallel the metacognitive CQ dimension of the cultural intelligence framework.

The second competency is *flexibility*, the ability to modify your behavior and adjust your assumptions. Flexibility has three dimensions:

- *Flexible behavior*, the degree to which you can adapt to different social and cultural situations by employing a wide repertoire of different behaviors that have proven effective in most circumstances. This dimension is equivalent to the behavioral CQ of the cultural intelligence framework.
- *Flexible judgments*, the degree to which you are able to suspend judgment, question assumptions, and avoid jumping to conclusions. You are aware of your biases and are open to new information to adjust your prejudices.

- *Learning languages*, the degree to which you are motivated to learn and employ different languages, beyond the lingua franca. This dimension corresponds to the socio-linguistics sub-dimension of cognitive CQ.

The third competency is *personal autonomy*. Working across the daily challenges and divergences that arise during cross-cultural encounters, it is easy to lose focus and a clear sense of direction. The two dimensions of personal autonomy are:

- *Inner purpose*, the degree to which you are able to retain strong personal values and beliefs that provide reliability and stability in unfamiliar and challenging situations.

- *Focus on goals*, the degree to which you believe you have control over the environment, setting specific goals and persevering in achieving them.

The fourth competency is *emotional strength*. Dealing with people with different behaviors, traditions, values, and norms can be highly demanding and stressful, and it requires a certain level of emotional strength.

Emotional strength has three dimensions:

- *Resilience*, the degree to which you are able to overcome embarrassment, criticism, or disapproval during cross-cultural encounters and are ready to bounce back after having made a mistake.

- *Coping*, the degree to which you are able to deal with unfamiliar, stressful, and hectic situations and remain calm under pressure.

- *Spirit of adventure*, the degree to which you look for change, new inputs, and situations in life, breaking from the status quo. The degree to which you seek uncomfortable and ambiguous situations.

The emotional strength competency is comparable to the motivational CQ dimension of the cultural intelligence framework.

The fifth dimension is *perceptiveness*. Understanding nonverbal communication and the hidden meaning of words given by the context requires the skill to "read between the lines."

Perceptiveness has two dimensions:

- *Attuned*, the degree to which you are able to isolate and interpret paraverbal and nonverbal signals such as tone, body language, and facial expression.

- *Reflected awareness*, the degree to which you are aware of how others perceive and interpret your communication patterns and behavior.

The perceptiveness competency is analogous to the paraverbal and nonverbal sub-dimensions of behavioral CQ.

The sixth competency is *listening orientation*, the capacity to focus on another person and really pay attention to what they are saying and communicating despite language and cultural barriers. Listening orientation has only one dimension: *active listening*, a proactive approach that aims to test out your assumptions and understand the views of others.

The seventh competency is *transparency*. Delivering information and communicating meaning clearly can be highly challenging in an international context. Even simple messages can potentially lead to misunderstandings when speaking in a foreign language or in the lingua franca.

Transparency has two key dimensions:

- *Clarity of communication*, the degree to which you are aware of the potential misunderstandings that can occur during cross-cultural interactions and the degree to which you are able to adapt how the message is delivered to be clearly understood by the audience.

- *Exposing intentions*, the degree to which you are able to build and develop trust in international relationships by clearly and unequivocally communicating your objectives and needs.

The eighth competency is *cultural knowledge*, the understanding of different values and norms and how they can shape relationships in an international context. Cultural knowledge has two dimensions:

- *Information gathering*, the degree to which you take time to gather information and learn about different cultures.

- *Valuing differences*, the degree to which you are sensitive to how people with diverse backgrounds see the world differently.

Cultural knowledge competency is comparable to the cognitive CQ dimension of the cultural intelligence framework.

The ninth competency is *influencing*. The ability to persuade, influence, and motivate people despite language and cultural barriers; influencing has three dimensions:

- *Rapport*, the degree to which you are able to display warmth and thoughtfulness when building relationships in a variety of contexts that can lead to trust-based relationships in the long term.

- *Range of styles*, the degree to which you are able to employ a range of styles to influence people across cultures.

- *Sensitivity to context*, the degree to which you are able to identify the informal organization that lies behind the nominal organizational chart, understand the decision-making process, and identify the key decision makers and influencers in the organization.

The last competency is *synergy*, the ability to combine and integrate different options and approaches to solve problems in a multicultural context. The only dimension of synergy is *creating new alternatives*, which involves the degree to which you are able to find novel and innovative solutions to problems, by merging different methodologies.

YIN AND YANG THEORY

Hofstede's paradigm ignores within-culture diversity as well as cultural change over time.

The ancient Chinese philosophy of Yin Yang suggests an alternative to Hofstede's bipolar and static model for defining cultures.

The yin-yang balance is an open system that accommodates both the either-or (Aristotle's deductive logic) and the both-or (Hegel's dialectical thinking) frameworks.[21]

According to Tony Fang's (2012) Yin and Yang theory, culture is learnt and not inbred, and cultural dimensions have intrinsically dynamic, opposite and paradoxical value orientations.[22] Interdependent and complementary opposites provide symmetry and dynamic equilibrium.

The theory affirms that each culture has specific values, that can cohabit with their opposites, depending on the situation, context, and time.

Depending on the context and time, a culture will promote certain values and restrain their opposite; according to the theory, the best analogy to understand culture is the ocean one: at any time, some cultural values may become more relevant, rising to the surface, while other cultural values may be temporarily inhibited, according to the specific situation.

In other words, the notion of culture, which Hofstede's conceptualized as a passport-based and nationality-embedded phenomenon, has acquired a dynamic and systemic implication in the yin yang model.

THE VOYAGER'S MIND-SET

In cross-cultural interactions, it is important to be aware and recognize *stereotypes* and *generalizations*. However, what is the difference between these two concepts?

Generalization is the starting point for further analysis. Stereotypes, on the other hand, are based on biased perceptions, prejudices, a judgmental mind-set, and an unwillingness to learn to change perspective and question assumptions. Generalizations become damaging when they fall into stereotypes.

We cannot remove stereotypes from our cognitive process because the stereotype is an intrinsic element of our brain and key feature of our cortex functioning (more on this in chapter 8).

We need to develop an open and tolerant attitude toward the large number of variables we come across in cross-cultural interactions. Developing a voyager's mind-set requires first recognizing our biases and prejudices and then questioning our assumptions, judgments, and abiding ambiguities to be open to new information and ideas and curious about individuals with backgrounds that differ from ours.

Here are some guidelines from Carlos Ghosn, chairman of the board and chief executive officer at Renault and Nissan:

- Don't let your passport determine your destination. Raise your hand for overseas postings.
- When you start a new foreign assignment, be humble. Don't assume you know best. Have a student's mind-set. Appreciate the differences. Be curious.
- Be multilingual. Study foreign languages (more on this in chapter 8).
- Don't over-plan. Accept the unaccepted. Move beyond your comfort zone.

DEVDUTT PATTANAIK

Devdutt Pattanaik, an Indian mythologist and leadership consultant, speaking at the first Ted Conference in India.[23]

"You have to hear a story of Ganesha, the elephant-headed god who is the scribe of storytellers, and his brother, the athletic warlord of the gods, Kartikeya. The two brothers one day decided to go on a race, three times around the world. Kartikeya leapt on his peacock and flew around the continents and the mountains and the oceans. He went around once, he went around twice, he went around thrice. But his brother, Ganesha, simply walked around his parents once, twice, thrice, and said,

"I won." "How come?" said Kartikeya. And Ganesha said, "You went around the world. I went around my world." What matters more?

If you understand the difference between the world and my world you understand the difference between logos and mythos. The world is objective, logical, universal, factual, scientific. My world is subjective. It's emotional. It's personal. It's perceptions, thoughts, feelings, dreams. It is the belief system that we carry. It's the myth that we live in.

The world tells us how the world functions, how the sun rises, how we are born. My world tells us why the sun rises, why we were born. Every culture is trying to understand itself: "Why do we exist?" And every culture comes up with its own understanding of life, its own customized version of mythology.

Culture is a reaction to nature, and this understanding of our ancestors is transmitted generation from generation in the form of stories, symbols and rituals, which are always indifferent to rationality. And so, when you study it, you realize that different people of the world have a different understanding of the world. Different people see things differently: different viewpoints.

There is my world and there is your world, and my world is always better than your world, because my world, you see, is rational and yours is superstition. Yours is faith. Yours is illogical. This is the root of the clash of civilizations. It took place, once, in 326 B.C. on the banks of a river called the Indus, now in Pakistan. This river lends itself to India's name. India. Indus.

Alexander, a young Macedonian, met there what he called a gymnosophist, which means the naked, wise man. We don't know who he was. Perhaps he was a Jain monk... Or perhaps he was just a yogi who was sitting on a rock, staring at the sky and the sun and the moon.

Alexander asked, "What are you doing?" and the gymnosophist answered, "I'm experiencing nothingness." Then the gymnosophist asked, "What are you doing?" and Alexander said, "I am conquering the world." And they both laughed. Each one thought that the other was a fool. The gymnosophist said, "Why is he conquering the world? It's pointless." And Alexander thought, "Why is he sitting around, doing nothing? What a waste of a life."

To understand this difference in viewpoints, we have to understand the subjective truth of Alexander, his myth, and the mythology that constructed it. Alexander's mother, his parents, his teacher Aristotle told him the story of Homer's Iliad. They told him of a great hero called Achilles, who, when he participated in battle, victory was assured, but when he withdrew from the battle, defeat was inevitable. Achilles was a man who could shape history, a man of destiny, and this is what you should be, Alexander. That's what he heard.

"What should you not be? You should not be Sisyphus, who rolls a rock up a mountain all day only to find the boulder rolled down at night. Don't live a life which is monotonous, mediocre, meaningless. Be spectacular!, like the Greek heroes, like Jason, who went across the sea with the Argonauts and fetched the Golden Fleece. Be spectacular like Theseus, who entered the labyrinth and killed the bull-headed Minotaur. When you play in a race, win! - because when you win, the exhilaration of victory is the closest you will come to the ambrosia of the gods."

Because, you see, the Greeks believed you live only once, and when you die, you have to cross the River Styx. And if you have lived an extraordinary life, you will be welcomed to Elysium, the heaven of the heroes. But these are not the stories that the gymnosophist heard. He heard a very different story. He heard of a man called Bharat, after whom India is called Bhārata. Bharat also conquered the world. And then he went to the top-most peak of the greatest mountain of the center of the world called Meru. And he wanted to hoist his flag to say, I was here first. But when he reached the mountain peak, he found the peak covered with countless flags of world-conquerors before him, each one claiming I was here first... that's what I thought until I came here. And suddenly, in this canvas of infinity, Bharat felt insignificant. This was the mythology of the gymnosophist.

You see, he had heroes, like Ram, Raghupati Ram and Krishna, Govinda Hari. But they were not two characters on two different adventures. They were two lifetimes of the same hero. When the Ramayana ends the Mahabharata begins. When Ram dies, Krishna is born. When Krishna dies, eventually he will be back as Ram.

You see, the Indians also had a river that separates the land of the living from the land of the dead. But you don't cross it once. You go to and fro endlessly. It was called the Vaitarani. You go again and again and again. Because, you see, nothing lasts forever in India, not even death. And so, you have these grand rituals where great images of mother goddesses are built and worshiped for 10 days ... And what do you do at the end of 10 days? You dunk it in the river. Because it has to end. And next year, she will come back. What goes around always comes around, and this rule applies not just to man, but also to the gods. You see, the gods have to come back again and again and again as Ram, as Krishna. Not only do they live infinite lives, but the same life is lived infinite times till you get to the point of it all. Groundhog Day.

Two different mythologies. Which is right? Two different mythologies, two different ways of looking at the world. One linear, one cyclical. One believes this is the one and only life. The other believes this is one of many lives. And so, the denominator of Alexander's life was one. So, the value of his life was the sum total of his achievements. The denominator of the gymnosophist's life was infinity. So, no matter what he did, it was always zero. And I believe it is this mythological paradigm that inspired Indian mathematicians to discover the number zero. Who knows?

And that brings us to the mythology of business... Take a look. If you live only once, in one-life cultures around the world, you will see an obsession with binary logic, absolute truth, standardization, absoluteness, linear patterns in design. But if you look at cultures which have cyclical and based on infinite lives, you will see a comfort with fuzzy logic, with opinion, with contextual thinking, with everything is relative, sort of, mostly.

… And then look at business. Standard business model: vision, mission, values, processes. Sounds very much like the journey through the wilderness to the promised land, with the commandments held by the leader. And if you comply, you will go to heaven.

But in India there is no "the" promised land. There are many promised lands, depending on your station in society, depending on your stage of life.

… You see, Indian music, for example, does not have the concept of harmony. There is no orchestra conductor. There is one performer standing there, and everybody follows. And you can never replicate that performance twice. It is not about documentation and contract. It's about conversation and faith. It's not about compliance. It's about setting, getting the job done, by bending or breaking the rules.

You see, this is what India is today. The ground reality is based on a cyclical world view. So, it's rapidly changing, highly diverse, chaotic, ambiguous, unpredictable. And people are okay with it. And then globalization is taking place. The demands of modern institutional thinking is coming in. Which is rooted in one-life culture. And a clash is going to take place, like on the banks of the Indus. It is bound to happen.

… So, then we come back to Alexander and to the gymnosophist. And everybody asks me, "Which is the better way, this way or that way?" And it's a very dangerous question, because it leads you to the path of fundamentalism and violence. So, I will not answer the question. What I will give you is an Indian answer, the Indian head-shake.

Depending on the context, depending on the outcome, choose your paradigm. You see, because both the paradigms are human constructions. They are cultural creations, not natural phenomena. And so the next time you meet someone, a stranger, one request: Understand that you live in the subjective truth, and so does he. Understand it. And when you understand it you will discover something spectacular. You will discover that within infinite myths lies the eternal truth.

(ENDNOTES)

1   Heraclitus

2   Kottak, C. (2006). Mirror for humanity. New York, NY: McGraw-Hill.

3   McSweeney, B. (2002). Hofstede's model of national cultural differences and their consequences: A triumph of faith - a failure of analysis. Human Relations, Vol. 55, N. 1, 89-118.

4   Ailon, G. (2008). Mirror, mirror on the wall: Culture's Consequences in a value test of its own design. The Academy of Management Review, Vol. 33, N. 4, 885-904.

5   Ying-yi, H., Ip, G., Chiu, C., Morris, M. W., & Menon, T. (2001). Cultural Identity And Dynamic Construction Of The Self: Collective Duties And Individual Rights In Chinese And American Cultures. Social Cognition, Vol. 19, N. 3, 251-268.

6   Douglas, M. (2003). Being fair to hierarchists. University of Pennsylvania Law Review, Vol. 151, N. 4, 1349-1370.

7   Apfelthaler, G., & Domicone, H. (2008). Drawing wrong borderlines: the concept of culture in a pluralist management world. Problems and Perspectives in Management, Vol. 6, N. 2, 44-58.

8   Triandis, H. C., Leung, K., Villareal, M. J., & Clack, F. I. (1985). Allocentric versus idiocentric tendencies: Convergent and discriminant validation. Journal of Research in Personality, Vol. 19, N. 4, 395-415.

9   Gullestrup, H. (2006). Cultural analysis, Towards cross cultural understanding. Copenhagen, Denmark: Copenhagen Business School Press.

10   Inglehart, R., & Welzel, C. (2005). Modernization, cultural change, and democracy. New York: Cambridge University Press.

11   Ying-yi, H., Chiu, C., Morris, M. W., & Benet-Martinez, V. (2000). Multicultural Minds, A Dynamic Constructivist Approach to Culture and Cognition. American Psychologist, Vol. 55, N. 7, 709-720.

12   Wu, L., Ray, F., & Ying-yi, H. (2009). Culture, Accountability, and Group Membership: A Dynamic Constructivist Approach to Cross-cultural Negotiation. 22nd Annual International Association of Conflict Management Conference, Kyoto, Japan.

13   Hughes, R. (2010). CULT-URE. London, UK: Fiell Publishing

14   Einstein, A. (1995). Relativity (great minds). New York, NY: Prometheus Books.

15   Feynman, R. P. (1959). Plenty of Room at the Bottom. Presentation to the American Physical Society, Pasadena, December.

16   Van Dyne, L., Ang, S., & Livermore, D. (2010). Cultural intelligence: A pathway for leading in a rapidly globalizing world. In K. M. Hannum, B. McFeeters, & L. Booysen (Eds.), Leadership across differences: Casebook. San Francisco, CQ: Pfeiffer.

17   Van Dyne, L., Ang, S., Ng, K. Y., Rockstuhl, T., Tan, M. L., & Kph, C. (2012). Sub-Dimensions of the Four Factor Model of Cultural Intelligence: Expanding the Conceptualization and Measurement of Cultural Intelligence. Social and Personality Psychology Compass, Vol. 6, N. 4, 295-313.

18   Livermore, D. (2011). The cultural intelligence difference: Master the one skill you can't do without in today's global economy. New York, NY: AMACOM.

19   Satirical article and parody available at http://dailycurrant.com/2013/04/22/sarah-palin-calls-inva-sion-czech-republic/

20   Trickey, D., Ewington, N., & Lowe, R. (2009). Being International: what do international managers and professionals really think is important - and do experts agree?. The Journal of Intercultural Mediation and Communication, Vol. 2, 49-78.

21   Croce, B. (1915). What is Living and What is Dead in the Philosophy of Hegel. Translated by D. Ainslie. London: Macmillan.

22   Fang, T. (2012). Yin Yang: A New Perspective on Culture. Management Organization Review, Vol. 8, N. 1, 25-50.

23   Pattanaik, D. (2009). East vs. West - the myths that mystify. Ted Conference in India, November. Retrieved from http://new.ted.com/talks/devdutt_pattanaik#

CHAPTER 4

Indigenous Perspective on Culture

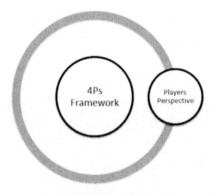

Stage 4: Players' Perspective

INTRODUCTION

There is rising acknowledgment that existing psychological theories developed in Europe and North America are not universal.

The etic approach, which was introduced through the cultural dimension models in chapter 2, is characterized by the process of description and comparison of psychological characteristics across different cultural groups.

However, because psychological theories are culture bound, it becomes necessary to study human behavior and human cognitive processes in their natural context, taking into account local sociopolitical, historical, religious, and ecological factors.

The emic approach that will be used in the current chapter aims to describe the psychosocial aspects of a particular culture that directly influence the behavior of individuals.

Indigenous psychology (the emic approach) can therefore be defined as the exploration of human functioning in a cultural context from the point of view of researchers from the specific culture.[1]

In the next paragraphs, we will introduce the emic approach of indigenous psychology applied to specific cultures.

Because indigenous psychology is an emerging field, the literature is only available for a limited number of nations.

CHINESE TRADITIONAL VALUES

The most important values representing traditional Chinese society are *face, high-context communication, trust, centrality and inadequacy,* and *thinking.*

FACE AND SHAME

The word face is used as a metaphor for an individual's public image.[2]

Face saving, face restoration, and face giving are fundamental values for Chinese people. Social reputation is considered a fundamental personal and family asset. The worst thing that can happen to the Chinese is to lose face, to experience a feeling of shame, to undergo social humiliation.

There are 113 core shame terms in Chinese, organized around three key concepts:

- The fear of losing face.
- The state of shame after having lost face.
- The associated feeling of guilt.

Shame in China can be considered a tool to teach right from wrong and to endeavor to improve.

Face may not only be increased or lost; it can also be exchanged. Trading face means giving face to the other person, who in turn must reciprocate. Social cohesion and social order in China are ensured by the concept of face. The Chinese culture can be considered a shame-socialized culture.

Two types of face can be identified in Chinese culture:

- *Mianzi*: Social status. Reputation achieved through success and ostentation. Emphasizes a person's power.
- *Lian*: Moral character. Reputation achieved through moral integrity and respect for social roles. Emphasizes a person's morality.

HIGH-CONTEXT COMMUNICATION

As we have seen in previous chapters, in high-context cultures where social harmony and relationships are essential, the meaning is suggested indirectly and implicitly and what is not said is often more important than what is said.

In China, where the whole society is expected to replicate family values, harmony must be preserved avoiding conflict and the expression of emotions and feelings must be restrained (an old Chinese saying is people have emotions like trees have worms). Maintaining control is a Confucian virtue.

TRUST

In China, suspicion is the rule and the imperative is to minimize the risk against tricks or deceit. Skepticism and distrust exemplify all encounters with strangers. Risk minimization is achieved through a shielding circle of long-lasting relationships based on trust.

Commitment to cooperation, fairness, and patience are essential to accomplish a relationship of trust in China.

CENTRALITY AND SENSE OF INADEQUACY

A strong perception of cultural superiority is deep-seated in Chinese people. The name China, Zhong Guo, literally translates as the Middle Kingdom.

During the Qing dynasty, the Euro-centric world map drawn by Jesuit Matteo Ricci was considered absolutely unacceptable because China was represented at the margin of the world. In 1600, Matteo Ricci was forced to revise his world map, placing China at the center, with Europe represented at its left and America at its right. The Imperial Records of that time documented any foreign mission to China as a tributary delegation.

According to the Chinese view, the Chinese culture and nation lie at the center of human civilization: everything in China is evaluated from a Sino-centric point of view.[3]

At the same time, the Chinese desire to state their place in the world can be attributed to the sense of subordination that originated with the invasion and occupation that occurred at the turn of the 19th century by Western troops and the following humiliating Boxer Protocol.

Over the following decades, the Chinese built up a sense of inadequacy and inferiority towards the West that was further reinforced by China being both ignored and isolated by the West following the 1949 communist revolution.

The current Chinese self-consciousness about the country's primacy can thus also be assessed from a different perspective: the desire to overcome decades of intellectual and cultural subordination to the old imperial powers.

CONFUCIANISM

In 1966, Mao embarked on what can be considered humanity's biggest ever experiment in management, the Cultural Revolution.[4]

During the Cultural Revolution, organizations were overturned, managers relegated to the factory floor, professors and doctors sent to cultivate farms, while revolutionary committees of workers and peasants took charge of universities, hospitals, and plants.

In the end, the Cultural Revolution clashed with enduring Confucian core values such as loyalty to one's social role (*zhong*), respect for elders (*xiao*), and rules of appropriate behavior (*li*) (more on Confucianism in chapter 2).

THINKING

Chinese culture can be described as the complex result of three systems of thought: *Confucianism, Taoism,* and *Buddhism.*

The Chinese perceive the world differently, mainly because of the characteristics of the Chinese language and the historical isolation in which Chinese society has developed.

Westerners have developed an analytical approach to problems by segmenting issues and identifying specific causes and effects, while the Chinese developed a holistic approach based on a global assessment of the problem and the links between the different issues.[5]

The Chinese way of thinking emphasizes perceptions of the concrete over abstract thought. Chinese thinking is highly consistent with the language because ideograms come from pictograms, which are simplified representations of reality.[6]

According to Western logic, a fact is either true or untrue. There is no ambiguity. In China, things are not black or white, but black and white (yin and yang) at the same time, and they can change according to the situation. Chinese thinking operates on the logic of both/and rather than either/or, with an inclusive perspective in relation to differences. Opposites are interdependent and complementary elements that provide symmetry, dynamic equilibrium, and harmony.

Think through the following statements about recent scientific discoveries:[7]

Statement A. Two mathematicians have discovered that the activities of a butterfly in Beijing, China, noticeably affect the temperature in the San Francisco Bay Area.

Statement B. Two meteorologists have found that the activities of a local butterfly in the San Francisco Bay Area have nothing to do with temperature changes in the same San Francisco Bay Area.

Theoretically, there are four possible psychological responses to the apparent contradiction of the two statements. The first is denial, acting as if there is no contradiction.

The second is to discount both statements because they contradict each other.

The third response is to compare both reports and decide which is right and which is wrong.

A fourth response is also possible: holding simultaneously the two opposing perspectives, tolerating contradiction and uncertainty. Such an attitude allows a person to believe that both statements are true and to attempt a reconciliation and integration of the two statements.

The cognitive tendency toward acceptance of contradiction is defined as dialectical or integrative thinking.

CHINESE CHANGING VALUES

The most important values exemplifying modern Chinese society are *individualism, time* and *rituals.*

INDIVIDUALISM

Although China is deemed to be a collectivistic country (according to Hofstede, China has a score of 20 in the Individualism / Collectivism dimension), Chinese society is becoming increasingly individualistic.

According to some Chinese scholars, the family in China is the reference group and all others are regarded as outsiders.

However, at the present time, even family values are challenged: Sons or daughters earn far more than their fathers, questioning the traditional family hierarchy. Another trend is supporting the notion of family values being questioned: the steady and continuous escalation in divorces.[8]

While the official moral code still refers to collectivistic values, the market economy and the boosting urbanization are increasingly fostering individuals to pursue their own interests and wealth. Openly displaying one's status is becoming a basic social requirement. Superstitions and worship are back in the hope that they will bring prosperity and wealth.

There is a consistent indication that in China life satisfaction has become mainly determined by financial satisfaction

However, this leads to another interesting Chinese dilemma: Rising incomes don't correspond to rising happiness. Subjective well-being is declining for all income groups.

One explanation is that despite absolute advances, most income groups find themselves in a more unfavorable relative position. People tend to compare themselves with other individuals or groups when assessing their own condition. Relative decline despite absolute increase has a major frustrating effect, generating financial dissatisfaction, which leads to life discontent.[9]

TIME AND RITUALS

Rituals have always had an important function in Chinese society. Becoming proficient at rituals was a sign of refinement. Today, ritualistic behaviors are becoming less and less relevant, with relations becoming more direct. Even repetition, the basic process of traditional education, is less valued.[10]

With rituals, time perception is also changing. Time was considered an unlimited resource. Contracts took months, or even years, before being signed. Today, time becomes money and the famous Chinese long-term orientation is shifting to a shorter term focus where planning is replaced by intuition.

JAPANESE CULTURE

The most important values representing Japanese society are *mentsu, religion and philosophy, le, wa, isolation and uniqueness*, and its *cultural paradox*.

THE CONCEPT OF MENTSU

Individuals all over the world are concerned about their reputation, which is represented by the face metaphor. However, in cultures such as China and Japan face becomes a fundamental value.[11]

Mentsu is an indigenous Japanese face concept that emphasizes an individual's fulfillment of his or her ascribed social roles. The Japanese lose face when they fail to meet the expectations of others with regard to their social position and roles. Because mentsu represents a person's public image, individuals in Japan are more concerned about their face when interacting with someone not close to them, above all during formal situations.

The perception of losing face in the presence of subordinates is far graver than the perception of losing face in front of a superior or peer.

Because public image is vital for individuals, risk aversion is culturally favored in Japan.

RELIGION AND PHILOSOPHY

Confucianism entered Japan via Korea in the 5th century.

Confucian philosophy influenced Japanese culture and social behavior through the promotion of personal virtues and harmony and respect for tradition and elders, establishing the society on a very firm hierarchy of relationships where every individual should fulfill his or her different social roles according to relative social position.[12]

Confucianism today is blended with two other religions and belief systems in Japan: *Buddhism* and *Shinto*. We introduced Buddhism in chapter 2.

Shinto can be defined as a set of codified rituals and practices, to be carried out meticulously, to establish a link between ancient and modern Japan. It is characterized by veneration of nature spirits (kami) and ancestors and influences every aspect of Japanese life: ethics, politics, family, society, art, sport, and spirit. Even profane events such as the construction of a new building involve a Shinto ceremony. Examples of rituals are purification rites, festivals, ceremonies for ancestors, Sumo events, theater dramas, ceremonies for a newborn, and ceremonies to secure the benediction of kami for a generous harvest.

LE

Le represents the concept of extended household in Japan. Japanese families are mostly patriarchal and are made up of grandparents and their son's family. The son inherits the house and with it the responsibility of taking care of his parents, all living under the same roof. An important aspect of le is the commemoration of ancestors, principally the ones who held the status of household chiefs.

Interdependence, respect for hierarchy, and closeness are critical in the Japanese family to preserve harmony, ensure continuity, and direct efforts toward in-group benefits.

WA

Wa originates from le; the concept symbolizes traditional Japanese family values and represents harmony, conformity, and affiliation within a social group. Wa, to a certain extent, expands the concept of le to the whole society.

Members of a group give priority to group interests over individual interests. Employees are traditionally provided with lifelong employment so as to foster the affiliation with the company and rewards and bonuses are given to the group, not to individuals, to reinforce group unity.

Wa is a core concept in Japanese culture that requires individuals to preserve and guard the unity and harmony of the group. Following are concepts that ensure wa preservation:

- *Enryo* refers to restrained behavior and communication to avoid conflict. Individuals are required to restrict explicit opinions and displays of personal feelings to preserve harmony. Expressing one's opinions is regarded as uncultured and rude.

- *Sasshi* refers to the ability to read between the lines and understand what the other person is implicitly and indirectly saying.

- *Amae* refers to a form of protective relationship and mutual dependence among the members of a group. The needs that motivate people to adopt amae behavior are mainly two: the need for unconditional acceptance (as in the newborn and mother relationship) and the need for control, in which the amae requester controls the situation by making an appropriate appeal to another person. For example, less powerful individuals can control the situation if they are able to make a proper request of the more powerful person, particularly when a solid relationship exists between the two individuals (more on this in chapter 13).[13]

- *Giri* refers to obligation, loyalty, and duty toward somebody who has done well by the person. An example is employees' sense of obligation toward their company to the point of consuming only products made by their conglomerate. It is a moral obligation to perform one's work obligations toward members of the group to the best of their ability.

- *Awase* refers to the ability to adapt to different situations, giving precedence to group goals over individual goals.

- *Kenson* refers to humble and modest behavior, discounting one's abilities and successes, avoiding standing out, and showing humility to preserve the status quo of a relationship and group harmony.

- *Honne and Tatemae.* Honne refers to a person's true feelings and needs, usually kept concealed if not matching what is considered appropriate behavior by the society. Tatemae (literally façade) refers to a person's public behavior and ideas. It is what is expected by society and required according to one's social role and the situation.

- *Jouge kankei* refers to the Confucian concept of respect for superiors, parents, and elders.

- *Kata* refers to the perpetual and accustomed way of doing something, from martial arts to tea ceremonies. Kata is the result of strict rules and instructions needed to cope with the Japanese high uncertainty avoidance. The goal is to adopt the movements and techniques of a kata to be able to apply them instinctively under different circumstances.

ISOLATION, DENSITY, AND UNIQUENESS

The belief in the superiority and uniqueness of Japan has weakened but not entirely disappeared in present-day Japan.

To understand Japanese culture, it is essential to comprehend that Japan was never united until the Meiji period (1868 - 1912). Because of its geographic characteristics (an isle surrounded by ocean), Japan has also been relatively isolated from the rest of Asia for more than 200 years, starting from the Tokugawa period until the mid-19th century. In 1825, an expulsion edict was implemented, interdicting all barbarians and Westerners from entering Japan.

Motoori Nogara, an 18th century Japanese scholar, revived ancient Japanese myths asserting the centrality and superiority of Japan and Japanese people: According to Nogara, even the sun goddess was born in Japan.

A last important point is the country's dense population, which results in close proximity among people, further enforcing the concept of interdependence.[14]

AKIO MORITA

Akio Morita, founder of Sony, speaking to Harvard's Kennedy School of Government:[15]

Sony has many lawyers in the company today, and is involved with many law firms in America and elsewhere, but if we listen to lawyers too much, we cannot do any business. The lawyer's role is very important for the businessman, but I also think that it poses a danger. Even if the lawyers think of all possible risks, an unpredictable thing may happen. If you have so many lawyers, they have to find business, which sometimes they have to create. Sometimes, nonsensical lawsuits are generated by lawyers. In the United States, everybody sues everybody.

In the United States, there are more than 500,000 lawyers, with 39,000 new graduates every year. In Japan (with roughly half the population of the United States), there are 17,000 lawyers with about 300 new graduates each year.

The integration of lawyers into the business climate of the United States is an impediment to efficiency, and creates a legalistic climate of mutual mistrust and loss of confidence. It creates an unnecessary handicap on entrepreneurial efforts.

JAPANESE CULTURAL PARADOX

During the Meiji period, between 1868 and 1912, the Japanese Industrial Revolution occurred, transforming Japan from a feudal to a modern society. At the end of the 19th century, Japan became the first Asian industrialized country.

As a developed Asian country, and as a non-Western modernized country, Japan faced a dilemma between Westernization and tradition: Should Japan obtain its own independence by modernizing and Westernizing or should it become the leader of East Asia in the battle against Western colonialism and imperialism?[16]

In 1885, influential scholar Yukichi Fukuzawa claimed that Japan should turn itself toward the civilized countries of the West, leaving behind its backward Asian neighbors, specifically Korea and China. Japan leaders' eventual goal was to be regarded as equal by Western powers (specifically, the US and UK). Fukuzawa's essay laid the grounds for later Japanese imperialism in the region.

During the Sino-Japanese war (1894-1895), to emphasize affiliation with the West and separation from East Asia, popular books portrayed Japanese soldiers with Western facial features and Chinese with grotesque faces and pigtails:[17] According to these perspectives, Japan was equal to Western nations and superior to the backward Chinese, Taiwanese, and Koreans, those living in countries where it was introducing civilization and modernity.[18]

On the other side, during the Meiji period, the concept of Pan-Asianism was also developed. It started as a reaction against the spread of European imperialism to East Asia and led to the Greater East Asia Co-Prosperity Sphere ideology of the 1940s. That ideology promoted the cultural and economic unity of East Asia with the purpose of creating a union of Asian nations led by the Japanese and free of Western powers that legitimized Japanese expansion as an act to free Asia from Western powers.

KOREAN CULTURE

Among the main features of Korean cultures we can find *inhwa, weness and jung, maum, kibun, nunchi* and *self-regulation*.

INHWA

Inhwa is a concept influenced by Confucian philosophy that emphasizes harmony in society through a reciprocal and mutually beneficial system of loyalty among people. Organizations are viewed as an extension of the family: subordinates defer to the judgment of their superiors, while superiors maintain a strong interest in the well-being of their subordinates.

WE-NESS AND JUNG

In Korea, family members and close friends belong to the we-ness category, which comprises people linked by an intimate relationship founded on jung, a concept that can be translated as attachment and affection between members of the we-ness category and caring, polite, and supportive behavior.

The prototype of the jung-based relationship is the relationship among family members.

A relationship without the we-ness category is instead based on rationality, social norms, personal interests, and equity.[19]

MAUM

The main currency in Korean relationships is a maum exchange rather than a behavioral exchange.

Maum is defined as a collection of emotions, thoughts, experiences, and relationships that create the individual's picture of the world, mind and soul. Relationships in Korea are evaluated according to the degree of maum that is communicated through the interaction.

The concept of maum is to a certain degree similar to the concept of face in China and mentsu in Japan.

KIBUN

Both professional and social relationships in Korea are based on kibun, a concept that can be defined as harmony, balance, and respect for other's feelings. According to kibun, criticism in public must be avoided and individuals must always endeavor to be polite and respectful.[20]

NUNCHI

Nunchi is the ability to listen, read between the lines, and determine other people's concealed feelings. The concept of nunchi is essential to understand the high-context communication dynamics in Korea.

SELF-REGULATION

Because academic failure is regarded as a painful disappointment by Korean families, there is strong pressure on students in Korea to endeavor for academic excellence.

Three important factors influence Korean students' academic achievement:

- *Support received from parents.* Support from parents helps promote students' self-efficacy (the belief a person holds regarding his or her ability to complete tasks and reach goals). Children also feel indebted to their parents, fostering achievement motivation and relational closeness.

- *Students' self-regulation,* a concept that includes persistence, patience, determination, and willpower. Koreans rarely emphasize innate talent as a motivation for academic achievement and often hold lack of self-regulation responsible for their failures.

- *Established behavior.* Established behavior is enforced through monitoring and sanctioning from institutions such as family and school, with no room for interpretation.

The influence of parents, self-regulation and monitoring, and sanctioning from institutions are factors that help explain not only Korean, but also Chinese, Indian, and other Asian students' academic success.[21]

INDIAN CULTURE

Some people even question the fact that India is a country. According to Winston Churchill, India is merely a geographical expression. The founder of Singapore, Lee Kuan Yew, recently argued that India is not a real country. Instead it is thirty-two separate nations that happen to be arrayed along the British rail line.

Regardless of major differences, many still believe in an essential coherence and singleness about India.[22] Because of its geographical features, the country has been relatively isolated from the rest of the world by the mountains in the north and the sea in the south.

The most important values characterizing Indian society are: *time, karma, cosmic collectivism, hierarchical order, spiritual orientation, idealistic thinking, independent and interdependent self, context sensitivity,* and *sport heroes.*[23]

TIME AND KARMA

Belief in rebirth defines and distinguishes all religions originated in India (Hinduism, Jainism, Buddhism, and Sikhism). Indians understand time as cyclical, with each cycle made of four stages: childhood (*Krita,* when we learn), youth (*Treta,* when we accumulate wealth), maturity *(Dvapar,* when we teach), and old age (*Kali,* when we withdraw).

Faith in reincarnation has vast repercussions:[24]

First, it means that birth is not the beginning and death is not the end. If you live only once, the value of your life is the sum of your accomplishments. However, when you live infinite lives, your aim is not achievement and control, but understanding and meditation.

Because the events of the past influence the present, we, and no one else, are answerable for what occurred, is occurring, and will occur to us.

Reincarnation requires that we accept different and contradictory contexts existing concurrently.

The concept of karma, the law of consequence, implies that every choice has a consequence. No action exists in isolation and every decision affects the self, the people around, and the environment surrounding us.

As a result, the individual alone is accountable for the implications of his or her choices and actions. The individual cannot blame anyone for the consequences of his or her decisions.

An arrow that has been released from the bow is an allegory for a decision that cannot be retracted. It has consequences that each archer must face.[25]

COSMIC ORDER

Cosmic collectivism represents the concept that all the different forms of animate and inanimate elements are interrelated and part of the *Brahman* (the ultimate spirit, the greatest and invariable reality). Everything within the cosmos is organized according to a relative hierarchical order. Animates are superior to inanimates, human beings are superior to other animates, and, among human beings, hierarchy is based on caste and within caste on age and gender.

Above humans are the gods led by Indra. Above Indra is Brahma (the Creator), above Brahma is Shiva (the Destroyer), and above Shiva is Vishnu (the Preserver). Above Vishnu is the Goddess.

The ancient Indian categorization of elements in the cosmos shows strong similarities with the Confucian concept of social harmony that requires individuals to appropriately play their role according to their place in the social order.

Indians worship different gods according to circumstances and context defines the status of each god. According to the notion *of kathenotheism,*[26] in the Vedas each divinity is regarded as superior in turn, not at all times.

SPIRITUAL ORIENTATION

Indians strive for perfection in the attempt to rise above animal instincts and material ambitions through a serene and detached experiential approach to life consisting of yogic exercises and meditation.

Two ancient sources provide clear examples of Indian spirituality:

From the Bhagavad-Gita: You have a right to perform your prescribed duty, but you are not entitled to the fruits of action. Never consider yourself to be the cause of the results of your activities, and never be attached to not doing your duty (Gita: Ch. 2, 47).

From the Mahabharata: He whose proposed actions are never obstructed by heat or cold, fear of attachment, prosperity or adversity, is considered wise. He whose judgment dissociated from desire, follows both virtue and profit, and who disregarding pleasure chooses such ends as are serviceable in both worlds, is considered wise (Udyoga Parva, section 33, verse 19 & 20).

IDEALISTIC THINKING

Idealistic thinking refers to people's introverted and idealistic approach to problem solving, as a consequence of people's spiritual orientation. Indians tend to patiently aim for the unattainable, and, while looking for the perfect solution, they are often unable to separate actual facts from extreme fantasies.[27] This approach persuades individuals to strive for the unachievable ideal while simultaneously recognizing that this ideal may be all but impossible to achieve. The Indian approach to problem solving is often much too grand to develop into tangible solutions for concrete problems.[28]

Another feature of Indian thinking, supported by introspection and meditation, is the ability to follow a non-sequential logic, holding opposite and contradictory concepts together and integrating them in a new solution.

INDEPENDENT AND INTERDEPENDENT SELF

A unique characteristic of the Indian mentality is that it blends both individualistic and collectivist features. As individualists, Indians are very goal oriented and competitive.[29]

Therefore, Indians possess both an independent self that aims to fulfill individualistic goals and an interdependent self-concerned with meeting social expectations.[30]

Indians' primary collectivistic mode of behavior, which emphasizes the interdependence between individuals, is influenced by Hindu values, while the secondary individualistic mode of behavior, which focuses on autonomy and independence, has been affected by American and British values.[31]

Furthermore, Indians display a collectivistic approach toward the extended family and a competitive and individualistic attitude toward out-group members. In other words, the Indians are very family-oriented individuals and restrict trust and loyalty to those who are close to them. This leads to an evident lack of cooperation and teamwork among Indians.

CONTEXT SENSITIVITY

Indians display a deep concern and understanding of the context and tend to present conflicting thoughts and behaviors, such as individualism vs. collectivism, cooperation vs. competition, and respect for hierarchy and seniority vs. meritocracy, depending on the specific situation.

They are likely to avoid extreme behaviors, assessing the implications of their actions and responses to the particular circumstance. For example, public places induce different norms and values than private settings such as family; interaction with out-group members brings different behaviors than dealings with in-group members.[32]

Rules can be followed or broken according to the circumstances. Honesty and virtue don't depend on rules, but on context. Decisions can be either right or wrong according to the situation and can be evaluated only in hindsight.

As a result, Indian negotiators display a primary mode of behavior based on traditional Hindu values, such as collectivism, high power distance, cooperation, and passivity and a secondary mode of behavior based on imported Western management practices, mainly from the US and UK, that emphasize individualism, egalitarianism, competitiveness, and proactivity. [33]

TENDULKAR: THE MIRROR OF INDIA

The career of Sachin Tendulkar (see Figure 1), Indian greatest cricket player, embodies India's ascension as the third economy in the world (in terms of purchasing power parity). His 24-year career mirrors the renovation of India from a developing country to a land optimistic about the future. No other sport person in the world has had a similar impact on his or her home country. Tendulkar united India for more than two decades, rising above its profound schisms created by language, religion, ethnicity, and caste.

Despite being an icon, Tendulkar always remained an unpretentious individual.

If cricket is a religion in India, Sachin is a god.[34]

Figure 1. Divinization of Tendulkar.

He also promoted the notion of individuals shaping their own destiny, without being constrained by fatalism and the traditional passive acceptance of events.

In the words of Shashi Tharoor, an Indian government minister, *Tendulkar became a symbol of what, as a nation, we collectively aspire to be.*

RUSSIAN CULTURE

The most important values typifying Russian society are *Russian identity, Eurasian perspective, creative survival, unwritten rules*, and *contradictions*.

RUSSIAN IDENTITY

Russian cultural identity is defined by language and religion. To be Russian is primarily to speak Russian, the language of the Muscovy state that unified Russia during the 14th century.[35]

At least to a certain extent, another unifying factor is religion. At the end of the 10th century, Vladimir Prince of Kiev felt the need to import a single state religion to bring together the different Russian tribes. The choice fell on Byzantine Christianity, which became Russian Orthodoxy during the Great Schism in 1054.[36] According the latest Russian census, a majority of Russian citizens, and as many as 80% of ethnic Russians, identified themselves as Russian Orthodox.

EURASIAN PERSPECTIVE

Russia has a unique position on the margins of both Europe and Asia.

During Peter the Great's reign at the end of the 17th and beginning of the 18th centuries, a program of economic, political, and cultural reforms was established to move Russia closer to Europe. Russian geographers proposed to set the continental demarcation between Europe and Asia on the Urals.

In this way, the cities west of the Urals became part of Europe, while Siberia, the land of fur, was relegated to Asia. The Asian territories were considered to be part of the Russian empire only in a political sense.

Starting from the 19th century, because of the lack of Western endorsement for Russia's European identity, a new nationalist perspective saw Asia as a ground to promote Russian superiority over the West and pursue Russian interests.[37]

Today, a unique Eurasian identity, not dissimilar from the one promulgated by the Muscovy state in the 14th century, that sets Russia apart from both the West and the East, has been reasserted.

CREATIVE SURVIVAL

Russian culture has been strongly influenced by the tough conditions the early Slavic settlers encountered: harsh climate, remoteness, and an unfriendly environment providing sporadic crops. The result was a culture that emphasizes caution, prudence, determination, patience, security, and survival.[38]

Traditionally, Russia has been considered a high power distance (PDI score of 93) and a high uncertainty-avoidance culture (UAI score of 95). These results have been confirmed by the World Values Survey, where Russians score very high on economic and physical security, and in terms of conservatism and hierarchy values.

A history of authoritarian and centralized leadership (the Orthodox Church, tsars, landowners, the communist party elite, the modern oligarchs) has promoted significant inequality between people in power and people not in power, great respect for hierarchy, and reluctance to take the initiative and challenge the status quo in the workforce.

Centuries of authoritarian and centralized leadership have also stimulated an attitude of *optimistic fatalism*: Life just carries on by itself and responsibility for change is passed to fate and people with authority.[39]

Because the past security system is no longer in place, today Russians are compelled to face uncertainty, a situation labeled creative survival, which requires them at least to take some level of initiative and to rapidly and resourcefully adapt to the changing environment.[40]

UNWRITTEN RULES

Russia is a country of unwritten rules. In the post-Soviet environment, a prevailing set of practices originating in the early Slavic community and reinforced throughout the following centuries, during the medieval Muscovy reign, the tsars' period, and the Soviet era, has undermined the rule of law:

* Risk aversion and stability are promoted over innovation and progress.
* Real power is in the hands of a leader and his inner circle (the prince and his boyars during the tsars' period, the general secretary and the politburo during the Communist era, the oligarch and his close personal network today).
* Decision making is secretive, ambiguous, opaque, and based on informal rules and personal connections.

A skeptical attitude, which sometimes grows into disregard, toward an inconsistent and rarely enforced legal framework has facilitated the rise of the logic of unwritten systems, in which the rule of law is subjugated to personal interests.[41]

CONTRADICTIONS

Understanding Russian contradictory behavior is not easy.

Orthodox Christianity had a remarkable role in shaping Russians' traditional negative attitudes toward money and material wealth, which is in sharp contrast to the current oligarchs' behavior.

Novels by Dostoyevsky, Tolstoy, and Goncharov, among others, traditionally depicted Russians as passive, procrastinators, and unwilling to take risks and responsibility or to make decisions, but at the same time, according to several recent surveys, foreign nationals perceive Russians as serious, hardworking, and assertive.

One possible explanation is that personality traits in older Russians have been more heavily influenced by the communist regime. However, research has not found any striking difference between younger and older Russians' values and behaviors (results are similar to those found around the world).

An old Orthodox religious maxim says: *We cannot see this reality with our eyes, but we perceive it with our minds.*[42]

Perhaps the best advice to comprehend Russians comes from poet Fyodor Tyutchev: *One cannot understand Russia by reason.*

POLISH CULTURE

The most important influences on Polish identity have been *Catholicism, foreign domination,* and *Humanism.*

CATHOLICISM

Historically, Poland has been characterized as the safeguard of Catholicism, from time to time against the Islamic world, the Tartars, Orthodox Russia, and Lutheran countries.

During the more than 200 years of foreign rule, from the end of the 18th century to the end of the 20th century, the Catholic Church has strongly shaped Polish identity, acting as a unifying element of the country.

FOREIGN DOMINATION

National insurrections were the norm during the 200 years of foreign domination, leading to a national mythology that inspired sacrifice for just causes and the romantic glorifying of heroes.

Each time, loss of independence, to Russia first and then from time to time to Prussia, Austria, Germany, and the Soviet Union, has resuscitated patriotic pride and camaraderie. The social movement of the 1980s, Solidarność, which fought against Soviet repression through civil resistance, is just the latest example of Polish rebellion during the last two centuries.[43]

HUMANISM AND LOW SOCIAL EFFECTIVENESS[44]

Three main historical reasons have contributed to the shaping of humanism and low social effectiveness in Polish culture:

- Anarchic freedoms over law and order because of historical instability and uncertainty.
- Centuries-long rural life.
- Religion highlighting human imperfection.

Humanism emphasizes close, cordial, and informal personal relations, with high status for women. It is an ethical perspective that highlights the value and agency of human beings, who are defined through actions and experience instead of doctrine and faith.

Low social effectiveness can be summarized by the following traits: improvisation preferred over planning, a belief that things will be resolved one way or another, little law enforcement, low trust in authority, and flexible time.

AFRICAN CULTURE

There is a tendency to consider the African continent as a homogeneous unit. However, significant diversity exists in several aspects: colonization legacy (e.g., the linguistic divide between Anglophone and Francophone blocs), level of economic development (South Africa and Nigeria make up over 50% of sub-Saharan Africa's gross domestic product), level of political development, and cultural and ethnic groups.

More than one billion people belonging to more than 2,000 different ethnic groups live in Africa. Nigeria, for example, is home to 3 major cultural groups, more than 200 ethno-linguistic groups, and 3 major religions.

Despite this strong historical, economic, political, ethnic, and cultural diversity in Africa, enough traits in common exist among the different cultures to authorize use of the term African for sub-Saharan African countries.[45]

The most important common values characterizing African society are *traditional religion, ubuntu, family and chief-ship,* and *heterogeneity.*

TRADITIONAL RELIGION

Religion is interpreted in Africa as spirituality rather than doctrine. Traditional African religions have been transmitted from one generation to the next orally through rituals, festivals, songs, dances, proverbs, and myths.

Traditional religion in Africa asserts the wholeness of all beings because all existing creatures originate from a single supreme being, embraces natural phenomena, and honors spirits, secondary deities, and ancestors.

The traditional African worldview is dynamic: The force that links all human beings is continuously changing, strengthening and weakening, influenced by natural phenomena and ancestors.

Religion plays a central and universal role in the lives of African people, and participation in the community's religious rituals and ceremonies is required to be part of the group.

Traditional religion is followed by only 12% of the African population (45% of Africans are Christians, 40% Muslims), but still has formidable influence in the African interpretation of Christianity and Islam.

UBUNTU

The African worldview emphasizes the concept of ubuntu, the sub-Saharan, predominantly South African, notion of humanity and morality that can be described as respect and compassion for others: the essence of being human. *I am, because we are; and since we are, therefore I am.*[46] According to a South African proverb, a person becomes human through others.

The community is seen as the context within which each individual can realize his or her potential. Reputation and status are influenced by the degree of thoughtfulness each individual displays in meeting the needs and fostering the well-being of the community.

It is also true that, on occasion, a wide gap has grown between the ideal and the real value of humanity and morality in Africa (e.g., with domestic slavery, human sacrifices, ethnic conflicts).

FAMILY AND CHIEF-SHIP

The notion of family in Africa encompasses all blood relatives with a common ancestor. Extended families are the pillars on which the community is built, and marriages are considered crucial to the development of kinship ties that ensure the group's welfare and perpetuation. African society is paternalistic and hierarchical: a system of seniority, ranking, and heredity selects the tribal chief, who is usually both the political and the religious leader.

The tribal chief must seek advice from the representatives of the community before any decision and should never abuse his power.

During assemblies, the principles of egalitarianism, mutual benefit, respect, and acceptance are employed: People are free to express their opinions without being interrupted in seemingly endless consultations and decisions are reached mostly through consensus to preserve harmony and relationships in the community.[47]

What made the Sierra Leonean civil war so destructive, was that boys, enlisted by both sides, killed elders. The elder's job is to protect the young; when they feared them instead, it made resuming normal life much more complicated.[48]

HETEROGENEITY

Taking into account various performance measures, African firms show significant disadvantages in all measures of firm performance compared to other continents' companies.

However, recent research has found that, contrary to common assumptions, using statistical adjustments that compensate for regional disadvantages, African companies possesses an inherent advantage and African entrepreneurs perform better because to survive in such a challenging environment, they must work harder and smarter.[49]

Therefore, no intrinsic curse on Africa due to self-loathing or perceptions of inferiority (as a consequence of traditional African cultural values being subjugated during colonization) impedes its development; there is only a need to overcome the poor political, business, and social environment, particularly the lack of infrastructure, inadequate access to finance, and scarce party competition.

According to the research, an important factor that can foster progress in Africa is ethnic fractionalization because it is positively correlated with labor productivity and growth. African ethnic fractionalization can create the same competitive advantage that immigrants provided to the United States: Heterogeneity nurtures creativity and cooperation.

ARAB CULTURE

The Arab world consists of around 420 million people living in 22 countries and extends from the Atlantic Ocean in the west to the Arabian Sea in the east and from the Mediterranean Sea in the north to the Horn of Africa and the Indian Ocean in the southeast (see Figure 2).

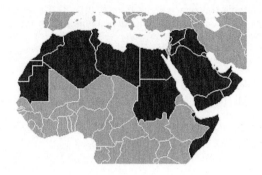

Figure 2. Arab World.

All members of the Arab League are commonly accepted as being part of the Arab world: Algeria, Bahrain, Comoros, Djibouti, Egypt, Iraq, Jordan, Kuwait, Lebanon, Libya, Mauritania, Morocco, Oman, Palestine, Qatar, Saudi Arabia, Somalia, Sudan, Syria, Tunisia, United Arab Emirates, Yemen.

The term Arab actually includes many different ethnic and racial groups, with two elements in common: the Arabic language and Islam.

The most important common values characterizing the Arab world are a *cult of personality, Bedouin tradition, fatalism, wasta,* and *oil.*

CULT OF PERSONALITY

Most Arabs are attracted and fascinated by strong personalities. These personages can be political, religious, organizational, or community figures. This is one of the reasons why many populist and authoritarian regimes have arisen in the Arab world. Conventional people tend to identify with leaders who have the qualities of charisma, self-confidence, purpose, and ambition and originate from modest families: Assad in Syria, Gadhafi in Libya, and Saddam Hussein in Iraq are just some examples of authoritarian leaders in the Arab world.

These figures are legitimized through pictures, posters, news, songs, biographies, and TV programs and corroborated through a cult of personality that often involves adoration and glorification.

BEDOUIN TRADITION

Bedouins (inhabitants of the desert) are nomadic tribes that for centuries have populated the desert regions of North Africa and the Middle East. The harsh desert environment has inspired the development of rigid rules and values: hospitality, generosity, honor, and a hierarchical and consultative style of leadership, expressed by the sheikh.

Even if most Bedouin tribes have settled, these values are still maintained in the present day by most Arabs.

The family, which is deeply correlated to the tribe, is the basic social structure of Arab society. Relationships between different families can still be influenced by agreements that are centuries old.

FATALISM

Islam is a fundamental trait of Arab society. As emphasized in chapter 2, while most Arabs are Muslims (although with some significant Christian minorities), not all Muslims are Arabs.

Islam is the third and most recent major religion that originated in what today is the Arab world.

The term Islam literally means submission; Muslims believe they are submitting to the will of God.

This aspect of Islam has contributed to the generation of highly hierarchical societies, with communities ruled by a leader making decisions through consultation.

Islamic values primary focus on helping each other, settling conflicts by the law of God, taking care of the needy and the weak in society, and being humble.

When speaking about future events, a commonly heard phrase throughout the Arab world is *Insha'Allah*, meaning if God wills. To some people, it may sound as if Insha'Allah specifies that an event will occur only if God takes a direct interest in it, indicating that individuals have no control over their environment. However, to Muslims, it only means that despite the person's best intentions and effort, if God has other plans, the individual will never be able to successfully complete the job.[50]

This aspect of Islam leads to a sense of fatalism about life, based on the postulation that outcomes are not always the result of a process. Planning, scheduling, and organizing are not synonymous with control of the environment and of the future in the Arab world.

WASTA

Wasta is derived from the Arabic word wasat, which means medium, intermediary, broker, or middle-man.

Today the word wasta is identified with connections and influence. As in many other cultures, Arabs prefer doing business with people they trust. Affiliation with the same tribe or family is a powerful connection. Many relationships between families have been in place for several generations.

The system of wasta was originally developed to protect the social structure of Bedouin tribes. The sheikhs allocated wealth, favors, and opportunities at their discretion to preserve the harmony of the tribe. Relationships and conflicts between families and tribes were managed through intermediaries, individuals respected by both parties.

Having wasta is fundamental to having access to key people, information, and scarce resources. Without wasta, it would be very difficult to complete any kind of task in the Arab world.

Thus, wasta is the most valuable form of currency in the Arab world.[51]

Oil

Most people of the Arab world have language, religion, and history in common, but their societies differ deeply in terms of economic wealth.

We can split the Arab world into three categories:

- A first group of countries that despite efforts to diversify their economies in recent years still mostly rely on oil to create wealth (among them the Gulf nations, Saudi Arabia, and Libya).

- Other countries, which account for almost 70% of the region's population, have modest oil reserves and have developed established higher education systems and economies (among them, North African countries, Lebanon, Jordan, and Syria). The Egyptian economy, for example, is based on agriculture, tourism, and fees deriving from the Suez Canal.

- A third group of countries that don't control any natural resource and have not been able to promote a solid higher education system or develop their economies (among them, Sudan, Somalia, and Yemen).

For Arab oil-exporting countries, oil is important not only for economic reasons, but also for political reasons. Oil is a scarce resource that is essential to all Western powers. The Organization of Arab Petroleum Exporting Countries (OAPEC) first exercised its power during the Yom Kippur War in 1973 when the United States supplied Israel with weapons. In response, the OAPEC announced an oil embargo that started in October 1973 and ended only after five months.

Oil has therefore served as a substitute for military power, obliging oil-importing nations to reconsider their foreign policies in the light of their long-term economic interests.

At the same time, oil has also implanted an artificial perception of power and economic security in oil-exporting states. Few of these countries have been able to diversify their economies using oil money to invest in new economic sectors.

In synthesis, oil meant and still means foreign involvement in internal affairs, political corruption, militarization, a distorted economy (fully reliant on oil), and authoritarian governments:[52] Oil wealth has the effect of hindering any economic, political, or social reform that might begin in Arab oil-exporting countries.

Mexican Culture

The most important values characterizing Mexican society are *simpatía, the relationship between state and church, family*, and *machismo*.

Simpatía

A simpático person is pleasant, friendly, easygoing, caring, polite, and in most circumstances modest.

Simpatía is a cultural script that is used to describe a typical Mexican (and Latin American in general) pattern of interaction aimed at promoting harmony in relationships by showing respect, avoiding conflict, and underscoring positive actions, while understating negative actions.[53]

In Mexican culture, being courteous and polite is a moral imperative. Traditional Mexicans will do everything in their power to accommodate the needs and wishes of their guests.

Beyond *politeness* and *loyalty*, another essential aspect of Mexican culture is *patience*, which helps to overcome the conflicts and challenges of interpersonal relationships and preserve harmony in the extended family that often lives under the same roof.

STATE-CHURCH RELATIONSHIP

Since 1519, when Cortes landed in Mexico accompanied by Roman Catholic clergy, the Roman Catholic Church has sustained a major role in Mexico. After independence, the government tried to limit the influence and the privileges of the Church, which acted as a state within the state, which led to a civil war between 1857 and 1860.

In the constitution of 1917, far-reaching restrictions on the role of the Church in political affairs were introduced. In the 1940s, the conflict between state and church officially ended, until the 1980s, when the Church demanded a more important role in national matters, criticizing government corruption, as well as the Mexican political system and its inability to implement an effective democracy in Mexico.

FAMILY

Family is the building block of Mexican society. Extended families are the norm, and members maintain very close relationships, with three or even four generations living under the same roof.

Families tend to gather to celebrate birthdays, public holidays, saints' days, funerals, marriages, rites of passage (such as the quinceañera, the 15th birthday of a young female), and births.

Mexicans consider their responsibility to support close and extended family members and place high value on hierarchy, authority, traditions (whether Maya, Huichol, or Catholic), and respect for seniors, with the father acting as the authority and decision maker within the family.

MACHISMO

During the mid-20th century the term macho became associated with aggression and virility, acquiring misogynist nuances and negative stereotyped connotations.

However, in pre-Columbian Mexico, the term was associated with wisdom and leadership: A macho individual was an admirable and commendable person.

When the Spanish arrived, the term changed its connotations, acquiring a strictly masculine meaning that stressed bravery, courage, and strength, even if still related to wisdom and leadership.

However, it is important to point out that machismo has multiple tiers, with positive connotations related to caballerismo, chivalry (honor, bravery, magnanimity, perseverance, courage, bravery), and also child care responsibilities and respect for women.

BRAZILIAN CULTURE

The most important influences in Brazilian culture are *a sense of separateness, jeitinho, novelas, religion,* and *short-termism.*

SENSE OF SEPARATENESS

Brazil is almost a continent on its own. There is a widespread feeling of autonomy because of the size of the country and its population (which constitutes approximately one third of the Latin American population) and also because Brazil is the only country in Latin America whose population doesn't speak Spanish.[54]

Another important factor in Brazil is its racial diversity: Originally, the Brazilian population was composed of Portuguese settlers, African slaves (mostly Bantu and West Africans), and indigenous populations. In the late 19th and early 20th centuries, new ethnic groups arrived from Portugal, Italy, Spain, Germany, Japan, and the Middle East.

JEITINHO

In a country where social norms, laws, and rules can be flexibly interpreted and dodged, jeitinho is defined as a special way to solve a problem or a creative solution to an emergency.

In economic terms, it is a means to overcome the excessive Brazilian bureaucracy. In social terms, it is a mechanism that provides a way to overcome unforeseen situations and circumvent impersonal rules.

In Brazil, it is difficult to draw a precise line between jeitinho, favor, and corruption. Jeitinho is a subjective concept that is situated somewhere in-between what is right and what is wrong.

Jeitinho is socially justifiable in Brazil because it provides the majority of the population with a means to meet their basic needs.

An important aspect of jeitinho is related to the concept of simpatía that we introduced in the previous paragraph: Because jeitinho is not based on financial or social resources, but on interpersonal relationships, the way jeitinho is requested becomes essential.

The person requesting jeitinho has to be pleasant, respectful, polite, and friendly; in short, the person has to be simpatico. To a certain extent in Brazil, it is more important to be nice than to be important. Simpatía is therefore a fundamental element of jeitinho.[55]

NOVELAS

TV soap operas, novelas, are a unifying factor in Brazil. The common novela configuration is made of three parallel stories with characters belonging to three different classes: upper, middle, and lower. The plots converge to create relationships between characters, stories, and social classes.

According to many Brazilian scholars, novelas represent a central element in Brazil's integration.

Another unifying element of Brazilian people from all social classes is certainly *football* (soccer to Americans). The fate of the Brazilian national team directly affects Brazil's citizens, and during major football matches, streets and offices are deserted.

RELIGION

Historically, Brazil has been, and still is, a strongly Catholic country, even if syncretism, the combination of different traditions and beliefs, is widespread and socially accepted.

The convergence of Catholicism with the religious traditions of African slaves and indigenous people has evolved in *syncretic religions* such as Candomblé (merger between Catholicism and African religions) and Pajelança (blend of Catholicism and native traditions).

Brazil is also the country where spiritualism inspired by the ideas of French mystic Allan Kardec is practiced. *Spiritualism* subscribes to the notion that the spirits of the dead can communicate with the world of the living. Another highly practiced syncretic religion in Brazil is Umbanda, originated from a combination of spirtualism and Candomblé, therefore with a strong Catholic orientation.

In Brazil, even football can be considered a religion.

With such a rich compendium of religions, it comes as no surprise that Brazilians are strongly superstitious.

SHORT-TERMISM

Brazilians live for the moment. Long-term planning is not relevant in Brazil and short-termism applies to every aspect of Brazilian society. Return on investment is expected to be almost immediate in every sector, from football to business ventures.

But living for the moment is not synonymous with indifference toward the future; it is only a consequence of the Brazilian *passive optimism*, an optimistic attitude toward life, associated with a fatalistic view about the future: *Amanhã tudo se resolve* (things will get better tomorrow).

US CULTURE

The most important values characterizing the United States are *religion, an Anglo-Saxon dominant culture, self-reliance*, and *egalitarianism*.

RELIGION

Religion is a strong cultural value in the U.S. According to a 2012 Gallup poll,[56] 94% of the population believes in God, 58% of Americans report that religion is very important in their lives, and 23% report that is fairly important.

Among Americans, 51% attend a religious service at least once a month (30% attend a religious service at least once a week). The level of religiosity in the United States is much higher than in any other developed country (in some cases, almost double any European country).

American theism has its foundation in the nation's Puritan-Protestant heritage.[57]

English colonists arrived as families and in several circumstances as entire religious congregations. Regarded as religious fanatics in Europe and subjected to persecution, these Puritan-Protestants pursued a religious utopia in the New World.

The result was exceptionally religious communities that exerted extreme influence on the culture of the English colonies; actually, the Puritan-Protestant settlers succeeded in establishing their values for what became the United States of America.

About 41% of all Americans classify themselves as Protestants, with 23% Catholics and 10% in Orthodox and other Christian religions. Jewish people make up only 2% of the population, the same percentage as Mormons.

The first Middle Atlantic independent states (such as New Jersey, Pennsylvania, and Maryland) were settled by immigrants persecuted in Europe for their religious beliefs.

Calvinists believed that only those who were predestined to be saved would be saved. Since it was impossible to know who was elected to be saved, the belief that hard work and frugality could bring social success and wealth were clear indicators of being elected and developed.

This view was not shared by all Protestants, but the Protestant work ethic emphasizing values such as hard work, frugality, and diligence became dominant in the U.S.

Anglo-Saxon Dominant Culture

The United States is a culturally diverse society with prevailing male, white, Anglo-Saxon, Protestant (WASP) cultural values.

Even if the WASP group's social and financial influence has diminished over the last decades, other ethnic groups (African Americans, Hispanics, Indians, Arabs, Asians) still have to give up their differences and match the dominant Anglo-Saxon cultural values and norms to became part of the mainstream society.[58]

According to Professor Fischer (1989),[59] American culture was shaped by four mass emigrations from four different regions of Britain and by four different socio-religious groups. New England was established between 1629 and 1640 by Puritans from East Anglia. Between 1640 and 1675, the next mass migration of southern English cavaliers settled the Chesapeake Bay. Then, between 1675 and 1725, Quakers settled the Delaware Valley. Finally, English, Scots, and Irish from the borderlands settled in Appalachia between 1717 and 1775. Each of these migrations produced a distinct regional culture that can still be seen in America today.

Self-Reliance

Self-reliance is confidence in one's own capabilities, decisions, judgments, and resources. The meaning can also be extended to include independence and unconventionality.

There is a time in every man's education when he arrives at the conviction that envy is ignorance; that imitation is suicide. Insist on yourself; never imitate.[60]

Self-reliance is the building block of individualism, the ideology and cultural value that fosters the precedence of individual goals and needs over group goals and needs.

Self-reliance also represents one of the U.S. initial core values. Many pioneers tried to take advantage of the huge opportunities in the West, such as land, gold, and natural resources: independent men of action who didn't rely on help from others.

Self-reliance comes with the belief that people can control and change the environment to fit their needs. There is an emphasis on action, success, ambition, competency, risk taking, development, transformation, and competition.

An ounce of action is worth a ton of theory, God will not have his work made manifest by cowards.[61]

In the U.S., fatalism is synonymous with laziness and indolence.[62]

Leaders must convey two crucial American qualities: *forcefulness* and *optimism*.

EGALITARIANISM

Being able to accomplish something by oneself is highly valued in the U.S. The Calvinist belief that each individual is equal in the eyes of God and can accomplish whatever is desired if he or she is prepared to work hard is the basis for the often abused statement that all people ought to be given an equal opportunity to succeed in life. Individuals have to take the responsibility to bring change and tackle the status quo.

Status in the U.S. is based on what an individual does and has achieved, not on who the individual is, and on inherited rights.

Because titles have historically been associated with hereditary status, Americans usually use their first name, emphasizing an extremely informal, open, and direct approach and communication style.

SOURCES

Following you'll find useful websites that provide an overview of national cultural differences, economic rankings, and articles on international affairs:

Culture Smart: http://www.culturesmartconsulting.com/
Global Sherpa: http://www.globalsherpa.org/world-rankings
Project Syndicate: http://www.project-syndicate.org/
Cyborlink: http://www.cyborlink.com/
Country Reports: http://www.countryreports.org/index.htm
World Business Culture: http://www.worldbusinessculture.com/
CIA World Factbook: https://www.cia.gov/library/publications/the-world-factbook/
IMF World Economic Database: http://www.imf.org/external/ns/cs.aspx?id=28

(ENDNOTES)

1   Berry, J. W., Poortinga, Y. H., Breugelmans, S. M., Chasiotis, A., & Sam, D. L. (2011). Cross-cultural psychology: Research and applications. Cambridge, UK: Cambridge University Press.

2   Lin, C. C., & Yamaguchi, S. (2011). Under What Conditions Do People Feel Face-Loss? Effects of the Presence of Others and Social Roles on the Perception of Losing Face in Japanese Culture. Journal of Cross-Cultural Psychology, Vol. 42, N. 1, 120-124.

3   Fang, T. (2006). The Chinese Negotiator. Journal of Business and Industrial Marketing, Vol. 21, N. 1, 50-60.

4   Hickson, D. J., & Pugh, D. S. (2003). Management Worldwide (2nd ed.). London: Penguin Business.

5   Chen, D. (1999). Three-dimensional Chinese rationales in negotiation. In D. M. Kolb. (Ed.), Negotiation Eclectics: Essays in Memory of Jeffrey Z. Rubin. Cambridge, MA: PON Books.

6   Faure, G. O. & Fang, T. (2008). Changing Chinese values: Keeping up with paradoxes. International Business Review, 17, 194-207.

7   Peng, K., & Nisbett, R. E. (1999). Culture, dialectics, and reasoning about contradiction. American Psychologist, Vol. 54, N. 9, 741-754.

8   Faure, G. O. (2012). China: New values in a changing society. Retrieved from http://www.ceibs.edu/ase/Documents/EuroChinaForum/faure.htm.

9   Brockmann, H., Delhey, J., Welzel, C., & Yuan, H. (2009). The China puzzle: Falling happiness in a rising economy. Journal of Happiness Studies, Vol. 10, N. 4, 387-405.

10 Faure, G. O. (2012). China: New values in a changing society. Retrieved from http://www.ceibs.edu/ase/Documents/EuroChinaForum/faure.htm.

11 Lin, C. C., & Yamaguchi, S. (2011). Under What Conditions Do People Feel Face-Loss? Effects of the Presence of Others and Social Roles on the Perception of Losing Face in Japanese Culture. Journal of Cross-Cultural Psychology, Vol. 42, N. 1, 120-124.

12 Hendry, J. (1998). Interpreting Japanese society (2nd ed.). Abingdon, UK: Routledge.

13 Yamaguchi, S., & Ariizumi, Y. (2006). Close Interpersonal Relationships among Japanese Amae as Distinguished from Attachment and Dependence. In U. Kim, K.-S. Yang, & K.-K. Hwang (Eds.), International and Cultural Psychology: Understanding people in context. New York: Springer.

14 Adachi, Y. (1997). Business Negotiations between the Americans and the Japanese. Global Business Languages, Vol. 2, 19-30.

15 Morita, A., Reingold, E. M., & Shimomura, M. (1986). Made in Japan: Akio Morita and Sony. New York, NY: Dutton.

16 Askew, W. K. (2004). The Cultural Paradox Of Modern Japan: Japan And Its Three Others. New Zealand Journal of Asian Studies, Vol. 6, N. 1, 130-149.

17 Henning, J. M. (2000). Breaking Company: Meiji Japan and East Asia. Education About Asia, Vol. 5, N. 3, 40-43.

18 Tanaka, S. (1993). Japan's Orient: Rendering pasts into history. Berkeley, CA: University of California Press.

19 Choi, S.-C., & Kim, K. (2006). Naïve Psychology of Koreans' Interpersonal Mind and Behavior in Close Relationships. In U. Kim, K.-S. Yang, & K.-K. Hwang (Eds.), Indigenous and Cultural Psychology, Understanding People in Context. New York: Springer.

20 Lee, C. Y. (2012). Korean Culture And Its Influence on Business Practice in South Korea. The Journal of International Management Studies, Vol. 7, N. 2, 184-191.

21 Park, Y., & Kim, U. (2006). Family, Parent-Child Relationship, and Academic Achievement in Korea. In U. Kim, K.-S. Yang, & K.-K. Hwang (Eds.), Indigenous and Cultural Psychology, Understanding People in Context. New York: Springer.

22 Zakaria, F. (2013). The rediscovery of India. In C. Chandler, & A. Zainulbhai (Eds.), Reimagining India: Unlocking the Potential of Asia's Next Superpower. New York: Simon & Schuster.

23 Sinha, J. B. P., & Kumar, R. (2004). Methodology for Understanding Indian Culture. The Copenhagen Journal of Asian Studies, 19, 89-104.

24   Pattanaik, D. (2013). Business Sutra: A Very Indian Approach to Management. New Delhi: Aleph Book Company.

25   Pattanaik, D. (2013). Business Sutra: A Very Indian Approach to Management. New Delhi: Aleph Book Company.

26   Müller, M. (1919). The Six Systems of Indian Philosophy. London: Longmans Green and Co.

27   Kumar, R. (2004). Brahmanical Idealism, Anarchical Individualism, and the Dynamics of Indian Negotiating Behavior. International Journal of Cross Cultural Management, 4, 39-58.

28   Kumar, R. (2004). Brahmanical Idealism, Anarchical Individualism, and the Dynamics of Indian Negotiating Behavior. International Journal of Cross Cultural Management, 4, 39-58.

29   Kumar, R. (2005). Negotiating with complex, Imaginative Indians. Ivey Business Journal, March/April, 1-6.

30   Markus, H. R., & Kitayama, S. (1991). Culture and the Self. Implications for Cognition, Emotion, and Motivation. Psychological Review, Vol. 98, N. 2, 224-253.

31   Sinha, J. B. P., & Kanungo, R. N. (1997). Context Sensitivity and Balancing in Organizational Behavior. International Journal of Psychology, Vol. 32, N. 2, 93-105.

32   Sinha, J. B. P., & Kumar, R. (2004). Methodology for Understanding Indian Culture. The Copenhagen Journal of Asian Studies, 19, 89-104.

33   Kumar, R. (2004). Brahmanical idealism, anarchical individualism, and the dynamics of Indian negotiating behavior, International Journal of Cross Cultural Management, 4, 39-58.

34   Vijay Santhanam & Shyam Balasubramanian.

35   Worth, D. S. (1998). Language. In N. Rzhevsky (Ed.), The Cambridge companion to modern Russian culture. Cambridge, UK: Cambridge University Press.

36   Likhachev, D. S. (1998). Religion: Russian orthodoxy. In N. Rzhevsky (Ed.), The Cambridge companion to modern Russian culture. Cambridge, UK: Cambridge University Press.

37   Bassin, M. (1998). Asia. In N. Rzhevsky (Ed.), The Cambridge companion to modern Russian culture. Cambridge, UK: Cambridge University Press.

38   Ledeneva, A. (2001). Unwritten rules: How Russia really works. London, UK: Centre for European Reform.

39   King, A. (2007). Culture smart: Russia. London, UK: Kuperard.

40   Alexashin, Y., & Blenkinsopp, J. (2005). Changes in Russian managerial values: a test of the convergence hypothesis?. International Journal of Human Resource Management, Vol. 16, N. 3, 427-444.

41   Ledeneva, A. (2001). Unwritten rules: How Russia really works. London, UK: Centre for European Reform.

42   King, A. (2007). Culture Smart: Russia. London: Kuperard.

43   Boski, P. (1993). Between West and East: Humanistic values and concerns in Polish psychology. In U. Kim, & J. Berry (Eds.), Indigenous psychologies: Research and experience in cultural context. Newbury Park: Sage.

44   Boski, P. (2012). Psychology of a Culture: Humanism and Social Ineffectiveness Embedded in Polish Ways of Life. Online Readings in Psychology and Culture, Vol. 3, N. 1. http://dx.doi.org/10.9707/2307-0919.1029.

45   Adeleye, I. (2011). Theorising human resource management in Africa: Beyond cultural relativism, African Journal of Business Management, Vol. 5, N. 6, 2028-2039.

46   Eze, M. O. (2010). Intellectual History in Contemporary South Africa. Basingstoke, UK: Palgrave Macmillan.

47   Gyekye, K. (1997). Tradition and Modernity: Philosophical Reflections on the African Experience. Oxford, UK: Oxford University Press.

48   Ishmael Beah, interviewed by Belinda Luscombe in Time Magazine, January 2014.

49   Harrison, A., Lin, J. Y., & Xu, L. C. (2013). Explaining Africa's (dis)advantage, National Bureau of Economic Research, retrieved from http://www.nber.org/papers/w18683.

50   Walsh, J. (2008). Culture smart: UAE. London, UK: Kuperard.

51   Whitaker, B. (2010). What is really wrong with the Middle East?. London, UK: Saqi Books.

52   Tetréault, M. A. (2004). The Political Economy Of Middle Eastern Oil. In D. J. Gerner, & J. Schwedler (Eds.), Understanding the Contemporary Middle East (2nd ed.). Boulder, CO: Lynne Rienner.

53   Ramírez-Esparza, N., Gosling, S. D., & Pennebaker, J. W. (2008). Paradox Lost, Unraveling the Puzzle of Simpatía. Journal of Cross-Cultural Psychology, Vol. 39, N. 6, 703-715.

54   Branco, S., & Williams, R. (2008). Culture smart: Brazil. London, UK: Kuperard.

55   Rodrigues, R. P., Milfont, T. L., Ferreira, M. C., Porto, J. B., & Fisher, R. (2011). Brazilian jeitinho: Understanding and explaining an indigenous psychological construct. Interamerican Journal of Psychology, Vol. 45, N. 1, 27-36.

56   Retrieved from http://www.gallup.com/poll/1690/religion.aspx

57   Uhlmann, E. L., Poehlman, A., & Bargh, J. A. (2008). Implicit Theism. In R. Sorrentino, & S. Yamaguchi (Eds.), Handbook of Motivation and Cognition Across Cultures. San Diego: Academic Press.

58   Weaver, G. R. (1999). American Cultural Values. Kokusai Bunka Kenshu (Intercultural Training), Special Edition, 9-15.

59   Fischer, D. H. (1989). Albion's Seed: Four British Folkways In America. New York: Oxford University Press.

60   Emerson, R. W. (1841). Self-Reliance. Retrieved from https://math.dartmouth.edu/~doyle/docs/self/self.pdf

61   Ralph Waldo Emerson.

62   Kohls, R. (1984). The Values Americans live by. Washington, DC: Washington International Centre.

CHAPTER 5:

Intercultural Communication

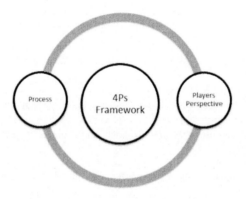

Stage 2: Process. Stage 4: Players Perspective

DEFINITIONS OF COMMUNICATION

Following are definitions of communication from leading academics and scholars:

Communication is the verbal interchange of thought or idea (Hoben, 1954).

Communication is a process which makes something which belongs to one person come to belong to two persons or more (Gode, 1959).

Communication is the process by which we understand others and in turn endeavor to be understood by them. It is dynamic, constantly changing and shifting in response to the total situation (Anderson, 1959).

Communication basely is a process which explains who says what, in which channel, to whom, with what effect (Lasswell, 1960).

Communication: the transmission of information, idea, emotion, skills, etc., by the use of symbols, words, pictures, figures, graphs, etc. It is the act or process of transmission that is usually called communication (Berelson & Steiner, 1964).

Communication arises out of the need to reduce uncertainty, to act effectively, to defend or strengthen the ego (Barnlund, 1964).

Communication is a symbolic process by which shared reality (Carey, 1989) and community (Cohen, 1985) are produced.

Communication is simply the exchange of meaning between individuals (Walker & Walker, 2002).

Communication stems from the Latin verb communicare, which means to make common or shared (Jönsson, 2002).

Two-way process of reaching mutual understanding, in which participants not only exchange (encode-decode) information, news, ideas, and feelings but also create and share meaning (Wikipedia).

The successful conveying or sharing of ideas and feeling (Oxford Dictionary).

A process by which information is exchanged between individuals through a common system of symbols, signs, or behavior (Merriam-Webster Dictionary).

THE PLAYERS PERSPECTIVE STAGE AND COMMUNICATION

Because at the negotiation table you constantly need to probe behind the stated position to identify the other party's real interests, understanding how to communicate with the other party is vital to recognizing the whys behind specific requests, behaviors, and positions.

You have to learn to filter, contextualize, and calibrate the information that is (and is not) provided to you.

Also, you must be able to convey your message effectively, knowing that the meaning you intend to deliver is often blocked, distorted, altered, and filtered on the receiver's side.

In international negotiations, how something is said is often more important than what is said, and what is not said is often more important than what is said.

Everything we do or make carries meaning. Any perceivable behavior, including the absence of action, has the potential to be interpreted by other people as having meaning. It is difficult to say nothing. *One cannot not communicate.*[1]

A COMMUNICATION MODEL

An effective way to understand the communication process is to build a communication model piece by piece, starting with the first three elements: sender, receiver, and message.

Figure 1. The communication process.

In its simplest form, communication can be viewed as a *sender* transmitting a message to a *receiver*. However, this one-way transmission is just information. For communication to be in place, we have to introduce *feedback* and move to two-way transmission.

Figure 2. Two-way transmission in communication.

You need feedback to understand whether your message was received clearly and correctly. Feedback enables the receiver to become the sender, concealing the distinction between the two roles.

At this stage, we can add a third element to our communication model: *Context*.

Communication is contextual; in other words, it doesn't occur in isolation, but within a specific context. The context is a combination of four elements:

- *The situational context*: The specific time and place where you are communicating.
- *The social context*: The occasion on which the communication is occurring (e.g., a party, a meeting, a dinner) and the social perception of the two participants, how they see each other (e.g., status, role, power, stereotypes).
- *The psychological context*: The needs, desires, and personality of the participants in the interaction.
- *The cultural context*: Values, norms, beliefs, and learned behaviors that influence the communication.

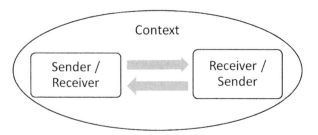

Figure 3. Context in communication.

The fourth element of our model is the *channel*. The channel is the mode used to transmit the message from the sender to the receiver. It can be a visual channel for a written message or an auditory channel for a spoken message. Body language, tone, and volume can also be considered communication channels.

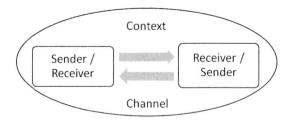

Figure 4. Communication channel as part of two-way communication.

The fifth and last element of our model is *interference*. No message is received precisely as the sender anticipated. Even very simple communication is often blocked, distorted, altered, generalized, filtered, and sometimes even deleted. Interference can be external (e.g., we can't see the speaker, we can't hear the sender) or internal (e.g., we are lost in our own thoughts, we lack confidence, we filter information according to our prejudices).

Values, beliefs, past experiences, stereotypes, prejudices, feelings, and environment are only some of the most probable forms of interference that can distort the meaning and obstruct the conveyance of the message.

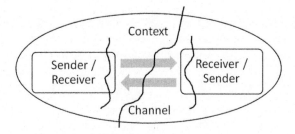

Figure 5. Communication distorted by internal and external factors.

Communication can be considered a method to reproduce a thought or idea. As with all methods of reproduction, it can be subject to distortion, noise, and misinterpretation.

The translation from thought to language may be distorted or inaccurate; similarly, it can be inaccurate in the reconversion from language to understanding in the mind of the receiver:

I know you think you understood what I said, but what you heard was not what I meant.[2]

Figure 6. The young and the old lady.

The purpose of communication is achieved only when the receiver has understood the intended message of the sender.

THE INTERNATIONAL LINGUA FRANCA

A lingua franca is a language that makes communication possible between people who do not share the same mother tongue. This working language can be a third language, different from both mother tongues, or one of the two mother tongues.

The term lingua franca was first coined during the Middle Ages to describe a combination of French and Italian that was developed by the Crusaders and traders. Various lingua francas have arisen around the world throughout human history for trade, diplomatic, and administrative reasons. Among them are Latin, Arabic, Chinese, Italian, French, Portuguese, and Malay.

Today, the international lingua franca is English. According to the Ethnologue database, 335 million people speak English as their first language (placing English in third position on the list of the top languages of the world, behind Spanish, with 406 million speakers, and Mandarin Chinese, with 848 million). However, more important, English has been adopted as the official first or second language in more than 70 countries, and in nations such as India, Pakistan, Bangladesh, the Philippines, the Scandinavian countries, and the Netherlands, it is widely and fluently spoken (the same can be said for Russian in Ukraine, Uzbekistan, Kazakhstan, and other ex-Soviet states and French in the Maghreb).

According to the Ethnologue database, more than 200 million Indians speak English as their second language; it is developing into a divergent Indian dialect, influenced by the other Indian languages, with its own jargon, expressions, and style.

English in effect became the international language of business (and not only business) after World War II for two main reasons:

- English is considered a neutral, flexible, direct, and detached language. Standard words and sentences are short and relatively easy to pronounce.
- US cultural, economic, and political dominance.

Both reasons have their shortcomings:

- A direct and detached language is not the best means to communicate in a world where most people speak in an indirect and formal style and where context and relationship are critical factors of the communication process.
- In many fields, particularly management theory and academics, unchallenged Anglophone views are too often uncritically adopted and researchers and managers from non-English-speaking countries sometimes neglect their own perfectly valid traditions.[3]
- In reality, the language of international business is broken English. Most global business is conducted in a linguistic variation of English, with different pronunciation, morphology, accents, cadences, and syntaxes. This is the reason why hiring our own translator is fundamental during International Negotiations.

In France, as in other places, there is strong debate whether to allow universities to teach courses in English to increase the country's intake of the best international students, especially those from China and India.

The Académie Française recently issued a statement against the attack on the status of the French language in universities, producing a *marginalization of our language*.

Chinese authorities are starting to de-emphasize the importance of English-language instruction in schools for two main reasons:[4]

- China is the number one economy in purchasing power parity and is steadily becoming more confident about its own identity. Studying Chinese is becoming popular in schools across the U.S., and Europe and Chinese education authorities are advancing Chinese language and culture globally through the opening of Confucius Institutes inside the main American and European universities.

- At the same time, more than 90% of Chinese have trouble remembering characters. The authorities are concerned that the Chinese are losing mastery of their written language.

So, what is the solution? According to Professor Pierre Frath, the use of a single lingua franca is not sufficient; people should be given the chance to select among different languages: English plus a choice of alternative languages according to the local environment (e.g., French, Spanish, Russian, Arabic, Mandarin, Malay, Hindi).

Studying different languages also brings additional benefits: Research shows that multilingual people are better at reasoning, at multitasking, and at integrative thinking; they also have the ability to reconcile conflicting ideas (more on this in chapters 8 and 11).

INTERCULTURAL COMMUNICATION

Psychologists and anthropologists have proposed that individuals from different cultures have different conceptions of self-identity and that these differences affect the expectations that players have as to the appropriate mode of interaction. In individualistic cultures, an independent view of the self prevails, whereas collectivistic cultures are characterized by a more interdependent view of the self. Members of individualistic cultures set clear and definite boundaries in the relationship, while in collectivistic cultures, individuals work within the context of tacit expectations and obligations.

In collectivist cultures the goal is to develop a social relationship, while in individualistic cultures it is one of task-related problem solving. This goal divergence implies a communicative conflict that leads to the emergence of negative emotions affecting the negotiation process.

As we'll see in chapters 8, 9, 12 and 13, negative emotions foster behavioral incompatibility and limit information processing.

Negative emotions such as frustration are expressed differently by individuals from different cultures: Members of individualistic cultures explicitly display their emotions, leading to aggressive behavior that evokes a desire to escape from the situation in members of collectivistic cultures, which usually tend to constrain the display of negative emotions.[5]

In reasoning about intercultural communication, we usually think of people from two different countries. However, geographic boundaries don't identify homogeneous cultures. The trickiest aspect of the notion of culture is when we are dividing people into groups, where do we draw the line?[6] Do we stop at the regional level? The city level? The neighborhood level? The family level? Or maybe at the individual level? The problem is that without generalization, we can't provide theories.

In addition to national group cultures, we also must consider other forms of culture, including:

- Religion.

- Technology.
- Education.
- Gender.
- Social class.
- Age.
- Organizational.
- Profession.

Intercultural communication between two people usually involves a portfolio of different cultures. Some of these cultures will be shared between the two parties, and some will not.

The intercultural communication literature pays very limited attention to *language*. The consequence is that international misinterpretations and disagreements due to language problems are often mistaken for cultural problems. *Culture has become a sort of passe-partout concept to justify differences between remote groups.*[7]

Think of an Italian and a Japanese negotiating in the official lingua franca, English. What are the odds that misunderstandings will be a consequence of language problems (often exacerbated by the presence of one or more interpreters) and what are the odds that it will be a consequence of cultural difficulties? Language is possibly the greatest barrier in communication, even when the two sides speak the same language.[8]

Language itself is fundamentally ambiguous.[9] All languages carry embedded constraints and limits that bound the meaning expressed with them. However, even more important, the meaning of the things we say is not only given by our words and sentences, but also by the interpretation that the receiver gives to them.

The interpretation is due not only to the different level of comprehension of the lingua franca between the two sides, but also to the fact that during the communication process, because language is ambiguous, we have to jump to conclusions about what the other person is meaning.[10]

Our extrapolations are based on our expectations (values, beliefs, prejudices, stereotypes, feelings: what we called interferences/noise in the previous paragraphs) of what other people would mean in similar situations.

Because perceptions are strongly influenced by expectations, it is very difficult to deliver messages that are inconsistent with what the other side already expects.

The problem with our extrapolations is that not only are they derived very quickly, but they also tend to be permanent deductions and not exploratory attempts to understand meaning.

Communication flows better the more the two sides share the same expectations and thus draw similar assumptions. Therefore, people with similar cultures (similar background and experiences) will often communicate better.

Two people speaking the lingua franca with high proficiency does not guarantee successful communication. If they don't share similar assumptions, communication will remain indefinite.

Figure 7 represents the intercultural communication model, which replaces the general interferences described in Figure 5 with the *language* barrier and the different *expectations* of the two sides.

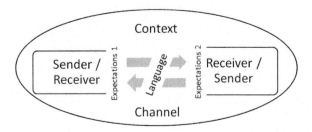

Figure 7. Language as a barrier to communication.

Our brain can be thought of as a memory system: To find solutions to problems, we use stored memories in the form of invariant representations (more on this in chapter 8). An important element of our sequential and associative memory is that unconsciously we are regularly completing patterns. For example, during a dialogue, we often end up completing patterns according to what we expect to hear.

EXPECTANCY VIOLATION THEORY

To comprehend nonverbal communication across cultures, it is useful to introduce the expectancy violation theory.[11] This theory suggests that we have subconscious expectations about how others should behave in specific situations; it attempts to explain how we will react if these expectations are violated.

Three factors affect our expectations during communication: speaker characteristics (age, gender, status, culture, personality), relational characteristics (relationship and background between the two parties), and the context (time, place, and social norms).

According to the context, the relationship, and the communicator's characteristics, we develop certain expectations of how our interlocutor should behave.

If an action is unpredicted and assigned a positive interpretation, it will produce more favorable outcomes than an expected act with the same interpretation.

HOW WE SAY THINGS IS AS IMPORTANT AS WHAT WE SAY

A king had a dream: All his teeth fell out except one. He called his oracle and asked him to interpret the dream.

The oracle said, "Your majesty, this is a bad omen. It means that all your relatives will die before you."

The king ordered his servant to cut off the oracle's head.

Then the king called in another oracle and recounted the dream to him. This oracle said: "Your majesty, this is cause for celebration. This means that you'll have a very long life. In fact, you'll live the longest among all your relatives."

The king showered him with treasures and land.[12]

The moral: How we say things is sometimes more important than what we say.

One often cited study on communication was conducted by Albert Mehrabian in 1967.[13] According to that study, words (verbal component) account for 7% of communication, tone, speed and volume (paraverbal component) for 38%, and body language and facial expressions (nonverbal component) for 55%.

It is important to emphasize that his findings were related to our liking of the channel that the person who expresses feelings and attitudes is using. Another limitation of the study is that the focus is on one word at a time, not on full sentences, creating an artificial context with a very simple communication model.

In mentioning the study, we often ignore its limitations, thereby contributing to its misinterpretation.

The study only establishes that for effective communication of emotions we have to rely mostly on the nonverbal component of communication. In addition, the three factors must be perceived as consistent.

As stated earlier, the different communication components' weight is at the feeling level, not at the informational level. Therefore, during negotiations, the percentages change and content (the verbal component) influence on communication increases. However, still, content doesn't represent the full communication. Our paraverbal and nonverbal communication influences the receiver's perception of the meaning of our message, chiefly when emotions become predominant during the talks.

According to psycholinguist David McNeill (1970),[14] the synchrony between speech and gesture stimulates thinking for speaking. Nonverbal and verbal skills maintain strong ties because they are used to adopt similar circuits in our brain that only in recent times separated into distinct behavioral sections.

Empirical research supports his view:

- People who could no longer move their arms after having suffered a brain injury also progressively lost their capability to communicate verbally.
- Children with normal hearing who took an American Sign Language class for nine months improved their scores in cognitive tests by as much as 50%.

Evidence suggests that the visual access to nonverbal behavior in face-to-face interaction facilitates the development of rapport and in so doing promotes mutually beneficial solutions to conflicts.[15]

What happens when we communicate by email? Certain information may be easy to communicate face-to-face but difficult to describe in an email. People pay attention to different elements when communicating electronically. Social status cues, for example, are less salient in computer-mediated than face-to-face communication. Communicating by email, we lose the paraverbal and nonverbal components of communication; consequently, we decrease our ability to influence the other side's perception of our message's value.

Furthermore, by email, the perceived social distance among negotiators increases, diminishing negotiators' social awareness of each other.[16]

Consequently, negotiators should adopt different information-sharing approaches when communicating electronically. As a result, because the messenger's social status may be less likely to influence how the message is interpreted, negotiators may focus more on the message content in electronic contexts.

Research suggests that the liabilities of e-mail in negotiation, might be overcome by social lubrication. Even a brief personal telephone conversation prior to e-mail negotiation, can help achieve better economic and social outcomes.[17]

HIGH- AND LOW-CONTEXT COMMUNICATION

Edward T. Hall (1973), an American cultural anthropologist,[18] developed a model of intercultural communication (introduced in chapter 2) based on his ethnographic studies in Germany, Japan, France, and the US.

His work has been strongly influenced by the following:

- Franz Boas's approach to the field of anthropology and his notion of culture as learned behaviors.

- Linguistics Benjamin Whorf and Edward Sapir's theory of linguistic relativity: the concept that language affects how its speakers conceptualize the world (a notion that will be further developed in the next paragraph of the chapter).

- Freud's unconscious level of communication in his psychoanalytic theory; according to Hall's interpretation of Freud's work, words conceal more than they disclose.

As seen in the communication model paragraph, communication doesn't occur in isolation, but within a specific context. The context can be situational (time and place), social (occasion and perception of each other), psychological (needs and personality), and cultural (values and norms).

Hall's intercultural communication model is based on the relative importance of the context of the message over the message itself.

In low-context communication, the context is less important than the message. The meaning is expressed directly through explicit statements. *"What I say is what I mean."* The verbal component is more important than the paraverbal and nonverbal components. The task at hand is more important than the relationship. Written communication is highly valued: Contracts protect us from uncertainty and speculation. Competence is separated from the person's character; feedback is accepted because it is focused on the task and not on the person.

In high-context communication, the context is important. The meaning is suggested indirectly through the context embodying the message. High-context communication requires reading "between the lines." What is not said is as important as what is said. *"Only kids are allowed to say what they think."* Paraverbal and nonverbal cues are fundamental components of communication. Silence is an essential part of the communication process. Relationships are more important than tasks at hand and disputes are resolved through in-group networks and not in court. A person's character is more important than his or her competencies and feedback is provided indirectly, without loss of face for any of the parties involved.

What do low-context communicators think of their high-context counterparts? They perceive them as ambiguous, confusing, complicated, unpredictable, and at times untrustworthy, unreliable, and even deceitful.

What do high-context communicators think of their low-context counterparts? They perceive them as distant, distrusting, suspicious, self-centered, sometimes arrogant and inconsiderate toward people, and too ordinary in finding new solutions.

Figure 8. High-/low-context cultures.

RICHARD LEWIS'S CULTURAL MODEL AND COMMUNICATION

Richard Lewis's cultural model, introduced in chapter 2, is useful in understanding different communication patterns across cultures. As highlighted in chapter 2, Lewis's model breaks away from the traditional classification system of polar opposites, organizing cultures into three groups, which he called *linear-active*, *multi-active*, and *reactive*.[19]

In a communication situation, linear-active people talk half of the time, in a direct and open manner. They rarely interrupt and tend to stick to facts even during conflicts. In conveying a message, they display limited body language. In influencing others, they regard facts and data. They are task-oriented and prefer to pursue one issue at a time, in a linear sequence. Examples include people in the US, the UK, Scandinavian countries, and Germany. According to Lewis, linear-active people represent around 10% of the world population.

Multi-active people tend to be talkative and relationship-oriented. During a conversation, they speak most of the time, tend to display feelings, and during confrontations are apt to become emotional. Communication is mainly nonverbal and paraverbal. In influencing others, they value charisma and eloquence. They tackle many things at once based on the priority of the moment. Multi-active people represent the largest group, about 56% of the world population. Examples are Southern Europeans, Latin Americans, some Africans, and Arabs.

People in reactive cultures are introverted and reserved, hesitant to be implicated in opinionated discussions. They usually listen most of the time, quietly and impassively, and react cautiously to the other side's propositions. In conflict, they communicate politely and indirectly, avoiding confrontation: They value respect and tend to not display emotions. In influencing others, they respect status, age, and experience. They display little nonverbal communication and are very sensible to face. Reactive people make up 29% of the world population. Examples are Chinese, Japanese, Vietnamese, and Koreans.

Figure 9. Lewis's model of cultural types.

As we can see from Figure 9, some of the countries can be represented as a combination of two of the three attributes.

FACIAL EXPRESSIONS AND LYING

Certain nonverbal communication can be considered universal; for example, a slight lifting of the eyebrow communicates acknowledgment not only among humans, but also among chimpanzees.

Many cross-cultural studies suggest that the facial expressions for seven basic emotions (happiness, sadness, disgust, fear, anger, contempt and surprise) are universal, being recognized by most cultural groups as having a similar meaning even though there are cultural differences in when these expressions are displayed.[20]

It is important to emphasize the difference between facial expressions and body language. Facial expressions show the emotion, the body shows how people cope with the emotion.

Micro facial expressions can reveal emotions a person is trying to cover: In reading faces, you should focus on temporary changes of expression, which usually last a fraction of a second.

While engaged in a conversation, we usually assemble information from verbal, paraverbal, and nonverbal sources.

Nonverbal sources are numerous: face, tilts of the head, posture, and movements of the arms, hands, legs, and feet. As a result, because most facial expressions of emotion are rapid, it is easy to miss important nonverbal messages.

Facial expressions of emotion are not easy to control. We are more fully trained in lying with words than with faces because words are easier to monitor, but also because facial expressions of emotion are involuntary and therefore require more attention to reverse.

The ability to deceive others is a complex mental skill: A large mental effort is required to suppress the instinctive and spontaneous honest reaction.

When lying, individuals also show an increase in reaction time (the time needed to respond) and a decrease in accuracy because of the conflict occurring in specific areas of the brain to subdue truthful information.

For that reason, on average, people tend to use 30% more words while lying. If somebody suddenly becomes verbose (compared to their baseline), he or she could be lying.

Bear in mind that the attempt to control facial expressions is not synonymous with lying. It simply tells you that something is out of place, not whether the other person is trying to mislead you. People manage their facial expressions for many reasons, such as cultural, personal, and gender display rules, professional requirements, or temporary needs.

When we lie, our brain responds to stress and anxiety, increasing its arousal level. The automatic nervous system is responsible for alterations in voice modulation, pupil dilatation, intensifications in respiratory and cardiac frequency, changes in the electrical properties of the skin, and an increase in the temperature of specific areas of the face. However, the same physiological alterations can simply signal an emotional perturbation rather than the cognitive act of lying. Therefore, these changes cannot be used to reliably identify deception.[21]

Emotions don't disclose their source. Don't make Othello's error. *Othello killed Desdemona because he thought that her signs of fear stemmed from being caught in a betrayal. However, she was afraid of not being believed. The fear of not being believed looked just like the fear of being caught in a betrayal. Fear is fear. You have to find out which type of fear you're dealing with. That's a little disappointing because people want to think, "Oh, if you look afraid, that means you did it." No, it doesn't mean that; it means you're afraid.*[22]

UNDERSTANDING NONVERBAL BEHAVIOR

Our brain is composed not only by the cortex but also by the emotional systems of the old brain. It is true that most of our actions are preprogrammed and our perceptions are based on a stored model of the world, which we continuously retrieve and update, but in trying to understand other people's nonverbal behavior, we must look at how they react under stressful conditions, when emotions develop.[23]

Therefore, first of all look for recurring patterns. Some actions can be easily modified, while others are coded into the brain by genetics and experience. Coded behavior is evident under stressful conditions, when we tend to switch into auto-pilot mode.

Second, look for behavior that conflicts with the standard baseline of the other person. Divergent behavior becomes noticeable particularly when emotions develop. Instinctive reactions interrupt our schemas because they are driven by a part of our old brain, particularly the *amygdalae*.

POLITENESS THEORY

Research on communication has supported the notion that most communication tends to be indirect. According to the politeness theory,[24] even in low-context cultures where people tend to say what they mean, communication is negotiated. The reason for the prevalence of indirect communication is the individual's need to preserve his or her public image, referred as *face*.

According to the theory, positive face refers to one's self-esteem, the desire to be approved of and admired by others; negative face refers to one's freedom to act without being forced by others.

Positive face and negative face exist universally in human culture. One difference is that while in some cultures losing face is a humiliation, in others it can be considered a simple, even if displeasing, setback. The second difference is that in some cultures speakers would rather risk threatening the relationship, and appearing detached, and in others they would prefer to risk threatening freedom, and appearing compelling.

In any social interactions, the two needs must be balanced. This is the reason for communication indirectness: People allude to what they would like to say, try to understand how the other person would receive it, and are ready to accommodate what they might have meant to avoid disagreement.

MANY WAYS OF SAYING NO

Because of the need to preserve harmony and avoid conflict, members of high-context environments rarely say no directly. Following are indirect ways of saying no in Japan that are unreadable by individuals from low-context cultures:[25]

- *Vague, ambiguous, or conditional no*: A soft no is used to decline a request without embarrassing the other side.
- *Yes but*: The real meaning is no because the focus of the response is on the but, not on the yes. Usually, the sentence continues with an apology or a regret.
- *Silence*: Silence can sometimes be used to decline requests.
- *Counter questions*: These bring the focus back to the question one doesn't want to answer. Sometimes, high-status individuals also question the content of the question.
- *Oblique responses*: Talking about a different issue implies a negative answer.
- *Leaving*: Exiting the room, refusing to answer without further explanations, is another way to say no.
- *Making an excuse or lying*: Bringing up false previous commitments or sickness allows for avoiding direct hurt to the other side's feelings.
- *I'll think about it*: Delaying the answer is a common technique for declining a request.

THE VALUE OF SILENCE

Silence is an essential part of the communication process in high-context cultures. Thoughtful and self-disciplined silence is often valued above speech. The value of silence in many Asian cultures can be seen in ancient philosophical traditions, such as Hinduism, Buddhism, and Taoism, where meditation, silence, and internal visualization are perceived as beneficial for thinking and even for highlighting authority and status.[26]

A number of proverbs portrays these principles: *Out of the mouth comes all evil, Silence is golden, Silence is the source of great strength, Nothing strengthens authority so much as silence, Silence never betrays you, In silence there is eloquence, Silence is the ultimate weapon of power, Silence makes idiots seem wise, and The tongue is sharper than the sword.*

In Japan, a very high context nation, the notion of silence can be associated with at least four different dimensions:[27]

- *Truthfulness*: Japanese aphorisms, expressions, poetry, and Buddhist tradition emphasize the notion that spoken words can't be trusted.

- *Face*: According to the politeness theory, silence improves one's social reputation and avoids disagreement, thereby maintaining the speaker's face.

- *Social distance*: Silence can be used to emphasize marginalization and detachment between individuals.

- *Hostility*: Silence can be used to communicate defiance and resentment, particularly in conjunction with other nonverbal communication, such as prolonged eye contact.

ASSERTIVENESS IN HIGH-CONTEXT CULTURES

Assertiveness means communicating our needs and positions confidently and explicitly.

Assertiveness can be placed between aggressiveness and passiveness as a combination of non-coercive and direct expression.[28]

Low-context cultures tend to get to the subject matter right away, with specifics following as needed.

High-context cultures, on the other hand, introduce the request after the explanations, complying with the following model: *salutation and preamble* (giving face), *reasons, request.* The result is that often low-context listeners become confused about the meaning of the message.[29]

In high-context cultures, assertiveness is frequently mistaken as aggressiveness. Direct communication is not always appreciated, and people try to avoid saying no directly, employing more restrained expressions such as "*I will try my best,*" "*it is difficult but we'll try,*" and "*many things are in place.*"

Speaking in English, people belonging to high-context cultures often end up being perceived as aggressive when trying to be assertive. The reason is that they tend to be more direct in their second language because of lack of vocabulary and language skills.

MISCOMMUNICATION WITH FOREIGNERS – THE JAPANESE CASE

There is a widespread perception that for most Japanese communication with foreigners is a demanding and often dreadful experience.[30]

Research has focused on the reasons behind this trend, trying to use a systemic approach to explain a phenomenon that needs to incorporate various factors. We will focus on some of them:

- *Geographic and cultural isolation*: Japan is an island with an extremely high degree of ethnic and cultural homogeneity. There is a strong degree of ethnocentrism, with a substantial focus on Japanese uniqueness. Cultural homogeneity leads to the Japanese having a shared nonverbal communication pattern. However, when they face completely different people (foreigners), their ability to guess at the other person's feeling becomes inadequate, creating a first reaction of astonishment.

  But why do populations of other island states not face the same experience? And why hasn't the situation improved in the 150 years since the isolation policy ended?

- *The Gaijin complex*: Japanese hold differing opinions toward Westerners, sometimes respect, occasionally frustration, often anxiety. The consequence is that Westerners end up being treated with suspicion and avoided for fear they may cause embarrassment. There is a strong emphasis on *we* versus *them*.

- *Japanese reticence*: Inhibition in speaking a foreign language could be a consequence of two factors related to face:

  The fear of making mistakes in front of other people, which prevents the Japanese from practicing a new language without restrictions.

  The fear of failure in communication in a language that the Japanese believe they should master. The two factors become even more considerable when communicating in the presence of other Japanese.

- *Status violation*: High hierarchy societies need to rank the other side. They need to know whether the other party is of higher or lower status. Communicating with low-context cultures, the Japanese are often unable to classify the other party. Another perception that Japanese have of low-context cultures is that they often violate their status, not listening enough and being too direct.

- *The paradox of using the Japanese language*: In most societies, foreigners are appreciated for their efforts to speak the local language, but not in Japan. As reported by some scholars, Japanese are reluctant to speak with foreigners in Japanese. According to Roy Andrew Miller (1980), an explanation for this paradox is the Japanese confusion between language and race. An attempt to master Japanese can be viewed as an attempt to acquire Japanese identity.

LANGUAGE UNIVERSALS AND PERCEPTION

Today, there are between 6,000 and 8,000 languages in the world and only about 500 have a description that includes grammar and vocabulary. If we go back to before Western colonization, there have probably been around 500,000 human languages.[31]

Some cognitive scientists have hypothesized that languages are all built according to a common structure,[32] but according to other researchers, confronting the 500 languages for which we have some valuable information, we can find very few universal language traits.

Therefore, the questions we have to ask, trying to understand the link between language and thought, are:

- Is our perception of the world shaped by the language we speak?
- Or do we all experience the world in the same way but have different ways of expressing our experiences?[33]

Different positions exist regarding the relationship between language and our perceptions.

According to the *nominalist position*, our perceptions are not determined by the language we speak. Different languages don't mean different cognitive processes.

On the other hand, the *relativist position* (the Sapir-Whorf hypothesis)[34] argues that our perception is defined by the language we speak. Language defines our cognitive process. For example:

- In some languages there are no possessives. Does this mean that the concept of possession is different in different languages?
- In English and Spanish, the continuous verb form is frequently used, while in French, it is used much less. Does this mean that speakers of different languages think differently about action?
- Many languages have a different number of words for different colors. Does this mean that speakers perceive colors differently?
- In some languages, there are no numerals. Does this mean that speakers have a different perception of any number greater than one?
- Through metaphors, we understand concepts and perform theoretical cognition.[35] Different languages use different metaphors to express similar concepts. Does this mean that speakers of different languages understand concepts differently?

Finally, we have the *qualified relativist position* that claims an intermediate standpoint: Language influences how we perceive, but there is no straightforward link between language and thought.[36]

As of today, growing new research definitely supports the Sapir-Whorf argument that linguistic differences affect thought.[37]

CONCLUSIONS

Two monks happened to be discussing the wind and flag problem. One was maintaining that the wind moves, the other was maintaining that the flag moves.

They were discussing it back and forth without coming to any conclusion. I came forward and said, "*Neither the wind nor the flag is moving, kind sirs, it is the mind that moves.*"[38]

(ENDNOTES)

1   Watzlawick, P., Beavin-Bavelas, J., & Jackson, D. (1967). Pragmatics of Human Communication. A Study of Interactional Patterns, Pathologies and Paradoxes. New York: Norton.

2   Hughes, R. (2010). CULT-URE. London, UK: Fiell Publishing.

3   Pierre Frath, 2009.

4   Roberts, D. (2014, May 22). China's war on English. BusinessWeek.

5   Kumar, R. (1999). Communicative Conflict in Intercultural Negotiations: The Case of American and Japanese Business Negotiations. International Negotiation, Vol. 4, N. 1, 63-78.

6   Scollon, R., Scollon, S., & Jones, R. H. (2012). Intercultural Communication A Discourse Approach (3rd ed.). Oxford: John Wiley & Sons.

7   Piller, I. (2007). Linguistics and Intercultural Communication. Language and Linguistic Compass, Vol. 1, N. 3, 208-226.

8   Medina Walker, D., Walker, T., & Schmitz, J. (2002). Doing business internationally (2nd ed.). New York: McGraw-Hill.

9   Levinson, S. C. (2000). Presumptive meanings: The theory of generalized conversational implicature. Cambridge: MIT Press.

10   Scollon, R., Scollon, S., & Jones, R. H. (2012). Intercultural Communication A Discourse Approach (3rd ed.). Oxford: John Wiley & Sons.

11   Burgoon, J. K. (1983). Nonverbal Violations of Expectations. In J. M. Wiemann, & R. R. Harrison (Eds.), Nonverbal Interaction. Beverly Hills, CA: Sage.

12   No source found.

13   Mehrabian, A. (1981). Silent messages: Implicit communication of emotions and attitudes (2nd ed.). Belmont, CA: Wadsworth.

14   McNeill, D. (2007). Gesture and Thought. Chicago: University of Chicago Press.

15   Drolet, A., & Morris, M. W. (2000). Rapport in Conflict Resolution: Accounting for How Face-to-Face Contact Fosters Mutual Cooperation in Mixed-Motive Conflicts. Journal of Experimental Social Psychology, 36, 26-50.

16   Narsness, Z. I., Bhappu, A. D. (2004). At the Crossroads of Culture and Technology social influence and information-sharing processes during negotiation. In M. J. Gelfand, & J. M. Brett (Eds.), The Handbook of Negotiation and Culture. Palo Alto, CA: Stanford University Press.

17   Morris, M., Nadler, J., Kurtzberg, T., & Thompson, L. (2002). Schmooze or Lose: Social Friction and Lubrication in E-Mail Negotiations. Group Dynamics: Theory, Research, and Practice, Vol. 6, N. 1, 89-100.

18   Hall, E. (1973). The silent language. New York, NY: Anchor Books.

19   Lewis, R. D. (2005). When cultures collide. (3rd ed.). London, UK: Nicholas Brealey Publishing.

20   Ekman, P., & Friesen, W. V. (2003). Unmasking the Face: A guide to recognizing emotions from facial clues. Cambridge, MA: Malor Books.

21   Proverbio, A. M., Vanutelli, M. E., & Adorni, R. (2013). Can You Catch a Liar? How Negative Emotions Affect Brain Responses when Lying or Telling the Truth. PLoS ONE, Vol. 8, N. 3, e59383.

22   Paul Ekman in an interview with Harry Kreisler of the Institute of International Studies, Berkeley. Jan. 2004.

23   Edwards, C. (2006). Mind reading. Old Windsor: Real Publishing.

24   Brown, P., & Levinson, S. C. (1987). Politeness: Some universals in language usage. Cambridge, UK: Cambridge University Press.

25   Ueda, K. (1974). Sixteen Ways to Avoid Saying No in Japan. In J. C. Condon, M. Saito, & K. K. Daikagu (Eds.), Intercultural Encounters with Japan. Perspectives from the International Conference on Communication Across Cultures, International Christian University, Tokyo.

26   Kim, H. S. (2002). We talk, therefore we think? A cultural analysis of the effect of talking on thinking. Journal of Personality and Social Psychology, 83, 828-842.

27   Lebra, T. (2007). The Cultural Significance of Silence in Japanese Communication. In T. Lebra (Ed.), Identity, gender, and status in Japan: collected papers of Takie Lebra. Folkestone, U.K.: Global Oriental.

28   Kawamoto, F. (2007). Assertive Communication in Japanese English Learners, Jiyugaoka Sanno College Bulletin, Vol. 1, N. 9, 57-64.

29   Scollon, R., Scollon, S., & Jones, R. H. (2012). Intercultural Communication A Discourse Approach (3rd ed.). Oxford: John Wiley & Sons.

30   Kowner, R., & Wiseman, R. L. (2003). Culture and Status-Related Behavior: Japanese and American Perceptions of Asymmetric Dyad-Interactions. Cross-Cultural Research, Vol. 37, N. 10, 178-210.

31   Evans, N., & Levinson, S. C. (2009). The myth of language universals: Language diversity and its importance for cognitive science. Behavioral and Brain Sciences, Vol. 32, N. 5, 429-448.

32   Chomsky, N. (1965). Aspects of the Theory of Syntax. Boston: MIT Press.

33   Martin, J. N., & Nakayama, T. K. (2010). Intercultural Communication in Contexts (5th ed.). New York: McGraw-Hill.

34   Whorf, B. L. (1967). Language, Thought and Reality (5th ed.). Edited by J. B. Carroll. Boston: MIT Press.

35   Lakoff, G. (1992). The contemporary theory of metaphor. In A. Ortony (Ed.), Metaphor and thought (2nd ed.). New York: Cambridge University Press.

36   Pinker, S. (2007). The Stuff of Thought: Language as a Window Into Human Nature. New York: Viking.

37   Nisbett, R. E., & Norenzayan, A. (2002). Culture and Cognition. In H. Pashler (Ed.), Stevens' Handbook of Experimental Psychology (3rd ed.). Hoboken, NJ: John Wiley & Sons.

38   Huineng (1964). The Sutra of the Sixth Patriarch on the Pristine Orthodox Dharma. Translated by P. Fung, & G. Fung. San Francisco: Buddha's Universal Church.

CHAPTER 6

Negotiation Basics

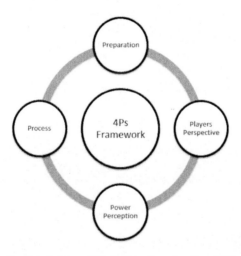

Stage 1: Preparation. Stage 2: Process. Stage 3: Power Perception. Stage 4: Players Perspective

DEFINITIONS OF NEGOTIATION

Following are definitions of negotiation from leading academics and scholars in the field:

Negotiation is a decision-making process in which people mutually decide how to allocate scarce resources (Pruitt, 1983).

Negotiation is a process in which two or more entities come together to discuss common and conflicting interests to reach an agreement of mutual benefit (Harris & Moran, 1987).

Negotiation is a fundamental form of social interaction which is necessary for individuals who must accomplish their social objectives in collaboration with others (Thompson & Hastie, 1990).

Negotiation is a field of knowledge that focuses on gaining the favor of people from whom we want things (Cohen, 1997).

Negotiation takes place any time two people are communicating, where one or both parties have a goal in mind (McRae, 1999).

Negotiation is a basic means of getting what you want from others. It is back-and-forth communication designed to reach an agreement when you and the other side have interests that are shared and others that are opposed (Fisher & Ury, 1999).

Negotiation can be considered a psychological process of setting up a kind of influence game between perceptions and expectations (Dupont & Faure, 2002).

Negotiation is a subclass of social communication (Jönsson, 2002).

Negotiation is basically a process of communication by which two or more persons seek to advance their individual interests through joint action (Salacuse, 2003).

Negotiation is an interpersonal decision-making process necessary whenever we cannot achieve our objectives single-handedly (Thompson, 2005).

Negotiation can be defined as back-and-forth communication designed to reach an agreement between two or more parties with some interests that are shared and others that may conflict or simply differ (Patton, 2005).

A negotiation is an interactive communication process that may take place whenever we want something from someone else or another person wants something from us (Shell, 2006).

Negotiation is a process of defining and reducing alternative positions until a unique combination is reached that is acceptable to all parties (William, 2008).

Negotiation is the process of combining divergent viewpoints to produce a common agreement (Zartman, 2008).

Negotiation is a means of getting what you want by working through others (Walch, 2012).

TYPES OF NEGOTIATION

There are two main categories of negotiation: *distributive* and *integrative*.

A distributive negotiation is a negotiation in which the parties compete over the distribution of a fixed sum of value. In distributive negotiations, a gain by one side is a loss for the other. It is a zero-sum or, better, a constant-sum negotiation (fixed pie). This type of negotiation is also referred to as win-lose. Each side's goal in a distributive negotiation is to get as much as possible of the fixed value at stake.

An example of a distributive negotiation is the sale of a carpet, where the buyer and the seller do not know each other. In this specific situation, the seller wants to obtain as high a price as possible, while the buyer wants to pay as low a price as possible.

Relationship and reputation are less important than claiming value in distributive negotiations.

An integrative negotiation is a negotiation in which the parties collab integrate their interests to achieve the maximum benefits for both the si also competing in the value division.

These deals are first about creating value and then claiming it. This type of negotiation is usually referred to as win-win. Negotiators make trade-offs to obtain the things they value the most, while giving up other, less critical elements.

In an integrative negotiation, parties cooperate to achieve maximum benefits by integrating their interests into an agreement while also competing to divide the value. In an integrative negotiation, the task is dual: Create as much value as possible for both sides, and then claim it.

Options that can increase the value of the negotiation (enlarge the size of the pie), other than price, include delivery date, payment terms, training, after sales, future agreements, services, and opportunities for new market entry. Integrative negotiation requires creativity to be effective.

THE TENSION IN CREATING AND CLAIMING VALUE

The tension between creating and claiming value is a crucial element of almost any negotiation. Creating value is the process of maximizing the value in the deal (integrative strategy); claiming value is the attempt to obtain as much of this value as possible (distributive strategy).

Negotiations are rarely entirely distributive or entirely integrative. Thus, negotiations can be more appropriately defined as a continuum between the win-lose and the win-win poles.

Deciding where to negotiate along that continuum implies a tension known as the negotiator's dilemma.

In this dilemma, the players can create value if both are forthcoming with information about their interests, constraints, and concerns. However, both will suffer if either shares information and the other does not. Thus, the negotiator's dilemma can be considered a specific inference of the prisoner's dilemma (examined in depth in chapter 8): Being the first to reveal important information is a risky strategy, while concealing information and persuading the other side to open up is the most beneficial approach. According to game theory, a player will choose the less risky strategy: concealing information.

FOUR KEY CONCEPTS

Any effective negotiation is based on the following four key concepts:

- The best alternative if no agreement can be reached (*BATNA*).
- Each party's walk-away point, the minimum acceptable level required to accept a solution (*reservation value*).
- The zone of possible agreement (*ZOPA*), the range of possible solutions acceptable by both the parties.
- *Value creation* through trades.

BATNA

BATNA is the acronym for best alternative to a negotiated agreement. The BATNA answers the question: What is your alternative if you fail to reach an agreement in the current negotiation?

If your BATNA is strong, then you can push for more positive conditions, knowing that if you don't reach an agreement, you have a better alternative on which to fall back.

If your BATNA is weak, then you can end up accepting an unfavorable deal, knowing that if you don't reach an agreement you don't have a better alternative as a fallback.

Always clearly identify your BATNA before entering into a negotiation. If not, you won't know whether you can accept a deal or not.

Without knowing your BATNA, you can end up rejecting an advantageous offer (that is better than your unidentified alternatives) because you are overly optimistic or accepting an unfavorable offer.

Remember that your BATNA is not what you think is reasonable, or the price you originally paid for the specific article you are selling, or the price you are willing to take for it. Your BATNA is the situation you'll play against if you don't reach a deal in the current negotiation.[1]

The concept of BATNA is straightforward when it involves only price. However, it becomes more complicated when it comprises different variables that can't easily be compared.

For example, if you are considering the purchase of a specific used car and are evaluating different options from different dealers, many issues other than price play an important role in your decision-making process, including mileage, warranty, mechanical and body condition, color, and transmission (automatic or manual).

One car can have a lower price but higher mileage, no warranty, and a color that is not exactly your favorite. Another can be more expensive but with lower mileage, a 12-month warranty, and a nice color. How can you compare different alternatives?

If price were the only issue, defining the BATNA would be easy: It would be the first car, the one with the lowest price. To define your BATNA, assign a weight and a score to the different factors. In the example in Fig. 1, scores range from 1 (low) to 4 (high). Option 3 is the alternative with the best score.

Factors	▾	Weight ▾	Option 1 ▾	Option 2 ▾	Option 3 ▾
Price		10%	4	2	3
Mileage		20%	2	3	3
Warranty		25%	4	2	4
Color		5%	1	3	4
Mechanical Condition		15%	4	3	3
Body Condition		15%	2	3	2
Transmission (A / M)		10%	1	4	4
total		**100%**	**2,85**	**2,75**	**3,25**

scores from 1 to 4

Figure 1. BATNA with weighted scores.

The prices of the different cars are as follows:

Option 1: $11,000; Option 2: $13,000; Option 3: $12,000.

To explain how the scores were assigned, let's take as an example Option 1. The price score is 4, meaning that the price is low. Warranty received a 4, meaning that an extended warranty is provided. Color got a 1, meaning that you really dislike the color of the car. Mechanical condition is very good (score of 4), and transmission is manual (you would prefer the automatic transmission that is available in the other two options).

RESERVATION VALUE

The reservation value (the walk-away point) is the least favorable point at which one will accept a deal: the maximum a buyer is willing to offer and the minimum a seller is willing to accept.

Your reservation value is assessed from the BATNA. If the negotiation is only about money, the reservation price should be equal to the BATNA.

Going back to the used car example, the best alternative is option 3. However, what happens if the price of the car is $12,000 and you only have $11,800 in the bank? In this situation, $11,800 becomes your reservation price, and you'll be forced to settle for Option 1 (the alternative with the second highest score), which has a manual transmission (you would have preferred an automatic) and a color you really dislike.

ZOPA

The ZOPA, zone of possible agreement, is the third key negotiation concept. ZOPA is the set of potential agreements that can satisfy both parties. In other words, the ZOPA is the range between the seller's reservation value and the buyer's reservation value.

Going back to the used car example, if your reservation value is $11,800 and option 1's reservation price is $10,500 (the listed price is $11,000, but the dealer is willing to accept a lower offer), the ZOPA is the following (Fig. 2):

ZOPA

$10,500 $11,800

Figure 2. ZOPA.

Your task in the negotiation is not only to reach an agreement, but also to claim as much value as possible. With foreknowledge of the other player's reservation value, you can strive for an agreement close to $10,500.

However, what would happen if the two reservation values were reversed (Fig. 3)?

ZOPA

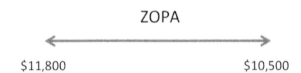

$11,800 $10,500

Figure 3. Impossible ZOPA.

There would be no ZOPA. No agreement would be possible in this case.

VALUE CREATION THROUGH TRADES

The fourth central concept of negotiation is value creation through trades. In the context of integrative negotiations, the parties collaborate to enlarge the size of the pie, creating value by integrating their interests into the process.

Value creation through trades can be defined as each party getting something wanted in return for something valued less. The act of making trade-offs across issues in a negotition is called *log-rolling.*

The first step of the process of value creation requires each party to carefully evaluate his or her own interests and clearly define the relative importance of each issue, that is, the priority ranking.

The second step is to assess issues complementary to the negotiation, increasing the possibility of trades across issues.

The third step is to negotiate multiple issues concurrently, not in sequence. The goal is to negotiate the best package deal, not the best result on only one or a few issues.

Options that can increase the value of the negotiation for a potential supplier are extended delivery terms, reduced payment terms, increased volumes, future potential orders, and opportunities for entry into new markets.

Options that can increase the value of the negotiation for a potential client include reduced delivery terms, extended payment terms, after sales, training, and risk reduction.

When negotiating multiple issues, the ZOPA can be defined as the set of overlapping and complementary interests between the parties, as represented in Fig. 4.

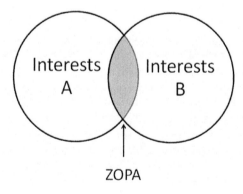

Figure 4 – ZOPA in Integrative Negotiations

TACTICS FOR DISTRIBUTIVE NEGOTIATIONS

In win-lose negotiations, the focus is on claiming value; therefore, collaboration and information exchange should be reduced to a minimum.

Following are important factors to consider during a distributive negotiation:

The first offer can become a strong psychological anchor point, one that establishes the negotiation range. Experiments indicate that negotiation outcomes often correlate to the first offer.

Do not reveal the whys behind your demands. Conceal your interests, priorities, concerns, and constraints.

Let the other party know that you have favorable alternatives if the deal falls through.

Learn as much as possible about the other party's interests, priorities, concerns, and constraints.

Hypothesize the ZOPA. If what you learn during the negotiation supports your assumptions, set the first offer.

In setting the first offer, don't go beyond what you can reasonably request. The other side may feel offended and walk away. However, at the same time, don't undershoot.

Make small concessions and *sell* them.

Anchoring

Anchoring is an attempt to establish a reference point around which negotiations will revolve. The first offer influences the negotiators' perceptions and expectations of possible outcomes, becoming a strong psychological anchor.

Studies indicate that the first party to place a number on the table acquires an important psychological advantage. Moreover, negotiation outcomes often correlate to the first offer.

When should a negotiator make the first offer? If you have a good estimate of the other party's reservation value, and therefore of the ZOPA, then make the first offer. Otherwise, don't.

When you place your offer, be prepared to justify it, offering a logical explanation of the reasons why you think your first offer is fair.

Anchoring with an offer or proposal produces three dangers.

First, if your first offer is too aggressive (too far outside the ZOPA), the other side may determine that a deal is impossible and, more important, may feel personally insulted, breaking the relationship (see Fig. 5, which illustrates an aggressive first offer of $8,000 in the used car example).

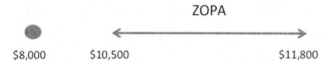

Figure 5. Aggressive first offer in the used car example.

Second, if your first offer is far outside the ZOPA, you risk losing credibility when you move toward less aggressive positions to find agreement. In this case, bring a backup line of reasoning to support your subsequent shift.

Third, if you made an erroneous estimate of the other side's reservation price, your offer can fall within the ZOPA and, therefore, you will immediately leave money on the table; Figure 6 illustrates a poor first offer of $11,000 in the used car example. The first offer falls within the ZOPA, and you instantly lose $500.

Figure 6 - Poor first offer.

COUNTER-ANCHORING

If the other side makes the first offer, you should refuse to accept the offer's potential influence as a psychological anchor. Anchors' influence is higher when there is strong uncertainty regarding the price and proposal.

For that reason, the best way to decrease the other side's anchoring power is to decrease the uncertainty surrounding the issue that is the focus of the negotiation by collecting impartial and unbiased information before entering the negotiation.

If the other party's first offer is unrealistic or unfavorable, steer the conversation away from numbers. Focus instead on interests, concerns, and constraints. Ignore the offer. Then, only after some time has passed and the effect of the anchor has diluted, place your counteroffer on the table, supporting it with rigorous arguments.

Keep away from a direct comparison between the other party's first offer and your counteroffer.

If the other party comes back to its initial offer, ask for the reasoning behind the number. This will help you understand if the first offer was realistic or not.

CONCESSIONS

After an anchor has been placed through the offer and subsequent counteroffer, you will enter the competitive phase of the negotiation process.

During the competitive phase, you attempt to obtain your goals and satisfy your interests. At this stage, you are competing with the other side.

Concession exchange usually takes place during the competitive stage. Concessions can be assessed from two distinct points of view: They can be considered a sign of goodwill or a sign of weakness. In the first case, they can follow the norm of reciprocation. In the second case, they can result in more competitive behavior from the other side because they set higher expectations (the other side will think that there is more room for bargaining).

After the offer and counteroffer have defined the anchor point, the parties engage in a set of concessions to reach an agreement.

According to the *norm of reciprocity*, for any concession from one side there must be a concession from the other side as a sign of goodwill.

A large concession is usually interpreted as a sign of considerable additional flexibility. A small concession, on the other hand, is generally interpreted as a sign that the other party is approaching his or her reservation price.

The following recommendations stand as useful guidelines when making concessions:

- Test the other party's willingness to comply with the norm of reciprocity. Reciprocity is considered a strong shaping factor of human behavior; it is a form of social obligation directed to the future and, therefore, it strongly influences the establishment and development of social relationships.[2]
- Make a small concession and verify whether the other side responds with a concession of the same value. If the norm of reciprocity is not respected, don't make any further concessions.
- Don't start with large concessions. The other side will perceive that you really need the deal.
- If the other side asks you to make another move, don't comply. Ask for the other party to make at least a symbolic move. Don't bid against yourself.
- Make strategic use of the law of diminishing rates of concessions: Gradually decrease the range of your concessions; as the negotiation progresses, make smaller and smaller concessions. This signals that you are approaching your reservation price.
- Be patient. Don't be eager to close the negotiation. Think twice before making any concession. Ask yourself: What signal am I conveying with this concession?

- Never make unilateral concessions. To avoid having the other party degrade or ignore your concession, label it; make it obvious that the concession has a cost for you.
- To increase the chances that the other party will conform to the norm of reciprocity, label your concessions and clearly assert what you expect in return for the concessions. Attach your concessions to specific actions on the other side.

An Example

Following is an example of a negotiation between a customer and a shopkeeper for the sale of a carpet.

Customer: How much do you want for this carpet?

Shopkeeper: That is a beautiful, handmade, and unique product. I can give it to you for just $350.

Customer: Oh, come on, it seems to be in very poor shape. I'll give you $150.

Shopkeeper: Sorry, but $150 certainly isn't a serious offer.

Customer: Well, I could go to $175, but I would never pay anything like $350. Give me a realistic price.

Shopkeeper: You are a tough negotiator; $300 cash, right now.

Customer: $200.

Shopkeeper: That doesn't even slightly cover my cost. Make me a serious offer.

Customer: $225. That's the highest I will go.

Shopkeeper: Have you noticed the texture and the colors of the carpet? It is a unique item. Two years from now, it will be worth three times what you pay today.

In this negotiation, a few issues can be highlighted:

Before making the counteroffer, did the customer ponder the reservation price of the shopkeeper and, therefore, the zone of possible agreement?

The customer makes a counteroffer of $150 and then a further concession of $25. The customer has bid against himself.

The shopkeeper makes a concession of $50, from $350 to $300. The customer may interpret this as an indication of additional flexibility.

The customer makes an offer of $200 and then bids again, making a further concession of $25. The shopkeeper can interpret the last concession as an indication of additional flexibility.

Closing

When you are ready to bring the negotiation to a close, adhere to the following maxims:[3]

- Don't unexpectedly declare that you have reached your reservation value. The other party will think you are bluffing. Signal that you are approaching your bottom line well in advance. Also, repeat the warning so the other party takes you seriously.

- If you are aware that the other player doesn't have full decision authority, leave yourself some flexibility for the final negotiation. Don't reach your reservation value. Stop earlier and leave some room for maneuvering in the final round.
- Dissuade the other side from seeking further concessions once a deal has been reached. If the other party asks for changes on a specific issue, explain that in such a case the whole package must be reopened or that further concessions on a specific issue must be matched by concessions from the other side on other issues.
- As soon as a deal is reached, write down the agreed terms and conditions. Draft a provisional agreement that details the main terms, make a copy, and have both parties sign them. Even if your draft agreement is not an official contract, it will still serve as a common reference for both parties if any complications occur.

TACTICS FOR INTEGRATIVE NEGOTIATIONS

Integrative negotiations require a different approach, a different mind-set, and a different strategy from distributive negotiations. The focus is on creating value while obtaining a significant quantity of the enlarged pie.[4]

While in distributive negotiations information exchange is kept to a minimum, integrative negotiations require both parties to disclose their interests and constraints to create value before claiming it.

During the first phase of integrative negotiations, players should look for creative options to enlarge the pie, supplementing issues for the negotiation to increase the value on the table.

Understanding your interests and their relative importance is fundamental during this phase, as is identifying the other side's interests, constraints, and priorities.

Finding opportunities for information sharing is important in integrative negotiations because it allows negotiators to create relationships based on trust, explain their interests in the deal, describe their constraints, talk about their concerns, evaluate additional issues to be included in the negotiation, and find creative options to solve both parties' problems.

Following are recommendations to enhance problem solving and collaboration during integrative negotiations:

ASK QUESTIONS AND LISTEN

Ask open-ended questions about the other side's interests, concerns, priorities, and constraints.

Don't fall prey to *fixed-pie bias*, entering the negotiation with a win-lose perspective, or assuming that a fixed value is to be negotiated.

Listen actively. The more people on the other side talk, the more they are likely to open up, and the more information you are likely to get. Adjust your assumptions based on what you learn.

Tell the other side your interests, concerns, priorities, and constraints. Identify shared interests and opportunities for trade.

BE PATIENT

Don't be enticed to close the deal too quickly. Spend time identifying common and conflicting interests and finding ways to create value. Learn as much as you can about the other side's interests, priorities, concerns, and constraints. Be patient. Avoid the pressure to close the deal too quickly.

Don't accept the first offer on the table. Dig more. Leave the creating-value phase only when you have run through all the options.

BUILD A RELATIONSHIP

Building a personal and organizational relationship with the other side is fundamental in negotiations. Relationships can increase payoffs in negotiations for several reasons:

- You can learn more about the other side's interests and constraints.
- You can proactively disclose your interests and constraints.
- You can jointly brainstorm and develop integrative solutions.
- You can negotiate as if the problem is a shared problem and the solution should satisfy both sides' interests.
- You can decrease the possibility of misperception and misunderstanding.
- You can better manage emotions and communication.

People tend to like and trust people who are similar, individuals with whom we share interests and background experiences such as education, age, sport, family, vacations, common foreign assignments, and memberships. Do your homework prior to the negotiation: Find some common interests, hobbies, or experiences unrelated to the specific negotiation.

Use small talk at the beginning of the negotiation: This helps drive out tension, lowers people's natural resistance, and starts the process of building relationships.

Always avoid personal attacks and maintain the other party's face and reputation.

Beware of negotiating with close friends. Research has confirmed that people negotiating with individuals with whom they have a personal relationship will seek to minimize conflict and try to find a compromise based on equality.

Always keep in mind that negotiation is about people, their goals, constraints, concerns, and interests. Establish, develop, and maintain a trust-based relationship with the other party.

PACKAGE OFFERS

In the integrative phase, always negotiate multiple issues simultaneously. Don't tackle one issue at a time; if you do, you'll lose the possibility of *log-rolling*, the act of trading across issues in a negotiation: If the other side values something more than you do, you should give it up in exchange for reciprocity on issues that are of higher priority to you.[5] Negotiations are built on the relative importance of each issue to each party and on the different priorities of each player.

Log-rolling requires that each party know his or her interests and priorities. This is why maximizing the value in the deal and claiming as much of its value as possible requires high competence and drive.

LOOK FOR OPTIONS THAT EXPLOIT DIFFERENCES

Negotiators are usually very good at creating value based on shared or overlapping interests. However, value creation is greater when the players build on their differences, trading unrelated or even conflicting issues. The aim is to generate options that neither party could have created on its own. Specifically, value can be created by leveraging factors such as access to resources, people, and technology, future expectations, time preference, and risk propensity.

Each party has different priorities. Leverage these differences to create value. This is how log-rolling works. People have different expectations about the future, different risk propensity, and different time preferences. Seek out the differences and develop integrative solutions.

IDENTIFY POTENTIAL BARRIERS

Identify potential obstacles that might prevent value-creating opportunities. Recognize and respond to the other party's potential limitations and constraints, including second-level actors, standard company procedures that don't allow for exceptions, and unrealistic expectations of the other side.[6]

Manage tolerance for different risk and ambiguity levels. Never underestimate the power of self-interest when negotiating an agreement.

Don't let emotions take charge of the negotiation. Separate problems from people; don't blame the other side.

Don't fall prey to threats and other pressure tactics. Focus on your goals and help the other side do the same. Be patient and always be ready to highlight the benefits for both parties of joint problem solving.

Identify potential relationship problems based on mistrust and misperceptions, such as power and status asymmetry or language and communication barriers. Manage face saving and giving.

Last, but perhaps most important, don't be a victim of the fixed-pie fallacy. Players' goals and interests are not always in opposition. Negotiation doesn't have to be a zero-sum game. Even when interests conflict and resources are scarce, many opportunities exist to expand the size of the pie by seeking out differences to exploit and creating value through trades.

IS WIN-WIN FOR REAL?

Negotiations develop on a continuum from purely distributive zero-sum games to purely integrative joint problem solving.

At one end of the scale, negotiations are entirely distributive, where a gain for one side represents a loss for the other.

At the other end of the scale, negotiations are entirely integrative or win-win. Between purely distributive and purely integrative, we find most of the real-world negotiations.

As seen in earlier paragraphs, deciding where to negotiate along that continuum between win-lose and win-win implies a tension known as the negotiator's dilemma.

To create value, players should transparently exchange information and reveal their interests, constraints, and concerns. However, what happens if one side shares information and the other does not? This is the dilemma that most negotiators face.

The concept of win-win has become almost a cliché. For some people, the term is almost synonymous with negotiation. However, how can the notion of win-win apply when the other party uses hardball tactics, behaves unethically, doesn't have the decision authority to negotiate an integrative deal, is under time pressure, or is not sufficiently skilled to negotiate an integrative solution?

In conclusion, negotiations don't have to be entirely distributive, but neither are they likely to be fully integrative. Negotiators must tailor their strategies to the type of negotiation, trying when possible to create value by trading differences and then claiming as much of that value as possible.

THE ATTIC NEGOTIATION

The attic game is a role-play exercise that simulates the sale of a small attic. Participants are split in two teams (buyers and sellers). Following are the instructions provided to each team.

SELLER

You are the owner of a 40-square-meter attic with a gable roof in Milan. The attic is situated just above the 200-square-meter penthouse where you and your family have lived for the past 10 years.

The attic is connected to the penthouse only through an external staircase and has always been used as your private office. It is located in a suburban but quite upscale area.

You are a professional consultant specialized in evaluating company assets. You are entering into a partnership with two of your friends who work in Rome. This is why after so many years you will move away from Milan. You have decided to sell your home in Milan to buy a new home in Rome.

You were able to sell your penthouse immediately for €930,000, while the attic is still unsold after three months.

In the meantime, you and your family have moved to Rome and you can't devote much time to the sale of the attic. Nevertheless, you urgently need the money to support the new venture (currently in the hole for €160,000, at an interest rate of 8% per annum).

You have asked for three different appraisals of your attic and received three different assessments, all between €160,000 and €240,000. The reason behind this price inconsistency is that rumors persist that the new city development plan will grant major contractors the possibility of developing new office buildings. A similar situation occurred in a neighboring district and house prices skyrocketed when the contractors started to purchase residential buildings for conversion into offices. Prices for attics in your area currently range between €4,000 and €6,000 per square meter.

For the moment, the only potential buyer is a young business graduate who responded to your advertisement in the local paper and a couple of days ago visited the attic, which came across as a bit unclean but at the same time very romantic and in good structural condition. He expressed his interest and asked you to call him as soon as you were back in Milan.

The only tangible offer you have received to date is from a building contractor offering €100,000 in cash.

Your job does not allow you to spend further time on the sale of the attic and even only €100,000 can be of service.

Before accepting the contractor's offer, you have decided to make one last attempt to call the young man who recently visited the attic. You tell him that you have had an offer and that you must provide an answer by tomorrow evening. He asks for a meeting for the next morning. You are determined to get rid of the attic by tomorrow.

If you can sell it to the young graduate, all the better; otherwise, you'll sell it to the contractor for €100,000 in cash without any further thought.

Deferred payments are of no interest for you. You need immediate cash for your firm.

BUYER

You are a young business graduate working in a multinational company in Milan.

You have been renting an attic for the past five years in a suburban but quite upscale area. Your office is only a five-minute walk from the attic; your fiancée and most of your friends live in the same neighborhood. You would really hate to move away from your current area.

Unfortunately, the owner is forcing you out of your home because he has decided to sell the attic to a relative for €160,000 in cash. You have to leave the apartment by the end of the month.

Finding an attic for rent is almost impossible. You have to buy one. Adding your savings and a loan from your parents, you can reach €160,000 in cash. Just in case, you are also prepared to take out a small mortgage on top of the €160,000.

Furthermore, rumors persist that the new city development plan will grant major contractors the possibility of developing new office buildings. A similar situation occurred in a neighboring district and house prices skyrocketed when the contractors started to purchase residential buildings for conversion into offices. This is just a possibility, but you can't afford to lose the opportunity to find a solid solution before the end of the month.

You are looking for a small and romantic attic because you are not planning a family in the near future. Prices for attics in the area fluctuate between €4,000 and

€6,000 per square meter, guided by property conditions and expectations on possible increases in value affected by the rumors of the new city development plan.

You have unsuccessfully combed the district for a suitable attic for days when you bump by chance into an interesting advertisement in the local paper. You call the owner, a very busy 50-year-old engineer. He tells you that he and his family lived in the underlying penthouse and he used the attic as an office. He easily sold the penthouse, and he is in negotiations to sell the attic. He is selling his properties in Milan because he is moving to Rome for business purposes.

You have visited the attic and had to force yourself not to display your delight. The attic is just like the one where you are living now, with an area of 40 square meters and a gable roof. It is a bit dirty, but it is located just 100 meters from your current apartment. To avoid exposing your position, you tell the owner that you want to think it over and ask him to call you when he returns to Milan.

He just called you after three days, telling you that he has an interesting offer and that he must provide an answer by tomorrow evening. You ask for a meeting for the next morning. You are determined to get the attic by tomorrow. In the meanwhile, you haven't found any alternative option: This seems to be your only and last chance.

Simulation Results

Each team must appoint two negotiators who will have 20 minutes to find a solution. Each team is also allowed to call for a time-out and change one or both the players.

Reading both the instructions, the established price range is between €160,000 and €240,000. Both the buyer and the seller have a very poor BATNA: The seller has an offer for €100,000, while the buyer has no alternatives.

The selling price should be around €200,000, being that the market price range is between €160,000 and €240,000 and both players have poor or even no alternatives. In reality, the price should be higher than €200,000 because the buyer has no BATNA, while the seller has one, even if quite poor.

The simulation was carried out with undergraduates, master's of business administration students, young talents, and executives from over 40 countries.

After approximately 600 simulations, the results are as follow:

• 87% of the teams reached an agreement.
• Surprisingly, the average price was just €169,000.
• Only one simulation ended with a price equal to €200,000.
• 21% of the negotiations ended with a price below €160,000.

Figure 7. Attic current price range and average solution.

There are two possible explanations:

- The €100,000 BATNA psychologically anchors the sellers to the very low end of the ZOPA.
- The sellers are usually more subject to the psychological burden of having to close the deal, which in turn provides buyers with a slight advantage in most bargaining situations.

An additional interesting constant across all the simulations is that in around 50% of the cases, sellers failed to provide a first offer outside the ZOPA.

Another interesting element is provided by the size of the concessions. Sellers tended to make very large concessions at the beginning (a leap from €240,000 to €200,000 was quite common) and then to make very small concession at the end, when approaching their reservation value.

Buyers, on the other hand, tended to make very small concessions at the beginning and increase the size of the concessions toward the end, when time pressure became significant.

(Endnotes)

1   Malhotra, D., & Bazerman, M. (2008). Negotiation genius. New York: Bantam.

2   Bell, D. (1991). Reciprocity as a generating process in social relations. Journal of Quantitative Anthropology, 3, 251-260.

3   Watkins, M., & Luecke, R. (2003). Harvard business essentials: Negotiation. Boston: Harvard Business School Press.

4   Lax, D., & Sebenius, J. (1992). The Manager as Negotiator: The Negotiator's Dilemma: Creating and Claiming Value. In S. Goldberg, F. Sander, & N. Rogers (Eds.), Dispute Resolution (2nd ed.). Boston: Little Brown and Co.

5   Malhotra, D., & Bazerman, M. (2008). Negotiation genius. New York: Bantam.

6   Wheeler, M. A. (2001). Negotiation Analysis: An Introduction. Business Fundamentals As Taught at the Harvard Business School. Harvard Business Publishing, 3-16.

CHAPTER 7:

The 4Ps Negotiation Framework

Negotiations are inherently systemic and dynamic[1]; they are a complex interaction of four dimensions.

Because negotiations are nonlinear, fragmented in time, complex social processes that take place under conditions of ambiguity and uncertainty,[2] the four negotiation stages are linked and overlapping, and a change in one element triggers changes in the others.

We will look at negotiations as systems in which the four stages influence one another and overlap.

The four interrelating stages (the four Ps) that we employ to describe and analyze negotiations are *preparation, process, power perception,* and *players' perspective* (see Figure 1).

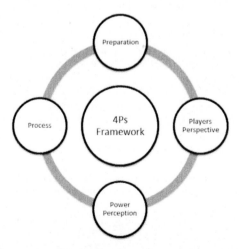

Figure 1. The Four Ps.

ᵎEPARATION STAGE

....ᵤ and cultivate the science.[3]

Most negotiators make their biggest mistake before even getting to the bargaining table: They don't reserve time to prepare for the negotiation.

A successful negotiation is like an iceberg. The fundamental part occurs below the waterline, where you can't see it, behind the scenes in the research, planning, and organizing phases or, in other words, in the preparation stage.[4]

At the end of the preparation stage (which often overlaps the process stage), you should know:

- Your MATNAs (Multiple Alternatives to a Negotiated Agreement).
- Your reservation value.
- Your goals.
- The other parties' MATNAs.
- Their reservation value.
- The ZOPA.
- Their interests.
- Options for an integrative negotiation.
- Their culture.
- The key players.
- Your first offer and the concession plan.

Your MATNAs

Most of the negotiation literature focuses on the concept of BATNA. To understand who has the most power at the negotiation table, you should answer the question: What is your BATNA, your best alternative to a negotiated agreement? That is: What is your alternative if no agreement can be reached?

Your BATNA sets a standard that tells you whether you should accept the terms of the agreement or walk away and pursue other options.

However, the question is: In preparing for multiparty, multidimensional, and unpredictable international negotiations in a volatile, uncertain, complex, and ambiguous (VUCA) world, is the notion of BATNA still relevant? The answer is yes, but.

The constantly shifting or kaleidoscopic nature of each party's best alternative to a negotiated agreement (BATNA)[5] in international contexts requires listing and evaluating all the alternatives to no agreement, without committing to only one course of action if the negotiation ends in an impasse.

There is also another reason why committing to only one course of action can be a mistake: The preparation phase often extends to the process phase; beforehand, in evaluating alternatives, we do not have all the needed information or facts to select the BATNA.

Therefore, a better preparation strategy for international negotiations asks for multiple feasible alternatives (MATNAs).

The better your MATNAs, the greater your power. Negotiation power is not (only) wealth, connections, authority, and status; the relative negotiation power of the parties depends mainly on how interesting to each is the option of no agreement.

If the real relative power in a negotiation lies in the alternative to a negotiate agreement, why should we choose only the alternative that we deem to be the best, but which could turn out to be not very promising during the talks?

Having different conceivable alternatives to a no agreement provides a compelling and flexible setting to approach the talks with the other side.

YOUR RESERVATION VALUE

Determine your reservation value (RV), or your walk-away point in the negotiation, according to your MATNAs.

YOUR GOALS

Setting goals motivates people by focusing their attention. According to research, you are more likely to achieve your goals if the goals are specific. You are also more persuasive if you are committed to achieving a specific target.

Goals are derived from your specific interests in the negotiation: your needs, ambitions, concerns, and constraints.

Goals differ from the bottom line (what we call reservation value), the minimum acceptable level you require to say yes in a negotiation. Goals are cogitated judgments about what you can reasonably achieve. They are your legitimate expectations.[6]

In complex and demanding situations, we have limited capacity to maintain concentration. We tend to gravitate toward a reference point (i.e., for most of us, the bottom line is the most natural focal point). Because we tend to make concessions until we get very close to our reference point, we often end up closing deals and achieving only a mediocre result that reflects our reservation value.

This is why it is important to establish a goal as a reference point; any offer below that reference point will be perceived as a potential loss, and loss avoidance is a powerful motivator.

Research shows that people who succeed in achieving their target goals are more likely to raise their goals the next time and therefore achieve better results.

Never take your eyes off your goals.[7]

INTERESTS AND CONCERNS

Every person has his or her own interests: needs, aspirations, wants, concerns, anxieties, and fears. Interests are what motivate people and shape their behavior. We tend to think that the only interest involved in negotiations is money, but the most intense interests are basic human needs, such as security, subsistence, understanding, a sense of belonging, recognition, protection, participation, and identity.

Understanding the interests of the other side is paramount to reach an agreement and achieve your objectives.

Ask questions and listen to what the other side is telling you. Don't pay attention only to the explicit words, but try to understand from what is not said and from the nonverbal and paraverbal communication, the hidden interests of the other side. Remember, often what is not said is more important than what is said, and how something is communicated is more important than the content itself.

To identify other people's interests, put yourself in their shoes. *Become your opponent.*[8] Ask yourself why they are behaving in such a way. Why are they taking this specific position? Why are they making this specific decision?

However, understanding their interests is not sufficient. A fundamental question to ask yourself is: *Why not?* Why did they not make the specific decision you envisioned? Which are their concerns and constraints? Why might the other side say no? Often the answer is related to non-financial personal needs, such as status, recognition, appreciation, and belonging.

Each member of the other team has his or her own multiple interests and concerns. Don't assume that all the team members on the other side have homogeneous interests. Identify the key players and put yourself in their shoes. Assess the interests and concerns of all the players (more on that in the Key Players paragraph and in the Player's Perspective section of this chapter).

During the preparation phase, always ask yourself the following questions: What obstacles might prevent an agreement? Which barriers will I be facing during the negotiation? Identify the other side's potential constraints and parameters, such as company policies, stakeholders' bearing, and unrealistic goal setting. Detect potential relationship problems grounded on mistrust, miscommunication, and misperceptions.[9]

Once you have identified their interests and concerns, identify options that can help members from the other side not only reach their goals, but also solve their problems.

The Other Side's MATNAs

Knowledge of the other side's MATNAs is particularly beneficial because it lets you know how far you can push during the negotiation.

Identify the other side's alternatives to a negotiated agreement by answering the following questions:

- How important is this deal to the other side at this time?
- Which benefits will the other side receive from reaching an agreement with you?
- Can your competitors deliver the same benefits?
- What are the alternatives to a negotiated agreement available to the other side?
- Has the other side already started informal or formal negotiations with anyone else?

Identify ways to weaken the other side's MATNAs. Anything that weakens their alternatives strengthens your relative position.

The Other Side's Reservation Value

What is the other side's walk-away point?

THE ZOPA

The zone of possible agreements (ZOPA) is the range of all possible deals included in the two reservation values. Any value outside the ZOPA will be rejected by one of the two sides.

OPTIONS FOR AN INTEGRATIVE NEGOTIATION

Identify opportunities for value creation that are not obvious. Negotiators are often subject to fixed-pie bias: Price becomes the only issue on the table.

During the preparation phase, discover issues that can be added to the negotiation. The goal of a negotiation is not to get the best possible outcome on any one issue, but to negotiate the best possible package deal based on consideration of all the issues.[10]

If the other side appears to be only focused on price, try to persuade them to take into consideration other negotiation issues, such as delivery date, payment terms, quality, technical specifications, contract length, penalties, service support, warranties, training, and supplementary business.

The following preparation strategies stand as useful for value creation:[11]

- *Identify your multiple interests*, issues other than price that can be discussed at the negotiation table.
- *Create a scoring system.* Identify priorities and rank your different interests; classify these interests along a continuum between non-negotiable elements and easily yielded elements. Establish what is more and what is less important to you in the negotiation.
- *Calculate a package reservation value.* The package reservation value is the least favorable total value at which you will accept a deal. The value is calculated in terms of dollars, if you can assign a monetary value to the different interests, or points, when the different elements cannot be assigned dollar value, with a scoring system that allows you to compare different packages.
- *Identify the other party's multiple interests.* Establish what is more and what is less important to the other party in the negotiation. Based on the available information, estimate a ranking for the other side's interests and isolate interests that can be important for the other side but that you can effortlessly concede.
- *Identify the other party's constraints.* Why might they say no to your proposal? Search options that can solve the other side's problems.
- *Outline your package concession plan* according to your priorities and the other party's interests.

Inventing options to expand the pie requires advice.

To devise creative alternatives, try to escape from early criticism of new ideas. Premature judgment hinders creativity. Look for as many options as possible before starting the screening process. Try to integrate different options to shape a better solution.

Furthermore, develop options that appeal not only to your self-interest, but also to the self-interest of the other side. Favorable agreements depend on the other party making the decision you want.

Chapter 11 will provide extensive material on integrative thinking and creativity.

THE OTHER SIDE'S CULTURE

What are the other side's cultural values (what a person deems important) and norms (what a person considers suitable behavior)?

What is the other side's organizational culture?

What language will be used during the negotiations? Is there a need for interpreters?

Chapters 2, 3 and 4 have provided extensive material on culture.

THE KEY PLAYERS

Every negotiation has at least three levels of participants.

First-level players are the actual negotiators.

In preparing for the meeting, you should answer the following questions:

• Who are first-level players (who will be at the negotiating table)?
• What are their formal titles and areas of responsibility?
• What is their decision authority? Do they have a broad mandate to close the deal or just an exploratory mandate?

Second-level players are those who directly affect the negotiators: bosses, shareholders, clients, colleagues, suppliers, external consultants and even spouses. Understanding the dynamics between first-level and second-level players helps in recognizing negotiators' decision-making authority, constraints, interests, thinking patterns, culture, and behavior.

Third-level actors are those who can affect the negotiation indirectly: shareholders, competitors, policy makers, unions (sometimes unions are second-level players), and journalists writing about the talks.

In negotiating with organizations, you should understand how the company is structured, its decision-making unit, and its decision-making process. Who are the key players that you must influence (sometimes away from the negotiation table) and what are each player's interests (more on that in the Players Perspective section of this chapter)?

Can any player outside the organization (such as competitors, legislators, customers, shareholders) influence the organizational decision-making process?

YOUR FIRST OFFER AND THE CONCESSION PLAN

Before entering the negotiation process, outline what your first offer (or counteroffer) will be and the concession plan you intend to adopt.

It is important to detail your concession plan in advance because in the heat of negotiation we often switch to automatic mode, and thus are apt to rely on intuition, and make costly mistakes (e.g., yielding when there is no need, conceding too much, compromising when the other side is not yet ready to close, not waiting for reciprocation and providing a further concession just after having made one).

An in-depth analysis of how and when to make the first offer, and how to manage concessions, will be provided in phase three of the negotiation process in this chapter (see Opening Moves).

The preparation stage does not end when you arrive at the negotiation table. It often protracts to the process phase: Some of the information we want to have is simply not available beforehand or is not accurate, and we must gather int during the process phase.

THE PROCESS STAGE

The second stage of the 4Ps framework is the process. During the process phase, the two or more parties meet (whether at the negotiation table, by phone, video conference, or at dinner) to find an agreement.

Although the different stages of the negotiation process may overlap, may not be sequential, may be confusing, and differ in duration, most negotiations can be broken down into the following seven distinct phases:

- Designing the game (off-the-table negotiation).
- Exchanging information.
- Opening moves.
- Competitive phase.
- Integrative phase.
- End game.
- Negotiation post-mortem analysis.

The precise division of phases is to some extent arbitrary because no negotiation process is as systematic and standard as this seven-phase model indicates.

PHASE 1: DESIGNING THE GAME (OFF-THE-TABLE NEGOTIATION)

Deals are often decided away from the negotiation table. Being able to involve the right parties in the right string at the right time is a vital skill for international negotiators.

Capable negotiators design the game in their favor even before they get to the table.[12] They also build alliances that influence key people to frame the outcome of the negotiations.

They change the negotiation's setup, involving additional or different players, introducing different interests than the obvious ones, managing the information flow among the different players, and improving their alternatives.

By working behind the scenes, a negotiator can plant the seeds of ideas and start to build consensus before formal decision making begins.[13]

To better design the game, ask yourself the following questions:

- Who outside the existing players has interest in the deal?
- Negotiating with organizations, which is the organization's decision-making unit and what is its decision-making process? More on this in chapters 12 and 13.
- Can you leverage complementary interests?
- Can additional players positively change the alternatives to a no agreement (e.g., additional bidders, competitors, suppliers, or customers)?

PHASE 2: EXCHANGING INFORMATION

Information exchange is the initial step in the ritual of negotiation; it always precedes the opening moves in the negotiation process.

Information exchange is a key factor for the following reasons:

- It is the link between the preparation and process phases. Underlying issues, interests, and perceptions that can arise in sharing initial information can provide valuable material for integrating and testing the hypothesis on which you built your preparation before the meeting, as well as your conclusions. Furthermore, you come to understand the scope of the other side's decision authority.
- It is the stage on which the relationship is built. You will find common interests (unrelated to the negotiation), experiences, and educational background that you share with the other party.
- In being cultures, the information exchange stage is the most important phase of the negotiation process. Establishing a personal relationship based on trust is crucial to move the negotiation to the next phase. Commitment to the relationship is tested in different contexts (e.g., meetings, social gatherings, dinners) and this is why negotiations in some parts of the world need months or years before they enter the opening moves stage.
- It is the testing field for your counterpart's commitment to the norm of reciprocity.

Phase 3: Opening Moves

After the initial ritual information exchange stage, the real negotiation process starts with the opening moves.

Opening moves refer to the first offer and consequent counteroffer.

Questions to address before entering the opening moves stage include:

- Should I be the first to open?
- If so, should I open fairly or aggressively?
- Should I start hard and then become more flexible, or should I start soft and then harden my position?
- Should I let the other side make the first offer?
- If so, how should I respond?

Several experiments have demonstrated that the final agreement tends to favor the negotiator who makes the first offer. In particular, the first offer establishes an anchor that focuses the other party's attention and expectations, especially when the other side is unclear about the ZOPA. Negotiations tend to revolve around the first offer. This suggests that making the first offer in a negotiation constitutes a powerful tool to influence the outcome of the negotiation. Anchoring effects are typically robust and very difficult to counteract even for experienced negotiators.[14]

Your opening offer often compels the other party to reconsider their goals and adjust expectations.

However, setting a general rule is not easy: In opening first, you could also lose some of the theoretical ZOPA. In general, abide by the following guidelines:

- If you have a clear idea of the ZOPA, then you gain an important advantage from opening, especially if the other side is uncertain about the appropriate outcome.

- If you don't know the exact market value of the product or service that you are negotiating, then let the other side open.

Let's assume you have a clear idea of the potential ZOPA: Should you open optimistically or reasonably?

If the relationship with the other side is more important than your goal(s), then a fair or sometimes even accommodating opening is the right move.

In all other situations, start with an optimistic opening: the highest (or lowest) number for which there is a supporting argument that allows you to build a factual and persuasive case.

The difference between an optimistic opening and an outrageous opening is this: The outrageous opening has no justification whatever to support it. The optimistic opening, in contrast, is a highly favorable interpretation of a standard or reference point.[15]

Optimistic openings won't work if you have no leverage and the other party knows it.

With your first offer, always make use of the full ZOPA. If your first offer is already inside the ZOPA, you have lost your chance to claim value that lies between your offer and the other party's reservation value.

In some cultures, such as those in South America, the Middle East, some Asian countries, and Africa, anything other than an optimistic opening becomes a serious social and negotiation mistake.

If you didn't make the first offer, how can you respond to it?

- First of all, ignore it. Shift the conversation to a different topic. Don't spend time refuting the other side's anchor.
- Second, separate reasonable information from the other side's attempt to influence your perception. Bring together the tangible facts behind the other side's justification.
- Third, focus on the other party's reservation price and alternatives to a no agreement, not on the other party's target. You have to concentrate on the information that is inconsistent with the other side's first offer: This allows you to neutralize the anchoring effect.
- Fourth, give the other side time to moderate its offer without losing face; otherwise, the other side will attach even more to its first offer. In other words, when reacting to very extreme offers, your goal should be to provide a new anchor for the negotiation, not to express your resentment. Re-anchoring requires helping the other side find a way to withdraw from radical demands without losing face. This takes patience.
- Last, provide a counteroffer that is at the edge of the ZOPA with strong justification and robust supporting arguments. Your aim is to make the counteroffer the new anchor.

Phase 4: The Competitive Phase

After the opening moves, offer, and counteroffer, you enter the competitive phase of the negotiation process.

During the competitive phase, you attempt to obtain your goals and satisfy your interests. At this stage, you are competing with the other side.

Concession exchanges usually take place during the competitive stage. Concessions can be assessed from two distinct points of view: They can be considered a sign of goodwill or a sign of weakness. In the first case, for any concession from one side, there must be a concession from the other side (norm of reciprocation). The second case results in more competitive behavior on the other side because it sets a higher expectation (the other side will think that there is more room for bargaining).

One experiment compared three different concession strategies:[16]

- Start high, and then turn down any request for concessions.
- Start reasonably, and then turn down any request for concessions.
- Start high, and then make progressive and steady concessions.

More agreements are accomplished using the last strategy.

Start optimistically, and after the other side's counteroffer, grant a small concession. Test the other side's commitment to reciprocity. Don't make unilateral concessions.

Keep in mind that optimistic openings won't work if you lack leverage and the other party knows it. Never show the other party that you don't have alternatives to a no agreement. Begin with the position that *you do not need this deal.*[17]

If the other side complies with the norm of reciprocity, then make gradual concessions. Start slowly. Don't make overly large concessions during the initial phase; if you do, the other party will perceive that you really want the deal and that the issues you concede are not important to you because people don't value concessions that are secured effortlessly. Always *sell* concessions. Never devaluate them. Make the other side work for them, establishing that they have a cost for you.

Make strategic use of the law of diminishing concession rates: Concession rates in negotiations follow a pattern where early concessions are larger than later concessions. The closer you move to the reservation value, the smaller the concessions become.[18]

If the other side is complying with the norm of reciprocity, but not delivering concessions of the envisioned significance, you can also specify what you expect in return.

One main factor that guides a negotiator's behavior is saving face. Face is the aspiration to project an image of competence and power or, on the other hand, to avoid projecting an image of incompetence, powerlessness, and weakness. In many cultures, the word face is used as a metaphor for an individual's reputation. Experiments show that face maintenance, particularly in front of an audience, can slow down concession making because a concession made in response to the other player's request can be perceived as a sign of weakness.[19]

PHASE 5: THE INTEGRATIVE PHASE

The competitive and integrative phases do not always follow in sequence. Sometimes, after an initial phase of positioning, the negotiation directly enters the problem-solving phase. On occasion, it doesn't leave the competitive phase; when the relationship becomes hostile and the negotiation reaches an impasse because neither party is willing to concede on fundamental issues, moving to the problem-solving stage becomes difficult. At times, the competitive and problem-solving phases run in tandem. Occasionally, the problem-solving phase even prec competitive phase.

Now and then, the negotiation doesn't move to the integrative stage because the other side appears entirely focused on price and you are not able to move the other party away from its fixed-pie bias.

In these cases, stage 1 of the negotiation process (designing the game: building coalitions and influencing key decision-making actors) is vital for entering the creating-value phase.

During the integrative phase, you test the assumptions about possible options for value creation that you identified during the preparation phase. The integrative stage requires a shift in mind-set, moving from a focus on *what* the other party wants to *why* the other party wants it.

There are various schools of thought about the appropriate sequence of issues to be tackled in the negotiation:[20]

- Start the negotiation with the easiest issue so you can get the negotiation off to an effective start.
- Deal with the most important issue at the beginning.
- Start with the most complicated issue.
- Resolve a manageable issue. Collaborative problem solving can foster relationship development.

We recommend the last strategy.

However, by negotiating one issue at a time, you remove any chance of log-rolling (i.e., yielding on low-priority issues in exchange for gains on high-priority issues). By negotiating one issue at a time, you also lose any opportunity for value creation. Attacking one issue at a time also carries high risk of reaching a stalemate because there are often issues on which one of the parties cannot yield (e.g., on payment terms or delivery time). Thus, you should negotiate multiple issues simultaneously, present package offers, and reach an agreement on one issue only after you have discussed all of them and understood the different priorities for each of the parties involved, leveraging these differences to expand the pie. Understanding the other side's interests and priorities is vital to find solutions that are beneficial for both parties.

During the integrative stage, make contingent concessions, concessions tied to specific actions by the other side. However, in international negotiations, where trust building is fundamental, be careful not to attach too many provisions to your concessions; otherwise, the other side could interpret your strategy as a reluctance to cooperate.

How does the integrative phase work?

After a discussion of all the issues, one side proposes a multiple-issue platform (that includes a demand on each issue). The other party responds with a platform, including a demand on each issue. In the next move, the side that opened could make a concession on one or two less important issues, demonstrating that the concession is meaningful (avoiding the danger of concession devaluation). The other side reciprocates, yielding on lower priority issues. After a number of rounds, each side begins to understand the other side's interests.

PHASE 6: ENDGAME

If you become deadlocked, then change your approach or use a different tactic.
Act as the sea when your opponent is like a mountain, and act like a mountain when
the enemy is like the sea.[21]

The negotiation process ends with closing the deal and gaining both parties' commitment.

However, how can you accelerate the last stage of the negotiation process to achieve your goals and strengthen the relationship?

First, try to instill urgency, making the other side perceive that it has something to lose from a no deal. The other side must feel that not closing the deal now will mean not having another opportunity to do so. You have to leverage the *scarcity effect*, the human tendency to want things more when they are in short supply.

You can introduce the scarcity effect in at least three ways:

- *Competition*: When many people want the same thing, stress that your product or service has many potential buyers; make the other side perceive that you have many alternatives.
- *Deadlines*: Impose a deadline; for example, tell the other side that the offer is valid only for the next hour.
- *Take it or leave it*: Walkouts work only if your position is perceived as credible.

Always be careful in adopting the walkout tactic or bluffing. If the other side calls your bluff, or doesn't accept the deadline or ultimatum, what is your plan B? Always leave an open back door through which to return to the negotiation table.

There is always a slim equilibrium between the credibility of your ultimatum and the fact that you want to maintain a communication link with the other side in case of stalemate.

In case of deadlock, and no back door, adopt the *trivial step technique*: Make a very small but detectable move in the other side's direction, waiting for a response. If there is a significant response, then make another small move and wait for reciprocation, and so on.

Scarcity effect strategies can be implemented if your relationship with the other party is less important than achieving your goal.

Another strategy to speed up the endgame phase is to leverage loss aversion and over-commitment to the negotiation process. As the other side invests more and more time and resources in the negotiation process, the party becomes progressively more committed to closing the deal. This constitutes one of people's many biases due to not thinking rationally (more on that in chapter 9).

If the relationship has a bearing, then think of adopting a softer closing technique, such as compromising or even yielding.

Compromise is often adopted during the final stages of a negotiation because it is a simple, fast, and fair way to split differences.

Be cautious in adopting a compromise tactic too early in the negotiation process. If you do, you will lose the opportunity to evaluate additional options to create value. Furthermore, resorting to splitting could lead to further requests for concessions when the other side is not yet ready to close and is still claiming its share of value.

Relationships in a negotiation depend on the actual final result, but more than that, they depend on both sides' *perception of the final result*. As a negotiator, you must manage the other side's perception of the deal.

This is why yielding too rapidly in a negotiation can weaken the relationship: The other party could question the final deal, wondering what if it had asked for more.

To close the deal, you sometimes have to help the other side with its behind-the-table challenges (challenges to overcome inside its own organization).[22] To overcome the other party's domestic opposition, you have to understand not only the other side's interests, but also its constraints and the obstacles it must confront within the company (e.g., other business units, bosses, colleagues, skeptical groups). You should try to map in advance the other side's domestic obstacles, understand the other side's concerns, and develop agreements that can help the other party with its behind-the-table challenges.

Draft arrangements that the other parties can present as a victory within their organization.[23]

After you close the deal, remember that the goal of all negotiations is to obtain commitment, not only agreement.[24]

There are four levels of commitment, with an increasing level of reassurance, but also a decreasing level of trust between the parties:

- The social ritual of a handshake (*highest trust, lowest reassurance*).
- A written agreement based on a few principles (*high trust, low reassurance*).
- A legally enforceable agreement or contract (*low trust, high reassurance*). Bear in mind that in some cultures, a handshake is more respected than a contract and that a contract with too many clauses can hinder the relationship between the parties. Also, contracts require perfect foresight to predict all of the possible occurrences and conditions that may affect the relationship in the future, and this is even more difficult in an ever changing international context. A further obstacle concerns international contracts: There is no assurance that a court will interpret the contract as it was intended due to different business practices, political systems, and laws.[25]
- An escrow account. An escrow account ensures a simultaneous exchange (usually of documents and money that were put into the custody of a third party) subject to the fulfillment of contractually agreed conditions by the parties (*lowest trust, highest reassurance*).

In international negotiations, the aim is to structure the agreement to balance the need to minimize future uncertainties and the need to build a relationship based on trust (more on this in chapter 13).

PHASE 7: NEGOTIATION POST-MORTEM ANALYSIS

The negotiation post-mortem is the last stage of the process phase. It is the evaluation of the negotiation and documentation of the lessons learned: what worked and what you would have done differently.

The post-mortem analysis requires you to run through the following checklist:

- Did you gather all the information required for each of the 11 elements of the preparation stage?

- Did you identify alternatives to a no agreement?
- Did you achieve the planned goals? Were your goals sufficiently ambitious?
- Did you correctly identify the ZOPA?
- Did you exploit the beginning of the negotiation process to gather further information and test your assumptions?
- Who made the first offer? Did it act as an anchor?
- Were the concessions made on an alternating basis?
- Was information transparently exchanged or did the negotiation not move from the competitive phase?
- Did either party obtain more favorable terms? If so, how?
- If no settlement was achieved, what might you have done differently during each of the different stages of the 4Ps framework?

The negotiation post-mortem is essential because it can activate experiential learning, the process of making meaning from discovery and direct experience, through four stages:[26]

- *Concrete experience*: The negotiation process.
- *Observation of and reflection on the negotiation*: Write a short report on what happened during the negotiation process, highlighting what worked and what must be improved.
- *Formation of abstract concepts based on reflection*: Make sense of the different episodes that occurred during the negotiation process and find the connections between them. Develop your theoretical model of the negotiation process.
- *Testing the new concepts*: Reflect on how you will implement the lesson learned for the next negotiation.

THE POWER PERCEPTION STAGE

Most negotiators think of negotiating power as defined by wealth, financial and human resources, social and political connections, status, and role. In reality, in any negotiation, power lies in the party that needs the agreement less.

Power is dynamic and it changes as the negotiation proceeds. A strong correlation exists between time and power. Offers, concessions, and alternatives change their significance over time.[27] If you ask for concessions when your power is high, you improve your chances of a favorable outcome.

POWER IMBALANCES

In international negotiations, it is vital to address power imbalances, such as dependence and the perception of fairness in the process. Experimental studies have shown that integrative agreements were achieved far more often when the perceived difference in relative power between the parties was small.[28]

When the asymmetry in dependence between the pairs is high (power asymmetry), there is less motivation on the stronger side to recognize the other side's interests, concerns, and constraints and less incentive on the weaker side to disclose information.

In addition, a perception of unfairness in the process often leads to less than optimal negotiation outcomes.

To resolve conflicting issues, you should agree with the other party on a standard, norm, principle, or objective criteria to regulate the matter in question. This will make your proposal more persuasive and convey a perception of fairness to the other side.[29]

Anticipate the other side's preferred standards and frame your proposal according to those standards.

Establish your credibility, which is the aggregate of your knowledge, your track record, and your reliability as a person. If the other player perceives you as a credible interlocutor, he or she will also perceive your proposal as more persuasive and fair or, in other words, trustworthy. Bear in mind that it takes ages to establish your credibility, but just one second to lose it. Credibility is extremely fragile (more on that in chapter 16).

Depending on the issue, you may propose a solution based on:[30]

- Market value.
- Precedent.
- Expert judgment.
- Professional standards.
- Efficiency.
- Costs.
- What a court would decide.
- Moral standards.
- Equal treatment.
- Tradition.
- Reciprocity.

Precedents are powerful standards because people have a deep need to act in consonance with their past actions and, accordingly, with widely shared values and beliefs.

It is also true that in international negotiations, contrary to general assumptions, the perceived weaker side often does better than the stronger side at the end of the negotiation.

Like the rich who take their wealth for granted, the stronger side in a negotiation often does not think much about power since power is something it already has whereas the weaker side is preoccupied with power.[31] This leads the weaker party to use other tactics and strategies in the negotiations to win, such as building coalitions, negotiating off the table, looking for alternatives, understanding the interests and roles of all the players, and preparing to wait and bargain longer, showing that it doesn't need an agreement, at least at the current stage.

MANAGING POWER PERCEPTION

To improve your power in international negotiations, employ the following strategies:

- Optimize your MANTAs. The better your MATNAs, the greater your power in international negotiations.

- Think about which side needs the deal more to achieve his or her goals or, even better, which side in any given moment has the most to lose from a failure to agree. That is the player who has less power in the negotiation.[32]
- Understand that power is dynamic and can change during the negotiation process, above all in an international context.
- Know that power is having something the other side needs.
- If you are in the position to do so, explicitly convey the message that you can worsen the other player's position. However, use threats with great caution to preserve the relationship and avoid conflict and acrimony.
- Frame your proposal according to the other party's preferred and affirmed principles or standards. Leverage the consistency principle (the human need to appear coherent in beliefs, values, and past actions and decisions).
- To achieve optimal negotiation outcomes, manage the perceived imbalance in power and process fairness during the negotiation.
- Be prepared. Preparation is power in negotiation.
- Understand that power is based on the other party's perception of the situation, not on facts.[33]
- Negotiations are often determined off the table. Map the other side's decision-making process and identify the key players. Build coalitions and develop relationships. Change the negotiation structure by introducing different players with complementary interests.

WHAT IF YOU DON'T HAVE POWER?

Summing up, to understand power in negotiation, think about which side at any moment has the most to lose from a failure to agree[34] and structure a negotiation process that is perceived as fair.

Because power lies on the side of the party that controls the status quo and that is not interested in changing the current situation, if you want to change the status quo, tangibly convey to the other party what it has to lose from a no deal.

But what if you don't have relevant MATNAs? Then, preparation becomes a key factor to overcome your weakness:

- Understand who the key players in the decision-making process of the other party are and recognize their interests, concerns, and constraints.
- Identify what you have that key players on the other side value.
- Negotiate off the table: Build coalitions and relationships. In ambiguous situations, people do what other people do. Influence the key players.
- Look for alternatives, shifting the balance of needs: new suppliers, new markets, and new customers.
- Make tangible to the other party that it has something to lose from a no deal.
- Don't show your eagerness to close the deal. Be ready to wait for the power imbalance to shift. Be patient.

What if the other party doesn't feel the need to negotiate?

- Find alternatives to make the status quo less attractive.
- Make the costs of not negotiating tangible and explicit.
- If you can, weaken the other party's BATNA.

- Don't wait for the other party to understand the value of negotiating with you. Make the benefits explicit.
- If the other party is risk averse, take one step at a time: Show the other party the benefits of moving just one step away from the status quo. When the other party sees the value, ask that party to make another move.
- Build a coalition to establish your credibility and support your proposal.
- Be patient. Remember that power is dynamic and shifts with time. In the meantime, look for alternatives and support.

In summary, during negotiations, your goal is to have the other party perceive that he or she has more to lose and/or you have less to lose from a no agreement.

THE PLAYERS' PERSPECTIVE

OFF-THE-TABLE PLAYERS

As we saw during the preparation stage, in every negotiation there are at least three levels of participants.

First-level players are the actual negotiators.

Second-level players are those who directly influence the negotiators: bosses, shareholders, clients, colleagues, suppliers, external consultants and even spouses. Understanding the underlying relationships between first-level and second-level players helps to identify negotiators' authority, concerns, limits, interests, constraints, norms, values, thinking patterns, and behaviors.

Third-level actors are those who can influence the negotiation indirectly.

In negotiating with organizations, it becomes vital to map their decision-making process, identify the key players involved, and understand their relationships.

Answering the following questions can help you better understand the other side's decision-making process: How are decisions made in the other organization? Are decisions made through consensus or majority? Who is the final decision maker? Who can influence decisions? How many players have a voice in decisions? Whose opinion will the final decision maker consider?

International negotiations usually involve multiple parties acting in specific contexts with divergent objectives, priorities, cultures, and personalities. Therefore, negotiators must build coalitions to progress their interests, bringing people with different interests on board.

Understanding the varying interests, concerns, and constraints of the different players involved (also the behind-the-scenes players) is a vital skill for any global negotiator.

THE DECISION-MAKING UNIT

The decision-making unit (DMU) consists of all the players that take part in the organizational decision-making process during a negotiation. Any DMU can be defined by six distinct roles (Fig. 2):[35]

Figure 2. The decision-making unit.

- *Users*: players who put the purchased good or service into use and work with it.
- *Influencers*: players who can influence the choice of the decision makers. They may be experts or consultants with in-depth knowledge and experience of the good or service or informal influencers such as friends, family, and colleagues.
- *Buyers*: players usually responsible for the actual negotiation and contract terms.
- *Initiators*: players who recognize a need to be satisfied or a problem to be solved.
- *Deciders*: player(s) ultimately responsible for the final choice.
- *Gatekeepers*: players who control the information to influencers and decision makers. They are responsible for the flow of information and knowledge within the DMU.

Within the DMU, the same players can play different roles. Individuals may be influencers and initiators or gatekeepers and users. The different roles are systemic and dynamic, and they change according to the organization. Conflicting interests among the different players must be taken into account during the off-the-table negotiation phase.

Mapping the decision-making unit and the relationships among the different players is a key element in the preparation phase. Establishing a trust-based relationship with initiators so as to be involved early in the decision-making process is a strategic factor, as is the ability to persuade gatekeepers and influencers and to minimize the perceived risk for users and buyers.

Another key element is understanding the decision-making process: What is the flow of information? Who are the key players? What is their voice in the final decision? Are they standing up for you or are they silent supporters? Do they have veto power? Are they going to exercise their veto power?

We can map the different players involved in the DMU along three axes (see Fig. 3):

- *Level of support*: Are they well-disposed or averse to your proposal?
- *Level of assertiveness*: Will they yell their support or opposition? Will they influence the process behind the scenes? Will they be proactive in supporting or opposing your proposal?
- *Level of influence in the decision-making process*: What is their position in the organization? What is their credibility within the DMU? Is their voice heard? Can they persuade people to change their minds? Are they recognized as leaders by the group?

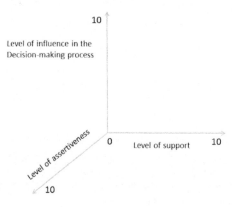

Figure 3. Players' positioning within the DMU.

RELATIONSHIPS

People are complex, multifaceted, impulsive, and erratic.

In international negotiations, maintaining relationships is often as important as achieving your goals. The ability to understand the other side's perspective, mental schemas, culture, cognitive processes, and constraints is therefore critical to reach integrative solutions perceived as favorable by both parties (see Fig. 4).

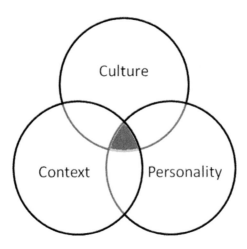

Figure 4 - Elements of relationships.

A basic fact about negotiation is that you are dealing with human beings.[36] They have emotions, different values, distinctive experiences, and individual points of view. They can also fail to correctly interpret what you intend to communicate. In short, they are irrational. Be equipped to deal with the other side's irrationality: Understand her interests and constraints. Educate the other side if necessary.

Every individual is the product of a combination of three elements:

- *Culture*, the invisible lens which filters how the person sees the world; the collective programming of the mind which distinguishes the members of one group from members of another.[37] Culture does not involve only national culture, but also other cultural influences such as gender, education, age, profession, social class, and technology.
- *The social context*: the immediate environment in which the person grew up (family, friends) and employs his or her skills (organization).
- *Personality*: a person's combined behavioral, emotional, and mental response patterns.

Culture, context, and personality affect people's behavior and cognitive processes.

We have dedicated multiple chapters of this book to understanding the influence of culture, personality, and cognition on people's mental schemas and behavior at the negotiation table.

The aim is a *role reversal*: putting yourself in the other side's shoes to understand the values, norms, prejudices, biases, social scripts, attitudes, and predispositions that regulate the other party's communication patterns, cognitive processes, and behavior so as to identify the other side's interests, constraints, and concerns.

Role reversal, the skill of seeing the situation as the other party perceives it, becomes even more important in an international context in which the factors involved in the negotiation process are even more elusive and difficult to pin down.

In international negotiation, it is important to pay attention also to social logical measures.

Negotiators judge the negotiation process according to four factors:[38]

- Feelings about the objective outcome of the negotiation.
- Feelings about the self (e.g., saving face and living according to one's own values and standards).
- Feelings about the fairness of the negotiation process.
- Feelings about the relationship with the other party.

Your goal at the negotiation table is not to understand the *what*, but rather the *why*. Shifting the perspective from what the other party does and says to what the other party thinks is fundamental. You constantly need to probe behind the stated position to identify the other party's real interests:

- Why is the other side making this specific demand?
- Why is the other side behaving in such a way?
- Why is the other side taking the stated position?

Never accept the other party's replies literally. Take up the habit of filtering and calibrating the information that is provided to you. Understand how to communicate with the other side (more on this in chapter 5).

If you understand why certain behaviors occur, you control the key to unlocking the potential of an integrative agreement.

CONCLUSION

Research has continually highlighted 11 common behaviors adopted by skilled international negotiators:

- They prepare. Preparation is key to increase your perceived power.
- They negotiate away from the table. They understand that international negotiations are often determined off the table during informal meetings among key players.
- They look for alternatives. They understand that power lies in the hands of the side that needs an agreement less (that has the most valuable MATNAs).
- They set higher goals. They have high expectations.
- They don't fall prey to the fixed-pie bias. They don't focus only on price.
- They listen more than they talk. And when they talk, they ask questions.
- They don't pay attention solely to positions (the whats). They look for interests (the whys).
- They see the situation as the other party sees it. They put themselves in the other side's shoes.
- They are curious. They welcome ambiguous situations to create integrative solutions.
- They are patient. They don't show their zeal to close the deal. They understand that impatience reduces their perceived power.
- They are reliable. They keep their promises.

(Endnotes)

1   Moty Cristal: The Negosystem™ Model.

2   Watkins, M. (1999). Negotiating in a Complex World. Negotiation Journal, Vol. 15, N. 3, 245-270.

3   Musashi, M. (1993). The book of five rings. Translated by T. Cleary. Boston: Shambhala Publications.

4   Camp, J. (2007). Start With No: The Negotiating Tools That the Pros Don't Want You to Know. New York: Crown Business.

5   Susskind, L., Mnookin, R., Rozdeiczer, L., & Fuller, F. (2005). What We Have Learned About Teaching Multiparty Negotiation. Negotiation Journal, Vol. 21, N. 3, 395-408.

6   Shell, G. R. (2006). Bargaining for Advantage: Negotiation Strategies for Reasonable People (2nd ed.). London: Penguin Books.

7   Diamond, S. (2010). Getting More: how to negotiate to achieve your goals in the Real World. New York: Crown Business.

8   Musashi, M. (1993). The book of five rings. Translated by T. Cleary. Boston: Shambhala Publications.

9   Wheeler, M. A. (2001). Negotiation Analysis: An Introduction. Business Fundamentals As Taught at the Harvard Business School. Harvard Business Publishing, 3-16.

10   Malhotra, D., & Bazerman, M. (2008). Negotiation genius. New York: Bantam.

11   Malhotra, D., & Bazerman, M. (2008). Negotiation genius. New York: Bantam.

12   Lax, D. A., & Sebenius, J. K. (2003). 3-D Negotiation: playing the whole game. Harvard Business Review, Vol. 81, N. 11, 65-74.

13   Kolb, D. M., & Williams, J. (2001). Breakthrough Bargaining. Harvard Business Review, Vol. 79, N. 2, 88-97.

14   Galinsky, A. D., & Mussweiler, T. (2001). First Offers as Anchors: The Role of Perspective-Taking and Negotiation Focus. Journal of Personality and Social Psychology, Vol. 81. N. 4, 657-669.

15   Shell, G. R. (2006). Bargaining for Advantage: Negotiation Strategies for Reasonable People (2nd ed.). London: Penguin Books.

16   Shell, G. R. (2006). Bargaining for Advantage: Negotiation Strategies for Reasonable People (2nd ed.). London: Penguin Books

17   Camp, J. (2007). Start With No: The Negotiating Tools That the Pros Don't Want You to Know. New York: Crown Business.

18   Shell, G. R. (2006). Bargaining for Advantage: Negotiation Strategies for Reasonable People (2nd ed.). London: Penguin Books

19   Dupont, C., & Faure, G. O. (2002). The Negotiation Process. In V. A. Kremenyuk (Ed.), International Negotiation: analysis, approaches, issues (2nd ed.). San Francisco: Jossey-Bass.

20   Vi-Ming Kok, A., & Pope, A. (2014). Legal Negotiation Skills Guide. Retrieved from http://www.routledge.com/cw/slapper-9780415639989/s2/negotiation/

21   Musashi, M. (1993). The book of five rings. Translated by T. Cleary. Boston: Shambhala Publications.

22   Sebenius, J. K. (2013). Level Two Negotiations: Helping the Other Side Meet Its "Behind the Table" Challenges. Negotiation Journal, Vol. 29, N. 1, 7-21.

23   Fisher, R., Ury, W. L., & Patton, B. (1991). Getting to yes: Negotiating Agreement Without Giving In (2nd ed.). London: Penguin Books.

24   Shell, G. R. (2006). Bargaining for Advantage: Negotiation Strategies for Reasonable People (2nd ed.). London: Penguin Books

25   Salacuse, J. W. (2003). The Global Negotiator: Making, Managing, and Mending Deals Around the World in the Twenty-First Century. New York: Palgrave Macmillan.

26   Kolb, D. A. (1984). Experiential Learning: experience as the source of learning and development. Englewood Cliffs, NJ: Prentice Hall.

27 Zartman, W. I. (2002). The Structure of Negotiation. In V. A. Kremenyuk (Ed.), International Negotiation: analysis, approaches, issues (2nd ed.). San Francisco: Jossey-Bass.

28 Wolfe, R., & McGinn, K. (2005). Perceived Relative Power and its Influence on Negotiations. Group Decision and Negotiation, 14, 3-20.

29 Salacuse, J. W. (2003). The Global Negotiator: Making, Managing, and Mending Deals Around the World in the Twenty-First Century. New York: Palgrave Macmillan.

30 Fisher, R., Ury, W. L., & Patton, B. (1991). Getting to yes: Negotiating Agreement Without Giving In (2nd ed.). London: Penguin Books.

31 Zartman, I. W., & Rubin, J. Z. (2000). Power and Negotiation. Ann Arbor, MI: The University of Michigan Press.

32 Shell, G. R. (2006). Bargaining for Advantage: Negotiation Strategies for Reasonable People (2nd ed.). London: Penguin Books.

33 Shell, G. R. (2006). Bargaining for Advantage: Negotiation Strategies for Reasonable People (2nd ed.). London: Penguin Books.

34 Shell, G. R. (2006). Bargaining for Advantage: Negotiation Strategies for Reasonable People (2nd ed.). London: Penguin Books.

35 Kotler, P., & Keller, K. L. (2011). Marketing Management (14th ed.). Upper Saddle River, NJ: Prentice Hall.

36 Fisher, R., Ury, W. L., & Patton, B. (1991). Getting to yes: Negotiating Agreement Without Giving In (2nd ed.). London: Penguin Books.

37 Hofstede, G. (2001). Culture's consequences: Comparing values, behaviors, institutions and organizations across nations (2nd ed). Thousand Oaks, CA: Sage.

38 Curhan, J. R., Elfenbein, H. A., & Xu, H. (2006). What Do People Value When They Negotiate? Mapping the Domain of Subjective Value in Negotiation. Journal of Personality and Social Psychology, Vol. 91, No. 3, 493-512.

CHAPTER 8:

Decision Making

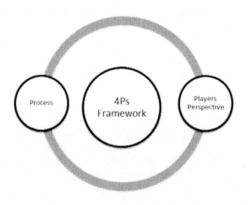

Stage 2: Process. Stage 4: Players' Perspective

... We never deal with reality per se, but rather with images of reality, that is, with interpretations. While the number of potentially possible interpretations is very large, our world image usually permits us to see only one, and this one therefore appears to be the only possible, reasonable, and permitted view. Furthermore, this one interpretation also suggests only one possible, reasonable, and permitted solution, and if we don't succeed at first we try and try again, or, in other words, we resort to the recipe of doing more of the same.[1]

INTRODUCTION

Decision making is a choice among gambles.[2]

Decision making is the cognitive process of selecting an optimal course of action among multiple alternatives.

According to rational choice (expected utility) theory, individuals consider values and probabilities of likely outcomes before making their final choice. The expected utility model supposes that people can forecast the payoff of each available option. However, in real-life situations, the rational choice framework is not a reliable predictive model for the outcome of the decision-making process.

When choosing between alternative courses of action, people rarely know with certainty what outcomes those actions will generate and multiple factors can influence the decision-making process and cause people to make irrational decisions.

Analyzing how individuals make decisions can provide fundamental insight into how to negotiate and influence across situations for at least two important reasons:

- Understanding how people think and make decisions allows us to improve our influencing skills.
- Understanding our biases and constraints allows us to improve our own decision-making ability.

Our journey through the decision-making process starts with game theory, continues with basic elements of how our brain functions, and how personality influences decision making. The voyage carries on in chapter 9 with the study of common cognitive biases, continues with strategies for improving our decision-making process and ends in chapter 10 with the analysis of decision making across cultures.

GAME THEORY

Game theory is the study of interdependent decision making. Game theory employs formal mathematical models to define, determine, and predict the behavior and actions of rational players whose decisions depend on the decisions made by another actor.[3]

Classic game theory entails players making rational choices to maximize their own gain, taking into consideration the strategic decisions made by the other party.

Game theory has application in all fields that involve decision making in complex social environments, including negotiation and influence.

Both negotiation and game situations consist of group decision making. Games involve interactive decision making. The payoffs for each individual are determined not only by the individual's own decision but also by the decisions of the other individuals.

Negotiations, on the other hand, involve joint decision making: Multiple players cooperate to attain a joint decision and consequently produce joint payoffs for each individual.[4]

There are three categories of games: games of skill, games of chance, and games of strategy.[5]

Games of skill are one-player games where the single player has complete control over all the outcomes and strategic choices lead to certain results. Solving a crossword puzzle is a game of skill. Since games of skill don't involve any other player, there is no interdependency. Consequently, games of skill are not part of game theory.

Games of chance are one-player games against nature, where the player does not completely control the outcomes and strategic choices do not lead to certain results. The outcomes of a game of chance depend partly on the player's choices and partly on nature, which is a second player. Games of chance are further categorized as involving either risk, where the probability of nature's response is known, or uncertainty, where the probability of nature's response is not known.

Games of strategy are games involving two or more players, not including nature, each of whom has partial control over the outcomes. Game of strategy can be further divided into three classes: games in which players' interests are completely coincidental, completely conflicting, or partially coincidental and partially conflicting.

Game theory's focus is mainly on games of strategy where players' interests are partially coincidental and partially conflicting because these games most realistically represent situations involving decision making in the context of social interactions.

Both negotiation and game situations involve group decision making. Games consist of multiple individuals making separate decisions that interact. The payoffs for each individual are determined not only by the individual's own decision but also by the decisions of the other individuals, and vice versa. Negotiations, on the other side, consist of multiple individuals cooperating to arrive at a mutual decision. The joint decision involves joint outcomes for each individual.[6]

NASH EQUILIBRIUM

Game theory is involved with games of strategy, in which the best strategy for each player depends on what he or she expects the other players to do.

As a first example of game theory, let's consider the well-known *prisoner's dilemma*: Two persons suspected of being fellows in a crime are arrested and placed in separate prison cells so that they cannot communicate with each other. Without a confession from at least one suspect, the prosecutor does not have sufficient evidence to convict. So he tells both suspects the potential consequences of their actions (see Table 1):

- If one confesses and the other does not, the one who confesses goes free but the other gets 10 years in prison.
- If both confess, each gets five years.
- If both remain silent, each gets one year on a reduced charge.

	A	
	Do not confess (Cooperate)	Confess (Defect)
B — Do not confess (Cooperate)	1 year / 1 year	10 years / 0 years
B — Confess (Defect)	0 years / 10 years	5 years / 5 years

Table 1. Prisoner's dilemma payoff matrix.

Table 1 represents the payoff matrix, a normal-form representation of the prisoner's dilemma in which players move simultaneously, or at least don't know the other player's decision before making their own.

In this specific game, if player A cooperates and player B cooperates, each gets one year in prison. If player A cooperates and player B defects, player A gets 10 years in prison, while player B goes free. If player A defects and player B defects, each gets five years in prison. If player A defects and player B cooperates, player A goes free, while player B gets 10 years in prison.

In summary, if player A thinks player B will cooperate, then she should defect to maximize the payoff (going free against one year in prison).

If player A thinks player B will defect, than she should again defect to maximize the payoff (5 years in prison against 10 years).

The same logic holds for player B.

The rational player will choose defection (to confess) in every situation because it is her best option, no matter what her opponent chooses.

Mutual defection (the block shaded in grey in Table 1) is therefore the unique Nash equilibrium of the prisoner's dilemma (the only stable solution of the game). This is true if the following conditions are met:

- Each player aims to maximize her own profit.
- The players know the Nash equilibrium strategy of all players.
- The players believe that a deviation in their own strategy will not cause deviations by any other players.
- There is a consensus that all players understand these conditions.

The more doubt each player has about the actions of the other side, the more likely she will choose the strategy corresponding to a Nash equilibrium, the less risky strategy.

However, such a result is sub-optimal because both players would be better off collaborating.

Trust may be built only in repetitive games through the occurrence of reliable and recurring patterns of behavior.

According to game theory, agreements are improbable because each party has an incentive to defect to maximize her own gains.

However, in real-world scenarios, a Nash equilibrium is not necessarily played because the aforementioned conditions of rational players with full and common knowledge of the Nash equilibrium are not always met. For example, in real-world negotiations, players often have imperfect or incomplete information about the other side's objectives.

In general, game theory does not reliably predict people's behavior in real-life situations.

MULTIPLE EQUILIBRIA GAMES

As a second example, let's consider the following:

Two radio stations (WIRD and KOOL) must choose formats for their programs. There are three possible formats: Country-Western (CW), Pop Music (IPM), and All News (AN). The audiences for the three formats are 50%, 30%, and 20%, respectively. If the stations choose the same format, they will split the audience for that format equally, while if they choose different formats, each will get the total audience for that format.[7] The payoffs (audience shares) are shown in Table 2.

		KOOL		
		Country Western	Pop Music	All News
WIRD	Country Western	25, 25	50, 30	50, 20
	Pop Music	30, 50	15, 15	30, 20
	All News	20, 50	20, 30	10, 10

Table 2. The radio stations' payoff matrix.

In this example, there are two Nash equilibria in which one of the two stations decides to choose CW and gets a 50% market share and the other chooses IPM and gets 30% (the blocks shaded in grey in Table 2). It is not important which station selects which format. The total payoff is the same in both cases: 80. And there is no larger total payoff than 80.

Having multiple equilibria produces a risk that both stations will choose the more profitable CW format, splitting the market's 50% share (25% each). There is an even more serious risk that each station, assuming the other station will choose CW, decides to choose IPM, thus splitting a smaller market and ending up with a market share of just 15% each.

Multiple Nash equilibria can provide possible solutions for coordination games such as in the radio stations example.

Game theory seems very compelling when we examine situations that have only one equilibrium.

But what happens when we analyze games with multiple equilibria, as with the example we saw before?

Acknowledging multiple equilibria in games reduces one of game theory's main benefits: its methodological determinism.[8]

However, according to Nobel Prize-winning economist Thomas Schelling (1960), multiple equilibria games are effective representations of real-life social situations.

When a game has two or more Nash equilibria, the players may find it difficult to settle on one. Among the different equilibria, people will tend to perceive as meaningful and likely only one specific solution: a *focal point.* Any piece of information, signal, or hint (e.g., standards, precedents, practices) that focuses the players' attention on one equilibrium may lead them to expect it, and so rationally to play it.

In the radio stations example, sources of information that could solve the coordination game are the stations' roots and history, their notable personalities, the mix of musical programs in the previous years, the preferences of the two program directors, and the predilection of advertisers, sponsors and audiences.

The concepts of multiple equilibria and focal point allow for social, cultural, and situational influences on rational behavior.[9] However, not all games with multiple equilibria have Schelling focal points.

CREDIBLE COMMITMENT

A second fundamental concept Schelling (1960) introduced is credible commitment.

Firm commitments (threats and promises) have the potential to alter the other player's expectations and consequently her choices.

Credible commitments can influence the central social problem of choosing among multiple equilibria, making some Nash equilibria more plausible than others and, therefore, creating a focal point for the other player.

A commitment to effectively influence the other player's behavior has to be credible: *The other side must believe that you'll do what you say you will do.*

A credible commitment is an irreversible course of action that intentionally excludes some options with the purpose of influencing the other player's choices.

Perhaps one of the most renowned metaphors of commitment in literature comes from the game of chicken.[10]

The game of chicken involves two drivers, both heading toward a single-lane bridge from opposite directions. The first to deviate relinquishes the bridge to the other. If neither player deviates, the outcome is a crash.

The payoff matrix for the game of chicken is presented in Table 3.

		A	
		Swerve	Straight
B	Swerve	Tie, Tie	Lose, Win
	Straight	Win, Lose	Crash, Crash

Table 3 - Payoff matrix for the game of chicken.

The best alternative for each driver is to stay straight while the other swerves. Additionally, because a crash is the worst result for both players, the rational strategy would be to deviate before a crash occurs. As a consequence, the game has multiple Nash equilibria (the blocks shaded in grey in Table 3). In each Nash equilibria, one player chooses a cooperative strategy (Swerve) while the other player chooses a non-cooperative strategy (Straight).

Using the game of chicken as an example, we will present possible strategies to ensure the irrevocability and therefore the credibility of threats and promises:[11]

- *Build reputation*: Maintaining a reputation over time for consistency, reliability, steadiness, and following through on threats and promises is valuable for confirming credibility with regard to threats and promises. For example, in the game of chicken, a reputation for never yielding would be effective.
- *Block communication*: Suspending communication is an effective stratagem to ensure commitment credibility. In the game of chicken, for example, you would ensure that your opponent sees you putting a brown paper bag over your head; because you can't see what the other driver is doing, you confirm your commitment to your course of action.
- *Burn bridges*: Examples include a general making an evident and irreversible commitment to fight rather than retreat by burning bridges behind his troops and a politician making public promises. Both the general and the politician, by committing to an irreversible course of action, exclude future options with the purpose of influencing their opponents. In the game of chicken, for example, such a commitment would be throwing away your steering wheel.

- *Brinkmanship*: This involves pushing events to the edge of disaster with the purpose of achieving the most advantageous result. A player can introduce an element of intense risk by, for example, displaying irrational and erratic behavior. The following story explains the concept of brinkmanship:

  So you're standing at the edge of a cliff, chained by the ankle to someone else. You'll be released, and one of you will get a large prize, as soon as the other gives in. How do you persuade the other guy to give in, when the only method at your disposal – threatening to push him off the cliff – would doom you both?

  Answer: You start dancing, closer and closer to the edge. That way, you don't have to convince him that you would do something totally irrational: Plunge him and yourself off the cliff. You just have to convince him that you are prepared to take a higher risk than he is of accidentally falling off the cliff. If you can do that, you win.[12]

Schelling (1960) taught us not only the strategic importance of credible commitments in negotiation and influence, and how to increase the credibility of our commitments, but also that in negotiations it is always wise to filter and calibrate the information provided to us, and to test the credibility of the other side's threats and promises.

THE ULTIMATUM GAME

The ultimatum game is a game where one player is given a certain amount of money (let's assume $50) and asked to split it between himself and an unknown other player. The first player proposes how to divide the sum between the two players, and the second player can either accept or reject this offer. If the second player rejects the offer, neither player receives any money. If the second player accepts the offer, the money is divided according to the offer. The game is played only once and therefore reciprocation is not a concern.

The question is: How much should the first player offer? If both the players are rational, then the first player should offer one penny, and the second player should accept the proposal, given that one penny is better than nothing. The homo economicus should only maximize his utility, without taking into consideration concepts such as fairness and justice.[13]

Several experimental studies have highlighted the gap between theory and real-world scenarios. In experiments, the average mean offer is in the range of 37%-50% of the total amount. About 50% of responders reject offers below 30% of the total amount.[14][15]

Do experimental results differ across cultures? The answer is: Mostly no.

According to several international experimental studies, ranging from the US to Japan and Indonesia, offers in the range of 44%-50% are the norm across most cultures. There are a few exceptions; for example, among the Machiguenga, a population from the Peruvian Amazon, proposers offered only 26%.[16]

It is also theorized that unfair allocations are rejected only because the absolute amount of the offer is low. Experimental results offer contradictory evidence regarding this last issue.

The aforementioned experimental results can been explained by a preference for fairness and integrity on the proposers' side, aversion toward injustice and inequity on the responders' side, and, more pragmatically, the proposers' desire to get at least half the stake ($25 in our case).

However, the explanation that proposers want to make sure they get at least half of the pie is partially contradicted by experimental studies using the *dictator game*, a version of the ultimatum game in which the responder plays a passive role: He simply accepts any balance of the stake left by the proposer. The results indicate that more than 60% of proposers hand out a positive amount of money, with an average allocation of roughly 20% of the pie.[17] As a result, the allocation in the dictator game is not more than 40% as in the ultimatum game, but it is still substantially higher than zero.

We can also provide a neurologic justification for the irrational behavior of proposers. In a 2007 experiment,[18] participants were infused with oxytocin (an hormone produced by the hypothalamus) or a placebo and engaged in a blinded ultimatum game. Several studies have shown that oxytocin enables a temporary connection between strangers, increasing empathy, trust, and reciprocity. The results of the experiment were staggering: Proposers on oxytocin were 80% more generous than those given a placebo.

The result indicates that oxytocin affects trust and, to an even greater degree, influences generosity.

SOCIAL DILEMMAS

A social dilemma is a situation in which a conflict exists between individual and collective interests. It is a situation in which individuals produce superior short-term outcomes by making selfish choices versus cooperative choices, regardless of the choices made by other players; everyone involved produces inferior long-term outcomes if everyone makes selfish choices versus cooperative choices.[19]

The proposed definition encompasses the time factor: Outcomes for the individual are often immediate or short term, while outcomes for the collective often develop over longer periods of time.

In summary, *a social dilemma occurs when individual rationality leads to collective irrationality.*[20]

Overgrazing of common property, overpopulation, environmental pollution, exhaustion of natural resources, and intergroup conflict are all examples of real-world social dilemmas.

We can think of social dilemmas as multi-player extensions of the prisoner's dilemma. In this case, they represent specific team decision-making situations in which individuals and collectivist interests are at odds.[21]

But how do people make decisions in social dilemmas? For years, the prevailing theoretical model applied to decision making in social dilemmas has been the expected utility (or rational choice) framework. Players predict the likely payoff associated with each alternative and then choose to maximize their outcome.

Recently, a different framework has been recommended; this framework encompasses the collective aspect of social dilemmas, as well as the influence of heuristics in the decision-making process.[22]

The appropriateness framework proposes that people making decisions ask themselves: What does a person like me do in a situation like this? This question categorizes three noteworthy elements: recognition and classification of the kind of situation faced, identity of the individual making the decision, and relevance of rules or heuristics in directing the decision-making process. What does a person like me (*identity*) do (*rules and heuristics*) in a situation like this (*recognition*)?

In defining the context of the game, decision makers are therefore influenced by personal experiences, personal and cultural values, their perceived social identity, the roles and rules of the game, and the specific situation.[23]

In a series of experiments designed to understand the role of culture within the appropriateness framework, Chinese and Japanese decision makers in an asymmetric social dilemma typically distributed financial resources more equally than U.S. and Australian decision makers.[24]

NEUROSCIENCE

Neuroscience is the interdisciplinary science that studies the brain and the nervous system and their relationship to behavior and learning (see Figure 1).

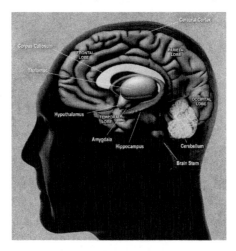

Figure 1. The human brain.[25]

Even though the brain corresponds to only 2% of our body weight, it receives 15% of our cardiac output, it consumes 20% of our total body oxygen, and it uses 25% of our total body glucose.

The primary element of the brain is the *neuron*. A typical neuron is constituted by a *soma* (the cell body), *dendrites* (long, diverging filaments attached to the cell), and a single *axon* (a cellular filament, which may be thousands of times the length of the soma).

Communication among neurons occurs through electrochemical signals. The signal travels along the axon and is transmitted through a connection known as a *synapse* to a nearby neuron, which receives it through its dendrites.

The brain's function is not simply a product of its complexity but of its connectivity[26] and the synapses represent the means by which signals are transferred from one neuron to another. Each of the 100 billion brain neurons has on average 7,000 synaptic connections to other neurons[27] (see Figure 2).

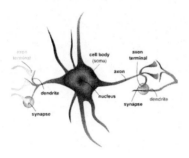

Figure 2. Neuron structure and synapses.[28]

Our brain is constantly evolving and is shaped not only by our culture and experiences, but also by chance: To a certain extent, the connected structure of our brain and the signals flowing among the neurons through the synapses are random.

Everything we think of as intelligence – language, creativity, music, mathematics, problem solving, and planning – occurs in the cortex, a 2 mm thick multilayered sheet of neural tissue that surrounds most of the our primordial brain.[29] A typical human cortex contains around 20 billion neurons and 240 trillion synapses.[30]

The human brain doesn't discriminate among vision, hearing, and motor control. The cortex associates, organizes, and processes, according to a common algorithm, different patterns regardless of their source. The same cortical areas can perform different functions according to the different signals involved (vision, hearing, and motor control).

The processes of perception, cognition, and action are not serial and distinct, but dynamic, overlapping, and continuous. The tentative results from the processing of perceptual signals continuously update the cognitive system, whose results constantly update the motor system[31] (see Figure 3).

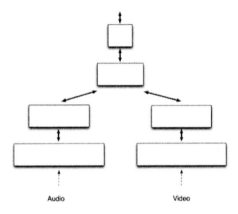

Audio   Video

Figure 3. Different patterns, same algorithm.[32]

As of this writing, we still know too little about the brain and how it is organized to fully understand how it works. However, there is something we do know: Our cortex can be thought of as a memory system.

To find solutions to problems, we don't compute as machines do; rather, we retrieve the answer from our memories. We use stored memories to solve problems and produce behavior. Looking for solutions, we cannot recall all the details of a memory simultaneously. Instead, we go through a sequential process of interrelated steps: Our memory system works through associative and sequential stages.

Because we don't always encounter the same situation, how can we handle variations in problems? Think of the task of receiving and kicking a ball in soccer and how each pass and each kick differs from the previous one. To handle these variations, the brain creates invariant representations that unconsciously identify patterns, even if they are modified. Our brain can identify modified patterns because memories are stored in a form that depicts the core of the relationship among events (invariant representations) and not the details of each event.

How our brain forms invariant representations is still unknown.

Recent developments in neuroscience have hypothesized that the key mission of our brain is to make predictions.[33] Our brains use stored memories to unconsciously and continuously anticipate what is going to happen. What is actually happening is constantly compared with what is expected and our attention is caught when an inconsistency appears between our prediction and our actual experience. Our brain is constantly comparing our model of the world against reality.

Our predictions are not always correct because we make probabilistic forecasts about what is going to happen based on our stored memories, combining previous experiences with what is actually happening. Each individual makes different predictions regarding similar events because our memories and therefore our model of the world are based on our experiences, education, context, culture, and personality.

Our cortex's hierarchical structure stores a model of the world's hierarchical structure; higher regions of our cortex follow the big picture (e.g., the principles on which a contract has been drafted), while lower levels control the small details (e.g., the punctuation of the last sentence of the second paragraph of the contract).

During education, we first learn the basics, the essential models. This knowledge, over time, moves down the cortical hierarchy, leaving the opportunity for additional learning in the higher levels of the cortex.

Experts can be defined as people who see structures and patterns in specific subjects, beyond what others are able to see.

When an unpredicted event (an unexpected pattern) occurs, the information climbs up the cortical hierarchy until it finds a region that can predict the pattern. If an event is absolutely new, it will ascend the cortical hierarchy; because all the regions will recognize an inconsistency, and none of them will be able to anticipate a pattern, the original event will enter the hippocampus, at the peak of the cortical hierarchy, forming new memories that thereafter will be either moved to the cortex or lost (see Figure 4).

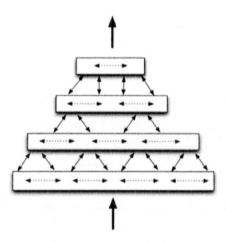

Figure 4. Cortex's hierchicarl structure.[34]

SOCIAL BRAIN

Brains are metabolically expensive. Because the average adult human brain weighs about 2% of body weight but consumes about 20% of total body oxygen, the question is: Why do humans need larger brains than other species?

Conventional theory has assumed that brains evolved to process factual information about the world and carry out complex ecological problem-solving tasks.

The social brain hypotheses suggested by Professor Dunbar (1995) claimed that the unusually large human brain evolved to manage complex social systems. As a result, human brains developed as social brains[35] and intelligence evolved to support typical within-large-group behaviors, such as altruism, empathy, rapport, deceptiveness, and sensitivity to context. These are traits that are, in general, more developed in women than men, and women exhibit greater attitude in structuring, categorizing, and combining information and data.

In other words, according to Dunbar, human brain size increased correspondingly with the proliferation of social interactions and the size and complexity of social groups.[36]

Recent research has confirmed that brain size and cognitive ability are correlated,[37] advancing the hypothesis that the large human brain is necessary not only to support social interactions, but also to perform cognitive tasks (learning, innovating, and problem solving).

In other words, social and ecological intelligence hypotheses should not necessarily be regarded as alternatives in explaining human brain evolution. A theory that embraces both hypotheses is better suited to answer our initial question: Why do humans need larger brains than other species?

MULTILINGUALISM

Studies have confirmed that knowing two or more languages improves reasoning, multitasking, problem solving, and the ability to reconcile different perspectives and ideas.

Scanning the brain of polyglots, before and after learning a new language, shows a measurable growth in the hippocampus, which helps the formation of new memories, and in areas of the cortex where systemic reasoning is processed.

NEUROECONOMICS

Neuroeconomics is a combination of experimental economics and neuroscience that intends to improve the predictions of game theory to better estimate how decisions are actually made in the real world by identifying the brain mechanisms and biological constraints involved in complex social decision-making processes.[38]

In short, neuroeconomics measures brain activity during decisions to predict behavior.

Researchers have investigated brain functioning in interdependent decision-making processes (games of strategy), reporting common topics that deserve further in-depth analysis.

SOCIAL REWARD

Neuroimaging studies have confirmed that a subcortical part of the forebrain, the striatum (see Figure 5), is involved in social decisions concerning reward and punishment.

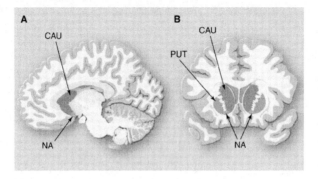

Figure 5. The striatum and its subcomponents; caudate nucleus (CAU), putamen (PUT), nucleus accumbens (NA).[39]

Reciprocated cooperation during strategic games is consistent with increased activation in the striatum, while unreciprocated cooperation is consistent with a decrease in activation in the striatum.

The striatum is activated not only by reciprocated cooperation, but also by the possibility of punishing non-reciprocators. The decision to punish a defector activates the striatum.

Another important element of the research is the indication of the existence of reinforcement-learning methods that improve choices over time by continually updating the outcomes according to the rewards and punishments encountered in the environment. In other words, the striatum records social prediction errors to inform future decisions about cooperation and reciprocity.[40]

In conclusion, recent research has confirmed the neural origin of social altruism: The striatum is highly activated by voluntary charitable donations.

The last research, coupled with the fact that oxytocin influences generosity, indicates a correlation between oxytocin and striatum.

EMOTIONS

Although classic models of decision making have ignored the influence of emotions in the choice among alternatives, in the previous chapter we introduced the major role that emotions play in the decision-making process, more specifically in negotiations (more on this in chapters 12 and 13).

Neuroscience presents the possibility of identifying the causal relationship between an emotional response and consequent interdependent decisions.

In the ultimatum game experiments, specific brain areas, such as the anterior insula (Figure 6c), are significantly activated by unfair behavior. Consequently, the activation of this area is a reliable predictor of whether the player will decide to accept or reject the offer. Because the anterior insula is also the region of the brain associated with primitive states such as disgust, we can assume that what we perceive as unfair behavior triggers a disgust response.

Even if fair behavior strongly influences social decision making, what we consider fair is a matter of perception and depends on cultural and contextual factors.[41]

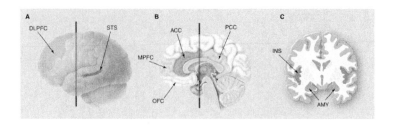

Figure 6. Map of brain areas activated in social decision making; DLPFC: dorsolateral prefrontal cortex. MPFC: medial prefrontal cortex. STS: superior temporal sulcus. INS: insula. AMY: amygdala.[42]

Another important brain area involved in the causal relationship between emotions and decision making is the amygdala. The amygdala is a collection of bundles of neurons concealed in the medial temporal lobes of the cerebral cortex. The amygdala is part of the limbic system and is involved with the processing of emotions and, even more important, the development of associations between emotions and salient stimuli. The amygdala has traditionally been associated with aversive emotions, such as anger or fear.

More recent research has investigated the role of the amygdala in decision making.[43] The amygdala acts as an impulsive system that activates autonomic (involuntary) responses to emotional stimuli.

A long tradition of research and philosophy has considered reason and emotion as being in opposition. However, is it true that successful decision making relies on suppressing the emotions arising from the limbic system of the brain? In some aspects yes, but the truth is that emotions provide us with motivation and meaning that are fundamental factors in making decisions.[44]

For example, patients with amygdala damage lack these autonomic responses to emotional stimuli and consequently display impaired decision-making capacity.

Emotions shouldn't be suppressed, but rather controlled. A reasonable dose of emotions improves our decision-making ability.

In some way, the amygdala is the equivalent of the hippocampus with regard to emotions. In other words, as the hippocampus is fundamental in creating new memories, the amygdala is essential for acquiring new emotional attributes associated with specific emotional stimuli.[45]

LYING

The capacity to deceive others is a complex and demanding mental skill that requires the ability to suppress truthful information.

According to recent research,[46] when lying, individuals show stronger activation of the prefrontal cortical areas, which implies an increase in mental workload of the posterior cingulate cortex, the area that processes visual information and its association with emotions, and of the left middle frontal gyrus, the right middle, inferior, and superior frontal gyri and the anterior cingulate cortex (see Figure 7).

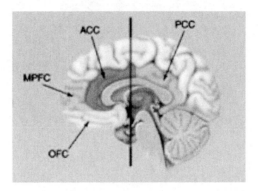

Figure 7 – Map of brain areas activated when lying; MPFC: medial prefrontal cortex. OFC: orbitofrontal cortex. PCC: posterior cingulate cortex. ACC: anterior cingulate cortex. [47]

THEORY OF MIND

Theory of mind is the branch of cognitive science that explores how we attribute mental states (beliefs, intents, desires) to other individuals and how we use these states to explain and predict the actions of other individuals.

According to research, several distinct brain regions are activated during theory of mind reasoning, thereby developing an integrated functional network. The core regions of the network are the prefrontal cortex and the superior temporal sulcus (Figure 6a, b), while other more peripheral regions contribute only marginally to theory of mind.[48]

Both behavioral and brain imaging research have proposed that some aspects of theory of mind may not be entirely universal. Differences exist among cultures with respect to how people understand others' behaviors.[49]

WHOLE BRAIN THINKING

Based on physicist Ned Herrmann's (1996) research, our brain can be described as organized into four distinct elements that represent our preferred thinking styles and influence the way we learn, interpret, process information, and interact with others.[50]

Every person's brain is made up of the same four highly specific functions and thought processes. The four quadrants represent a metaphorical model for how the brain works (see Figure 8). Each individual tends to preferably exploit one of the quadrants.

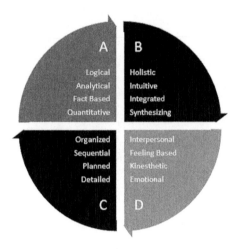

Figure 8. Whole Brain Quadrants. © 1981-2014 Herrmann Global, LLC.

- *Quadrant A* refers to the rational, logical, factual, and present-oriented function of the brain, concerned with analysis and processing of information. It answers the what question.
- *Quadrant B* refers to the sequential and quantifying function of the brain, concerned with risk minimization, reliability, and planning. It answers the how question.
- *Quadrant C* refers to the feeling-based, intuitive, and emotional function of the brain, mainly concerned with interpersonal relations. It answers the who question.
- *Quadrant D* refers to the holistic, innovative, and future-oriented function of the brain, concerned with a systemic view, risk predisposition, and long-term goals. It answers the why question.

Our purpose is to use all the quadrants, even the less preferred ones, and to adapt our thinking styles to the other party while negotiating and influencing.

PERSONALITY AND DECISION MAKING

Every individual nature has its own beauty.[51]

Personality is defined as a complex of behavioral and emotional characteristics that distinguishes an individual[52] and uniquely influences his or her cognitions, emotions, motivations, and behaviors in various situations.[53]

Personality also refers to the relatively enduring pattern of thoughts, feelings, and behaviors that influences people's expectations, self-perceptions, values, and attitudes and predicts individuals' reactions to other people, when facing problems, or under pressure.[54]

It is important to emphasize that personality traits don't exist in isolation. Each individual is a combination of at least three factors: *culture, personality,* and *context* (see Figure 9).

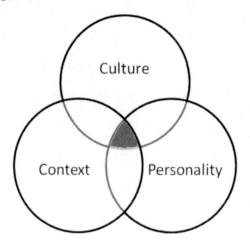

Figure 9. Context, culture and personality.

THE FIVE FACTOR MODEL

The Five Factor Model provides a common language to describe individuals and human personality. The model is based on five major dimensions of personality and six facets that define each dimension.[55]

The Five Factor Model has been validated across 56 nations, and a variety of economic, cultural, religious, and linguistic contexts.[56]

The first dimension, *neuroticism*, identifies individuals' propensity for psychological distress. The stimulus that triggers neuroticism is stress, and an individual's neuroticism score is an estimation of the level of stress that triggers her sympathetic nervous system and activates her automatic fight or flight response mode.

The neuroticism domain is composed of the following six facets:

- *Anxiety*: Tendency to feel concern and apprehension.
- *Angry hostility*: Tendency to experience anger, frustration, and resentment.
- *Depression*: Tendency to experience feelings of guilt, sadness, hopelessness, and loneliness.
- *Self-consciousness*: Tendency to feel shyness or social anxiety.
- *Impulsiveness*: Tendency to act on cravings and urges rather than reining them in and delaying gratification.
- *Vulnerability*: General exposure to stress.

A low score on neuroticism identifies *resilient* individuals, who tend to respond to stressful situations in a calm, secure, steady, and rational way. Resilient people have a habit of handling problems in an analytical and logical manner, sometimes being perceived by others as detached, relaxed, or insensitive.

A high score on neuroticism identifies *reactive* individuals, who tend to respond to stressful situations in a nervous, anxious, excited, and concerned way. Reactive people have a habit of handling problems emotionally and sensitively, sometimes being perceived by others as erratic, agitated, involved, and easily discouraged.

The second dimension, *extraversion*, detects individuals' tendency to search for sensory stimulations and interaction with people. The stimulus that triggers extraversion is sensation (humans' five senses). Conventionally, extraversion has been associated with sociability, the tendency to favor the company of other people. However, the primary cause of extraversion is the need for sensory stimulation, and other people are the most common source of such stimulation.

The extraversion domain is composed of the following six facets:

- *Warmth*: Interest in and friendliness toward others.
- *Gregariousness*: Preference for the company of others.
- *Assertiveness*: Tendency for social preeminence and vigor of expression.
- *Activity*: Fast pace of living.
- *Excitement seeking*: Need for strong environmental stimulation.
- *Positive emotions*: Tendency to experience positive sensations.

A low score on extraversion identifies *introverts*, thoughtful, quiet, and reserved people who prefer to work alone in a weak sensory stimulation context. An introvert can sometimes be perceived by others as cold, inaccessible, and isolated.

A high score on extraversion identifies *extroverts*, loquacious, passionate, sociable, and friendly people who prefer to work with people in strong sensory stimulation situations. An extrovert may sometimes be perceived as outspoken, arrogant, forceful, and superficial.

The third dimension, *openness to experience*, identifies individuals' pursuit of new experiences. The stimulus that triggers openness to experience is curiosity for the novel and unfamiliar, and an individual's openness to experience score is an estimation of the level of novelty needed to activate her dopaminergic system.

Openness to experience is composed of the following six facets:

- *Fantasy*: Accessibility to the inner world of imagination.
- *Aesthetics*: Appreciation of art and beauty.
- *Feelings*: Openness to inner feelings and emotions.
- *Actions*: Openness to new experiences on a practical level.
- *Ideas*: Intellectual curiosity.
- *Values*: Inclination to reassess one's own values and those of authority figures.

A low score on openness to experience identifies *preservers*, practical and concrete individuals who tend to possess expert knowledge about a specific topic or domain and are comfortable with repetitive tasks. A preserver can sometimes be perceived as conservative, conventional, and rigid.

A high score on openness to experience detects *explorers*, curious, absorbed, and contemplative individuals seeking new experiences and continuously planning their future. Explorers are comfortable with theory and concepts and always need new circumstances to escape boredom. An explorer can sometimes be perceived as unrealistic, unconventional, and idealistic.

The fourth dimension, *agreeableness*, identifies individuals' preference for cooperation and conflict avoidance. The stimulus that triggers this system into action is the dominance challenge, and an individual's agreeableness score is an estimation of the serotonin and testosterone levels affecting this trigger point: Higher levels of serotonin and lower levels of testosterone are associated with relaxation and placidity, lower levels of serotonin and higher levels of testosterone with aggression and hostility.

The agreeableness domain is composed of the following six facets:

- *Trust*: Belief in the honesty and trustworthiness of others.
- *Straightforwardness*: Candor in expression.
- *Altruism*: Active concern for the welfare of others.
- *Compliance*: Passive response to interpersonal conflict.
- *Modesty*: Tendency to underplay one's own achievements and be modest.
- *Tender-mindedness*: Attitude of sympathy for others.

A low score on agreeableness identifies *challengers*, individuals who tend to relate to authority in a skeptical, arrogant, and challenging way. Challengers are independent, competitive people who pursue their self-interests and can be perceived by others as being aggressive, reserved, offensive, and confrontational.

A high score on agreeableness identifies *adapters*, individuals who relate to authority by being patient, humble, and compliant. Adapters are cooperative, empathic, and interdependent people who pursue group welfare and can sometimes be perceived as spineless, passive, innocent, and conflict-averse.

The fifth dimension, *conscientiousness*, identifies individuals' level of motivation, organization, and persistence in goal-directed behavior. Distractions are stimuli that cause individuals to lose focus and concentration.

The consciousness domain is composed of the following six facets:

- *Competence*: Belief in own self-efficacy.
- *Order*: Personal organization and method.
- *Dutifulness*: Emphasis on fulfilling moral obligations.
- *Achievement striving*: Need for personal achievement and purpose.
- *Self-discipline*: Ability to complete tasks despite obstacles, boredom, or distractions.
- *Deliberation*: Propensity to ponder things before acting or speaking.

A low score on conscientiousness identifies *flexible* individuals, who tend to procrastinate and switch between tasks. They are likely to approach goals casually and in a relaxed way. Flexible people can be perceived by others as disorganized, careless, and unreliable.

A high score on conscientiousness identifies *focused* individuals, who tend to pursue goals diligently, systematically, and thoroughly. They are likely to tackle one task at a time, carefully allocating time and resources to each activity. Focused people can be perceived by others as obsessive, pedantic, controlling, and stubborn.

CULTURAL INFLUENCES ON PERSONALITY

The Five Factor Model has been validated across 56 different cultures. After having grouped these 56 nations into 10 geographic world regions, specific trends in the worldwide distribution of personality dimensions emerged from research.[57] They are:

- *Extraversion*: The lowest scores were located in East Asian countries. Furthermore, South America, South Asia, and Southeast Asia scored lower than other regions.

- *Agreeableness*: African countries scored considerably higher and East Asian countries scored significantly lower than other world regions.

- *Conscientiousness*: As with agreeableness, African countries scored considerably higher and East Asian countries scored significantly lower than other world regions.

- *Neuroticism*: African countries scored considerably lower and East Asian countries scored significantly higher than other world regions.

- *Openness*: East Asian and African countries scored considerably lower and South American countries scored significantly higher than other world regions.

Some of these regional personality profiles may seem mistaken or counterintuitive. However, it is important to emphasize that when comparing the mean scores of different cultures on a personality dimension scale, any observed differences may exist not only because of a real cultural disparity but also because of incorrect translations, biased sampling (e.g., college students), or the non-identical response styles of people from different cultures. For example, East Asians tend to be humble when making a self-assessment. This could explain their low score on conscientiousness.

Another explanation is provided by Hsu (2006):[58] *The Western concept of personality represents a Ptolemaic view of human nature, where the individual is situated at the center of the universe. In contrast to this, the Chinese, and more generally East Asian, concept of Jen (the word meaning man in Mandarin) places the individual within a context in which everyone has to maintain one's relationships with others at an acceptable level of dynamic equilibrium, so representing a Galilean view of human nature.*

IDIOCENTRISM AND ALLOCENTRISM

Individualism and collectivism describe the cultural dimension, whereas at the individual level of analysis, the equivalent terms are *idiocentrism* and *allocentrism*.[59]

Idiocentrism and allocentrism can be defined as personality attributes that are often orthogonal to each other.

Idiocentrism emphasizes self-reliance, competition, uniqueness, hedonism, and emotional distance from in-groups.

Allocentrism highlights interdependence, sociability, family integrity, and concern for the needs and welfare of in-group members.

In all cultures, we can find both idiocentrics and allocentrics, but in different magnitudes.

All individuals have access to both individualist and collectivist cognitive structures, but the accessibility to these structures varies. In individualist cultures, people have more access to the individualist cognitive structures and tend to be more idiocentric, whereas in collectivist cultures people have more access to the collectivist cognitive structures and tend to be more allocentric.

PERSONALITY AND NEGOTIATION

Even if most studies confirm that personality moderately affects negotiation payoffs, empirical evidence for the role of personality in negotiation is sometimes inconclusive, other times contradictory.

In a recent study, researchers found that extroverts (high score on extraversion) and adapters (high score on agreeableness) tend to achieve worse outcomes in distributive negotiations.[60]

Furthermore, extraversion and agreeableness have no effect on outcomes in integrative negotiations.

On the other hand, focused individuals (high score on conscientiousness) achieve better outcomes in integrative negotiations, but have no benefit in distributive bargaining.

According to a different set of studies, negotiators high in agreeableness achieve better payoff in integrative negotiations and negotiators low in agreeableness achieve better outcomes in distributive negotiations.[61]

Explorers, individuals with a high score on openness to experience, are inclined to be better suited for integrative negotiations. These results have been confirmed in both an American and a Chinese context.[62]

One reason why personality does not consistently and strongly predict bargaining behavior may be that personality dimensions are broad constructs.

A new and narrower personality construct that can help explain distributive negotiation outcomes, and the reason why some negotiators make concessions and accommodate their counterparts' requests whereas others in the same position stand firm and get what they want, is *unmitigated communion (UC)*, an orientation involving high concern for and anxiety about one's relationships coupled with low self-concern.

Relational concerns of individuals high in UC lead them to give away too much at the bargaining table.[63]

PERSONALITY EMOTIONAL STYLES

According to recent neuroscience research, personality is composed of six basic emotional dimensions.[64] These emotional dimensions, or styles, describe how people react to problems and challenges. They are:

- *Resilience*: The ability to quickly recover from adversity.
- *Outlook*: The ability to sustain enduring positive emotions.
- *Social intuition*: The ability to detect and recognize social cues from others.
- *Self-awareness*: The ability to detect and recognize one's own bodily feelings that reflect emotions.

- *Sensitivity to context*: The ability to regulate emotions and behavior according to the context.
- *Attention*: The ability to stay focused.

People respond differently to difficulties and task because each individual is a unique combination of these six dimensions. Furthermore, while these dimensions tend to be quite stable over time in most adults, they can still be changed through systematic practice of specific mental exercises.[65]

(ENDNOTES)

1   Watzlawick, P. (1993). The Situation Is Hopeless But Not Serious (The Pursuit of Unhappiness). New York: Norton.

2   Daniel Kahneman.

3   Aumann, R. J. (2008). Game Theory. In S. N. Durlauf, & L. E. Blume (Eds.), The New Palgrave Dictionary of Economics (2nd ed). New York: Palgrave Macmillan.

4   Raiffa, H., Richardson, J., & Metcalfe, D. (2007). Negotiation Analysis: The Science and Art of Collaborative Decision Making. Cambridge, MA: Belknap Press.

5   Kelly, A. (2003). Decision making using game theory: An introduction for managers. Cambridge, UK: Cambridge University Press.

6   Raiffa, H., Richardson, J., & Metcalfe, D. (2007). Negotiation Analysis: The Science and Art of Collaborative Decision Making. Cambridge, MA: Belknap Press.

7   McCain, R. A. (2010). Game theory: A nontechnical introduction to the analysis of strategy (Revised Edition). Singapore: World Scientific Publishing.

8   Determinism is a philosophical doctrine stating that for every human event, act, and decision, there exist conditions that could cause no other event, act, or decision because they are the result of antecedent states of affairs.

9   Schelling, T. C. (1960). The strategy of conflict. Cambridge, MA: Harvard University Press.

10   Jacque Russell, B. W. (1959). Common sense and nuclear warfare. London: George Allen and Unwin.

11   Dixit, A. K., & Nalebuff, B. (1990). Making strategies credible. New Haven: Yale School of Organization and Management.

12   Kinsley, M. (2014, October 23). A Nobel laureate who's got game. Washington Post. Retrieved from http://www.washingtonpost.com/wp-dyn/content/article/2005/10/11/AR2005101101336.html

13   Thaler, R. H. (1988). Anomalies: The Ultimatum Game. Journal of Economic Perspectives, Vol. 2, N. 4, 195-206.

14   Güth, W., Schmittberger, R., & Schwarze, B. (1982). An experimental analysis of ultimatum bargaining. Journal of Economic Behavior and Organization, Vol. 3, N. 4, 367-388.

15   Kahneman, D., Knetsch, J. L., & Thaler, R. H. (1986). Fairness and the assumptions of economics. Journal of Business, Vol. 59, N. 4, 285-300.

16   Henrich, J. (2000). Does culture matter in economic behavior? Ultimatum game bargaining among the Machiguenga of the Peruvian Amazon. American Economic Review, Vol. 90, N. 4, 973-979.

17   Camerer, C. F. (2003). Behavioral game theory: Experiments in strategic interaction. Princeton, NJ: Princeton University Press.

18   Zak, P. J., Stanton A. A., & Ahmadi S. (2007). Oxytocin increases generosity in humans. PLoS ONE, Vol. 2, N. 11, e1128.

19   Van Lange, P. A., Joireman, J., Parks, C. D., & Van Dijk, E. (2013). The Psychology of Social Dilemmas: A Review. Organizational Behavior and Human Decision Processes, Vol. 120, N. 2, 125-141.

20   Weber, J. M., Kopelman, S., & Messick, D. M. (2004). A Conceptual Review of Decision Making in Social Dilemmas: Applying a Logic of Appropriateness. Personality and Social Psychology Review, Vol. 8, N. 3, 281-307.

21   Denis, A. (2002). Collective and individual rationality: Maynard Keynes's methodological standpoint and policy prescription. Research in Political Economy, Vol. 20, 187-215.

22   Weber, J. M., Kopelman, S., & Messick, D. M. (2004). A Conceptual Review of Decision Making in Social Dilemmas: Applying a Logic of Appropriateness. Personality and Social Psychology Review, Vol. 8, N. 3, 281-307.

23   Kopelman, S. (2008). The Herdsman and the Sheep, Mouton, or Kivsa? The Influence of Group Culture on Cooperation in Social Dilemmas. In A. Biel, D. Eek, T. Garling, & M. Gustafsson, M. (Eds.), New issues and paradigms in research on social dilemmas. New York: Springer.

The 4 Ps Framework

24 Brett, J. M., & Kopelman, S. (2004). Cross-cultural perspectives on cooperation in social dilemmas. In M. J. Gelfand, & J. M. Brett (Eds.), Handbook of Negotiation and Culture. Palo Alto: Stanford University Press.

25 NIA National Institute on Aging: http://www.nia.nih.gov/sites/default/files/01_brainside_lg.jpg

26 Hughes, R. (2010). CULT-URE. London: Fiell Publishing.

27 Drachman, D. (2005). Do we have brain to spare? Neurology, Vol. 64, N. 12, 2004-2005.

28 http://ssbstephaniesmid.wordpress.com/2012/09/04/the-ecological-city-and-the-brain/neuron/

29 Hawkins, J. (2004). On intelligence. New York, NY: Owl Books.

30 Koch, C. (1998). Biophysics of Computation: Information Processing in Single Neurons. New York: Oxford University Press.

31 Freeman, J. B., Ambady, N., Midgley, K. J. & Holcomb, P. J. (2011). The real-time link between person perception and action: Brain potential evidence for dynamic continuity. Social Neuroscience, Vol. 6, N. 2, 139-155.

32 Numenta Platform for Intelligent Computing http://numenta.org/resources/HTM_CorticalLearningAlgorithms.pdf

33 Hawkins, J. (2004). On intelligence. New York, NY: Owl Books.

34 Numenta Platform for Intelligent Computing http://numenta.org/resources/HTM_CorticalLearningAlgorithms.pdf

35 Dunbar, R. (1995). Neocortex size and group size in primates: a test of the hypothesis. Journal of Human Evolution, 28, 287-296.

36 Baron-Cohen, S. (2003). The Essential Difference. Men, Women and the Extreme Male Brain. London: The Penguin Press.

37 Reader, S. M., & Laland, K. N. (2002). Social intelligence, innovation, and enhanced brain size in primates. PNAS, Vol. 99, N. 7, 4436-4441.

38 Sanfey, A. G. (2007). Social Decision-Making: Insights from Game Theory and Neuroscience. Science, Vol. 318, N. 5850, 598-602.

39 Sanfey, A. G. (2007). Social Decision-Making: Insights from Game Theory and Neuroscience. Science, Vol. 318, N. 5850, 598-602.

40 Sanfey, A. G. (2007). Social Decision-Making: Insights from Game Theory and Neuroscience. Science, Vol. 318, N. 5850, 598-602.

41 Lee, D. (2011). Game theory and neural basis of social decision making. Nature Neuroscience, Vol. 11, N. 4, 404-409.

42 Sanfey, A. G. (2007). Social Decision-Making: Insights from Game Theory and Neuroscience. Science, Vol. 318, N. 5850, 598-602.

43 Gupta, R., Koscik, T. R., Bechara A., & Tranel D. (2011). The amygdala and decision making. Neuropsychologia, Vol. 49, N. 4, 760-766.

44 Seth, A. (Ed.) (2014). 30-Second Brain. London: Icon Books.

45 Bechara, A., Damasio, H., & Damasio, A. R. (2003). Role of the amygdala in decision making. Annals of the New York Academy of Sciences, 985, 356-369.

46 Proverbio, A. M., Vanutelli, M. E., & Adorni R. (2013). Can You Catch a Liar? How Negative Emotions Affect Brain Responses when Lying or Telling the Truth. PLoS ONE, Vol. 8, N. 3, e59383.

47 Sanfey, A. G. (2007). Social Decision-Making: Insights from Game Theory and Neuroscience. Science, Vol. 318, N. 5850, 598-602.

48 Carrington, S. J., & Bailey, A. J. (2009). Are there theory of mind regions in the brain? A review of the neuroimaging literature. Human Brain Mapping, Vol. 30, N. 8, 2313-2335.

49 Kobayashi F. C., & Temple, E. (2009). Cultural effects on the neural basis of theory of mind. Progress in Brain Research, 178, 213-223.

50 Herrmann, N. (1996). The Whole Brain Business Book. New York: McGraw-Hill

51 Ralph Waldo Emerson.

52 Merriam-Webster, retrieved from http://www.merriam-webster.com/dictionary/personality

53   Ryckman, R. (2012). Theories of Personality (10th ed.). Boston: Cengage Learning.

54   Krauskopf, C. J., & Saunders, D. R. (1994). Personality and Ability: The Personality Assessment System. Lanham, MD: University Press of America.

55   Howard, P. J., & Howard, J. M. (2001). The Owner's Manual for Personality at Work: how the Big Five Personality traits affect performance, communication, teamwork, leadership, and sales. Marietta, GA: Bard Press.

56   Schmitt, J., Allik, D. P., McCrae, R. R., & Benet-Martinez, V. (2007). The Geographic Distribution of Big Five Personality Traits: Patterns and Profiles of Human Self-Description Across 56 Nations. Journal of Cross-Cultural Psychology, Vol. 38, N. 2, 173-212.

57   Schmitt, J., Allik, D. P., McCrae, R. R., & Benet-Martínez, V. (2007). The Geographic Distribution of Big Five Personality Traits: Patterns and Profiles of Human Self-Description Across 56 Nations. Journal of Cross-Cultural Psychology, Vol. 38, N. 2, 173-212.

58   Hsu, C. (2006). Development of an indigenous Chinese personality inventory based on the principle of Yin-Yang and the five elements and on the ancient Chinese text "Jen Wu Chih". (Electronic Thesis or Dissertation). Retrieved from https://etd.ohiolink.edu/

59   Triandis, H. C., & Suh, E. M. (2002). Cultural Influences on Personality. Annual Reviews of Psychology, 53, 133-160.

60   Barry, B., & Friedman, R. A. (1998). Bargainers Characteristics in Distributive and Integrative Negotiation. Journal of Personality and Social Psychology, Vol. 74, N. 2, 345-359.

61   Dimotakis, N., Conlon, D. E., & Ilies, R. (2012). The mind and heart (literally) of the negotiator: Personality and contextual determinants of experiential reactions and economic outcomes in negotiation. Journal of Applied Psychology, Vol. 97, N. 1, 183-193.

62   Ma, Z., & Jaeger, A. (2005). Getting to Yes in China: Exploring Personality Effects in Chinese Negotiation Styles. Group Decision and Negotiation, Vol. 14, 415-437.

63   Amanatullah, E. T., Morris, M. W., & Curhan, J. R. (2008). Negotiators Who Give Too Much: Unmitigated Communion, Relational Anxieties, and Economic Costs in Distributive and Integrative Bargaining. Journal of Personality and Social Psychology, Vol. 95, N. 3, 723-738.

64   Davidson, R. J., & Begley, S. (2012). The Emotional Life of your Brain. New York: Hudson Street Press.

65   Davidson, R. J., & Begley, S. (2012). The Emotional Life of your Brain. New York: Hudson Street Press.

CHAPTER 9:

System 1 and System 2 Thinking

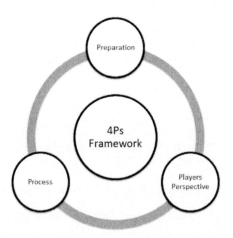

Stage 1: Preparation. Stage 2: Process. Stage 4: Players' Perspective

The difficulty lies not so much in developing new ideas as in escaping from old ones.[1]

Intuition simply corresponds to recognition.[2]

SYSTEM 1 AND SYSTEM 2 THINKING

INTRODUCTION

In his study of chess masters, Herbert Simon (1973) found that after thousands of hours of practice they see the pieces on the board strategically. Through preparation, they learn to identify familiar constituents in a new and complex situation and to take action in a way that is appropriate to that situation.

The same happens to negotiators when they face unusual or multifaceted circumstances. They come up with a quick answer guided by experience. The problem is that sometimes intuition fails us and, instead of an expert answer, we retrieve a heuristic solution.

Because we are indolent machines built to jump to conclusions, and our ability to concentrate is limited, we tend to over-rely on intuition and we switch to a more deliberate and effortful form of thinking only when we are forced to do so.

When confronted with a difficult problem, to simplify the task, we often address an easier substitute problem instead. However, this does not provide an answer to the original question.

Two distinct cognitive systems underlie thinking and reasoning: *System 1* and *System 2*.[3]

System 1 refers to our intuitive system, which is, as a rule, fast, instinctive, effortless, implicit, parallel, associative, contextualized, and emotional.

Attaining the result of multiplying 6 x 7 mainly involves System 1 thinking because the product of the multiplication is stored in our memory from primary school and thus the number 42 intuitively jumps to mind as a possible answer.

System 2 refers to our rational system, which is slower, conscious, effortful, explicit, serial, rule based, abstract, and logical.[4]

System 2 enables abstract reasoning and hypothetical thinking, but it is limited by the brain's working memory capacity.

Finding the result of multiplying 24 x 17 mainly involves System 2 thinking because, for most of us, the number 408 doesn't intuitively jump to mind as a possible answer. To reach the correct answer, we undertake mental processes that call for determination, motivation, and focus (for example 24 x 20 – 24 x 3 or 24 x 10 + 24 x 7).

System 1 cannot keep track of options and when uncertain, guided by experience, it bets on an answer. The betting rules are intelligent: Recent events and the current context have the most weight in determining an interpretation. When no recent events come to mind, more distant memories govern.

System 1 is like a machine for jumping to conclusions because it is not comfortable with uncertainty and complexity, which are the exclusive domain of System 2.

System 1 is also an incredibly sensitive pattern-recognition machine. Our brain fills in the gaps in raw information with interpolated assumptions.[5]

THE INTERACTION BETWEEN THE TWO SYSTEMS

The partition of work between System 1 and System 2 is highly efficient: It minimizes effort and improves performance.

Most of the time, when we do not face any complexity, System 2 accepts the proposals of System 1 without alteration.

System 2 comes into play when System 1 meets a challenge that needs a rational processing system to be solved (e.g., the 24 x 17 multiplication problem).

The process frequently runs smoothly because System 1 is generally very good at reacting to familiar situations and making accurate short-term extrapolations.

Nevertheless, System 1 is susceptible to biases and systematic errors in specified circumstances: It sometimes answers easier and different questions than those it is asked, it has little comprehension of statistics, and it cannot identify multiple and complex relationships.

What is important for System 1 is the coherence of the decision it generates, not the quantity or quality of the information on which the decision is based.

One further constraint of System 1 is that it cannot be turned off.

Because System 1 operates automatically, preventing errors in spontaneous thought is difficult; this would require a continuously alert System 2 and, consequently, a lot of energy and effort.

However, we can learn to recognize situations in which mistakes are plausible and employ System 2 thinking when the risk involved is high.

SELF-CONTROL

Another fundamental purpose of System 2 is self-control, the continuous monitoring of our own behavior, particularly when under pressure; *the most effortful forms of slow thinking are those that require you to think fast.*

That we dispose of a limited budget of attention also explains why we cannot do several things at once unless the tasks are easy and straightforward.

While walking with a friend, try the following: Ask her to immediately multiply 24 x 17 in her head. She will almost definitely have to stop walking.

Now ask her to speed up walking and then to multiply 9 x 7. Her attention will be drawn to keeping the faster pace and her ability to think will be weakened accordingly.

Self-control and deliberate thought use the same limited budget of effort.

For example, people who are cognitively engaged also tend to make superficial judgments in social situations.

The need-for-closure factor, the desire for definite solutions and the avoidance of confusion and ambiguity, is a key indicator of our degree of self-control. People with a high need for closure:

- Do not look for alternative options.
- Feel pressure to reach a decision quickly and to stick with it.
- Are not comfortable with ambiguity.
- Rely on heuristic judgment.

Individuals with a high need for closure are therefore represented by cognitive impatience, a tendency to jump to conclusions on the basis of insufficient information, and inflexibility. Because they find cognitive effort unpleasant, they also tend to be hasty and overconfident in their intuitions.

There is a direct correlation between degree of self-control and thinking. People who display more self-control score substantially higher on tests of intelligence.

PATH OF LEAST RESISTANCE

In physics, the path of least resistance among a set of alternative routes is the path that provides the least resistance to forward motion by a given object. A law of least effort also applies to cognitive thinking. According to this principle, if the same task can be completed in a number of ways, people will eventually chose the least demanding course of action. In other words, effort is a cost, and laziness is built deep into our nature.[6]

When we acquire skills in a specific task, the effort required to complete that task diminishes. Talent has analogous effects. Talented individuals require less effort to solve problems.

The notion of mental energy is not merely a metaphor. It is analogous to the idea of a runner using glucose stored in her muscles during a sprint. Effortful thinking increases glucose and oxygen consumption.[7]

THE ASSOCIATIVE MACHINE

Our brain doesn't follow a sequence of conscious ideas, one at a time. According to current research, ideas can be thought of as nodes of a vast network, our associative memory, in which each node (idea) is linked to many others. Links associate ideas, which in turn activate other ideas.

An important feature of associative thinking is that it primarily occurs unconsciously.

The fact that our thinking is associative has some interesting corollaries.

The first corollary is the priming effect. Exposure to a word causes instant differences in the ease with which many associated words can be called to mind. If you have just seen or heard the word EAT, you will be temporarily more likely to complete the word fragment SO_P as SOUP rather than SOAP: The opposite would happen if you had just seen WASH. The idea of EAT primes the idea of SOUP, and WASH primes SOAP.[8]

Research on the effect that money has on people's behavior has yielded interesting results.[9] Money-primed participants become more individualistic: They ask for more and give less help to others, they prefer to work alone, and they require a good deal of physical space between themselves and others. On the other hand, reminders of respect foster interdependent and supporting behavior.

Other studies have suggested that reminding people of their mortality increases the attractiveness of authoritarian ideas, which may offer a sort of relief when confronting the notion of death.

Research on the priming effect has yielded results emphasizing that frequently our choices and decisions are not wholly autonomous or conscious.

The second corollary is that our System 1 associates familiarity with veracity. Frequent repetition is a consistent way to make people believe in lies. As a consequence, to be credible in front of an audience, it is always better to use simple and familiar language.

The third corollary is the direct and reciprocal correlation between associative thinking and mood, whereby positive mood improves associative thinking ability and broad associative thinking increases mood. According to research, patients with major depressive disorder (MDD) have impaired associative processing ability since they are susceptible to increased, self-focused, and narrow cogitation. Even just being in a bad mood can reduce our ability to make broad connections among different ideas.[10]

The fourth corollary is that our brain doesn't like surprises. Violations of our model of the world, made of associations among ideas, events, situations, actions, and consequences that occur with predictability and consistency, are immediately spotted. Surprises disrupt our interpretation of the present and our expectations of the future, built on patterns of associated ideas.

NEED FOR COGNITION

The need for cognition in psychology is a personality variable indicating the degree to which individuals are disposed toward effortful cognitive activities.

A higher need for cognition is associated with increased appreciation of debate, idea evaluation, and problem solving (System 2 thinking). Those with a high need for cognition tend to elaborate information. Those with a lower need for cognition tend to process information more heuristically, often through low elaboration (System 1 thinking).[11]

Individuals with low cognitive motivation tend to trust simple information cues and to adopt cognitive heuristics. They also tend to be easily stressed by complex cognitive tasks.

Individuals with high cognitive motivation tend to actively search for and use new and relevant information. As a result, they are usually more effective decision makers in situations of risk and uncertainty than individuals with a low need for cognition.

DECISION MAKING UNDER STRESS AND PRESSURE

When under stress or pressure, our brain significantly restricts the range and amount of information we have to deal with.

A 1987 study exposed participants to either controllable (performance-based potential electric shocks) or uncontrollable (arbitrary potential electric shocks) stress and no stress at all. The results indicate that participants exposed to stress showed a significantly stronger tendency to offer answers before all available options had been considered (premature closure) and to scan their alternatives in a nonsystematic fashion than did participants who were not exposed to stress.[12]

One possible explanation is that participants devoted part of their conscious attentional capacity to the threat and to the autonomous reactions elicited by the threat.

The partial consideration of options could therefore be interpreted as the result of a temporarily narrowed attentional capacity or a defense mechanism designed to prevent information overload.

Other research findings have shown that individuals subject to a tight deadline not only feel pressure, but they also feel more anxious and more energetic.[13]

According to the study, anxiety is associated with the extra demand placed on participants by time pressure. A higher energy level reflects the greater task involvement and the need to work harder that is involved when a deadline is imposed.

The optimal state in which stress improves performance is when the heart rate is between 115 and 145 beats per minute.

At 145, our cognitive abilities quickly decrease. At 175, there is an almost complete interruption of cognitive processing. The same happens under time pressure: We tend to withdraw to our stereotypes and prejudices.[14]

The only way to overcome cognitive shutdown is through training and rehearsal. Our ability to function under pressure in a specific domain improves with practice.

HEURISTICS

It ain't so much the things we don't know that get us into trouble. It's the things we know that just ain't so.[15]

We expect other reasonable and attentive people to perceive the same reality we do.[16]

Heuristic is defined as a simple procedure that helps find acceptable, though often limited, answers to demanding questions.

Heuristics are simple, efficient, and experience-based rules that people use to form judgments, solve problems, and make decisions. They are mental shortcuts that reduce the cognitive effort involved in the decision-making process and usually consist of focusing on one specific trait of a complex problem, ignoring other important elements. These rules, based on our System 1 thinking, work well in most circumstances, but in certain situations they can lead to systematic errors, called *cognitive biases.*

Following are examples of psychological heuristics.

FIRST IMPRESSIONS

When we meet a new person, we always build hypotheses (often based on inadequate information) that lead to preconceptions.[17] Most people tend to persist with their first impressions, discarding contradictory evidence and favoring information that confirms their prejudices.

This is the first and main reason why first impressions, particularly negative impressions, are so hard to rectify. *People don't want information, they want confirmation.*

Bad emotions and bad feedback have more impact than good emotions and good feedback. Bad impressions and bad stereotypes are faster to form and more resilient to disconfirmation than good ones.

According to research, people produce inferences from the facial appearance of other individuals, even with only 100 milliseconds of exposure.[18] When exposure time increases from 100 milliseconds to 500 milliseconds, judgment accuracy doesn't improve significantly; what rises is confidence in the deduction.

According to the same research, we assess two traits of a stranger's face: how *dominant* (and therefore potentially threatening) he is and how *trustworthy* he is (whether his intent is more likely to be friendly or hostile).

The shape of the face provides the clues for assessing dominance (e.g., a strong square chin). Facial expressions provide the cues for assessing the stranger's intentions.

Even in assessing competence, we tend to fall back on a simple and quick evaluation: We combine the two dimensions of strength and trustworthiness.

According to another experiment, social status changes our perception of race.[19]

Participants in one study were asked to categorize the race of individuals along a white to black continuum, presented with high or low status clothing. When categorization along a white-black continuum was uncertain, low status clothing increased the probability of classification as black, whereas high status clothing increased the odds of classification as white.

When faces with high status clothing were classified as black or faces with low status clothing were categorized as white, participants' hand movements showed hesitation before selecting a race within the continuum.

A widely used measure designed to identify the strength of a person's automatic association between mental representations in memory is the Implicit Association Test (IAT).[20] The IAT is a computer-based measure that requires the user to promptly classify two target concepts with an attribute in a seven-step procedure. Faster responses are interpreted as more strongly associated implicit memories than slower responses.

The IAT is used to understand implicit cognition and the processes that lead to memory creation and recollection, attitude, and stereotypes.

Our brain makes predictions by analogy, recalling stored memories in the form of invariant representations. Because stereotypes can be assumed to be synonymous with invariant representations, prediction by analogy can be considered comparatively the same as reasoning by stereotype. Stereotypes are therefore intrinsic components of our cortex and key elements of our brain functioning. The only way to limit their repercussions is to recognize our prejudices and make a habit of continuously adjusting them according to updated information.

Halo Effect

Running through the Fortune 500 list, it comes as no surprise that most of the chief executive officers (CEOs) are white men. The almost absence of women and minorities among the chief executives might be explained by inequity, discrimination, or cultural biases. However, another statistic is more puzzling: In the U.S. population, about 14.5% of all men are 6' (1.83 meters) or taller. Among CEOs of Fortune 500 companies, the figure is 58%. Even more markedly, in the U.S. population, 3.9% of all men are 6'2" (1.88 meters) or taller. Among the CEO sample, 30% were 6'2" or taller. The chiefs of big companies are nearly all tall. When companies look for a new CEO with the required experience and skills, they can find only a few women or minorities for the short list because of the above mentioned prejudices. However, this is not true of short people. There are far more short people than tall people (85.5% vs. 14.5%).[21]

Here is another example. What do you think of Jim and Sam?[22]

Jim: Smart, hard-working, spontaneous, judgmental, obstinate, resentful

Sam: Resentful, obstinate, judgmental, spontaneous, hard-working, smart

Most of us would regard Jim much more positively than Sam. The early attributes in the list change the implication of the traits that appear later.

The obstinacy of a smart person is justified and can even become a positive trait. On the other hand, a smart but resentful and obstinate individual can be regarded as dangerous.

The halo effect is one of the means that System 1 thinking employs to create a model of the world that is far simpler and more comprehensible than the real world. The halo effect amplifies the importance of first impressions, often to the point that successive information is mostly disregarded. As a consequence, because the sequence in which we discern a person's traits is key, chance plays a vital role in our assessment of other individuals.

JOSHUA BELL

Joshua David Bell is one of the world's greatest violinists. He has recorded more than 40 albums, and he won a Grammy in 2000 for best classical performance. Bell always performs on the same instrument, a 1713 Stradivari called the Gibson ex Huberman.

On Friday, January 12, 2007, at 7:51 a.m., Bell, wearing a baseball cap and an ordinary T-shirt, staged an incognito concert in the Washington, D.C., metro. In the next 43 minutes, the violinist performed six classical pieces.

Of the 1,097 people who passed by, only 7 (accounting for 0.64% of the total) stopped to listen for more than a minute. Bell earned $32 in tips.[23]

Why people didn't stop? Was it because they thought Bell was just another auditioner for a TV show or a student trying to earn some money?

Or was it because of his humble clothes and performance stage?

Another interesting outcome of the experiment was the anxiety Bell felt before the test, even though he was accustomed to playing before monarchs, celebrities and in all the most prominent theaters of the world. In his own words:

When you play for ticket-holders you are already validated. I have no sense that I need to be accepted. I'm already accepted. Here, there was this thought: What if they don't like me? What if they resent my presence?

CONFIRMATION BIAS

If a man is offered a fact which goes against his instincts, he will scrutinize it closely, and unless the evidence is overwhelming, he will refuse to believe it. If, on the other hand, he is offered something which affords a reason for acting in accordance to his instincts, he will accept it even on the lightest evidence.[24]

The human understanding, once it has adopted an opinion, collects any instances that confirm it, and though the contrary instances may be more numerous and more weighty, it either does not notice them or else rejects them, in order that this opinion will remain unshaken.[25]

Confirmation bias is a tendency for individuals to favor information that confirms their preconceptions or assumptions regardless of whether the information is true. Consequently, people gather evidence and recall information from memory selectively and interpret that information through a biased lens.

The associative memory process is predisposed to testing its assumptions by looking for confirming proof. The confirmatory bias of System 1 is also why we tend to exaggerate the prospect of extreme and unlikely events.

Contrary to the rules of science that instruct on testing hypotheses by trying to refute them, people search for facts that are consistent with their presumptions.

Because we can often anticipate other people's beliefs and preferences, we tend to carefully choose the right people to consult, thereby increasing our chances of hearing what we want to hear.

People's inclinations influence not only the type of information they take into account, but also the amount they study. When the initial evidence supports our preferences, we are pleased and conclude our search; when the initial evidence is unfavorable, however, we often dig deeper, hoping to find more reassuring information or to reveal reasons why the original evidence was unreliable.[26]

An important consequence of confirmation bias is that when people are given evidence against their beliefs they tend to believe even more strongly in their preconception.

EMOTIONS AND COGNITIVE PROCESS

Fear and euphoria are dominant forces, and fear is many multiples the size of euphoria.[27]

Emotion is dominated primarily by the possibility, by what might happen, and not so much by the probability.[28]

Emotions are biologically based responses to situations that are seen as personally relevant. They are shaped by learning and usually involve changes in peripheral physiology, expressive behavior, and subjective experience.

Emotions are produced in the limbic system of the brain, and some negative emotions, such as fear, are generated specifically in the amygdala. According to some researchers, emotions hinder our ability to make predictions, which is the primary function of our cortex.[29]

Historically, research has focused on cognitive processes excluding emotions. However, recent studies have advanced the hypotheses that emotions shape our motivation and goals and are therefore fundamental elements of our cognitive process.

Emotions shouldn't be blocked, but rather regulated. A moderate amount of emotions increases our decision-making capability.

Recent research has called attention to the role of steroid hormones in our brain.[30] Specific steroid hormones, such as *cortisol* and *testosterone*, can influence neural functions in regions involved in economic decision making.

Cortisol increases risk aversion, while testosterone increases risk propensity.

An interesting outcome of the recent work on steroid hormones is the *winner effect*.

While studying animals, biologists observed a widespread phenomenon: An animal winning a first fight is more likely to win the next fight.

Taking into consideration and then ruling out alternative reasons (e.g., size, strength, quickness, motivation, age) a single explanation became apparent: a self-enhancing positive loop in which the positive outcome provides a competitive advantage, thereby raising testosterone levels which in turn leads to further victories.

Athletes, traders, managers, and animals on a winning streak have a different body chemistry than those on a losing streak; on a losing streak, cortisol levels increase, leading to risk aversion and lower competiveness.

Another interesting study analyzed the association between *sadness* and *impatience*: According to that research, sadness generates a myopic focus on immediate gratification. The same association has not been verified with other negative emotions such as disgust, which suggests motivational features unique to sadness in creating the phenomenon of myopic misery.[31]

THE SUPERIORITY ILLUSION

The superiority illusion is a cognitive bias that induces individuals to overestimate their positive traits and abilities and to underestimate their negative qualities in relation to others.[32] For example, most people judge themselves as more intelligent, desirable, and skilled than the average person.

However, this amount of superiority is mathematically impossible because in a normally distributed population more than 50% of the people cannot be above average.

For example, in a survey of faculty at the University of Nebraska, 90% of faculty members rated themselves as above average teachers, and 68% rated themselves among the top quarter in teaching ability.[33]

In a 1981 survey, 90% of Swedes described themselves as above-average drivers.[34]

In another more recent study, 87% of MBA students at Stanford University rated their academic performance as above the median.[35]

A survey of a million high school seniors found that 70% thought they were above average in leadership ability and only 2% thought they were below average. In terms of ability to get along with others, all students thought they were above average, 60% thought they were in the top 10%, and 25% thought they were in the top 1%.[36]

Recent studies have determined that the superiority illusion is biologically regulated by the level of the neurotransmitter dopamine: Increasing dopamine levels promotes a person's superiority bias.[37]

The most recent research challenges the generalization of the superiority illusion: People don't always perceive themselves as better than others. As a general rule, individuals believe that they are better than others on familiar tasks and worse than others on unusual tasks.[38]

OPTIMISM BIAS

The superiority illusion belongs to a class of biases that includes the optimism bias, in which people tend to have an unrealistically promising expectation of the future.

From a neurological point of view, thinking about the future and about the past is the same because the brain activates the same neural area in both cases.[39]

However, forecasting the future requires more energy.

One outcome of the optimism bias is the *planning fallacy*, a tendency to underestimate the time needed to complete a task, even when knowing that the best part of similar projects has run late.[40]

When building plans, we tend to underestimate how long it will take to complete a task.

The definition of planning fallacy can be expanded to the tendency to underestimate the time, costs, and risks of future actions and at the same time overestimate the benefits of the same actions.[41]

The bias only affects predictions about one's own tasks; when disinterested observers predict task completion times, they show a pessimistic bias, overestimating the time needed.

AFFECT HEURISTIC

Affect plays a fundamental role in the relationship between perceived risk and perceived benefit when making judgments. The affect heuristic is a type of heuristic in which emotional response plays a central role.[42]

People judge the perceived risk and perceived benefit of an activity not only by what they think about it but also by how they feel about it. If their feelings toward an activity are favorable, they tend to judge the risks as low and the benefits as high; if their feelings toward the activity are negative, they tend to judge the risks as high and the benefits as low.

According to psychologist Paul Slovic (1995), people let their likes and dislikes determine their beliefs about the world.

For example, when assessing a project, we tend to underestimate the risks involved and overestimate the benefits if we like the project and to make the opposite judgment if we dislike the project.

RANDOMNESS

We look for pattern in chaos, and see order in random events.[43]

When facing information scarcity, our System 1 tends to find causal correlations between the various fragments of information available.

Our associative brain is disposed to see patterns even when none exist, particularly when evaluating random events.

Sport represents one of many examples where we perceive order and causality in randomness.

When a basketball player sinks three or four baskets in a row, we are unable to refrain from developing a causal judgment that the player is hot or, in other words, has a temporarily increased predisposition to score. Analysis of thousands of sequences of shots has led to the conclusion that the sequence of successful and missed shots fulfills all criteria of randomness: *There is no such thing as a hot hand in basketball.* A player's performance on a given shot is independent of his performance on previous shots.[44] (n.b.: The winner effect introduced in the Emotions and Cognitive Process paragraph marginally disputes Gilovich's (1993) conclusions).

Even if we are quick to identify rules and patterns, we must understand that most of what occurs to us is random.

People tend to apply causal thinking to situations that require statistical reasoning. The problem is that System 1 does not have the capability for this mode of reasoning, and System 2 needs training to think statistically.

An example of causal thinking is the tendency to overestimate the relationship between a company's performance and its CEO. However, because economic and social systems are essentially dynamic, we must accept the intrinsic randomness that drives companies' performance: *A company's results are the product of several factors, some of them beyond the CEO's control.*[45]

THE LAW OF SMALL NUMBERS

Capricious similarities can cause careless conjectures, and early exceptions eclipse eventual essentials.[46]

We are prone to assign causal patterns to random events because we often choose to assess samples that are too small.

Using a sufficiently large sample is the only way to minimize the risk of reaching the wrong conclusion. Picking a sample that is too small leaves us at the mercy of chance.

Because we strive for coherency and consistency, we tend to exaggerate the certainty and reliability of the causal pattern we identify in the random event, even if the considered sample doesn't appropriately represent the population from which it is drawn.

The law of small numbers is an indicator of a general bias that favors certainty over doubt.

The exaggerated confidence of investigators in what can be discovered from a few observations is closely related to the halo effect.

ANCHORING

Anchoring is a cognitive bias that illustrates the common human propensity to rely on an initial piece of information when making a decision.

Two different mechanisms produce cognitive anchoring. In System 2, there is a deliberate *process of adjustment*, while anchoring in System 1 occurs by an *automatic priming effect*.

Adopting System 2 thinking, individuals tend to make decisions by adjusting away from the initial anchor, but various studies have shown that these additional adjustments based on supplementary information are usually inadequate. System 2 falls prey to the anchoring effect because it tends to interpret all additional information with reference to the initial anchor. This is the mechanism we outlined in the chapter 6 while illustrating the basic concepts of negotiation.

The second mechanism, the automatic priming effect, is pervasive, robust, and very difficult to avoid.

For example, in one study,[47] students were given anchors that were obviously wrong. They were asked whether Mahatma Gandhi died before or after age 9 or before or after age 140.

Neither of these anchors is correct, but the two groups still made significantly different guesses. According to the first group, Gandhi died at 50, while according to the second group, he died at 67. (By the way, the correct answer is 78.)

The *focusing illusion* is another feature of anchoring that occurs when individuals focus on one aspect of an event, experience, circumstance, problem, or object and ignore the significance of other traits.

Every painting, every photograph, every point of view can be as much about what is omitted as what is included.[48]

The focusing illusion is particularly relevant in comparisons: We often place importance on a small and relevant number of features, disregarding the remaining important attributes. The focusing illusion is for events and things what the halo effect is for people.

In organizations, to ensure better quality control over decision making during meetings, where the opinions of those who speak early and assertively determine the flow of the discussion (priming effect), before discussing an issue, ask all members to write down a very brief outline of their perspective.[49]

Nothing in life is as important as you think it is when you are thinking about it.[50]

CONTRAST EFFECT

Research indicates that a preference between options is influenced by the presence or absence of other, even irrelevant, options.

For example, individuals are more likely to select an option in the presence of a similar inferior alternative than in the absence of the inferior alternative.

In a 1992 study, the likelihood that participants would choose an elegant Cross pen versus $6 in cash was increased by offering a third option, a less attractive second pen.[51]

The inference is that a negotiator's preference for one potential agreement over another might be influenced by the addition of other options that make the proposed agreement seem more attractive in contrast.

AVAILABILITY

The availability heuristic is based on the concept that if something can be easily recalled then it must be important and occur more frequently.

Some events and occurrences attract significant attention and can be easily retrieved from memory. This is why we are more likely to exaggerate the frequency of political corruption, VIP divorces, plane crashes, or earthquakes.

We are also more likely to exaggerate our personal impact on projects, housework, and childcare. We remember much more clearly our contribution than that of others, and the difference in availability leads to a difference in judged frequency.[52]

According to research, people's impressions of the frequency of a category are influenced by two factors:[53]

- The number of instances retrieved.
- The ease with which the instances come to mind.

An interesting corollary of the above mentioned proposition is that people tend to be less confident in a choice when asked to produce more arguments to support it. The first few cases are easy to recall, but before long the task becomes much harder. The reason is that retrieving many examples requires putting effort into the task. Putting effort into the task means switching to System 2. Switching to System 2 decreases the availability bias.

If I'm having so much more trouble than expected coming up with advantages of my television, then the television can't be so good.[54]

If you want to improve your chances of influencing somebody, ask the person to produce more than five arguments to support his or her proposal or to list five arguments to oppose your proposal. Because recalling many instances is difficult, the person's confidence in the original choice will be weakened.

REPRESENTATIVENESS

Representativeness heuristics is a tendency to assess the similarity and association of categories along salient dimensions.[55]

For example, we expect effects to look like their causes.

Judgment by representativeness is often reasonable and helpful because objects, occurrences, and categories are often similar.

It is the over-application of representativeness that gets us into trouble.[56]

One fundamental feature of System 1 is that it characterizes categories as norms and prototypal models. When the categories are social, these representations are called stereotypes.

Stereotypes are how we think of social categories. Stereotypes are valid in most cases, but not in all cases.

Here is an example:

You see a person reading the New York Times on the New York subway. Which of the following is a better guess about the reading stranger?[57]

- She has a PhD.
- She does not have a college degree.

Representativeness would suggest that you consider the PhD option, but it would be better to bet on the second alternative because many more non-graduates than PhDs ride the New York subway.

Here is another example:[58]

Linda is 31 years old, single, outspoken, and very bright. She majored in philosophy. As a student, she was deeply concerned about issues of discrimination and social justice and also participated in anti-nuclear demonstrations.

Now, based on the above description, rank the following statements about Linda, from most to least likely:

- Linda is a bank teller.
- Linda is a bank teller and is active in the feminist movement.

Most of us would think that it is more likely that Linda is a bank teller and is active in the feminist movement than that Linda is a bank teller. A feminist bank teller is much more representative of the description of Linda than just a bank teller.

We judge a conjunction of two events (bank teller and feminist) to be more probable than one of the events (bank teller) in a direct evaluation, even if the category bank teller and feminist is a sub-category of the category bank teller, and therefore the latter has to be more likely than the former.[59]

Contrary to logic, adding details to a situation makes it more plausible and therefore more persuasive.

REGRESSION TO THE MEAN

Regression to the mean is the statistical tendency of a variable to gravitate toward the average on its second measurement, provided it was extreme in the first measurement, and the tendency to be extreme in the second measurement if it was close to the average on its first.[60]

When two variables are imperfectly related, extreme values on one of the variables tend to be matched by less extreme values on the other.

As a result, very tall parents tend to have tall children, but not as tall (on average) as they are themselves;[61] a company's unsuccessful year tends to be followed by a more profitable one, and an excellent year tends to be followed by a worse one.[62]

The statistical phenomenon of regression to the mean must be taken into account whenever we assess events and interpret results; otherwise, we could end up finding too much meaning in chance events.

Regression to the mean also helps to explain why usually a good performance is typically followed by a deterioration regardless of whether the performance was praised and a bad performance is usually followed by an improvement regardless of whether it was punished.

The first good performance may be just due to a stroke of luck and therefore likely to worsen, being closer to the average on its second measurement. Similarly, a bad performance may be just due to bad luck and therefore likely to improve, being closer to the average on its second measurement.

The following example better explains the relationships among performance, skill, luck, and regression to the mean.

In the first two days of a golf tournament, let's assume that the average score of the players was at par 72.[63]

We concentrate on a player who did very well on the first day, ending with a score of 66 (6 under par).

What can we infer from that exceptional score? The first immediate reading is that the golfer is more skilled than the average player. However, we can also infer that the golfer enjoyed better than average luck on day 1.

Now let's concentrate on a player who scored 77 (5 over par). What can we infer from that less than ordinary score? As we did with the first player, the first immediate reading is that the golfer is less skilled than the average player, but we can also infer that the golfer enjoyed worse than average luck on day 1.

From day 1 scores, we can draw the following plausible (even if not definite) conclusions:

Above-average score on day 1 = above-average skill + good luck on day 1

Below-average score on day 1 = below-average skill + bad luck on day 1

Now that we know the two golfers' day 1 scores, how can we predict their scores for day 2?

Our suppositions will be based on the following two assumptions:

- We anticipate that the golfers will preserve the same skill on the second day.
- Because we have no means to foresee the golfers' luck, we predict the golfers will enjoy average luck (neither good nor bad) on the second day.

As a result, we expect that the first player will still be under par, but with a worse score than on day 1, and the second player will still be over par, but with a better score than on day 1 (see Figure 1).

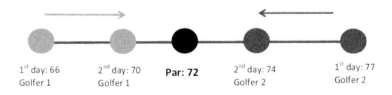

1st day: 66   2nd day: 70   **Par: 72**   2nd day: 74   1st day: 77
Golfer 1   Golfer 1   Golfer 2   Golfer 2

Figure 1. Golfers' scores and regression to the mean.

Based on the regression to the mean phenomenon, we expect the difference between the two players to decrease in the second day, even though we predict that the first player will still do better than the second.

SURVIVORSHIP BIAS

Survivorship bias is the tendency to focus on survivors of some process over-looking those that did not survive. When assessing events, individuals tend to focus on winners instead of losers or on successes instead of failures. Because we are prone to remove failures (non-survivors) from our view, we end up missing potentially important information, often without recognizing that we are missing information at all.

If we think about launching a start-up because there are so many examples of successful start-ups in the world, we ignore the fact that only successful start-ups survive to become cases in point.[64]

Because of survivorship bias, we tend to see only the successes and ignore the failures. We focus on a few salient events that occurred rather than on the numerous events that failed to occur.

HINDSIGHT BIAS

Forecasting is almost impossible: reality emerges from the interaction of many different and often unpredictable agents and forces, including blind luck.[65]

Hindsight bias occurs when individuals believe that an event is more predictable after it becomes known than it was before it became known.

Research indicates that if an event actually occurred, people tend to overstate the probability that they had assigned to it before it occurred.[66]

Hindsight bias may cause memory distortion, where the recollection and reconstruction of events can lead to incorrect outcomes. The concept of *narrative fallacy* defines how inconsistent stories of the past affect our views of the world and our expectations for the future. The descriptive stories tend to ascribe a larger role to skill, talent, and plans than to luck and fail to recognize the conceivability of events that failed to occur.[67]

Hindsight bias leads to *outcome bias*: Decision makers tend to assess the quality of a decision only by the outcome and not by the process. However, owing to luck, at times even ill-advised decisions can work out well.

This is why stories of success and failure constantly overstate the impact of leadership practices on organizational results. As seen in the Randomness paragraph, the impact of CEOs on firm performance is usually limited.

We think we understand the past, which implies that we can also predict the future, but in fact we understand the past less than we believe we do.

LOSS AVERSION

Ask yourself the following question:

What would you prefer to receive as a present?

$80 for sure or a gamble stating that you have a 75% chance to win $100 and a 25% chance to win $30?

The expected value of the gamble is $(0.75 \times 100 + 0.25 \times 30) = (75 + 7.5) = \$82.5$. That is higher than $80.

However, most of us would select the sure option.

Let's look at another example. Assume you are presented a gamble on the toss of a coin.

If the coin shows tails, you lose $100. If the coin shows heads, you win $140.

To make a decision, you must balance the psychological benefit of winning $140 against the psychological cost of losing $100. Although the expected value of the gamble is evidently positive by $40, most people have an aversion to it. For most people, the fear of losing $100 is more powerful than the prospect of winning $140.

But what is the minimum expected gain that we require to offset the chance to lose $100?

For most people, it is around $200. The average loss aversion ratio has been estimated in the range of 1.5 to 2.5.

An interesting corollary of loss aversion is the *endowment effect*, the theory that people assign more value to things only because they own them. The endowment effect is based on the premise that once an individual owns a piece, giving it up feels like a loss, and individuals are loss averse. Forgoing a bottle of nice wine is more painful than getting an equally good bottle is gratifying.[68]

The role of loss aversion in negotiation has been recurrently verified: Making concessions hurts because we place a higher value on the concessions than the other party does.

Decisions are greatly biased in favor of the reference point and usually biased to favor small rather than large changes.

GOALS AS REFERENCE

A reference point is usually the status quo, but it can also be a goal: Not reaching a goal is a loss, beating the goal is a gain.

Loss aversion suggests that aversion to the disappointment of not reaching a goal is much stronger than the desire to achieve the goal.

A recent study analyzed professional golfers' putting performance (the putt is a light golf stroke that propels the ball into or near the hole in the green).[69] Golf provides a perfect example of a reference point with *par*, the number of strokes set as a standard for a specific hole or a complete golf course in expert play. Every hole on the golf course is associated with a standard number of strokes.

To test the loss aversion hypothesis, the researchers analyzed more than 2.5 million putts, focusing on two situations:

Putt to avoid a bogey and putt to achieve a birdie.

In golf, a *birdie* (one stroke under par) is a gain, and a *bogey* (one stroke over par) is a loss.

They found that golfers are significantly influenced by the reference point of par.

Golfers are much less accurate when stroking a birdie putt that would earn them a stroke under par than when they attempt similar putts for par or bogey.

Another interesting result of the research is that, controlling for putt characteristics, players tend to be more risk averse when putting for birdie than when putting for par or bogey.

When putting, golfers balance two objectives. One objective is to hit the ball into the hole. The second is to limit the difficulty of the following shot should they miss the putt. Risk-averse putts sacrifice the likelihood of hitting the ball into the hole to limit the difficulty of a follow-on shot. Therefore, shots for risk-averse putts tend to be short.

THE STATUS QUO BIAS

Very often, option for the default is just one less obstacle to cross when making a decision. In a world of uncertainty, defaults also signal what is the right thing to do.[70]

Most decisions have a status quo alternative: doing nothing or maintaining the current or previous decision. Various studies have shown that people tend to unduly choose the status quo. The advantage of the status quo increases with the number of options.[71]

The status quo bias can be considered a consequence of loss aversion: Individuals have a strong tendency to maintain the current state of affairs because the status quo is taken as a reference point, and any change from the standard is perceived as a loss.[72] *We tend to follow the path of least resistance.*

The status quo bias, the aversion to loss, and the endowment effect all contribute to inadequate strategy decisions. For example, they make CEOs hesitant to sell businesses. McKinsey research has shown that divestments are a major potential source of value creation but a largely disregarded one.[73]

FEAR OF REGRET

Fear of regret plays a crucial role in our decision-making process.

Facing the choice between a 90% chance to win $1 million or $170,000 with certainty, if you chose the first option and lose the gamble, you will surely regret the decision of not selecting the $170,000 option.

According to *regret theory*, in a situation of uncertainty, individuals anticipate feelings of regret if they make the wrong choice and take this anticipation into consideration when making decisions.[74]

Fear of regret is a key factor in most of the decisions we make: The experience of an outcome is subject to the choice we could have selected but did not.

PROBABILITY AND CHOICES

The decision weight that people assign to outcomes is not equal to the probability of these outcomes.

Improbable outcomes tend to be overweighed, and almost definite outcomes tend to be underweighted.[75]

Research has provided evidence that we cannot separate the evaluation of uncertain outcomes and the likelihood of their causing events.[76]

In a situation where there is a 95% chance of winning $10,000, people tend to be risk averse for fear of regret and agree to a disadvantageous option.

If the situation offers a 95% chance of losing $10,000, individuals tend to be risk seeking in the hope of avoiding loss and discard an advantageous option.

In a situation where there is a 5% chance of winning $10,000, people tend to be risk seeking in the hope of a large gain and discard an advantageous option.

If the situation offers a 5% chance of losing $10,000, individuals tend to be risk averse for fear of a large loss and agree to a disadvantageous option.

SUNK COSTS FALLACY

Sunk costs are those that have already been sustained and cannot be recovered. Consequently, sunk costs do not change regardless of any subsequent course of action.[77]

Once individuals have made a large sunk investment, they tend to invest more to prevent their previous investment from being lost.

The sunk cost fallacy is the tendency of individuals to invest additional resources in a losing option once an investment in time, effort, or money has already been made.

Even if according to mainstream theory individuals should ignore sunk costs to make a rational choice, people are nonetheless influenced by sunk costs in their decision making.

One explanation is based on loss aversion: We would rather spend an additional $1 million to complete an unprofitable $10 million project than forget $10 million.

Another explanation relies on anchoring: Once the brain has been anchored at $10 million, spending an additional $1 million doesn't look so bad.

One more explanation relies on our need to conform to the behavior and opinions of others. For most individuals, there is only one thing worse than making a huge strategic mistake: being the only person to make it.[78]

The sunk cost fallacy keeps people for too long in poor jobs, unhappy marriages, unpromising projects and partnerships without prospect.[79]

Nevertheless, there are times when honoring sunk costs is a rational choice (e.g., when past investments are relevant and reputation concerns or financial and time constraints are significant).[80]

FRAMING EFFECT

A framing effect occurs when equivalent descriptions of decision problems lead to systematically different decisions.[81] People respond to a specific option in different ways depending on whether it is described as a loss or a gain.

The following example illustrates the framing effect.[82]

The statistics about the results of a surgery for the treatment of lung cancer were provided to surgeons using two equivalent descriptions:

- The one-month survival rate is 90%.
- There is 10% mortality in the first month.

Surgery was much more popular in the former frame (84% of physicians chose it) than in the latter (where 50% favored the alternative option of radiation).

FALSE CONSENSUS EFFECT

The false consensus effect refers to the propensity of individuals to overestimate the degree to which other people share their beliefs, values, attitudes, habits, and behaviors.

When we have a specific belief, we tend to estimate that belief to be more common than it is.

For example, although religious fundamentalists do not believe that most people are radicals, their assessments of the percentage of religious fundamentalists in the general population can be higher than similar evaluations made by nonreligious individuals.[83]

According to research, the false consensus effect is partially motivated by our desire to maintain a positive opinion of our own convictions, supported by the fact that our beliefs are shared by most people.

Another explanation of the false consensus effect focuses on the fact that individuals tend to be exposed to and process information that supports their beliefs.

One more explanation of the false consensus relies on our socializing with people who share our beliefs and behaviors; in these circumstances, we rarely receive corrective feedback telling us when our assumptions are off the mark.

LESS IS MORE

Research has suggested that the more information decision makers have, the less they are able to make an optimal decision. Often the extra information is not only useless, but even detrimental because it confuses the issue and makes decision makers more confident in the accuracy of their inadequate decisions.

Frugality improves decision making. Take a complex problem and reduce it to its basic elements: Even very complex problems have an identifiable underlying pattern. Overloading the decision makers with information makes identifying the problem's signature more difficult.[84]

THE ROLE OF LUCK

Those who have succeeded at anything and don't mention luck are kidding themselves.[85]

Chance favors only the prepared mind.[86]

In the search for robust general laws of behavior, the social sciences tend to suppress the role of luck in shaping the course of events.[87] However, chance definitely plays a prominent role in defining the consequences and outcomes of our actions (and consequently our successes and failures).[88]

The fact that the differential skill is narrowing or, in other words, that skill improves, particularly in competitive markets, means that luck plays an even more important role in defining outcomes.[89]

It is also true that chance events do not just occur autonomously. Luck is not entirely unpredictable and uncontrollable. Furthermore, even though people have marginal influence over the occurrence of chance events, they can exert at least some control over their outcome.[90]

If we believe that luck is the result of an individual deliberately interacting with chance, the consequence is that some people are certainly better at interacting with chance than others.[91]

Those we call unlucky people tend to be more narrowly focused, controlling, impatient, and risk averse. Lucky people, on the other hand, tend to tolerate ambiguity well, constantly changing habits and seeking out new experiences. They are more risk prone and ready to expose themselves to random chance than unlucky people. They try more and different things.

In general, lucky people find emerging fields where there is differential skill or adopt disruptive strategies in competitive areas.[92]

In conclusion, what we call luck corresponds to the outcome of a pattern of behaviors that individuals adopt when interacting with events and people.

THE COGNITIVE REFLECTION TEST

Consider the following problem:

A bat and a ball cost $1.10. The bat costs $1.00 more than the ball.

How much does the ball cost? _____ cents.

In this case, a spontaneous answer jumps to mind: 10 cents. However, this answer is not correct. If the ball costs 10 cents, then the bat would cost $1.10 (the bat costs $1.00 more than the ball, $1.00 + $0.10 = $1.10) and therefore the bat and the ball would cost $1.20 ($1.10 + $0.10 = $1.20). The only correct solution is 5 cents.

A short three-item cognitive reflection test (CRT)[93] that includes the bat and ball challenge, can be used as a straightforward measure of an individual's cognitive ability to switch from System 1 to System 2 thinking when required.

The CRT[94] is composed of three problems:

- A bat and a ball cost $1.10. The bat costs $1.00 more than the ball. How much does the ball cost? _____ cents.

- If it takes 5 machines 5 minutes to make 5 widgets, how long would it take 100 machines to make 100 widgets? _____ minutes.
- In a lake, there is a patch of lily pads. Every day, the patch doubles in size. If it takes 48 days for the patch to cover the entire lake, how long would it take for the patch to cover half of the lake? _____ days.

The majority of people will give the intuitive wrong answers: 10, 100, and 24. Even among those who provide the correct answers, the intuitive wrong answers were the first to jump to mind.

In a survey of 3,428 people, one third of the respondents missed all three questions, and even among MIT-sampled students, less than half was able to correctly answer all questions.

An interesting corollary of the CRT is that respondents do much better if the problem is presented in a way that encourages computation. For example, respondents miss the bat and ball problem as presented earlier far more often than they miss the same problem presented in a different way:

A bat and a ball cost $1.23. The bat costs $1.07 more than the ball.

How much does the ball cost? _____ cents.

Many studies have supported the notion that both willingness to take risks and patience are systematically related to cognitive ability.[95]

Individuals with higher CRT scores are more patient and forgo immediate benefits for the sake of long-term reward.

Individuals with higher CRT scores are also more willing to take risks. According to the theory, people are more willing to take risks to avoid losses than to achieve gains. Individuals with higher cognitive ability display higher risk propensity than people with lower CRT scores, particularly in situations when they can achieve gains.[96]

Recent studies have also confirmed the link between patience and altruism[97] and even between cognitive ability and cooperation: Higher cognitive ability is related not only to patience, but also to cooperative behavior.[98] These findings come as no surprise, considering that it is quite intuitive that win-win strategies lead to higher long-term rewards.

The CRT has also highlighted another interesting result: Men tend to score significantly higher than women, suggesting that men are more likely to ponder their answers (System 2 thinking), while women tend to go with their intuition (System 1 thinking).

THE UNCONSCIOUS THOUGHT THEORY

The unconscious thought theory makes a distinction between two modes of thought: unconscious and conscious.[99]

Conscious thought is deliberate, methodical, effortful, logical, and analytical. The concept of conscious thought is analogous to the System 2 thinking approach seen in earlier paragraphs.

Unconscious thought is intuitive, effortless, instinctive, and associative. The concept of unconscious thought is similar but not identical to the System 1 thinking approach. The main difference is that while System 1 thinking is fast and emotional and tends to jump to conclusions, unconscious thought, to be effective, requires reactions to be delayed in time.

Unconscious thought can be defined as a slow and deliberate process that happens subconsciously.[100]

Even if counterintuitive, according to research, conscious thought leads to better decisions on simple issues, but worse choices on complex issues because of its low capacity to process multiple factors and its tendency to focus on specific factors.

On the other hand, unconscious thought leads to better choices when facing complex and ambiguous issues that require us to weigh multiple factors because of its capacity to integrate and process different attributes of choice against the importance of different weights and criteria. As a result, after some delay, unconscious thought will produce a definite intuition indicating the most appropriate option.

Unconscious thinking also facilitates divergent thinking and thus creativity because of its capacity to discover multiple associations between different ideas (more on this in chapter 11, Incubation).

It must be emphasized that *because unconscious processes require time the quality of decisions increases with the extent of unconscious thought.*

Conscious thinking is superior when individuals need to apply specific rules and generate accurate solutions to specific problems, such as an answer to 8 x 7.2. A conscious, analytical process is likely to produce the answer of 57.6. In contrast, an unconscious, intuitive process is likely to generate a more approximate answer, such as 60.[101]

When a decision strategy warrants the careful and strict application of one specific rule, as in a lexicographic strategy, use conscious thought. When matters become more complicated and weighting is called for, as in the weighting strategy, use unconscious thought.[102]

Recent research has partially disconfirmed the unconscious thought theory,[103] showing little if any difference in quality between decisions made under conscious deliberation conditions and those made unconsciously.

HOW CAN WE IMPROVE OUR DECISION-MAKING PROCESS?

The last and most comprehensive strategy when facing complex decisions is to adopt the following five-step approach:

- Be careful not to jump to conclusions. Be patient.
- Don't be overloaded with information. Identify the underlying pattern and reduce the problem to its basic elements without losing sight of the big picture and of the relationships among the different parts.
- Rely on simple algorithms when making statistical predictions. Equations perform significantly better than human judgment in making extrapolations.[104]
- Take time to organize and process all the options and weigh multiple factors.
- Learn to combine conscious deliberation with unconscious processing[105] and to balance between rational and intuitive thinking.[106]

(ENDNOTES)

1   John Maynard Keynes.

2   Simon, H. A., & Chase, W. G. (1973). Skill in chess. American Scientist, 61, 394-403.

3   Stanovich, K. E., & West, R. F. (2000). Individual difference in reasoning: Implications for the rationality debate?. Behavioural and Brain Sciences, 23, 645-726.

4   Kahneman, D. (2011). Thinking fast and slow. New York, NY: Farrar, Strauss, & Giroux.

5   Hughes, R. (2010). CULT-URE. London: Fiell Publishing.

6   Kahneman, D. (2011). Thinking fast and slow. New York, NY: Farrar, Strauss, & Giroux.

7   Forgas, J. P., Baumeister, R. F., & Tice, D. M. (2009). Psychology of self-regulation: Cognitive, affective, and motivational processes. New York, NY: Psychology Press.

8   Kahneman, D. (2011). Thinking fast and slow. New York, NY: Farrar, Strauss, & Giroux.

9   Vohs, K. D., Mead, N. L., & Goode, M. R. (2006). The psychological consequences of money. Science, 314, 1154-1156.

10   Bar, M. (2009). A cognitive neuroscience hypothesis of mood and depression. Trends in Cognitive Sciences, Vol. 13, N. 11, 456-463.

11   Cacioppo, J. T., & Petty, R. E. (1982). The need for cognition. Journal of Personality and Social Psychology, 42, 116-131.

12   Keinan, G. (1987). Decision Making Under Stress: Scanning of Alternatives Under Controllable and Uncontrollable Threats. Journal of Personality and Social Psychology, Vol. 52, N. 3, 639-644.

13   Maule, A. J., Hockey, G. R. J., & Bdzola, L. (2000). Effects of time-pressure on decision-making under uncertainty: Changes in affective state and information processing strategy. Acta Psychologica, 104, 283-301.

14   Gladwell, M. (2007). Blink: The power of thinking without thinking. New York, NY: Back Bay Books.

15   Artemus Ward.

16   Pronin, E., Gilovich, T., & Ross, L. (2004). Objectivity in the Eye of the Beholder: Divergent Perceptions of Bias in Self Versus Others. Psychological Review, Vol. 111, N. 3, 781-799.

17   Edwards, C. (2006). Mind reading. Old Windsor: Real Publishing.

18   Willis, J., & Todorov, A. (2006). First impressions: Making up your mind after a 100-ms exposure to a face. Psychological Science, Vol. 17, N. 7, 592-598.

19   Freeman, J. B, Penner, A. M., Saperstein, A., Scheutz, M., & Ambady, N. (2011). Looking the Part: Social Status Cues Shape Race Perception. PLoS ONE, Vol. 6, N. 9, e25107.

20   https://implicit.harvard.edu/implicit/

21   Gladwell, M. (2007). Blink: The power of thinking without thinking. New York, NY: Back Bay Books.

22   Kahneman, D. (2011). Thinking fast and slow. New York, NY: Farrar, Strauss, & Giroux.

23   Weingarten, G. (2007, April 8). Pearls before breakfast. Washington Post. Retrieved from http://www.washingtonpost.com/wp-dyn/content/article/2007/04/04/AR2007040401721.html

24   Russell, B. (2004). The proposed roads to freedom. New York, NY: Cosimo Classics.

25   Francis Bacon.

26   Gilovich, T. (1993). How we know what isn't so: The fallibility of human reason in everyday life. New York, NY: Free Press.

27   Greenspan, A. (2013). The map and the territory: Risk, human nature, and the future of forecasting. London: Penguin Press.

28   Loewenstein, G. F., Weber, E. U., Hsee, C. K., & Welch, N. (2001). Risk as a feeling. Psychological Bulletin. Vol. 127, N. 2, 267-286.

29   Hawkins, J. (2004). On intelligence. New York, NY: Owl Books.

30   Coates J. (2012). The hour between dog and wolf. Risk taking, gut feelings, and the biology of boom and bust. New York, NY: Random House.

31   Lerner, J. S., Li, Y., & Weber, E. U. (2013). The Financial Cost of Sadness. Psychological Science, Vol. 24, N. 1, 72-79.

32   Hoorens, V. (1993). Self-enhancement and Superiority Biases in Social Comparison. European Review of Social Psychology, Vol. 4, N. 1, 113-139.

33   Cross, K. P. (1977). Not can, but will college teaching be improved?. New Directions for Higher Education, 17, 1-15.

34   Roxburh, C. (2003). Hidden flaws in Strategy. McKinsey Quarterly, N. 2, 26-39.

35   Zuckerman, E. W., & Jost, J. (2001). What Makes You Think You're So Popular? Self -Evaluation Maintenance and the Subjective Side of the "Friendship Paradox". Social Psychology Quarterly, Vol. 64, N.3, 207-223.

36   Gilovich, T. (1993). How we know what isn't so: The fallibility of human reason in everyday life. New York, NY: Free Press.

37   Superiority illusion arises from resting-state brain networks modulated by dopamine, retrieved from www.pnas.org/cgi/doi/10.1073/pnas.1221681110

38   Moore, D. A. (2007). Not so above average after all: When people believe they are worse than average and its implications for theories of bias in social comparison. Organizational Behavior and Human Decision Processes, Vol. 102, N. 1, 42-58.

39   Bernsten, D., & Bohn, A. (2010). Remembering and forecasting: The relation between autobiographical memory and episodic future thinking. Memory & Cognition, Vol. 38, N. 3, 265-278.

40   Buehler, R., Griffin, D., & Ross, M. (2002). Inside the planning fallacy: The causes and consequences of optimistic time predictions. In T. Gilovich, D. Griffin, & D. Kahneman (Eds.), Heuristics and biases: The psychology of intuitive judgment. Cambridge, UK: Cambridge University Press.

41   Lovallo, D., & Kahneman D. (2003). Delusions of success. How optimism undermines executives' decisions. Harvard Business Review, Vol. 81, N. 7, 56-63.

42   Finucane, M. L., Alhakami, A., Slovic, P., & Johnson, S. M. (2000). The affect heuristic in judgments of risks and benefits. Journal of Behavioral Decision Making, 13, 1-17.

43   Hughes, R. (2010). CULT-URE. London: Fiell Publishing.

44   Gilovich, T. (1993). How we know what isn't so: The fallibility of human reason in everyday life. New York, NY: Free Press.

45   Ormerod, P. (2007). Why most things fail, New York, NY: John Wiley & Sons.

46   Guy, R. K. (1988). The strong law of small numbers. American Mathematical Monthly, Vol. 95, N. 8, 696-712.

47   Strack, F., & Mussweiler, T. (1997). Explaining the enigmatic anchoring effect: Mechanisms of selective accessibility. Journal of Personality and Social Psychology, Vol. 73, N. 39, 437-446.

48   Hughes, R. (2010). CULT-URE. London: Fiell Publishing.

49   Kahneman, D. (2011). Thinking fast and slow. New York, NY: Farrar, Strauss, & Giroux.

50   Kahneman, D. (2011). Thinking fast and slow. New York, NY: Farrar, Strauss, & Giroux.

51   Tversky, A., & Simonson, I. (1993). Context-Dependent Preferences. Management Science, Vol. 39, N. 10, 1179-1189.

52   Kahneman, D. (2011). Thinking fast and slow. New York, NY: Farrar, Strauss, & Giroux.

53   Schwarz, N., Strack, F., Bless, H., Klumpp, G., Rittenauer-Schatka, H., & Simons, A. (1991). Ease of retrieval as information: Another look at the availability heuristic. Journal of Personality and Social Psychology, Vol. 61, N. 2, 195-202.

54   Kahneman, D. (2011). Thinking fast and slow. New York, NY: Farrar, Strauss, & Giroux.

55   Gilovich, T., & Savitsky, K. (1996). Like goes with like: The role of representativeness in erroneous and pseudoscientific beliefs. Skeptical Inquirer, Vol. 20, N. 2, 34-40.

56   Gilovich, T. (1993). How we know what isn't so: The fallibility of human reason in everyday life. New York, NY: Free Press.

57   Kahneman, D. (2011). Thinking fast and slow. New York, NY: Farrar, Strauss, & Giroux.

58   Kahneman, D. (2011). Thinking fast and slow. New York, NY: Farrar, Strauss, & Giroux.

59   Gilovich, T., & Savitsky, K. (1996). Like goes with like: The role of representativeness in erroneous and pseudoscientific beliefs. Skeptical Inquirer, Vol. 20, N. 2, 34-40.

60   Bland, J. M., & Altman, D. G. (1994). Statistics notes: Regression towards the mean. British Medical Journal, 308, 1499.

61   Galton, F. (1886). Regression towards mediocrity in hereditary stature. The Journal of the Anthropological Institute of Great Britain and Ireland, Vol. 15, 246-263.

62   Gilovich, T. (1993). How we know what isn't so: The fallibility of human reason in everyday life. New York, NY: Free Press.

63   Kahneman, D. (2011). Thinking fast and slow. New York, NY: Farrar, Strauss, & Giroux.

64   Taleb, N. N. (2007). The black swan: The impact of the highly improbable. New York, NY: Random House.

65   Kahneman, D. (2011). Thinking fast and slow. New York, NY: Farrar, Strauss, & Giroux.

66   Roese, N. J., & Vohs, K. D. (2012). Hindsight Bias. Perspectives on Psychological Science, Vol. 7, N. 5, 411-426.

67   Taleb, N. N. (2007). The black swan: The impact of the highly improbable. New York, NY: Random House.

68   Kahneman, D., Knetsh, J. L., & Thaler, R. H. (1990). Experimental Tests of the Endowment Effect and the Coase Theorem. The Journal of Political Economy, Vol. 98, N. 6, 1325-1348.

69   Pope, D. G., & Schweitzer, M. E. (2011). Is Tiger Woods Loss Averse? Persistent Bias in the Face of Experience, Competition, and High Stakes. American Economic Review, 101, 129-157.

70   Cartwright, E. (2011). Behavioral economics. New York, NY: Routledge.

71   Samuelson, W., & Zeckhauser, R. (1988). Status Quo Bias in Decision Making. Journal of Risk and Uncertainty, 1, 7-59.

72   Kahneman, D., Knetsch, J. L., & Thaler, R. H. (1991). Anomalies: The Endowment Effect, Loss Aversion, and Status Quo Bias. Journal of Economic Perspectives, Vol. 5, N. 1, 193-206.

73   Roxburh, C. (2003). Hidden flaws in Strategy. McKinsey Quarterly, N. 2, 26-39.

74   Loomes, G., & Sugden, R. (1982). Regret theory: An Alternative Theory of Rational Choice Under Uncertainty. The Economic Journal, Vol. 92, N. 368, 805-824.

75   Kahneman, D., & and Tversky, A. (1979). Prospect Theory: An Analysis of Decision under Risk. Econometrica, Vol. 47, N. 2, 263-292.

76   Weber, E. U. (1994). From Subjective Probabilities to Decision Weights: The Effect of Asymmetric Loss Functions on the Evaluation of Uncertain Outcomes and Events. Psychological Bulletin, Vol. 115, N. 2, 228-242.

77   McAfee, R. P., Mialon, H. M., & Mialon, S. H. (2010). Do Sunk Costs Matter?. Economic Inquiry, Vol. 48, N. 2, 323-336.

78   Roxburh, C. (2003). Hidden flaws in Strategy. McKinsey Quarterly, N. 2, 26-39.

79   Kahneman, D. (2011). Thinking fast and slow. New York, NY: Farrar, Strauss, & Giroux.

80   Kelly, T. (2004). Sunk Costs, Rationality, and Acting for the Sake of the Past. Noûs, March, Vol. 38, N. 1, 60-85.

81   Sher, S., & McKenzie, C. R. M. (2008). Framing effects and rationality. In N. Chater, & M. Oaksford (Eds.), The Probabilistic mind: Prospects for Bayesian cognitive science. Oxford: Oxford University Press.

82   Kahneman, D. (2011). Thinking fast and slow. New York, NY: Farrar, Strauss, & Giroux.

83   Gilovich, T. (1993). How we know what isn't so: The fallibility of human reason in everyday life. New York, NY: Free Press.

84   Gladwell, M. (2007). Blink: The power of thinking without thinking. New York, NY: Back Bay Books.

85   Larry L. King.

86   Louis Pasteur.

87   Krantz, D. L. (1998). Taming Chance: Social Science and Everyday Narratives. Psychological Inquiry, Vol. 9, N. 2, 87-94.

88   Bandura, A. (1982). The Psychology of Chance Encounters and Life Paths. American Psychologist, Vol. 37, N. 7, 747-755.

89   Mauboussin, M. J. (2012). The Success Equation: Untangling Skill and Luck in Business, Sports, and Investing. Cambridge, MA: Harvard Business Review Press.

90   Bandura, A. (1998). Exploration of fortuitous determinants of life paths. Psychological Inquiry, 9, 95-99.

91   Wiseman, R. (2003). The Luck Factor. Skeptical Inquirer, Vol. 27, N. 3, 26-30.

92   Mauboussin, M. J. (2012). The Success Equation: Untangling Skill and Luck in Business, Sports, and Investing. Cambridge, MA: Harvard Business Review Press.

93   Frederick, S. (2005). Cognitive Reflection and Decision Making. Journal of Economic Perspectives. Vol. 19, N. 4, 25-42.

94   Frederick, S. (2005). Cognitive Reflection and Decision Making. Journal of Economic Perspectives. Vol. 19, N. 4, 25-42.

95   Dohmen, T., Falk, A., Huffman, D., & Sunde, U. (2010). Are risk aversion and impatience Related to Cognitive Ability?. American Economic Review, Vol. 100, N. 3, 1238-1260.

96   Frederick, S. (2005). Cognitive Reflection and Decision Making. Journal of Economic Perspectives. Vol. 19, N. 4, 25-42.

97   Curry, O. S., Price, M. E., & Price, J. G. (2008). Patience is a virtue: cooperative people have lower discount rates. Personality and Individual Differences, Vol. 44, N. 3, 780-785.

98   Chia-Ching, C., I-Ming, C., Smith J., & Yamada, T. (2012). Too smart to be selfish? Measures of cognitive ability, social preferences, and consistency. Munich Personal RePEc Archive, Paper N. 41078.

99   Dijksterhuis, A., & Nordgren, L. F. (2006). A theory of unconscious thought. Perspectives on Psychological Science, 1, 95-109.

100 Bos, M. W., Dijksterhuis, A., & van Baaren, R. B. (2011). The benefits of sleeping on things: Unconscious thought leads to automatic weighting. Journal of Consumer Psychology, Vol. 21, N. 1, 4-8.

101 Moss, S. (2008). Unconscious thinking theory, retrieved from http://www.psych-it.com.au/psychlopedia/article.asp?id=59

102 Dijksterhuis, A., & Nordgren, L. F. (2006). A theory of unconscious thought. Perspectives on Psychological Science, 1, 95-109.

103 Huizenga, H. M., Wetzels, R., van Ravenzwaaij, D., & Wagenmakers, E. J. (2012). Four empirical tests of Unconscious Thought Theory. Organizational Behavior and Human Decision Processes, 117, 332-340.

104 McAfee, A. (2014, January 7). The Future of Decision Making: Less Intuition, More Evidence. Harvard Business Review Blog Network, retrieved from http://blogs.hbr.org/2010/01/the-future-of-decision-making/

105 Bos, M. W., Dijksterhuis, A., & van Baaren, R. B. (2011). The benefits of sleeping on things: Unconscious thought leads to automatic weighting. Journal of Consumer Psychology, Vol. 21, N. 1, 4-8.

106 Gladwell, M. (2007). Blink: The power of thinking without thinking. New York, NY: Back Bay Books.

CHAPTER 10:

Decision Making Across Cultures

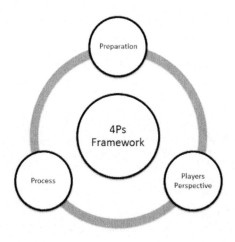

Stage 1: Preparation. Stage 2: Process. Stage 4: Players' Perspective

INTRODUCTION

If we study individuals without regard for their environments (physical, social, and cultural), we may not understand many of the reasons that guide their cognitive process and behavior.

A large body of research today supports cognitive differences between cultures.

Differences in decision making across cultures are the result of dissimilarities in values, beliefs, philosophies, and social orientation.

The main difference is in *analytical* (Western) thinking versus *holistic* (Eastern) thinking, but there is also remarkable dissimilarity in the decision-making patterns between cultures with an *independent* vs. *interdependent* orientation. Research has confirmed that different views of the self across cultures influence individuals' cognition, motivation, and behavior.

IMPLICIT MOTIVES AND BEHAVIOR

Three main factors affect and shape an individual's mental processes and behavior: (a) *personality traits*, (b) *cognitions* such as attitudes, beliefs, goals, and values, and (c) *motivations*.

According to research, goal-directed behavior is generated by two types of motives: *implicit* and *explicit*.

Each type of motive is associated with different information processing:[1] [2]

Implicit motives are fairly enduring, unconscious needs, linked to System 1 thinking, which automatically, quickly, effortlessly, and efficiently processes information.

Explicit motives are tangible rewards affected by social norms, associated with System 2 thinking, our rational system, which actively, slowly, deliberately, and logically processes information.

Implicit motivations are thus central in understanding and predicting human behavior.

Individuals are different, and their behavior can be explained by taking into account variables such as values, motives, skills, circumstances, and personality traits.

As a generalization, we can say that in most individualistic cultures behavior is mainly affected by the individual's needs and personality traits, while in most collectivistic cultures, it is influenced by the socio-cultural context and the requirements of a specific circumstance.[3]

SELF-VERIFICATION MOTIVES

Self-verification theory focuses on people's need to be known and understood by others.

According to the theory, individuals universally tend to prefer others who confirm their self-views; the psychological comfort derived from their self-views reflecting social reality provides them with a sense of coherence, certainty, order, and control.[4]

According to most theories, the need for psychological consistency and security is universal.

Across cultures, the satisfaction and durability of our relationships depend on the self-verification process. Individuals select a social environment that provides them with constancy regarding their self-views.

To maintain a sense of psychological coherence, individuals consider self-verifying information to be more reasonable than non-verifying information. Therefore, they tend to disregard, interpret, or misunderstand disconfirming feedback.

Interdependence encourages members of collectivistic societies to develop stable, meaningful, and distinct context-specific selves, which are shaped to conform to different relationship partners and different situations. Members of collectivistic cultures will seek confirmation for each of their different and situational selves.

Independence, on the other hand, encourages members of individualistic cultures to seek confirmation of their comprehensive and universal self.

AGENCY AND SELF-EFFICACY

In sociology and philosophy, agency is the capacity of individuals to make choices and act. Self-efficacy is the ability to persist and succeed with a task.

Agency, people's capacity to make decisions and act accordingly, is highly affected by beliefs regarding self-efficacy.

The belief that one has the ability to produce the desired outcomes through one's actions is crucial in motivating individuals to persevere in the face of difficulties.[5]

A high degree of personal efficacy is just as important in collectivistic societies as it is in individualistic societies.

In addition, group goals are as demanding as individual goals. The difference is that in collectivistic cultures the focus is on *duty*, while in individualistic societies the focus is on *rights*. In collectivistic societies, duty is crucial to the conception of the collective self, while in individualistic cultures, rights are important components of the individual self.[6]

People who work interdependently in collectivistic societies need to successfully perform their role, as do people who work independently in individualistic societies.

In collectivistic cultures, members are respected for their personal contributions to group achievements.

In a study on students' perceived self-efficacy, adolescents in Hong Kong and Japan obtained the lowest self-efficacy scores, while Costa Ricans and Russians obtained the highest.[7]

The self-efficacy belief of students in most East Asian cultures is influenced by socio-cultural attributes such as high achievement standards, an emphasis on hard work, effort, and performance, and the trivial importance assigned to ability and talent.

In Hong Kong, for example, high standards of achievement are associated with high parental expectations; students are infrequently praised for good work, but they are commonly reprimanded for poor performance. Furthermore, performance feedback is usually private, hindering the possibility for social comparison.

Average students, therefore, come across fewer events that can contribute to the development of strong self-efficacy beliefs.

East Asian students have lower agency beliefs related to innate ability and higher agency beliefs related to effort. They tend to attribute successes and failures to effort rather than ability, in contrast to students from Western countries who tend to make more ability-based attributions.[8]

In general, self-efficacy tends to be lower in cultures that place little emphasis on self-reliance and independence.

Self-efficacy is also lower in *tight cultures*, where social norms are explicit and obligatory and conventional behavior is enforced through monitoring and sanctioning from institutions such as family and school with no room for interpretation.[9]

On the other hand, self-efficacy tends to be higher in *loose cultures*, where social norms are flexible and informal and individuals have to set goals and find ways to implement them.

SELF-IMPROVING PATTERNS

Research has confirmed that although the self-enhancement motive is universal, its magnitude is influenced by cultural factors: East Asians tend to self-enhance less and to view themselves more critically than do North Americans.[10]

Research has also revealed marked self-improving motivations among East Asians.

These differences in self-critical and self-improving motivations are considerable and consistent.

A recent study confirmed that similar patterns also emerge in non-Asian collectivist cultures.[11]

The authors found a self-enhancing orientation among North Americans, where people persisted longer on a task if they had earlier received success feedback for that task. Americans are more likely to switch to a new task after failing on one than they are after succeeding.

In contrast, the Japanese exhibited a self-improving pattern, in which people persisted longer following failure than success. The same self-improving pattern was found among Chileans, confirming that self-critical and self-improving motivations are not limited to East Asian societies but may generalize to other collectivist cultures.

Like the Japanese, Chileans are more likely to switch to a new task after succeeding on one than they are after failing.

MODES OF THINKING

Our mind is capable of passing beyond the dividing line we have drawn for it. Beyond the pairs of opposites of which the world consists, other, new insights begin.[12]

Researchers have constantly found different patterns of thinking and perception in different societies, with some cultures indicating a more analytic pattern and others a more holistic pattern.

The division between what can be known and reasoned logically versus what can only be experienced and apprehended has been described in different ways: rational vs. intuitive, analytical vs. holistic, differentiative vs. integrative, Western vs. Eastern.

Western modes of thinking are mainly rooted in Greek and Aristotelian logic and the European traditions of rationalism, idealism, and enlightenment. The main features of Aristotelian thinking are:

- *Linearity*: The whole can be understood in term of its parts.

- *Synthesis-orientation*: Emphasis is on consistency and stability through integration and synthesis.
- *Universalism*: There is an inclination toward logical and analytical thinking, including a predisposition for universal, context-independent rules and categories.[13]

Aristotelian thinking aims to resolve contradiction by combining separate elements to form a coherent whole (Hegelian dialectic of thesis, antithesis, and synthesis).

To avoid cognitive dissonance[14] (the feeling of discomfort when simultaneously holding two or more conflicting ideas or beliefs), contradictory phenomena are understood as being separate and dichotomous. In other words, according to Aristotelian either-or thinking, conflicting factors cannot occur simultaneously.

Asian modes of thinking are mainly based on Hinduism, Buddhism, Confucianism, and Taoism. Asian dialectical thinking emphasizes the following notions:[15]

- *Change*: All phenomena are fluid and constantly evolving.
- *Holism*: All elements are interconnected and mutually dependent.
- *Contradiction*: All phenomena consist of opposing, complementary, and balanced elements.
- *Relativism*: There is an inclination toward concrete perception and direct experience and a greater tendency to rely on context, relationships, and situational factors when making decisions.[16]

Examples of the concepts of contradiction, holism, and change are the yin and yang symbol of Taoism that represents mutually dependent, complementary, and harmonious opposites and the notion of Trimurti in Hinduism: The cosmic functions of creation, maintenance, and destruction are personified by Brahma the creator, Vishnu the preserver and Shiva the destroyer.[17]

Asian dialectical thinking is focused on context and situation, which makes the simultaneous occurrence of conflicting elements possible.

We have broadly defined Western and Eastern modes of thinking, but what about nations that are positioned in the midpoint, such as Middle East countries?

According to research, Middle Eastern people display a higher level of integrative and holistic thinking than the Euro-Canadian group.[18]

One study focused on discourse and decision-making tasks that measured the number and diversity of topics linked together in a thought unit. Middle Eastern individuals were able to link different topics, while Euro-Canadian individuals showed a tendency to focus on one topic at a time.

According to the research,[19] differentiative and analytical thinking is predominant among industrial societies with highly dense sedentary populations, relatively low levels of social stratification, and low socialization emphasis.

On the other hand, integrative and holistic thinking is prevalent in agricultural societies with moderate populations, high levels of social stratification, and strong socialization emphasis.

An old Jewish story tells about two litigants appearing before the town's rabbi. The first litigant having presented his case, the rabbi tells him: You are right. Then the second litigant presents his case, and the rabbi tells him, too: You are right. After the litigants had gone, the rabbi's wife reproaches him: How can they both be right? The rabbi listens to her attentively, and says: You know what? You are right, too.[20]

HEURISTICS ACROSS CULTURES

As seen in the previous chapter, heuristics are mental shortcuts that reduce the cognitive effort involved in the decision-making process and usually consist of focusing on one specific trait of a complex problem, ignoring other important elements.

The following paragraphs present the results of several studies that have determined how heuristic thinking differs across cultures.

PROBABILITY JUDGMENT AND OVERCONFIDENCE

As seen in the previous chapter, individuals tend to overestimate their knowledge, underestimate risks, and exaggerate their ability to control events.

According to research, probability judgments, or confidence about the certainty of an outcome, differ across cultures.[21]

Studies among Japanese, Chinese, and American respondents have confirmed that overconfidence tends to be particularly strong in Chinese culture and weak among the Japanese.[22]

The Japanese not only displayed less overconfidence, but also demonstrated more systematic decision-making behavior, taking more time to answer questions and generating more counterarguments, than Chinese and American participants.

Two plausible explanations for Chinese overconfidence can be brought forward:

- The Chinese are not taught how to make probability judgments. They would rather answer a problem under conditions of uncertainty through trial and error.
- The Chinese are taught to follow specific rules for approaching various cognitive tasks and, among them, to memorize specific cases.

As a result, because the Chinese educational system promotes respect for tradition, individuals tend to search for confirming evidence of their initial judgment and, consequently, be overly confident in their conclusions.

Another recent study found that overconfidence not only affects participants in studies, it also affects scientists who are trained to present unbiased results.[23]

Chinese researchers were more overconfident in their conclusions and less able to generate arguments against their research than other researchers.

CORRELATION IS NOT CAUSATION

The correlation implies causation fallacy claims that if two events occur concurrently, they must have a cause and effect relationship. Furthermore, events and their causes must correspond in magnitude.

One famous example of correlation that doesn't imply causation is provided by the comparison between the total US highway fatality rate and the metric tons of fresh lemons imported from Mexico.[24]

The data show an almost perfect correlation between the two variables: As the amount of imported lemons increases, so do the traffic fatalities. However, it is evident that there is no causal relationship between the two: Importing lemons does not cause traffic fatalities and stopping the import of lemons would not decrease the number of traffic fatalities.

Possibly the most famous example of a correlation being evident but causation being unclear is from smoking and lung cancer in the 1950s. There was no doubt that a correlation existed between lung cancer and smoking, but proving the causality was not easy. The increase in the rate of lung cancer could have, for example, been the result of better diagnosis or more pollution.[25]

It took a study first published in 1956, involving more than 40,000 doctors in the UK, to irrefutably link tobacco smoking to a number of serious diseases, including lung cancer.[26]

According to research involving Canadian and Chinese participants, Canadians expected events and their causes to correspond in magnitude to a greater degree than did the Chinese.

Furthermore, Canadians primed to reason holistically expected less cause-effect magnitude correspondence than did those primed to reason analytically.[27]

As a result, we can state that analytical thinking favors the correlation implies causation fallacy.

RISK PERCEPTION

In one study, American, German, Polish, and Chinese participants were asked to assess a set of financial investment options, measuring their willingness to pay and their risk perception.[28]

The Chinese showed the lowest risk perception and the highest willingness to pay, and Americans were at the opposite pole.

According to the *cushion hypothesis*,[29] Chinese managers are part of a large and tight relationship network that provides individuals with economic support against financial worst-case outcomes. As a result, the Chinese perceive the same financial situation as being less risky than Americans do.

However, the same collectivist cushion that protects the Chinese from financial loss cautions them from seeking social support in the face of adverse conditions, out of fear of disrupting social harmony and losing face.[30]

Risk perception differences are thus specific to the financial domain. In the social domain, the pattern reversed, with the Chinese being less risk seeking.

Another study compared the content of Chinese, German, and American proverbs to collect further evidence on cultural differences in risk taking. Regardless of the nationality of the raters, Chinese proverbs were judged to recommend greater risk taking than American and German proverbs, suggesting that differences in risk-taking are rooted in traditional teachings.[31]

Similar research has shown that Singaporeans and Chinese participants are less risk averse than Dutch and New Zealanders over both gain- and loss-framed situations when making a personal financial decision. A second study has displayed that Singaporeans and Japanese are less risk averse than New Zealanders and Americans when deciding whether to switch supplier, under both a gain and a loss frame.[32]

Another study assessed cross-cultural differences in the perception of financial risks among participants from Hong Kong, Taiwan, the US, and the Netherlands.

The results demonstrated that the perception of risk among respondents from Hong Kong and Taiwan was affected by the magnitude of the potential loss, while the perception of respondents from the US and the Netherlands was influenced by the probability of the potential loss.[33]

Another important factor influencing risk perception and motivation is how cultures cope with uncertainty.

Individuals from uncertainty-oriented cultures (such as Canada and the US) tend to accept and manage uncertainty and therefore are more likely driven by the possibility of a positive outcome.

Individuals form certainty-oriented cultures (such as Japan) tend to avoid uncertainty and therefore are more likely driven by the fear of a possible failure.[34] When negotiating with certainty-oriented individuals, it is crucial to minimize the risks involved in the deal.

ENDOWMENT EFFECT

Endowment occurs when an owner places greater value on a possession than potential buyers do.

In one study, all participants validated the endowment effect; however, European-American and European-Canadian participants displayed a greater endowment effect than Asian, Asian-American, and Asian-Canadian participants.

The researchers assigned these cultural differences to the more independent self-construal of individualistic societies versus the more interdependent self-construal of collectivistic cultures.[35]

ATTRIBUTION BIAS

A fundamental challenge facing social perceivers is identifying the cause underlying other people's behavior.

In social psychology, attribution is the process of explaining the causes of events or behaviors. Evidence indicates that East Asian perceivers are more likely than Western perceivers to reference the social context when attributing a cause to target a person's actions.[36]

Three main *attribution* biases affect the way we determine the reasons behind an action or occurrence:[37]

- *Fundamental attribution error*: The tendency to overestimate dispositional (internal or personality-based) causes of others' behavior while underestimating situational (external) explanations.
- *Actor-observer effect*: The tendency to attribute own behavior to situational factors and, on the other hand, others' actions to dispositional causes.
- *Self-serving bias*: The tendency to attribute dispositional factors for success and situational causes for failure.

Athletes tend to attribute their successes to themselves but to blame their losses on external factors, such as the weather or bad luck.

Students who do well on an exam tend to attribute their performance to dispositional factors and to assess the examination process as fair; those who fail tend to blame their failure on situational factors and to judge the exam as arbitrary and unfair.

Teachers tend to attribute a student's success to the quality of instruction the student received but to blame a student's failure on the student's lack of ability or effort.[38]

Research has shown that culture affects how people make attributions.[39]

People from individualistic cultures are more inclined to make fundamental attribution errors than people from collectivistic cultures. Individualistic cultures tend to attribute a person's behavior to dispositional factors, while collectivistic cultures tend to attribute a person's behavior to situational factors.

Individualistic cultures engage in self-serving bias more than do collectivist cultures: Individualist cultures tend to attribute success to dispositional factors and to attribute failure to situational factors.

On the other hand, collectivistic cultures engage in *self-effacing bias*, the opposite of self-serving bias: Collectivistic cultures tend to attribute success to situational factors and blame failure on dispositional factors.

Research has also shown that while North Americans experience more biases than East Asians, East Asians make attribution errors that North Americans do not. When assessing an action or decision made by a group or organization (and not by an individual), East Asians display a stronger dispositionist bias than do North Americans; they explain the success or failure of an organization in terms of internal dispositions, such as its discipline, authority, or harmony, rather than in terms of external factors, such as the competition or the environment.[40]

Research has verified that attribution, the process by which individuals explain the causes of behaviors and events, has three fundamental causal dimensions that have cross-situational generality:[41] *locus, stability,* and *controllability.*

Locus refers to the position of a cause, which can be either inside or outside the actor. For example, ability and effort are considered dispositional (internal) causes of success, whereas chance and support from the family are interpreted as situational (external) causes.

Locus influences feelings of accomplishment and self-esteem. If the locus of the cause is internal, for example, with success due to effort and ability, the consequence is an increase in pride and self-esteem.

Self-esteem would not increase if the success was due to an external factor, such as chance or help from fellow students.

Causal stability refers to the duration of a cause. Some causes, such as aptitude for geometry, are perceived as invariable, while causes such as chance are considered unpredictable and temporary.

If a cause is considered stable, then the same result will be expected following either a success or a failure. If failure is perceived as due to lack of ability or an unfair boss, then another assessment from the same boss will be expected to result in one more failure.

In contrast, failure perceived as due to unstable factors, such as bad luck or lack of preparation, is not an indicator that there will be more failure.

Finally, some causes are under our control and others are not. Effort is controllable, while chance and ability are not.

Controllability, in combination with locus, defines whether guilt or shame is experienced following failure to reach a goal. Attribution of failure to scarce effort, which is internal and controllable, often produces guilt in combination with regret.

On the other hand, an attribution of failure to lack of ability, which is internal but uncontrollable, tends to induce feelings of shame and embarrassment.

Expectancy of success, as a consequence of the causal stability dimension, combined with feelings of pride, guilt, regret, shame, and anxiety are believed to define following behavior.

In other words, *behavior is a function of thoughts and feelings.*[42]

We have discussed cultural influences on attribution biases. Culture and other situational factors can also concern the goals for which one is striving, the perception of a success or failure, and the dimensions of locus, stability, and controllability of causes.

PERCEIVED CONSENSUS

As much as we like to think of ourselves as individuals, the fact is that we're driven to fit in and to conform to be liked and accepted by others.

This is why most individuals tend to conform and align their attitudes, beliefs, and behaviors to group norms and to change their behavior to match the responses of others.[43]

In many cases, when people strive for consensus within a group, they not only align their beliefs to group norms, but even dismiss their own personal beliefs and adopt the opinion of the rest of the group. In groupthink, contrary evidence is quickly rejected, and individuals who are opposed to the decisions or prevailing opinion of the group, frequently suppress their beliefs to minimize conflict and avoid disrupting relationships.[44]

A key factor that influences social cognition across cultures is individuals' perceptions of their culture's consensual beliefs: People's thoughts and behaviors are motivated by their perceptions of what the majority in their society believes.

In other words, *what others think affects our cognition and behavior.*

Research has confirmed that perceived cultural consensus has considerable influence in predicting social judgment and, even more important, the influence of perceived cultural consensus is similarly robust across cultures.[45]

BASIC VALUES

Shalom Schwartz (2012) identified 10 universal human values that reflect individuals' universal needs, social motives, and social institutional demands.[46]

The values theory defines 10 comprehensive values, distinguishing one from another according to the goal or motivation that underlies each of them.

As in chapter 2, Schwartz also introduced the value type theory, suggesting that seven cultural dimensions (types of values) address the three basic problems with which all societies must cope. According to Schwartz, individual and cultural levels of analysis are conceptually independent.

Individual-level dimensions reflect the psychological dynamics that individuals experience when acting on their values in everyday life, while cultural-level dimensions reflect the solutions that societies find to regulate human actions.

The 10 basic values that we discuss here are part of an individual level of analysis. The human values identified are:

- *Self-Direction*: The defining motivation is independent and action-oriented thought (creativity, curiosity, selecting own goals, independence).
- *Stimulation*: The defining motivation is excitement, novelty, and challenge in life.
- *Hedonism*: The defining motivation is pleasure and enjoying life.
- *Achievement*: The defining motivation is personal success associated with social approval (success, capability, ambition, influence).
- *Power*: The defining motivation is social status and prestige, control, or dominance over people and resources (authority, wealth, social power).
- *Security*: The defining motivation is safety, harmony, and stability of society, of relationships, and of self (social order, group security, reciprocation of favors).
- *Conformity*: The defining motivation is restraint of actions, inclinations, and impulses likely to upset or harm others and violate social expectations or norms (self-discipline, obedience, politeness, honoring parents and elders).
- *Tradition*: The defining motivation is respect, commitment, and acceptance of the customs and ideas that traditional culture or religion provides (respect, devotion, modesty).
- *Benevolence*: The defining motivation is preservation and improvement of the welfare of people with whom one is in frequent personal contact, the in-group (assistance, honesty, forgiveness, loyalty, responsibility).
- *Universalism*: The defining motivation is understanding, appreciation, tolerance, and protection for the welfare of all (tolerance, social justice, equality, wisdom, unity with nature). This value conflicts with the in-group focus of benevolence.

In addition to identifying 10 basic values, the theory explains the structure of dynamic relationships among them. The quest is for any value that has corollaries that conflict with some values but fit with others.

An example of this is pursuing achievement conflicts with pursuing benevolence. However, pursuing both achievement and power values is usually congruent.

The circular structure illustrated in Figure 1 represents the pattern of relationships of conflict and compatibility among values.

Figure 1. Schwartz's (2012) basic values.

Adjacent values are conceptually close to one another, while opposite values convey conceptually diametrical goals in life.

Even though the theory categorizes 10 values, it suggests that, basically, the values form a continuum of correlated motivations that create the circular structure.

The relationships among the 10 values can be summarized in two fundamental conflicts (analogous to the two dimensions of the World Values Survey introduced in chapter 3):

self-enhancement versus *self-transcendence* and *openness to change* versus *conservation.*

Self-enhancement values include power and achievement. These values conflict with self-transcendence values such as benevolence and universalism.

Openness-to-change values are represented by stimulation and self-direction. These values conflict with conservation values such as tradition, conformity, and security.

Hedonism shares elements of both openness to change and self-enhancement.

An alternative structure categorizes values into *person-focused* (self-direction, stimulation, hedonism, achievement, power) versus *social-focused* (universalism, benevolence, tradition, conformity, security).

The theory has been validated across 82 countries. Even if individuals differ substantially in the importance they attribute to the 10 values, the structure of relationships among values is shared across all cultures.

Social Axioms

As seen in chapter 2, most cross-cultural research has been based on value dimensions (e.g., Hofstede (2001), Schwartz (1999), Trompenaars (1997), and others). Searching for a complementary framework, some researchers have selected a construct based on beliefs, defined as assumptions and convictions that are held to be true by an individual or group.

More precisely, the model is based on social axioms, general, context-free beliefs that people acquire through social experiences. These beliefs are essential to people's cognitive processing and are assumed to be pan-cultural because of their functionality and because of the universal problems that humans must tackle to survive.[47]

Social axioms guide people to function effectively in two broad domains, *social interaction* and *problem solving*, based on a five-factor model substantiated across 40 cultures.

The first factor, *social cynicism*, proposes a negative view of human nature, a prejudice against some social groups, distrust toward social institutions, and a belief that individuals are disposed to ignore ethical means in pursuing their goals. Social cynicism is related to the detection of deception and is concerned with the potential for exploitation.

Dutch, Canadians, and Caucasian Americans reported the lowest scores (positive view of human nature) and Greeks, Germans, and Georgians reported the highest scores (negative view of human nature) in this dimension.

The second factor, *social complexity*, suggests that there are no rigid rules but rather multiple ways to solve a problem and that people behave differently according to the situation.

Peruvians, Romanians, and Pakistanis reported the lowest scores (rigid rules and few ways to solve problems) and Taiwanese, Germans, and Norwegians reported the highest scores (no rigid rules and multiple ways to solve problems) in this dimension.

The third factor, *reward for application*, asserts that the investment of effort, knowledge, and careful planning will lead to positive results and help avoid negative outcomes

Dutch, Italians, and Czechs reported the lowest scores (investment of effort and careful planning don't necessarily lead to positive outcomes) and Pakistanis, Indians, and Malaysians reported the highest scores (investment of effort and careful planning lead to positive outcomes).

The fourth factor, *religiosity*, validates the existence of supernatural forces and the beneficial functions of religious beliefs, institutions, and practices.

Spaniards, Norwegians, and Belgians reported the lowest scores (no supernatural being and no value in religious beliefs) and Indonesians, Malaysians, and Pakistanis reported the highest scores (a supernatural being and value in religious beliefs).

The fifth factor, *fate control*, states that life events are predetermined by external forces and that people can influence the negative impact of these forces.

Norwegians, Spaniards, and Italians reported the lowest scores (events are not predetermined and fate doesn't influence outcomes) and Nigerians, Thais, and Pakistanis reported the highest scores (events are predetermined and fate influences outcomes).

According to the researchers, the five axiom dimensions can be applied to different contexts and are good predictors of individuals' social behavior.

Table 1 includes the results for the 40 cultures.

Citizen	Social Cynicism	Social Complexity	Reward for Application	Religiosity	Fate Control
American (Caucasian)	2.65	4.10	3.66	3.18	2.46
Belgian	2.97	4.03	3.36	2.58	2.58
Brazilian	2.81	3.98	3.54	3.39	2.49
British	2.75	4.11	3.46	2.81	2.35
Canadian	2.63	4.20	3.74	3.10	2.43
Chinese	3.03	4.08	3.74	2.92	2.90
Czech	2.77	4.10	3.29	3.10	2.62
Dutchman	2.62	4.18	3.18	2.73	2.56
Estonian	3.16	4.11	3.81	2.70	2.81
Filipino	2.84	4.09	4.03	3.52	2.60
Finn	2.76	4.08	3.59	3.07	2.54
French	3.05	4.08	3.56	2.60	2.62
Georgian	3.37	3.88	3.69	3.65	3.00
German	3.32	4.33	3.76	2.93	2.77
Greek	3.32	4.02	3.73	3.13	2.37
Hong Kong Chinese	3.13	4.08	3.70	3.44	2.69
Hungarian	2.96	4.13	3.40	2.99	2.67
Indian	3.04	3.92	4.19	3.37	2.97
Indonesian	2.72	3.96	4.14	4.22	2.91
Iranian	2.89	3.79	4.12	4.15	2.85
Israeli	2.76	4.16	3.60	2.60	2.53
Italian	2.74	4.01	3.28	2.72	2.29
Japanese	3.16	4.04	3.50	2.65	2.59
Korean	3.16	3.98	3.85	3.10	2.98
Latvian	3.05	4.02	3.58	3.10	2.77
Lebanese	3.05	4.11	3.77	3.10	2.47
Malaysian	2.88	3.93	4.29	4.30	2.96
New Zealander	2.77	4.14	3.59	2.83	2.34
Nigerian	2.98	3.89	4.04	3.67	3.08
Norwegian	2.66	4.37	3.53	2.55	2.01
Pakistani	3.29	3.77	4.15	4.40	3.15
Peruvian	3.29	3.67	3.88	3.21	2.48
Portuguese	2.87	3.90	3.61	3.09	2.43
Romanian	3.23	3.72	3.74	3.29	2.55
Russian	3.09	3.86	3.82	3.12	2.97
Singaporean	2.93	4.14	3.78	3.24	2.52
Spaniard	2.89	4.14	3.48	2.40	2.27
Taiwanese	3.30	4.22	3.87	3.22	3.01
Thai	3.22	3.80	3.98	3.43	3.14
Turk	2.94	4.14	3.97	3.48	2.68

Table 1. Social axiom scores.[48]

LANGUAGE AND COGNITION

Language plays a crucial role in sustaining an agent-oriented versus context-oriented emphasis across cultures.

A classic example is the English language, with *I* and *you* as singular first and second person pronouns. Research has confirmed that the frequency of using first and second person pronouns is directly associated with the cultural dimension of individualism.[49]

Individualism is also inversely correlated to the number of second person pronouns.

Some languages, such as Italian, Spanish, French, Hindi, and other Asian languages, display a greater variety in second person pronouns, suggesting individuals' understanding of the context and relationship in which those individuals behave.

A more formal language is used when speaking to elder people or to individuals with a higher social status.

Language also directs the person's attention toward different traits of the context. For example, significant differences exist in gender marking across cultures. In English, gender marking is minimal, while in other languages such as Italian and French, there are two distinct gender categories and in German and Russian there are even three.

Gender assignment tends to be random in many languages, even if grammatical gender affects the perception of the object, associating it with stereotyped masculine versus feminine traits.

Furthermore, in most languages, generic plurals tend to be masculine in gender, decreasing the visibility of feminine versus masculine characteristics.

Systematic differences also exist in the use of verbs versus adjectives in communication among different cultures. Analytic cultures tend to use more adjectives than verbs, while the opposite is true of holistic cultures.

Some languages are written horizontally from left to right (such as English) or from right to left (such as Arabic, Hebrew, Farsi, and Urdu), others vertically in columns from left to right or from right to left (such as Chinese), and still other languages use mixed systems (such as Japanese). Researchers have claimed that the way we usually read and write language affects our way of thinking.

According to research, the predominant left-right trajectory involves large areas of cognition. For example, when asking people to draw scenes corresponding to minimal subject-verb-object phrases (e.g., Fabio feeds the dog), a vast majority of respondents raised in left-right languages will envisage the agent (Fabio) to the left of the receiver (dog).

The opposite pattern is true for languages that are written/read from right to left, such as Arabic, Hebrew, Farsi, and Urdu.

Writing direction also influences social cognition. Violent film scenes were perceived as more aggressive and more harmful to the victim when the aggressor was positioned to the left of the victim than when the exact same scenes were observed with an opposite spatial arrangement. Along the same line, the same soccer goal was perceived as more powerful, faster, and more beautiful when the player was observed as acting in a left–right rather than a right–left fashion. Notably, this bias was reversed for Arabic speakers who observed the same scenes.

We can therefore affirm that observers assign greater strength to the action and greater agency to the actor when the trajectory mirrors the direction in which language is written in a given culture.

This also has remarkable implications for stereotyping. Studies of artwork generally show that men are more likely to be portrayed facing right than are women, who are usually portrayed facing left.

The 4 Ps Framework

(ENDNOTES)

1   McClelland, D. C. (1985). Human motivation. Glenview, IL: Scott, Foresman

2   Schultheiss, O. C. (2008). Implicit motives. In O. P. John, R. W. Robins, & L. A. Pervin (Eds.), Handbook of personality: Theory and research (3rd ed.). New York: Guilford Press.

3   Hofer, J. & Bond, M. H. (2008). Do Implicit Motives Add to Our Understanding of Psychological and Behavioral Outcomes Within and Across Cultures?. In R. Sorrentino, & S. Yamaguchi (Eds.), Handbook of Motivation and Cognition Across Cultures. San Diego: Academic Press.

4   English, T., Chen, S., & Swann Jr., W. B. (2008). A Cross Cultural Analysis Of Self-Verification Motives. In R. Sorrentino, & S. Yamaguchi (Eds.), Handbook of Motivation and Cognition Across Cultures. San Diego: Academic Press.

5   Bandura, A. (2002). Social Cognitive Theory in Cultural Context. Applied Psychology: An International Review, Vol. 51, N. 2, 269-290.

6   Ying-yi H., Y., Ip, G., Chiu, C., Morris, M. W., & Menon, T. (2001). Cultural Identity And Dynamic Construction Of The Self: Collective Duties And Individual Rights In Chinese And American Cultures. Social Cognition, Vol. 19, N. 3, 251-268.

7   Oettingen, G., & Zosuls, K. M. (2006). Culture and self-efficacy in adolescents. In F. Pajares, & T. Urdan (Eds.), Self-efficacy in adolescents. Greenwich, CT: Information Age Publishing.

8   Kim, U., & Park, Y. (2008). Cognitive, Relational and Social Basis of Academic Achievement in Confucian Cultures: Psychological, Indigenous, and Cultural Perspectives. In R. Sorrentino, & S. Yamaguchi (Eds.), Handbook of Motivation and Cognition Across Cultures. San Diego: Academic Press.

9   Oettingen, G., Sevincer, A. T., & Gollwitzer, P. M. (2008). Goal Pursuit in the Context of Culture. In R. Sorrentino, & S. Yamaguchi (Eds.), Handbook of Motivation and Cognition Across Cultures. San Diego: Academic Press.

10   Heine, S., & Takeshi, H. (2007). In Search of East Asian Self-Enhancement. Personality and Social Psychology Review, Vol. 11, N. 1, 4-27.

11   Heine, S. J., & Raineri, A. (2009). Self-Improving Motivations and Collectivism: The Case of Chileans. Journal of Cross-Cultural Psychology, Vol. 40, N. 1, 158-163.

12   Herman Hesse.

13   Miyamoto, Y., Nisbett, R. E., & Masuda, T. (2006). Culture and the Physical Environment: Holistic Versus Analytic Perceptual Affordances. Psychological Science, Vol. 17, N. 2, 113-119.

14   Gawronski, B., Peters, K. R., & Strack, F. (2008). Cross-Cultural Cognitive Dissonance. In R. Sorrentino, & S. Yamaguchi (Eds.). Handbook of Motivation and Cognition Across Cultures. San Diego: Academic Press.

15   Goetz, J. L., Spencer-Rodgers, J., & Peng, K. (2008). Dialectical Emotions: How Cultural Epistemologies Influence the Experience and Regulation of Emotional Complexity. In R. Sorrentino, & S. Yamaguchi (Eds.). Handbook of Motivation and Cognition Across Cultures. San Diego: Academic Press.

16   Buchtel, E. E., & Norenzayan, A. (2009). Thinking across cultures: Implications for dual processes. In J. Evans, & K. Frankish (Eds.), In two minds: Dual processes and beyond. Oxford, UK: Oxford University Press.

17   Flood, G. (1996). An introduction to Hinduism. Cambridge, UK: Cambridge University Press.

18   Zebian, S., & Denny, J. P. (2001). Integrative Cognitive Style in Middle Eastern and Western Groups: Multidimensional Classification and Major and Minor Property Sorting. Journal of Cross-Cultural Psychology, Vol. 32, N. 1, 58-75.

19   Nisbet, R. E. (2003). The Geography of Thought. New York, NY: The Free Press.

20   Elqayam, S. (2011). Grounded rationality: A relativist framework for normative rationality. In K. I. Manktelow, D. E. Over, & S. Elqayam (Eds.), The Science of Reason: A Festschrift in Honour of Jonathan St. B.T. Evans. Hove, UK: Psychology Press.

21   Ji, L., & Kaulius, M. (2013). Judgement and Decision Making across Cultures. Advances in Psychological Science, Vol. 21, No. 3, 381-388.

22   Yates, J., Lee, J., & Shinotsuka, H. (1996). Beliefs about overconfidence, including its cross national variation. Organizational Behavior and Human Decision Processes, 65, 138-147.

23   Li, S., Bi, Y.-L., & Rao, L.-L. (2011). Every Science/Nature potter praises his own pot - Can we believe what he says based on his mother tongue?. Journal of Cross-Cultural Psychology, Vol. 42, N. 1, 125-130.

24   Johnson, S. R. (2008). The Trouble with QSAR (or How I Learned to Stop Worrying and Embrace Fallacy). Journal of Chemical Information and Modeling, Vol. 48, N. 1, 25-26.

25   Green, N. (2012, January 6). Correlation is not causation. The Guardian. Retrieved from http://www.theguardian.com/science/blog/2012/jan/06/correlation-causation

26   Doll, R., & Hill, A. B. (1956). Lung cancer and other causes of death in relation to smoking; a second report on the mortality of British doctors. British Medical Journal, 5001, 1071-1081.

27   Spina, R. R., Ji, L. J., Guo, T., Zhang, Z., Li, Y., & Fabrigar, L. (2010). Cultural Differences in the Representativeness Heuristic: Expecting a Correspondence in Magnitude Between Cause and Effect. Personality and Social Psychology Bulletin, Vol. 36, N. 5, 583-597.

28   Weber, E. U., & Morris, M. W. (2010). Culture and Judgment and Decision Making: The Constructivist Turn. Perspectives on Psychological Science, Vol. 5, N. 4, 410-419.

29   Weber, E. U., & Hsee, C. K. (1998). Cross-cultural differences in risk perception, but cross-cultural similarities in attitude towards perceived risk. Management Science, 44, 1205-1217.

30   Ji, L., & Kaulius, M. (2013). Judgement and Decision Making across Cultures. Advances in Psychological Science, Vol. 21, No. 3, 381-388.

31   Weber, E. U., Hsee, C. K., & Sokolowska, J. (1998). What folklore tells us about risk and risk taking: A cross-cultural comparison of American, German, and Chinese proverbs. Organizational Behavior and Human Decision Processes, 75, 170-186.

32   Marshall, R., Huan, T.-C., Xu, Y., & Nam, I. (2011). Extending Prospect Theory Cross-Culturally by Examining Switching Behavior in Consumer and Business-to-Business Contexts. Journal of Business Research, Vol. 64, N. 8, 871-878.

33   Bontempo, R. N., Bottom, W. P., & Weber, E. U. (1997). Cross-cultural differences in risk perception: A model-based approach. Risk Analysis, 17, 479-488.

34   Sorrentino, R. M., Szeto, A., Nezlek, J. B., Yasunaga, S., Kouhara, S., & Ohtsubo, Y. (2008). Uncertainty regulation: the master motive?. In R. Sorrentino, & S. Yamaguchi (Eds.), Handbook of Motivation and Cognition Across Cultures. San Diego: Academic Press.

35   Maddux, W., Yang, H., Falk, C., Adam, H., Adair, W., Endo, Y., Carmon, Z., & Heine, S. (2010). For Whom is Parting from Possessions More Painful: Cultural Differences in the Endowment Effect. Psychological Science, Vol. 21, N. 12, 1910-1917.

36   Mason, M. F., & Morris, M. W. (2010). Culture, attribution and automaticity: a social cognitive neuroscience view. SCAN, 5, 292-306.

37   Gilovich, T., Keltner, D., & Nisbett, R. E. (2011). Understanding Others. In T. Gilovich, D. Keltner, & R. E. Nisbett (Eds.), Social psychology (2nd ed.). New York: W. W. Norton & Company.

38   Gilovich, T. (1993). How we know what isn't so: The fallibility of human reason in everyday life. New York, NY: Free Press.

39   Weber, E. U., & Morris, M. W. (2010). Culture and Judgment and Decision Making: The Constructivist Turn. Perspectives on Psychological Science, Vol. 5, N. 4, 410-419.

40   Morris, M. W., & Gelfand, M. J. (2004). Cultural Differences and Cognitive Dynamics: expanding the cognitive perspective on negotiation. In M. J. Gelfand, & J. M. Brett (Eds.), The Handbook of Negotiation and Culture. Palo Alto, CA: Stanford University Press.

41   Weiner, B. (2008). An attribution theorist addresses the co-existence of theoretical generality and cultural specificity. In R. Sorrentino, & S. Yamaguchi (Eds.), Handbook of Motivation and Cognition Across Cultures. San Diego: Academic Press.

42   Weiner, B. (1995). Judgments of responsibility: A foundation for a theory of social conduct. New York, NY: Guilford.

43   Cialdini, R. B., & Goldstein, N. J. (2004). Social influence: Compliance and conformity. Annual Review of Psychology, 55, 591-621.

44   McCauley, C. (1989). The nature of social influence in groupthink: Compliance and internalization. Journal of Personality and Social Psychology, Vol. 57, N. 2, 250-260.

45   Zou, X., Tam, K., Morris, M. W., Lee, S., Yee-Man Lau, I., & Chiu, C. (2009). Culture as Common Sense: Perceived Consensus Versus Personal Beliefs as Mechanisms of Cultural Influence. Journal of Personality and Social Psychology, Vol. 97, N. 4, 579-597.

46   Schwartz, S. H. (2012). An overview of the Schwartz theory of basic values. Online Readings in Psychology and Culture, Unit 2, Subunit 1. Retrieved from http://dx.doi.org/10.9707/2307-0919.1116

47   Leung, K., & Zhou, F. (2008). Values and social axioms. In R. Sorrentino, & S. Yamaguchi (Eds.), Handbook of Motivation and Cognition Across Cultures. San Diego: Academic Press.

48   Leung, K., & Bond, M. H. (2004). Social axioms: A model of social beliefs in multi-cultural perspective. In M. P. Zanna (Ed.), Advances in Experimental Social Psychology, Vol. 36. San Diego: Academic Press.

49   Karasawa, M., & Maass, A. (2008). The role of language in the perception of person and group. In R. Sorrentino, & S. Yamaguchi (Eds.), Handbook of Motivation and Cognition Across Cultures. San Diego: Academic Press.

CHAPTER 11:

Creativity and Integrative Thinking

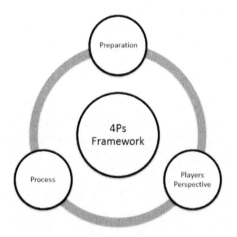

Stage 1: Preparation. Stage 2: Process. Stage 4: Players' Perspective

I am neither especially clever nor especially gifted. I am only very, very curious. I stay longer on problems, without giving up.[1]

INTEGRATIVE NEGOTIATION PHASE

In negotiation, creating value describes the process of maximizing the value in a deal (integrative strategy), but identifying opportunities for value creation during the negotiation process is not an easy task.

Creating options for expanding the pie and recognizing potential integrative solutions requires guidance.

A conventional analytical approach to negotiation can limit the potential of joint gains because the standard problem-solving method tends to be subject to the fixed-pie bias, hinders the possibilities of finding new alternatives, uncritically follows only established patterns, and often falls prey to early judgments of unconventional and original options.

There are often several issues to be negotiated in an integrative negotiation, and the only way to exploit the different options is to come up with peculiar and innovative solutions.

Concessions are not necessary. Focus on enlarging the pie through trades. Look for creative options.[2]

This is why we have introduced a chapter on creativity and integrative thinking; the aim is to present guidelines for how to produce new and unique alternatives during the negotiation process that can lead to an integrative agreement.

Contrary to the common assumption, creativity can be developed and taught. People can be trained to be more creative.

I would say creativity can be re-kindled in people: all children are creative. They just lose their capability to be creative by growing up.[3]

WHAT IS CREATIVITY?

Creativity is seeing what everyone else has seen, and thinking what no one else has thought (Szent-Gyorgi, n. d.).

Creativity is a type of learning process where the teacher and pupil are located in the same individual (Koestler, 1964).

Creativity is the ability to see relationships where none exist (Disch, 1967).

Creativity involves breaking out of established patterns in order to look at things in a different way (De Bono, 1973).

Creativity is any act, idea, or product that changes an existing domain, or that transforms an existing domain into a new one (Csikszentmihalyi, 1996).

Creativity is primarily an ability to challenge the status quo and come up with new and better solutions (Wind, 2014).

We know creativity when we see it, but we are not able to describe the mental processes involved.

Creative people view things from different perspectives and produce new and distinctive alternatives. Creativity is associated with other cognitive attitudes and areas of knowledge, encountered in the International Profiler in chapter 3, such as flexible judgment, new thinking, creating new alternatives, and tolerance of ambiguity and unpredictability (spirit of adventure).[4]

WHAT IS INTEGRATIVE THINKING?

The test of a first-rate intelligence is the ability to hold two opposed ideas in the mind at the same time, and still retain the ability to function.[5]

Integrative thinking is the ability to constructively face the tensions of opposing alternatives and, instead of choosing one at the expense of the other, generate a creative resolution of the tension in the form of a new model that contains elements of both alternatives, but is superior to each.

Integrative thinkers rarely rush into a decision. They keep all the possibilities in mind without rejecting any. They don't choose among options, but try to combine different elements to come up with a new idea.[6]

Integrative thinking, based on the logic of both/and rather than either/or, is comparable to the yin and yang perspective of the Chinese worldview, introduced in chapters 3 and 4, where mutually dependent and balancing opposites provide symmetry and dynamic equilibrium.

Combining topics from distinct fields or multiple perspectives often leads to original ideas. Bronowski (a Polish-Jewish British mathematician, biologist, historian of science, theater author, poet, and inventor) claimed that *a genius is a person who is able to combine two great ideas.*

Bohm (an American theoretical physicist who made important contributions to the fields of quantum theory, philosophy of mind, and neuropsychology) believed that creative individuals are able to tolerate ambivalence between opposite or incompatible subjects.

Professor Albert Rothenberg (1971) was perhaps the first scholar to link creativity and integrative thinking.[7]

He coined the term *Janusian thinking*, referring to the creative process of concurrently conceiving and combining multiple opposite thoughts. The process is named after Janus, a Roman god with two faces, each looking in the opposite direction.

BRAIN ACTIVITY IN CREATIVE THINKERS

The brain activity of integrative and analytical thinkers differs. According to a 2007 study, integrative problem solvers display greater activity in right hemisphere regions, possibly due to right hemisphere disposition in processing remote associations among elements of a problem.[8]

The study also reveals a distinct pattern of brain activity at rest; even spontaneous thought, like daydreams, contains more remote associations in integrative thinkers.

A second difference is that creative and integrative thinkers exhibit different activity in areas of the brain that process visual information. For example, a word spoken in an overheard conversation can spark a correlation that can lead to a solution.

Thus, the study shows that fundamental differences in brain activity between integrative and analytical problem solvers are apparent, not only when individuals work on a problem, but even when they are at rest.

HOW CAN WE FOSTER CREATIVITY?

Look, there is one side of an argument, but wait there is another side of the argument. That is a great case for saying, look, the world is a lot messier than we think it is.[9]

Following are suggestions to promote creativity and integrative thinking.

A SOLUTION EXISTS

First, you need to believe that a solution to the problem exists, and you need to persevere in finding that solution. As Albert Einstein once stated, "I am neither especially clever nor especially gifted. I am only very, very curious. I stay longer on problems, without giving up."

Newton claimed that he could concentrate absorbedly on a problem for days. Research shows that experts in any creative field take at least 10 years of practice, starting from the moment when the specific domain basic skills and knowledge are acquired, before producing a masterwork.

Any creative solution comes only after a long search with little or no evident improvement; however, apparently inactive periods preceding a triggering event can lead to comprehension of the problem (more on this in chapter 9, The Unconscious Thought Theory).

Inventions involve false starts, dead ends, and several endeavors.

THINK PRODUCTIVELY

To have a great idea, have a lot of them.[10]

As we have seen in previous sections, because all memories are sequential and associative, absolutely random thoughts don't exist. Creativity can therefore be defined as making predictions by analogy. We forecast the future by comparison to the past.[11]

Usually we think reproductively, based on past experiences; once we have a solution that has worked in the past, it becomes hard for us to contemplate alternative positions.

In contrast, integrative individuals think productively, not reproductively. When tackling a problem, they ask themselves how many different ways they can look at the problem, how many different ways they can reorganize it, and how many different ways they can explain it, instead of asking how they have solved it in the past. They tend to come up with many different answers, some of which are original.

A distinctive feature of creative people is their vast productivity. Thomas Edison held 1,093 patents and Mozart produced more than 600 pieces of music. Einstein published 249 papers; Freud published 330. Picasso executed more than 20,000 works. In fact, most esteemed geniuses produce not only great works, but also more average works. Out of their immense quantity of work comes quality.[12]

According to Thomas Edison, invention is 1% inspiration and 99% perspiration; discovery is the outcome of systematically examining large numbers of options.[13] Creativity is a Darwinian process: Seek out different possibilities that can compete and integrate with each other.[14]

When producing ideas, be careful not to judge, define, label, and categorize. Don't constrain your thoughts. Be at ease in ambiguity, uncertainty, disorder, and chaos. Don't judge an idea when it comes to your mind. Rely on divergent thinking, where criticism and judgment are temporarily suspended while exploring different possibilities.

One of the biggest obstacles to your creativity is the adoption at an early stage of convergent thinking that uses analysis, criticism, logic, argument, and reasoning to narrow down the options and select the preferred choice.

Let's use an example: How many ways of halving 13 can you find?[15]

An integrative thinker would find many different ways to express 13 and many different ways to halve 13.

$13 / 2 = 6.5$

$13 = 1$ and 3

THIR TEEN = 4 (4 letters on each side)

XI|II = 11 and 2

~~XIII~~ = 8 and 8 (halving horizontally gives us 8 on top and 8 on bottom)

When asked about the difference between him and the average person, Einstein replied that if you asked the average person to find a needle in a haystack the person would stop when he or she found a needle. He, on the other hand, would pull apart the entire haystack looking for all the possible needles.[16]

USE DIFFERENT PERSPECTIVES

A guesstimate is that the human brain has approximately 60,000 thoughts a day. The problem is that 95% (57,000) of today's thoughts will be the same ones we'll have tomorrow.

Because our mind recognizes sequences, similarities, and patterns, our initial perspective on problems tends to be constricted and superficial. The problem arises when we settle on one specific initial perspective: We shut down all but one line of thought, without recognizing that other views may be more appropriate.

We could be far more creative just by switching from System 1 to System 2 thinking.

To gain different perspectives on a problem, begin by restructuring it; the goal is not to obtain the right problem definition, but alternative problem definitions:

- Separate the different elements from the whole and focus on the relationships among the various parts and the key factors that can influence each element.
- Rephrase a problem in your own words. Restructuring a problem in words reinforces the development of new thoughts. Even better, write down the problem you are attempting to solve.
- Shift your perspective by putting yourself in the shoes of other stakeholders. Write the problem statement from the perspectives of at least two other people who are close to or involved in the problem. Next synthesize the different perspectives. For example, Walt Disney was able to identify with both the characters in his animated films and the audience. If you are developing a new product, look at your idea from the potential customer's point of view, from the manufacturing point of view, and from the sales point of view. Then synthetize the different views.

Art can provide a vivid example of what we mean by shifting perspectives.

In painting, since the Renaissance, the focus has been on a fixed point of view and on balanced proportions. Pablo Picasso, with his *Les Demoiselles d'Avignon*, broke all established conventions and introduced multiple and discordant perspectives and styles in representing angular and abstracted female body shapes, with Iberian and African influences and inspiration from Cezanne, Gauguin, and El Greco (see Figure 1).

Figure 1. Les Demoiselles d'Avignon, Pablo Picasso.

In writing, one of the best examples of double perspective is provided by Joseph Conrad. He used the narrator/character double narrative technique in many of his books, such as *Heart of Darkness, Lord Jim*, and *Chance*. The narrator's role is to interpret the events for the reader from a distant and detached point of view, while the character provides his experience, state of mind, and own personal version of events.

MAKE IT VISUAL

The increase in creativity in the Renaissance was closely tied to the recording and conveying of knowledge through drawings, diagrams, and graphs.

Leonardo da Vinci used drawings, diagrams, charts, and graphs to capture information, record ideas and observations, and articulate and solve problems.[17]

Drawings provide a context to the problem, highlight the relationships between the elements, and force us to look at the problem differently.[18]

One way to represent diagrams, before thoughts lose their activity, is *mind mapping*.

Mind mapping is an organized brainstorming method that allows you to represent thoughts through key words: Write the problem or idea at the center of a piece of paper. Then spontaneously write down ideas and concepts associated with the central idea or with the new concepts that you just recorded on the paper. Don't worry about structure, cause, and effect. Use lines to connect different nodes in the map and to make associations among different words.

Mind maps are powerful because they allow for parallel mental processing, capturing thoughts before they evaporate and stimulating connections and associations between different ideas.

Figure 2 shows an example of a mind map representing the structure of the book you are reading.

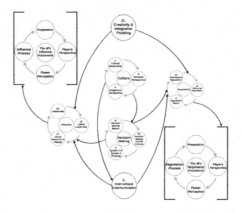

Figure 2. Book Mind Map.

According to Picasso, the artist paints to unload feelings, visions, and thoughts. We can replicate Picasso's way of working by expanding our knowledge related to a specific problem and searching and reading material until we are filled with the subject. Then, like Picasso did with his art, we can start from the central idea or problem and let thoughts, ideas, associations, and connections flow.

Leonardo used a similar technique, listing and cataloging his thoughts in little notebooks that he carried everywhere. He would then use the written words to generate new patterns, combinations, and associations.[19]

CHALLENGE ASSUMPTIONS

Challenge the most basic assumption you have about the problem you are facing. For example, assume you want to grow the business of your company, but your main product has been made obsolete by a new technology. What would you do? Can any idea, or its variations, be used in today's world?

Another example: Assume you want to find a favorable agreement in a negotiation. The basic assumptions are that members of the other side are interested in your current product and that you have a trusting relationship with them, having been their certified supplier for years. If you challenge these assumptions, how then can you close the deal if your product is of no interest to the other parties or they didn't have any prior experience with you? Ask yourself, how can you close the deal despite these difficulties?

With reversal, you turn your problem inside-out. Using the same previous example, how can you sink your business? To generate ideas with this technique, work them in their opposites. Having developed ways to kill your business, how can you remove these obstacles or turn them into their opposites? New ideas can be generated by considering the opposite of any topic or action. Reversal is an original technique because it breaks conventional patterns of thought, creating new thoughts.

If we use the second example, then what can you do to not achieve an agreement? How can you find an unfavorable agreement? List all the possible solutions to the reverse problem and think how they can be applied to your real situation.

Another valuable technique is regressive logic. Instead of converting a question (3 x 3 = ?) into an answer (9), start from the result and find the different ways to get the answer (e.g., 6 + 3, 7 + 2, 9 x 1, 192 - 183).

Einstein envisioned his theory of relativity as a given and then worked backward to what he knew. Thus, you should visualize the answer. Then work backward to the problem and look for ways to achieve the result.[20]

With regressive logic, you imagine an ideal solution and then work backward to work out how to achieve that solution: What gaps need to be filled? What should precede each step?

In the year 333, Alexander the Great attempted to solve the famous Gordian Knot, tied to the shaft of an ox cart in the palace of the former kings of Phrygia. It was prophesied that whoever managed this feat would go on to become king of Asia.

Unable to see how the tangle could be undone, Alexander sliced it apart with a stroke of his sword.

This became known as the *Alexandrian solution*.[21]

CONNECTING THINGS

Creativity is just connecting things. When you ask creative people how they did something, they feel a little guilty because they didn't really do it, they just saw something. It seemed obvious to them after a while. That's because they were able to connect experiences they've had and synthesize new things. And the reason they were able to do that was that they've had more experiences or they have thought more about their experiences than other people.[22]

A wonderful Harmony arises from joining together the seemingly unconnected.[23]

Creativity is not only genetic; it is an ability that can be acquired. The key skill in creativity is developing associative thinking, which is the ability to link previously independent ideas.[24]

Learn to observe and to be curious about different domains. Different areas of knowledge can provide associations and insights into your problem. Curiosity and knowledge trigger associations.

Read, read a lot, on different subjects, even on topics in which you have no interest. Learn about things outside your domain. An interdisciplinary approach that promotes cross-fertilization among different domains of knowledge brings ideas and concepts from one field or specialty to another. Combining them in a new way stimulates interactions across different disciplinary boundaries[25] (i.e., integrative thinking).

Also, meet people who are not like you. Develop weak ties that can connect you to different social domains and therefore to different experiences and perspectives. As we'll see in the next paragraphs, the simple attempt to accept and reconcile different points of view leads to integrative thinking.

QUESTIONING

The important and difficult job is never to find the right answers; it is to find the right question.[26]

Integrative thinkers are curious and inquiring. They ask a lot of questions. Don't refrain from asking obvious, childlike questions. Asking the right question often releases a flow of ideas and associations that can lead to the solution.

Next time, try to ask every possible question that comes to your mind related to a specific problem within a limited time frame, for example, 15 minutes. Professor Gregersen (2011) named this process *questionstorming.*[27]

I have six honest serving men
They taught me all I knew
I call them What and Where and When
And How and Why and Who.[28]

Use the questions introduced by Kipling in his short poem to trigger ideas and associations. A planned sequence of questions could be similar to the following:

What is the problem? Where is it happening? When is it happening? Why is it happening? How can you overcome this problem? Who do you need to get involved? When will you know you have solved the problem?

Never forget the most important question: What if? Use your imagination, without premature judgments and constraints.

Don't stop with the first answer. Try to come up with as many responses as possible.

INCUBATION

Boredom is often the precursor to creativity.[29]

Discoveries are usually preceded by seemingly quiet periods in which no apparent progress is made. The best way to find new ideas on a specific subject is first to study and read as much as possible about the topic. Then let it incubate: Read about unrelated matters, visit a museum or an art gallery, watch a movie, play sports.

Recording ideas fixes the information in our long-term memory and, because our subconscious mind never rests, it allows for novel connections between different subjects, even when our consciousness is directed elsewhere (more on this in chapter 9, The Unconscious Thought Theory).[30]

Constantly keeping track of ideas is necessary because ideas come at unusual moments, and if they are not written down, they are usually forgotten within 24 hours.

The more complex and comprehensive the network of information in our mind (information about different topics), the more likely we are to find new ideas and associations about a specific subject.

BRAHMA'S MEAL

The Upanishads, a collection of Indian Vedic texts, tell the story of Brahma inviting his children to a meal. After serving the food, Brahma imposes a restriction: no one can bend their elbows while getting the food. As a result, the food cannot be picked and brought to the mouth.

Some children complain. Others get creative: they pick up the food and start serving the person next to them by swinging the arm. Others provide for them in reciprocation.[31]

MULTICULTURAL EXPERIENCES AND CREATIVITY

Recent studies have determined that metacognitive cultural intelligence (CQ) enhances creative collaboration because people high in CQ strategy are able to adapt their interaction style to create rapport with other individuals. Also, the sharing of feelings, experiences, and values that follows a relationship based on trust is the prelude of transparent communication and the flow and acceptance of new ideas.[32]

Multicultural experiences increase individuals' sensitivity to different knowledge and ideas, resulting in a positive correlation between multicultural experiences and integrative thinking: Exposure to different cultures' ideas enhances the individuals' attitudes we introduced in the International Profiler in chapter 3, such as openness to novel perspectives and ideas, flexible judgment, new thinking, creating new alternatives, and spirit of adventure.[33]

A corollary of the previous statement is that multicultural teams with high cultural heterogeneity are potentially more creative than homogenous teams, not taking into account factors such as time pressure and individual propensity for cognitive closure that tend to limit acceptance of novel ideas.[34]

Another study highlighted biculturals' (individuals concurrently exposed to two cultures) ability to employ more integrative and complex solutions in solving problems than single-culture individuals. According to the researchers, the ability is an outcome of greater internal conflict resulting from an attempt to reconcile inconsistent cognitions of the two different cultures.[35]

IMAGINEERING

The term imagineering is a combination of the words *imagination* and *engineering*. Imagineering is often associated with Walt Disney because it describes his ability to convert fantasies, thoughts, and ideas into real and concrete creations and achievements.

However, the term imagineering was originally coined by Alcoa, the aluminum company. *Imagineering is letting your imagination soar, and then engineering it down to earth.*[36]

Walt Disney's integrative thinking strategy was based on three different and distinct perspectives (see Figure 3).

He would shift his perspective three times by performing three independent roles: The dreamer, the realist, the critic.

Figure 3. Walt Disney's thinking process.

Walt Disney would first play the *dreamer*. He would let his imagination work without worrying about how to implement his ideas. He would conceive apparently absurd and irrational concepts, connecting seemingly unrelated thoughts. He would also describe his ideas in detail, representing all the different features of the concept.

Next, he would try to make his thoughts more pragmatic by playing the *realist*. He would figure out how to make his ideas work in the real world. As a realist, he would look for ways to make his conceptions into something workable and practical, without losing the core of the dreamer's idea.

Finally, he would play the part of the *critic*, the devil's advocate, asking distressing and uncomfortable questions such as: Is it really feasible? If yes, can the idea's features be translated into customer benefits? What would users think? Do we have the capabilities to implement the concept? What is the return on investment? How long it will take the competition to catch up? Will it provide us with a real competitive advantage? Does the concept fulfill real customer needs?

IS CREATIVITY GENETIC?

Individuals on the autistic spectrum have a kind of intelligence untouched by tradition or culture - unconventional, unorthodox, strangely pure and original.[37]

According to some scholars, the *social brain* (a concept introduced in chapter 7), the ability to manage complex social interactions, is not well suited for radical creativity in fields that require the ability to systematize and organize information, data, and concepts, such as mathematics, physics, sciences, and engineering.[38]

Great mathematicians and scientists display the ability to intensely concentrate on a specific subject and become detached from the environment for long periods, matched with the incapacity to entertain normal social relations.[39]

A typical example in the literature is Isaac Newton, whose autism is commonly acknowledged by psychiatrists and psychologists. Autism is a general term defining a group of neuro-developmental disorders, characterized, in differing degrees, by impairments in social interactions, verbal and nonverbal communication, and behavior.[40]

According to Professor Fitzgerald, because these developmental disorders are mainly hereditary and mostly concern men, creativity can be primarily considered as the product of genetic rather than environmental factors.[41]

The differences between standard and autistic routes to creativity can be summarized as follows:[42]

- A standard brain forms thoughts and mental models that capture the whole picture, while an autistic brain is more focused on the parts rather than the whole.
- A standard brain works mainly on intuition and preconceived ideas, while an autistic brain works on logic and facts.
- As a result, standard brains process information based on System 1 thinking and autistic brains process information based on System 2 thinking.

CREATIVE PROBLEMS

When confronted with a problem, creative people ask: In how many different ways can I look at the problem? How can I rethink the way I see it? In how many different ways can I solve it? They do not ask: What have I been taught by someone else about how to solve this? How did I solve something similar in the past? They tend to come up with many different responses, some of which are unconventional and possibly unique.

Following are examples of problems that require an unconventional approach, using some of the techniques noted previously. The first four examples (the coin, Sahara, the equation, the card players) are entirely derived from David Perkins (2000). [43]

THE COIN

Someone brings an old coin to a museum director and offers it for sale. The coin is stamped 540 B.C.E. (Before Common Era or Before Christ). Instead of considering the purchase, the museum director calls the police. Why?

SAHARA

You are driving a jeep through the Sahara desert. You encounter someone lying face down in the sand, dead. There are no tracks anywhere around. There has been no wind for days to destroy any tracks. You look in a pack on the person's back. What do you find?

THE EQUATION

The equation:

$$2 + 7 - 118 = 129$$

This is not a valid mathematical statement. The challenge: Add one straight line anywhere in the equation to make it a true statement.

THE CARD PLAYERS

Four people are seated at a table playing cards. However, all four lose. No other people are present. How can this be?

THE MONEY LENDER

The following tale is completely derived from De Bono's (1973).[44]

Many years ago when a person who owed money could be thrown into jail, a merchant in London had the misfortune to owe a huge sum to a money lender. The money lender, who was old and ugly, was attracted to the merchant's beautiful teenaged daughter. He proposed a deal. The money lender said he would cancel the merchant's debt if he could have the girl instead.

Both the merchant and his daughter were shocked at the request. So, the money lender proposed that they let chance decide the matter. He told them that he would put a small black rock and a small white rock into an empty money bag and then the girl would have to withdraw one of the stones. If she chose the black stone, she would become his wife and her father's debt would be canceled. If she chose the white stone, she would stay with her father and the debt would be canceled. However, if she refused to withdraw a stone, her father would be thrown into jail and she would starve.

Unwillingly, the merchant agreed. They were standing on a stone-strewn path in the merchant's garden as they talked and the money lender bent forward to pick up the two stones. As he picked up the stones, the girl noticed that he picked up two black stones and put them into the money bag. He then asked the girl to pick out the stone that was to decide her fate and that of her father.

Put yourself in the shoes of the unfortunate girl. What would you have done?

CREATIVE SOLUTIONS

THE COIN

If the coin were authentic, the makers of the coin, working in B.C.E. (Before Common Era or Before Christ), would not have known that Christ would be born.

SAHARA

In the person's backpack, you would find an unopened parachute.

THE EQUATION

The first two and easiest solutions come from recognizing that the equation doesn't need to create an equality:

$$2 + 7 - 118 \neq 129$$
$$2 + 7 - 118 \leq 129$$

The third involves reframing the problem, changing the + to a 4:

$$2\ 4\ 7 - 118 = 129$$

THE CARD PLAYERS

The four people are each playing solitaire.

THE MONEY LENDER

Vertical thinkers would envisage only three options:

- The girl should refuse to withdraw a stone.
- The girl should show that there are two black stones in the bag and expose the money lender as a cheat.
- The girl should take a black stone and sacrifice herself to save her father from prison.

None of these suggestions is very helpful because if the girl does not withdraw a stone her father goes to prison; if she does, she has to marry the money lender.

Vertical thinkers are affected by the fact that the girl has to withdraw a stone. Integrative thinkers consider the stone that is left behind; they attempt to explore all the different ways of looking at something, rather than narrowing the options.

The girl put her hand into the money bag and pulled out a stone. Without looking at it, she let it drop to the path where it got lost among all the others.

"Oh, how clumsy of me," she said, "but never mind, if you look into the bag you will be able to tell which stone I took by the color of the one that is left."

Since the remaining stone is, of course, black, it must be presumed that she has taken the white stone. In this way, by using creativity, the girl changes what seems an impossible situation into an extremely advantageous one. The girl is actually better off than if the money lender had been honest and put one black and one white stone into the bag because then she would have had only an even chance of being saved. As it was, she was sure of remaining with her father and at the same time having his debt canceled.

(ENDNOTES)

1   Albert Einstein.

2   Ertel, D., & Gordon, M. (2007). The Point of the Deal: How to Negotiate When 'Yes' is Not Enough. Cambridge, MA: Harvard Business Review Press.

3   John Maeda.

4   Franken, R. E. (1999). Human motivation (3rd ed.). Pacific Grove, CA: Brooks/Cole.

5   F. Scott Fitzgerald.

6   Martin, R. L. (2007). The opposable mind: How successful leaders win through integrative thinking. Boston, MA: Harvard Business School Press.

7   Rothenberg, A. (1971). The process of Janusian thinking in creativity. Archives of General Psychiatry, 24, 195-205.

8   Kounios, J., Fleck, J. I., Green, D. L., Payne, L., Stevenson, J. L., Bowden, E. M., & Jung-Beeman, M. (2008). The origins of insight in resting-state brain activity. Neuropsychologia, Vol. 46, N. 1, 281-291.

9   Malcolm Gladwell.

10 Thomas Edison.

11 Hawkins, J. (2004). On intelligence. New York, NY: Owl Books.

12 Michalko, M. (2001). Cracking creativity: The secrets of creative genius. Berkeley, CA: Ten Speed Press.

13 Perkins, D. (2000). Archimedes' bathtub: The art and logic of breakthrough thinking. New York, NY: W. W. Norton & Company.

14 Brown, T. (2009). Change by design: How design thinking transforms organizations and inspires innovation. New York, NY: HarperCollins.

15 Michalko, M. (2001). Cracking creativity: The secrets of creative genius. Berkeley, CA: Ten Speed Press.

16 Michalko, M. (2001). Cracking creativity: The secrets of creative genius. Berkeley, CA: Ten Speed Press.

17 Michalko, M. (2001). Cracking creativity: The secrets of creative genius. Berkeley, CA: Ten Speed Press.

18 Brown, T. (2009). Change by design: How design thinking transforms organizations and inspires innovation. New York, NY: HarperCollins.

19 Birch, P., & Clegg, B. (2000). Imagination engineering: A toolkit for business creativity. London, UK: Pearson Education.

20 Michalko, M. (2001). Cracking creativity: The secrets of creative genius. Berkeley, CA: Ten Speed Press.

21 Hughes, R. (2010). CULT-URE. London, UK: Fiell Publishing.

22 Steve Jobs interviewed by Gary Wolf on Wired, February 1996.

23 Heraclitus.

24 Dyer, J., Gregersen, H., & Christensen, C. M. (2011). The innovators's DNA, Mastering the five skills of disruptive innovators. Boston, MA: Harvard Business School Press.

25 Robinson, K. (2011). Out of our minds: Learning to create. Chichester, UK: Capstone Publishing.

26 Peter Drucker.

27 Dyer, J., Gregersen, H., & Christensen, C. M. (2011). The innovators's Dna, Mastering the Five Skills of Disruptive Innovators. Boston: Harvard Business School Press.

28 Rudyard Kipling.

29 Kim John Payne.

30 Perkins, D. (2000). Archimedes' bathtub: The art and logic of breakthrough thinking. New York, NY: W. W. Norton & Company.

31   Pattanaik, D. (2013). Business Sutra: A Very Indian Approach to Management. New Delhi: Aleph Book Company.

32   Chua, R. Y. J., & Morris, M. W. (2012). Collaborating across cultures: Cultural metacognition and affect-based trust in creative collaboration. Organizational Behavior and Human Decision Processes, http://dx.doi.org/10.1016/j.obhdp.2012.03.009.

33   Trickey, D., Ewington, N., & Lowe, R. (2009). Being International: what do international managers and professionals really think is important - and do experts agree?. The Journal of Intercultural Mediation and Communication, Vol. 2, 49-78.

34   Chua, R. Y. J. (2011). Innovating at the world's crossroads: how multicultural networks promote creativity. HBS Working Papers 11-085. Cambridge, MA: Harvard University Press.

35   Tadmor, C. T., Tetlock, P. E., & Peng, K. (2009). Acculturation Strategies and Integrative Complexity: The Cognitive Implications of Biculturalism. Journal of Cross-Cultural Psychology, 40, 105-139.

36   Time Magazine. February 16, 1942.

37   Hans Asperger.

38   Baron-Cohen, S. (2003). The Essential Difference. Men, Women and the Extreme Male Brain. London: The Penguin Press.

39   Fitzgerald, M. (2004). Autism and Creativity: Is there a link between autism in men and exceptional ability?. New York: Brunner Routledge.

40   Caronna, E. B., Milunsky, J. M., & Tager-Flusberg, H. (2008). Autism spectrum disorders: clinical and research frontiers. Archives of Disease in Childhood, Vol. 93, N. 6, 518-523.

41   Fitzgerald, M. (2004). Autism and Creativity: Is there a link between autism in men and exceptional ability?. New York: Brunner Routledge.

42   Snyder, A. (2004). Autistic Genius. Nature, Vol. 428, 470-471.

43   Perkins, D. (2000). Archimedes' bathtub: The art and logic of breakthrough thinking. New York, NY: W. W. Norton & Company.

44   De Bono, E. (1973). Lateral thinking: Creativity step by step. New York, NY: Harper Colophon.

CHAPTER 12:

Advanced Negotiation

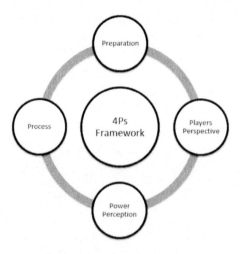

Stage 1: Preparation. Stage 2: Process. Stage 3: Power Perception. Stage 4: Players Perspective

THE NEGOTIATOR'S DILEMMAS

Like it or not, you are a negotiator. Negotiation is a fact of life.[1]

Negotiators find themselves trapped in a dilemma. They recognize only two ways to negotiate: Should I push to get what I want or concede to maintain the relationship with the other person?

The hard negotiator sees any situation as a competition. She goes after her goals by maintaining extreme positions to persuade the other party to concede. This strategy ends up damaging the relationship with the other side.

The soft negotiator wants a quick and harmonious solution. Because she sees conflict as dangerous for the relationship, she yields swiftly to reach an agreement. This strategy doesn't allow the negotiator to fully achieve her goals.

261

When there is time pressure, yielding (soft style) is by far the strategy most commonly adopted.

People have a propensity to adopt a hard style when they negotiate on issues that involve strong emotions such as basic rights, self-esteem, honor, public image, or values (see Table 1).

Negotiator's strategy	Chances of reaching any agreement	Chances of reaching a favorable agreement
Hard	Low	High
Soft	High	Low

Table 1. The negotiator's dilemma.

The hard negotiator has a lower possibility of reaching an agreement than a softer negotiator, but if she reaches an agreement, it will, in most of the cases, be a favorable one.

Other standard negotiating strategies fall between hard and soft, but each involves a trade-off between achieving one's goals and preserving the relationship.

A third negotiation strategy involves joint problem solving. The integrative negotiator tries to identify alternatives that satisfy both parties' goals. In doing so, she also strengthens the relationship with the other person (see Figure 1).

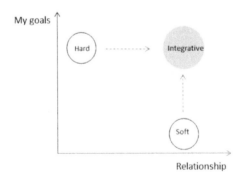

Figure 1. The negotiator's dilemma.

Negotiators also face a second dilemma: Should I deceive the other person about my interests and stand firm on my positions or be transparent about my interests and flexible about demands to create options that can help both parties achieve their goals, while strengthening the relationship?

Despite the two strategies requiring paradoxical mind-sets, it is often ne to adopt both styles in the same negotiation: It is necessary to compete ____ the other party has different goals, but it is also necessary to collaborate to exploit whatever integrative potential may exist in the situation, finding new options that are better for both parties than those that are obvious at first.

The integrative phase is not always part of the negotiation process: It requires joint problem-solving with the other party, which can't happen if the other player is playing hard ball, behaving unethically, providing misleading information, or adopting a very competitive strategy, focusing only on his or her own self-interests. Or perhaps the other party doesn't have the authority to negotiate different options from those on the table. In negotiations where emotions and irrationality play a primary role, problem-solving strategies often don't work. *We therefore dismiss the notion that every negotiation should be win-win.*

If a relationship is not fundamental and the other party is not willing to participate in the joint decision-making process, than every negotiator should try to claim as much value as possible.

Perhaps the best approach to negotiation is *co-opetition*, a strategy that combines competition and cooperation, thereby developing complex relationships with multiple players, taking advantage of overlapping interests, and at the same time claiming as much value as possible.

POSITIONS AND INTERESTS

In negotiations, each player usually takes an extreme position, makes a case for it, contends with the other side's rationale, and makes concessions to reach a compromise.

As seen in the example of the negotiation between a customer and a shopkeeper in chapter 6, bargaining is usually built around a sequence of positions, where players start with an extreme position and continue with negotiators obstinately supporting and defending it.

However, bargaining over positions doesn't produce optimal payoffs, and it often harms the relationship between the parties.

When negotiators bargain over positions, they are more likely to confine themselves within the boundaries of those positions. The more they support their position, the more they become committed to it.

Positional bargaining is also ill suited for negotiations involving multiple parties. Tactics built around reciprocal concessions can't lead to agreements. And altering positions becomes exponentially harder than in bilateral negotiations, not only for the number of first-level actors involved, but also because key decision makers are not usually at the negotiation table.

During negotiations, the focus is usually on demands (positions) and not on interests.

Interests are peculiar needs, desires, uncertainties, constraints, and concerns that explain why a player has adopted a specific position.

As we'll see in the following example, conflicting positions don't always imply conflicting interests.

The Six-Day War

The 1978 Egyptian-Israeli peace treaty after the Six-Day War of 1967 is a perfect example of positional bargaining leading to a stalemate. A solution was created only after moving beyond stated positions and carefully looking at each side's interests.

During the Six-Day War, Israel occupied the Egyptian Sinai Peninsula (see Figure 2).

Figure 2. The Sinai Peninsula.

When Egypt and Israel started discussions in an attempt to reach an agreement, their positions were irreconcilable. Israel's position was to keep some of the Sinai. Conversely, Egypt maintained that all the Sinai had to return to Egyptian sovereignty.

A solution in which the Sinai was split between the two countries was unacceptable to Egypt. Going back to the conditions prior to the Six-Day War was unacceptable to Israel.

However, looking beyond their positions to their interests opened the door for a solution.

Israel's interest was security and protection. The Sinai represented a perfect cushion between Egypt and Israel, holding Egyptian tanks far from Israeli borders.

On the other hand, Egypt's interest was sovereignty. The Sinai had been under Egyptian control since the time of the pharaohs. Egypt had just reclaimed authority over the peninsula after centuries of foreign domination, and it was not ready to relinquish it again.

At Camp David in September 1978, President Sadat of Egypt and Prime Minister Begin of Israel agreed to the following proposal:

The Sinai would return to Egyptian sovereignty and most of the Sinai would be demilitarized; as a result, Israeli security would be safeguarded.

Systematic Questioning Mind-Set

Understanding the context of the game and the interests and concerns of the other player requires a systematic approach. Most negotiators focus on what the other side wants, on the other side's demands and positions, and while understanding what the other party wants is important, more critical is identifying why the other party is formulating a specific demand, and why the other party is sustaining a particular position.

The purpose of any negotiation is to resolve interests, not demands. As a negotiator, you need to shift from a behavioral to a cognitive perspective. You must understand what the other party is thinking.

Your goal is not to compromise, but to maximize value. And the only way to do this is to clearly define your interests and priorities and to learn the other side's interests and the relative importance of the different issues to the other side.

Remember two key facts while negotiating:

- *Demands are something to learn from*: Always ask yourself why the other side is making this specific demand. Why is the other side holding this specific position?
- *The other party's problems are your problems*: The only way to reconcile interests and achieve an optimal payoff for both parties is to find a solution to the other side's interests, constraints, and concerns.

OFF-THE-TABLE NEGOTIATION

As we have highlighted in chapter 7, deals are often determined away from the negotiation table.

Negotiators must understand how to transform the negotiation scope and structure by exploring complementary interests and concerns of behind-the-scenes players and how to alter the negotiation power dynamics by broadening the playing field.

Adding and subtracting issues and parties can change the perceived structure of the negotiation and therefore its outcomes.

Therefore, negotiators must identify all three levels of players: the actual negotiators, the parties directly affecting the negotiations, and the parties indirectly influencing the negotiations.

They must involve all the players in the right sequence.

In addition, they must recognize the different complementary interests and concerns of all the parties involved, paying careful attention to the needs of second- and third-level players, those not sitting at the negotiation table.

Going back to the 1978 Egyptian-Israeli peace treaty, the agreement was fostered by Henry Kissinger's (US secretary of state) role in the back channel pre-negotiation talks. The United States needed to improve its image with oil-producing Arab countries and Egypt, as a member of the Arab League, represented the perfect channel through which to achieve this goal. Israel needed military and financial support that the United States could provide. Egypt wanted to reclaim authority over the Israeli-occupied Sinai.

Back-channel negotiations sometimes circumvent and sometimes complement official negotiations. In this specific case, the agreement was achieved by broadening the negotiation perspective and involving a third player with overlapping interests: Trilateral negotiations were needed to close the circle of reciprocation and accommodate the parties' different interests and concerns (Figure 3).

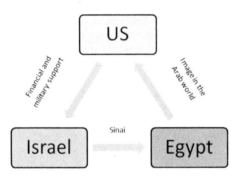

Figure 3. Trilateral negotiations.

TATA ACQUIRES JAGUAR AND LAND ROVER[2]

In 2006, the Ford Motor Company, the world third largest automobile manufacturer, reported losses of $12.7 billion, the worst performance in the company's history. It lost around $6 billion in the American operations, and a further investment of $12 billion was required to make those operations profitable by the year 2009.

By the time the results for 2006 were out, analysts believed that to salvage the North American business Ford needed to sell Jaguar and Land Rover (JLR). Strategic reviews conducted by Ford on the two brands ended with recommendations to sell. However, some analysts voiced the perspective that both brands were on the path to revival. Jaguar, even if still losing money, had several new models lined up and had introduced the XK in 2006. Land Rover was on its way to profits and recorded sales of 192,000 units in 2006.

JLR had three manufacturing sites and two advanced design centers in the UK. The design centers employed approximately 5,000 of the total 16,000 workforce in JLR.

When it acquired Jaguar in 1989 for $2.5 billion, Ford had plans to produce around 400,000 units a year to compete with Mercedes, Audi, and BMW. However, in 2007, Jaguar sales were only 60,485 units, with Europe accounting for 57% of the sales and North America for 26%.

Land Rover was acquired from BMW in 2000 for $2.7 billion. By 2007, Europe accounted for 60% of the sales and North America for 23%.

Since 2002, the activities of both Jaguar and Land Rover had been fully integrated. They had a single engineering team, shared technologies and power trains, and functioned through co-managed engineering facilities. Most of the back-office functions like purchasing, human resources, information technology, quality, and finance were also integrated.

Over the years, Ford found that it was failing to derive the desired benefits from these acquisitions, even after spending more than $10 billion just on Jaguar since acquiring it.

Jaguar and Land Rover customers were seen as highly nationalistic and brand loyal. Jaguar customers were considered traditionalists. Analysts cited the case of the X-Type launched by Ford, which consumers did not accept as they did not like the design. Consumers felt that it was more like a Ford Mondeo than a Jaguar. To control costs, Ford built Jaguar on the Mondeo platform, but this only served to dilute Jaguar's premium image.

After a preliminary evaluation of JLR, six companies expressed an interest in acquiring Jaguar and Land Rover.

In November 2007, Ford announced the three preferred bidders: two Indian industrial conglomerates, Tata Motors (part of Tata Group) and Mahindra & Mahindra, and one equity firm, One Equity Partners (fronted by former Ford chief executive officer Jac Nasser).

FORD PERSPECTIVE

At the moment talks initiated, Ford's main priority was to maintain its image in the UK, which was its second largest market. This was more important than maximizing the financial side of the deal.

During negotiations, Ford had to consider the union's concerns because any misstep in this direction could adversely affect its image in the UK.

Ford had also to consider the British public's (and government's) reaction to the sale of two British symbols to either an equity firm or an Indian company.

Ford decided to sell JLR as a package, without separating the two brands, for two main reasons:

- Jaguar and Land Rover operations were fully integrated. Therefore, the interests of the workers would be more easily met if the two brands were sold together.
- Land Rover's outlook was brighter than Jaguar's. Jaguar would be harder to sell as a standalone company.

UNION PERSPECTIVE

In early July 2007, Unite, Britain's largest trade union, sent a five-point charter to Ford demanding, among other things, that the union be involved in the sale process.

Union members were present in the early stages of presentations and negotiations between Ford and the bidders.

Unite requests were the following:

- No jobs will be shed at the three JLR factories and the two JLR engineering sites, protecting a total of 16,000 workers.
- Jaguar and Land Rover will still be produced in Britain in the future.
- Employee terms and conditions (including pensions) will be maintained.
- The status quo will be maintained in sourcing agreements (with Ford's UK plants).

TATA PERSPECTIVE

Tata Motors is a leading industrial group (part of Tata Group, with $21.5 billion in sales in 2007) that manufactures cars and light trucks; in recent years, it is best known for its innovative launch of the Tata Nano, the least expensive car in the world at about $3,000.

Many analysts believed that Tata's main goal was Land Rover and that it would try to persuade Ford to negotiate the two brands separately. Another objective was to increase Tata's international presence through the JLR global dealer network: By the end of 2007, Jaguar had 859 dealers and a presence in 93 markets across the world; Land Rover had a presence in 175 markets through 1,397 dealers.

Takeovers are often associated with layoffs and factory closings. Tata, instead, has a history of merging in a different way, more as a strategic partner than vulture capitalist.

Tata has applied this approach to $18 billion in overseas deals since 2000, when it acquired Tetley Tea for $400 million. After buying British and Italian engineering and design houses, Korean truck makers, American hotels, Asian and European steelmakers, and software companies around the globe, Tata now has 333,000 employees worldwide, 26% of whom are outside India. Tata's unique shareholder structure makes it more focused on long-term goals, thus insulating its employees from short-term gains pressure.

In all its deals, Tata has been careful to signal its respect for workers, leaving executives in place and setting up joint management boards. Following its overseas acquisitions, layoffs and factory closings are exceptions.

THE NEGOTIATIONS

Ravi Kant, Tata Motors managing director, was quick to understand the interests of the different players.

Ford wanted to maintain its image in the UK and sell JLR as a package. The union wanted to retain the status quo for its workers (job security, salaries, benefits, and production volumes).

Kant also explored the interests and concerns of the British government and public opinion.

A massive public relations effort was put together and Tata began to make presentations to workers, unions, members of parliament, and local and government officials to diffuse widespread skepticism over an Indian company acquiring such iconic and luxury brands.

Kant decided to proactively answer questions such as Will these brands remain British? Will an Indian company which has never manufactured/marketed a luxury car be able to manage the challenges of a high-end car business? Why should we have confidence that Tata will succeed where Ford failed?

Tata involved all the players in the right sequence: First was the union (meeting all its demands). Then came the government and public opinion (diffusing skepticism). And finally, only after having secured the support of Unite and opinion leaders and government, Tata approached Ford for direct talks.

At that stage, Tata had already defined the structure of the negotiation, diminishing the leeway for Ford and setting the range of potential outcomes. In other words, Tata wiped out all Ford's alternatives: If Ford wanted to meet its primary interest of not damaging its image in the UK, it had to sell to Tata.

On March 26, 2008, Tata Motors entered into an agreement with Ford for the purchase of JLR. Tata Motors agreed to pay $2.3 billion in cash for a 100% and totally debt free acquisition of JLR.

Today JLR sells 429,000 cars (79,000 Jaguars and 350,000 Land Rovers), employs 28,000 workers, with a turnover of $32,1 billion and a profit before tax of $4,1 billion.

DECISION AUTHORITY

During international negotiations, recognizing the key decision maker among the people sitting in front of you can be difficult. One golden rule is to focus on body language. Watch at whom everybody on the other side looks when there is an unexpected or equivocal moment.

Status and influence are primordially expressed by the head: Pushing the chin up and raising the eye level conveys confidence and bravery. Putting the head down is a primitive defensive reaction to a potential punch to a vulnerable spot such as the throat. It is a display of fear that reveals deference and submission, and it is a key clue to understanding team ranking.

Identify the negotiator's authority and constraints, as well as the relationship between the different levels of participants. If the other player lacks decision authority, and you anticipate a further round of negotiations, leave yourself room for flexibility and further concessions with the final decision maker.

Because sometimes the decision maker is not sitting at the negotiation table, you have to find a way to influence her decisions. Therefore, mapping the other side's decision-making process and identifying the key decision makers becomes a key exercise during the preparation phase of the negotiation.

RT OF DIPLOMACY

5, Francois de Callieres, a French diplomat, wrote a manual that is still considered a reference for modern diplomacy.[3] Following are five guidelines for present-day negotiators:[4]

- *Negotiations do not end with the signature of a contract.* Continual negotiation is needed to foster the relationship between parties and adapt the agreement to changing circumstances.
- *Put yourself in the position of others.* Listen, recognize, and understand the other side's perspective.
- *Be patient.* Negotiations usually take longer than initially planned. Learn the art of patience; take out obstacles, resist hardball tactics, identify options for an integrative solution, and claim value without rushing to a conclusion.
- *Prepare.* Study thoroughly for every negotiation.
- *Show respect.* Above all in international negotiations, show respect, and willingness to learn from the other side's values and norms. Never adopt arrogant or disrespectful behaviors.

ETHICS IN NEGOTIATION

Ethical standards in negotiation have always raised contrasting opinions from researchers and scholars.

According to many negotiators, deception is to be expected in negotiation and is morally acceptable. According to others, deception is always ethically undesirable.[5]

The main problem with the debate regarding ethics in negotiation is that individuals subjectively interpret what is fair in negotiation: Their standards can unconsciously differ according to the culture, the context, and their personality. Even within the same culture, depending on age, experience, education level, and gender, individuals hold different views of what is perceived as ethical behavior.

According to the arguments put forward by the advocates of *moral relativism,* ethical propositions are relative to social, cultural, historical, and personal references and do not reflect universal truths.[6]

DECEPTION

A significant difference between those who are effective negotiators and those who are not lies in their capacity to mislead and not to be misled.[7]

Negotiators often face an important dilemma: Should I deceive the other person about my interests and stand firm on my positions or be transparent about my interests and flexible about demands to create options that can increase the size of the pie and help both parties achieve their goals, while strengthening the relationship?

In every negotiation, after the integrative, value-creation phase, there is always a moment when the pie needs to be allocated. Sharing information can allow for value creation. However, deceiving and hiding information can ensure a larger share of the pie. This stalemate cannot be totally determined, but can be managed.

Among the most common deceptive and unethical negotiation tactics, we can identify the following:[8]

- *Traditional competitive bargaining* (intentionally use time pressure, threats, extreme opening demands).
- *Bluffing* (intentionally display false intentions to commit an action).
- *False promises* (in return for concessions now, offer future concessions, which you know you can't deliver).
- *Misrepresentation or falsification of information* (intentionally providing flawed or inaccurate information).
- *Misrepresentation or falsification of own role* (intentionally exaggerating own decision authority within the organization or demeaning the other party).
- *Omissions* (intentionally omitting relevant information).

When it comes to ethical behavior in negotiation, there are three main schools of thought:[9]

- *Negotiation as a poker game school*: Negotiation is analogous to a poker game, where information asymmetry exists between the parties[10] and, thus, it must be played according to certain rules. All negotiators should be aware of these rules. Only conduct that falls outside the rules must be considered unethical. Most deceptive behaviors fall within the game rules and must therefore be deemed acceptable during negotiations.
- *Negotiation as an aspect of social life school*: This viewpoint rejects the analogy between negotiation and game; bargaining doesn't have its own set of rules and should obey the same set of ethics that applies to everyday social meetings.[11]
- *The pragmatist negotiation school*: According to the pragmatist school, unethical and deceptive behavior should be avoided not only because it's unprincipled, but mainly because of the consequences for long-term relationships.

The prisoner's dilemma represents the starting point in understanding an individual's behavior in negotiation, particularly when the stakes are high, information regarding the other party is limited, and there is no certain way for each side to predict whether the other side will lie (more on game theory in chapter 8). The result is that incentives to lie are very high in negotiation.

Therefore, it is fundamental to probe all the information you receive: Don't take for granted that what other people are telling you is true.

If you discover that the other side is acting unethically, don't immediately call her on it. Wait and see if explicit embarrassment is really required. Uncover the deception only if it is useful to your goals. In negotiation, it doesn't matter who is right; the focus must always remain on the goals.

Incentives to lie can be reduced by increasing the flow of information between the parties.

Information is power in negotiation and the only way to promote information exchange is to relentlessly ask questions, attentively listen to replies, and continuously filter and calibrate the facts and evidence provided by the other party.

During the preparation phase, write down the questions you want to have answered and during the negotiation process check whether each question has been satisfactorily addressed. If not, continue pressing, and probe all information provided. If numbers are provided, validate them against industry standards or market values and, if they are not available, ask for the reasoning behind the result.

Establishing long-term relationships is another effective way to decrease incentives to lie and to raise ethical standards in the negotiation.

However, because one of the most reliable indicators of lying is a sudden change in behavior, establishing a baseline for behavior is fundamental in trying to detect deception (although, as seen in chapter 5, discovering when others are lying and recognizing what they are lying about is very difficult). Establishing a concrete baseline is easier if we have known a person over a long period of time. This is another reason why long-term relationships can be useful in negotiation.

How to Combat Hardball Tactics

If your opponent's aggressive intentions are clearly perceptible, move to an empty-mind attitude. Real emptiness is the state where there is no obscurity and any clouds of confusion have cleared away. Place your intellect on a broad plane. Learn to be unmoved in mind even in the heat of battle.[12]

In going up against a challenging opponent, most people respond in one of two ways. The first is to give in, hoping the other side will not demand further concessions. However, often the other party will request additional yielding. The second common response is to react in a tough way, making threats, being deceptive, bluffing, and making extreme demands. If neither party compromises, then the negotiation will break off.[13]

Generally, most negotiators, when they believe they are going to face a competitive negotiator, tend to avoid conflict so as to reach an agreement, enter the negotiation with lower expectations, and accommodate the other party demands.[14]

When the other side appears to be using a deceitful tactic, the first step is to identify the tactic.

After recognizing the scheme, bring it up with the other side, being careful not to question the person, but only the specific situation.[15] Don't get the other player defensive; otherwise, it will be more difficult to move the other side from its position, making a possible agreement more challenging.

Uncovering a deceptive tactic serves the purpose of setting the ground rules and boundaries of the game. Attacking the other side personally doesn't usually help obtain our goals.

In general, unless you have good reasons to trust somebody, don't.[16] Probe; verify facts and affirmations. Don't accept being a victim. Be ready to play hard bargaining. Before entering a negotiation, lower your expectations for the other party's behavior. It is not important who is right and who is wrong. Focus on your goals. Always remember, there are things you can control, and others you can't. Focus on those you can control. You have no control over what happened in the past. Focus on the present and the future.

Don't let your emotions cloud your judgment. Never respond to questions and demands under time pressure. Detach yourself from the situation: If necessary, take a break. Sometimes it pays to look at things from the outsider's point of view.

Focus on your goals and try to separate the people from the problem.[17] Separate the relationship from the issue. Don't fall into the blame trap. Blaming is counter-productive because it makes the other side defensive and distracts from the real issue: achieving your goals.

If a person upsets you and you stay upset, they have gotten you twice. Every time you remember and feel angry, they get you again.[18]

COMMON DIRTY TRICKS

Ambiguous authority: You decide to negotiate with the other side, reaching what you believe is a final agreement only to discover that the other party doesn't have full decision authority and has to take the deal to the boss for approval. This technique is intended to provide the parties' with a second round of negotiation.

Before starting to give any concession, investigate the decision authority on the other side.

Diminishing your status: The other side can make you wait, decide to defer the talks to handle more urgent matters, or interrupt the negotiations to deal with other persons. All these tactics are aimed at attacking your status.

Personal attack: The other side can imply that you are uninformed or unfamiliar with the object of the negotiation. The other side can pretend to not listen to you or to not care about what you are saying.

The good-guy/bad-guy routine: During a negotiation, two people on the same side will stage an argument. One will bring a tough and inflexible stance to the table. The other will make small concessions that look like a favor.

The humble negotiator: Some individuals induce sympathy, admitting the outstanding skills and experience of the other side, which creates a false sense of security in the opponents. Every time they receive a concession, they ask for further accommodations, highlighting their lack of experience and competence, and placing themselves in the hands of the other party.

In each case, recognize the tactic and bring it up explicitly to moderate its impact. Unequivocally raising the issue can prevent further recurrences.

The Bully: The other side can be very aggressive in convincing you that its take-it-or-leave-it tactic is serious and its position is not flexible. When you negotiate with a bully, don't make concessions. Keep the meeting short, and don't lose your temper. Your goal is to create a breach in the iron curtain built by the other side.

Use silence. Long sentences dilute the importance of the message. Using silence, you'll show the other side that you are ready to be competitive but are not willing to tolerate aggressive behavior.

:r and calibrate the information provided by the other party. Test the credibility of threats and promises (further information on credible commitment is provided in chapter 8).

Above all else, be patient. Don't focus on the other side's behavior; concentrate on the information provided to you. How you respond is more important than what you say. Don't become prey to possible personal attacks. Keep your composure and stay focused on your goal.[19]

WHAT IF YOU ARE WEAK?

Power in negotiations is not defined by wealth, financial resources, political networks, or status. Power is in the hands of the player who needs the agreement less. Power lies in the player who has the strongest alternative.

If you are weak and have few or even no alternatives, don't show it. Don't disclose that you are weak. Focus on improving your available alternatives (MATNAs). Any alternative that can decrease your dependence on the current negotiation can increase your power.

If you have no alternatives, try to focus the conversation on the other party's desire to minimize risk by closing the deal now and not having to look for other options. This strategy is particularly effective if you already have an established relationship with the other side. Be careful not to make your eagerness to close too obvious.

Focus on the other side's alternatives. You know that your MATNAs are weak, but what about the other player's? Having weak MATNAs is not a problem, if the other side also has frail MATNAs.

Leverage the fact that powerful negotiators usually don't allocate sufficient time for preparation before a negotiation.

If the other side is focused only on price, try to emphasize what you bring to the table, which differentiates you from your competitors. This is not an easy task. Following are strategies that can be employed:

- Submit two proposals, one with the lowest possible price, the other one with a higher price that includes additional elements that you know the other party values. Connect apparently isolated issues into a single package.
- Lower you price enough to enter the final rounds of negotiation, which sometimes take place face to face, allowing for different elements to be evaluated.
- Negotiate off the table; map the decision-making process and influence the different key players. Understand each player's interests and draft a proposal that includes different elements. Understanding the decision-making process, you can also recognize how to make the price issue less relevant.
- The previous activity cannot be employed when there is an auction or a request for offer. Consequently, you must learn to communicate with the other party when there is no potential deal on the table or in between requests for offer. Take the initiative. Be proactive. Try beforehand to identify the other side's needs and make proposals to influence the negotiation process. Your objective is to get your interests integrated into the organization's

decision-making process and subsequently into the final specifications and technical documents, before reaching the bargaining table.[20]

- Mapping the decision-making process allows you to identify the key players involved in the decision. Understand the links and the degree of influence among the different players, and try to move away from low-level officials with limited authority and limited access to their organization's leadership.

- Most international negotiations involve in some way third-level players (competitors, customers, suppliers). There are few strictly bilateral negotiations. Thus, it is wise to build coalitions and alliances with third-level players that can influence the other side.[21]

Another tactic that can be employed is bluffing. The problem is that this is a risky strategy because it can lead to no deal and a broken relationship.

If the other party knows that you are weak, then acknowledge the other party's power and individualize the meeting, appealing to the relationship between the parties and, if required, relinquishing any power left: It's up to you. What would it take for you to say yes? Write your number and conditions. Any help would be appreciated.

Bear in mind that if you are too narrowly focused in the current negotiation you can lose sight of your entire portfolio of negotiations. Sometimes not accepting a deal makes good sense considering your overall portfolio.

As seen in the following example, recognizing your weaknesses and finding ways to diminish them and leverage the other side's interests and weaknesses can increase your power in a negotiation.

THE ROOSEVELT CAMPAIGN

The year was 1912. During the presidential campaign, three million copies of Roosevelt's photograph had been printed for circulation with a campaign speech when Roosevelt's campaign manager, George Perkins, discovered a terrible error: Mr. Moffet, the photographer, had not been asked for permission to use the photograph.

Copyright law allowed the photographer to demand as much as $1 per copy of the photograph. The potential loss of $3 million would have easily killed the campaign.[22]

Mr. Perkins had very weak MATNAs:

- Destroying the pamphlets.
- Threatening the photographer.
- Promising the photographer future important political or professional roles when and if Roosevelt became president.
- Negotiating a lump-sum payment.
- Risking Roosevelt's reputation and millions in liability.

Put yourself in Mr. Perkins' shoes: How would you manage the negotiation with Mr. Moffet?

After analyzing the problem, Perkins contacted Moffet with the following telegram:

We are planning to distribute millions of pamphlets with Roosevelt's picture on the cover. It will be great publicity for the studio whose photograph we use. How much will you pay us to use yours? Respond immediately.

Moffet replied that although he'd never done something like that before he'd be willing to pay $250.

Perkins evaluated the photographer's MATNAs and the information available to him at that moment. Mr. Moffet perhaps did not know that Perkins' MATNAs were so weak, but his alternative of missing out on a great opportunity for publicity wasn't good either.

In other words, Perkins put himself in Moffet's shoes.

The telegram's tone implied that the campaign had good alternatives. By ending the message with *Respond immediately* Perkins conveyed a tight deadline, highlighting that Moffet was at risk of losing the deal. He also denied the photographer the chance to gather information and perhaps discover that the campaign speech had already been printed.

BEHAVIORS AND EMOTIONS IN NEGOTIATION

Cognitive decision making is not the only factor shaping negotiators' behavior; emotions, as a consequence of the conflict embedded in bargaining situations, are fundamental in understanding how people think and behave during negotiations (as seen in chapters 8 and 9).

Emotions are subjective and conscious mental experiences (such as anger and fear) directed toward a specific object or situation and typically characterized by physiological and behavioral changes in the body.

Emotions can also be viewed as high-intensity affective states caused by the ability or inability to achieve our goals.[23]

Emotions differ from mood because they are related to specific situations (they are directed toward something) and usually have a shorter duration. What is interesting is that both *integral emotions* (emotions triggered by events related to the negotiation) and *incidental emotions* (emotions triggered by events unrelated to the negotiation) influence negotiators' cognitive processes and, as a result, their behaviors.[24]

THE SOCIAL FUNCTIONALIST PERSPECTIVE

According to recent research, emotions in negotiation have the specific function of solving social problems that arise in dyad and group relations.[25]

The first kind of problem negotiators face is *creating and sustaining mutual cooperation based on trust and reciprocity*. Some emotions can facilitate the establishment of collaborative conduct. Liking is often the premise for the foundation of collaborative ties. Appreciation rewards the other side for employing cooperative behavior.

On the other side, emotions can also act as precautions against non-cooperative behavior. Anger occurs in response to non-collaborative actions. Manifestations of discomfort, sadness, and guilt over others' and own behavior stimulate the employment of cooperative behavior.

The second type of problem is *maintaining status hierarchies within the dyad or groups*. Social hierarchical structures have the purpose of allocating resources within a group. Specific emotions related to dominance, such as contempt and anger, signal negotiators' claims to particular resources.

The third category of problem is *preserving group norms*. Embarrassment and shame convey compliance, acting as an expression of regret following behaviors that disrupt social relationships with the purpose of resuming collaborative behavior.

Emotions differ according to the different negotiation stages.

As seen in chapters 1 and 7, the negotiation process stage can be divided into seven phases:

- Designing the game; off-the-table negotiation.
- Exchanging information.
- Opening moves.
- Competitive phase.
- Integrative phase.
- End game.
- Negotiation post mortem analysis.

Most negotiation research concurs on a fundamental assumption with regard to negotiations: *the importance of first impressions*.

During the exchanging information phase, gestures and emotions help us understand whether the other side is worth talking to, communicating that you are worth talking to, breaking the ice, and creating the premises for a cooperative negotiation. Head nods, smiles, physical proximity, and hand gestures convey liking, while leaning forward, lifting the head, and raising the eyebrow convey interest. Liking and interest prompt compliance and positive feeling in addition to accomplishing the above mentioned exchanging information stage functions.

During the opening moves and the competitive phases, negotiators face the dilemma between claiming and creating value. Usually individuals begin by pursuing value claiming during the initial stages of a negotiation, asserting their power and authority. Emotions that fulfill the function of conveying dominance are anger, toughness, stubbornness, and contempt. Anger aims at changing others' behavior or obtaining a concession. Anger is still associated with authority and power in many cultures. Toughness and stubbornness convey the information that you care about the specific topic and are ready to leave the negotiation if you don't receive the required concession, inducing emotions of fear in the counterpart. Contempt communicates to the other party that he or she is not a worthy opponent, resulting in low self-confidence and in some cases submission in the other side.

It is important to emphasize that while anger and contempt fulfill an important role in the opening moves and competitive phases of negotiation, they can also have negative repercussions, leading to conflict spirals and limiting the options for collaborative negotiation (integrative phase).

During the integrative phase, negotiators pursue value creation, shifting from competitive to cooperative positions. To build a relationship and create trust, the first step is to convey behaviors associated with embarrassment, to communicate regret and guilt for the conduct adopted during the competitive phase. The second step is to establish rapport. As seen in chapter 3, in the International Profiler paragraph, rapport can be defined as the degree to which you are able to display warmth and thoughtfulness when building relationships in a variety of contexts that can lead to trust-based relationships in the long term and mutual cooperation.

During the end game phase, the focus is on closing the deal and achieving your goals. The aim is to convince the other side that no more concessions will be yielded. Two emotions play a fundamental role at this stage: pain and exasperation.

Pain is conveyed in response to further demands for concessions to stress that you have reached your reservation value.

Exasperation implies that certain requests are not consistent with the established relationship and that, if further concessions are requested, you will implicitly consider the other side to be acting in bad faith.

COGNITION AND BEHAVIOR ASSOCIATED WITH EMOTIONS

Emotions can influence both the scope and the depth of the information a negotiator is able to process.[26]

Negotiators encountering negative emotions tend to focus only on specific information and, therefore positions, limiting their ability to generate new ideas and options. In contrast, positive emotions boost the ability to produce integrative and creative solutions.

Both negative and positive emotions restrict the ability to exert cognitive effort and use careful information processing. In other words, negotiators experiencing anger or happiness will rely more on heuristics when making decisions.

When experiencing anger, individuals are more likely to blame others for the situation and as a result evaluate the other side more negatively. Negotiators experiencing negative emotions are also more likely to take retaliatory actions; they are therefore more risk-seeking and more likely to adopt competitive strategies than happy negotiators.

A display of negative emotions can lead to a conflict spiral because the other side can decide to mirror the negotiator's behavior by making extreme counteroffers as an act of ill will.[27]

Even if happy negotiators are more likely to share information and adopt collaborative strategies, the heuristic behavior associated with positive emotions can lead individuals to complacency, setting less ambitious goals, accepting a deal too quickly, and thus leaving value on the table.

As seen in chapter 7, process fairness is key to managing the perceived power asymmetry during negotiations. Negotiators who believe in the fairness of the negotiation process are more likely to experience positive emotions during and after the negotiation.

Ultimatum game experiments have demonstrated that perceptions of unfairness and anger are correlated: Responders reject unfair offers because they wish to punish proposers who make inequitable offers. Higher rejection rates occur when a time constraint is applied to the experiment: Unfair offers activate the anterior insula area of the brain, and time pressure doesn't allow for activation of the dorso-lateral prefrontal cortex that should mediate the emotional response of the insula.[28]

Not only cultural and contextual factors, but also personality can influence our perception of fairness. In recent experiments based on the Five-Factor Personality Model, extraverts were more likely to remember positive words and situations and make more positive judgments, while high-neuroticism individuals recalled more negative words and situations and made more negative judgments.[29]

Personality can thus affect players' perception of the fairness of the negotiation process, influencing their emotions and consequently their behavior during the bargaining process.

Also emotional expressivity, the extent to which people outwardly display their emotions, and the ability to control it may affect negotiations. Negotiators high in expressivity tend to express both positive and negative emotions, while negotiators low in expressivity, because of their ability to regulate the explicit display of their emotions, tend to express only positive feelings.

Therefore, during negotiations, highly emotionally expressive players can chose to display specific emotions according to the situation, such as pretending to be pleased or angry when they are not, whereas less emotionally expressive players may rather chose to conceal their emotions.

APPRAISAL THEORY

Appraisal theory states that emotions are caused by people's interpretations and evaluations of a specific situation. Emotions reveal the occurrence of a discrepancy between a desired outcome and the actual outcome. This is why different people react differently to the same circumstance.[30]

EMOTIONAL INTELLIGENCE

Emotional intelligence is the ability to recognize, monitor, and regulate your own and others' emotions, discriminate between these emotions, and then use this information to guide your thoughts and actions.[31]

In situations of impasse, negotiators tend to react in three ways: They become angry, leave the table, or avoid the source of the conflict.[32] The problem is that these responses often intensify the conflict.

According to the emotional intelligence framework, negotiators are more effec-tive if they respond counter-intuitively, first by regaining emotional balance and then by skillfully interacting with the other player(s).

To regain emotional balance, the four central competencies are:

- *Self-Awareness*: The ability to recognize your emotions and their effects on your behavior and decision-making ability.
- *Self-Regulation*: The ability to channel your emotions into appropriate behav-ior. Self-regulation is less like concealing your emotions and more like having the capability to control unsettling emotions. As a result, self-regulation

should be understood as mastering your emotions so that, for example, one can contain extreme anger when it is important to do so, while at the same time being able to convey it when it is strategically necessary.[33]

• *Self-Motivation*: The ability to be persistent in pursuing your goals despite difficulties and setbacks.

• *Patience*: The ability to tolerate frustration, irritation, provocation, adversity, delays, and pain with composure, perseverance, and diligence. Patience implies the capacity to make decisions only when emotions are fully under control, carefully evaluating the different options, without falling victim to pressure tactics. Remember: Emotions are momentary; decisions are often long-lasting.

To effectively interact with other negotiators, the two primary competencies are:

• *Empathy*: The ability to read others' emotions, understand them, and take into account others' feelings and perspectives.

• *Social Skills*: The ability to effectively communicate and interact with others.

THE IMPORTANCE OF RITUALS

Recent research has suggested that rituals may be exceptionally effective for managers engaged in high-value tasks, such as international negotiations.[34]

Despite the lack of a direct causal connection between the ritual and the anticipated result, performing rituals with the objective of obtaining a specific result is sufficient for that result to occur. To be effective, rituals don't have to be rational. Indeed, most everyday rituals are nonsensical.

These results are consistent with research in sport psychology indicating that routines increase performance, reduce anxiety and stress, and improve focus, emotional stability, and confidence.[35]

Examples of famous sport rituals are:

• The New Zealand rugby team performs the Haka, a Maori dance, before every match.

• Michael Jordan always wore his North Carolina college shorts under his Chicago Bulls uniform.

• Usain Bolt, the 100- and 200- meter World and Olympic champion, makes a show for the crowd before the start of a sprint.

• Valentino Rossi, the nine-time motorcycle Grand Prix World Champion, before the race, kneels beside his bike and has a small chat with it.

• F1 drivers and downhill skiers, before their competitions, rehearse all the elements of the track.

Rituals put individuals in the right mind-set to approach high-stress tasks, deliver a sense of shared identity, and reinforce desired behaviors.[36]

COMMON MISTAKES AT THE NEGOTIATION TABLE

Negotiators can make many mistakes at the negotiation table.

First, we often fail to prepare:

• We don't set goals.

- We don't prioritize interests.
- We don't explore different alternatives (MATNAs).
- We don't take time to ponder the other players' interests and their potential alternatives.
- We fail to recognize opportunities for value creation.
- We don't map the other party's decision-making process and don't collect information on the role of second- and third-level players and their specific interests.
- We don't define in advance our first offer (or counteroffer) and our concession plan.

Second, we often make errors during the negotiation process:

- We focus only on claiming value and not on creating value. We are affected by the fixed-pie bias that causes us to focus only on one issue, usually price, failing to address opportunities for value creation through trade-offs among multiple issues.
- We make concessions that are too large.
- We don't process, filter and calibrate the information provided to us.
- We focus on positions and not interests. We lose opportunities for value creation by not exploring the whys behind specific demands.
- We fail to gain firm commitments on the deal.
- We do not maintain a balance between relationships and issues: Sometimes we focus too much on the relationship and set aside the negotiation issues; in other cases, we focus too much on the issues to the detriment of the relationship.
- We fall prey to emotions and lose sight of our goals.
- Under pressure, we are not able to delay our reactions[37] and balance between rational and intuitive, conscious and unconscious thinking.[38]

(ENDNOTES)

1   Fisher, R., Ury, W. L., & Patton, B. (1991). Getting to yes: Negotiating Agreement Without Giving In (2nd ed.). London: Penguin Books.

2   Columbia Business School, Program on Social Intelligence, Workshop December 9, 2011, Negotiating International Acquisitions. Morris, M. W. & Rana, Y. S. Retrieved from http://www8.gsb.columbia.edu/psi/workshops/culture

3   de Callières, F. (2000). On the Manner of Negotiating With Princes. Translated by. A. F. Whyte, introduction by C. Handy. New York: Houghton Mifflin.

4   Salacuse, J. W. (2003). The Global Negotiator: Making, Managing, and Mending Deals Around the World in the Twenty-First Century. New York: Palgrave Macmillan.

5   Banaji, M. R., Bazerman, M. H., & Chugh, D. (2003). How (un)ethical are you?. Harvard Business Review, Vol. 81, N. 12, 56-64.

6   Carr, A. (1968). Is Business Bluffing Ethical?. Harvard Business Review, Vol. 46, N.1, 143-153.

7   Reilly, P. R. (2009). Was Machiavelli Right? Lying in Negotiation and the Art of Defensive Self-Help. Ohio State Journal on Dispute Resolution, Vol. 24, N. 3, 481-533.

8   Lewicki, R. J., & Robinson, R. (1998). A factor analysis study of ethical and unethical bargaining tactics. Journal of Business Ethics, 18, 211-228.

9   Shell, G. R. (2006). Bargaining for Advantage: Negotiation Strategies for Reasonable People (2nd ed.). London: Penguin Books.

10 Carr, A. (1968). Is Business Bluffing Ethical?. Harvard Business Review, Vol. 46, N.1, 143-153.

11 Provis, C. (2000). Ethics, Deception, and Labor Negotiation. Journal of Business Ethics, Vol. 28, N. 2, 145-158.

12 Musashi, M. (1993). The book of five rings. Translated by T. Cleary. Boston: Shambhala Publications.

13 Fisher, R., Ury, W. L., & Patton, B. (1991). Getting to yes: Negotiating Agreement Without Giving In (2nd ed.). London: Penguin Books.

14 Field, A. (2003). How to Negotiate With a Hard-Nosed Adversary. Harvard Management Update (U0303A).

15 Shell, G. R. (2006). Bargaining for Advantage: Negotiation Strategies for Reasonable People (2nd ed.). London: Penguin Books.

16 Shell, G. R. (2006). Bargaining for Advantage: Negotiation Strategies for Reasonable People (2nd ed.). London: Penguin Books.

17 Fisher, R., Ury, W. L., & Patton, B. (1991). Getting to yes: Negotiating Agreement Without Giving In (2nd ed.). London: Penguin Books.

18 Edwards, C. (2006). Mind Reading. Old Windsor: Real Publishing.

19 Lewicki, R. J., Saunders, D. M., & Barry, B. (2010). Essentials of Negotiation (5th ed.). New York: McGraw Hill.

20 Sebenius, J. K. (2002). The Hidden Challenge of Cross-Border Negotiations. Harvard Business Review, Vol. 80, N. 3, 76-85.

21 Salacuse, J. W. (2003). The Global Negotiator: Making, Managing, and Mending Deals Around the World in the Twenty-First Century. New York: Palgrave Macmillan.

22 Lax, D. A., & Sebenius, J. K. (2006). 3-D Negotiation: Powerful Tools to Change the Game in Your Most Important Deals. Boston: Harvard Business Press.

23 Kumar, R. (2004). Culture and Emotions in Intercultural Negotiations: An Overview. In M. J. Gelfand, & J. M. Brett (Eds.), The Handbook of Negotiation and Culture. Palo Alto, CA: Stanford University Press.

24 Barry, B., Fulmer, I. S., & Van Kleef, G. (2004). I laughed, I cried, I settled: The role of emotion in negotiation. In M. J. Gelfand, & J. M. Brett (Eds.), The Handbook of Negotiation and Culture. Palo Alto, CA: Stanford University Press.

25 Morris, M. W., & Keltner, D. (2000). How Emotions Work: The Social Functions Of Emotional Expression In Negotiations. Research in Organizational Behaviour, Vol. 22, 1-50.

26 Kopelman, S., Gewurz, I., & Sacharin, V. (2007). The Power of Presence: Strategic Response to Displayed Emotions in Negotiations. Ross School of Business Paper N. 1061, IACM 20th Annual Conference.

27 Kopelman, S., Rosette, A. S., & Thompson L. (2006). The three faces of Eve: Strategic displays of positive, negative, and neutral emotions in negotiations. Organizational Behavior and Human Decision Processes, 99, 81-101.

28 Knight, S. (2012). Fairness or anger in Ultimatum Game rejections?. Journal of European Psychology Students, Vol. 3, 2-14.

29 Barry, B., Fulmer, I. S., & Van Kleef, G. (2004). I laughed, I cried, I settled: The role of emotion in negotiation. In M. J. Gelfand, & J. M. Brett (Eds.), The Handbook of Negotiation and Culture. Palo Alto, CA: Stanford University Press.

30 Aronson, E., Wilson, T. D., & Akert, R. M. (2005). Social Psychology (7th ed.). Upper Saddle River, NJ: Pearson Education.

31 Goleman, D. (1996). Emotional Intelligence: Why it can matter more than IQ?. London: Bloomsbury Publishing PLC.

32 Salovey, P., & Mayer, J. D. (1990). Emotional intelligence. Imagination, Cognition, and Personality, 9, 185-211.

33 Benoliel, M. (2010). Master Negotiators: Intelligences and Competencies. Research Collection Lee Kong Chian School Of Business. Paper 3690.

34 Norton, M. I., & Gino, F. (2013). Rituals Alleviate Grieving for Loved Ones, Lovers, and Lotteries. Journal of Experimental Psychology: General. Advance online publication. February. doi: 10.1037/a0031772.

35 Mamassis, G., & Doganis, G. (2004). The Effects of a Mental Training Program on Juniors Pre-Competitive Anxiety, Self-Confidence, and Tennis Performance. Journal of Applied Sport Psychology, Vol. 16, N. 2, 118-137.

36 Guenzi, P., & Ruta, D. (2013). Leading Teams: Tools and Techniques for Successful Team Leadership from the Sports World. San Francisco: Jossey-Bass.

37 Dijksterhuis, A., & Nordgren, L. F. (2006). A theory of unconscious thought. Perspectives on Psychological Science, 1, 95-109.

38 Gladwell, M. (2007). Blink: The power of thinking without thinking. New York, NY: Back Bay Books.

CHAPTER 13:

International Negotiation

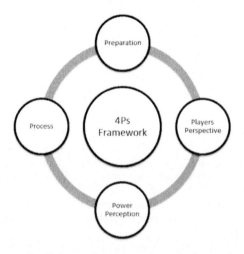

Stage 1: Preparation. Stage 2: Process. Stage 3: Power Perception. Stage 4: Players Perspective

In our culture it takes three cups of tea to do business. On the first cup you are a stranger. With the second cup you become a friend, and with the third cup you become family. The process takes years.[1]

INTRODUCTION

Assessing the impact of culture in intercultural negotiations is not easy. Culture is an artificial and abstract notion often adopted as an explanation for differences in behavior among people from different parts of the world. However, assessing human behavior only through a cultural lens is not sufficient.

Furthermore, culture is not monolithic: Cultural variations are significant and cultures are dynamic.[2] Additionally, all cultures display both dominant and recessive characteristics.

If we ascribe behavior only to culture, we end up disregarding other important factors that can affect decision-making, such as gender, age, role, religion, corporate culture, social class, education, and international experiences.[3]

The relationship between culture and an individual's behavior is therefore not straightforward.[4] We must also consider two other key elements: the individual's personality and motivation and the social context in which the individual operates.

Nevertheless, as we have seen in chapter 8 and 9, when making decisions, we often rely on schemas, cognitive templates that provide low effort and quick responses. Above all, time pressures, multitasking, and stress often lead us to rely on mental shortcuts and, among them, when conducting business across the globe, on *cultural schemas*.

Understanding these triggering factors can help us predict the degree to which culture will influence the other party's behavior.[5]

Consequently the real question is not *does culture matter?* but *when does culture matter?* Our aim is to understand why the influence of culture is fundamental in some cases but irrelevant in others.[6]

COGNITIVE PROCESSES

Negotiation can be considered a psychological process that builds based on a contest between perceptions and expectations. A change in one player's behavior will alter the perceptions and expectations of the other party, which will in turn affect the player's behavior.[7]

What ultimately matters in negotiation are the perceptions, beliefs, and assumptions that the players bring to the table rather than their objective contrasts.[8]

Cognitive processes take a prominent role in international negotiations because situations are frequently characterized by structural uncertainty: They are often atypical, complex, and incongruous.

The cognitive approach is centered on the resistance to change among the different players, the human predisposition to stand by predetermined beliefs in the face of differing evidence.

Prior to a negotiation, players generate expectations based on available information. These expectations are then either confirmed or disconfirmed during the negotiation process. What usually happens during the negotiation is that negative beliefs remain unchanged even in the face of objective contradictory evidence.

However, what can be done to overcome negative assumptions on the other side?

Adopting voluntary and costly conciliatory actions can help break down negative beliefs. Going back to the 1978 Egyptian-Israeli peace treaty, Sadat's (the Egyptian president) visit to Jerusalem is a perfect example of a voluntary and costly, in terms of political losses, conciliatory action.[9]

Another factor that can increase the impact of conciliatory actions is the element of surprise: Unexpected actions can erode negative assumptions, particularly if they are implemented without assuming immediate reciprocation on the other side, as Sadat did with his visit to Jerusalem.

HOW CULTURE AFFECTS NEGOTIATIONS

We presented the main theories regarding the impact of culture on business encounters in chapters 2, 3, and 4.

Following is a summary of the main cultural dimensions that can influence negotiators' behavior:

- Individualism and collectivism.
- Hierarchy.
- High and low context.
- Time.

Individualism and collectivism: People in all cultures distinguish between in-group and out-group members. However, while in individualistic cultures, self-identity is independent from in-group membership, in collectivistic cultures, self-identity is interdependent with in-group membership. Individuals from collectivistic cultures emphasize interdependence, social obligations, and group welfare. Individuals from individualistic cultures promote autonomy and individual accomplishments.

Psychologists and anthropologists have proposed that individuals from different cultures have different conceptions of their self-identity and that these differences affect the expectations that players have as to the appropriate mode of interaction. In individualistic cultures, an independent view of the self prevails, whereas collectivistic cultures are characterized by a more interdependent view of the self. Members of individualistic cultures set clear and definite boundaries in the relationship, while in collectivistic cultures, individuals work within the context of tacit expectations and obligations.

In collectivist cultures the goal is to develop a social relationship, while in individualistic cultures the goal is one of task-related problem solving. This goal divergence implies a communicative conflict that leads to the emergence of negative emotions affecting the negotiation process.

Negative emotions foster behavioral irreconcilability and limit information processing.

Negative emotions, such as frustration, will be expressed differently by individuals from different cultures: Members of individualistic cultures will explicitly display their emotions, exposing an aggressive behavior that will induce a desire to escape from the situation in members of collectivistic cultures who usually constrain the display of negative emotions.[10]

Hierarchy: In hierarchical cultures, the social structure is stratified and based on an uneven distribution of power, resources, wealth, and authority. Social status often means long-term social power in hierarchical societies. In egalitarian cultures, the emphasis is on fairness, justice, responsibility, and independence, leading to a uniform distribution of wealth, power, resources, and authority. Members of hierarchical cultures avoid conflict because confrontation indicates a lack of deference for social status. On the other hand, members of egalitarian cultures challenge higher status individuals because social rank is temporary and context related.

In hierarchical cultures, where power gaps are marked and social stratification accepted, a power strategy (getting what you want through coercion) represents a more significant and accepted alternative in resolving conflicts and disputes.

Power strategy, because it favors the most powerful party, tends to preserve the status quo, ensuring stability and tradition. Power strategy is therefore relevant in cultures that value social order and quick conflict resolution.

On the other hand, in hierarchical cultures, with social power often comes the obligation to look after those at the bottom of the pyramid. Social obligations can therefore restrain the most powerful negotiator from disregarding the interests of the less powerful party.[11]

Even though individualism and power distance are two distinct dimensions, they are correlated. Highly individualistic cultures, in general, tend to be low in power distance and vice versa.[12]

High and low context: As seen in chapter 5, members of low-context cultures tend to communicate directly, explicitly, and unambiguously. Members of high-context cultures are likely to communicate indirectly and implicitly. Meaning is embedded in the context of the message and must be deduced to be comprehended.

A low-context individual perceives a high-context person as ambiguous, fuzzy, and unreliable. A high-context individual will perceive a low-context person as arrogant, distant, and disrespectful.

According to research, during international encounters, members of high-context cultures may be more likely to adapt to low-context norms for direct information for the following two reasons:[13]

- Low-context communication is easier to master than high-context communication, as it relies only on the meaning of the words, and not on the context.
- Members of high-context cultures are more aware of social obligations for hospitality and harmony and, therefore, are more willing to adapt than low-context negotiators.

The problem is that English, the recognized international lingua franca, is a direct and detached language, unsuitable for conveying the typical nuances of high-context communication, above all when adopted by negotiators with limited vocabulary.

Time: We can identify three general orientations toward time across cultures.[14]

People with a linear orientation perceive time as a straight line that includes the past, present, and future. Time is valuable and separable into discrete units. Individuals with a circular orientation perceive time and events as repeated in a cyclical pattern. The future is expected to be the same as the past, and the focus is on the present. People with a procedural time orientation perceive time as irrelevant. Tasks are procedural rather than time driven. Activities must to be performed correctly; they are not shaped by deadlines.

Scholars sometimes overemphasize the impact of individualism and collectivism on intercultural negotiation. Luckily, research has begun to bring into the picture indigenous concepts and to expand the scope of cultural values relevant to international negotiations.

According to studies, the Chinese avoiding style of negotiation and conflict management is captured by the societal conservatism (e.g., conformity and tradition) dimension in Schwartz's model, while an orientation toward Schwartz's value of self enhancement, and specifically achievement, underlies the tendency of U.S. managers to adopt a competing style of negotiation and conflict management.[15]

SITUATIONAL FACTORS

As in chapter 3, most research emphasizes only the main influences of culture on negotiation, without taking situational factors into consideration.

According to the dynamic constructivist theory, because culture is specific and situational, we have to take social contexts into consideration to understand when specific cultural patterns and behaviors are activated.[16]

Many studies have highlighted that members of collectivistic cultures feel more compelled to be cooperative with in-group members than do members of individualistic cultures, but are even more competitive than individualists when interacting with out-group members.

Accountability and social norms that support cooperation trigger a greater relationship-oriented approach in members of collectivistic cultures when negotiating with in-group members.

Other situational factors, such as noise, time pressure, emotions, or fatigue, can increase reliance on cognitive heuristics and reduce the motivation to search and process information when making decisions.

As a consequence, individuals under time pressure and fatigue will be prone to conform to cultural norms because norms provide fast, recognized, and shared solutions that obey the in-group values.

Cultural norms can thus provide security, consensus, and effort-minimizing solutions to individuals under pressure, stress, and exhaustion.[17]

MOTIVATION

Social context and situational factors are fundamental in understanding when specific cultural behaviors are triggered.

Other factors that can influence the activation of specific cultural patterns are individual-level elements.

Specifically, we focus on the *need for closure factor*,[18] the desire for definite solutions and the avoidance of confusion and ambiguity. People with a high need for closure:

- Need definite order and structure in their lives and despise unrestrained chaos and disorder.
- Favor solutions that are established and shared by the in-group.
- Require knowledge that can be used across situations without exception.
- Do not accept alterative options to their knowledge.
- Feel an urgency to reach a decision and stick with their judgments, without challenging them.
- Are not comfortable with ambiguity.
- Rely on heuristic judgment.

Individuals with a high need for closure are exemplified by cognitive impatience, jumping to conclusions on the basis of inadequate substantiation, and rigidity of thought.

At the other end of the continuum, individuals with a low need for closure are characterized by extensive searches and processes for information. In other words, individuals with a high need for closure may be more prone to use cognitive heuristics in making judgments and decisions than individuals with a low need for cognitive closure.[19]

As a consequence, individuals with a high need for closure will tend to conform to cultural norms because norms provide quick, established, and shared solutions that abide by in-group values.

In other words, some individual-level factors, such as high need for closure, can foster cultural conformity.

Consequently, to understand when cultural patterns and behaviors are activated, we need to focus not only on macro cultural dimensions, such as individualism and collectivism, hierarchy, low and high context, and situational factors, but also on individual-level variables, such as need for closure.

EMOTIONS IN INTERNATIONAL NEGOTIATIONS

As seen in chapters 8, 9 and 12, emotions represent a key factor in understanding people's thinking and behavior during negotiations.

International negotiators are more susceptible to negative emotions because of the degree of divergence in cultural values and beliefs across cultures, defined as *cultural distance*.[20]

Cultural distance is more likely to produce negative feelings and low trust prior to negotiations for the following reasons:

- First, dissimilarity in values and beliefs makes it difficult for negotiators to retrieve a common frame of reference and draws attention to the other individual not belonging to the in-group.

- Second, ambiguous and demanding situations caused by cultural distance can produce negative emotions in negotiators as a consequence of the perceived lack of control in the environment.

Because emotions are often caused by the ability or inability of negotiators to achieve their goals, cultural distance is a key factor in assessing the frequency and intensity of emotions at the negotiation table.

According to various studies, individuals from different cultures tend to judge emotions based on similar visual cues, despite facial physiognomy differences and cultural norms dissimilarities.[21] In other words, we can affirm that the facial expressions for seven basic emotions (happiness, sadness, disgust, fear, anger, contempt, and surprise) are universal.[22] What changes across cultures is the level of emotional expressivity of individuals, the degree to which people from a specific culture openly express their emotions.

Social norms known as *display rules* are learned early in life and determine the management of an emotional response contingent on the individual's social role and social context.[23]

Display rules perform a crucial function in society by helping to regulate emotional behaviors related to social roles and norms, supporting within-group social coordination and eventually group and individual persistence.

Members of specific cultures may try to keep emotions from influencing their behavior, either because their emotions have a low frequency or intensity or because cultural norms require emotions to be concealed. In these cultures, openly displaying emotions is considered an indication of weakness and thus is inappropriate.

EMOTIONAL PERSUASION

The most distinctive and commonly adopted form of social interchange for conflict resolution and persuasion in Japan is called *naniwabushi*, an emotional appeal referring to popular ballads from the Edo period (1600-1868). The appeal relies on three stages:

- *Kikkake*: the opening, which gives the general background of the story, recounting the central character's feeling about the relationship.
- *Seme*: the narrative of critical events that made the social relationship problematic.
- *Urei*: an expression of great sorrow or self-pity intended to persuade the other side to be compassionate.

Naniwabushi is always planned and designed to convey a dramatic and tragic narrative that relies on values such as long-term relationship, harmony, and most of all *amae*, a form of protective relationship and mutual dependence among members of the group.[24]

PLAYERS IN INTERNATIONAL NEGOTIATIONS

International negotiations are generally multiplayer, multi-issue, and multi-stage events.

International negotiations rarely involve unitary players on each side; it is fundamental to understand the complex interactions among different pawns, knights, and bishops within the organization and their often-conflicting interests.[25]

As highlighted in chapters 1, 7 and 12, most corporate decisions involve at least eight individuals. When you are negotiating with organizations, you are always interacting with individuals bringing a diverse set of interests to the table:[26]

Map the other side's decision-making process and identify the key players. Isolate the relationship and the degree of influence among the different players. Avoid making concessions to relatively low-level agents who function as important messengers or gatekeepers, but not as decision makers.

Chart your steppingstone strategy to influence the key decision maker(s) (more on this in chapters 14 and 17).

Identify the second-level players. The ones not sitting at the negotiation table that can still directly influence the first-level players. Leverage the different interests of the different players.

For example, fundamental when negotiating with the Japanese is the concept of *nemawashi*, a gardening term that can be translated as preparing the roots before transplanting. Japanese negotiators rarely change their minds during the negotiation because the decision-making process in Japanese organizations usually involves a consensus among many second-level players through informal conversations outside the negotiation table. Consequently, in Japan, off-the-table groundwork prior to the negotiation is more important than the negotiation itself in determining the agreement.[27]

TICE AND FAIRNESS IN INTERNATIONAL NEGOTIATIONS

Justice can be considered a macro concept referring to general criteria of what is right and what is wrong. Fairness, on the other hand, can be considered a micro concept which suggests what is right and wrong in specific situations.

As seen in chapter 8, ultimatum game experiments suggest that perceived unfair allocations are often rejected, and that the mean average offer is in the range of 37% to 50%. Experimental results don't differ across cultures. Justice and fairness therefore play a key role in international negotiations.[28]

The concept of distributive justice is based on several fundamental principles:[29]

- *Mutual advantage*: Negotiations have to deliver benefits to both sides.
- *Reciprocity*: Parties have to respond to each other's concessions.
- *Equality*: Parties have to receive identical resources, benefits, and obligations.
- *Equity*: Resources, benefits, and obligations should be allocated to each party in proportion to the party's relevant inputs (resources, efforts, actions).
- *Need*: Resources, benefits, and obligations should be allocated to the parties according to their needs.
- *Compensatory justice*: Resources, benefits, and obligations should be allocated to the parties that have mostly suffered from the situation.

According to research, members of collectivistic societies seem generally to prefer the equality norm when negotiating with in-group members and the equity norm when negotiating with out-group members.[30]

Cross-cultural research has confirmed that Americans associate themselves with fair behavior and others with unfair behavior to a greater extent than do the Japanese. Research has also shown that American disputants believe more strongly than the Japanese that an objective third party will consider their behavior as fair and judge offers from the counterparty as unfair.[31]

In structuring negotiations and agreements, the interests and concerns of all parties must be represented and guarded. Furthermore, every party should have a chance to present his or her case and provide input into all stages of the negotiation process. Fair input and a fair hearing are fundamental for effective negotiations. Multiplayer negotiations are often based on package deals to accommodate the different needs of the different parties.

Last but no less important is the notion of fair play: All parties must have the chance to play according to agreed rules and procedures, without intimidation and pressure.

INTERNATIONAL DYADIC RELATIONSHIPS

The in-group and out-group dichotomy is not appropriate to fully understand the complexity of relationships in collectivistic cultures. We need to add a third category.

If we describe the relational categories by two concentric circles, the innermost circle (*in-group*) includes members with a total sense of interdependence. In these relationships, duty, obligation, and need shape behavior. Trust is therefore intrinsic in the relationship.

The outermost circle includes the *out-group*, which comprises strangers. Among these individuals, the relationship is managed through equity values, with no relational expectations and no assumption of trust.

Both in the innermost and outermost circles, communication can be direct and conflict accepted.

Between the inner and outer circles exists a middle circle comprising relationships that may become in-group. This *middle group* includes friends, neighbors, classmates, and colleagues with whom we are in the process of establishing trust.

Most important, it is within this middle circle, and not the inner or the outer circle, that consideration of relational issues such as giving and protecting face and avoiding conflict is particularly important (see Figure 1).[32]

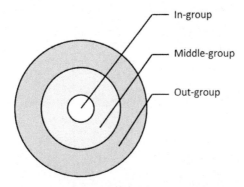

Figure 1. Relationship complexity.

TRUST IN INTERNATIONAL NEGOTIATIONS

Value creation can be challenging without information sharing. Nevertheless, information sharing requires some level of trust.

Trust is therefore a fundamental factor in international negotiations, but negotiators from different cultures display different trust propensities.[33]

In *tight cultures*, where social norms are unambiguous and imposed, acceptable behavior is enforced through monitoring and sanctioning from institutions such as family and social groups, with no room for interpretation.

In *loose cultures*, where social norms are flexible and informal, acceptable behavior is defined within a range that is left to the interpretation of each individual.

Because negotiators from tight cultures (such as Malaysia, India, Japan, Pakistan, and South Korea) usually rely on institutional guarantors, they display relatively low interpersonal trust.

On the other hand, negotiators from loose cultures (such as Israel, the Netherlands, Venezuela, New Zealand, Brazil, Australia, and the US) display high interpersonal trust (see Table 1).

Country	Score
Ukraine	1.6
Estonia	2.6
Israel	3.1
Netherlands	3.3
Brazil	3.5
Venezuela	3.7
Greece	3.9
New Zealand	3.9
Australia	4.4
United States	5.1
Spain	5.4
Belgium	5.6
Poland	6.0
France	6.3
Hong Kong	6.3
Germany	6.5
Austria	6.8
Italy	6.8
United Kingdom	6.9
Mexico	7.2
Portugal	7.8
China	7.9
Japan	8.6
Turkey	9.2
Norway	9.5
South Korea	10.0
Singapore	10.4
India	11.0
Malaysia	11.8
Pakistan	12.3

(Right side annotations: Loose Cultures —— Tight Cultures; High Trust Cultures —— Low Trust Cultures)

Table 1. Cultural tightness-looseness (Gelfand et al., 2010).

According to research,[34] negotiators from tight cultures tend to assume little trust, rely more on single issue offers, and adopt more frequently deceptive tactics.

Conversely, negotiators from loose cultures tend to assume high trust, rely more on the norm of reciprocity, and ask more questions, thereby fostering information sharing.

In sum, in tight cultures interpersonal trust requires time, while in loose cultures it is more immediate. Negotiating with members from tight cultures establishing rapport during the non-task-related interaction phase of the negotiation is funda-mental. Initial impressions, often based on marginal information and perceived similarities (such as rank, sex, age, religion, education, experiences, and member-ships) form the basis for interpersonal trust.[35]

SOCIAL FACTORS INFLUENCING TRUST

Real-world international negotiations are rarely socially bound and temporally confined.[36] This is why it is important to understand the influence of social factors on the negotiator's behavior.

Research supports the tendency for individuals to display preference for other in-group members and comparatively negative prejudices toward out-group members.

Preference for in-group members is primarily motivated by the expectation of competitive, unfair, and untrustworthy behavior from the other side that leads to distrust, suspicion, self-protective conduct, and sometimes intense negative reac-tions toward out-group members.

What is interesting is that any classification of individuals into distinct groups, even when those group boundaries are founded on completely random and transito-ry criteria, can lead individuals to perceive out-group members as less trustworthy, less honest, and less cooperative than members of their own in-group.

This predicted antagonism and untrustworthiness generates a self-fulfilling dynamic: Believing that the other player will be competitive, we tend to increase our competitiveness to avoid a potential loss and safeguard the in-group's welfare.[37] Anticipating their opposition, we tend to adopt coercive strategies when trying to influence out-group members, generating a cycle of destructive action-reaction as each player responds in a self-protective fashion to the aggressive and confronta-tional actions of the other side.

THE COOP-COMP NEGOTIATOR

Chinese negotiators tend to employ at least two different strategies according to the circumstances.[38]

When mutual trust is high, they usually adopt the *Confucian gentleman's ap-proach*. They seek mutual benefit through cooperation and morality. They discuss matters and issues, but at the same time are careful to avoid conflict. The negotiation process develops usually into a smooth and brief win-win game.

When the relationship is not established and mutual trust is low (e.g., with foreign managers) because of strong feelings of suspicion and skepticism, Chinese negotiators adopt the *Chinese stratagem's approach*. They employ competitive strategies descended from Sun Tzu's Art of War and the Thirty-Six Stratagems: The negotiation table becomes a battlefield where negotiators must overcome the enemy. Chinese stratagems emphasize wisdom and indirect means rather than direct physical displays of power and strength to gain advantages over the opponent. The negotiation develops into a tactless and lengthy zero-sum game, based on the *wu wei* principle, which can be translated into act without acting.

Some of the Thirty-Six Stratagems are:[39]

Hide a knife in a smile; lure the tiger to leave the mountains; play dumb; feint to the east while attacking in the west; relax and wait for the adversary to tire himself out; pretend to advance down one path while taking another hidden path; conceal a dagger in a smile; sacrifice the plum for the peach; remove the ladder after your ascent; decorate the tree with fake blossoms; inflict pain on oneself to infiltrate the adversary's camp and win the confidence of the enemy; and retreat is the best option.

At the center of these bargaining tactics is the idea of defeating the opponent without fighting.[40]

When mutual trust is low, employing deceiving, manipulating, and oblique actions is therefore not only ethically justified but also a prerequisite for effective negotiations in China.[41]

The coop-comp negotiation approach is also current in Japan, due to the extensive dissemination of the Chinese Stratagems and the Art of War, as well as the influence of Musashi's The Book of Five Rings.

Concepts such as if you are getting into a deadlock then change the approach and use a different tactic; act as the sea when your opponent is like a mountain, and act as a mountain when the enemy is like a sea; and become the opponent: put yourself in an opponent's place and think from the opponent's point of view,[42] from the Book of the Five Rings, are analogous to the notions offered by the Art of War.

The term *kosho* is the closest Japanese equivalent to negotiation.[43] In its typical connotation, kosho has a very similar meaning to the concepts derived from the The Chinese Stratagems and the wu wei principle: adopting deceptive, manipulating, and indirect tactics to overcome the enemy, particularly when it's a foreigner.

The coop-comp negotiation style is prevalent in most societies. Also, Indian negotiators display different behaviors according to the context, emphasizing the traditional Hindu values when interacting with family members and the imported individualistic and competitive principles when negotiating with out-group members.

RE-ESTABLISHING TRUST ACROSS CULTURES

Apologies can be a useful means of restoring or building trust in negotiations. However, the function, meaning, and norms associated with an apology diverge extensively across cultures.

According to research, apologies are main contributors to cultural misunderstandings in international negotiations.

As seen in chapter 10, in collectivistic cultures, the main locus of agency is at the group level. Groups and situational contexts are seen as primary causal agents in collectivistic societies, and apologies are therefore assumed to be an expression of general remorse, serving to operate as a normative social lubricant rather than a means of assigning blame or responsibility to individual players.

In individualistic cultures, there is a fundamental assumption of individual agency with the locus of control for events and actions being located within individuals. This is why there is an almost total absence of apologies in disputes in individualistic cultures: Apologies are understood as a way of assigning blame and responsibility to individual players and re-establishing personal credibility.

A study of Japanese and American managers observed that, compared to Americans, the Japanese apologized more frequently and were more prone to apologize for actions in which they were not involved; on the other hand, Americans were more likely than the Japanese to associate apologizing with personal responsibility.[44]

FACE NEGOTIATION THEORY

Faces are the various facets of an individual that all societies perceive and evaluate based on cultural norms and values.[45]

Face is composed of six domains:

- *Autonomy*: the need for others to acknowledge our independence.
- *Inclusion*: the need to be recognized as friendly, pleasant, and cooperative.
- *Status*: the need for others to acknowledge our appearance, position, and power.
- *Reliability*: the need for others to recognize our consistency, trustworthiness, and dependability.
- *Competence*: the need for others to acknowledge our skills, expertise, knowledge, and leadership.
- *Moral:* the need for others to recognize our integrity, nobility, and ethics.

One might forgo one domain to satisfy the need in another area. For example, to satisfy the need for inclusion, one might sacrifice some of the autonomy or status face.

Faces can be lost, saved, or protected, and conflict occurs when the individual or group face is endangered.

Facework can be employed prior to, during, and after a conflict situation. Preventive facework is an attempt to minimize loss of face before the actual conflict occurs. Protective strategies include referrals, recommendations, credentialing, and qualifications.

In general, collectivistic cultures put more emphasis on preventive strategies than individualistic cultures.

Restorative facework attempts to repair face that has been lost. Restorative strategies include excuses, justifications, aggression, avoidance, and apologies.

In general, individualistic cultures are more likely to adopt restorative facework than collectivistic cultures.

CONFLICT RESOLUTION

Research has highlighted that different cultures adopt different strategies to resolve conflict.[46]

The use of different conflict management strategies is based on the notion that arguments used to persuade individuals differ across cultures.

The first strategy is to focus on *interests*. The interests strategy supports the resolution of impasses through cognitive problem-solving, focusing on the underlying interests of each side.

The interests-based conflict management notion relies on three key assumptions:

- Individual interests are more important than collective interests.
- All parties are equal, and their interests equally rightful.

- All parties can effortlessly break and form relationships.

The second strategy is to rely on mutually acknowledged, objective, independent *standards* or regulations that can increase the legitimacy of the line of reasoning. To reduce the chances of being perceived as arbitrary, the standards conflict management notion has to rely on two basic hypotheses:

- Standards have to be independent and recognized.
- Standards have to be universally applicable.

The third strategy is to force a solution based on *status power*. As previously highlighted, this approach has the advantage of quickly resolving conflict without disrupting social order.

Power strategies based on social status rely on the two key assumptions:

- Status differences exist and are broadly accepted.
- Different rules apply for different actors, according to their social status.

According to research, different cultures tend to adopt a combination of different approaches to manage conflict despite some cultures displaying an inclination toward a specific strategy (e.g., German managers on regulations and Japanese managers on status power).

TIMING

While most research is focused on negotiation content, the timing of the negotiation is also a vital factor in negotiations.

In game theory terms, a conflict is assumed to be *ripe for resolution* when both players recognize that the status quo (a conflict situation with no negotiation) is a negative sum (lose-lose) situation, not a zero sum (win-lose) situation.

Put in other terms, a conflict is assumed to be ripe for resolution only when both players recognize they cannot win, and the conflict becomes too costly or too painful for both of them. A decision to negotiate is therefore often caused by increasing pain with the current situation.[47] Parties, therefore, put an end to their conflict only when they are ready to do so.[48]

A conflict is *ready for resolution* only if the situation is symmetrical: Both parties are motivated to cease conflict escalation and are confident about reaching a settlement.[49]

The concepts of ripeness and readiness can also be extended to business negotiations: Choosing the appropriate time for the negotiation can increase the odds of an integrative outcome. Doing the right thing at the right moment is of essence in international negotiations.

RISK PROPENSITY

According to prospect theory, people are risk averse when they perceive themselves to be in the sphere of gain and risk seeking in the sphere of loss. Therefore, risk is situational. Risk propensity augments when income and wealth increase.

Risk propensity can also be different in different life domains. Individuals can be more risk seeking in certain areas of their lives and less in others. They can also have different risk propensity according to their life stage. Risk propensity is inversely related to age. Higher risk propensity is also correlated with greater frequency of career changes and reported business start-ups.

Other scholars view risk as associated with trans-situational factors, such as personality. According to these studies, risk is an individual more than a situational characteristic.

Men tend to be more prone to risk than women. Generally, risk propensity is directly associated with extraversion and openness and inversely related to neuroticism, agreeableness, and conscientiousness.[50]

Finally, according to a recent study on the role that marital status plays in chief executive officers' risk propensity, bachelors tended to be more aggressive in their investment decisions, while married chief executive officers tended to be more risk averse.[51]

How does culture affect our risk preferences?

Research maintains the assumption that particular cultures are more risk averse than others.

According to a research based on self-assessment questionnaires,[52] French, Indians, British, Chinese, and US-Americans deem themselves to be highly risk tolerant. Germans choose a median position, while Brazilians, Mexicans, and Spaniards believe themselves to be risk averse. Japanese assess themselves as highly risk averse because their complex group decision-making process requires a large amount of information.

According to research, risk propensity, and negotiation behavior in general, is highly affected by personality in American individuals and by cultural norms in Chinese negotiators:[53]

Extraversion and agreeableness are inversely associated with competitive behavior in American negotiators, while face, harmony, and ren qing (reciprocity, hospitality, good manners) are inversely associated with competitive behavior in Chinese negotiators.

Assessing the impact of religion, religious individuals are more risk averse than atheists. Protestants tend to display higher risk propensity than people with other religions.[54]

When dealing with risk-averse individuals, we should take into consideration the following:[55]

- Don't rush the negotiating process. Advance step by step in a string of increments, rather than all at once. Speed is directly associated with risk in risk-averse negotiators.
- Set up procedures that may decrease the apparent risks in the deal for the other side.
- Establish a trust-based relationship. Don't rush. Make small concessions as a sign of goodwill. Be present before and after the signature of the deal.

NEGOTIATING WITH IRRATIONAL NEGOTIATORS

North Korea's nuclear program has been a great concern to the world in recent years. Launched in 2003, the Six Party Talks were intended to terminate North Korea's nuclear efforts through negotiations involving China, the United States, North and South Korea, Japan, and Russia.

The negotiation process has been continuously fragmented and sometimes stalled by North Korea's provocations (such as performing missile tests and defying UN resolutions) and by the conflicting interests of the other five players.

DIVERGING INTERESTS

The US main concern is Pyongyang's nuclear program and the possible sale of nuclear materials and technology to inimical states, or even worse to terrorist groups.

South Korea's ultimate goal is the reunification of the Korean peninsula. Intermediate goals are North Korea's denuclearization and economic development, minimizing the possibilities of a great flow of evacuees from North Korea.

China is a longstanding North Korea ally whose main concern is a flow of refugees across its border. The main Chinese interest is to reassert its influence in Northeast Asia, mainly in contrast to Japan.

Like China, Russia's main interest is also to reaffirm its influence in Northeast Asia.

Japan's main concern is that North Korea's missile tests could potentially reach Japan. Another concern for Japan is the potential flow of refugees from North Korea. The main interest on the Japanese side is to use the Six Party Talks as a forum for negotiating a resolution to the abduction of Japanese citizens by North Korean spies in the 1970s and 1980s.

While Japan and the United States have over and over again pushed for strong sanctions, China, South Korea, and Russia have supported less severe actions from concern that a sudden collapse of the regime would generate major refugee floods.

Progress reached a stalemate when Pyongyang walked out of negotiations in 2009, only to be back in early 2012, when under new leader Kim Jong-un, North Korea declared it would stop nuclear tests and allow international inspections to monitor the moratorium in exchange for food aid from the United States. However, a long-range missile launch in late 2012 and another test in early 2013 that defied UN resolutions halted the negotiation process once again.[56]

AN UNPREDICTABLE REGIME

From the US point of view, North Korea's behavior is capricious, unpredictable, and puzzling.

Rationally, North Korea shouldn't be provoking the countries it relies on for assistance and to provide food and medicines to its impoverished and starving population.

However, this is exactly what it has been doing for nearly the last two decades.

A more careful assessment reveals that North Korean behavior is far from irrational when we take into account three main concerns that shape Pyongyang's strategy and behavior:[57]

- The first and most important interest is the *perpetuation of the hereditary regime*, the reins of which were inherited by Kim Jong-il upon the death of Kim Il-sung, his father, and today are in the hands of his third son, Kim Jon-un.

- Then there is the notion of *national face*, the preservation of North Korean international status and reputation during negotiations. Consequently, the formulation of the concessions is often more important than the essence of the concessions.
- Last is the *rejection of a conditional approach* in which one side takes action to achieve progress without reciprocal measures by the other side. For example, whenever asked to honor past commitments to dismantle its nuclear technology, to resume negotiations, North Korea has consistently rejected the request, asking all sides to take simultaneous action.

Another hurdle to the progress of the talks is US reluctance toward bilateral negotiations.

North Korea has repeatedly demanded separate talks with the US, while not addressing inter-Korean tensions with South Korea, as a condition to terminating its nuclear program. However, the US resisted direct negotiations, so that any compromise or concession to the North Korean regime would be framed as a multilateral decision and not as a yielding granted solely by the US.

REAL INTERNATIONAL NEGOTIATION CASES

To better understand the interests behind international mergers and acquisitions (M&As) and partnerships, and the reasons for their success or failure, we'll illustrate and analyze actual negotiations in the automotive sector.

We have chosen the automotive industry for three main reasons: It is one of the most competitive sectors, requiring heavy investments in new product development, is afflicted by overcapacity, with very slim margins in most segments, and is heavily suffering the actual volatile, uncertain, complex, and ambiguous (VUCA) environment.

THE DAIMLERCHRYSLER MERGER

In the mid-1990s, Chrysler Corporation was the most profitable automotive producer in the world. It was renowned for bold and risk-taking design that translated into original and groundbreaking vehicles. Unlike other auto manufacturers, which focused on cutting costs, Chrysler's profits came from the introduction of new models.

It had 16% of the US market share, even if only 1 out of 13 cars was sold abroad. In other words, more than 92% of Chrysler's sales were in the US.

In 1995, Chrysler held $7.5 billion in cash and a full range of best-selling minivans, pickup trucks, and sport utility vehicles (SUVs).

However, Chrysler's future was threatened by a potential takeover. In April 1995, Kirk Kerkorian, the biggest Chrysler's shareholder, announced intention to acquire the remaining stock of Chrysler, paying a 40% premium over the previous day's closing to Chrysler's stockholders. Even worse for Chrysler's current management, Lee Iacocca, former Chrysler chairman and chief executive officer (CEO) was an investor in this transaction. According to Kerkorian, Chrysler's stock was undervalued and the company needed a stock buyback program and an increase in dividends to lift its share value.[58]

This event triggered the first talks between Helmut Werner, Mercedes Benz's CEO, and Bob Eaton, Chrysler's CEO.

Daimler-Benz AG was the largest industrial group in Germany with revenues of over $60 billion. Even though known mainly for its luxury Mercedes cars, Daimler operated in four business segments: automotive (passenger and commercial vehicles), aerospace, services, and directly managed businesses.

First Contacts

Werner proposed a joint venture (JV) to share the risk of entering the new emerging markets with low-cost cars. He outlined a joining between Mercedes' engineering expertise and heavy truck distribution network and Chrysler's innovative and low-cost product line to take advantage of the bottom-of-the-pyramid segment of developing countries.

Negotiations came to a standstill when Werner's boss, Daimler-Benz CEO Jürgen Schrempp stepped into the picture and methodically pulled to pieces the premises on which the JV plan was based.

At the same time, Jürgen Schrempp started talks with Alex Trotman, CEO of Ford. These talks came to a full stop because neither party was willing to accept a subordinate position in a potential alliance. The Ford family wasn't willing to dilute its 40% shares in Ford, and Daimler was not willing to become a subsidiary of Ford as Jaguar.

Negotiation Resume

Negotiations between Chrysler and Daimler-Benz resumed two years later, in 1997, with a completely different perspective: not a limited scope JV, but a full merger between the two companies, with the direct involvement of Jürgen Schrempp. The rationale behind the change of scale and outlook can be explained by at least six main reasons:

- The industry was afflicted by excess capacity. According to some studies, the automotive industry production capacity exceeded 70 million cars per year, but only 60 million cars were sold worldwide.
- Chrysler made 92% of its sales in the volatile US market that had already reached its apex.
- Every segment in which Chrysler was leader and making high profits was under fierce attack from competitors.
- Daimler-Benz relied almost entirely on its Mercedes business unit for its profits. Mercedes-Benz, although renowned for its luxury cars, was absolutely absent from the lower segments of the market. Another factor was that the limited number of premium vehicles sold didn't allow Daimler to achieve economies of scale.
- Daimler and Chrysler products and markets did not overlap.
- Chrysler's stock traded at about 9 times its earnings per share; Daimler's stock traded at 26 times earnings.

Through consolidation, assembly plants could be streamlined and Chrysler and Mercedes individual strengths, if joined, could create a strong global player in every segment of the market.

On May 7, 1998, Eaton announced that Chrysler would merge with Daimler-Benz. The $37 billion stock-swap deal was the largest trans-Atlantic merger ever. The transaction was structured as a merger of equals, with Daimler-Benz paying a 28% premium to Chrysler shareholders.

Problems Surface

During the negotiations, Jürgen Schrempp obtained three major concessions from Bob Eaton that shaped the future of the merger:[59]

- *Name*: The name was DaimlerChrysler, with Daimler before Chrysler.
- *Location*: The company was incorporated in Germany, with a two-tier board structure based on a supervisory board and a management board.
- *Long-term leadership*: Eaton would step down as co-CEO of DaimlerChrysler within three years.

Two major events revealed that the transaction was in fact more an acquisition than a merger of equals:

- Bob Eaton publicly announced that he would step down as co-CEO within three years, making people in Chrysler perceive that the dominant player in the management of DaimlerChrysler would be Daimler-Benz and its CEO Jürgen Schrempp.
- Because the parent company was German, Chrysler was removed from the Standard & Poor's 500 stock index. US money managers avoid holding a stock not represented in the S&P 500; therefore, mutual funds in the US were forced to unload their Chrysler shares. The result was that the percentage of US shareholders quickly fell from the initial 43% to 25%. This incident fostered the perception that it was actually an acquisition.

The problems between the two companies were obvious from the beginning:

- Daimler was a conglomerate building not only cars, but also trucks, jets, buses, satellites, engines, and railroad cars. Chrysler was just focused on cars.
- Daimler had a formal and hierarchical organization, with a complex decision-making process. Chrysler, on the other hand, was more informal, promoting cross-functional teams and involving different organizational layers in the decision-making process.
- Daimler had larger staffs and therefore many more resources involved in post-merger integration meetings.
- Chrysler managers earned much bigger salaries. Chrysler executives earned double-digit figures (in millions) for merging with Daimler.
- Germans spoke English. Americans didn't speak German (with few exceptions). Germans were accustomed to traveling and living abroad and were willing to relocate to Auburn Hill. Very few Americans were eager to relocate to Stuttgart.
- Jürgen Schrempp, just a few days after announcement of the merger, began to evaluate the possibility of adding Nissan to the partnership between Daimler and Chrysler. From his point of view, this was the best opportunity to gain a foot in Asia and make the company truly global (the DamilerChrysler board eventually did not support the merger with Nissan).

- High-profile defections further weakened Chrysler's position in the partnership and supported the image of German control.
- Bob Eaton slowly detached himself from the co-CEO role, assigning to Jürgen Schrempp the position of de facto CEO of the company.
- The friction provided by Mercedes' perception of Chrysler brands as inferior to its premium brand. This was coupled with different perceptions of the brands among customers: Chrysler's image was built on innovation and boldness, while Mercedes relied on disciplined engineering and quality.
- In autumn 2000, DaimlerChrysler CEO Jürgen Schrempp admitted in an interview with the German financial daily Handelsblatt that he always intended Chrysler to be a subsidiary of Daimler and that the merger of equals announcement was essential to gain the support of Chrysler's workers, board, and the American public.

In late 2005 Jürgen Schrempp stepped down from his position as DaimlerChrysler's CEO, having failed to deliver what he promised.

In May 2007, DaimlerChrysler sold an 80% stake in Chrysler to Cerberus Capital Management, a private equity investment firm, receiving $1.4 billion.

RENAULT-NISSAN NEGOTIATIONS[60]

Today the Renault-Nissan alliance is the fourth largest automotive group in the world.

However, the marriage between the second largest French and the second largest Japanese automaker was initially dismissed by analysts as impracticable due to cultural distance, difficulty of the issues to be resolved, and complexity of the various stakeholders involved.

In 1998, when the preliminary talks started, Renault was in good financial shape despite still heavily relying on its home and European markets and having a majority shareholder in the French government.

Nissan, on the other hand, was a global company with sales in more than 180 countries. However, at the same time, it was losing money and heavily indebted (particularly Nissan Diesel, the truck and bus manufacturer division of Nissan Motor).

Analysts at the time classified automakers in three categories: attackers, prey, and unfit.

Renault fell in the prey group, while Nissan was in the unfit category. Analysts were skeptical about an alliance between a potential prey and an unfit automaker.

Renault and Nissan Interests

Schweitzer, Renault's CEO, has been assessing the long-term strategy for Renault for some time when the megamerger between Daimler and Chrysler accelerated the need for an answer regarding the company's future.

Renault had a very weak presence in all non-European markets. It was absent in the US and had very weak standing in Asia and South America. At that moment, it had two viable options: Stay alone and use the cash to finance new market entries or find a partner.

Evaluating potential partners, Schweitzer immediately acknowledged that Renault had little to offer any of the major players (GM, Toyota, Ford, VW, and DaimlerChrysler).

Thus, he turned his attention to the number two Japanese automaker: Nissan.

In 1999, besides a heavy debt burden, Nissan was suffering from declining market share in the US and Europe and a reputation for boring and costly cars.

Another constraint that Nissan faced was the Japanese business environment, which was committed to lifetime employment, unreceptive to change, and in general protective of the status quo.

On the other side, French companies were perceived in Japan as arrogant, unpredictable, and on the margins of the world economic picture.

Evaluating potential partners, Hanawa, Nissan's CEO, after spending all his working life in the company, had very few options. The only potential partner besides Renault was DaimlerChrysler.

The two companies had overlapping and complementary strengths and interests:
- Renault was renowned for its unconventional products, which could improve Nissan's recent reputation for dull cars.
- Renault could contribute $2 billion in cash to provide some debt relief for Nissan.
- Renault was strong in Europe, while Nissan relied on the US and Asia. There was no market overlap.
- Nissan had the production volumes and the global span to help Renault reach critical size and increase competitiveness.

Designing the Game

In addition to the two main actors, Schweitzer and Hanawa, the CEOs of Renault and Nissan, respectively, and the other first-level players directly involved in the talks, composed from the two executive teams, it was important to take into account second- and third-level players.

Second-level players are those that can directly influence the negotiators. Second-level players on the Renault side were:
- Renault's board of directors, which had to authorize any strategic decision.
- The French unions, which represented approximately 60% of the Renault workforce.
- The French government, which had veto power over board decisions.
- Merrill Lynch, the investment banker that acted as Renault's advisor.

Second-level players on the Nissan side were:
- Fuji Bank, Industrial Bank of Japan, and Dai-Ichi Mutual Insurance, members of Nissan's industrial group, the Fuyo keiretsu, which at the same time were both Nissan's shareholders and creditors.
- Salomon Smith Barney, the investment banker that acted as Nissan's advisor.
- The Nissan labor union.

Third-level players are those that can indirectly influence the negotiations.

In this specific negotiation, third-level players included:

- The Japanese government, which had no direct stake in Nissan, but could affect the decisions.
- Japanese public opinion, which would oppose a foreign takeover of a company with Nissan's history.
- Jurgen Schrempp, DaimlerChrysler's CEO, who wanted Nissan to improve his company's limited presence in Asia.

The Negotiations

From the beginning, Schweitzer didn't consider the possibility of a typical acquisition or merger with Nissan. To accommodate the interests of the various players on Nissan's side, and overcome the skepticism reflected in Japanese public opinion, he had to find a new form of alliance that could balance the interests and the roles of the two companies. He also had to obtain support from the French prime minister to start the discussion.

Another problem Schweitzer faced was the presence of a potential second bidder, DaimlerChrysler.

Nissan management considered Daimler as a more appealing and superior potential partner for the future of the company.

Schweitzer tried to include in the letter of intent a lock-in clause that prevented Hanawa from carrying on talks with other potential partners until the completion or end of talks with Renault. Hanawa refused to sign the clause.

On the other side, Hanawa fixed four pre-conditions for a deal: retaining the Nissan name, protecting jobs, support for the organizational restructuring already underway at Nissan with Nissan management leading the effort, and selection of a CEO from Nissan's ranks.

After having reached an impasse, the negotiations hit the turning point when Schrempp, forced by the lack of support from the DaimlerChrysler's board, formally withdrew his bid for Nissan Motor.

At that point, Schweitzer didn't change his offer. The reasoning behind his decision was to reaffirm the fact that Renault did not intend to exploit Nissan. The move was fundamental in establishing the basis for the future cooperative relationship.

The final agreement was signed on the basis of Renault's investment of $5.4 billion for 36.8% of Nissan Motor and stakes in other Nissan entities.

Schweitzer's decision was essential to provide Carlos Ghosn, Renault's executive vice president, appointed after the deal as chief operating officer (COO) of Nissan, full authority to cut costs as a primary step for reviving Nissan. In other words, Schweitzer's decision not to lower the bid was crucial in persuading Hanawa to forgo some of his pre-conditions for the deal.

In October 1999, Ghosn announced the termination of five plants in Japan, 21,000 layoffs, and other cost reductions. By the end of the 2000, when Ghosn became chairman of Nissan, the company turned a profit

The deal was a good choice. If Renault hadn't taken it now, in a few years Renault would have been acquired and Nissan would have closed down. Renault seized an opportunity that may never be seen again.[61]

FIAT AND GM ALLIANCE

In 2000, General Motors (GM) was the world largest automaker, with an annual production of more than 8.5 million vehicles, 386,000 employees, and turnover of $184 billion.

The company had a strong international presence, with market share of 26.7% in North America, 9.3% in Europe, 16.3% in Latin America, Africa, and the Middle East areas combined, and 3.7% in the Asia-Pacific zone.

Fiat is an Italian conglomerate, still for the most part owned by the founding Agnelli family, with turnover of $48 billion (the car business unit contributed half of the total turnover), a strong presence in Italy and Brazil, a relevant market share in the major European markets, and an annual car production of 2.4 million vehicles in 2000.

The Industrial Partnership

In March 2000, Fiat and GM reached an agreement to forge a strategic alliance focused on Europe, Latin America, and Asia (the US was excluded from the contract).

The business deal, signed by GM Chairman Jack Smith and Fiat Chairman Paolo Fresco, was based on an industrial partnership aimed at pursuing mutual synergies in two key areas:

- ·Purchasing and procurement.
- Joint development of engines and gearboxes.

The two companies decided to develop an alliance and not a full merger as in the DaimlerChrysler case for at least four main reasons:[62]

- Circumvent the cultural problems that arise with standard M&As.
- Reduce capital and human resources commitment.
- Prevent agreements of the partner with other competitors (according to rumors, Fiat was in talks with DaimlerChrysler).
- Because Fiat is mainly a private company, an alliance sidesteps possible negative reactions from the Italian public opinion and government arising from a full merger or acquisition.

The transaction was based on a stock swap deal (GM received 20% of Fiat shares, while Fiat got 5% of GM shares) and a put option that allowed Fiat to sell the remaining 80% of its shares to GM. GM had the ability to exercise a priority option only by offering a price which was not lower than any other competing buyer. GM agreed to the put option to prevent Fiat from partnering with DaimlerChrysler and thus becoming a potential competitor for Opel (GM's European arm) in Germany.

The Divorce

In the following years, the alliance failed to deliver the planned $2 billion per year in cost savings and after the partnership was established, GM's European arm and Fiat packed massive losses.

In 2003, GM refused to put more money into Fiat.

The put option seemed a very good move in 2000, primarily because it prevented Fiat from partnering with DaimlerChrysler and because it created opportunities for joint technology development and cost savings.

On the other hand, the same put option became a heavy liability for GM in the following years. It was a marriage between two weak partners: GM's European division and Fiat.

After more than 20 months of negotiations, Fiat's new CEO, Sergio Marchionne, was able to persuade GM's CEO Rick Wagoner to pay $2 billion, a figure higher than industry analysts expected, to give up the put option agreed to five years earlier in exchange for a half share in a diesel-engine factory in Poland and the acquisition of intellectual property rights in diesel technology, an area where Fiat was very strong and GM very weak.

Sergio Marchionne succeeded in obtaining this high figure from GM by leveraging three key factors:

- Primarily the risk of having to incorporate such a heavily indebted and money-losing company as Fiat.
- Ancillary acquisition of diesel technology from Fiat.
- The consolidation wave originated by the DaimlerChrysler merger in 1998 had stopped. The prospect that Fiat could fall prey to a competitor was not an issue for GM in 2005.

As a result of the previously outlined factors, Marchionne had a very strong alternative: Exercise the put option and force GM to acquire Fiat's car division.

On the other side, he also faced a daunting constraint: Selling Fiat to a foreign company would have triggered a wave of criticism by the Italian public and establishment.

GM CEO Rick Wagoner was sure that Marchionne would back down and decide not exercise the put option, but Fiat's CEO strategy worked and GM decided to pay the money rather than discover whether Marchionne would carry his bluff through to the very end, forcing GM to enter a threatening court battle or, even worse, to acquire a company on the verge of bankruptcy. Marchionne leveraged on holding both Canadian and Italian citizenship and having spent most of his life outside Italy; thus, he was an outsider in the Italian political and business system and therefore immune to its pressures and constrictions.

According to some sources,[63] Marchionne was also able to exploit a particular circumstance: Before the meeting started, the GM CEO, a former Duke University basketball player, asked for a television so he could follow a big game between his alma mater and Maryland.

Geely Buys Volvo

Geely is a private company and the tenth largest car manufacturer in China. In 2009, when the talks with Ford started, it sold 329,000 cars, mainly in the Chinese market. Therefore, even in China, Geely was still a relatively small player in the automotive arena.

Volvo is a Swedish luxury car manufacturer owned by Ford. In 2009, it sold 335,000 cars through 2,300 dealers in more than 100 countries, with US, Sweden, and Great Britain its largest markets.

Li Shufu, founder of Chinese Geely Group, had long wanted to buy Volvo.

In 2007, Li sent a letter to the US headquarters of Ford, Volvo's owner, stating his interest in purchasing Volvo. No one at Ford took Li's letter into consideration.

In 2008, Li met Ford's CEO at the Detroit auto show. Ford politely discounted Li, not considering his company a credible potential buyer for Volvo.

The main difficulty Li had to face was his company's lack of reputation and credibility in the global arena. He had to find a way to ensure that his proposal was considered by Ford and Volvo.

Since Ford purchased Volvo in 1999 for $6.4 billion, Volvo's sales have been continually dropping and the brand has seldom turned a profit. In 2008, Volvo was deeply in deficit and became a heavy burden to Ford, which was facing reorganization on its own to avoid bankruptcy after having reported losses of $12.7 billion in 2006 and $2.7 billion in 2007. This was exactly the window of opportunity that Li has been envisioning for years.[64]

Skepticism and Lack of Credibility

During the 2009 Detroit auto show, Li visited Ford for a second time. This time, a senior executive promised that Geely would be immediately informed if Ford decided to sell Volvo.

However, Li first had to overcome six overwhelming obstacles:

- Lack of credibility with Ford. Geely sold fewer cars than Volvo, and its market was limited to China, where it was only the 10th largest car manufacturer.
- Gain the support of the Chinese government. Geely was a private company, without the influential backing of the Chinese government that a state-owned enterprise enjoyed.
- Widespread skepticism existed that a small manufacturer of cheap cars would be able to manage a premium brand.
- Fear of potential production relocation in China also arose.
- Intellectual property rights were another concern.
- Potential competitors, particularly Chinese contenders, had to be considered.

The Movie Star Marries the Peasant[65]

To address the first obstacle, Li assembled an impressive acquisition team. He invited the investment bank Rothschild, the most renowned advisor in M&A in the auto industry, to help with the deal.[66]

The Rothschild team was led by Jennifer Yu, the bank's top investment banker in greater China, and Meyrick Cox, the bank's co-head of the automotive team.

Yu, being married to the adopted son of former Chinese President Jiang Zemin, had wide and deep connections within the Chinese establishment. She helped develop strong ties with the Chinese government, submitted regular reports to the National Development and Reform Commission, and addressed therefore the second issue that Li was facing. By creating a strong communication bridge with regulators, and informing the Chinese government of its plans early, Li established himself as the prime candidate (at least among Chinese competitors) in the regulators' eyes, partially addressing issue number 6 (potential Chinese competitors).

Cox was key in addressing Li's fifth concern: negotiating complex intellectual property issues. After agreement on all major commercial clauses of the purchase, negotiations continued for eight more months, particularly on concerns about intellectual property. Safeguards had to be agreed upon to limit potential intellectual property leaking. Contributory to dealing with the intellectual property issue was also Li's track record of respect for intellectual property in all his previous agreements with foreign companies.

Instrumental in addressing the third and fourth concerns (skepticism over Geely and fear of production relocation) were Hans-Olov Olsson and Pehr Gyllenhammar, two former chairmen of Volvo, and now members of the Rothschild-Geely team.

Their role was central in gaining support from Volvo employees, unions, and suppliers. They reassured that production would stay in Sweden and Belgium, promised that Volvo's culture of safety and efficiency would be maintained and safeguarded, and outlined Volvo's potential development in China, which represented the world's fastest growing luxury car market.

After nearly two years of talks, in August 2010, Ford agreed to sell Volvo to Geely for $1.8 billion.

THE FIAT CHRYSLER AGREEMENT

After the divorce from GM, Fiat, the Italian carmaker, started a robust turnaround led by its CEO Sergio Marchionne, and in 2008, despite the global economic crisis, the company delivered profits.

Chrysler, on the other hand, after the failed merger with Daimler-Benz and the acquisition by Cerberus Capital Management (with Daimler-Benz retaining a minority stake), began a constant and steady decline. As a result, the company ended 2008 selling just 1.4 million vehicles (in 1999 Chrysler sold more than 2.6 million cars).

Talks between the two companies started after the funding Chrysler received from the US government in late 2008 to cover its substantial debt was tied to the definition of a turnaround plan to be executed with an industrial partner that could provide environmentally friendly technologies.

In January 2009, Fiat and Chrysler announced the following agreement:

- Fiat would provide know-how and technologies for fuel-efficient vehicles in exchange for 35% of Chrysler's share capital and an option to increase its stake by an additional 20% in the next 12 months.
- Fiat would share its dealer network in Europe and Chrysler its dealer network and production sites in the US and Canada.

The agreement allowed Fiat to regain access to the US market after many years and acquire economies of scale by sharing its technology with the new partner and permitted Chrysler to fulfill the conditions required by the US government in providing the funds: corporate restructuring and development of new environmentally friendly vehicles.

Negotiation Stalemate

Right after the agreement was reached, the situation immediately presented a deadlock because of three important concerns:[67]

- Chrysler needed additional capital to guarantee business continuity and Fiat had no intent of investing cash in the deal.
- Public opinion criticized US government financing of the company associated with a handover to Fiat.
- Creditors of Chrysler had no intention of giving up their entitlements.

At this stage, the negotiation involved five players: Chrysler (specifically its two main shareholders, Cerberus Capital and Daimler-Benz), Fiat, the US government, the unions, and the creditors.

Fiat's CEO Sergio Marchionne negotiated an agreement with President's Obama staff based on the US government providing the required additional financing in exchange for a more radical restructuring plan and a more gradual entry of Fiat in the stake of Chrysler, reduced from the previously agreed 35% to 20%, which could increase up to 49% with the planned transfer of technologies. A majority stake would be made available to Fiat only following the full reimbursement of the public lending by Chrysler.

President Obama's staff insisted that Fiat make at least a token investment, so that Marchionne wouldn't walk away from Chrysler after few months, creating as a result an adverse reaction in public opinion toward the US government.

However, Marchionne stood firm and sidestepped the issue, knowing that Fiat was at that moment the only concrete alternative for Chrysler. In other words, President Obama's staff had no alternatives to Fiat and had to yield to Marchionne's terms.

It is also true that Fiat needed Chrysler almost as badly as Chrysler needed Fiat for two main reasons:

- Fiat needed a partner to achieve economies of scale.
- Fiat had no presence in the US.

However, time pressure was acting against President's Obama task force. The US government had to find a solution for Chrysler as soon as possible.

The agreement between Fiat and the US government addressed the first two issues that led to the impasse: It provided additional funding for Chrysler and relieved the controversy over President Obama's involvement in the rescue of Chrysler (Fiat made a concession on the entry stake in Chrysler, which was reduced from 35% to 20%).[68]

For the negotiations to proceed, the unions needed to support the deal between Fiat and President Obama's staff and creditors' claims had to be attended.

Subsequently, two negotiation tables opened simultaneously between Chrysler and the unions and Chrysler and the creditors.

The unions approved the restructuring plan presented by Marchionne to President Obama, accepting a salary reduction in exchange for a stake in the new company, which acted as a guarantee for the $10.6 billion Chrysler obligation to the union's health care and pension trusts. The union unsuccessfully attempted to have the pension credits paid in cash instead of stock that could be worth nothing in the future, but nevertheless was able to obtain a majority stake in the new company.

On the other hand, negotiations between Chrysler and creditors ended for a second time in an impasse because of the creditor's firm request to recover the full credit of $6.9 billion.

The Solution

At this stage, Chrysler, with consent from the US government, decided to file for Chapter 11 bankruptcy protection (Chapter 11 is a chapter of the United States Bankruptcy Code that involves a reorganization of a debtor's business affairs and assets. It is generally filed by corporations that require time to restructure their debts. Under Chapter 11, debtors are also protected from other litigation against the business through the imposition of an automatic stay, an automatic injunction that stops actions by creditors).

By filing for Chapter 11, Chrysler in effect eliminated the creditors from the negotiation table, leaving only four players in the negotiation process: Chrysler, Fiat, the US government, and the unions.

The final agreement was based on the creation of a new post-bankruptcy company which included the assets of Chrysler, with the following shareholding structure: 68.5% to the unions (as a guarantee for the pension credits), 20% to Fiat (with the option to increase the share to 35% upon achievement of specific pre-established targets), 9.2% to the US government, and 2.3% to the Canadian government, which also contributed with additional funding to Chrysler's survival.

The agreement did not contemplate any investment in cash by Fiat. Fiat would also have the right to acquire a majority interest in Chrysler once all government loans were fully repaid.

The alliance provided both companies with economies of scale and a complementary range of products and markets.

Chrysler was able to expand its product portfolio with the addition of low environmental impact models. Chrysler also had access to Fiat's international distribution network.

Fiat was able to return to the US market and introduce new models in Europe.

Today, Fiat Chrysler Automobiles is the world's seventh-largest auto maker, established as a Netherlands-based holding group with a primary listing on the New York Stock Exchange.[69]

INTERNATIONAL CONTRACTS

Contracts are usually negotiated when there are good relations between the parties.

However, clarifying potentially ambiguous issues and planning in advance for a breakdown in relations is an important part of contract negotiations. International business transactions are no exception.

ARBITRATION

First, every contract should include the process of resolving disputes.

In most international business contracts, it is standard procedure to specify the law that governs the contract.

Most contracts fall into two categories: specifying that disputes will be determined either by *litigation* or by using a *third-party agent*.

Litigation is using a lawyer to defend one's rights in the negotiation. This is an application of a rights-based approach to resolve the differences before a court of law.

Options for using a third-party agent include *arbitration, mediation,* and *conciliation.*

Arbitration, mediation, and conciliation are all defined as a process of settling an argument or disagreement in which the people or groups on both sides present their opinions and ideas to a third person.[70]

Arbitration differs from mediation and conciliation in that in mediation and conciliation both parties have the option of accepting or rejecting the intermediary's solution. Mediation and conciliation are voluntary and non-binding processes. In arbitration, the two parties agree to submit a dispute to a third person and further agree that they will carry out that third person's decisions. The arbitrator determines the outcome of the case.

In the event of a future dispute before they try other means of dispute settlement such as arbitration and litigation, parties might agree to use mediation or conciliation.

Conciliation is a term often used interchangeably with mediation, but it differs fundamentally from mediation in the following ways:

- Conciliation is a method employed in civil law countries (among them, most European countries, East Asia, Turkey, and Russia).
- The conciliator actively drives the negotiation, directing the parties toward a satisfactory agreement by developing solutions and the terms of settlement.
- The mediator at all times must maintain her impartiality, facilitating communication between the parties and acting as a partner to find a satisfactory solution, without ever assuming sole responsibility for developing solutions.

Many arbitration institutions, offer a service of conciliation. The conciliator will invite both sides to state their views of the dispute and will then make a report proposing an appropriate settlement. The parties may reject the report and proceed to arbitration or they may accept it. In many cases, they will use the conciliator's report as a basis for a negotiated settlement.

Arbitration is often favored over litigation because it is perceived as being faster and cheaper.

In most international business contracts, it is also standard procedure to specify the court that has jurisdiction to hear disputes arising under the contract.

Each party, understandably, would choose the courts of its own country to hear such disputes and would prefer to avoid the other's courts due to suspicions of bias. To find a neutral decision maker for potential future disputes, negotiating parties tend to choose international commercial arbitration to the exclusion of national courts. The best known arbitration institutions include the International Chamber of Commerce, the American Arbitration Association, the London Court of Arbitration, the Stockholm Chamber of Commerce, and the Zurich Chamber of Commerce. Each has its own rules and procedures.

Most international business contracts include a clause dictating that if a dispute occurs between the parties they will not go to court but will use mediation or conciliation to find a solution. If a satisfactory solution is not found through mediation or conciliation, they will refer the matter to an arbitrator located in a third country to hear the dispute and make a decision.[71]

LETTER OF CREDIT

To overcome payment risks in international business, banks and businesses have developed the letter of credit.

In international sales of goods/services between unaffiliated parties, neither payment in advance nor payment on account is commonly used, chiefly because of the intensified risks created by the international environment.[72]

A letter of credit is a document issued by a bank that essentially acts as an irrevocable guarantee of payment to a beneficiary: The letter of credit serves as a guarantee to the seller that it will be paid regardless of whether the buyer ultimately fails to pay. Basically, the objective of the letter of credit is to shift payment risks inherent in an international sale of goods/services from the buyer and the seller to a bank. Obviously, there is a cost in issuing a letter of credit.

A letter of credit proves that the seller has performed the duties specified by an underlying contract and the goods/services have been supplied as agreed. In return for these documents, the beneficiary receives payment from the financial institution that issued the letter.

FOREIGN EXCHANGE RISK

In conducting business internationally, the inclusion of a foreign currency in a deal creates a risk. Between the time the agreement is signed and the time payment is received, the value of the foreign currency in relation to the company's main currency may decrease, changing the value of the good/service.[73]

To avoid foreign exchange risk, a party can insist on being paid or on making payment in its own currency, thereby shifting the foreign exchange risk to the other side.

A second solution adopted by companies to protect themselves against adverse fluctuations in exchange rates is to use a foreign exchange hedge, which transfers the foreign exchange risk from the company to a financial institution.

Two common hedges are *forward contracts* and *options*.[74]

A forward contract will lock in an exchange rate today at which the currency transaction will occur on a future date.

An option sets an exchange rate at which the company may select to exchange currencies. If the current exchange rate is more favorable, then the company will not exercise this option.

A third solution is for the parties to agree on a procedure that allows for sharing the foreign exchange risk, for example, negotiating an agreement in which a share of the payment is to be made in one side's currency and another share is to be paid in the other side's currency.

(ENDNOTES)

1   Mortenson, G., & Relin, D. O. (2007). Three Cups of Tea: One Man's Mission to Promote Peace One School at a Time. London: Penguin Books.

2   Docherty, J. S. (2004). Culture And Negotiation: Symmetrical Anthropology For Negotiators. Marquette Law Review, Vol. 87, N. 4, 711-722.

3   Sebenius, J. K. (2002). Caveats for Cross-Border Negotiators. Negotiation Journal, Vol. 18, N. 2, 121-133.

4   Brett, J. M. (2001). Negotiating Globally: How to Negotiate Deals, Resolve Disputes, and Make Decisions Across Cultural Boundaries. San Francisco: Jossey-Bass.

5   Morris, M. W. (2005). When Culture Counts - and When It Doesn't. Harvard Business Publishing Newsletters, June, 3-5.

6   Ho-ying Fu, J., Morris, M. W., Lee, S., Chao, M., Chiu, C., & Hong, Y. (2007). Epistemic Motives and Cultural Conformity: Need for Closure, Culture, and Context as Determinants of Conflict Judgments. Journal of Personality and Social Psychology, Vol. 92, N. 2, 191-207.

7   Dupont, C., & Faure, G. O. (2002). The Negotiation Process. In V. A. Kremenyuk (Ed.), International Negotiation: analysis, approaches, issues (2nd ed.). San Francisco: Jossey-Bass.

8   Rubin, J. Z. (2002). Psychological Approach. In V. A. Kremenyuk (Ed.), International Negotiation: analysis, approaches, issues (2nd ed.). San Francisco: Jossey-Bass.

9   Jönsson, C. (2002). Cognitive Theory. In V. A. Kremenyuk (Ed.), International Negotiation: analysis, approaches, issues (2nd ed.). San Francisco: Jossey-Bass.

10   Kumar, R. (1999). Communicative Conflict in Intercultural Negotiations: The Case of American and Japanese Business Negotiations. International Negotiation, Vol. 4, N. 1, 63-78.

11   Tinsley, C. H. (2004). Culture and Conflict enlarging our dispute resolution framework. In M. J. Gelfand, & J. M. Brett (Eds.), The Handbook of Negotiation and Culture. Palo Alto, CA: Stanford University Press.

12   Ting-Toomey, S. (2005). The Matrix of Face: An Updated Face-Negotiation Theory. In W. B. Gudykunst (Ed.), Theorizing About Intercultural Communication. Thousand Oaks, CA: Sage Publications.

13   Adair, W. L., & Brett, J. M. (2004). Culture and Negotiation Processes. In M. J. Gelfand, & J. M. Brett (Eds.), The Handbook of Negotiation and Culture. Palo Alto, CA: Stanford University Press.

14   Graham, R. J. (1981). The role of perception of time in consumer research. Journal of Consumer Research, 7, 335-342.

15   Morris, M. W., Williams, K. Y., Leung, K, Larrick, R., Mendoza, T., Bhatnagar, D., Li, J., Kondo, M., Luo, J., & Hu, J. (1998). Conflict Management Style: Accounting for Cross-National Differences. Journal of International Business Studies, Vol. 29, N. 4, 729-748.

16   Wu, L., Ray, F., & Ying-yi, H. (2009). Culture, Accountability, and Group Membership: A Dynamic Constructivist Approach to Cross-cultural Negotiation. 22nd Annual International Association of Conflict Management Conference, Kyoto, Japan.

17   De Dreu, C. K. W. (2004). Motivation in Negotiation: a social psychological analysis. In M. J. Gelfand, & J. M. Brett (Eds.), The Handbook of Negotiation and Culture. Palo Alto, CA: Stanford University Press.

18   Ho-ying Fu, J., Morris, M. W., Lee, S., Chao, M., Chiu, C., & Hong, Y. (2007). Epistemic Motives and Cultural Conformity: Need for Closure, Culture, and Context as Determinants of Conflict Judgments. Journal of Personality and Social Psychology, Vol. 92, N. 2, 191-207.

19   De Dreu, C. K. W. (2004). Motivation in Negotiation: a social psychological analysis. In M. J. Gelfand, & J. M. Brett (Eds.), The Handbook of Negotiation and Culture. Palo Alto, CA: Stanford University Press.

20   Kumar, R. (2004). Culture and Emotions in Intercultural Negotiations: An Overview. In M. J. Gelfand, & J. M. Brett (Eds.), The Handbook of Negotiation and Culture. Palo Alto, CA: Stanford University Press.

21   Matsumoto, D., & Juang, L. (2007). Culture and Psychology. Belmont: Wadsworth/Thomson.

22   Ekman, P., & Friesen, W. V. (2003). Unmasking the Face: A guide to recognizing emotions from facial clues. Cambridge, MA: Malor Books.

23   Matsumoto, D., & Wilson, J. (2008). Culture, Emotion and Motivation. In R. Sorrentino, & S. Yamaguchi (Eds.). Handbook of Motivation and Cognition Across Cultures. San Diego: Academic Press.

24   March, R. M. (1990). The Japanese negotiator: Subtleties and strategy beyond Western logic. Tokyo, Japan: Kodansha International.

25   Rubin, J. Z. (2002). The Actors in Negotiation. In V. A. Kremenyuk (Ed.), International Negotiation: analysis, approaches, issues (2nd ed.). San Francisco: Jossey-Bass.

26   Sebenius, J. K. (2002). The Hidden Challenge of Cross-Border Negotiations. Harvard Business Review, Vol. 80, N. 3, 76-85.

27   Koldau, C. (1996). Meanings of Cross-Cultural Differences in Establishing Relationships in Japanese-American Business Negotiations. ISBM Report 14.

28   Leung, K., & Tong, K. K. (2004). Justice across cultures: A three-stage model for intercultural negotiation. In M. J. Gelfand, & J. M. Brett (Eds.), The Handbook of Negotiation and Culture. Palo Alto, CA: Stanford University Press.

29   Albin, C. (2001). Justice and fairness in international negotiation. Cambridge, UK: Cambridge University Press.

30   Zhang, Z.-X. (2006). Chinese Conceptions of Justice and Reward Allocation. In U. Kim, K. Yang, & K. Hwang (Eds.), Indigenous and Cultural Psychology, Understanding People in Context. New York: Springer.

31   Morris, M. W., & Gelfand, M. J. (2004). Cultural Differences and Cognitive Dynamics: expanding the cognitive perspective on negotiation. In M. J. Gelfand, & J. M. Brett (Eds.), The Handbook of Negotiation and Culture. Palo Alto, CA: Stanford University Press.

32   Gelfand, M. J., & Cai, D. A. (2004). Cultural Structuring of the Social Context of Negotiation. In M. J. Gelfand, & J. M. Brett (Eds.), The Handbook of Negotiation and Culture. Palo Alto, CA: Stanford University Press.

33   Gunia, B. C., Brett, J. M., & Nandkeolyar, A. (2014). Trust me, I'm a negotiator: Using cultural universals to negotiate effectively, globally. Organizational Dynamics, 43, 27-36.

34   Gunia, B. C., Brett, J. M., Nandkeolyar, A., & Kamdar, D. (2011). Paying a price: Culture, trust, and negotiation consequences. Journal of Applied Psychology, Vol. 96, N. 4, 774-789.

35   Simintiras, A. C., & Thomas, A. H. (1998). Cross-cultural sales negotiations - A literature review and research propositions. International Marketing Review, Vol. 15 N. 1, 10-28.

36   Kramer, R. M. (2004). The "Dark Side" of Social Context: the role of intergroup paranoia in intergroup negotiations. In M. J. Gelfand, & J. M. Brett (Eds.), The Handbook of Negotiation and Culture. Palo Alto, CA: Stanford University Press.

37   Brewer, M. B., & Brown, R. J. (1998). Intergroup relations. In D. T. Gilbert, S. T. Fiske, & G. Lindzey (Eds.), The Handbook of Social Psychology. New York: Oxford University Press.

38   Fang, T. (2006). The Chinese Negotiator. Journal of Business and Industrial Marketing, Vol. 21, N. 1, 50-60.

39   Barkai, J. (2008). Cultural Dimension Interests, the Dance of Negotiation, and Weather Forecasting: A Perspective on Cross-Cultural Negotiation and Dispute Resolution. Pepperdine Dispute Resolution Law Journal, Vol. 8, N. 3, 403-448.

40   Tzu, S. (1991). The art of war. Translated by T. Cleary. Boston: Shambhala Publications.

41   Faure, G. O. (1999). The Cultural Dimension of Negotiation: The Chinese Case. Group Decision and Negotiation, Vol. 8, N. 3, 187-215.

42   Musashi, M. (1993). The book of five rings. Translated by T. Cleary. Boston: Shambhala Publications.

43   De Mente, B. L. (2004). Japan's Cultural Code Words: 233 Key Terms That Explain Attitudes & Behavior of the Japanese. North Clarendon, VT: Tuttle Publishing.

44   Maddux, W. W., Kim, P. H., Okumura, T., & Brett, J. (2011). Cultural Differences in the Function and Meaning of Apologies. International Negotiation, 16, 405-425.

45 Ting-Toomey, S. (2005). The Matrix of Face: An Updated Face-Negotiation Theory. In W. B. Gudykunst (Ed.), Theorizing About Intercultural Communication. Thousand Oaks, CA: Sage Publications.

46 Tinsley, C. H. (2001). How Negotiators get to yes: Predicting the constellation of conflict management strategies used across cultures. Journal of Applied Psychology, Vol. 86, N. 4, 583-593.

47 Zartman, W. I. (2002). Regional Conflict Resolution. In V. A. Kremenyuk (Ed.), International Negotiation: analysis, approaches, issues (2nd ed.). San Francisco: Jossey-Bass.

48 Zartman, I. W. (2001). The Timing of Peace Initiatives: Hurting Stalemates and Ripe Moments. The Global Review of Ethnopolitics, Vol. 1, N. 1, 8-18.

49 Pruitt, D. G. (2005). Escalation, readiness for negotiation, and third party functions. In I. W. Zartman, & G. O. Faure (Eds.), Escalation and negotiation. Cambridge, England: Cambridge University Press.

50 Nicholson, N., Soane, E., Fenton-O'Creevy, M., & Willman, P. (2005). Personality and domain-specific risk taking. Journal of Risk Research, Vol. 8, N. 2, 157-176.

51 Roussanov, N. L., & Savor, P. G. (2013). Marriage and Manager's attitudes to risk. AFA San Diego Meetings Paper, December.

52 Salacuse, J. W. (2003). The Global Negotiator: Making, Managing, and Mending Deals Around the World in the Twenty-First Century. New York: Palgrave Macmillan.

53 Liu, L. A., Friedman, R. A., & Chi, S. (2005). 'Ren Qing' versus the 'Big Five': The Role of Culturally Sensitive Measures of Individual Difference in Distributive Negotiations. Management and Organization Review, Vol. 1 N. 2, 225-247.

54 Weber, E. U., & Hsee, C. (1998). Cross-Cultural Differences in Risk Perception, but Cross-Cultural Similarities in Attitudes towards Perceived Risk. Management Science, Vol. 44, N. 9, 1205-1217.

55 Salacuse, J. W. (2003). The Global Negotiator: Making, Managing, and Mending Deals Around the World in the Twenty-First Century. New York: Palgrave Macmillan.

56 Bajoria, J., & Xu, B. (2013). The Six Party Talks on North Korea's Nuclear Program. New York: Council on Foreign Relations. Retrieved from http://www.cfr.org/proliferation/six-party-talks-north-koreas-nuclear-program/p13593.

57 Shih, M. (2013). A Method to the Madness: North Korean Negotiating Strategy in the Six-Party Talks. WWS Case 3/09. New Jersey: Princeton University, Woodrow Wilson School of Public and International Affairs. In P. Kerr, & G. Wiseman (Eds.), Diplomacy in a Globalizing World: Theories and Practices. Oxford: Oxford University Press.

58 Finkelstein, S. (2002). The DaimlerChrysler Merger. Tuck School of Business at Dartmouth. Case Study n. 1-0071.

59 Vlasic, B., & Stertz, B. A. (2000). Taken for a Ride: How Daimler-Benz drove off with Chrysler. New York: HarperCollins Publishers.

60 Weiss, S. E. (2011). Renault-Nissan Negotiation. In M. Benoliel (Ed.), Negotiation and Persuasion. Singapore: World Scientific Publishing.

61 Jean-Michel Prillieux, industry consultant with Mavel SA in Paris.

62 Camuffo A., & Volpato G. (2002). Partnering in the global auto industry: the Fiat-GM strategic alliance. International Journal of Automotive Technology and Management, Vol.2, N. 3., 335-352.

63 Clark, J. (2011). Mondo Agnelli: Fiat, Chrysler, and the Power of a Dynasty. Hoboken, NJ: John Wiley & Sons.

64 Nueno, P., & Liu, G. (2012). How Geely won over Volvo. CEIBS Case Center.

65 Li Shufu, founder of the Chinese automotive manufacturer Geely Group: the Geely-Volvo deal was equivalent to a world famous movie star marrying a peasant in China.

66 Webb, Q. (2010, March 29). Rothschild quartet helped China's Geely snare Volvo Cars. Reuters, Retrieved from http://www.reuters.com/article/2010/03/29/volvo-geely-bankers-idUSL-DE62S17C20100329?feedType=RSS&feedName=everything&virtualBrandChannel=11563

67 Caputo, A. (2012). Integrative Agreements in Multilateral Negotiations: The Case of Fiat and Chrysler. International Journal of Business and Social Science, Vol. 3, N. 12, 167-180.

68 Clark, J. (2011). Mondo Agnelli: Fiat, Chrysler, and the Power of a Dynasty. Hoboken, NJ: Wiley.

69   Wikipedia. Retrieved from http://en.wikipedia.org/wiki/Fiat_Chrysler_Automobiles

70   Merriam-Webster, retrieved from http://www.merriam-webster.com/dictionary/arbitration

71   Salacuse, J. W. (2003). The Global Negotiator: Making, Managing, and Mending Deals Around the World in the Twenty-First Century. New York: Palgrave Macmillan.

72   Salacuse, J. W. (2003). The Global Negotiator: Making, Managing, and Mending Deals Around the World in the Twenty-First Century. New York: Palgrave Macmillan.

73   Salacuse, J. W. (2003). The Global Negotiator: Making, Managing, and Mending Deals Around the World in the Twenty-First Century. New York: Palgrave Macmillan.

74   Hull, J. C. (2011). Options, Futures and Other Derivatives (8th ed.). Upper Saddle River, NJ: Prentice Hall.

CHAPTER 14:

The 4Ps Influence Framework

As in negotiations, influencing (getting others to choose to do what you need them to do) is also inherently systemic and dynamic;[1] it is a complex interaction of four dimensions.

Because influencing is a nonlinear, multi-step, fragmented in time, complex social process that takes place under conditions of ambiguity and uncertainty,[2] the four negotiation stages are linked and overlapping, and a change in one element triggers changes in the others.

We will look at the influencing process as a system in which the four stages influence one another and overlap.

The four interrelating stages (the four Ps) that we employ to describe and analyze influence are *preparation, process, power perception,* and *players' perspective* (see Figure 1).

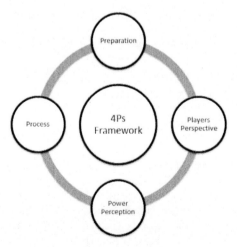

Figure 1. The Four Ps.

THE PREPARATION STAGE

Map out your future, but do it in pencil.[3]

As seen in negotiation, reserving time for preparation is a crucial element of successful influencing.

The preparation stage activities, which include behind-the-scenes research, planning, and organizing, are the foundation for effective influencing.

We can identify three distinct steps in the preparation stage of the 4Ps framework:
- Step 1: Identify your goals.
- Step 2: Identify the target.
- Step 3: Identify relevant exchange currencies.

STEP 1: IDENTIFY YOUR GOALS

Determine your goals and your priorities.

What do you want to achieve? What are your goals? What are your short-term and long-term objectives? What are your priorities? Rank them.

Goals can be divided in six broad categories:[4]
- *Facilitative goals*: You need to gain access to a player in the decision-making process.
- *Attitude goals*: You try to gain a positive opinion toward your initiative. You need the other person to say: This is a good idea.
- *Authorization goals*: You need approval for resources to progress your initiative to the next step.
- *Endorsement goals*: You try to gain active support for your initiative.
- *Decision goals*: You need approval for your initiative from a decision maker. This entails both positive opinions and active support (attitude + endorsement goals).
- *Implementation and action goals*: You want to move to the implementation phase, involving definite steps on a timetable. This entails both approval and commitment of resources (decision + authorization goals).

Never take your eyes off your goals.[5]

STEP 2: IDENTIFY THE TARGET

In every organization, regardless of its size, even uncomplicated decisions require the engagement of an average of 8 people, and complex decisions usually involve as many as 20 people.

Progress in organizational decision making is often a multi-stage, non-linear process.

Consider a chessboard. Each piece has a specific position on the board and distinct moves it can make.[6] The same is true for organizations.

We need to understand not only the position on the board but also the relationships among all the relevant individuals who can assist in achieving our goal.

Influence requires knowledge of the decision-making process and criteria, and of the relationship among the key decision makers. It also requires the ability to contact the right person at the right time using the most appropriate communication style.

We have to be able to identify the informal organization that lies behind the official organizational chart, recognize sub-groups that can be affected by our proposal, understand the decision-making process, and identify the key decision makers and influencers in the organization.

And, finally, we need to develop a steppingstone influence strategy to gradually gain the support of influencers and key decision makers. How can we gain access to those key players? Are there any gatekeepers, key individuals who can grant or withhold permission to access key players?

Step 3: Identify Relevant Currencies

If there is any secret in success, it lies in the ability to understand the other person's point of view and see things from that person's angle, as well as your own.[7]

Now that you have determined the individuals you need to influence to reach your goal, the next step is to identify their interests, priorities, and constraints. Understanding an individual's context is fundamental to identifying her interests.

Examples of contextual factors are organizational reward systems, her boss's expectations, her peers' expectations, education, career history (how long she has been with the company, whether she is high potential, contented, or dead-ended).

Collaboration depends on finding appropriate arrangements.

After you understand what the other person values, you should identify among your available resources what can serve as a suitable currency of exchange. If you have no currencies that the other person values, you have nothing to exchange.

Some such currencies are easy to identify, such as financial, human, or physical resources. Others are less obvious, or even less valuable in your eyes, because they are easy to provide. Nevertheless, they can still be valuable to the other person. For instance, an offer to provide timely information or introductions to one's connections may be highly valued.

Examples of currencies are important roles in projects, access to resources, chances through which to learn new skills, signs of public recognition and appreciation, flexible work schedules, and lower bureaucratic and procedural barriers.

Influence is possible when you have what others want.[8]

We can divide currencies relevant to organizational level into five broad categories:[9]

- *Inspiration-related currencies*: Having a chance to get involved in a strategic or potentially groundbreaking project.
- *Task-related currencies*: Obtaining resources such as money, people, and space. Having a chance to learn new skills or receiving support in a complex task. Receiving timely information or obtaining technical or organizational knowledge.
- *Position-related currencies*: Recognition of effort, results, and abilities. Visibility, reputation, and connections with key decision makers.
- *Relationship-related currencies*: Being listened to, feeling of belonging, and receiving personal and emotional support.

- *Personal-related currencies*: Receiving appreciation, obtaining ownership over important projects, getting troubles out of the way, and affirmation of self-esteem and identity.

A final important concept about exchanging currencies is *equivalence*. It is not so important how we value a specific currency, but how others value it is. Equivalence is basically a matter of perception, and the value attached to specific currencies differs according to the individual and the context. In the absence of this perceived equivalence, people may lose the motivation to continue the exchange.

Two corollaries can be derived from the equivalence principle:

- It is fundamental to accurately identify the interests of the target person.
- Because currencies obtained effortlessly tend to be depreciated and devalued, it is important to sell one's efforts to the target person.

THE INDIAN GRADUATE DILEMMA

The following example is entirely derived from Shell and Moussa (2007).[10]

Raj, the oldest son of a wealthy Indian family, was the heir to his family's large printing business. His father was eager for him to return home from the US after graduation from college and take up his duties with the family firm. Raj, on the other hand, wanted to stay in America for a few more years and gain what he thought would be valuable business experience working for a global consulting company.

How could Raj persuade his father to bless a decision to stay in America without trampling on this all-important relationship?

Make your recommendations taking into account the following information gathered during an interview with Raj:

Question 1: How are decisions made in the family?

My mother, father, grandmother, and grandfather will all sit down together and discuss it (grandfather and grandmother are from my father's side of the family).

Question 2: And of those four, who would be most sympathetic to your view?

My mother.

Question 3: Does she have influence inside the family?

In Indian families, the wife is supreme inside the house. But the issue is both inside and outside the house. And she may be afraid that if I stay in America, I will meet an American girl and want to marry. She would be very opposed to that. There is also my grandfather. He founded the business and thinks some experience working on lots of projects for the consulting firm might be useful, but he cannot oppose my father.

Question 4: And your grandmother?

She will agree with my grandfather.

How can Raj persuade his father to bless a decision to stay in America without trampling on this all-important relationship? See Figure 2 for a diagram of the problem.

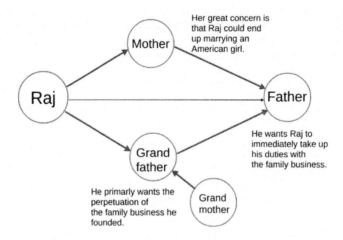

Figure 2. The family decision-making process.

First we would discourage Raj from talking directly to his father. That could be counterproductive because a veto from his father would leave no room for further talks.

We would, instead, build a coalition with his mother and grandparents.

His grandfather's main interest is to see Raj successfully running the family business. So, he would be very motivated to support a postponement of his return for Raj to gain valuable experience that he could bring to the business. Another important element is that it is true that the grandfather can't oppose the father, but it is not said that he cannot influence him.

The grandmother will agree with the grandfather.

His mother is also sympathetic to Raj's view and has a very important role inside the house. Her only concern is that Raj could marry an American girl.

For Raj to meet his primary objective to stay longer in the US, to influence his mother and gain her full support he will have to provide something valuable to her in the exchange, for example, the promise that he will get engaged (or even married) shortly to a Indian girl of whom his mother approves.

Now that Raj has gained his mother and grandparent's support, he can have all the family sit down to discuss the issue so as to persuade his father. In preparing for the meeting, Raj could even ask his mother and grandfather to privately speak to his father and introduce their line of reasoning in support of his decision.

The father wants him to return as soon as possible and take up his duties with the family firm.

With the support of his mother and grandparents, he can try to persuade his father that he will certainly take up his duties, but not now.

THE PROCESS STAGE

The second stage of the 4Ps framework is the process. During the process phase, two or more players meet to exchange currencies to achieve their objectives. We can identify five key potential barriers to the influencing process:[11]

* Negative relationships.
* Poor credibility.
* Communication gaps.
* Conflicting interests.
* Diverging belief systems.

BARRIER N. 1: NEGATIVE RELATIONSHIPS

Trust is the utility through which knowledge flows.[12]

The first barrier to the influencing process is negative relationship. The enduring success of collaboration depends mainly on the quality of interpersonal relationships.

Most effective relationships share three features:[13]

* *Perception of similarity*: The finding of shared experiences, background facts and events, hobbies, affiliations, education, and lifestyle can trigger identification, value congruence, and the perception of similarity.

* *Reciprocity*: A relationship established to constantly meet the needs of both parties. This is why the norm of reciprocity is one of the most robust social psychological norms in all societies. Reciprocity can take the form of mutual exchanges of obligations, resources, services, support, information, contacts, and status.

* *Face time matters*: Familiarity as a key element of functioning relationships. There is no substitute for in-person interaction and face-to-face meetings.

This is why when starting a new project with international and virtual teams the project manager should spend most of his travel budget early in the project life to meet the different team members and their bosses. Planned recurrent gatherings among all team members can foster in-person social-related conversations that result in a perception of similarity and create the basis for a reciprocity-based relationship.

Poor or nonexistent relationships make it almost impossible to exchange currencies and therefore to influence people. Relationships must be established before they are needed. If even one relationship is damaged, the result is a gap in the network and therefore in the information flow.

Never let relationships get to the breaking point. If feasible, find a way to restore them before the point of no return.

Do not burn bridges.[14] You may need the other person's support someday.

This is why most influential people are meticulous in broadening their networks regularly, developing existing connections, and doing small favors for people whenever possible. They invest current resources with a view to meeting future needs.

More important than the number of individuals in a network are the quality and structure of the network.[15] Networks should be open, where the people we know are not all connected to each other; they should be diverse, deep, and high quality. Open, diverse, and deep networks allow for greater exchange of information, ideas, resources, opportunities, and knowledge.

Relationship Modes

We can identify three distinct relationship modes:

- *Rapport level*: A casual relationship based on seeming similarity and social signals, such as acknowledging people or holding doors.
- *Reciprocity level*: A relationship in which two people agree to do something similar (in perceived value) for each other.[16] The underlying principle of reciprocity is giving something valued by the other(s) in return for what you want or need.[17] We tend to do things for people who do things for us, and vice versa. It is also important to emphasize that the sense of a relationship being fair is basically a matter of perception.
- *Trust level*: Individuals in a reciprocity-level relationship have the chance to evaluate the reliability and the skills of the other person. The trust level arises when people develop stable positive beliefs about the other person's disposition, intentions, and traits. Interestingly, people in trust-level relationships no longer have to prove themselves to each other. Actually, they tend to give each other the benefit of the doubt. A failure to keep a promise, which would hurt a reciprocity-level relationship, is more likely to be tolerated by individuals who trust each other.

BARRIER N. 2: POOR CREDIBILITY

The credibility of the teller is the ultimate test of the truth of a proposition.[18]

The word credibility derives from the Latin *crēdibilis*, meaning to be believed, worthy of belief.

Credibility is defined as the quality or power of inspiring belief.[19]

An individual's credibility descends from her skills, her knowledge, and her ability to set and achieve goals and keep commitments.[20]

Credibility is derived from three fundamental sources: expertise, results, and consistency.

- *Expertise*: A combination of skills, knowledge, abilities, and attitude; the way an individual approaches challenges.

  A person's knowledge of the details of a specific subject is often perceived as a reliable demonstration of her expertise.[21] Concrete details provide credibility not only to the expert, but also to the idea itself. In negotiations, and while influencing, details can make a demand or an assertion more tangible and concrete and, therefore, more credible.

- *Results*: A strong track record of achieving goals. Getting things done by focusing on a few critically important goals and consistently delivering measureable results is a key element of credibility.[22]

- *Consistency*: A combination of reliability, keeping one's promises and doing what one says, and personal integrity. When leaders match their words and actions and do what they say they will do, they place a high value on their commitments.

An important feature of credibility is that it takes time to build, but it can be lost in a few moments. And, finally, once it is lost, it takes a lot of effort to win it back.

Self-Confidence

Believe in yourself. Believe in your dreams. If you don't, who will?[23]

Self-confidence is an essential element of credibility because it defines both the confidence in one's abilities and the belief that those abilities will allow task completion and goal achievement.

Self-confidence is a combination of two factors: *self-esteem* and *self-efficacy*.

The dictionary definition of self-esteem is a feeling of confidence, satisfaction, and respect for oneself and one's abilities.[24]

In psychology, the term self-esteem describes a person's overall sense of self-worth or personal value. Self-esteem is often seen as a personality trait, which means that it tends to be stable and enduring.

Self-efficacy is the extent of one's belief in the ability to complete tasks and achieve goals.

Self-confidence represents the basis on which the first two sources of credibility, expertise and results, are established.

What convinces is conviction. Believe in the argument you are advancing. If you don't, you're as good as dead. The other person will sense that something isn't there, and no chain of reasoning, no matter how logical or elegant or brilliant, will win your case for you.[25]

Assertiveness

The dictionary definition of assertiveness is confidence and directness in claiming your rights or putting forward your views.[26]

While aggressive behavior is based on winning, on doing what is in your best interest without regard for the rights, wants, or needs of other people, assertiveness is based on balance: It involves being straightforward about your rights, wants, and needs and still being able to take into consideration the rights, needs, and wants of others.

It's not always easy to identify assertive behavior. This is because there is a fine line between assertiveness and aggression. Assertiveness is the opposite of passive behavior, compliance with other people's demands that can undermine your rights, self-confidence, and, even more important, credibility.

Assertiveness is a key element of credibility because assertive communication projects a confident and credible image that can support the ideas and proposals you are conveying.

In other words, if you are assertive, people will be inclined to believe that you know what you are talking about.

Pulchronomics

As seen in chapter 9, when building credibility with people we don't know, initial impressions count for a great deal. Because most people tend to persevere with their first impressions, rejecting contradictory evidence and choosing information that confirms their prejudices, negative first impressions are quicker to form and more resistant to disconfirmation than good impressions.

The halo effect further amplifies the importance of first impressions and the tendency of people to create biased judgments about the target individual based on specific traits. As a consequence, it becomes vital to present our most positive traits early during encounters to create a favorable first impression.

According to the results of a survey conducted among randomly selected people in the US, discrimination based on looks exceeded discrimination on ethnicity/ national background.[27]

Pulchronomics is defined as the economics of beauty. According to research, better-looking men earn more than average-looking men of similar education and experience, and uglier men earn even less.

But what can average and worse-looking people do to overcome this discrimination? Appearance is just one of many factors that affect one's credibility and career. People can leverage the halo effect and emphasize other traits, such as personality, strength, and intelligence (more on this in chapter 9, first impressions and halo effect).

While this all sounds incredibly unfair, it is a simple fact of life.[28]

BARRIER N. 3: COMMUNICATION GAPS

If you don't ask, you don't get.[29]

We dealt with the main communication barriers in chapter 5.

In this paragraph, we'll only recap a summary of the key concepts.

Because communication can be considered a method to reproduce a thought or idea, as with all methods of reproduction, it can be subject to distortion, noise, and misinterpretation.

The translation from thought to language may be distorted or inaccurate; similarly, it can be inaccurate in the reconversion from language to understanding in the mind of the receiver:

I know you think you understood what I said, but what you heard was not what I meant.[30]

Values, beliefs, past experiences, stereotypes, prejudices, feelings, and environment are only some of the most probable forms of interference that can distort the meaning and obstruct the conveyance of a message.

In an international context, other than cultural values, norms, beliefs, and stereotypes, language probably represents the greatest barrier in communication. This is especially true when interactions across countries are conducted using the unofficial language of international business, broken English, a linguistic variation of English with different pronunciation, morphology, accents, cadences, and syntaxes.

Always bear in mind that the purpose of communication is achieved only when the receiver has understood the sender's intended message.

BARRIER N. 4: CONFLICTING INTERESTS

There is some self-interest behind every friendship. There is no friendship without self-interests. This is a bitter truth.[31]

Self-interest makes some people blind, and others sharp-sighted.[32]

Negotiations, both inside and outside the organization, are based on complementary interests.

The most important barrier facing any new proposal is the possibility that someone somewhere in the organization will perceive it as a threat to her turf. This is particularly pertinent in change initiatives aimed at dismantling organizational silos.

Never underestimate the power of self-interest in shaping people's cognition and behavior.

Identify the other people's interests. Show them that your idea can promote their objectives. Frame your proposal in terms of their needs and concerns.

Interests can be shaped either by explicit motives, conscious and transitory goals shaped by social norms and tangible rewards (money, position, benefits), or by implicit motives, unconscious and enduring goals, such as a need for affiliation and belonging, a need to enhance one's performance, and a need for power.[33]

Obviously, people tend to favor ideas that benefit them and oppose those that carry significant personal costs to them.[34]

Another barrier to influence is the bias in favor of the status quo: People have a strong propensity to preserve the current state of affairs because any change from the status quo is perceived as a loss.

When there are conflicting interests, you can either resort to your negotiation skills or leverage your sensitivity to the organizational context, forming alliances with influencers and key players.

Conflict Management

Following are two definitions of conflict:

A state of disharmony between incompatible or antithetical persons, ideas, or interests.[35]

Competitive or opposing action of incompatibles ideas, interests, or persons.[36]

According to the *contingency approach*, most people have a preferred style of handling conflict, but are likely to use different styles corresponding to the situation.[37]

According to conflict management theory, conflict management styles can be differentiated along two main dimensions (see Figure 3):[38]

- *Assertiveness, or concern for self*: The degree to which individuals pursue their own interests.
- *Cooperation, or concern for others*: The degree to which people seek to encompass the interests of others.

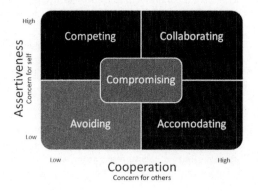

Figure 3. Conflict management styles (Rahim, 2002).

The five conflict management styles are:
- *Competing*: High concern for self, low concern for others. Assertive and not cooperative.
- *Accommodating*: Low concern for self and high concern for others. Cooperative and not assertive.
- *Avoiding*: Low concern for both self and others. Neither assertive nor cooperative.
- *Compromising*: Moderate concern for self and others. Moderately assertive and cooperative.
- *Collaborating*: High concern for self and others. Assertive and cooperative.

The competing style has a win-lose and assertive orientation that ignores the needs and concerns of the other party, often with the result of damaging the relationship.

The accommodating style has a cooperative approach that seeks to satisfy the needs and concerns of the other party, often with the aim of preserving the relationship.

The avoiding style tends to elude and sidestep conflict, with the result of not satisfying either self or others' needs and concerns. Avoiding can only be effective in the short term, when conflict is emotionally charged or the issue is trivial compared to the importance of the relationship with the other side.

The compromising style requires both parties to give up something to reach a mutually acceptable agreement. At the end, neither party fully meets her interests. This style is appropriate when the parties need a temporary solution, when the negotiation process has reached an impasse or when the parties are under extreme time pressure.

Compromising often provides a quick, easy, and acceptable outlet when collaborating would produce a better solution.

The collaborating style seeks a win-win solution, displaying high concern for self and others. It requires a certain degree of trust to exchange information and evaluate alternatives.

Collaborating is a demanding, laborious, and time-consuming process that involves the adoption of integrative thinking to challenge the status quo and identify novel solutions.

Effective conflict management requires individuals to adapt their style according to the context, the counterpart, and the issue.

During conflicts, individuals must continuously manage assertiveness versus cooperation tension. As in negotiation, conflict management requires the ability to be both assertive and cooperative to equally claim and create value.

Still, adding the separate skill of creativity to the dichotomy of assertiveness versus cooperation allows individuals to move from basic compromise to a more comprehensive collaborative outcome. The result is the triangle of effectiveness (see Figures 4 and 5).[39]

Figure 4. Triangle of effectiveness. Adapted from Schneider, 2012.

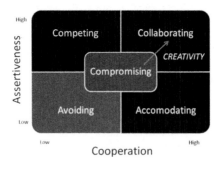

Figure 5. From compromising to collaborating. Adapted from Schneider, 2012.

Furthermore, an individual with the ability to be assertive, cooperative, and creative will be better equipped to move among the different styles, according to the context, the importance of the issue, and the counterpart conflict management style.

Nonviolent Communication

Observing without evaluating is the highest form of human intelligence.[40]

Communication is not only one of the main sources of conflict, but also an important means for conflict prevention and resolution. Words can be used to de-escalate a potentially critical situation.

Careful communication prevents alienating people and burning bridges. This is important during all exchanges, but even more crucial for low-context individuals who are interacting with high-context people.

During negotiations and conflicts, if you behave inappropriately or have made a mistake, don't get defensive. Instead just acknowledge your behavior and apologize.

Following are examples of how slight changes in sentence construction, words choice, and positioning can help convey a totally different message. The examples are derived from Edwards (2006).[41]

I am pleased with your progress but I need to talk with you today.

The but contradicts the compliment and suggests a problem. Changing the word but to and makes the request look positive.

I always seem to have a problem completing tasks with you.

Substituting the always with often opens the door for a potential solution.

I just want to talk with you.

You are reducing the contribution of the other person before she speaks.

I need you to stop what you are doing and come with me to see the director because we want to ask your opinion.

Provide the context first; otherwise, the other person will start guessing what the request is about and stop listening to the second part of the sentence.

The director and I would like your opinion, so could you stop what you are doing and come and help us now?

A crucial skill in negotiating and influencing across cultures is the ability to observe without evaluating.

Labeling, judging, comparing, criticizing, blaming, and insulting are all forms of evaluation.

Most of us find it difficult to observe people without making evaluations.

Observations and evaluations have to be distinct. Moreover, evaluations must be based on observations specific to time and context.[42]

Following are examples of evaluations and observations (derived from Rosenberg, 2003) that help explain the differences between the two actions:[43]

John was angry with me yesterday for no reason. Evaluation.

John told me he was angry. Observation.

John pounded his fist on the table. Observation.

John works too much. Evaluation.

John spent more than 60 hours at the office last week. Observation.

Pay attention to use of the words always, never, ever, whenever, and frequently. At times such words are used as exaggerations, in which case observations and evaluations are being integrated.

Following is a list of seven sentences that should be avoided when managing conflict:[44]

- *You wouldn't understand:* We are prejudging the other person's ability to understand.
- *Because these are the rules:* Explain the rationale behind the rule you are enforcing. The other person might not agree, but at least he or she understands your point of view.
- *It's none of your business:* This labels the other person as an outsider. Instead explain why you can't disclose the information.
- *What do you want me to do?*: This is an evasion of responsibility. Instead, offer to think of a solution. Even an apology could work: I'm sorry, but I really don't know what else to do.
- *Calm down:* This is a criticism of the other person's behavior and, even more important, implies that he or she has no right to be upset.
- *I'm not going to say this again:* This is a threat that we often can't sustain, thus losing credibility in the eyes of the other person.
- *Be more reasonable:* All people think they are right. So, first try to reassure the other person that you understand his or her point of view (this lowers the tension) and then help the person to move along your line of reasoning.

Conflict and Culture

Culture and conflict are inextricably connected. In addition, value orientations affect perceptions and expectations of conflict management behavior.

According to research, the Confucian avoiding style of conflict management can best be explained by the *societal conservatism* (e.g., conformity, interdependence, tradition) dimension in Schwartz's model, while the tendency of Anglo-Saxon individuals to adopt a competing style of conflict management is described as an orientation toward Schwartz's values of *self-enhancement, independence,* and *achievement.*[45]

Cultures that emphasize embeddedness of an individual in the group will therefore tend to seek harmony and avoid conflict.

In contrast, societies that emphasize self-reliance, independence, and autonomy will display a higher drive for success and will adopt a more competitive conflict management style.[46]

Status is another important factor when analyzing conflict management. Members of hierarchical cultures avoid conflict because individuals are expected to comply with the roles assigned to them in the hierarchy and are subjected to sanctions if they fail to comply.

In hierarchical cultures, where social stratification is conventional, a power strategy represents a viable alternative in resolving conflicts and disputes. A power strategy is adopted in cultures where social order and quick conflict resolution are important because it tends to preserve the status quo and the social fabric of the society.

On the other hand, in hierarchical cultures, with social power also comes the duty to care for those at the bottom of the pyramid. Social obligations can therefore influence the most powerful individual to meet the interests of the less powerful party.[47]

Conversely, members of egalitarian cultures challenge higher status individuals because social rank is temporary and context related.

BARRIER N. 5: DIVERGING BELIEF SYSTEM

A journey of a thousand miles begins with a single step.[48]

Beliefs can be defined as assumptions and convictions that are held to be true by an individual or group. Social beliefs are the expectations around which we organize our social life. Beliefs are acquired through social experience and guide individuals' cognitive processing and behavior.

If one's initiative might collide with a key player's core belief, don't force the situation. The other person will easily fall prey to confirmation bias, the tendency to favor information that confirms one's assumptions, regardless of whether the information is true or false.

Possible strategies to adopt include the following:[49]

- *Patience*: Changing people's beliefs takes time. Be persistent without being insistent.
- *Shift target*: If you hit a wall, change the target player.
- *Position your idea as irrelevant*: Introduce your idea so that it is not perceived as a threat to the accepted belief system.
- *Inconsequence:* Proceed one step at a time. Break your initiative into small steps that demand less commitment from the other person. Decisions tend to be influenced by the reference point (core beliefs in this case) and usually biased to favor small rather than large changes. Starting with the easy things provides a feeling of accomplishment and commitment.[50] After some small ideas have worked out, you will have a feeling of momentum and further small actions can be put in place. Furthermore, people will persevere in their action to be seen as consistent. The inconsequence strategy requires not only commitment but also immediate results to break the status quo inertia.[51]
- *Adapt your idea*: If the above strategies don't work, revise your initiative to incorporate the other party's core beliefs.

THE POWER PERCEPTION STAGE

Power is a key factor in influencing people. The actual success we experience while influencing is directly associated with the power others give to us.

People perceive that you have power when you have what others want or need.

Power is dynamic. There is a strong correlation between time and power. Currencies change their value over time.[52]

SOURCES OF POWER

The capacity a leader has to influence comes from six main sources (more on this in chapter 15):[53]

- *Legitimate power*: Essentially, this type of power is founded exclusively on position. Legitimate power is based on the importance people give to the role we play in the organization. Legitimate power can differ across cultures and can be based either on ascription (status, social class, family background) or merit (skill, track record).

- *Reward/coercive power*: Reward power is attained by giving others what they want and taking away from others what they do not want. The opposite is punishing: having the power to take away from others what they want and not providing what they want.
- *Information power*: Access to valuable and nearly unavailable information.
- *Relationship power*: Access to valuable and relevant people; who you know and the level of your relationship with important individuals.
- *Expert power*: Specific talents, abilities, knowledge, or skills that are needed by others. This is reinforced by a robust track record.
- *Referent power (charisma):* This is essentially a personal source of power. Charisma is based on a high degree of association, admiration, respect, and identification with another person.

POWER-DEPENDENCE THEORY

Power-dependence theory provides a framework for characterizing relative and total power, based on the dependence between two players.

More specifically, the power of A over B is equal to and based on the dependence of B upon A.[54]

The concept of dependence is based on two factors:

- It is directly correlated to the value ascribed to the outcome at stake.
- It is inversely correlated to the availability of this outcome through alternative sources.

Consequently, A's power over B is directly correlated to the degree to which B is dependent on A or, in other words, to the degree to which B obtains greater benefit from the relationship with A than B can receive from alternative relationships.

It is important to emphasize that, because each player's power is independently determined by the other's dependence, an increase in A's power does not necessarily decrease B's power, and vice versa.

THE PLAYERS' PERSPECTIVE STAGE

As seen previously, most organizational decision making requires contact with 8 to 20 people.

Influencing is therefore a dynamic, complex, and multi-stage process, requiring one to persuade different people to do different things at different stages.[55]

Planning a steppingstone strategy is a six-step process:

- Map the decision-making process in the organization.
- Categorize the key players comprising the decision-making unit.
- Who has power (not only positional power)? Who is favorable to your idea? Who is opposed?
- Enlist a champion, giving something in exchange.

- Ask your champion to approach other members of the decision-making unit (DMU) and build a coalition.
- Then ask the coalition to speak to the decision maker.

Bypassing the initial steps and speaking directly to the decision maker could be counterproductive (as we have seen in the Indian Graduate Dilemma we encountered earlier in this chapter).

INFORMAL ORGANIZATION PLAYERS

Social network experts have identified five distinct and recurring types of actors within the informal organization.

The first are the *hubs*, those with the most direct connections within the group. They are typically highly social and very good communicators. They tend to rapidly disseminate information and centralize work processes. They are usually the influencers and decision makers of the DMU.

The second are the *bridges*, shortcuts that connect different clusters. They are fundamental in accelerating the flow of information between different networks. Bridges differ from hubs: While hubs are directly connected to many individuals, bridges connect two or more clusters. Organizations can methodically create bridges, for example, by having people within the company move from one country or one department to another.

The third are the *gatekeepers*, players who control access to the influencers and decision makers. They are responsible for the flow of information and knowledge within the group.

The fourth are the *information brokers*, the primary sources of information within the group.

The fifth are the *peripheral players*, individuals at the edges of the informal organization. They can be connected to other players via indirect routes because they have some source of power (such as expertise, information, or position).

THE DECISION-MAKING UNIT

The DMU comprises all the players who participate in the organizational decision-making process.

Its composition is very similar to that of the 4 Ps negotiation framework (see Figure 6).

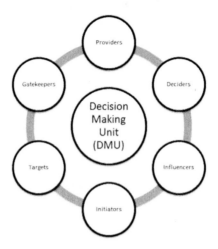

Figure 6. The decision-making unit.

- *Targets*: Players who are directly or indirectly affected by your proposal.
- *Influencers*: Players who can influence the choice of decision makers (experts with in-depth knowledge or experience of the good/service or informal influencers such as friends, family, and colleagues).
- *Providers*: Players in charge of resources (financial, physical, human).
- *Initiators:* Players who see the need to be satisfied or problem to be solved.
- *Deciders*: Player(s) responsible for the final choice.
- *Gatekeepers*: Players who control the information that influencers and decision makers receive. These people manage the flow of information and knowledge within the DMU.

The same players in the DMU can take on different roles. Individuals can act as influencers and initiators or gatekeepers and providers. These roles are systemic and dynamic, and they change according to the organization. Conflicting interests among these players must be considered in the influencing process.

Mapping the decision-making unit and the relationships among the different players is critical in the preparation phase. Strategic tactics associated with these efforts involve building trust-based relationships with initiators that allow for early involvement in the decision-making process, persuading gatekeepers and influencers, and minimizing the perceived risk for targets and providers.

It is also critical to understand the decision-making process: How does information flow through the organization? Who are the key players? What is their role in the organization? What is their main source of power? Can they influence other players? How strong is their voice in the final decision? Will they speak up on your behalf or be silent supporters? Do they see your proposal as a threat to their turf? Do they have veto power? Are they likely to exercise their veto power?

As in negotiations, the different players participating in the DMU can be mapped along three axes (Figure 7):

- *Level of support*: Are they well-disposed or averse to your proposal?
- *Level of assertiveness*: Will they voice their support or opposition? Will they exert influence behind the scenes? Will they actively support or oppose your proposal?
- *Level of influence* in the decision-making process: What is their position in the organization? Do they have credibility within the DMU? Do people listen to them? Can they persuade people to change their minds? Does the group recognize them as leaders?

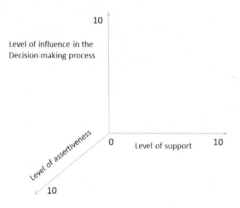

Figure 7. - Players' positioning within the DMU.

RELATIONSHIPS

People are complex, multifaceted, impulsive, and erratic.

When influencing across cultures, maintaining relationships is important to achieving your goals. Understanding the other side's perspective, mental schemas, culture, cognitive processes, and constraints is thus critical to devise integrative solutions that are seen as favorable by both parties

Basic to influence is that it involves people; people experience emotions and have different values, distinctive experiences, and individual points of view. They can also incorrectly interpret what you intend to communicate. In short, they are irrational. Be equipped to deal with this irrationality: You must strive to understand the other parties' interests and constraints, even if it involves educating them.

Every individual is the product of a combination of three elements (see Figure 8):

- *Culture* is the invisible lens filtering how a person sees the world; it is the collective programming of the mind which distinguishes members of one group from members of another.[56]

Culture involves more than national culture; it also involves cultural influences such as gender, education, age, profession, social class, and technology.

337

- *The social context* is the immediate environment in which the person grows up (family, friends) or employs his or her skills (organization).
- *Personality* refers to a person's combined behavioral, emotional, and mental response patterns.

Culture, context, and personality influence people's behavior and cognitive processes.

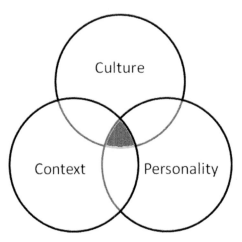

Figure 8. Elements of relationships.

We have dedicated multiple chapters of this book to understanding the influence of culture, personality, and cognition on people's mental schemas and behavior.

The aim is a *role reversal*: taking up the other side's position to understand the values, norms, prejudices, biases, social scripts, attitudes, and predispositions that regulate the other party's communication patterns, cognitive processes, and behavior so as to identify the other side's interests, constraints, and concerns.

Role reversal, the skill of seeing the situation as the other party sees it, is even more important in an international context in which the factors involved in the influencing process are even more elusive and difficult to pin down.

In international influence, it is also important to consider social psychological measures.

People judge the exchange process based on four factors:[57]
- Feelings about the objective outcome of the exchange.
- Feelings about the self (e.g., saving face, living according to one's own values and standards)
- Feelings about the fairness of the exchange process.
- Feelings about the relationship with the other party.

The last two factors are crucial in influencing.

Your goal when influencing is to determine the thinking of the other party and why specific behaviors occur and to identify the other party's real interests, concerns, and constraints.

(ENDNOTES)

1   Moty Cristal: The Negosystem™ Model.

2   Watkins, M. (1999). Negotiating in a Complex World. Negotiation Journal, Vol. 15, N. 3, 245-270.

3   Jon Bon Jovi.

4   Shell, G. R., & Moussa, M. (2007). The Art of Woo: Using Strategic Persuasion to sell your ideas. New York: Penguin Group.

5   Diamond, S. (2010). Getting More: how to negotiate to achieve your goals in the Real World. New York: Crown Business.

6   Shell, G. R., & Moussa, M. (2007). The Art of Woo: Using Strategic Persuasion to sell your ideas. New York: Penguin Group.

7   Henry Ford.

8   Cohen, A. R., & Bradford, D. L. (2005). Influence without authority (2nd ed.). Hoboken: John Wiley & Sons.

9   Cohen, A. R., & Bradford, D. L. (2005). Influence without authority (2nd ed.). Hoboken: John Wiley & Sons.

10   Shell, G. R., & Moussa, M. (2007). The Art of Woo: Using Strategic Persuasion to sell your ideas. New York: Penguin Group.

11   Shell, G. R., & Moussa, M. (2007). The Art of Woo: Using Strategic Persuasion to sell your ideas. New York: Penguin Group

12   Karen Stephenson.

13   Shell, G. R., & Moussa, M. (2007). The Art of Woo: Using Strategic Persuasion to sell your ideas. New York: Penguin Group.

14   Uchil, A. (2007). Relationship Selling: The Fine Art of Consultative Sales. Parker, CO: Outskirts Press.

15   Willburn, P., & Cullen, K. L. (2013). A Leader's Network: How to Help Your Talent Invest in the Right Relationships at the Right Time. Centre for Creative Leadership, White Paper, October.

16   Merriam-Webster, retrieved from http://www.merriam-webster.com/dictionary/recirpocity

17   Cohen, A. R., & Bradford, D. L. (2005). Influence without authority (2nd ed.). Hoboken: John Wiley & Sons.

18   Neil Postman.

19   Merriam-Webster, retrieved from http://www.merriam-webster.com/dictionary/credibility

20   Covey, S. R. (2006). The SPEED of Trust: The One Thing That Changes Everything. New York: Free Press.

21   Heath, C., & Heath, D. (2008). Made to Stick. London: Arrow Books.

22   Krames, J. (2005). Jack Welch and the 4 E's of Leadership: How to Put GE's Leadership Formula to Work in Your Organization. New York: McGraw-Hill.

23   Jon Bon Jovi.

24   Merriam-Webster. Retrieved from http://www.merriam-webster.com/dictionary/self-esteem

25   Lyndon B. Johnson.

26   Collins Dictionary. Retrieved from http://www.collinsdictionary.com/dictionary/english/assertiveness

27   Hamermesh, D. S. (2013). Beauty pays: Why Attractive People Are More Successful. Princeton: Princeton University Press.

28   Lakhani, D. (2005). Persuasion: the art of getting what you want. Hoboken: John Wiley & Sons.

29   Guy Kawasaki

30   Hughes, R. (2010). Culture. London, UK: Fiell Publishing.

31   Chanakya.

32   Francois de La Rochefoucauld.

33   Hofer, J., & Chasiotis, A. (2011). Implicit Motives Across Cultures. Online Readings in Psychology and Culture, Unit 4. Retrieved from http://scholarworks.gvsu.edu/orpc/vol4/iss1/5

34   Shell, G. R., & Moussa, M. (2007). The Art of Woo: Using Strategic Persuasion to sell your ideas. New York: Penguin Group.

35   The Free Dictionary, retrieved from http://www.thefreedictionary.com/conflict

36   Merriam-Webster, retrieved from http://www.merriam-webster.com/dictionary/conflict

37   Rahim, M. A. (2002). Toward A Theory Of Managing Organizational Conflict. The International Journal of Conflict Management, Vol. 13, N. 3, 206-235.

38   Shell, R. G. (2001). Bargaining Styles and Negotiation: The Thomas-Kilmann Conflict Mode Instrument in Negotiation Training. Negotiation Journal, Vol. 17, N. 2, 155-174.

39   Schneider, A. K. (2012). Teaching a New Negotiation Skills Paradigm. Washington University Journal of Law & Policy, Vol. 39, 13-38.

40   Jiddu Krishnamurti.

41   Edwards, C. (2006). Mind reading. Old Windsor: Real Publishing.

42   Rosenberg, M. B. (2003). Nonviolent communication: A language of life. Encinitas, CA: Puddledancer Press.

43   Rosenberg, M. B. (2003). Nonviolent communication: A language of life. Encinitas, CA: Puddledancer Press.

44   Thompson, G. J. (2004). Verbal judo: The gentle art of persuasion. New York, NY: William Morrow Paperbacks.

45   Morris, M. W., Williams, K. Y., Leung, K, Larrick, R., Mendoza, T., Bhatnagar, D., Li, J., Kondo, M., Luo, J., & Hu, J. (1998). Conflict Management Style: Accounting for Cross-National Differences. Journal of International Business Studies, Vol. 29, N. 4, 729-748.

46   Schwartz, S. H. (2006). A Theory of Cultural Value Orientations: Explication and Applications. Comparative Sociology, Vol.5, N. 2-3, 137-182.

47   Tinsley, C. H. (2004). Culture and Conflict enlarging our dispute resolution framework. In M. J. Gelfand, & J. M. Brett (Eds.), The Handbook of Negotiation and Culture. Palo Alto, CA: Stanford University Press.

48   Lao-Tzu.

49   Shell, G. R., & Moussa, M. (2007). The Art of Woo: Using Strategic Persuasion to sell your ideas. New York: Penguin Group.

50   Diamond, S. (2010). Getting More: how to negotiate to achieve your goals in the Real World. New York: Crown Business.

51   Lakhani, D. (2005). Persuasion: the art of getting what you want. Hoboken: John Wiley & Sons.

52   Zartman, W. I. (2002). The Structure of Negotiation. In V. A. Kremenyuk (Ed.), International Negotiation: analysis, approaches, issues (2nd ed.). San Francisco: Jossey-Bass.

53   Raven, B. H. (1992). A power/interaction model of interpersonal influence: French and Raven 30 years later. Journal of Social Behavior and Personality, 7, 217-244.

54   Emerson, R. M. (1962). Power-Dependence Relations. American Sociological Review, Vol. 27, N. 1, 31-41.

55   Shell, G. R., & Moussa, M. (2007). The Art of Woo: Using Strategic Persuasion to sell your ideas. New York: Penguin Group.

56   Hofstede, G. (2001). Culture's consequences: Comparing values, behaviors, institutions and organizations across nations (2nd ed). Thousand Oaks, CA: Sage.

57   Curhan, J. R., Elfenbein, H. A., & Xu, H. (2006). What Do People Value When They Negotiate? Mapping the Domain of Subjective Value in Negotiation. Journal of Personality and Social Psychology, Vol. 91, No. 3, 493-512.

CHAPTER 15:

Leadership

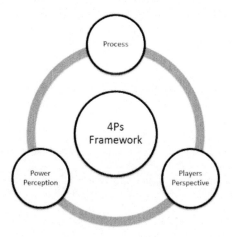

Stage 2: Process. Stage 3: Power Perception. Stage 4: Players Perspective

INTRODUCTION

Despite possibly being one of the most recurrently studied topics, the link between leadership and objective variables remains unclear: Researchers and managers are still in pursuit of the characteristics that make a good leader.

Following are definitions of leader and leadership from foremost academics and scholars:

A leader sets a direction, aligns people to the vision and motivates them (Kotter, 1990).

Leadership is the sum of the actions that focus resources to create desirable opportunities (Campbell, 1991).

The only definition of a leader is someone who has followers (Drucker, 1996).

343

A leader is a person who sets attractive goals and has the ability to attract followers who share those goals (Bower, 1997).

A leader's singular job is to get results (Goleman, 2000).

A leader's most important job is to develop people (Peters, 2014).

Leadership is defined as the ability of an individual to influence, motivate, and enable others to contribute toward the effectiveness and success of the organizations of which they are members (House, 2002).

Leadership is about making things happen, contingent on a context (Ancona, 2005).

Leadership does remain pretty much of a black box or unexplainable concept (Luthans, 2005).

Leadership is a process of social influence, which maximizes the efforts of others, towards the achievement of a goal (Kruse, 2013).

It is important to emphasize that although we have traditionally associated leadership with position, Leadership is not the same as authority.[1]

If you want to build a ship, don't drum up people together to collect wood and don't assign them tasks and work, but rather teach them to long for the endless immensity of the sea.[2]

A LEADER AND A FOLLOWER

Following is a tale entirely derived from Devdutt Pattanaik (2013)[3] that describes the difference between a leader and a follower:

One day, the sage Narad asks Vishnu (the Indian deity): *Why do you insist that the image of Garud (Vishnu's eagle and vehicle) be placed before you in the temples? Why not me? Am I not your greatest devotee?*

Before Vishnu can reply a crash is heard outside the main gate of Vaikuntha (the home of Vishnu). *What was that?* asks Vishnu. Garud, who usually investigates such events, is nowhere to be seen. *I have sent Garud on an errand. Can you find out what happened, Narad?* asks Vishnu. Eager to please Vishnu, Narad runs out to investigate. *A milkmaid tripped and fell,* he says when he returns.

What was her name? asks Vishnu. Narad runs out, speaks to the maid, and returns with the answer: *Sharda.*

Where was she going? asks Vishnu. Narad runs out once again, speaks to the maid, and returns with the answer: *She was on her way to the market.*

What caused her to trip? asks Vishnu. *Why didn't you ask this question the last time I went?* mumbles an irritated Narad. He then runs out, speaks to the maid once again. *She was startled by a serpent that crossed her path,* he says on his return. *Anything else?* he asks.

Are all her pots broken? asks Vishnu. *I don't know,* snaps Narad. *Find out,* insists Vishnu. *Why?* asks Narad. *Find out, Narad. Maybe I would like to buy some milk,* says Vishnu patiently. With great reluctance, Narad steps out of Vaikuntha and meets the milkmaid. He returns looking rather pleased, *She broke one pot. But there is another one intact. And she is willing to sell the milk but at double the price.*

So how much should I pay her? asks Vishnu. *Oh, I forgot to ask. I am so sorry,* says Narad, running out again. *Do not bother. Let me send someone else,* says Vishnu.

Just then, Garud flies in. He has no idea of what has transpired between Vishnu and Narad. Vishnu tells Garud, *I heard a crashing sound outside the main gate. Can you find out what happened?* As Garud leaves, Vishnu whispers, *Let us see how he copes.*

Garud returns and says, *It is a milkmaid called Sharda. She was on her way to the market. On the way, a snake crossed her path. Startled she fell down and broke one of the two pots of milk she was carrying. Now she wonders how she will make enough money to pay for the broken pot and the spilt milk. I suggested she sell the milk to you.*

And the price of the milk? asks Vishnu. Impeccably comes Gardu's reply, *Four copper coins. One actually, but I think she hopes to make a handsome profit when dealing with God.*

Vishnu's eye caught Narad's and Narad understood in that instant why Garud's statue, and not his, was always placed before the image of Vishnu in Vishnu's temple.

SOURCES OF POWER

Psychologists John French and Bertram Raven (1959) conducted a noteworthy study on social power, identifying five bases of power:[4] legitimate, reward, expert, referent, and coercive.

Raven (1965) later added a sixth: information power.[5]

- *Legitimate power* is the formal authority that derives from a person's title or position in a group or an organization: Elections, social hierarchies, cultural values, and organizational structure provide the foundation for legitimate power.
- *Reward power* is the authority that derives from a person's ability to reward individuals for obeying principles or meeting expectations. Raises, promotions, challenging assignments, training opportunities, and acknowledgment are all forms of reward.
- *Expert power* is the authority that derives from a person's knowledge in a specific domain. It involves the ability to understand a problem and provide reliable solutions.
- *Referent power* is the authority that derives from a person's style, persona, appearance, attractiveness, and appeal. It is often characterized as charisma, a special charm or appeal that causes people to feel attracted and excited by someone.[6]
- *Coercive power* is the authority that derives from a person's ability to sanction individuals for failure to conform to principles or meet expectations. Threats and punishment are common means of coercion.
- *Information power* is the authority that derives from a person's ability to access and control information needed by others to reach their goals.

Recently, a seventh crucial base of power was introduced:

- *Relationship power* is the authority that derives from a person's ability to build trust-based relationships and develop valuable networks both inside and outside the organization.

We should think of the different bases of power as separate factors. Leaders should be able to adopt different sources of power in changing circumstances, according to the specific situation.

THE MAKING OF AN EXPERT

Even if an individual is naturally very talented, achieving an exceptional level of performance requires more than 10 years of practice starting from the moment when the specific domain basic skills and knowledge are acquired. One of the most popular studies of expertise followed international chess masters, observing that the time between chess players' first learning the basic rules and attaining the level of grandmaster was longer than 10 years.[7]

Other studies have confirmed these results: For musicians, an average of 20 years after starting to study music is necessary to compose their first prominent work.

A study on poets and scientists determined that more than 10 years on average intervened between the publication of their first work and their masterpiece.[8] The same rule applies to the domains of mathematics and sports.

All these studies emphasize that motivation and perseverance are key ingredients in achieving outstanding performance and that expert performance is the result of a very long time of practice.

However, expert performance is not only the result of the amount but also the quality of the practice.

We answered the first question: What amount of time is needed to achieve exceptional performance?

But one important question remains unanswered: What kind of practice improves performance to the level of an expert?

Most people focus on the things they know best. However, the practice required to improve one's performance is different: It requires focusing on one's weaknesses. This is where self-assessment comes into play.

Not all practice makes perfect. It is only by working at what you can't do that you turn into the expert you want to become.[9]

This kind of practice implies two sorts of learning: improving the skills one already has and increasing the reach and range of one's skills. The concentration needed to carry out this kind of practice explains why most experts, across multiple domains, are not able to engage in more than 3 or 4 hours a day of high-concentration training. It also explains the importance of mentors and coaches in the development of true experts.

Because experts with a lot of experience are prone to respond automatically to specific situations, and therefore to make mistakes by relying exclusively on their intuition, once you become an expert in a specific domain, it is important to move outside your traditional comfort zone and analyze each specific situation to find the correct response. In other words, to become a true expert, you need to switch from System 1 to System 2 thinking.

Becoming a true expert requires the ability and the motivation to shift away from training what you can do well to practicing things that you don't do well, outside your comfort zone.

CONTINGENCY THEORY AND SITUATIONAL THEORY

Contingency and situational theories offer two distinct models that rely on the same fundamental concept: There is no single best style of leadership.

According to the contingency model, effective leadership is contingent on matching a leader's style to the right situation: A single leadership style does not suit every context, and effective leadership requires adjusting one's behavior according to the specific circumstance.[10]

According to situational theory, the most successful leaders adapt their leadership style to the task and the people they are trying to lead.[11]

The leadership styles originated from four basic behaviors are (see Figure 1):

- *Directing*: This is a highly directive and weakly supportive behavior, characterized by one-way communication in which the leader defines the roles of the individual or group and provides the what, how, why, when, and where to do the task. The directing leadership style is highly effective with people who have low competence and high commitment.
- *Supporting*: Supporting is a weakly directive and highly supportive behavior, characterized by shared decision making in which the leader provides socio-emotional support to the individual or group. The supporting leadership style is highly effective with people who have high competence and little commitment.
- *Delegating*: Delegating is a weakly directive and weakly supportive behavior, characterized by responsibility and accountability being allocated to the individual or group. The delegating leadership style is highly effective with people who have high competence and high commitment.
- *Coaching*: Coaching is a highly directive and highly supportive behavior, characterized by two-way communication in which the leader provides both direction and socio-emotional support to the individual or group. The coaching leadership style is adopted with people who have little competence and little commitment.

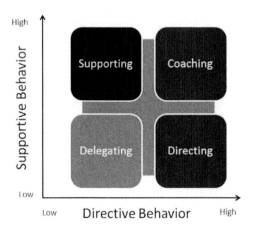

Figure 1. Leadership styles (adapted from Hersey-Blanchard situational theory).

Recent studies have provided further support for the contingency and situational leadership models: Effective leadership is founded on the application of distinct leadership styles at the right time and at the right place.[12]

BALANCE IN LEADERSHIP

The idea that ineffective leadership results from underdoing any of the essential skills, such as delegating, providing direction, communicating, collaborating, and evaluating performance, is well established.[13]

Less acknowledged is the notion that ineffective leadership can also result from overdoing essential skills. The outcome is a distortion produced by an excess of any specific *core quality*.[14] Core qualities are our innate and distinctive strengths (e.g., determination) that if pushed to the extreme can turn into weaknesses, or *pitfalls*. For example, a determined person's pitfall is pushiness (Figure 2). Core qualities and pitfalls are two sides of the same coin.

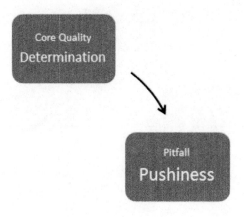

Figure 2. Core quadrant - Pitfall (source: Daniel Ofman).

The pitfall's polar opposite is the *challenge*. Following our example, the opposite of pushiness is patience (see Figure 3).

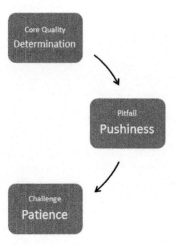

Figure 3. Core quadrant - Challenge (source: Daniel Ofman).

The core quality (determination) and the challenge (patience) complement each other. The purpose is to find a balance between the core quality and the challenge, between determination and patience, without incurring an *allergy*, an excess of the challenge. In our case, too much patience can lead to passiveness; this is the allergy of a determined person (see Figure 4).

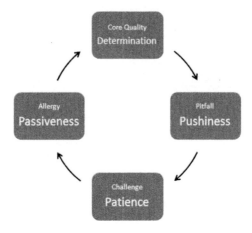

Figure 4. Core quadrant - Allergy (source: Daniel Ofman).

The lack of balance in leadership is the result of people's tendency to polarize and overemphasize one approach, and neglect the opposing one, because of uneven skill development, habit, fear of inadequacy, or mental models. In defining leadership skills and qualities, it is therefore useful to consider both approaches, which together form a balanced whole.[15]

Examples of opposite and complementary approaches include controlling and delegating, competing and cooperating, directing and consulting, being resolute and patient, being consistent and adaptable.

Leaders should be able to adjust their behavior and apply the most appropriate approach in any given situation. They must also constructively face the tensions of opposing alternatives by employing integrative thinking: *Leadership is the mastery of opposites, the balancing act between tensions and trade-offs* (more on this in chapter 11, integrative thinking).[16]

TRAITS OF LEADERSHIP

The number-one trait of an effective leader is that they do one thing at a time.[17]

More than 1,000 studies have been conducted in the last 60 years in an attempt to determine the definitive styles, characteristics, or personality traits of great leaders. However, none of these studies has provided a definitive profile of the ideal leader. There is no single set of indicators that render a person a leader.

Leadership personality, leadership style, and leadership traits do not exist.[18]

Nevertheless, research has confirmed that some universal traits are recurrently, even if not always, associated with effective leadership, including persistence, tolerance for ambiguity, self-confidence, drive, honesty, integrity, internal locus of control, achievement motivation, and cognitive ability.[19]

Furthermore, according to Dr. Chamorro-Premuzic (2013), three psychological qualities can improve people's ability to manage complexity:[20]

- *Intelligence quotient (IQ):* IQ refers to our mental ability. According to several studies, higher level IQs help people solve novel and complex problems faster. IQ is a much stronger predictor of performance on complex activities than on simple ones.
- *Emotional quotient (EQ):* EQ refers to our ability to feel, control, and express emotions. Individuals with higher EQ are less disposed to stress and anxiety. Additionally, EQ is a key element for developing and maintaining relationships in complex contexts. Finally, individuals with higher EQ are more proactive in exploiting opportunities.
- *Curiosity quotient (CQ):* CQ refers to our need to learn or know about something or someone. People with higher CQ are more open to new experiences and more tolerant of ambiguity. According to research, higher CQ is also directly correlated with higher IQ.[21]

Taking into account the previously defined qualities, in this book, we decided to emphasize the following five leadership traits, which we think best describe the qualities that most recurrently can be linked to effective leadership:

- The ability to establish trust-based relationships.
- Self-awareness.
- Self-control.
- Persistence.
- Intellectual Curiosity.

TRAIT N. 1: ESTABLISH TRUST-BASED RELATIONSHIPS

The ability to establish, grow, extend, and restore trust is the key leadership competency.[22]

Trust can be broadly defined as the mutual confidence that no party to an exchange will exploit another's vulnerabilities.[23]

Another valuable definition of trust is the following: confident positive expectations about another's motives with respect to oneself in situations entailing risk.[24]

Trust describes a bond that is established between and among individuals.[25]

Trust is an attribute of a relationship between exchange partners, while *trustworthiness* is an attribute of individual exchange partners.

An exchange partner is trustworthy when it is worthy of the trust of others.

An exchange partner worthy of trust is one that will not exploit other's exchange vulnerabilities.[26]

Trust is a crucial element in all domains of social life. Trust is also essential for successful cooperation and effectiveness in organizations.

ORGANIZATIONAL TRUST

Trust is an important social lubricant across businesses.[27]

Trust is the social glue that holds organizations together.[28]

Organizational trust can be defined as the positive expectations individuals have about the intentions and behaviors of various organizational members based on organizational processes, roles, relationships, and capabilities.[29]

Organizational trust is the sum of *interpersonal* and *institutional trust*.

Organizations cannot rely on interpersonal trust only; they have to put in place complementary tools to support collaboration, as well as knowledge creation and transfer.

Expertise, demographic similarity, both gender and age, perceived value congruency, defined as perceived homogeneity between individuals' values, and behavioral consistency, defined as consistency and predictability in behavior pattern, are positively correlated with individuals' disposition to trust.[30]

Six factors affect interpersonal trust within organizations:[31]

- *Competence*: the ability to perform as expected.
- *Reliability*: consistency and predictability in keeping promises and meeting expectations.
- *Integrity*: adherence to moral and ethical principles; honesty and reciprocity.
- *Benevolence*: concern, care, respect, and interest toward people.
- *Openness:* proactive, transparent, and comprehensive access to relevant information.
- *Identification*: value congruence and the perception of similarity.

Interpersonal trust between an employee and a boss, as well as between team members, is an important predictor of team performance and effectiveness.

The notion of reciprocity in the conceptualization of trust is fundamental: Leader-member and member-member exchange is not always mutual and equivalent.

If organizational collaboration, performance, and knowledge transfer is to improve, trust has to be reciprocal.[32]

In cross-cultural and virtual teams, trust doesn't develop slowly through steps, but is likely to be established, or not, right at inception. This is why the first interactions among the team members are critical.[33]

The institutional element of organizational trust refers to organizational members' trust in shared and established values and norms and consistent and predictable governance systems, such as reputation, contracts, rules, roles, processes, and structures.[34]

Institutional trust is based on an organization's systems, processes, structures, and rewards alignment with a common and consistent goal.[35]

Research has confirmed that higher levels of trust are linked to higher levels of commitment, motivation, collaboration, performance, knowledge transfer, productivity in virtual and distant teams, innovation, organizational commitment and morale, support for change initiatives, and, above all, leadership effectiveness in organizations.[36]

According to Stephen Covey (2006), trust affects two measurable organizational variables: *speed* and *cost*.[37]

Speed is directly correlated to trust, while cost is inversely correlated. When trust decreases, speed falls and cost increases, generating a trust charge.

When trust increases, speed surges and cost declines, generating a trust bonus.

Trust lowers organizational transaction costs because it operates as a social decision heuristic (an effortless behavioral rule to deal with complex problems) that increases decision making and implementation speed.

On the other hand, in the absence of trust, organizations must put costly and often inefficient preemptive monitoring systems in place, such as procedures and control mechanisms that cause the organization to become bureaucratic, inefficient, and slow.[38]

Independent studies have supported the role of trust in improving organizational performance, showing that publicly traded Fortune *100 Best Companies to Work For* constantly outperform major stock indexes by a factor of 2.[39]

The main element that moves a company onto the 100 Best Companies list is the level of trust between employees and management. Trust is thus the central concept of great workplaces, built on management's credibility and the degree to which employees expect to be treated fairly and with respect.[40]

Based on the Great Place to Work® model, trust can be measured along five dimensions:

- *Credibility*: the degree to which employees perceive management as trustworthy and reliable.
- *Respect*: the degree to which employees feel valued by management.
- *Fairness*: the degree to which employees perceive that management practices are just and impartial.
- *Pride*: employees' perception of satisfaction and self-esteem in their work.
- *Camaraderie:* employees' perception of solidarity and fellowship in their workplace.

DIMENSIONS OF TRUST

We can categorize trust according to two main dimensions: *cognitive* and *affective*.

The first is confidence in the ability of others, based on competence, with an emphasis on the cognitive component.

The second is faith in the trustworthy intentions of others, based on emotional bonds between individuals, with an emphasis on the affective component.[41]

Research has confirmed the key role of the amygdala in trust evaluation. Determining whether an unknown person is trustworthy is one of the most important decisions in social environments. The amygdala automatically categorizes faces according to face traits normally perceived to indicate untrustworthiness. The amygdala activation level increases as perceived trustworthiness decreases.[42]

Individuals are inclined to spontaneously trust people based only on a few dimensions, and among those dimensions, facial features are one of the most significant (more on this in chapter 9, First Impressions).[43]

BARRIERS TO TRUST

According to studies, we can identify three barriers to trust building.

The first is a corollary of the fact that trust building is an interactive process that involves (at least) two individuals learning about each other's trustworthiness: Establishing a trust based relationship between and among individuals requires time and determination.

Second, trust involves a certain degree of risk: There is no absolute confidence that trust will be honored.

Third, trust and distrust are asymmetric: Trust is built up slowly, gradually, and incrementally; distrust is usually sudden. Three main cognitive factors contribute to the asymmetry between trust building and trust destroying:[44]

- Negative events are more evident and more easily recalled than positive events.
- Negative events carry more impact on trust judgments than positive events.
- Sources of bad news are perceived as more credible than sources of good news.

THREE TYPES OF TRUST

We can identify at least three forms of trust: *weak, semi-strong,* and *strong.*[45]

In the weak form of trust, no significant vulnerabilities can be exploited; therefore, the trustworthiness of exchange partners will be high, and trust will be the norm in the exchange. In this type of exchange, trust develops because of limited opportunities for opportunism.

In the semi-strong form trust, although significant exchange vulnerabilities exist, trust can be developed through various governance devices that can impose costs on parties that behave opportunistically. If the appropriate governance devices are in place, the cost of opportunistic behavior will be greater than its benefit. Costs can be both social (reputation) and economic.

Examples of governance devices with different levels of commitment are intention ascription, intention declaration, promises, promises in front of a witness, and specific contingent claim contracts.[46]

In the strong form of trust, trust develops despite significant exchange vulnerabilities, independent of whether or not complex social and economic governance mechanisms exist, because opportunistic behavior would infringe on values, principles, and standards that guide the behavior of the exchange partners.

DEVELOPMENTAL MODEL OF TRUST

The developmental model of trust is based on the assumption that once trust has been established at one level it will move to the next level.[47]

The three levels of trust are *calculus-based, knowledge-based,* and *identification-based.*

At the calculus-based level, trust is established on a cost and benefit basis. At this level, usually deterrent elements tend to be more effective than rewards. This is why calculus-based trust is often based on a party's capability and commitment to impose sanctions for defection.

At the knowledge-based level, trust is built on confidence in another's predictability, dependability, and reliability and develops over time with recurrent interactions.

At the identification-based level, trust comes from a full understanding of each other, knowledge of the others' needs and wants, and support in pursuit of those goals. Eventually, identification-based trust implies the expectation that the relationship will endure over time.

TRUST ACROSS CULTURES

Trust is the currency of the new economy.[48]

Even if trust propensity varies across cultures,[49] research confirms how trust helps fill the gap in misunderstandings in an international context.

Members of high-trust societies usually promptly trust their countrymen until they prove untrustworthy. They assume that their countrymen will follow the rules and the laws. They are mostly linear active cultures, such as Germany, the UK, the US, Switzerland, and Sweden. In these countries, trust is fairly impersonal and based on facts, performance, consistency, and integrity. To maintain trust, members of these societies must keep their promises.

Japan, Finland, Denmark, Germany, and the US are high-trust cultures. Britain can be considered a medium-trust culture.

Members of low-trust cultures are initially guarded and suspicious of their compatriots. Members of these societies display an inconstant observance of rules, regulations, and laws. China, Korea, France, Italy, Taiwan, and Mexico are examples of low-trust cultures.[50]

In highly reactive cultures such as Japan, Korea, and China, trust is gained through respectful behavior, protecting the other's face, exchanging face, reciprocating favors, and displaying ritual courtesies.

In multi-active societies (e.g., Italian, Spanish, Brazilian, Greeks, Turk, Slav), trust is based on in-group membership (e.g., family, close friends). Citizens of these countries trust people who show them consideration and protection and those who are ready to bend the rules to maintain the relationship.

TRAIT N. 2: SELF-AWARENESS

A high self-awareness score is the strongest predictor of executives' overall success.[51]

Self-awareness can be defined as a psychological catalyst that enables other qualities (such as charisma, vision, and eloquence) to work effectively.[52]

Self-awareness is constituted by two factors:

- A realistic assessment of our own strengths and weaknesses.
- A clear understanding of our impact on other people.

Knowing our strengths and abilities allow us to identify the gaps that need to be filled. The best leaders continuously work to build up their strengths and improve their weaknesses.

Furthermore, they tend to hire complementary subordinates who perform better in domains where the leader is weaker.

Tools like the 360 Degree Review, a process in which employees receive direct, confidential, and comprehensive feedback from their subordinates, peers, and boss, can provide leaders with an objective and comprehensive look at the impact their behavior is having on others.

Usually the leader's self-perception is different from the perception of others, with the main discrepancy being the contradiction between what the leader says and what he or she does.

One explanation for this is that under pressure or emotional strain leaders tend to be affected by the *performance gap*: a disparity between what one should do and what one actually does in the specific circumstance.

According to Erica Ariel Fox (2014), most managers are unable to produce the very behavior they wish to employ when it matters most. *They know what to say, they know what to do, but they just can't say or do it at that moment.*[53]

Most self-assessment profiles are based on a combination of five distinct elements (see chapter 8, the Whole Brain Training):

- The rational, logical, factual, and present-oriented function of the brain, concerned with analysis and processing of information.
- The sequential and quantifying function of the brain, concerned with risk minimization, reliability, and planning.
- The feeling-based and emotional function of the brain, mainly concerned with interpersonal relations.
- The innovative, intuitive, and future-oriented function of the brain, concerned with a holistic view, risk predisposition, and long-term goals.
- The executing, implementing, and performing function of the brain, concerned with accomplishment and completion.

We all possess, to a certain degree, all five qualities, but each individual has a preferred thinking style, and the purpose is to effortlessly be able to adapt our profile according to the context, shifting from one style to another when required.

TRAIT N. 3: SELF-CONTROL

If you conquer yourself, then you conquer the world.[54]

As seen in chapter 9, there is a direct correlation between degree of self-control and thinking. People who have more self-control score substantially higher on tests of intelligence.

The dictionary definition of self-control is "restraint exercised over one's own impulses, emotions, or desires."[55] Self-control is directly associated with System 2 thinking and cognitive effort.

Professor Roy Baumeister (2002) defined self-control as the ability to alter one's own states and responses, overruling one initial pattern of response in favor of another.[56]

Daniel Goleman (2007) defined self-control as putting one's attention where one wants it and keeping it there in the face of temptation to wander.

In this chapter, even if not all scholars agree, we will use the terms self-control, patience, and willpower interchangeably.

According to the American Psychological Association, willpower is the ability to resist short-term temptations to meet long-term goals.

Patience is the ability to tolerate frustration, irritation, provocation, adversity, delays, and pain with composure and serenity. It involves the capacity to make decisions only when emotions are fully under control, carefully evaluating the different options without falling victim to pressure tactics.[57]

Self-control is a key leadership competency because it not only affects logical reasoning, but also interpersonal processes: Self-control is needed both for switching from intuitive (System 1) thinking to deliberate and effortful (System 2) thinking and for managing cross-cultural encounters.

Insufficient self-control has been associated with behavioral and impulse-control problems, such as overeating, alcohol and drug abuse, smoking, crime and violence, lavishness, and sexually impulsive behavior.

It is also associated with school and task failure, lack of persistence, and emotional problems.[58]

In the late 1960s and early 1970s, psychologist Walter Mischel (1972) conducted a series of studies on delayed gratification, known as the Stanford marshmallow experiment.[59]

Delayed gratification is the degree to which an individual can resist the desire for immediate gratification.

A person's ability to delay gratification is associated with other similar skills such as patience and self-control.

In Mischel's studies, a child was offered a choice between getting one marshmallow immediately or, if she was able to wait 15 minutes until the tester returned, receiving two marshmallows.

Interestingly, the children who waited longer, when re-evaluated as teenagers and adults, still performed better on the self-control task. Moreover, they were able to attain better outcomes in their life, confirmed by higher Scholastic Aptitude Test (SAT) scores, advanced educational accomplishments, and lower body mass index.[60]

Furthermore, these children were better able to cope with stress, were more likely to plan ahead, displayed higher levels of social competence and self-efficacy, and were less prone to addictive behaviors and conduct disorders.

In follow-up studies, the researchers examined brain activity using functional magnetic resonance imaging. They found that the prefrontal cortex (the region concerned with planning complex cognitive behavior, decision making, and moderating social behavior) was more active in subjects with higher self-control. In addition, the ventral striatum (a region associated with reward delivery) displayed higher activity in those with lower self-control.[61]

SELF-CONTROL AS A MUSCLE

Since the 1990s, research has uncovered a correspondence between self-control and muscle behavior.

The strength model suggests that self-control resembles a muscle in the sense that it is a limited resource whose confines can be expanded over time.[62]

Self-control, resembling a muscle that gets tired, is susceptible to decline over time from reiterated efforts. According to studies, self-control depends on a limited energy supply: Repeated endeavors of self-control cause reductions in blood glucose.

We have a limited stock of mental energy for applying self-control.

Furthermore, just as training can make muscles stronger and more resistant, regular actions of self-control can improve willpower resiliency, so that self-control declines at a slower rate.

Self-control is like a muscle that can be trained and strengthened by regular exercise in the long term.[63]

Studies have confirmed that regularly exercising one's willpower, for example, with physical workouts, leads to stronger self-control in almost all spheres of one's life.

Furthermore, research has verified that aerobic exercise increases gray and white matter density in the self-control system in old adults.[64]

According to McConigal (2011), willpower has a physiological basis, rooted in our instincts and analogous to the fight or flight response, where an external stressor elicits increased blood pressure and heart rate, focused attention, and inhibition of the prefrontal cortex to enable automatic response to the potential threat.[65]

Similarly, the *pause and plan* response is the instinct for self-control that prevents automatic action when an external impulse threatens our welfare and long-term goals; it mobilizes energy to the prefrontal cortex and decreases blood pressure and heart rate.

Because self-control, like a muscle, becomes exhausted from overuse and our store of mental energy is limited, an important corollary of the strength model is that tasks that require willpower are better accomplished in the morning.

Suggestions to improve self-control are:

- *Direct attention*: Focus on one goal at a time, filtering distractions.
- *Unlearn old habits*: Make one good habit a routine before tackling the next target. Unlearning old habits and replacing them with new ones takes time, determination, and practice.[66]
- *Plan ahead*: Having a plan in place ahead of time helps in making decisions without having to draw from the stock of mental energy.
- *Prioritize, and consciously discern the important from the urgent*: We spend more than 70% of our workday on low-priority activities (crises, urgencies, problems).[67]
- *Regularly exercise willpower*: For example, engage in physical workouts, mental activities (such as writing a book), meditation, or yoga.
- *Practice to overcome setbacks and adversity:* Think of them as opportunities to learn, develop and try new approaches.
- *Adopt rituals*: As seen in chapter 12, research in sport psychology indicates that rituals increase performance, reinforce desired behaviors, reduce anxiety and stress, and improve focus, emotional stability, and confidence,
- *Learn to count to 10 and evaluate your options:* Do this before making any important decision (be patient).

Karma is the beginning of knowledge. Next is patience. Patience is very import-
ant. The strong are the patient ones. Patience means holding back your inclination
to the seven emotions: hate, adoration, joy, anxiety, anger, grief, fear.[68]

It is not necessary for all men to be great in action. The greatest and sublimest
power is often simple patience.[69]

Trait N. 4: Persistence

According to a study conducted on more than 300 chief executive officer (CEO) candidates,[70] execution-related skills (persistence, efficiency, and proactivity) are the most important predictors of CEO success.

Leaders get the right things done.[71]

Also, among the three qualities, persistence was ranked as the top ability.

Persistent individuals demonstrate tenacity and are determined and obstinate in working toward their goals. They don't give up and they do stick with tasks until they are completed.

John Grisham is an American lawyer and author, famous for his legal thrillers. His first book, A Time to Kill, was rejected by 27 publishers before being printed by Wynwood Press.[72]

Also, J. K. Rowling's first Harry Potter was rejected by nine publishers.

A question comes to mind immediately: How many John Grishams quit after 15, 20, or 25 rejections?

Maybe many. But how many authors persevere despite a lack of ability or talent?

Persistence is a key leadership feature that can even be counterproductive if not associated with self-awareness.

Trait N. 5 Intellectual Curiosity

Curiosity is one of the permanent and certain characteristics of a vigorous mind.[73]

I have no special talents, I'm only passionately curious.[74]

As seen in chapter 11, curiosity is a crucial factor to trigger associations between different domains and employ integrative thinking.

Curiosity is defined as the desire to learn or know about something or someone.[75] Curiosity drives the acquisition of new information and the creation of new connections and, despite popular wisdom, curiosity is a learnable personality trait. It can be cultivated and developed like any other competency.

Children are curious. In a world that is strange and novel for them, a lot that is new waits to be discovered.

Once the structure of the frontal lobe is completed, adults tend to form well-established thinking patterns that dictate their response in most foreseeable situations.

Once these stable cell connectivities are formed, adults stop being inquisitive. They have created a world in which everything is under control and nothing unpredictable can happen. They observe and react to situations according to established standards.

They stop looking at the world from different perspectives, challenging conventional assumptions, learning about different areas of knowledge, and making associations between different domains.

Through education and socialization, all human beings learn, at first as a child and later as an adult, to use their brains in a certain culturally specific way. Thus, within each of their communities they are required, encouraged, and occasionally forced to develop certain capabilities and skills rather than others, to pay more attention to certain things rather than others, to allow certain feelings more than others, and therefore to gradually use their brains as is considered useful and customary by their community.

The social dimension and the precise knowledge of the socio-cultural structuring of the human brain can be well described with the metaphor of the construction site:

If everyone from a certain cultural circle builds their house according to their tradition, the foundations, the building heights, and stability of the houses will be similar in the region.[76]

Established thinking patterns provide security and are shared by the community. This is why challenging conventional assumptions, and trying new routes, calls for two fundamental preconditions:

- *Self-confidence,* the belief in one's own capabilities, skills, experiences, and knowledge.
- *Courage,* the ability to persevere and withstand danger, fear, or difficulty;[77] the willingness to take risks, express one's own opinions, and experiment.[78]

It must be stressed that, although necessary, self-confidence and courage are not sufficient for curiosity and leadership in general.

According to recent experiments, curiosity obeys a U-shaped curve. We are most curious when we know a little about a specific subject, but not too much. Curiosity activates an area of the brain called the caudate, which has been associated with dopamine reward. In other words, curiosity is rooted in the same primal pathway that also responds to addictions such as sex, drugs, and alcohol.[79]

These findings support the *information gap theory* developed by George Loewenstein (1994): Curiosity is a form of cognitively induced deprivation that arises from the perception of a gap in knowledge or understanding.[80]

Pushing ourselves to learn something new, or to know somebody new, overcoming the initial uncertainty and insecurity, is a good way to foster curiosity. *Be interested.*[81]

CROSS-CULTURAL LEADERSHIP

In addition to the previously described traits (ability to build trust, self-awareness, self-control, persistence, and curiosity), global leaders must develop three fundamental skills (which we encountered in Chapter 3): *motivational CQ, emotional strength,* and *sustaining and restoring energy.*

Motivational CQ is the first sub-dimension of cultural intelligence. It is the ability to function effectively across cultures and more specifically refers to our confidence, drive, motivation, level of interest, and curiosity during cross-cultural encounters.

Emotional strength is the fourth competency of the international profiler, composed of three factors: (a) *resilience,* the ability to bounce back after embarrassments and criticism, (b) *coping,* the ability to deal with unfamiliar and stressful situations, and (c) *spirit of adventure,* the degree to which one seeks uncomfortable and ambiguous situations.

Sustaining and restoring energy has emerged now that companies are more global. *So, you have jet lag, you are tired, the food is different.*[82]

Just to give you an idea of my calendar for the next 10 days: Berlin tomorrow, then Seoul, then Munich, then Frankfurt, then Singapore, then the Middle East. I'm almost constantly on a plane. With all this traveling, physical stamina has become much more important.[83]

Today's leaders must systematically reestablish their own physical, mental, and emotional energy levels by being disciplined in their food and sleep intake and by allocating time to work out, pursue their hobbies, meditate, and devote some quality time to their families and friends.[84]

You have to be very disciplined about schedules and about organizing everything. Physical discipline is crucial, for food, exercise, sleep. I live like a monk, well, maybe not a monk, but a Knight Templar. I wake at a certain hour, sleep at a certain hour. There are certain things I won't do past a certain time.[85]

I'm pretty energetic. I start at five in the morning. I don't even think about it anymore; the alarm goes off and I'm up. I go for a 30-minute run. I do weight training three mornings a week. I try to eat well, but not too much. I'm a big walker—that's my favorite thing.[86]

LEADERSHIP STYLES AND CULTURAL DIMENSIONS

We can identify four main leadership styles across cultures, based on two basic dimensions: *power distance* and *uncertainty avoidance*.

The four leadership styles are (see Figure 5):

- *Paternalistic*: A high power distance and uncertainty acceptance leadership style. It is common and very effective in countries like India, Malaysia, and China, where there is a preference for a dependent, nurturing, and personal relationship with the leader.[87] Paternalism is a cultural characteristic, more than just a leadership style. The paternalistic leader acts as a father figure, maintaining authority, controlling, protecting, and taking care of his subordinates, even outside the work domain, in exchange for loyalty, compliance, and commitment from his employees.[88]

- *Authoritarian*: A high power distance and uncertainty avoidance leadership style. It is common in countries like Mexico, Russia, and South Korea. The authoritarian leader directs and controls all activities and dictates policies and procedures, keeping close supervision on subordinates. Input from subordinates is neither solicited nor valued.

- *Democratic*: A low power distance and uncertainty acceptance leadership style. It is common in countries like the US, Great Britain, and Sweden. The democratic leader promotes debate and the sharing of ideas and involves subordinates in the decision-making process.

- *Bureaucratic*: A low power distance and uncertainty avoidance leadership style. It is fairly common in countries like Germany, and to a certain degree, France, and Switzerland. The bureaucratic leader follows rules and procedures scrupulously and makes certain that his or her subordinates follow guidelines and established methods accurately.

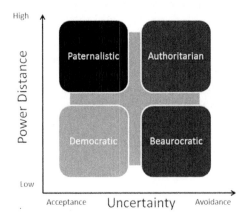

Figure 5. Leadership style across cultures.

THE GLOBE STUDY

Earlier, we discussed the GLOBE study, the Global Leadership and Organizational Behavior Effectiveness Research Project, an international assessment of how cultural differences influence leadership behavior and effectiveness.[89]

In chapter 2, we focused on the cultural dimensions identified by the research based on the results collected from more than 17,000 managers in 62 countries.

In addition to identifying nine cultural dimensions, and based on the proposition that leadership is contextual, GLOBE's second major outcome shows how different cultures conceptualize exceptional leaders. This conceptualization is based on people's expectations about what great leadership is.[90]

Starting with 112 leadership traits, GLOBE eventually identified 21 characteristics that represent the foundation of six leadership styles:

- *The charismatic and value-based style* comprises visionary, inspirational, self-sacrificial, integrity, decisive, and performance-oriented facets. It emphasizes high standards, determination, and innovation, inspiring people around a vision, and holding them to core values.
- *The team-oriented style* involves collaborative team orientation, team integrator, diplomatic, (reverse scored) malevolence, and administrative competence. It emphasizes collaboration, team cohesiveness, and common goals.
- *The participative style* includes (reverse scored) autocratic and (reverse scored) non-participative facets. It fosters shared decision making and promotes a professional context based on delegation and fairness.
- *The humane style* comprises modesty and humane-oriented facets. It is related to the well-being of others, emphasizing factors such as concern, generosity, patience, and understanding.

- *The self-protective style* involves a self-centered, status-conscious, conflict inducer, face saver, and procedural approach. It focuses on the protection and security of the individual and the group, emphasizing ritual, status-conscious, and face-saving behaviors.
- *The autonomous style* includes only the facet of autonomy. It is characterized by an independent, individualistic, and self-centric approach to leadership.

Tables 1 and 2 provide scores for the six leadership styles. The potential score for each style is from 1 (lowest) to 7 (highest). Scores below 3.5 show that a style is perceived as inhibiting outstanding leadership, while scores higher than 4.5 indicate that a style is perceived as contributing to outstanding leadership. Scores between 3.5 and 4.5 indicate a style that is perceived as ordinary or average.[91]

Countries	Charismatic	Team Oriented	Participative	Humane Oriented	Autonomous	Self-Protective
Albania	5,79	5,94	4,50	5,24	3,98	4,62
Argentina	5,98	5,99	5,89	4,70	4,55	3,45
Australia	6,09	5,81	5,71	5,10	3,95	3,05
Austria	6,02	5,74	6,00	4,93	4,47	3,07
Bolivia	6,01	6,10	5,29	4,56	3,92	3,83
Brazil	6,00	6,17	6,06	4,84	2,27	3,49
Canada (English)	6,15	5,84	6,09	5,20	3,65	2,96
China	5,56	5,57	5,04	5,19	4,07	3,80
Colombia	6,04	6,07	5,51	5,05	3,34	3,37
Costa Rica	5,95	5,81	5,54	4,99	3,46	3,55
Denmark	6,00	5,70	5,80	4,23	3,79	2,81
Egypt	5,57	5,55	4,69	5,15	4,49	4,21
El Salvador	6,08	5,95	5,40	4,69	3,47	3,43
Equador	6,46	6,21	5,51	5,13	3,53	3,62
Finland	5,94	5,85	5,91	4,30	4,08	2,55
France	4,93	5,11	5,90	3,82	3,32	2,81
Georgia	5,65	5,85	4,88	5,61	4,57	3,89
Germany East	5,84	5,49	5,88	4,44	4,30	2,96
Germany West	5,87	5,51	5,70	4,60	4,35	3,32
Greece	6,01	6,12	5,81	5,16	3,98	3,49
Guatemala	6,00	5,94	5,45	5,00	3,37	3,77
Hong Kong	5,66	5,58	4,86	4,89	4,38	3,67
Hungary	5,91	5,91	5,22	4,73	3,23	3,24
India	5,85	5,72	4,99	5,26	3,85	3,77
Indonesia	6,15	5,92	4,60	5,43	4,19	4,12
Iran	5,81	5,90	4,97	5,75	3,85	4,34
Ireland	6,08	5,81	5,64	5,06	3,95	3,00
Israel	6,23	5,91	4,96	4,68	4,26	3,64
Italy	5,98	5,87	5,47	4,38	3,62	3,25
Japan	5,49	5,56	5,07	4,68	3,67	3,60
Kazakhstan	5,54	5,73	5,10	4,26	4,58	3,35

Table 1. Scores for GLOBE leadership styles A.[92]

Countries	Charismatic	Team Oriented	Participative	Humane Oriented	Autonomous	Self-Protective
Kuwait	5,90	5,89	5,03	5,21	3,39	4,02
Malaysia	5,89	5,80	5,12	5,24	4,03	3,49
Mexico	5,66	5,74	4,64	4,72	3,86	3,86
Morocco	4,81	5,15	5,32	4,10	3,34	3,26
Namibia	5,99	5,81	5,48	5,10	3,77	3,36
Netherlands	5,98	5,75	5,75	4,82	3,53	2,87
New Zealand	5,87	5,44	5,50	4,78	3,77	3,19
Nigeria	5,76	5,65	5,18	5,49	3,62	3,89
Philippines	6,33	6,06	5,40	5,53	3,75	3,32
Poland	5,67	5,98	5,04	4,56	4,34	3,52
Portugal	5,75	5,92	5,48	4,62	3,19	3,10
Qatar	4,51	4,74	4,75	4,66	3,38	3,91
Russia	5,66	5,63	4,67	4,08	4,63	3,69
Singapore	5,95	5,76	5,30	5,24	3,87	3,31
Slovenia	5,69	5,91	5,42	4,44	4,28	3,61
South Africa (Black)	5,16	5,23	5,04	4,79	3,94	3,62
South Africa (White)	5,99	5,80	5,62	5,33	3,74	3,19
South Korea	5,53	5,52	4,92	4,87	4,21	3,67
Spain	5,90	5,93	5,11	4,66	3,54	3,38
Sweden	5,84	5,75	5,54	4,73	3,97	2,81
Switzerland	5,93	5,61	5,94	4,76	4,13	2,92
Switzerland (French)	5,90	5,62	5,30	4,55	4,02	2,94
Taiwan	5,58	5,69	4,73	5,35	4,01	4,28
Thailand	5,78	5,76	5,29	5,09	4,28	3,91
Turkey	5,95	6,01	5,09	4,90	3,83	3,57
United Kingdom	6,01	5,71	5,57	4,90	3,92	3,04
United States	6,12	5,80	5,93	5,21	3,75	3,15
Venezuela	5,72	5,62	4,88	4,85	3,39	3,81
Zambia	5,92	5,86	5,29	5,27	3,43	3,66
Zimbabwe	6,11	5,97	5,57	5,18	3,37	3,20

Table 2. Scores for GLOBE leadership styles B.[93]

Based on a 7-point scale, we can also rank the five most universally desirable leadership characteristics and the five least universally desirable characteristics, as shown in Table 3.[94]

Most desirable traits	score
Integrity	6,07
Inspirational	6,07
Visionary	6,02
Performance-oriented	6,02
Team-integrator	5,88

Least desirable traits	score
Face saver	2,92
Non-participative	2,66
Autocratic	2,65
Self-centered	2,17
Malevolent	1,80

Table 3. Most and least desirable leadership traits.95

As we can see, the top four universally most desirable leadership traits are facets of the charismatic leadership style. Participative is the second universally most desirable leadership style (reverse scored for autocratic and non-participative).

On the other hand, self-protective (specifically in the self-centered and face-saver facets) was found universally to impede leadership.

GLOBE researchers divided the 62 countries into 10 cultural clusters based on:
- Geographic proximity.
- Ethnicity.
- Religious and linguistic commonalities.
- Similarities in social and psychological variables such as values, beliefs, and attitudes.
- Degree of modernity and economic development.
- Degree of socio-political development.

The 10 clusters are:
- *Anglo cultures*: England, Australia, South Africa (white sample), Canada, New Zealand, Ireland, and the US.
- *Latin Europe*: Israel, Italy, Portugal, Spain, France, and Switzerland (French-speaking).
- *Nordic Europe*: Finland, Sweden, and Denmark.
- *Germanic Europe*: Austria, Switzerland, the Netherlands, and Germany.
- *Eastern Europe*: Hungary, Russia, Kazakhstan, Albania, Poland, Greece, Slovenia, and Georgia.
- *Latin America*: Costa Rica, Venezuela, Ecuador, Mexico, El Salvador, Colombia, Guatemala, Bolivia, Brazil, and Argentina.
- *Sub-Sahara Africa*: Namibia, Zambia, Zimbabwe, South Africa (black sample), and Nigeria.

- *Arab cultures*: Qatar, Morocco, Turkey, Egypt, and Kuwait.
- *Southern Asia*: India, Indonesia, the Philippines, Malaysia, Thailand, and Iran.
- *Confucian Asia*: Taiwan, Singapore, Hong Kong, South Korea, China, and Japan.

Compared to other clusters:

Anglo societies expect relatively high charismatic, humane-oriented, and participative leaders with a relatively low self-protective style.

Latin Europe favors relatively low humane-oriented, autonomous, and self-protective leaders.

Nordic European societies expect relatively high participative and low humane-oriented and self-protective styles.

Germanic European societies prefer relatively high participative and autonomous leaders with a relatively low self-protective style.

Eastern European societies expect relatively high autonomous and low participative leaders.

Latin American societies favor relatively high charismatic and team-oriented leaders with a relatively low autonomous style.

Sub-Saharan societies prefer relatively high humane-oriented and low autonomous leaders.

Arab cultures expect relatively low charismatic, team-oriented, and participative leaders with a relatively self-protective style.

Southern Asia societies favor relatively high charismatic, humane-oriented, and self-protective leaders.

Confucian Asia societies prefer relatively low charismatic, team-oriented, and participative leaders with a relatively high autonomous, humane-oriented, and self-protective style.

To understand how to decode the GLOBE leadership scores, we'll compare the results from the 20 major world economies against the world average and the US. Because we don't have GLOBE scores for Saudi Arabia (one of the G20 members), we include Kuwait in the sample.

Compared to the world average, Argentinian managers expect their leaders to be more team participative and autonomous. Compared to the US, Argentinian managers expect their leaders to be less humane oriented and more autonomous.

Compared to the world average, Australian managers expect their leaders to be slightly more charismatic and participative and less self-protective. Compared to the US, Australian managers expect their leaders to be slightly more autonomous and less participative.

Compared to the world average, Brazilian managers expect their leaders to be more team oriented and participative. On the other hand, they greatly disapprove of autonomous (independent and self-centric) leaders. Compared to the US, Brazilian managers expect their leaders to be more team oriented and significantly less autonomous.

Compared to the world average, Canadian (English-speaking) managers expect their leaders to be more charismatic and participative and less self-protective.

Differences between US and Canadian (English-speaking) managers' expectations are negligible.

Compared to the world average, Chinese managers expect their leaders to be slightly less charismatic and participative and marginally more humane oriented and self-protective. Compared to the US, Chinese managers expect their leaders to be rather less charismatic and significantly less participative and more self-protective.

Compared to the world average, French managers expect their leaders to be significantly less charismatic, team oriented, humane oriented, and self-protective. Compared to the US, French managers expect their leaders to be significantly less charismatic, team oriented, and humane oriented.

Compared to the world average, German (West) managers expect their leaders to be more autonomous and slightly more participative. Compared to the US, German (West) managers expect their leaders to be less humane oriented and more autonomous.

Compared to the world average, Indian managers expect their leaders to be slightly less participative and somewhat more humane oriented and self-protective. Compared to the US, Indian managers expect their leaders to be more self-protective and significantly less participative.

Compared to the world average, Indonesian managers expect their leaders to be more humane oriented and self-protective and less participative. Compared to the US, Indonesian managers expect their leaders to be significantly more self-protective and less participative.

Compared to the world average, Italian managers expect their leaders to be less humane oriented. Compared to the US, Italian managers expect their leaders to be less participative and significantly less humane oriented.

Compared to the world average, Japanese managers expect their leaders to be slightly less charismatic and participative. Compared to the US, Japanese managers expect their leaders to be less charismatic and humane oriented and significantly less participative.

Compared to the world average, South Korean managers expect their leaders to be slightly less participative and somewhat more autonomous. Compared to the US, South Korean managers expect their leaders to be significantly less participative, more autonomous and self-protective, and less charismatic.

Compared to the world average, Kuwaiti managers expect their leaders to be less autonomous and more self-protective. Compared to the US, Kuwaiti managers expect their leaders to be significantly less participative and more self-protective.

Compared to the world average, Mexican managers expect their leaders to be less participative and slightly more self-protective. Compared to the US, Mexican managers expect their leaders to be significantly less participative, more self-protective, and somewhat less humane oriented.

Compared to the world average, Russian managers expect their leaders to be less participative and humane oriented and more autonomous. Compared to the US, Russian managers expect their leaders to be significantly less participative and humane oriented, more autonomous, somewhat more self-protective, and less charismatic.

Compared to the world average, South African (black sample) managers expect their leaders to be less charismatic and team oriented. Compared to the US, South African (black sample) managers expect their leaders to be significantly less charismatic and participative, more self-protective, and less team oriented.

Compared to the world average, Spanish managers expect their leaders to be slightly less autonomous, participative, and humane oriented. Compared to the US, Spanish managers expect their leaders to be less participative and humane oriented.

Compared to the world average, Turkish managers expect their leaders to be slightly less participative and more team oriented. Compared to the US, Turkish managers expect their leaders to be less participative, slightly more self-protective, and less humane oriented.

Compared to the world average, UK managers expect their leaders to be less self-protective and slightly more participative. Compared to the US, UK managers expect their leaders to be slightly less participative and humane oriented.

Compared to the world average, US managers expect their leaders to be more participative, slightly less self-protective, and more humane oriented and charismatic.

The essence of global leadership is the ability to influence people who are not like the leader and who come from different cultural backgrounds. To succeed, global leaders need to have a global mind-set, tolerate high levels of ambiguity, and show cultural adaptability and flexibility.[96]

In conclusion, it is important to emphasize that the GLOBE study is subject to at least three limitations:

- GLOBE results are based on within-country homogeneity.
- GLOBE results present a snapshot of culture and leadership in the world, as it was more than 15 years ago.
- GLOBE results are founded on a limited sample of the population in each country.

CARLOS GHOSN: A TRANSCULTURAL LEADER

As seen in chapter 13, after Renault invested $5.4 billion for 36.8% of Nissan Motor, Carlos Ghosn, a Brazilian-born French citizen of Lebanese origin and Renault's executive vice president, was appointed as chief operating officer (COO) of Nissan.

It became clear that [Nissan] wanted results, but it didn't want change. Every idea I had was resisted. The Japanese people are very polite, so they wouldn't directly oppose any decision of mine; instead, they would propose something else to avoid it.

I knew that if I wanted to have any chance to be successful, I had to change all of it at once. I played to the sense of commitment that the Japanese have. I made it clear that I was personally committed to Nissan's revival.

I had to close down plants in a country where the plant is a sacred place. I had to reduce head count in a culture that expects lifetime employment. I had to challenge seniority, when everything was based on the oldest guy getting the job. I had to undo the keiretsu system (business groups linked by shared values, business ties and cross shareholdings), traditionally used to tie suppliers, manufacturers and distributors in the Japanese auto industry.

Every single thing that was needed for Nissan went against their values. It was a complete clash with the culture.

I was non-Nissan, non-Japanese. I knew that if I tried to dictate changes from above, the effort would backfire, undermining morale and productivity. But if I was too passive, the company would simply continue its downward spiral. The solution: cross-functional teams. The employee inside Nissan had solutions to the problems of the company. I only had to find them.

The cross-functional teams were limited to ten members and had three months to provide their specific recommendations to restore profitability and ensure future growth. Nothing was off limits to discuss and explore: there were no sacred cows, no taboos, no constraints.[97]

In October 1999, Ghosn announced the termination of five plants in Japan, 21,000 layoffs, and other cost reductions. By the end of the 2000, when Ghosn became chairman of Nissan, the company had turned a profit.

(ENDNOTES)

1   Linsky, M., & Heifetz, R. A. (2002). Leadership on the line: Staying alive through the dangers of leading. Boston, MA: Harvard Business School Press.

2   Antoine de Saint-Exupery.

3   Pattanaik, D. (2013). Business Sutra: A Very Indian Approach to Management. New Delhi: Aleph Book Company.

4   French, J. R. P., & Raven, B. H. (1959). The bases of social power. In D. Cartwright (Ed.), Studies in Social Power. Ann Arbor, MI: Institute for Social Research.

5   Raven, B. H. (1965). Social influence and power. In I. D. Steiner, & M. Fishbein (Eds.), Current studies in social psychology. New York: Holt, Rinehart, Winston.

6   Merriam-Webster, retrieved from http://www.merriam-webster.com/dictionary/charisma

7   Simon, H. A., & Chase, W. G. (1973). Skill in chess. American Scientist, 61, 394-403.

8   Ericsson, K. A., Krampe, R. T., & Tesch-Römer, C. T. (1993). The Role of Deliberate Practice in the Acquisition of Expert Performance. Psychological Review, Vol. 100, N. 3, 363-406.

9   Ericsson, K. A., Prietula, M. J., & Cokely, E. T. (2007). The Making of an Expert. Harvard Business Review, July-August, 114-121.

10   Fiedler, F. E. (1967). A Theory of Leadership Effectiveness. New York: McGraw-Hill.

11   Hersey, P., & Blanchard, K. H. (1969). Life cycle theory of leadership. Training and Development Journal, Vol. 23, N. 5, 26-34.

12   Goleman, D. (2000). Leadership that Gets Results. Harvard Business Review, March-April, 78-90.

13   Kaplan, R. E., & Kaiser, R. B. (2006). The versatile Leader: make the most of your strengths without overdoing it. San Francisco: Pfeiffer.

14   Ofman, D. (2004). Core Qualities: a Gateway to Human Resources. London: Cyan Communications.

15   Kaplan, R. E., & Kaiser, R. B. (2006). The versatile Leader: make the most of your strengths without overdoing it. San Francisco: Pfeiffer.

16   Kaplan, R. E., & Kaiser, R. B. (2006). The versatile Leader: make the most of your strengths without overdoing it. San Francisco: Pfeiffer.

17   Peter Drucker.

18   Drucker, P. F. (1996). Your leadership is unique. Christianity Today International Leadership Journal, Vol. 17, N. 4, 54-55.

19   Avolio, B. J. (2007). Promoting More Integrative Strategies for Leadership Theory-Building. American Psychologist, Vol. 62, N. 1, 25-33.

20   Chamorro-Premuzic, T. (2013). Confidence: Overcoming Low Self-Esteem, Insecurity, and Self-Doubt. New York: Hudson Street Press.

21   Kashdan, T. B. (2010). Curious?: Discover the Missing Ingredient to a Fulfilling Life. New York: Harper Perennial.

22   Covey, S. R. (2006). The Speed of Trust: The One Thing That Changes Everything. New York: Free Press.

23   Barney, J. B., & Hansen, M. H. (1994). Trustworthiness as a Source of Competitive Advantage. Strategic Management Journal, Vol. 15, Special Issue: Competitive Organizational Behavior, 175-190.

24   Lewicki, R. J., & Bunker, B. B. (1996). Developing and Maintaining Trust in Work Relationships. In R. M. Kramer, & T. R. Tyler (Eds.), Trust in Organizations, Frontiers of Theory and Research. Thousand Oaks, CA: Sage.

25   Lyman, A. (2012). The Trust Worthy Leader: Leveraging the Power of Trust to Transform you Organization. San Francisco: Jossey-Bass.

26   Barney, J. B., & Hansen, M. H. (1994). Trustworthiness as a Source of Competitive Advantage. Strategic Management Journal, Vol. 15, Special Issue: Competitive Organizational Behavior, 175-190.

27   Arrow, K. J. (1974). The limits to organizations. New York NY: Norton.

28   Atkinson, S., & Butcher, D. (2003). Trust in managerial relationships. Journal of Managerial Psychology, Vol. 18, N. 4, 282-304.

29   Shockley-Zalabak, P., Ellis, K., & Winograd, G. (2000). Organizational trust: What it Means, Why it Matters. Organizational Development Journal, Vol. 18, N. 4, 35-48.

30   D'Amico, L. C. (2003). Examining Determinants of Managerial Trust: Evidence from a Laboratory Experiment. Presented at The 7th National Public Management Research Conference, Oct. 10th, Washington, D.C.

31   Pirson, M., & Malhotra, D. (2007). What Matters to Whom? Managing Trust Across Multiple Stakeholder Groups. Hauser Center Working Paper No. 39.

32   Schoorma, F. D., Mayer, R. C., & Davis, J. H. (2007). An Integrative Model Of Organizational Trust: Past, Present, And Future. Academy of Management Review, Vol. 32, N. 2, 344-354.

33   Jarvenpaa, S. L., & Leidner, D. E. (1999). Communication and Trust in Global Virtual Teams. Organization Science, Vol. 10, N. 6, 791-815.

34   Blomqvist, K. (2008). Trust in a Knowledge-based organization. Presented at the Conference for Organizational Knowledge, Competences and Learning, April 30th- May 1st, Copenhagen, Denmark.

35   Covey, S. R. (2006). The Speed of Trust: The One Thing That Changes Everything. New York: Free Press.

36   Pirson, M., & Malhotra, D. (2007). What Matters to Whom? Managing Trust Across Multiple Stakeholder Groups. Hauser Center Working Paper No. 39.

37   Covey, S. R. (2006). The Speed of Trust: The One Thing That Changes Everything. New York: Free Press.

38   Kramer, R. M. (1999). Trust and distrust in Organizations: Emerging Perspectives, Enduring Questions. Annual Review of Psychology, 50, 569-598.

39   Great Place to Work® Institute, Inc.

40   Lyman, A. (2012). The Trust Worthy Leader: Leveraging the Power of Trust to Transform you Organization. San Francisco: Jossey-Bass.

41   Paliszkiewicz, J. O. (2011). Trust Management: Literature Review. Management, Vol. 6, N. 4, 315-331.

42   Engell, A. D., Haxby, J. V., & Todorov, A. (2007). Implicit Trustworthiness Decisions: Automatic Coding of Face Properties in the Human Amygdala. Journal of Cognitive Neuroscience, Vol. 19, N. 9, 1508-1519.

43   Vuilleumier, P., & Sander, D. (2008). Trust and valence processing in the amygdala. SCAN, 3, 299-302.

44   Slovic, P. (1993). Perceived Risk, Trust, and Democracy. Risk Analysis, Vol. 13, N. 6, 675-682.

45   Barney, J. B., & Hansen, M. H. (1994). Trustworthiness as a Source of Competitive Advantage, Strategic Management Journal, Vol. 15, Special Issue: Competitive Organizational Behavior, 175-190.

46   Castelfranchi, C., & Falcone, R. (2001). Social Trust: A cognitive approach. In C. Castelfranchi, & Y.-H. Tan (Eds.), Trust and Deception in virtual societies. Norwell, MA: Kluwer Academic Publishers.

47   Lewicki, R. J., & Bunker, B. B. (1996). Developing and Maintaining Trust in Work Relationships. In R. M. Kramer, & T. R. Tyler (Eds.), Trust in Organizations, Frontiers of Theory and Research. Thousand Oaks, CA: Sage.

48   Covey, S. R. (2006). The Speed of Trust: The One Thing That Changes Everything. New York: Free Press.

49   Lewis, R. D. (2005). When cultures collide (3rd ed.). London: Nicholas Brealey Publishing.

50   Fukuyama, F. (1995). Trust: The Social Virtues and the Creation of Prosperity. London: Penguin.

51   Green Peak Partners.

52   Lipman, V. (2013, November 18). All successful leaders need this quality: Self-Awareness, Forbes. Retrieved from http://www.forbes.com/sites/victorlipman/2013/11/18/all-successful-leaders-need-this-quality-self-awareness/

53   Boaz, N., & Fox, E.A. (2014). Change leader, change thyself. The McKinsey Quarterly, March.

54   Paulo Coelho.

55   Merriam-Webster, retrieved from http://www.merriam-webster.com/dictionary/self-control

56   Baumeister, R. F. (2002). Yielding to Temptation: Self-Control Failure, Impulsive Purchasing, and Consumer Behavior. The Journal of Consumer Research, Vol. 28, N. 4, 670-676.

57   Merriam-Webster, retrieved from http://www.merriam-webster.com/dictionary/patience

58   Baumeister, R. F., Vohs, K. D., & Tice, D.M. (2006). The Strength Model of Self-Control. Current Directions In Psychological Science, Vol. 16, N. 6, 351-355.

59   Mischel, W., Ebbesen, E. B., & Zeiss, A. R. (1972). Cognitive and attentional mechanisms in delay of gratification. Journal of Personality and Social Psychology, Vol. 21, N. 2, 204-218.

60   Mischel, W., Ayduk, O., Berman, M. G., Casey, B. J., Gotlib, I. H., Jonides, J., Kross, E., Teslovich, T., Wilson, N. L., & Shoda, Y. (2011). 'Willpower' over the life span: Decomposing self-regulation. Social Cognitive and Affective Neuroscience, Vol. 6, N. 2, 252-256.

61   Casey, B. J., Somerville, L. H., Gotlib, I. H., Ayduk, O., Franklin, N., Askren, M. K., Jonides, J., Berman, M. G., Wilson, N. L., Teslovich, T., Glover, G., Zayas, V., Mischel, W., & Shoda, Y. (2011). Behavioral and neural correlates of delay of gratification 40 years later. Proceedings of the National Academy of Sciences, Vol. 108, N. 36, 14998-15003.

62   Baumeister, R. F., Vohs, K. D., & Tice, D. M. (2006). The Strength Model of Self-Control. Current Directions In Psychological Science, Vol. 16, N. 6, 351-355.

63   American Psychological Association.

64   Colcombe, S. J., Erickson, K. I., Scalf, P. E., Kim, J. S., Prakash, R., McAuley, E., Elavsky, S., Marquez, D. X., Hu, L., & Kramer, A. F. (2006). Aerobic exercise training increases brain volume in aging humans. Journals of Gerontology, Series A - Biological Sciences and Medical Sciences, 61, 1166-1170.

65   McConigal, K. (2011). The Willpower Instinct: How Self-Control Works, Why it Matters and What you can Do to Get more of It. New York: Avery Publishing.

66   Goleman, D. (2004). What Makes a Leader?. Best of HBR on Emotionally Intelligent Leadership, 2nd ed., Harvard Business Review, January, 2-13.

67   Source: Franklin Covey Time Matrix Survey.

68   James Clavell.

69   Horace Bushnell.

70   Kaplan, S. N., Klebanov, M. M., & Sorensen, M. (2012). Which CEO Characteristics and Abilities Matter?. Journal of Finance, Vol. 67, N. 3, 973-1007.

71   Drucker, P. F. (2006). The Effective Executive: the Definitive Guide to Getting the Right Things Done. New York: Harper Business.

72   Mlodinov, L. (2008). The drunkard's walk, London: Penguin Books.

73   Samuel Johnson.

74   Albert Einstein.

75   Merriam-Webster, retrieved from http://www.merriam-webster.com/dictionary/curiosity

76   Hüther, G. (2008). The neurobiological preconditions for the development of curiosity and creativity. In H. von Seggern, J. Werner, & L. Grosse-Bächle (Eds.), Creating Knowledge. Berlin: Jovis Verlag.

77   Merriam-Webster, retrieved from http://www.merriam-webster.com/dictionary/patience

78   Warrell, M. (2013). Stop Playing Safe: Rethink Risk. Unlock the Power of Courage. Achieve Outstanding Success. Hoboken, NJ: John Wiley & Sons.

79   Lehrer, J. (2010, August 3). The itch of curiosity, Wired. Retrieved from http://www.wired.com/2010/08/the-itch-of-curiosity/

80   Loewenstein, G. (1994). The Psychology of Curiosity: A Review and Reinterpretation. Psychological Bulletin, Vol. 116, N. 1, 75-98.

81   John W. Gardner.

82   Carlos Ghosn in D. Barton, A. Grant, & M. Horn (2012). Leading in the 21st century. McKinsey Quarterly, June.

83   Josef Ackermann in D. Barton, A. Grant, & M. Horn (2012). Leading in the 21st century. McKinsey Quarterly, June.

84   Barsh, J., Mogelof, J., & Webb, C. (2010). How centered leaders achieve extraordinary results. The McKinsey Quarterly, October.

85   Carlos Ghosn in D. Barton, A. Grant, & M. Horn (2012). Leading in the 21st century. McKinsey Quarterly, June.

86   Moya Greene in D. Barton, A. Grant, & M. Horn (2012). Leading in the 21st century. McKinsey Quarterly, June.

87   Erben, G. S., & Güneşer A. B. (2008). The Relationship Between Paternalistic Leadership and Organizational Commitment: Investigating the Role of Climate Regarding Ethics. Journal of Business Ethics, 82, 955-968.

88   Aycan, Z. (2006). Paternalism. In U. Kim, K.-S. Yang, & K.-K. Hwang (Eds.), Indigenous and Cultural Psychology, Understanding People in Context. New York: Springer.

89   House, R. J., Hanges, P. J., Javidan, M., Dorfman, P. W., & Gupta, V. (Eds.). (2004). Culture, leadership, and organizations: The GLOBE Study of 62 Societies. Thousand Oaks, CA: Sage.

90   Javidan, M., Dorfman, P. W., Sully de Luque, M., & House, R. J. (2006). In the eye of the beholder: Cross Cultural lessons in leadership from project GLOBE. Academy of Management Perspectives, February, 67-90.

91   House, R. J., Hanges, P. J., Javidan, M., Dorfman, P. W., & Gupta, V. (Eds.). (2004). Culture, leadership, and organizations: The GLOBE Study of 62 Societies. Thousand Oaks, CA: Sage.

92   House, R. J., Hanges, P. J., Javidan, M., Dorfman, P. W., & Gupta, V. (Eds.). (2004). Culture, leadership, and organizations: The GLOBE Study of 62 Societies. Thousand Oaks, CA: Sage.

93   House, R. J., Hanges, P. J., Javidan, M., Dorfman, P. W., & Gupta, V. (Eds.). (2004). Culture, leadership, and organizations: The GLOBE Study of 62 Societies. Thousand Oaks, CA: Sage.

94   House, R. J., Hanges, P., Javidan, M., Dorfman, P., & Gupta, V. (2002). Leadership and Cultures Around the World: Findings from GLOBE. Journal of World Business, Vol. 37, N. 1, 3-10.

95   House, R. J., Hanges, P., Javidan, M., Dorfman, P., & Gupta, V. (2002). Leadership and Cultures Around the World: Findings from GLOBE. Journal of World Business, Vol. 37, N. 1, 3-10.

96   Javidan, M., Dorfman, P. W., Sully de Luque, M., & House, R. J. (2006). In the eye of the beholder: Cross Cultural lessons in leadership from project GLOBE. Academy of Management Perspectives, February, 67-90.

97   Magee, D. (2003). Turnaround: How Carlos Ghosn Rescued Nissan. New York: HarperCollins.

TOYOTA'S UNINTENTIONAL ACCELERATIONS

Over the past several decades, Toyota has developed an exceptional reputation for manufacturing excellence. This status was severely compromised between 2009 and 2010 following reports of accidental acceleration events in Toyota vehicles: Inadequately placed or unfitting floor mats under the driver's seat in some cases led to uncontrolled acceleration in a range of models.

Since 2009, more than 20 million cars have been recalled, placing Toyota under careful public scrutiny and government investigation.

One of Toyota's various responses to the problem was to commission a panel of professionally diverse individuals to survey Toyota's quality and safety processes and procedures and to make recommendations for a road forward for the company.[11]

To perform the task, the panel focused on a limited number of issues affecting Toyota's decision-making process and information sharing: *balance between global and local organizations, nemawashi,* and *overconfidence.*

Balance between global and local management control: Toyota currently sells vehicles in more than 170 countries. It manufactures vehicles and parts at 51 production sites spread around 26 countries. Toyota has historically structured its global operations to maximize control from Japan to attain global consistency and leverage its global scale. Toyota's North American operations are divided into independent operating companies with differing functions and responsibilities; they report directly to Toyota in Japan. North American operations don't have a single executive with overall authority.

The structure separates decision making from execution, with important decisions made in Japan and then implemented by regional managers.

This global structure has a severe impact on knowledge and information sharing across the organization. For example, the accelerator pedal issue was the main reason for a recall in 2000 in the UK on a Lexus model. However, the problem was never communicated and the information never shared with other regions, among them North America.

In Toyota, most of the information travels one way: from regional markets back to Japan.

All important decisions are made in Japan. *Instead of globalizing, Toyota colonized.*

Nemawashi: Toyota's decision-making process is based on consensus. Nemawashi is the process of discussing problems and potential solutions with all of those involved to collect their ideas and secure agreement on the future direction. This consensus process, although time-consuming, enhances the depth of the analysis and the breadth of the search for solutions, and once consensus is reached, implementation is faster.

The problem is that today, given Toyota's size, complexity, and global presence, the decision-making process based on consensus has become unfeasible and inefficient in circumstances that require quick decisions.

Overconfidence: A mix of condescension and arrogance, a result of being one of the most admired companies in the world for the last 25 years, has encouraged Toyota to be willing to listen to and take action on negative feedback coming from inside sources. However, Toyota tends to respond defensively to criticism from outside sources.

The three aforementioned factors, global vs. local structure, nemawashi, and overconfidence, combined with the increasing overall product complexity and the pursuit of growing sales, deeply affected Toyota's decreasing quality perception.

Breaking the regional silo structure, strengthening information sharing among regions, creating cross-regional and functional teams, and balancing global and local control are just some of the solutions that Toyota is implementing to improve its performance.

GENERAL MOTORS IGNITION SWITCH RECALL

In February 2014, General Motors commenced a massive recall campaign involving tens of millions of its cars over the next several months.[12]

The cause of the recalls is faulty ignition switches which could shut off the engine during driving and thereby prevent the airbags from inflating. As of this writing, twenty-seven people have died in car crashes as a result of the faulty switches.

The expected charge for General Motors is more than $1.2 billion, but it could further increase due to ongoing lawsuits and multiple investigations, including a federal criminal probe.

Because the fault had been known to General Motors for at least a decade prior to the recall start, the question is: Why didn't the company try to resolve the faulty ignitions earlier?

Former U.S. Attorney Anton Valukas produced a 325-page report on the problem, which General Motors made public on June 5, 2014.[13]

The report illustrates that General Motors (GM) made three tragic mistakes:

- First, it approved the use of an ignition switch that didn't meet its specifications.
- Second, it didn't understand that a consequence of the switch failing was non-deployment of the airbags.
- Third, it wasn't able to fix its ignition-switch issues quickly because of a complete absence of communication among the company's departments and employees.

These blunders led to shocking consequences: GM has identified at least 54 frontal impact crashes involving the deaths of 27 people in which the airbags did not deploy as a possible result of the faulty ignition switch.

While GM was made aware of ignition switch problems by customers, dealers, the press, and its own employees, it failed to take any action. Those outside General Motors, including, in 2007, a trooper from the Wisconsin Safety Patrol and a research team from Indiana University, figured out the connection between the switch and the airbag non-deployment.

This was an example of what is described as the *GM nod*, when everyone nods in agreement to a proposed plan of action, but then exits the room and ends up doing nothing about it.

Because the company didn't make the connection between switch failure and airbag functioning, General Motors engineers regarded the problem as a customer convenience issue, instead of a safety defect, a trivial but not substantial concern.

Once the failure was defined as a customer convenience issue, it received less attention, fewer resources, and less effort.

Though the question of the ignition switch passed through numerous engineers, investigators, and lawyers at General Motors, nobody escalated the issue to the highest levels of the company.

Even if procedures and processes were generally in place, nobody was accountable for the issue.

Breakdowns in communication between and within groups were a critical part of the failures described in this report.[14]

PROCESSES AND BEHAVIORS

Research has confirmed that when talking about organizational change, behaviors reinforce processes, not the other way around.[15] Changes in processes don't automatically generate changes in behavior. And there is no change without change in behavior.

Information silos are a systemic problem in most organizations. Decision making in complex companies is disconnected according to function, location, and product.

Furthermore, organizational silos are usually deep-seated and sheltered by executives' personal interests, which tends to reduce the prospect of crossing functional and geographic boundaries in information sharing and decision making.[16]

PERSUASION ACCORDING TO ARISTOTLE

According to Aristotle's Rhetoric, persuasion relies on the interaction of three fundamental elements, called *artistic proofs*. The three modes of persuasion are ethos, pathos, and logos.[17]

- *Ethos or the ethical appeal*: Ethos refers to the credibility and authority of the speaker, her expertise, her reputation, her integrity. Without credibility, there can't be persuasion.
- *Pathos or the emotional appeal*: Language, tone, stories, examples, and overall empathy serve the purpose of appealing to the emotions of the audience. Pathos engages and invokes the needs, beliefs, hopes, and fears of the audience to create involvement.
- *Logos or the appeal to logic*: By testing evidence, introducing facts, and using analogies and metaphors, the speaker determines the status and the substance of the argument. How the information is presented matters as much as what the information is.

Persuasion is a balance among the three elements. Aristotle's model states that effective persuasion appeals to both the cognitive (informational) and affective (emotional) sides of our brain. Furthermore, effective persuasion can't occur without ethos.

Aristotle's triad reminds us of a deceptively simple truth: Putting too much weight on one leg eventually lands you on the floor.[18]

EMOTIONAL PERSUASION

As seen in chapter 13, a commonly adopted form of persuasion and conflict resolution is the *naniwabushi*, a three-stage emotional appeal from the Edo period (1600-1868) in Japan:

- *Kikkake*: The opening, which gives the general background of the story, recounting the central character's feeling about the relationship.
- *Seme*: The narrative of critical events that made the social relationship problematical.
- *Urei*: An expression of great sorrow or self-pity intended to persuade the other side to be compassionate.

Naniwabushi is always planned and designed to appeal to the emotional side of the audience, relying on values such as relationships, harmony, and mutual dependence.[19]

Chinese rhetorical tradition is based on Confucian *ren tao*, the prescribed moral codes that regulate the five key relationships between ruler and subject, neighbor and neighbor, father and son, husband and wife, and brother and brother.

The five moral codes are: *jen* (benevolence), *yi* (righteousness), *li* (modesty), *zhi* (wisdom), and *shin* (faithfulness).[20]

According to the situation and to one's role in the relationship, effective persuasion requires the adoption of different approaches, appealing to different moral codes.

Furthermore, effective persuasion entails the moral concept of *zhong yong*: moderation, harmony, and reconciliation of differences.

PERSUASION TECHNIQUES

What is distinctively human at the most fundamental level is the capacity to persuade and be persuaded.[21]

To persuade people, we must have two conditions in place.

First, we have to overcome the *credibility barrier*.

The target person has to sense our credibility, meaning that he or she must have confidence in our knowledge, track record, and reliability.

Personal credibility can be established through expertise, resume, reputation, role, title, and status symbol (e.g., car, clothing, accessories).[22]

Credibility makes it easier for the target person to comply with our request.

Second, we have to *make our proposal relevant* to the target person: What is in it for him or her? What does the person get by accepting our request? During the preparation stage, one must understand the specific interests, concerns, and constraints of the other person and identify relevant exchange currencies.

Following are persuasion techniques that can be employed in different contexts and with different individuals.[23] Most of these techniques have their foundation in the tendency of individuals to adopt heuristic thinking.

THE POWER OF BECAUSE

The word because can trigger automatic response patterns in individuals.

Research has demonstrated that people are more likely to comply with a request if they are given a reason, even if the reason that justifies the request is futile.[24]

The experimenters approached people standing in line to use a photocopier with one of three requests:

- Excuse me, I have 5 pages. May I use the Xerox machine?
- Excuse me, I have 5 pages. May I use the Xerox machine because I am in a rush?
- Excuse me, I have 5 pages. May I use the Xerox machine because I have to make copies?

When given the request without a reason, only 9 of 15 people (60%) complied.

When given the request plus a sound reason, 15 of 16 people (94%) complied.

When given the request plus a "placebo" reason, 14 of 15 people (93%) complied.

According to the researchers, most human behavior falls into automatic response patterns (System 1 thinking) and therefore just hearing the word because, even if it is not followed by a sound reason, triggers compliance.

It is also interesting to see that 60% of people complied even without any reason.

When it comes to small favors, most people want to be helpful if they can be, as long as it does not significantly disrupt their own needs and provided that people make the requests in a polite way.

The same experiment was repeated with a larger request:

- Excuse me, I have 20 pages. May I use the Xerox machine?
- Excuse me, I have 20 pages. May I use the Xerox machine because I am in a rush?
- Excuse me, I have 20 pages. May I use the Xerox machine because I have to make copies?

In this case, the compliance rate sharply decreased.

When given the request without a reason, only 6 of 25 people (24%) complied.

When given the request plus a sound reason, 10 of 24 people (42%) complied.

When given the request plus a "placebo" reason, only 6 of 25 people (24%) complied.

When the request is large, people don't fall into an automatic response pattern; they move to System 2 thinking and expect a sound reason before complying.

And because in this case the request is large, and the potential disruption significant, the rate of compliance when given a request without a reason falls sharply (from 60% to 24%), as does compliance when given a request plus a "placebo" reason (from 93% to 24%).

CONTRAST PRINCIPLE

The contrast principle indicates that when we experience two similar things in succession, our perception of the second is affected by our perception of the first.

We make judgments comparing things, people, and events to other things, people, and events.

For example, if we lift a light object first and then a heavy object, we will guesstimate the second object to be heavier than if we had picked it up without first lifting the light one.

The contrast principle applies to all sorts of perceptions: colors, height or likability of a person, music, food, temperature, fragrances, sport performances, and salaries.

For the principle to work, the objects, people, or events being compared need to be similar.

To ride the contrast principle, a salesperson should present the expensive product first and then the less expensive one. Assume a man enters a fashionable men's store and says he wants to buy a three-piece suit and a sweater. Salespersons are instructed to sell the most expensive item first (the suit) and only then to present the sweater. If a man has just bought a $500 suit, spending $90 on a sweater doesn't seem disproportionate.[25]

THE NORM OF RECIPROCITY

There is no duty more indispensable than that of returning a kindness.[26]

The norm of reciprocity fulfills important social functions in ongoing relationships: It improves social stability in groups or systems and it shapes and preserves social relationships.

Furthermore, reciprocity facilitates the development of new relationships.

The norm of reciprocity is a universal and generalized concept across cultures.

Almost all societies endorse some form of the reciprocity norm; only a few members are exempt from it: the very young, the sick, and the old.[27]

The norm states that an individual who acts in a specific way toward us is eligible for a similar return act.

One corollary of the norm is an obligation to repay favors we have received.

Another consequence of the rule is an obligation to make a concession to someone who has made a concession to us.[28]

If someone gives us something, we feel obligated to give something in return.[29]

When you see a way to help people, take the opportunity to create a relationship. You can't expect strangers to jump at the opportunity to help you, but you can expect people to reciprocate because of what you have done for them.[30]

According to Wharton's Professor Adam Grant (2014), people can be divided based on their preferences for reciprocity into three groups: *givers, takers,* and *matchers.*[31]

Takers, in an attempt to quickly achieve their goals, try to get as much as possible from a person and contribute as little as they can in return.

Givers, on the other hand, give more than they take back. Matchers try to maintain a balance between give and take; they make sure the relationship is fair, keeping score of exchanges.

Professor Grant conducted a study in organizations across industries and countries, finding that givers are overrepresented both at the bottom and at the top of the pyramid.

Givers being overrepresented at the bottom of organizations can be explained by the fact that they put themselves at risk of being exploited by takers.

However, how can we explain givers being overrepresented at the top of organizations?

Matchers play an important role in lifting givers at the top of the pyramid. Matchers tend to dislike takers climbing with exploitation and, at the same time, tend to reward givers by promoting and supporting their rise.

Takers tend to win in the short run, but they often lose in the long run. Takers may also have more opportunities to succeed in stable and hierarchical organizations, but givers accomplish more in interdependent and cross-functional situations.

To judge a person, don't look at how he treats you. Look at how he treats his servants.[32]

CONSISTENCY

We are more likely to do something after we have agreed to it verbally or in writing. Once we have made a choice, we tend to behave consistently with that commitment.[33]

The need for consistency is a key factor in shaping our behavior.

Two main reasons can help explain why the need for consistency is so important for people:[34]

- Inconsistency is an undesirable personal trait across all cultures.
- Consistency provides a mental shortcut that allows us not to think any more about the matter.

Whenever someone makes a public commitment, he or she generates a need to maintain that position to look like a consistent person.

When influencing, ask for even small commitments to a specific course of action. This will enhance the probabilities of having your request accepted.

SIMILARITY

Induce the jurors to identify with you, to believe you are similar to them and, therefore, a person whom they can trust. If the jury identifies with you and likes your client, the probability of a favorable verdict is materially enhanced.[35]

We tend to like and trust people who are like us.

During the preparation phase, gather as much information as possible about your target person. Find some common ground: shared experiences, roles, background, lifestyle, education, affiliations. Most of all, find shared connections.

Recent research has shown that feelings of similarity toward others expand beyond social familiarity: When a person looks similar to us, we automatically believe they are trustworthy.

When a person is deemed trustworthy, we perceive that person's face to be more similar to our own.[36]

LIKABILITY

The main work of a trial attorney is to make a jury like his client.[37]

We prefer to agree to requests made by people we like, and we prefer doing business with people we like.

We also want people to like us. Consequently, we are more disposed to reward people we like and who like us in return.

Several factors can enhance likability:[38]

- *Physical attractiveness*: As seen in the concept of pulchronomics, the economics of beauty, good-looking people have an advantage not only in social interactions, but also in retributions. We tend to automatically assign to good-looking individuals traits such as ability and integrity (halo effect).
- *Similarity*: We like people who are similar to us.
- *Compliments*: We like people who like us. Value the other person. Acknowledge her power (even if she is not the CEO), and value what she does, her position, and her abilities.[39]
- *Recognition*: Research has confirmed that recognition, defined as acknowledging or giving special attention to people's's actions, efforts, behavior, or performance, is directly correlated with individuals' engagement and motivation.[40]
- *Association*: Common bonds (fraternities, people, group memberships, teams) can influence how people feel about us.

SCARCITY

According to the scarcity principle, options seem more valuable to us when their availability is limited.

The scarcity concept is based on the idea that if something is difficult to achieve, then it must be better than something easier to achieve.

Factors that can provide exclusivity and scarcity are:

- *Quantity (limited number)*: A specific product or service is in short supply.
- *Time (deadline)*: There is a time limit after which the option will expire.

For an event to be exclusive, opportunity to attend must be limited.[41]

If you want to position a product as exclusive, limit its availability. Make it a desirable but scarce resource.

If you want a promotion to succeed, fix a deadline.

SOCIAL PROOF

Social proof is a powerful persuasion strategy under conditions of uncertainty and ambiguity.

A high need for closure, for example, can foster conformity.

We view a behavior as more acceptable in a given situation to the extent that we see others adopting it.

According to the principle, the greater the number of people who find a proposal to be beneficial, the more the proposal will be beneficial. An initiative becomes even more acceptable not only if the number of people supporting it is large, but also if the individuals supporting it are perceived as credible.

In socially conservative cultures, conformity, the restraint from actions and behaviors that can violate social expectations and adherence to conventional norms, is a basic societal value. In these societies, the influence of social proof is even more significant.

DON'T FORCE A DECISION

People like to buy; they don't like to be sold.[42]

When persuading, don't tell the target person what the decision should be. Give the other person ownership of the decision by leading her to where you want her to go.[43]

After that, reassure her that she is making the right choice. Reassurance provides her with a mental shortcut similar to the consistency principle, so she doesn't have to think any more about the issue.[44]

GYROSCOPIC LEADERSHIP

A gyroscope is a mechanical device used to maintain orientation during motion; it consists of a rapidly spinning wheel set in a framework that permits it to tilt freely in any direction or to rotate about any axis.[45]

Gyroscopic leadership is therefore defined as the ability to assert one's own needs and requests while understanding and meeting the needs of others.[46] It allows individuals to maintain direction during international assignments and to resolve the tension between global standards, procedures, and targets and local specific needs and requirements.

The ability to balance (and integrate when required) push and pull competencies according to the specific situation is a crucial skill for global leaders.[47]

Push refers to moving forward personal/organizational goals, values, and standards in a confident, assertive way despite pressures to compromise. Push provides direction and purpose.

Example of push competencies are:[48]

- *Inner purpose*, a clear focus on long-term goals.
- *Spirit of adventure*, the search for change and novelty, breaking from the status quo.
- *Conviction*, a passionate and deep belief in one's own ideas.
- *Strategic linkage*, the focus on the organizational big picture and the development of networks of influence.

Pull, on the other hand, refers to accepting and adapting to different behaviors and ideas, showing a personal interest, and establishing trust-based relationships.

Example of pull competencies are:

- *Flexibility,* the ability to adapt one's own behavior to the person and the context.
- *Openness,* the recognition of others' ideas and perspectives.
- *Exploration,* active listening skills and non-verbal focus.
- *Rapport and trust*, the ability to quickly establish trust-based relationships.

Successful influencing in international contexts requires the ability to balance the two styles, resolve the tension between the two conflicting approaches, and adopt the required competency according to the context.

How to Present the Proposal

To understand how to best present our proposal to the target person or audience, we first have to comprehend how people make decisions.

As seen in chapter 9, for important and complex decisions, unconscious thinking leads to better decisions because of its ability to integrate and process different attributes of choice against the importance of different weights and, after some time, to identify the best alternative through an associative and intuitive approach.

The quality of decisions increases if an adequate amount of time is committed to the unconscious thinking process.

However, people tend to jump to conclusions and when making decisions are subject to systematic errors. Most of us make quick decisions based on heuristics, mental shortcuts that reduce the cognitive effort involved in the decision-making process, and usually focus on one specific trait.

Furthermore, even if individuals are not always rational, they are often *rationalizing*.

Individuals make decisions based on intuition and then, once they make their decision, they have to explain it to themselves and, more important, to others.

This is why individuals need reliable, concrete, and rational reasons to justify (rationalize) their decisions, even if they make the decision following an intuitive and unconscious process.

An important component of the influencing process is providing the target person or audience with coherent, consistent, and logical arguments, both because they back your reasoning and serve your purpose of persuading and because they give your audience members a means to explain their decision when their real motivations may be self-serving or difficult to formulate.[49]

In summary, to persuade people, adopt the following three-step approach:

- Identify the relevant exchange currency.
- Underline the benefits for the other party.
- Support your presentation with concrete facts and evidence.

The PCASB Model

According to the Wall Street Journal, more than 30 million PowerPoint presentations are delivered in the world every day.[50] And this is a 2006 estimate! I would guess that today this number is much higher.

Additionally, 3 of 4 executives admit they have slept during a recent corporate presentation.[51]

These two facts help explain why during a presentation it is fundamental to capture immediately the audience's attention, emphasizing the importance and urgency of the issue.

Furthermore, research has confirmed that given a list of things to remember people tend to recall the first and last items in a series better than the items in the middle.[52]

Things early in the list have the time to be transferred into long-term memory through rehearsal (*primacy effect*). Words from the end of the list enter the short-term memory (*recency effect*), which can typically hold between 5 and 7 items for a limited amount of time.[53] Words in the middle of the list are removed from short-term memory after a while, without having the chance to access long-term memory through rehearsal.

When people recall primary and recent information, it is thought that they are recalling information from two separate stores: the long-term and short-term memories.

To get the benefit of both primary and recent effects, state your best points early and then summarize them explicitly and briefly at the end.

Presentations should follow a template built around three main elements: the *introduction*, the *body* and the *conclusions*.

The Introduction leverages the primacy effect by answering the 3W questions:

- *Why you* (why are you speaking about the specific topic, what makes you credible)?
- *What* (what is the problem or the subject of the presentation)?
- *Why them* (what are the benefits for your audience; why should they listen to you)?

The body of the presentation must provide the audience members with concrete facts and evidence that has to substantially and logically back their decision-making process and provide them with a means to explain why they made the decision. The body follows the *PCASB (Problem, Cause, Alternatives, Solution, Benefits)* structure:[54]

- A short and concise statement defining the *Problem.*
- An explanation of the *Cause* of the problem or the need.
- A description of the *Alternatives* available beyond the status quo to solve the problem or meet the need.
- A presentation of your *Solution*, highlighting the *Benefits* for the audience and the feasibility of the solution.
- A concrete validation of why your solution is better than the alternatives, highlighting strengths and weaknesses of the different options and clarifying your assumptions.

  This step is particularly important when one of the alternatives is the status quo or when one of the alternatives is supported by highly influential people in the organizations.

Conclusions leverage on the recency effect by providing:

- *A short summary* of why your solution is the best choice, taking into account all other options (no more than two or three sentences)
- *A brief action plan*, requesting a commitment from the audience toward a concrete small action within an agreed deadline

In general, keep the presentation simple, clear, and engaging. Limit the number of points composing your argument to three or even fewer. Make the presentation salient to the audience using examples, stories, and analogies. Emphasize how the solution can directly benefit the audience. Provide evidence and facts. Force your audience to think.

THE ELABORATION LIKELIHOOD MODEL

The elaboration likelihood model suggests that individuals with high cognitive motivation (see chapter 9, Need for Cognition) have both the ability and the motivation to process information meticulously. They make decisions based on a systematic evaluation of data and evidence (*central cues*).

Individuals with low cognitive motivation (because, for example, of time pressure, stress, or low degree of issue importance) will process information heuristically, making decisions based on *peripheral cues* such as the credibility of the source or the quantity of information presented.[55]

The model states that when the issue is of high importance to the other party, and strong justifications exist, you will be more likely to have your proposal accepted when strong bases and justifications are presented early (rather than late) in the discussion.

In addition, when the issue is of low importance to the other party, or when only weak justifications exist, you will be more likely to have your proposal accepted when motivations and justifications are presented late (rather than early) in the discussion.[56]

According to the elaboration likelihood model, the credibility of the source affects decision making mostly when motivation or ability to think about a message is low.

THE CAGE FRAMEWORK

The CAGE distance framework, developed by Professor Pankaj Ghemawat (2001), identifies differences between countries that companies must address when developing international strategies. The framework is also useful in understanding patterns of trade, capital, information, and people flows across countries.[57] An appropriately corrected model based on the CAGE framework can also be applied to identify barriers to intercultural influence.

The CAGE distance framework classifies differences into four major groupings: *cultural, administrative, geographic,* and *economic.*

- *Cultural distance* includes differences in religion, race/ethnicity, language, and social norms, values, and beliefs.
- *Administrative distance* encompasses historical and political ties between countries, colonial heritage, free trade agreements, and the state of current relationships.
- The *geographic dimension* includes the distance between two countries, a country's physical size, within-country distances to borders, access to the ocean, topography, and time zones.

• *Economic distance* encompasses variables such as consumer income, cost of labor, differences in availability (or lack) of resources, inputs, infrastructure, and complements, as well as human and organizational capabilities.

The CAGE framework takes into consideration both bilateral and unilateral factors.

Table 1 provides a more detailed description of the four CAGE categories, depending on whether one is comparing two countries or looking at a specific country.

	Cultural Differences	Administrative Differences	Geographic Differences	Economic Differences
Bilateral Measures	– Different languages – Different ethnicities/lack of connective ethnic or social networks – Different religions – Differences in national work systems – Different values, norms and dispositions	– Lack of colonial ties – Lack of shared regional trading bloc – Lack of common currency – Different legal system – Political hostility	– Physical distance – Lack of land border – Differences in climates (and disease environments)	– Differences in consumer incomes – Differences in availability of: – Natural resources – Financial resources – Human resources – Intermediate inputs – Infrastructure – Information or knowledge
Unilateral Measures	– Traditionalism – Insularity – Spiritualism – Inscrutability	– Nonmarket/closed economy (home bias versus foreign bias) – Nonmembership in international orgs. – Weak legal institutions/corruption – Lack of govt. checks and balances – Societal conflict – Political/expropriation risk	– Landlockedness – Geographic size – Geographic remoteness	– Economic size – Low per capita income – Low level of monetization – Limited infrastructure, other specialized factors

Table 1. CAGE framework.[58]

Of interest is the effect on bilateral trade of specific factors of the CAGE framework:[59]

• Sharing the same language can increase trade by 42%.
• Being a member of the same regional trading bloc can increase trade by 47%.
• A colony-colonizer link can increase trade by 188%.
• Sharing the same currency can increase trade by 114%.
• Being landlocked (having no access to open seas) can decrease trade by 48%.
• Sharing a common land border can increase trade by 125%.
• In general, an increase of 1% in physical distance corresponds to a 1% decrease in trade.

A conveniently adjusted model based on the CAGE framework can be used to identify obstacles that individuals must overcome in efforts to influence across countries.

Factors that can potentially decrease barriers to influencing are:

- *Cultural distance*: Sharing the same language, having a common religion
- *Physical distance*: A limited physical distance between locations (derived from sharing a common land border)
- *Administrative distance*: Having a similar background (derived from the colony-colonizer link), being members of the same association/fraternity/ organization (derived from being members of the same regional trading bloc)
- *Economic distance*: Having a similar lifestyle and being a member of the same social class (derived from differences in consumer income)

WHAT WE CAN LEARN FROM LOBBYING

Lobbying is the process of influencing public and government policy.

The art of political persuasion is one of the world's oldest professions.

Whenever an individual, or group of individuals, exercises power over society, there will be other individuals or groups of individuals who will try to persuade them to exercise that power in a particular way.[60]

Leaders at all levels in organizations can learn a great deal from the lobbying process.

The first step in the lobbying process is *profile raising*, the activity of making politicians and civil servants aware of who you are and what you do.

You are much more likely to be listened to if you create a high level of recognition and appreciation of who you are and what you do.

This activity is easily transferable to an organizational context; if people don't know you or don't know what you do, it will be very difficult for you to be heard by them and consequently to influence them.

The second stage is a *contact building program*: It is not a great strategy to approach for the first time a politician or official the moment you need his or her assistance. It is better to begin establishing connections prior to the time when you actually need them.

Also, in organizations, it is fundamental to start establishing connections ahead of the time when you'll need them.

The third step of the process is *research and intelligence gathering*. You need to analyze the decision-making process and identify the people who will be in a position to make decisions.

Those who draft the decision are often more important than those who ultimately sign off on it. You need to identify the actors who practically, and not formally, are the most important contributors to the decision to be approved.

These are the people you need to contact to establish a relationship before the moment of need arrives. Bear in mind that people can be promoted, moved to another department, be given new responsibilities, or resign or retire. So, keep your contact records updated.

Research and monitoring is fundamental in identifying politicians who are active in a specific issue, identifying potential supporters and challengers, and promptly recognizing new regulations that could affect your goals.

The same goes for organizations: Often, second- and third-level players shape the decision-making process, and identifying the hubs and bridges of the informal network can provide valuable information on the people who can most influence a specific decision.

The fourth stage of the lobbying process is *making contact*: The normal procedure is to send a detailed briefing, with a one-page summary at the beginning, which states who you are and what you do. It is advisable to follow up with a phone call. Remember that the first obstacle you must overcome is the person's assistant or secretary, who often acts as gatekeeper. Therefore, the first step is to have your correspondence opened: Use high-quality white envelopes and write the address by hand. In the one-page summary, describe who you are and what you do, outline the issue, propose a potential solution, and define the next step.

Once you are able to set up a meeting, get straight to the point: The other party's schedule is very busy and his or her level of focus is quite low; therefore, you have to quickly gain the other party's interest. Because the other party might be forced to interrupt the meeting at any time, bring a briefing note with you to be distributed if the meeting is cut short.

Be sure to highlight the advantage for the other party. Without a supply side, you will easily be ignored.

The fifth stage of the lobbying process is *building coalitions*: Coalitions are crucial when lobbying decision makers in larger arenas, such as state and federal governments. Politics is about compromise; every time you take a position, you gain and lose allies.

To build coalitions, you have to identify the factors that influence the other parties' behavior and meet their different and aggregate interests to pursue your goal.

For example, pharmaceutical multinationals, to create a new market for nicotine replacement and anti-smoking products, backed specific health- and environment-conscious lobby groups pushing European Union (EU) anti-tobacco legislation.[61]

The sixth stage is a summary of the previous five: The lobby group, focusing on the desired result, implements a strategy to engineer the most promising circumstances right from the beginning. In the game of *Triple P*, you try to place the friendliest persons in the best positions in the most beneficial procedures.[62]

PERSONAL BRANDING

Big companies understand the importance of brands. Today, in the Age of the Individual, you have to be your own brand. Here's what it takes to be the CEO of Me Inc. Regardless of age, regardless of position, regardless of the business we happen to be in, all of us need to understand the importance of branding. We are CEOs of our own companies: Me Inc.[63]

Personal branding is defined as the process by which individuals differentiate themselves by identifying and articulating their professional unique value proposition to establish their reputation, expertise, and credibility.[64]

According to personal branding specialists, individuals shouldn't be constrained by their job title or their job description, but should be able to identify the attributes that make them distinctive.

Don't try to stand out from the crowd; avoid crowds altogether.[65]

The first step is to identify your *distinctive value*. To do so, individuals should answer the following questions:

- What makes you different from your competitors, colleagues, and co-workers? What is your distinctive value?
- If asked, what would your colleagues, boss, customers, and suppliers say is your greatest and distinct strength?
- How do these attributes translate to benefits for your customers (both internal and external to the organization)?
- What have you accomplished in your professional life that you are proud of and that you can take credit for?

The second step is to ensure *visibility*: Signing up for extra projects, creating new relationships, and displaying your skills inside the organization, working on freelance projects and getting acquainted with new people, participating in conferences, events, trade shows, and professional associations, teaching in your company, writing for a trade magazine, and making presentations at conferences are just some of the means that individuals can use to enhance their profile and establish their credibility and expertise.

In summary, the first step is to become expert at something that has value and get results. The next step is to develop relationships, inside and outside the organization, to enhance your visibility and profile.

THE PERSONAL BRANDING CANVAS

The Personal Branding Canvas,[66] developed by personal branding strategist Luigi Centenaro (2014), is a visual tool based on the business model canvas, which supports individuals in identifying their distinct value and gaining visibility with the right audience (see Figure 1).

Figure 1. The personal branding canvas.

The canvas is split into three sections.

The first describes your qualities (expertise, knowledge, experience), what you offer and what makes you credible (track record, publications, certifications, awards; see Figure 2).

Figure 2. Personal branding canvas – section 1.

The second section describes who needs to know your distinct value, which channels you use to increase your visibility, what benefits you bring to your audience (which problems you solve and which benefits you provide), and, finally and most important, why you; what is the distinctive feature that makes you different? (See Figure 3.)

Figure 3. Personal branding canvas - section 2.

The third section describes which investments are required to develop your brand and which results you expect from your personal brand (see Figure 4).

Figure 4. Personal branding canvas - section 3.

(ENDNOTES)

1   Palus, C. J., McGuire, J. B., & Ernst, C. (2012). Developing Interdependent Leadership. In S. Snook, N. Nohria, & R. Khurana (Eds.), The Handbook Leadership, Knowing, Doing, and Being. Thousand Oaks, CA: Sage Publications.

2   Mintzberg, H. (2009). Managing. San Francisco, CA: Berrett-Koehler Publishers.

3   Ernst, C., &, Chrobot-Mason, D. (2010). Boundary Spanning Leadership: Six Practices for Solving Problems, Driving Innovation, and Transforming Organizations. New York: McGraw-Hill Professional.

4   Conger, J. A. (1998). The Necessary Art of Persuasion. Harvard Business Review, May-June, 84-95.

5   Jarvenpaa, S. L., Leidner, D. E. (1999). Communication and Trust in Global Virtual Teams. Organization Science, Vol. 10, N. 6, 791-815.

6   Kuhl, S., Schnelle, T., & Tillmann, F.-J. (2005). Lateral Leadership: An Organizational Approach to Change. Journal of Change Management, Vol. 5, N. 2, 177-189.

7   Fisher, R., & Sharp, A. (2004). Lateral Leadership (2nd ed.). London: Profile Books.

8   Merriam-Webster, retrieved from http://www.merriam-webster.com/dictionary/influence

9   David G. Javitch.

10   Fisher, R., & Sharp, A. (2004). Lateral Leadership (2nd ed.). London: Profile Books.

11   Slater, R., Martin, R., Augustine, N., O'Neill, B. Goldman, P., Widnall, S., & Good, M. (2011). A Road Forward: The Report of the Toyota North American Quality Advisory Panel. Retrieved from http://www.changinggears.info/wp-content/uploads/2011/05/EMBARGOED_COPY_Toyota_Quality_Advisory_Panel_Report.pdf on June 7th 2014

12   Foroohar, R. (2014). We've All Got GM Problems. Time Magazine, June 23.

13   Valukas, A. R. (2014). Report to the Board of Directors of General Motors Company regarding Ignition Switch recalls. Retrieved from http://www.nytimes.com/interactive/2014/06/05/business/06gm-report-doc.html?_r=0 on the 16th June 2014

14   Valukas, A. R. (2014). Report to the Board of Directors of General Motors Company regarding Ignition Switch recalls. Retrieved from http://www.nytimes.com/interactive/2014/06/05/business/06gm-report-doc.html?_r=0 on the 16th June 2014

15   Herrero, L. (2008). Viral Change (2nd ed.). Bucks, Beaconsfield, UK: Meetingminds.

16   Gulati, R. (2007). Silo Busting: How to Execute on the Promise of Customer Focus. Harvard Business Review, Vol. 85, N. 5, 98-108.

17   Aristotle (2004). Rethoric. Translated by W. R. Roberts. Mineola, NY: Dover Publications.

18   Orren, G. (2000). Gore vs. Bush: Why It's All Greek to Me. Kennedy School Bulletin, Autumn, 36-39.

19   March, R. M. (1990). The Japanese negotiator: Subtleties and strategy beyond Western logic. Tokyo, Japan: Kodansha International.

20   Zhu Yunxia, Z., & Hildebrandt, H. W. (2003). Greek and Chinese classical rhetoric: the root of cultural differences in business and marketing communication. Asia Pacific Journal of Marketing and Logistics, Vol. 15, N.1, 89-114.

21   Bertrand Russell.

22   Bickman, L. (1974). The Social Power of a Uniform. Journal of Applied Social Psychology, Vol. 4, N. 1, 47-61.

23   Cialdini, R. B. (1993). Influence: The psychology of Persuasion. New York: HarperCollins Publishers.

24   Langer, E. J. (1989). Minding matters: The consequence of mindlessness-mindfulness. In L. Berkowitz (Ed.), Advances in experimental social psychology. Vol. 22, 137-174. San Diego: Academic Press.

25   Cialdini, R. B. (1993). Influence: The psychology of Persuasion. New York: HarperCollins Publishers.

26   Cicero.

27 Gouldner, A. W. (1960). The Norm of Reciprocity: A Preliminary Statement. American Sociological Review, 25, 161-178.

28 Cialdini, R. B. (1993). Influence: The psychology of Persuasion. New York: HarperCollins Publishers.

29 Lakhani, D. (2005). Persuasion: the art of getting what you want. Hoboken: John Wiley & Sons.

30 Guy Kawasaki.

31 Grant, A. (2014). Give and take: Why helping others drives our success. London: Penguin Books.

32 Mahatma Gandhi.

33 Greenwald, A. G., Carnot, C. G., Beach, R., & Young, B. (1987). Increasing Voting Behavior by Asking People if They Expect to Vote. Journal of Applied Psychology, Vol. 72, N. 2, 315-318.

34 Cialdini, R. B. (1993). Influence: The psychology of Persuasion. New York: HarperCollins Publishers.

35 Darrow, C. (1996). The story of my life. Boston, MA: Da Capo Press.

36 Farmer, H., McKay, R., & Tsakiris, M. (2014). Trust in Me: Trustworthy Others Are Seen as More Physically Similar to the Self. Psychological Science, Vol. 25, N. 1, 290-292.

37 Darrow, C. (1996). The story of my life. Boston, MA: Da Capo Press.

38 Cialdini, R. B. (1993). Influence: The psychology of Persuasion. New York: HarperCollins Publishers.

39 Diamond, S. (2010). Getting more: How to negotiate to achieve your goals in the real world. New York, NY: Crown Business.

40 Human Capital Institute.

41 Lakhani, D. (2005). Persuasion: The art of getting what you want. Hoboken, NJ: John Wiley & Sons.

42 Uchil, A. (2007). Relationship selling: The fine art of consultative sales. Parker, CO: Outskirts Press.

43 Diamond, S. (2010). Getting more: How to negotiate to achieve your goals in the real world. New York, NY: Crown Business.

44 Lakhani, D. (2005). Persuasion: The art of getting what you want. Hoboken, NJ: John Wiley & Sons.

45 Merriam-Webster, retrieved from http://www.merriam-webster.com/dictionary/gyroscope

46 David Trickey, Nigel Ewington. TCO International.

47 Ewington, N., & Hill, T. (2012). Push and Pull (The competencies required for working internationally). Cultus Journal, Training for a transcultural world.

48 David Trickey.

49 Shell, G. R., & Moussa, M. (2007). The Art of Woo: Using Strategic Persuasion to sell your ideas. New York: Penguin Group.

50 Sandberg J. (2006, November 14). Tips for PowerPoint: Go easy on the text; please, spare us. Wall Street Journal.

51 Shell, G. R., & Moussa, M. (2007). The Art of Woo: Using Strategic Persuasion to sell your ideas. New York: Penguin Group.

52 Frensch, P. A. (1994). Composition during serial learning: a serial position effect. Journal of Experimental Psychology: Learning, Memory, and Cognition, Vol. 20, N. 2, 423-443.

53 Atkinson, R. C., & Shiffrin, R. M. (1968). Chapter: Human memory: A proposed system and its control processes. In K. W. Spence, & J. T., Spence (Eds.), The psychology of learning and motivation (Vol. 2). New York: Academic Press.

54 Aristotle (1932). The Rhetoric of Aristotle. Translated by L. Cooper. New York: Appleton Century Crofts.

55 Cacioppo, J. T., Petty, R. E., Kao, C. F., & Rodriguez, R. (1986). Central and Peripheral Routes to Persuasion: An Individual Difference Perspective. Journal of Personality and Social Psychology, Vol. 51, N. 5, 1032-1043

56 Malhotra, D., & Bazerman, M. H. (2008). Psychological Influence in Negotiation: An Introduction Long Overdue. Journal of Management, Vol. 34, N. 3, 509-531.

57   Ghemawat, P. (2007). Redefining global strategy: Crossing borders in a world where differences still matter. Cambridge, MA: Harvard Business Review Press.

58   Ghemawat, P. (2007). Redefining global strategy: Crossing borders in a world where differences still matter. Cambridge, MA: Harvard Business Review Press.

59   Ghemawat, P., & Mallick, R. (2003). The Industry-Level Structure of International Trade Networks: A Gravity Based Approach. Harvard Business School, working paper, February.

60   Zetter, L. (2008). Lobbying: The Art of Political Persuasion. Petersfield, UK: Harriman House Ltd.

61   Duina, F., & Kurzer, P. (2004). Smoke in your eyes: The struggle over tobacco control in the European Union. Journal of European Public Policy, Vol. 11, N. 1, 57-77.

62   Van Shendelen, R. (2007). Macchiavelli in Brussels. The Art of Lobbying the EU. (2nd ed.). Amsterdam, Netherlands: Amsterdam University Press.

63   Peters, T. (1997, August 31). The brand called you. Fast Company.

64   Schwabel, D. (2013). Promote yourself: The new rules for career success. New York, NY: St. Martin's Press.

65   Hugh MacLeod.

66   http://personalbrandingcanvas.com/

CHAPTER 17:

Social Networks & Change

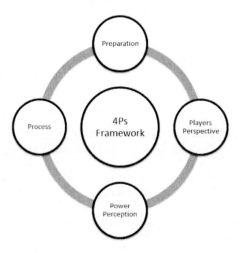

Stage 1: Preparation. Stage 2: Process. Stage 3: Power Perception. Stage 4: Players Perspective

INTRODUCTION

Knowledge and information flow along existing pathways in organizations. If we want to understand how to improve the flow of knowledge and information, we need to understand those pathways.[1]

Organizations are collective organisms which often have a life of their own. An organization is not simply a collection of homogeneous people, nor is it a set of individuals aligned behind a single mission. An organization is composed of sub-groups which interact with their own objectives and their own specific view of the situation.

Individuals must develop the ability to look beyond the organizational chart to see, understand, and engage the informal, invisible structure supporting their organization. This invisible structure is built on relationships, which create channels that often differ from those identified by policies and procedures and that cross functional divisions, managerial levels, and organizational boundaries. They also know the key players in the network who do not hold formal titles but nonetheless are important influencers because of their relationships with others. Understanding these connections is critical to implementing ideas and change and aligning strategy and work across organizational boundaries.[2]

The official organizational chart, with its roles, processes, procedures, and functions, doesn't always represent how an organization works.

Most of the work is not performed through the formal organizational structure but through informal channels.

How information flows between individuals is determined by the social network of which they are a part. Understanding how the social networks operate is a crucial step in fostering the flow of information in organizations, in identifying how decisions are made within a company, and, even more important, in bringing about cultural change in organizations.

Social Networks

Social networks are interpersonal information networks that connect people.

In a small network of just 100 people, there are 4,950 possible links. In a network with 1,000 members, there are potentially 495,000 links. And, even more important, networks are dynamic: People form new connections, change jobs, and move.[3]

But let's take a step back by first defining a network.

A network is the description of a set of nodes and the relationships between these nodes.[4]

In analyzing organizations, nodes represent individuals. Therefore, an organizational network consists of individuals and the relationships between these individuals.

The simplest network contains two nodes, 1 and 2, and one non-directional relationship that links them (see Figure 1).

1 ———————————————— **2**

Figure 1. Two-node network.

There are also directional relationships between nodes, for example, 1 likes 2 (see Figure 2).

1 ————————————————▶ **2**

Figure 2. Two-node relationship.

The relationship can also be symmetrical, such as 1 and 2 like one another (see Figure 3).

Figure 3. Two-node symmetrical relationship.

SOCIAL NETWORK ANALYSIS

Social network analysis maps organizational social relationships and the degrees of connectedness within a network to better understand how relationships work, information flows, and people collaborate (see Figure 4).

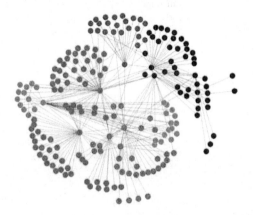

Figure 4. Social network. Source: Daniel Tenerife.

According to research, social network analysis represents a reliable predictor of people's behavior. *The network of relationships in which an individual is embedded shapes her cognitive processes, defines her goals, and imposes specific constraints.*[5]

Information is collected through surveys that ask employees about their interactions with colleagues. Typical questions are:

- Who do you turn to for professional advice regarding your daily work?
- Who do you turn to for information that you need in your daily job?
- Who do you turn to for help with technical work-related problems in your daily job?
- Who do you turn to for support with a difficult situation in your daily job?
- Who is the most acknowledged professional in your field?
- Who has knowledge or information you might need in your daily work but you do not ask?

The result is a diagram that exemplifies the information flow and identifies the connections and gaps in the network, the specific roles different individuals play, and the opportunities for improving collaboration across the organization (see Figure 5).[6]

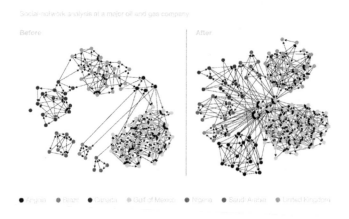

Figure 5. Social network analysis: Before and after.[7]

Social network analysis is based on three fundamental principles:[8]
- The focus of analysis is on the relationships between units, rather than the units themselves. A sample should be defined relationally rather than categorically.
- Dyadic ties are not sufficient to understand a social network. The flow of information and resources between two individuals is also influenced by other nodes in the network.

  A dyad is defined as two individuals maintaining a sociologically significant relationship.[9]
- Networks are overlapping rather than isolated and network boundaries are vague rather than stable.

PRINCIPLES OF SOCIAL NETWORKS

At an organizational level of analysis, fundamental principles make it more probable that a relationship will exist between two nodes and that the nodes will be connected to one another.[10]

Following we introduce the two key assumptions underlying social networks at an organizational level: *proximity* and *homophily*.

Proximity

All other conditions being equal, nodes are more likely to be connected with one another if they are geographically close to one another.

Physical proximity shapes networks. The closer people are physically, the more they tend to interact.

This principle explains why coordinating and managing a distant team can be particularly demanding.

Homophily

Homophily is the tendency for people to interact with individuals who are similar to them. Homophily is defined as having one or more common social attributes.

An implication of the homophily principle is that people who are similar to each other form *clusters*.

Clusters are formed according to dimensions such as interests, education, sex, age, social class, geography, background, and common goals.

PRIMARY NETWORKS

Two primary networks, *awareness* and *access*, are vital to an organization to effectively adapt and react to new opportunities and challenges.[11]

The awareness network reveals the degree to which individuals in an organization know the skills, knowledge, and experience of others. A mismatch between the expertise available and its employment is often due to a lack of awareness. A simple solution is to share the skills and experiences of individuals through a website that includes short bios and profiles.

Awareness is a necessary, but not sufficient condition for effective collaboration.

The access network reveals the degree to which individuals in an organization have access to people with the required skills and expertise. It is not about knowing the phone number or the email address, but about being able to make an effective exchange with the specific person.

We need both awareness and accessibility to create a flow of information among individuals and to establish effective collaboration.

SOCIAL NETWORK ACTORS

Social network experts have identified five distinct and recurring types of actors within the informal organization.

The first are the *hubs*, those with the most direct connections within the group. They are typically highly social and very good communicators. They tend to rapidly disseminate information and centralize work processes (see Figure 6).

Holding a central position in a network is analogous to having status and power in a group.

Power is not an attribute of an individual, but it is an attribute of a relationship between two individuals. This is why it is important to identify the circumstances under which one person has power over another, rather than simply stating that a specific individual has power.[12]

Power is often a function of the social network in which the two people are embedded. An individual is more powerful in a specific relationship because she occupies a more central position in the social network, with greater access to opportunities outside this single relationship.

Centrality and therefore hierarchy in networks is identified by two factors:
- The position of a given node relative to other nodes.
- The number of incoming connections, defined as the number of other nodes that flow into a given node.

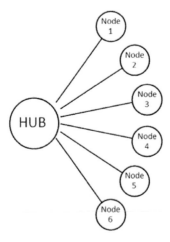

Figure 6. Network centrality.

The second are the *bridges*, shortcuts that connect different clusters. They are fundamental in accelerating the flow of information between different networks. Bridges differ from hubs: While hubs are directly connected to many individuals, bridges connect two or more clusters. Organizations can methodically create bridges, for example, by having people within the company move from one country or one department to another.

The third are the *gatekeepers*, players who control access to influencers and decision makers. They are responsible for the flow of information and knowledge within the group.

Gatekeepers can open the doors to decision makers, but they can also seal any opportunity to access key players.

The fourth are the *information brokers*, the primary sources of information within the group.

The fifth are the *peripheral players*, individuals at the edges of the informal organization. They can be connected to other players via indirect routes because they have some source of power (such as expertise, information, or position).

DISTANCE BETWEEN NODES

The region of nodes directly linked to a hub is called the first-order zone. The nodes two steps from a hub occupy the second-order zone, the nodes three steps from a hub are defined as the third-order zone, and so on.[13]

The influence of each zone on a node declines exponentially. For our purposes, the number of significant zones is between two and three.

The number of people in the first-order zone varies from about 300 to 1,000 individuals, depending on how this is calculated and the organizational role of the hub person.

The number of people who can be directly reached by any individual is therefore limited.

Two fundamental metrics are used to assess networks:[14]

• *Density*, the number and concentration of connections within a group. In other words, the number of individuals who have connections with each other. Density defines a group's cohesiveness and the amount and quality of information flow among nodes.

• *Cohesion*, the shortest path between each pair of individuals in the network. In other words, the number of people an individual has to go through to reach another person.

A Small World

In the early 1950s, mathematician Manfred Kochen and social scientist Ithiel de Sola Pool wrote a manuscript, not published until 1978, called *Contacts and Influences*; they said that if there were no overlap in people's personal networks, then any individual could reach the entire population of the United States in two or three steps.[15]

Because personal networks overlap, the distance between the nodes can be further reduced.

Despite the theoretical number of two to three steps between any two persons in the United States, experiments have estimated the actual number of steps to be six. The *small world* concept states that any two people are connected through a string of six or even fewer other people.[16]

The main point is not the number of individuals connecting any two people, but that any individual can be accessed through a limited number of steps.

When we speak about five or six brokers, we are talking about an enormous psychological distance between the starting and final points. The five intermediaries are not five persons apart, but five networks, five structures apart. This helps to place the small world concept in perspective.

STRUCTURAL HOLES AND GAPS

Social network analysis not only maps the information flow and the connections, but also identifies the missing links in a network.

The two basic metrics, density and cohesion, can help identify holes in the communication flow within or between networks.

A very low local concentration of connections and a very lengthy path between local pairs means there are structural holes in the network.

Finding and restoring the gaps between parts of the network that interact very little with each other can help foster collaboration between different clusters and across the organization.

On the other hand, *brokerage*, the ability to exploit and bridge gaps in the structure, can provide payoffs to individuals within an organization.

THE STRENGTH OF WEAK TIES

According to a renowned experiment,[17] more than 50% of people find jobs not through advertising, but from a personal contact, and in more than 80% of the cases, this personal contact is not a close friend or family member, but an acquaintance. The strength of weak ties principle applies to every situation. Your close friends have access to similar sources of information as you do while your social contacts can gain access to different information to which you otherwise wouldn't have access.

Weak ties, therefore, enable the flow of information from remote parts of a network and facilitate the integration of different networks.

Unluckily, we tend to gather around people who are similar to us, and this tendency limits our exposure to different information and different perspectives.

The internet can facilitate the development and maintenance of hundreds of weak ties, but at the same time, don't forget that our brain structure allows us to have an authentic social relationship with a limited number of people (around 200).[18] Today, the number of ties we can maintain is still limited, as it was in the past, but what has increased is the number of bridges, connectors between different clusters, that facilitate the extent and speed of information exchange.

Empirical studies of managers in large corporations show that an individual's achievement within a company is directly associated with that individual's access to a large number of weak ties.[19]

SOCIAL CAPITAL

Social capital refers to resources and benefits for an individual or group resulting from the creation, maintenance, and development of a social network.[20]

Individuals consider the creation of ties as an investment in the accumulation of social resources or social capital.[21]

Social capital provides opportunities for individuals to employ their financial and human (skills, abilities, experiences) capital.[22]

Individuals invest in establishing and maintaining connections to others with whom they can exchange valued resources. *Whether a relationship will be sustained over time depends on the payoffs to each of the two parties.*[23] Social capital is founded on the norm of reciprocity.

The concept of social capital is therefore based on two key factors:

- Individuals' ability to use their position in the network to gain resources and benefits.
- Individuals' ability to use their position in the network to provide the expected resources and benefits to the other nodes in the network.

For example, individuals can receive payoffs by exploiting structural holes and bridging gaps in the network.[24]

To increase social capital, you should constantly practice social arbitrage, the exchange of favors and intelligence, and find solutions to other people's problems, needs, and concerns.[25]

Frequent use of the reservoir of social trust without replenishment (e.g., through selfish exploitation of the stock for one's own advancement) will lead to faster depletion with a resulting loss in social cohesion[26] and therefore will harm ones' position in the network (a concept introduced in chapter 16, The Norm of Reciprocity - Takers).

OBESITY IN A LARGE SOCIAL NETWORK

The incidence of obesity in the United States has increased from 23% to 35% over recent years, and 69% of adults today are overweight.[27]

The obesity upsurge can be explained by the lifestyle changes that promote inactivity and food consumption. Furthermore, because an increase in obesity is widespread among all socioeconomic groups, researchers performed a study to determine whether obesity might spread from person to person and, if so, how the spread occurs.[28]

The study evaluated a network of 12,067 people who went through recurring measurements over a period of 32 years. The researchers examined several factors that could have affected the spread of obesity, including the existence of clusters of obese persons within the network, the association between one person's weight gain and weight gain among her social contacts, the correlation of this association with the nature of the social ties (e.g., ties between friends of different kinds, siblings, spouses, and neighbors), and the influence of variables such as sex, smoking behavior, and geographic distance between the domiciles of persons in the social network.

The researchers determined that when a study participant's friend became obese, the participant had a 57% greater chance of becoming obese herself. If the friend who became obese was a close friend, the study participant's chances of becoming obese increased to 171%.

Geographic distance between friends seems to have no bearing: Friends who lived many miles apart and saw each other occasionally were just as influenced by each other's weight gain as those who lived close and shared similar lifestyles.

The study also confirmed that friendship is the main cause of weight gain.

If a spouse became obese, the participant had a 37% greater chance of becoming obese.

If a sibling became obese, the participant had a 40% greater chance of becoming obese.

According to the researchers, the explanation for why friends bear more influence on us than spouses or siblings is related to social norms, whomever we look to when considering appropriate behavior, and usually we tend to look to our friends and not to our spouse or brother / sister.

We get to choose our friends. We don't get to choose our families.

In summary, because people are embedded in social networks and influenced by the behavior of their friends, the research suggests that weight gain in one person might influence weight gain in others.

CHANGE

People don't resist change. They resist being changed.[29]

Never doubt that a small group of thoughtful, committed citizens can change the world. Indeed, it is the only thing that ever has.[30]

Research confirms that when talking about organizational change, behaviors reinforce processes, not the other way around.[31] Change in processes doesn't automatically generate change in behavior. And there is no change without change in behavior.

Because an organization can be considered a loose network of links between people, organizational change is a non-linear process. It is neither top-down nor bottom-up, but implicit and distributed across the organization.

As seen in the previous paragraphs, the organizational network is composed of a few nodes with many connections (hubs) and other nodes with fewer connections. Even more interesting, hubs tend to acquire more connections, while nodes with fewer connections have difficulty in acquiring new connections.

The research into obesity in a large social network supports the notion that a relatively small number of individuals within any organization has great influence in the conception of change.

This influence is based on factors such as high connectivity with others, high level of trust, innovation seizure, popularity, and expertise. The role of management is to facilitate and support the change process by removing barriers and enabling resources.

But how can these influencers be identified?

One simple way is to adopt a survey technique, used originally by social scientists to study hidden populations such as street gangs, criminals, drug users, prostitutes, and individuals with HIV/AIDS.

Snowball sampling is a technique for finding hidden subjects unwilling to participate in formal research. One subject gives the researcher the name of another subject, who in turn provides the name of a third, and so on.[32] Trust is developed because referrals are made by acquaintances, and the chain of referrals quickly identifies a set of influencers once the names of candidates start to recur.[33]

CASCADING EFFECT

At a certain stage, a *tipping point* occurs, and nodes stop behaving as individual nodes and adopt a collective single behavior. Once a threshold has been reached, and a specific behavior has achieved a certain level of adoption throughout a network, all the nodes join in the behavior or phenomenon.[34]

We can therefore achieve *cascading effects*, where a new behavior starts with a small number of initial adopters and then spreads radially through the network.

Cascading behavior in a network is sometimes called social contagion because it spreads from one person to another in the same way as a biological epidemic.

There are important differences between social and biological contagion: Social contagion tends to involve decision making on the part of the affected individuals, whereas biological contagion is based on the chance of catching a disease-causing pathogen through contact with another individual.

Network-level dynamics are similar, and insights from the study of biological epidemics are also useful in thinking about the processes by which ideas and behaviors spread on networks.[35]

Weak ties and bridges are fundamental in conveying information, but they don't excel at transmitting behaviors that are risky or costly to adopt. *In adopting a new behavior, individuals tend to be influenced by strong rather than weak ties.*

This is why a behavior can rapidly spread in a cascading fashion through the network after the tipping point has been reached; a behavior can also be blocked at the edge of a densely connected cluster in the network.

A high-density network with very few bridges to external clusters can endure against outside influences and therefore block social contagion.

It is true that brokers, defined as bridges among different sub-groups within the organization, are weak in transmitting new behaviors. Nevertheless, without influential brokers, there would be no diffusion of knowledge or information across different clusters. Brokers are thus a necessary, but not sufficient condition for change. They can't foster behavior adoption, but they can ensure that new information and knowledge is transmitted within the cluster.[36]

(ENDNOTES)

1   Davenport, T. H., & Prusak L. (2000). Working Knowledge: How Organizations Manage What they Know (2nd ed.). Cambridge, MA: Harvard Business Review Press.

2   Cullen, K. L., Palus, C. J., & Appaneal, C. (2013). Developing Network Perspective: Understanding the Basics of Social Networks and their Role in Leadership. Centre for Creative Leadership, White Paper, March.

3   Rosen, E. (2009). The Anatomy of Buzz Revisited. Real-life Lessons in Word-of-mouth Marketing. New York: Doubleday.

4   Wasserman, S., & Faust, K. (1994). Social Network Analysis: Methods and Applications. Cambridge, UK: Cambridge University Press.

5   Katz, N., Lazer, D., Arrow, H., & Contractor, N. (2004). Network Theory And Small Groups. Small Group Research, Vol. 35, N. 3, 307-332.

6   Cross, R., & Parker, A. (2004). The Hidden Power of Social Networks, Understanding How Work Really Gets Done in Organizations. Cambridge, MA: Harvard Business School Press.

7   Gibbs, T., Heywood, S., & Weiss, L. M. (2012). Organizing for an emerging world. The McKinsey Quarterly, June.

8   Katz, N., Lazer, D., Arrow, H., & Contractor, N. (2004). Network Theory And Small Groups. Small Group Research, Vol. 35, N. 3, 307-332.

9   Merriam-Webster, retrieved from http://www.merriam-webster.com/dictionary/dyad

10 Kadushin, C. (2011). Understanding Social Networks: An Introduction to Social Network Concepts, Theories and Findings. Oxford, UK: Oxford University Press.

11 Cross, R., & Parker, A. (2004). The Hidden Power of Social Networks, Understanding How Work Really Gets Done in Organizations. Cambridge, MA: Harvard Business School Press.

12 Easley, D., & Kleinberg, J. (2010). Networks, crowds, and markets: Reasoning about a highly connected world. Cambridge, UK: Cambridge University Press.

13 Kadushin, C. (2011). Understanding Social Networks: An Introduction to Social Network Concepts, Theories and Findings. Oxford, UK: Oxford University Press.

14 Cross, R., & Parker, A. (2004). The Hidden Power of Social Networks, Understanding How Work Really Gets Done in Organizations. Cambridge, MA: Harvard Business School Press.

15 de Sola Pool, I., & Kochen, M. (1978). Contacts and influence. Social Networks, Vol. 1, N. 1, 5-51.

16 Milgram, S. (1967). The Small World Problem. Psychology Today, Vol. 1, N. 1, 61-67

17 Granovetter, M. (1995). Getting a Job: A Study of Contacts and Careers (2nd ed.). Chicago: University of Chicago Press.

18 Dunbar, R. (1995). Neocortex size and group size in primates: a test of the hypothesis. Journal of Human Evolution, 28, 287-296.

19 Easley, D., & Kleinberg, J. (2010). Networks, Crowds, and Markets: Reasoning about a Highly Connected World. Cambridge, UK: Cambridge University Press.

20 Bourdieu, P., & Wacquant, L. J. D. (1992). An Invitation to Reflexive Sociology. Chicago: University of Chicago Press.

21 Katz, N., Lazer, D., Arrow, H., & Contractor, N. (2004). Network Theory And Small Groups. Small Group Research, Vol. 35, N. 3, 307-332.

22 Burt, R. S. (1992). Structural holes: the Social Structure of Competition. Cambridge, MA: Harvard University Press.

23 Homans, G. C. (1958). Social Behavior as Exchange. American Journal of Sociology, Vol. 63, N. 6, 597-606.

24 Goyal, S., & Vega-Redondo, F. (2007). Structural holes in social networks. Journal of Economic Theory, 137, 460-492.

25 Ferrazzi, K. (2005). Never Eat Alone: And Other Secret to Success, One Relationship at a Time. New York: Currency Doubleday.

26 Giorgos Cheliotis.

27   Source: Centers for Disease Control and Prevention.

28   Christakis, N. A., & Fowler, J. H. (2007). The Spread of Obesity in a Large Social Network over 32 Years. The New England Journal of Medicine, Vol. 357, N. 4, 370-379.

29   Peter M. Senge.

30   Margaret Mead.

31   Herrero, L. (2008). Viral Change (2nd ed.). Bucks, Beaconsfield, UK: Meetingminds.

32   Atkinson, R., & Flint, J. (2001). Accessing hidden and hard-to-reach populations: Snowball research strategies. University of Surrey, Department of Sociology, Social Research Update, N. 33.

33   Duan, L., Sheeren, E., & Weiss, L. M. (2014). Tapping the power of hidden influencers. The McKinsey Quarterly, March.

34   Kadushin, C. (2011). Understanding Social Networks: An Introduction to Social Network Concepts, Theories and Findings. Oxford, UK: Oxford University Press.

35   Easley, D., & Kleinberg, J. (2010). Networks, Crowds, and Markets: Reasoning about a Highly Connected World. Cambridge, UK: Cambridge University Press.

36   Cross, R. L., Parise, S., & Weiss, L. M. (2007). The role of networks in organizational change. The McKinsey Quarterly, April.

Selected Bibliography

The bibliography is designed primarily to assist all readers who want to learn more on the field of intercultural negotiation and influence.

PREFACE

- Atsmon, Y., Child, P., Dobbs, R., & Narasimhan, L. (2012). Winning the $30 trillion decathlon: Going for gold in emerging markets. *Mckinsey Quarterly*, Vol. 4, 20-35.
- International Monetary Fund, World Economic Outlook Databases.
- KPMG: *Future State 2030,* retrieved from http://www.kpmg.com/PH/en/PHConnect/ArticlesAndPublications/Investors-Guide/Documents/future-state-2030-v1.pdf

CULTURAL DIMENSIONS - DYNAMIC CONSTRUCTIVIST APPROACH

- Ailon, G. (2008). Mirror, mirror on the wall: Culture's Consequences in a value test of its own design. *The Academy of Management Review*, Vol. 33, N. 4, 885-904.
- Ang, S., & Van Dyne, L. (2008). *Handbook of Cultural Intelligence: Theory Measurement and Application.* Armonk, NY: M. E. Sharpe.
- Apfelthaler, G., & Domicone, H. (2008). Drawing wrong borderlines: the concept of culture in a pluralist management world. *Problems and Perspectives in Management*, Vol. 6, N. 2, 44-58.
- Bennett, M. J. (1986). A developmental approach to training for intercultural sensitivity. *International Journal of Intercultural Relations*, Vol. 10, N. 2, 179-195.
- Bhagat, R. S., & Steers, R. M. (Eds.) (2011). *Cambridge Handbook of Culture, Organizations, and Work.* Cambridge, UK: Cambridge University Press.
- Bhawuk, D. P. S. (2001). Evolution of culture assimilators: toward theory-based assimilators. International Journal of Intercultural Relations, Vol. 25, N. 2, 141-163.
- Boyarin, D., & Boyarin, J. (2002). *Powers of Diaspora: Two Essays on the Relevance of Jewish Culture.* Minneapolis, MN: University of Minnesota Press.
- Chua, R. Y. J., & Morris, M. W. (2012). Collaborating across cultures: Cultural metacognition and affect-based trust in creative collaboration. *Organizational Behavior and Human Decision Processes*, http://dx.doi.org/10.1016/j.obhdp.2012.03.009.
- Clifford, J. (1988). *The Predicament of Culture: Twentieth Century Ethnography, Literature and Art.* Cambridge, MA: Harvard University Press.
- Croce, B. (1915). *What is Living and What is Dead in the Philosophy of Hegel.* Translated by D. Ainslie. London: Macmillan.

- Deutscher, G. (2010). *Through the Language Glass: Why the World Looks Different in Other Languages.* New York: Metropolitan Books.
- Douglas, M. (1970). *Natural Symbols. Explorations in Cosmology.* New York: Routledge.
- Douglas, M. (1978). Cultural Bias. Occasional Paper N. 35, *Royal Anthropological Institute of Great Britain and Ireland.*
- Douglas, M. (2003). Being fair to hierarchists. *University of Pennsylvania Law Review,* Vol. 151, N. 4, 1349-1370.
- Douglas, M., & Wildavsky, A. (1982). *Risk and Culture.* Berkeley: University of California Press.
- Fang, T. (2012). Yin Yang: A New Perspective on Culture. *Management Organization Review,* Vol. 8, N. 1, 25-50.
- Faure, G. O. (1999). The Cultural Dimension of Negotiation: The Chinese Case. *Group Decision and Negotiation,* Vol. 8, N. 3, 187-215.
- Faure, G. O. (2002) *International Negotiation: The Cultural Dimension.* In V. A. Kremenyuk (Ed.), *International Negotiation: analysis, approaches, issues* (2nd ed.). San Francisco: Jossey-Bass.
- Gesteland, R. R. (2005). *Cross-Cultural Business Behavior* (4th ed.). Copenhagen, Denmark: Copenhagen Business School Press.
- Gullestrup, H. (2006). *Cultural Analysis, towards Cross Cultural understanding.* Copenhagen, Denmark: Copenhagen Business School Press.
- Hall, E. (1973). *The Silent Language.* New York: Anchor Books.
- Hall, E. (1976). *Beyond Culture.* New York: Anchor Books.
- Hall, E. (1982). *The Hidden Dimension.* New York: Anchor Books.
- Hall, E. (1984). *The Dance of Life: the other dimension of time.* New York: Anchor Books.
- Hampden-Turner, C., & Trompenaars, F. (1997). *Riding the Waves of Culture: Understanding Diversity in Global Business.* (2nd ed.). New York: McGraw-Hill.
- Hickson, D. J., & Pugh, D. S. (2003). *Management Worldwide* (2nd ed.). London: Penguin Business.
- Hills, M. D. (2002). Kluckhohn and Strodtbeck's Values Orientation Theory. *Online Readings in Psychology and Culture, Unit 4.* Retrieved from http://scholarworks.gvsu.edu/orpc/vol4/iss4/3. Bellingham, Washington: Center for Cross-Cultural Research, Western Washington University.
- Hofstede, G. (2001). *Culture's consequences: Comparing values, behaviors, institutions and organizations across nations* (2nd ed). Thousand Oaks, CA: Sage.
- Hofstede, G. (2002). Dimensions do not exist: A reply to Brendan McSweeney. *Human Relations,* Vol. 55, N. 11, 1355-1361.
- Hofstede, G., Hofstede, G. J., & Minkov, M. (2010). *Culture and Organizations: Software of the Mind* (3rd ed.). New York: McGraw-Hill.
- Hughes, R. (2010). *CULT-URE.* London: Fiell Publishing.
- Inglehart, R., & Welzel, C. (2005). *Modernization, cultural change, and democracy.* New York: Cambridge University Press.

- Jackson, T. (2002). The Management Of People Across Cultures: Valuing People Differently. *Human Resource Management*, Vol. 41, N. 4, 455-475.
- Katz, D., & Kahn, R. (1978). *The Social Psychology of Organizations* (2nd ed.). New York: John Wiley & Sons..
- Klostermaier, K. K. (2007). *A Survey of Hinduism* (3rd ed.). Albany, NY: Suny Press.
- Kluckhohn, F. R., & Strodtbeck, F. L. (1961). *Variations in Value Orientations*. Evanston, IL: Row, Peterson & Company.
- Kottak, C. (2006). *Mirror for Humanity*. McGraw-Hill, New York.
- Lewis, R. D. (2005). *When cultures collide* (3rd ed.). London: Nicholas Brealey Publishing.
- Livermore, D. (2011). *The Cultural Intelligence Difference: master the one skill you can't do without in today's global economy*. New York: AMACOM.
- McSweeney, B. (2002). Hofstede's model of national cultural differences and their consequences: A triumph of faith - a failure of analysis. *Human Relations*, Vol. 55, N. 1, 89-118.
- Medina Walker, D., Walker, T., & Schmitz, J. (2002). *Doing business internationally* (2nd ed.). New York: McGraw-Hill.
- Nardon, L., & Steers, R. M. (2009). The culture theory jungle: divergence and convergence in models of national culture. In R. S. Bhagat, & R. M. Steers (Eds.), *Cambridge Handbook of Culture, Organizations, and Work*. New York: Cambridge University Press.
- Schneider, S. C., & Barsoux, J. L. (1997). *Managing Across Cultures*. London: Prentice Hall.
- Schwartz, S. (2004). Mapping and Interpreting Cultural Differences around the World. In H. Vinken, J. Soeters, & P. Ester (Eds.), *Comparing Cultures, Dimensions of Culture in a Comparative Perspective*. Leiden, the Netherlands: Brill.
- Schwartz, S. H. (1999). A theory of Cultural Values and Some Implications for Work. *Applied Psychology: An International Review*, Vol. 48, N. 1, 23-47.
- Schwartz, S. H. (2006). A Theory of Cultural Value Orientations: Explication and Applications. *Comparative Sociology*, Vol. 5, N. 2-3, 137-182.
- Sundararajan, L. (2011). Chinese Notions of Harmony, With Implications for the Development of Indigenous Psychology. In James Liu (chair), *Indigenous and cultural psychology, Harmonization and Differentiation in Theory and Practice*, symposium conducted at the 9th Biennial Conference of Asian Association of Social Psychology, Kunming, China.
- Sundararajan, L. (2011). Lost in the Translation: *"Chi"* and Related Terms of Shame in the Confucian Tradition. *The Emotion Researcher*, Vol. 26, N. 3, 9-11.
- Trickey, D., Ewington, N., & Lowe, R. (2009). Being International: what do international managers and professionals really think is important - and do experts agree?. *The Journal of Intercultural Mediation and Communication*, Vol. 2, 49-78.
- Van Dyne, L., Ang, S., & Livermore, D. (2010). Cultural intelligence: A pathway for leading in a rapidly globalizing world. In K. M. Hannum, B.

McFeeters, & L. Booysen (Eds.), *Leadership across differences: Casebook.* San Francisco, CQ: Pfeiffer.

- Van Dyne, L., Ang, S., Ng, K. Y., Rockstuhl, T., Tan, M. L., & Koh, C. (2012). Sub-Dimensions of the Four Factor Model of Cultural Intelligence: Expanding the Conceptualization and Measurement of Cultural Intelligence. *Social and Personality Psychology Compass,* Vol. 6, N. 4, 295-313.
- Whorf, B. L. (1967). *Language, Thought and Reality* (5th ed.). Edited by J. B. Carroll. Boston: MIT Press.
- Williams Jr., R. M. (1970). *American society: A sociological interpretation* (3rd ed.). New York: Knopf.
- Ying-yi H., Y., Chiu, C., Morris, M. W., & Benet-Martinez, V. (2000). Multicultural Minds, A Dynamic Constructivist Approach to Culture and Cognition. *American Psychologist,* Vol. 55, N. 7, 709-720.

INDIGENOUS PSYCHOLOGY

- Adair, J. G. (1999). Indigenization of Psychology: The Concept and its Practical Implementation. *Applied Psychology: An International Review,* Vol. 48, N. 4, 403-418.
- Adeleye, I. (2011). Theorising human resource management in Africa: Beyond cultural relativism. *African Journal of Business Management,* Vol. 5, N. 6, 2028-2039.
- Ajzen, I. (1991). The theory of Planned Behavior. *Organizational Behavior and Human Decision Processes,* 50, 179-211.
- Alexashin, Y., & Blenkinsopp, J. (2005). Changes in Russian managerial values: a test of the convergence hypothesis?. *International Journal of Human Resource Management,* Vol. 16, N. 3, 427-444.
- Allik, J., Realo, A., Mottus, R., Pullmann, H., Trifonova, A., McCrae, R. R., & 56 Members of the Russian Character and Personality Survey (2009). Personality traits of Russians from the observer's perspective. *European Journal of Personality,* 23, 567-588.
- Askew, W. K. (2004). The Cultural Paradox Of Modern Japan: Japan And Its Three Others. *New Zealand Journal of Asian Studies,* Vol. 6, N. 1, 130-149.
- Bassin, M. (1998). Asia. In N. Rzhevsky (Ed.), *The Cambridge companion to modern Russian culture.* Cambridge, UK: Cambridge University Press.
- Bedford, O. A. (2004). The Individual Experience of Guilt and Shame in Chinese Culture. *Culture Psychology,* Vol. 10, N. 1, 29-52.
- Berry, J. W., Poortinga Y. H., Breugelmans S. M., Chasiotis A., & Sam D. L. (2011). *Cross-Cultural Psychology: Research and Application.* Cambridge, UK: Cambridge University Press.
- Boski, P. (1993). Between West and East: Humanistic values and concerns in Polish psychology. In U. Kim, & J. Berry (Eds.), *Indigenous psychologies: Research and experience in cultural context.* Newbury Park: Sage.
- Boski, P. (2012). Psychology of a Culture: Humanism and Social Ineffectiveness Embedded in Polish Ways of Life. *Online Readings in Psychology and Culture,* Vol. 3, N. 1. http://dx.doi.org/10.9707/2307-0919.1029. Bellingham,

Washington: Center for Cross-Cultural Research, Western Washington University.

- Branco, S., & Williams, R. (2008). *Culture Smart: Brazil*. London: Kuperard.
- Brockmann, H., Delhey, J., Welzel, C., & Yuan, H. (2009). The China Puzzle: Falling Happiness in a Rising Economy. *Journal of Happiness Studies*, Vol. 10, N. 4, 387-405.
- Brown, J. L., Wang, L., & Fisher, K. W. (2004). The Organization of Chinese Shame Concepts. *Cognition and Emotion*, Vo. 18, N. 6, 767-797.
- Chang, W. C., & Lee, L. (2012). The Concentric Circle Revisited: Allocentrism and Self in a Contemporary Chinese Community. *Psychology*, Vol. 3, N. 4, 297-303.
- Choi, S.-C., & Kim, K. (2006). Naïve Psychology of Koreans' Interpersonal Mind and Behavior in Close Relationships. In U. Kim, K.-S. Yang, & K.-K. Hwang (Eds.), *Indigenous and Cultural Psychology, Understanding People in Context*. New York: Springer.
- Condon, J. C. (1984). *With Respect to the Japanese*. Yarmouth, ME: Intercultural Press.
- Dia, M. (1996). *Africa's Management in the 1990s and Beyond: Reconciling Indigenous and Transplanted Institutions*. Washington, DC: World Bank.
- Eze, M. O. (2010). *Intellectual History in Contemporary South Africa*. Basingstoke, UK: Palgrave Macmillan.
- Faure, G. O. & Fang, T. (2008). Changing Chinese values: Keeping up with paradoxes. *International Business Review*, 17, 194-207.
- Faure, G. O. (2012). *China: new values in a changing society*. Retrieved from: http://www.ceibs.edu/ase/Documents/EuroChinaForum/faure.htm.
- Fischer, D. H. (1989). *Albion's Seed: Four British Folkways In America*. New York: Oxford University Press.
- Flood, G. (1996). *An Introduction to Hinduism*. Cambridge: Cambridge University Press.
- Forster, D. (2007). Identity in relationship: The ethics of ubuntu as an answer to the impasse of individual consciousness. In C. du Toit (Ed.), *The impact of knowledge systems on human development in Africa*. Pretoria, South Africa: UNISA.
- Gyekye, K. (1997). *Tradition and Modernity: Philosophical Reflections on the African Experience*. Oxford, UK: Oxford University Press.
- Harrison, A., Lin, J. Y., & Xu, L. C. (2013). Explaining Africa's (dis)advantage. *National Bureau of Economic Research*, retrieved from http://www.nber.org/papers/w18683.
- Heine, S. J., & Raineri, A. (2009). Self-Improving Motivations and Collectivism: The Case of Chileans. *Journal of Cross-Cultural Psychology*, Vol. 40, N. 1, 158-163.
- Helfrich, H. (1999). Beyond the Dilemma of Cross-Cultural Psychology: Resolving the Tension between Etic and Emic Approaches. *Culture Psychology*, Vol. 5, N. 2, 131-153.
- Hendry, J. (1998). *Interpreting Japanese Society* (2nd ed.). Abingdon, UK: Routledge.

- Henning, J. M. (2000). Breaking Company: Meiji Japan and East Asia. *Education About Asia*, Vol. 5, N. 3, 40-43.
- Hook, D. (2005). A critical psychology of the postcolonial. *Theory and Psychology*, Vol. 15, N. 4, 475-503.
- Hu, H. C. (1944). The Chinese Concept of "Face". *American Anthropologist*, Vol. 46, N. 1, 45-64.
- Jensen, A. F. (1991). *India: its Culture and People*. New York: Longman Publishing.
- Joos, J. (2004). A Stinking Tradition: Tsuda Sokichi's View Of China. *East Asian History*, 28, 1-26.
- Kim, U., & Park, Y. S. (2005). Integrated analysis of indigenous psychologies: Comments and extensions of ideas presented by Shams, Jackson, Hwang and Kashima. *Asian Journal of Social Psychology*, 8, 75-95.
- King, A. (2008). *Culture Smart: Russia*. London: Kuperard.
- Kohls, R. (1984). *The Values Americans Live by*. Washington: Meridian House International.
- Lassiter, J. E. (2000). African Culture And Personality: Bad Social Science, Effective Social Activism, Or A Call To Reinvent Ethnology?. *African Studies Quarterly*, Vol. 3, N. 3, 1-21.
- Ledeneva, A. (2001). *Unwritten rules: How Russia really works*. London: Centre for European Reform.
- Lee, C. Y. (2012). Korean Culture And Its Influence on Business Practice in South Korea. *The Journal of International Management Studies*, Vol. 7, N. 2, 184-191.
- Likhachev, D. S. (1998). Religion: Russian orthodoxy. In N. Rzhevsky (Ed.), *The Cambridge companion to modern Russian culture*. Cambridge, UK: Cambridge University Press.
- Lim, S. L. (2009). "Loss of Connections Is Death": Transnational Family Ties Among Sudanese Refugee Families Resettling in the United States. *Journal of Cross-Cultural Psychology*, Vol. 40, N. 6, 1028-1040.
- Lin, C. C., & Yamaguchi, S. (2011). Under What Conditions Do People Feel Face-Loss? Effects of the Presence of Others and Social Roles on the Perception of Losing Face in Japanese Culture. *Journal of Cross-Cultural Psychology*, Vol. 42, N. 1, 120-124.
- Markus, H. R., & Kitayama, S. (1991). Culture and the Self. Implications for Cognition, Emotion, and Motivation. *Psychological Review*, Vol. 98, N. 2, 224-253.
- Matsumoto, D., & Juang, L. (2007). *Culture and Psychology*. Belmont: Wadsworth/Thomson.
- Mavor, G. (2005). *Culture Smart: Mexico*. London: Kuperard.
- Morita, A., Reingold E. M., & Shimomura M. (1986). *Made in Japan: Akio Morita and Sony*. New York: Dutton.
- Müller, M. (1919). *The Six Systems of Indian Philosophy*. London: Longmans Green and Co.

• Niemann, Y. F., Romero, A. J., & Arredondo, J. (1999). What Does It Mean to Be "Mexican"? Social Construction of an Ethnic Identity. *Hispanic Journal of Behavioral Sciences*, Vol. 21, N. 1, 47-60.

• Okazaki, S., David, E. J. R., & Abelmann, N. (2008). Colonialism and Psychology of Culture. *Social and Personality Psychology Compass*, Vol. 2, N. 1, 90-106.

• Park, Y., & Kim, U. (2006). Family, Parent-Child Relationship, and Academic Achievement in Korea. In U. Kim, K.-S. Yang, & K.-K. Hwang (Eds.), *Indigenous and Cultural Psychology, Understanding People in Context*. New York: Springer.

• Pattanaik, D. (2013). *Business Sutra: A Very Indian Approach to Management*. New Delhi: Aleph Book Company.

• Peng, K., & Nisbett, R. E. (1999). Culture, Dialectics, And Reasoning About Contradiction. *American Psychologist*, Vol. 54, N. 9, 741-754.

• Ramírez-Esparza, N., Gosling, S. D., & Pennebaker, J. W. (2008). Paradox Lost, Unraveling the Puzzle of Simpatía. *Journal of Cross-Cultural Psychology*, Vol. 39, N. 6, 703-715.

• Rodrigues, R. P., Milfont, T. L., Ferreira, M. C., Porto, J. B., & Fisher, R. (2011). Brazilian jeitinho: Understanding and explaining an indigenous psychological construct. *Interamerican Journal of Psychology*, Vol. 45, N. 1, 27-36.

• Scollon, C. N., Diener, E., Oishi, S., & Biswas-Diener, R. (2004). Emotions Across Cultures and Methods. *Journal of Cross-Cultural Psychology*, Vol. 35, N. 3, 304-326.

• Sinha, J. B. P., & Kanungo, R. N. (1997). Context Sensitivity and Balancing in Organizational Behavior. *International Journal of Psychology*, Vol. 32, N. 2, 93-105.

• Steele, L. G., & Lynch, S. M. (2013). The Pursuit of Happiness in China: Individualism, Collectivism, and Subjective Well-Being During China's Economic and Social Transformation. *Social Indicators Research*, Vol. 114, N. 2, 441-451.

• Tanaka, S. (1993). *Japan's Orient: Rendering Pasts into History*. Berkeley, CA: University of California Press.

• Tarakeshwar, N., Stanton, J., & Pargament, K. I. (2003). Religion: An Overlooked Dimension in Cross-Cultural Psychology. *Journal of Cross-Cultural Psychology*, Vol. 34, N. 4, 377-394.

• Tetréault, M. A. (2004). The Political Economy Of Middle Eastern Oil. In D. J. Gerner, & J. Schwedler (Eds.), *Understanding the Contemporary Middle East* (2nd ed.). Boulder, CO: Lynne Rienner.

• Van de Vijver, F. J. R. (2010). On the elusive nature of high Chinese achievement. *Learning and Individual Differences*, Vol. 20, N. 6, 574-576.

• Walsh, J. (2008). *Culture Smart: UAE*. London: Kuperard.

• Weaver, G. R. (1999). American Cultural Values. *Kokusai Bunka Kenshu* (Intercultural Training), Special Edition, 9-15.

• Whitaker, B. (2010). *What is really wrong with the Middle East*. London: Saqi Books.

- Worth, D. S. (1998). Language. In N. Rzhevsky (Ed.), *The Cambridge companion to modern Russian culture*. Cambridge, UK: Cambridge University Press.
- Yamaguchi, S., & Ariizumi, Y. (2006). Close Interpersonal Relationships among Japanese Amae as Distinguished from Attachment and Dependence. In U. Kim, K.-S. Yang, & K.-K. Hwang (Eds.), *International and Cultural Psychology: Understanding people in context*. New York: Springer.
- Yetim, F. (2001). A Meta-Communication Model for Structuring Intercultural Communication Action Patterns. *Proceedings of the Sixth International Workshop on the Language-Action Perspective on Communication Modelling* (LAP 2001).
- Zakaria, F. (2013). The rediscovery of India. In C. Chandler, & A. Zainulbhai (Eds.), *Reimagining India: Unlocking the Potential of Asia's Next Superpower*. New York: Simon & Schuster.

COMMUNICATION

- Bloch, B. (1996). The Language-Culture Connection in International Business. *Foreign Language Annals*, Vol. 29, N. 1, 27-36.
- Brown, P., & Levinson, S. C. (1987). *Politeness: Some universals in language usage*. Cambridge: Cambridge University Press.
- Burgoon, J. K. (1983). Nonverbal Violations of Expectations. In J. M. Wiemann, & R. R. Harrison (Eds.), *Nonverbal Interaction*. Beverly Hills, CA: Sage.
- Cai, D. A., & Rodriguez, J. I. (1996). Adjusting to Cultural Differences: The Intercultural Adaptation Model. *Intercultural Communication Studies*, Vol. 6, N. 2, 31-42.
- Chomsky, N. (1965). *Aspects of the Theory of Syntax*. Boston: MIT Press.
- Dance, F. E. X. (1970). The 'Concept' of Communication. *Journal of Communication*, Vol. 20, N. 2, 201-210.
- Evans, N., & Levinson, S. C. (2009). The myth of language universals: Language diversity and its importance for cognitive science. *Behavioral and Brain Sciences*, Vol. 32, N. 5, 429-448.
- Gudykunst, W. B. (2003). *Cross-Cultural and Intercultural Communication*. Thousand Oaks, CA: Sage Publications.
- Gudykunst, W. B., & Kim, Y. Y. (2003). *Communicating with strangers* (2nd ed). Boston: McGraw Hill.
- Hartkey, P. (1999). *Interpersonal Communication* (2nd ed.). London: Routledge.
- Huineng (1964). *The Sutra of the Sixth Patriarch on the Pristine Orthodox Dharma*. Translated by P. Fung, & G. Fung. San Francisco: Buddha's Universal Church.
- Kawamoto, F. (2007). Assertive Communication in Japanese English Learners. *Jiyugaoka Sanno College Bulletin*, Vol. 1, N. 9, 57-64.

- Kowner, R., & Wiseman, R. L. (2003). Culture and Status-Related Behavior: Japanese and American Perceptions of Asymmetric Dyad-Interactions. *Cross-Cultural Research*, Vol. 37, N. 10, 178-210.
- Krauss, R. M., & Fussell, S. R. (1996). Social Psychological Models Of Interpersonal Communication. In E. T. Higgins, & A. W. Kruglanski (Eds.), *Social psychology: Handbook of basic principles*. New York: Guilford Press.
- Kumar, R. (1999). Communicative Conflict in Intercultural Negotiations: The Case of American and Japanese Business Negotiations. *International Negotiation*, Vol. 4, N. 1, 63-78.
- Lakoff, G. (1992). The contemporary theory of metaphor. In A. Ortony (Ed.), *Metaphor and thought* (2ⁿᵈ ed.). New York: Cambridge University Press.
- Lebra, T. (2007). The Cultural Significance of Silence in Japanese Communication. In T. Lebra (Ed.), *Identity, gender, and status in Japan: collected papers of Takie Lebra*. Folkestone, U.K.: Global Oriental.
- Levinson, S. C. (2000). *Presumptive meanings: The theory of generalized conversational implicature*. Cambridge: MIT Press.
- Lustig, M., & Koester, J. (2012). *Intercultural Competence* (7ᵗʰ ed.). London: Pearson.
- Martin, J. N., & Nakayama, T. K. (2010). *Intercultural Communication in Contexts* (5ᵗʰ ed.). New York: McGraw-Hill.
- McNeill, D. (2007). *Gesture and Thought*. Chicago: University of Chicago Press.
- Mehrabian, A. (1981). *Silent messages: Implicit communication of emotions and attitudes* (2ⁿᵈ ed.). Belmont, CA: Wadsworth.
- Piller, I. (2007). Linguistics and Intercultural Communication. *Language and Linguistic Compass*, Vol. 1, N. 3, 208-226.
- Pinker, S. (1991). Rules of Language. *Science*, 253, 530–535.
- Pinker, S. (2007). *The Stuff of Thought: Language as a Window Into Human Nature*. New York: Viking.
- Schiffrin, D., Tannen, D., & Hamilton, H. E. (2003). *The Handbook of Discourse Analysis*. Hoboken: Wiley-Blackwell.
- Scollon, R. (1996). Discourse Identity, Social Identity, and Confusion in Intercultural Communication. *Intercultural Communication Studies*, Vol. 6, N. 1, 1-18.
- Scollon, R., Scollon, S., & Jones R. H. (2012). *Intercultural Communication A Discourse Approach* (3ʳᵈ ed.). Oxford: John Wiley & Sons.
- Street, B. V., Thompson, L. (1993). Culture is a verb: Anthropological aspects of language and cultural process. In D. Graddol, & M. Byram (Eds.), *Language and culture*. Clevedon, UK: BAAL in association with Multilingual Matters.
- Watzlawick, P., Beavin-Bavelas, J., & Jackson, D. (1967). *Pragmatics of Human Communication. A Study of Interactional Patterns, Pathologies and Paradoxes*. New York: Norton.
- Yetim, F. (2002). Designing "communication action patterns" for global communication and cooperation: a discourse ethical approach. *ECIS*, June 6-8, Gdańsk, Poland.

- Zhang, L. (2011). How Business Professionals Perceive Intercultural Differences: A Survey. *Global Business Languages*, 16, 15-26.

BODY LANGUAGE AND FACIAL EXPRESSIONS

- Edwards, C. (2006). *Mind Reading*. Old Windsor: Real Publishing.
- Ekman, P., & Friesen, W. V. (2003). *Unmasking the Face: A guide to recognizing emotions from facial clues*. Cambridge, MA: Malor Books.
- Proverbio, A. M., Vanutelli, M. E., & Adorni R. (2013). Can You Catch a Liar? How Negative Emotions Affect Brain Responses when Lying or Telling the Truth. *PLoS ONE*, Vol. 8, N. 3, e59383.
- Willis, J., & Todorov, A. (2006). First impressions: Making up your mind after a 100-ms exposure to a face. *Psychological Science*, Vol. 17, N. 7, 592-598.

NEGOTIATION

- Aumann, R. J. (2008). Game Theory. In S. N. Durlauf, & L. E. Blume (Eds.), *The New Palgrave Dictionary of Economics* (2nd ed). New York: Palgrave Macmillan.
- Banaji, M. R., Bazerman, M. H., & Chugh, D. (2003). How (un)ethical are you?. *Harvard Business Review*, Vol. 81, N. 12, 56-64.
- Barry, B., Fulmer, I. S., & Van Kleef, G. (2004). I laughed, I cried, I settled: The role of emotion in negotiation. In M. J. Gelfand, & J. M. Brett (Eds.), *The Handbook of Negotiation and Culture*. Palo Alto, CA: Stanford University Press.
- Bazerman, M. H., & Neale, M. A. (1992). *Negotiating rationally*. New York: Free Press.
- Bell, D. (1991). Reciprocity as a Generating Process in Social Relations. *Journal of Quantitative Anthropology*, 3, 251-260.
- Brandenburger, A. M., & Nalebuff, B. J. (1997). *Co-opetition*. New York: Currency Doubleday.
- Camp, J. (2007). *Start With No: The Negotiating Tools That the Pros Don't Want You to Know*. New York: Crown Business.
- Carnevale, P. J., & Pruitt, D. G. (1992). Negotiation and Mediation. *Annual Reviews of Psychology*, 43, 531-582.
- Carr, A. (1968). Is Business Bluffing Ethical?. *Harvard Business Review*, Vol. 46, N. 1, 143-153.
- Carson, T. L. (1993). Second thoughts about bluffing. *Journal of Business Ethics*, Vol. 3, N. 4, 317-341.
- Clausewitz, C. von. (1989). *On War*. Translated by P. Paret, & M. Howard. Princeton, N.J.: Princeton University Press.
- Curhan, J. R., Elfenbein, H. A., & Xu, H. (2006). What Do People Value When They Negotiate? Mapping the Domain of Subjective Value in Negotiation. *Journal of Personality and Social Psychology*, Vol. 91, N. 3, 493-512.
- de Callières, F. (2000). *On the Manner of Negotiating With Princes*. Translated by A. F. Whyte, introduction by C. Handy. New York: Houghton Mifflin.

- Dixit, A, K., & Nalebuff, B. (1990). *Making Strategies Credible*. New Haven: Yale School of Organization and Management.
- Drolet, A., & Morris, M. W. (2000). Rapport in Conflict Resolution: Accounting for How Face-to-Face Contact Fosters Mutual Cooperation in Mixed-Motive Conflicts. *Journal of Experimental Social Psychology*, 36, 26-50.
- Ertel, D., & Gordon, M. (2002). *The Point of the Deal: When 'Yes' is not enough*. Cambridge, MA: Harvard Business Review Press.
- Field, A. (2003). How to Negotiate With a Hard-Nosed Adversary. *Harvard Management Update* (U0303A).
- Fisher, R., Ury, W. L., & Patton, B. (1991). *Getting to yes: Negotiating Agreement Without Giving In* (2nd ed.). London: Penguin Books.
- Flynn, F. J., & Ames, D. R. (2006). What's Good for the Goose May Not Be as Good for the Gander: The Benefits of Self-Monitoring for Men and Women in Task Groups and Dyadic Conflicts. *Journal of Applied Psychology*, Vol. 91, No. 2, 272-281.
- Galinsky, A. D., & Mussweiler, T. (2001). First Offers as Anchors: The Role of Perspective-Taking and Negotiation Focus. *Journal of Personality and Social Psychology*, Vol. 81. N. 4, 657-669.
- Gino, F., & Shea, Catherine (2012). Deception in Negotiations: The Role of Emotions. In R. Croson, & G. Bolton (Eds.), *The Oxford Handbook of Economic Conflict Resolution*. Oxford, UK: Oxford University Press.
- Kim, P. H., Pinkley, R., & Fragale, A. R. (2005). Power Dynamics in Negotiation. *Academy of Management Review*, Vol. 30, N. 4, 799-822.
- Kolb, D. M., & Williams, J. (2001). Breakthrough Bargaining. *Harvard Business Review*, Vol. 79, N. 2, 88-97.
- Kolb, D., & Williams, J. (2000). *The shadow negotiation: how women can master the hidden agendas that determine bargaining success*. New York: Simon & Schuster.
- Kopelman, S., Gewurz, I., & Sacharin, V. (2007). The Power of Presence: Strategic Response to Displayed Emotions in Negotiations. *Ross School of Business Paper*, N. 1061, IACM 20th Annual Conference.
- Kopelman, S., Rosette, A. S., & Thompson L. (2006). The three faces of Eve: Strategic displays of positive, negative, and neutral emotions in negotiations. *Organizational Behavior and Human Decision Processes,* 99, 81-101.
- Korobkin, R. (2009). *Negotiation Theory And Strategy* (2nd ed.). New York: Aspen Publishers.
- Kotler, P., & Keller, K. L. (2011). *Marketing Management* (14th ed.). Upper Saddle River, NJ: Prentice Hall.
- Lax, D. A., & Sebenius, J. K. (2003). 3-D Negotiation: playing the whole game. *Harvard Business Review*, Vol. 81, N. 11, 65-74.
- Lax, D. A., & Sebenius, J. K. (2006). *3-D Negotiation: Powerful Tools to Change the Game in Your Most Important Deals*. Boston: Harvard Business Press.
- Lax, D., & Sebenius, J. (1992). The Manager as Negotiator: The Negotiator's Dilemma: Creating and Claiming Value. In S. Goldberg, F. Sander, & N. Rogers (Eds.), *Dispute Resolution* (2nd ed.). Boston: Little Brown and Co.

- Lewicki, R. J. (1983). Lying and Deception: A behavioral model. In M. H. Bazerman, & R. J. Lewicki (Eds.), *Negotiating in Organizations*. Beverly Hills, CA: Sage.
- Lewicki, R. J., & Robinson, R. (1998). A factor analysis study of ethical and unethical bargaining tactics. *Journal of Business Ethics*, 18, 211-228.
- Lewicki, R. J., Saunders, D. M., & Barry, B. (2010). Essentials *of Negotiation* (5th ed.). New York: McGraw Hill.
- Li, S., & Roloff, M. E. (2006). Strategic Emotion in Negotiation: Cognition, Emotion, and Culture. In G. Riva, M. T. Anguera, B. K. Wiederhold, & F. Mantovani (Eds.), *From Communication to Presence: Cognition, Emotions and Culture towards the Ultimate Communicative Experience. Festschrift in honor of Luigi Anolli*. Amsterdam, Netherlands: IOS Press.
- Malhotra, D., & Bazerman, M. (2008). *Negotiation Genius*. New York: Bantam.
- McCain, R. A. (2010). *Game Theory: A Nontechnical introduction to the Analysis of Strategy* (Revised Edition). Singapore: World Scientific Publishing.
- Moran, S., & Ritov, I. (2002). Initial Perceptions in Negotiations: Evaluation and Response to 'Logrolling' Offers. *Journal of Behavioral Decision Making*, 15, 101-124.
- Morris, M., Nadler, J., Kurtzberg, T., & Thompson, L. (2002). Schmooze or Lose: Social Friction and Lubrication in E-Mail Negotiations. *Group Dynamics: Theory, Research, and Practice*, Vol. 6, N. 1, 89-100.
- Musashi, M. (1993). *The book of five rings*. Translated by T. Cleary. Boston: Shambhala Publications.
- Olekalns, M., & Smith, P. L. (2009). Mutually dependent: Power, trust, affect and the use of deception in negotiation. *Journal of Business Ethics*, 85, 347-365.
- Provis, C. (2000). Ethics, Deception, and Labor Negotiation. *Journal of Business Ethics*, Vol. 28, N. 2, 145-158.
- Raiffa, H. (1982). *The Art and Science of Negotiation*. Cambridge, MA: Harvard University Press.
- Raiffa, H., Richardson, J., & Metcalfe, D. (2007). *Negotiation Analysis: The Science and Art of Collaborative Decision Making*. Cambridge, MA: Belknap Press.
- Reilly, P. R. (2009). Was Machiavelli Right? Lying in Negotiation and the Art of Defensive Self-Help. *Ohio State Journal on Dispute Resolution*, Vol. 24, N. 3, 481-533.
- Saorín-Iborra, M. C. (2007). Negotiation behaviour. Dichotomy or continuum?. *EsicMarket*, 129, 125-152.
- Schelling, T. C. (1960). *The strategy of conflict*. Cambridge, MA: Harvard University Press.
- Schneider, A. K. (2012). Teaching a New Negotiation Skills Paradigm. *Washington University Journal of Law & Policy*, Vol. 39, 13-38.
- Sebenius, J. K. (2001). *Six Habits of Merely Effective Negotiators*. Harvard Business Review, Vol. 79, N. 4, 87-95.

- Sebenius, J. K. (2013). Level Two Negotiations: Helping the Other Side Meet Its "Behind the Table" Challenges. *Negotiation Journal*, Vol. 29, N. 1, 7-21.
- Shell, G. R. (2006). *Bargaining for Advantage: Negotiation Strategies for Reasonable People* (2nd ed.). London: Penguin Books.
- Sinaceur, M. (2009). Suspending Judgment to Create Value: Suspicion and Trust in Negotiation. *Journal of Experimental Social Psychology*, doi: 10.1016/j.jesp.2009.11.002.
- Susskind, L., Mnookin, R., Rozdeiczer, L., & Fuller, F. (2005). What We Have Learned About Teaching Multiparty Negotiation. *Negotiation Journal*, Vol. 21, N. 3, 395-408.
- Thompson, L. (2011). *The Mind and Heart of the Negotiator* (5th ed.). Upper Sadler River, NJ: Pearson Prentice Hall.
- Thompson, L., & Lowenstein, J. (2003). Mental Models of Negotiation: Descriptive, Prescriptive, and Paradigmatic Implications. In M. A. Hogg, & J. Cooper (Eds.), *The Sage Handbook of Social Psychology* (3rd ed.). London: Sage Publications Ltd.
- Tzu, S. (1991). *The art of war*. Translated by T. Cleary. Boston: Shambhala Publications.
- Watkins, M. (1999). Negotiating in a Complex World. *Negotiation Journal*, Vol. 15, N. 3, 245-270.
- Watkins, M. (2002). *Breakthrough Negotiations: A Toolbox for Managers*. New York: John Wiley & Sons.
- Watkins, M., & Luecke, R. (2003). *Harvard Business Essentials: Negotiation*. Boston: Harvard Business School Press.
- Wheeler, M. A. (2001). Negotiation Analysis: An Introduction. Business Fundamentals As Taught at the Harvard Business School. *Harvard Business Publishing*, 3-16.
- White, J. (1984). The Pros and Cons of "Getting to Yes". *Journal of Legal Education*, 34, 115-124.
- Wolfe, R., & McGinn, K. (2005). Perceived Relative Power and its Influence on Negotiations. *Group Decision and Negotiation*, 14, 3-20.
- Young, H. P. (Ed.) (1991). *Negotiation Analysis*. Ann Arbor: University of Michigan Press.
- Zartman, I. W., & Rubin, J. Z. (2000). *Power and Negotiation*. Ann Arbor, MI: The University of Michigan Press.

SOCIAL COGNITION & DECISION MAKING

- Avenhaus, R. (2002). Game Theory. In V. A. Kremenyuk (Ed.), *International Negotiation: analysis, approaches, issues* (2nd ed.). San Francisco: Jossey-Bass.
- Bandura, A. (1982). The Psychology of Chance Encounters and Life Paths. *American Psychologist*, Vol. 37, N. 7, 747-755.
- Bandura, A. (1998). Exploration of fortuitous determinants of life paths. *Psychological Inquiry*, 9, 95-99.

- Bar, M. (2009). A cognitive neuroscience hypothesis of mood and depression. *Trends in Cognitive Sciences*, Vol. 13, N. 11, 456-463.
- Bazerman, M. H., & Moore, D. A. (2013). Improving Decision Making. In M. H. Bazerman, & D. A. Moore (Eds.), *Judgment in Managerial Decision Making* (8th ed.). New York: John Wiley & Sons.
- Bland, J. M., & Altman, D. G. (1994). Statistics notes: Regression towards the mean. *British Medical Journal*, 308, 1499.
- Bolton, G. E., Katok, E., & Rami Zwick, R. (1998). Dictator game giving: Rules of fairness versus acts of kindness. *International Journal of Game Theory*, 27, 269-299.
- Bos, M. W., Dijksterhuis, van Baaren, R. B. (2011). The benefits of *sleeping on things*: Unconscious thought leads to automatic weighting. *Journal of Consumer Psychology*, Vol. 21, N. 1, 4-8.
- Brett, J. M., & Kopelman, S. (2004). Cross-cultural perspectives on cooperation in social dilemmas. In M. J. Gelfand, & J. M. Brett (Eds.), *Handbook of Negotiation and Culture*. Palo Alto: Stanford University Press.
- Buehler, R., Griffin, D., & Ross, M. (2002). Inside the planning fallacy: The causes and consequences of optimistic time predictions. In T. Gilovich, D. Griffin, & D. Kahneman (Eds.), *Heuristics and biases: The psychology of intuitive judgment*. Cambridge, UK: Cambridge University Press.
- Cacioppo, J. T., & Petty, R. E. (1982). The need for cognition. *Journal of Personality and Social Psychology*, 42, 116-131.
- Cacioppo, J. T., Petty, R. E., Kao, C. F., & Rodriguez, R. (1986). Central and Peripheral Routes to Persuasion: An Individual Difference Perspective. *Journal of Personality and Social Psychology*, Vol. 51, N. 5, 1032-1043.
- Camerer, C. F. (2003). *Behavioral Game Theory: Experiments in Strategic Interaction*. Princeton, NJ: Princeton University Press.
- Cartwright, E. (2011). *Behavioral Economics*. New York: Routledge.
- Chia-Ching, C., I-Ming, C., Smith, J., & Yamada, T. (2012). Too smart to be selfish? Measures of cognitive ability, social preferences, and consistency. *Munich Personal RePEc Archive*, Paper N. 41078.
- Chugh, D. (2004). Why Milliseconds Matter: Societal and Managerial Implications of Implicit Social Cognition. *Social Justice Research*, Vol. 17, N. 2, 203-222.
- Coates J. (2012). *The Hour Between Dog and Wolf. Risk Taking, Gut Feelings, and the Biology of Boom and Bust*. New York: Random House.
- Cross, K. P. (1977). Not can, but *will* college teaching be improved?. *New Directions for Higher Education*, 17, 1-15.
- Denis, A. (2002). Collective and individual rationality: Maynard Keynes's methodological standpoint and policy prescription. *Research in Political Economy*, Vol. 20, 187-215.
- Dijksterhuis, A., & Nordgren, L. F. (2006). A theory of unconscious thought. *Perspectives on Psychological Science*, 1, 95-109.
- Dohmen, T., Falk, A., Huffman, D., & Sunde, U. (2010). Are risk aversion and impatience Related to Cognitive Ability?. *American Economic Review*, Vol. 100, N. 3, 1238-1260.

- Evans, J. (2003). In two minds: dual-process accounts of reasoning. *Trends in Cognitive Sciences,* Vol. 7, N. 10, 454-459.
- Finucane, M. L., Alhakami, A., Slovic, P., & Johnson, S. M. (2000). The affect heuristic in judgments of risks and benefits. *Journal of Behavioral Decision Making,* 13, 1-17.
- Forgas, J. P., Baumeister, R. F., & Tice, D. M. (2009). *Psychology of Self-Regulation: Cognitive, Affective, and Motivational Processes.* New York: Psychology Press.
- Frederick, S. (2005). Cognitive Reflection and Decision Making. *Journal of Economic Perspectives.* Vol. 19, N. 4, 25-42.
- Freeman, J. B., & Ambady, N. (2011). A Dynamic Interactive Theory of Person Construal. *Psychological Review,* Vol. 118, N. 2, 247–279.
- Galton, F. (1886). Regression towards mediocrity in hereditary stature. *The Journal of the Anthropological Institute of Great Britain and Ireland,* Vol. 15, 246-263.
- Gilovich, T. (1993). *How we know what isn't so: The Fallibility of human reason in everyday life.* New York: The Free Press.
- Gilovich, T., & Savitsky, K. (1996). Like goes with like: The role of representativeness in erroneous and pseudoscientific beliefs. *Skeptical Inquirer,* Vol. 20, N. 2, 34-40.
- Gladwell, M. (2007). *Blink: The Power of Thinking Without Thinking.* New York: Back Bay Books.
- Goleman, D. (1996). *Emotional Intelligence: Why it can matter more than IQ?.* London: Bloomsbury Publishing PLC.
- Goleman, D. (2007). *Social Intelligence: the new science of human relationship.* London: Arrow Books.
- Greenspan, A. (2013). *The Map and the Territory: Risk, Human Nature, and the Future of Forecasting.* London: The Penguin Press.
- Güth, W., Schmittberger, R., & Schwarze, B. (1982). An experimental analysis of ultimatum bargaining. *Journal of Economic Behavior and Organization,* Vol. 3, N. 4, 367-388.
- Guy, R. K. (1988). The strong law of small numbers. *American Mathematical Monthly,* Vol. 95, N. 8, 696-712.
- Hammond, J. S., Keeney R. L., & Raiffa H. (1998). The hidden Traps in Decision Making. *Harvard Business Review,* Vol. 76, N. 5, 47-59.
- Han, S., Lerner, J. S., & Keltner, D. (2007). Feelings and Consumer Decision Making: The Appraisal-Tendency Framework. *Journal of Consumer Psychology,* Vol. 17, N. 3, 158-168.
- Heath, C., & Heath, D. (2013). *Decisive: How to Make Better Choices in Life and Business.* New York: Crown Business.
- Herrmann, N. (1996). *The Whole Brain Business Book.* New York: McGraw-Hill.
- Hoorens, V. (1993). Self-enhancement and Superiority Biases in Social Comparison. *European Review of Social Psychology,* Vol. 4, N. 1, 113-139.

- Huizenga, H. M., Wetzels, R., van Ravenzwaaij, D., & Wagenmakers, E. J. (2012). Four empirical tests of Unconscious Thought Theory. *Organizational Behavior and Human Decision Processes*, 117, 332-340.
- Jones, B. D. (1999). Bounded Rationality. *Annual Review of Political Science*, Vol. 2, 297-321.
- Kahneman, D. (2011). *Thinking Fast and Slow*. New York: Farrar, Strauss & Giroux.
- Kahneman, D., & Tversky, A. (1979). Prospect Theory: An Analysis of Decision under Risk. *Econometrica*, Vol. 47, N. 2, 263-292.
- Kahneman, D., Knetsch, J. L., & Thaler, R. H. (1986). Fairness and the assumptions of economics. *Journal of Business*, Vol. 59, N. 4, 285-300.
- Kahneman, D., Knetsch, J. L., & Thaler, R. H. (1991). Anomalies: The Endowment Effect, Loss Aversion, and Status Quo Bias. *Journal of Economic Perspectives*, Vol. 5, N. 1, 193-206.
- Kahneman, D., Knetsh, J. L., & Thaler, R. H. (1990). Experimental Tests of the Endowment Effect and the Coase Theorem. *The Journal of Political Economy*, Vol. 98, N. 6, 1325-1348.
- Keinan, G. (1987). Decision Making Under Stress: Scanning of Alternatives Under Controllable and Uncontrollable Threats. *Journal of Personality and Social Psychology*, Vol. 52, N. 3, 639-644.
- Kelly, A. (2003). *Decision Making using Game Theory: An introduction for managers*. Cambridge, UK: Cambridge University Press.
- Kelly, T. (2004). Sunk Costs, Rationality, and Acting for the Sake of the Past. *Noûs*, Vol. 38, N. 1, 60-85.
- Kirst-Ashman, K. K. (2011). Organizational Structure and Dynamics. In K. K. Kirst-Ashman (Ed.), *Human Behavior in the Macro Social Environment: An Empowerment Approach to Understanding Communities, Organizations, And Groups* (3rd ed.). Belmont, CA: Brooks/Cole.
- Knight, S. (2012). Fairness or anger in Ultimatum Game rejections?. *Journal of European Psychology Students*, Vol. 3, 2-14.
- Kolb, D. A. (1984). *Experiential Learning: experience as the source of learning and development*, Englewood Cliffs, NJ: Prentice Hall.
- Kopelman, S. (2008). The Herdsman and the Sheep, Mouton, or Kivsa? The Influence of Group Culture on Cooperation in Social Dilemmas. In A. Biel, D. Eek, T. Garling, & M. Gustafsson, M. (Eds.), *New issues and paradigms in research on social dilemmas*. New York: Springer.
- Krantz, D. L. (1998). Taming Chance: Social Science and Everyday Narratives. *Psychological Inquiry*, Vol. 9, N. 2, 87-94.
- Lerner, J. S., Li, Y., & Weber, E. U. (2013). The Financial Cost of Sadness. *Psychological Science*, Vol. 24, N. 1, 72-79.
- List, J. A. (2007). On the Interpretation of Giving in Dictator Games. *Journal of Political Economy*, Vol. 115, N. 3, 482-494.
- Loewenstein, G. F., Weber, E. U., Hsee, C. K., & Welch, N. (2001). Risk as a feeling. *Psychological Bulletin*. Vol. 127, N. 2, 267-286.

- Loomes, G., & Sugden, R. (1982). Regret theory: An Alternative Theory of Rational Choice Under Uncertainty. *The Economic Journal*, Vol. 92, N. 368, 805-824.
- Lovallo, D., & Kahneman D. (2003). Delusions of success. How optimism undermines executives' decisions. *Harvard Business Review*, Vol. 81, N. 7, 56-63.
- Lucy, J. A. (1992). *Language Diversity and Thought: A Reformulation of the Linguistic Relativity Hypothesis*. Cambridge: Cambridge University Press.
- Mamassis, G., & Doganis, G. (2004). The Effects of a Mental Training Program on Juniors Pre-Competitive Anxiety, Self-Confidence, and Tennis Performance. *Journal of Applied Sport Psychology*, Vol. 16, N. 2, 118-137.
- Manktelow, K., Over, D., & Elqayam, S. (Eds.) (2011). *The Science of Reason*. New York: Psychology Press.
- Mauboussin, M. J. (2012). *The Success Equation: Untangling Skill and Luck in Business, Sports, and Investing*. Cambridge, MA: Harvard Business Review Press.
- Maule, A. J., Hockey, G. R. J., & Bdzola, L. (2000). Effects of time-pressure on decision-making under uncertainty: Changes in affective state and information processing strategy. *Acta Psychologica*, 104, 283-301.
- McAfee, R. P., Mialon, H. M., & Mialon, S. H. (2010). Do Sunk Costs Matter?. *Economic Inquiry*, Vol. 48, N. 2, 323-336.
- Milkman, K. L., Rogers, T., & Bazerman, M. H. (2010). I'll have the ice cream soon and the vegetables later: A study of online grocery purchases and order lead time. *Marketing Letters*, Vol. 21, N. 1, 17-36.
- Milkman, K., Chugh, D., & Bazerman, M. H. (2009). How Can Decision Making Be Improved?. *Perspectives in Psychological Science*, Vol. 4, N. 4, 379-383.
- Mlodinov, L. (2008). *The drunkard's walk*. London: Penguin Books.
- Norton, M. I., & Gino, F. (2013). Rituals Alleviate Grieving for Loved Ones, Lovers, and Lotteries. *Journal of Experimental Psychology: General*. Advance online publication, February, doi: 10.1037/a0031772.
- Ormerod, P. (2007). *Why Most Things Fail*. New York: John Wiley & Sons.
- Pennington, D. C. (2000). *Social cognition*. London: Routledge.
- Pope, D. G., & Schweitzer, M. E. (2011). Is Tiger Woods Loss Averse? Persistent Bias in the Face of Experience, Competition, and High Stakes. *American Economic Review*, 101, 129-157.
- Pronin, E., Gilovich, T., & Ross, L. (2004). Objectivity in the Eye of the Beholder: Divergent Perceptions of Bias in Self Versus Others. *Psychological Review*, Vol. 111, N. 3, 781-799.
- Robeyns, I. (2011). The Capability Approach. In E. N. Zalta (Ed.), *The Stanford Encyclopedia of Philosophy*, Summer Edition. Available at http://plato.stanford.edu/archives/sum2011/entries/capability-approach/
- Roese, N. J., & Vohs, K. D. (2012). Hindsight Bias. *Perspectives on Psychological Science*, Vol. 7, N. 5, 411-426.
- Roxburh, C. (2003). Hidden flaws in Strategy. *McKinsey Quarterly*, N. 2, 26-39.

- Russell, B. (2004). *The Proposed Roads to Freedom.* New York: Cosimo Classics.
- Russell, B. W. (1959). *Common Sense and Nuclear Warfare.* London: George Allen and Unwin.
- Salovey, P., & Mayer, J. D. (1990). Emotional intelligence. *Imagination, Cognition, and Personality,* 9, 185-211.
- Samuelson, W., & Zeckhauser, R. (1988). Status Quo Bias in Decision Making. *Journal of Risk and Uncertainty,* 1, 7-59.
- Schacter, D. L., Gilbert, D. T., & Wegner, D. M. (2011). *Psychology.* New York: Worth Publishers.
- Schelling, T. C. (2006). *Strategies of Commitment and Other Essays.* Cambridge, MA: Harvard University Press.
- Schwartz, S. H. (2012). An Overview of the Schwartz Theory of Basic Values. *Online Readings in Psychology and Culture,* Unit 2, Subunit 1. Retrieved from http://dx.doi.org/10.9707/2307-0919.1116. Bellingham, Washington: Center for Cross-Cultural Research, Western Washington University.
- Schwarz, N., Strack, F., Bless, H., Klumpp, G., Rittenauer-Schatka, H., & Simons, A. (1991). Ease of retrieval as information: Another look at the availability heuristic. *Journal of Personality and Social Psychology,* Vol. 61, N. 2, 195-202.
- Sher, S., & McKenzie, C. R. M. (2008). Framing effects and rationality. In N. Chater, & M. Oaksford (Eds.), *The Probabilistic mind: Prospects for Bayesian cognitive science.* Oxford: Oxford University Press.
- Stanovich, K E., & West, R F. (2000). Individual difference in reasoning: implications for the rationality debate?. *Behavioural and Brain Sciences,* 23, 645–726.
- Strack, F., & Mussweiler, T. (1997). Explaining the enigmatic anchoring effect: Mechanisms of selective accessibility. *Journal of Personality and Social Psychology,* Vol. 73, N. 39, 437-446.
- Taleb, N. N. (2007). *The Black Swan: The Impact of the Highly Improbable.* New York: Random House.
- Thaler, R. H. (1988). Anomalies: The Ultimatum Game. *Journal of Economic Perspectives,* Vol. 2, N. 4, 195-206.
- Trope, Y., & Liberman, N. (2010). Construal-Level Theory of Psychological Distance. *Psychological Review,* Vol. 117, No. 2, 440–463.
- Tversky, A., & Simonson, I. (1993). Context-Dependent Preferences. *Management Science,* Vol. 39, N. 10, 1179-1189.
- Tversky, A., & Kahneman, D. (1986). Rational Choice and the Framing of Decision. *The Journal of Business,* Vol. 59, N. 4, Part 2: The Behavioral Foundations of Economic Theory, S251-S278.
- Van Lange, P. A., Joireman, J., Parks, C. D., & Van Dijk, E. (2013). The Psychology of Social Dilemmas: A Review. *Organizational Behavior and Human Decision Processes,* Vol. 120, N. 2, 125-141.
- Vohs, K. D., Mead, N. L., & Goode, M. R. (2006). The Psychological Consequences of Money, *Science,* 314, 1154-1156.

- Watzlawick, P. (1993). *The Situation Is Hopeless But Not Serious (The Pursuit of Unhappiness)*. New York: Norton.
- Weber, E. U. (1994). From Subjective Probabilities to Decision Weights: The Effect of Asymmetric Loss Functions on the Evaluation of Uncertain Outcomes and Events. *Psychological Bulletin*, Vol. 115, N. 2, 228-242.
- Weber, J. M., Kopelman, S., & Messick, D. M. (2004). A Conceptual Review of Decision Making in Social Dilemmas: Applying a Logic of Appropriateness. *Personality and Social Psychology Review*, Vol. 8, N. 3, 281-307.
- Wiseman, R. (2003). The Luck Factor. *Skeptical Inquirer*, Vol. 27, N. 3, 26-30.
- Zuckerman, E. W., & Jost, J. (2001). What Makes You Think You're So Popular? Self-Evaluation Maintenance and the Subjective Side of the "Friendship Paradox". *Social Psychology Quarterly*, Vol. 64, N.3, 207-223.

NEUROSCIENCE

- Atkinson, R. C., & Shiffrin, R. M. (1968). Human memory: A proposed system and its control processes. In K. W. Spence, & J. T. Spence (Eds.), *The psychology of learning and motivation* (Vol. 2). New York: Academic Press.
- Bechara, A., Damasio, H., & Damasio, A. R. (2003). Role of the amygdala in decision making. *Annals of the New York Academy of Sciences*, 985, 356-369.
- Bernsten, D., & Bohn, A. (2010). Remembering and forecasting: The relation between autobiographical memory and episodic future thinking. *Memory & Cognition*, Vol. 38, N. 3, 265-278.
- Carrington, S. J., & Bailey, A. J. (2009). Are there theory of mind regions in the brain? A review of the neuroimaging literature. *Human Brain Mapping*, Vol. 30, N. 8, 2313-2335.
- Drachman, D. (2005). Do we have brain to spare?. *Neurology*, Vol. 64, N. 12, 2004-2005.
- Freeman, J. B., Ambady, N., Midgley, K. J., & Holcomb, P. J. (2011). The real-time link between person perception and action: Brain potential evidence for dynamic continuity. *Social Neuroscience*, Vol. 6, N. 2, 139-155.
- Frensch, P. A. (1994). Composition during serial learning: a serial position effect. *Journal of Experimental Psychology: Learning, Memory, and Cognition*, Vol. 20, N. 2, 423-443.
- Glimcher, P. W., Camerer, C. F., Fehr, E., & Poldrack, R. A. (Eds.) (2009). *Neuroeconomics: Decision Making and the Brain*. London: Elsevier Academic Press.
- Gupta, R., Koscik, T. R., Bechara, A., & Tranel, D. (2011). The amygdala and decision making. *Neuropsychologia*, Vol. 49, N. 4, 760-766.
- Hawkins, J. (2004). *On Intelligence*: New York: Owl Books.
- Koch, C. (1998). *Biophysics of Computation: Information Processing in Single Neurons*. New York: Oxford University Press.
- Kurzweil, R. (2012). *How to Create a Mind: The Secret of Human Thought Revealed*. New York: Viking Penguin.
- Lee, D. (2011). Game theory and neural basis of social decision making. *Nature Neuroscience*, Vol. 11, N. 4, 404-409.

- Reader, S. M., & Laland, K. N. (2002). Social intelligence, innovation, and enhanced brain size in primates. *PNAS*, Vol. 99, N. 7, 4436-4441.
- Sanfey, A. G. (2007). Social Decision-Making: Insights from Game Theory and Neuroscience. *Science*, Vol. 318, N. 5850, 598-602.
- Seth, A. (Ed.) (2014). *30-Second Brain*. London: Icon Books.
- Zak, P. J., Stanton A. A., & Ahmadi S. (2007). Oxytocin increases generosity in humans. *PLoS ONE*, Vol. 2, N. 11, e1128.

PERSONALITY

- Alessandra, T., O'Connor, M. J., & Van Dyke, J. (2006). *People Smart: In Business*. Garden City, NY: Morgan James Publishing.
- Amanatullah, E. T., Morris, M. W., & Curhan, J. R. (2008). Negotiators Who Give Too Much: Unmitigated Communion, Relational Anxieties, and Economic Costs in Distributive and Integrative Bargaining. *Journal of Personality and Social Psychology*, Vol. 95, N. 3, 723-738.
- Barry, B., & Friedman, R. A. (1998). Bargainers Characteristics in Distributive and Integrative Negotiation. *Journal of Personality and Social Psychology*, Vol. 74, N. 2, 345-359.
- Curry, O. S., Price, M. E., & Price, J, G. (2008). Patience is a virtue: cooperative people have lower discount rates. *Personality and Individual Differences*, Vol. 44, N. 3, 780-785.
- Davidson, R. J., & Begley, S. (2012). *The Emotional Life of your Brain*. New York: Hudson Street Press
- Dimotakis, N., Conlon, D. E., & Ilies, R. (2012). The mind and heart (literally) of the negotiator: Personality and contextual determinants of experiential reactions and economic outcomes in negotiation. *Journal of Applied Psychology*, Vol. 97, N. 1, 183-193.
- Howard, P. J., & Howard, J. M. (2001). *The Owner's Manual for Personality at Work: how the Big Five Personality traits affect performance, communication, teamwork, leadership, and sales*. Marietta, GA: Bard Press.
- Hsu, C. (2006). *Development of an indigenous Chinese personality inventory based on the principle of Yin-Yang and the five elements and on the ancient Chinese text "Jen Wu Chih"*. Retrieved from https://etd.ohiolink.edu/.
- Krauskopf, C. J., & Saunders, D. R. (1994). *Personality and Ability: The Personality Assessment System*. Lanham, MD: University Press of America.
- Ma, Z., & Jaeger, A. (2005). Getting to Yes in China: Exploring Personality Effects in Chinese Negotiation Styles. *Group Decision and Negotiation*, Vol. 14, 415-437.
- McCrae, R. R., & Costa Jr., P. T. (1997). Personality trait structure as a human universal. *American Psychologist*, 52, 509-516.
- Nicholson, N., Soane, E., Fenton-O'Creevy, M., & Willman P. (2005). Personality and domain-specific risk taking. *Journal of Risk Research*, Vol. 8, N. 2, 157-176.
- Ryckman, R. (2012). *Theories of Personality* (10th ed.). Boston: Cengage Learning.

- Schmitt, J., Allik, D. P., McCrae, R. R., & Benet-Martínez, V. (2007). The Geographic Distribution of Big Five Personality Traits: Patterns and Profiles of Human Self-Description Across 56 Nations. *Journal of Cross-Cultural Psychology,* Vol. 38, N. 2, 173-212.
- Triandis, H. C., & Suh, E. M. (2002). Cultural Influences on Personality. *Annual Reviews of Psychology,* 53, 133-160.

SOCIAL COGNITION AND CULTURE

- Aronson, E., Wilson, T. D., & Akert, R. M. (2005). *Social Psychology* (7th ed.). Upper Saddle River, NJ: Pearson Education.
- Bandura, A. (2002). Social Cognitive Theory in Cultural Context. *Applied Psychology: An International Review,* Vol. 51, N. 2, 269-290.
- Berry, J. W., Poortinga, Y. H., & Dasen, P. R. (2002). *Cross-Cultural Psychology - Research and Applications.* Cambridge: Cambridge University Press.
- Bontempo, R. N., Bottom, W. P., & Weber, E. U. (1997). Cross-cultural differences in risk perception: A model-based approach. *Risk Analysis,* 17, 479-488.
- Briley, D. A., Morris, M. W., & Simonson, I. (2005). Cultural Chameleons: Biculturals, Conformity Motives, and Decision Making. *Journal Of Consumer Psychology,* Vol. 14, N. 4, 351-362.
- Buchtel, E. E, & Norenzayan, A. (2009). Thinking across cultures: Implications for dual processes. In J. Evans, & K. Frankish (Eds.), *In two minds: Dual processes and beyond.* Oxford, UK: Oxford University Press.
- Chiao, J. Y., & Bebko, G. M. (2011). Cultural Neuroscience of Social Cognition. S. Han, & E. Pöppel (Eds.), *Culture and Neural Frames of Cognition and Communication.* Berlin: Springer-Verlag Gmbh.
- Cialdini, R. B., & Goldstein, N. J. (2004). Social influence: Compliance and conformity. *Annual Review of Psychology,* 55, 591-621.
- Dasen, P. R. (2013). Emics and etics in cross-cultural psychology: towards a convergence in the study of cognitive styles. In T. M. S. Tchombe, A. B. Nsamenang, H. Keller, & M. Fülöp (Eds.), *Cross-cultural psychology: An Africentric perspective.* Stockholm, Sweden: Design House.
- Doll, R., & Hill, A. B. (1956). Lung cancer and other causes of death in relation to smoking; a second report on the mortality of British doctors. *British Medical Journal,* 5001, 1071-1081.
- Dong, Y., & Lee, K. P. (2008). A cross-cultural comparative study of users' perceptions of a webpage: With a focus on the cognitive styles of Chinese, Koreans and Americans. *International Journal of Design,* Vol. 2, N. 2, 19-30.
- Elqayam, S. (2011). Grounded rationality: A relativist framework for normative rationality. In K. I. Manktelow, D. E. Over, & S. Elqayam, S. (Eds.), *The Science of Reason: A Festschrift in Honour of Jonathan St. B.T. Evans.* Hove, UK: Psychology Press.
- English, T., Chen, S., & Swann Jr., W. B. (2008). A Cross Cultural Analysis Of Self-Verification Motives. In R. Sorrentino, & S. Yamaguchi (Eds.), *Handbook of Motivation and Cognition Across Cultures.* San Diego: Academic Press.

- Evans, J. & Frankish, K. (Eds.) (2009). *In two minds: Dual processes and beyond.* Oxford: Oxford University Press.
- Freeman, J. B, Penner, A. M., Saperstein, A., Scheutz, M., & Ambady, N. (2011). Looking the Part: Social Status Cues Shape Race Perception. *PLoS ONE,* Vol. 6, N. 9, e25107.
- Gawronski, B., Peters, K. R., & Strack, F. (2008). Cross-Cultural Cognitive Dissonance. In R. Sorrentino, & S. Yamaguchi (Eds.), *Handbook of Motivation and Cognition Across Cultures.* San Diego: Academic Press.
- Gilovich, T., Keltner, D., & Nisbett, R. E. (2011). Understanding Others. In T. Gilovich, D. Keltner, & R. E. Nisbett (Eds.), *Social psychology* (2nd ed.). New York: W. W. Norton & Company.
- Goetz, J. L., Spencer-Rodgers, J., & Peng, K. (2008). Dialectical Emotions: How Cultural Epistemologies Influence the Experience and Regulation of Emotional Complexity. In R. Sorrentino, & S. Yamaguchi (Eds.), *Handbook of Motivation and Cognition Across Cultures.* San Diego: Academic Press.
- Guss, C. D. (2002). Planning in Brazil, India, and Germany: A cross-cultural study, a cultural study, and a model. In W. J. Lonner, D. L. Dinnel, S. A. Hayes, & D. N. Sattler (Eds.), *Online Readings in Psychology and Culture* (Unit 4, Chapter 2), (http://www.wwu.edu/~culture). Bellingham, Washington: Center for Cross-Cultural Research, Western Washington University.
- Heine, S. J., Harihara M., & Niiya, Y. (2002). Terror Management in Japan. *Asian Journal of Social Psychology,* Vol. 5, N. 3, 187-196.
- Heine, S., & Takeshi, H. (2007). In Search of East Asian Self-Enhancement. *Personality and Social Psychology Review,* Vol. 11, N. 1, 4-27.
- Henrich, J. (2000). Does Culture Matter in Economic Behavior? Ultimatum Game Bargaining Among the Machiguenga of the Peruvian Amazon. *The American Economic Review,* Vol. 90, N. 4, 973-979.
- Hofer, J., & Bond, M. H. (2008). Do Implicit Motives Add to Our Understanding of Psychological and Behavioral Outcomes Within and Across Cultures?. In R. Sorrentino, & S. Yamaguchi (Eds.), *Handbook of Motivation and Cognition Across Cultures.* San Diego: Academic Press.
- Hofer, J., & Chasiotis, A. (2011). Implicit Motives Across Cultures. *Online Readings in Psychology and Culture, Unit 4.* Retrieved from *http://scholarworks.gvsu.edu/orpc/vol4/iss1/5.* Bellingham, Washington: Center for Cross-Cultural Research, Western Washington University.
- Hong, Y., & Chiu, C. (2001). Toward a paradigm shift: from cross-cultural differences in social cognition to social-cognitive mediation of cultural differences. *Social Cognition,* Vol. 19, N. 3, 181-196.
- Hong, Y., & Chiu, C. (2001). Toward A Paradigm Shift: From Cross-Cultural Differences In Social Cognition To Social-Cognitive Mediation Of Cultural Differences. *Social Cognition,* Vol. 19, N. 3, 181-196.
- Hong, Y-y, Chiu, C., Morris, M. W., & Benet-Martinez, V. (2000). Multicultural Minds, A Dynamic Constructivist Approach to Culture and Cognition. *American Psychologist,* Vol. 55, N. 7, 709-720.
- Hong, Y-y, Ip, G., Chiu, C., Morris, M. W., & Menon, T. (2001). Cultural Identity And Dynamic Construction Of The Self: Collective Duties And

Individual Rights In Chinese And American Cultures. *Social Cognition*, Vol. 19, N. 3, 251-268.

- Huang, X., & Michael, H. B. (Eds.) (2012). *The handbook of Chinese organizational behavior: Integrating theory, research and practice.* Cheltenham, UK: Edward Elgar Publishing Ltd
- Ji, L., & Kaulius, M. (2013). Judgement and Decision Making across Cultures. *Advances in Psychological Science*, Vol. 21, No. 3, 381-388.
- Johnson, S. R. (2008). The Trouble with QSAR (or How I Learned to Stop Worrying and Embrace Fallacy). *Journal of Chemical Information and Modeling*, Vol. 48, N. 1, 25-26.
- Karasawa, M., & Maass, A. (2008). The role of language in the perception of person and group. In R. Sorrentino, & S. Yamaguchi (Eds.), *Handbook of Motivation and Cognition Across Cultures.* San Diego: Academic Press.
- Kim, U., & Park, Y. (2008). Cognitive, Relational and Social Basis of Academic Achievement in Confucian Cultures: Psychological, Indigenous, and Cultural Perspectives. In R. Sorrentino, & S. Yamaguchi (Eds.), *Handbook of Motivation and Cognition Across Cultures.* San Diego: Academic Press.
- Kobayashi, F. C., & Temple, E. (2009). Cultural effects on the neural basis of theory of mind. *Progress in Brain Research*, 178, 213-223.
- Leung, K., & Bond, M. H. (2004). Social axioms: A model of social beliefs in multi-cultural perspective. In M. P. Zanna (Ed.), *Advances in Experimental Social Psychology, Vol. 36.* San Diego: Academic Press.
- Leung, K., & Zhou, F. (2008). Values and social axioms. In R. Sorrentino, & S. Yamaguchi (Eds.), *Handbook of Motivation and Cognition Across Cultures.* San Diego: Academic Press.
- Levinson, J. D., & Peng, K. (2007). Valuing Cultural Differences In Behavioral Economics. *The Icfai Journal Of Behavioral Finance*, Vol. 4, N. 1, 32-47.
- Li, S., Bi, Y.-L., & Rao, L.-L. (2011). Every Science/Nature potter praises his own pot - Can we believe what he says based on his mother tongue?. *Journal of Cross-Cultural Psychology*, Vol. 42, N. 1, 125-130.
- Luszczynska, A., Gutierrez-Doña, B., & Schwarzer, R. (2005). General self-efficacy in various domains of human functioning: Evidence from five countries. *International Journal Of Psychology*, Vol. 40, N. 2, 80-89.
- Maddux, W. W., Kim, P. H., Okumura, T., & Brett, J. (2011). Cultural Differences in the Function and Meaning of Apologies. *International Negotiation*, 16, 405-425.
- Maddux, W., Yang, H., Falk, C., Adam, H., Adair, W., Endo, Y., Carmon, Z., & Heine, S. (2010). For Whom is Parting from Possessions More Painful: Cultural Differences in the Endowment Effect. *Psychological Science*, Vol. 21, N. 12, 1910-1917.
- Marshall, R., Huan, T.-C., Xu, Y., & Nam, I. (2011). Extending Prospect Theory Cross-Culturally by Examining Switching Behavior in Consumer and Business-to-Business Contexts. *Journal of Business Research*, Vol. 64, N. 8, 871-878.
- Mason, M. F., & Morris, M. W. (2010). Culture, attribution and automaticity: a social cognitive neuroscience view. *SCAN*, 5, 292-306.

- Matsumoto, D., & Wilson, J. (2008). Culture, Emotion and Motivation. In R. Sorrentino, & S. Yamaguchi (Eds.), *Handbook of Motivation and Cognition Across Cultures.* San Diego: Academic Press.
- Matsumoto, D., Yoo, S. H., & Fontaine, J. (2008). Mapping Expressive Differences Around the World: The Relationship Between Emotional Display Rules and Individualism Versus Collectivism. *Journal of Cross-Cultural Psychology*, Vol. 39, N. 1, 55-74.
- McCauley, C. (1989). The nature of social influence in groupthink: Compliance and internalization. *Journal of Personality and Social Psychology*, Vol. 57, N. 2, 250-260.
- McClelland, D. C. (1985). *Human motivation.* Glenview, IL: Scott, Foresman.
- Miyamoto, Y., Nisbett, R. E., & Masuda, T. (2006). Culture and the Physical Environment: Holistic Versus Analytic Perceptual Affordances. *Psychological Science*, Vol. 17, N. 2, 113-119.
- Moore, D. A. (2007). Not so above average after all: When people believe they are worse than average and its implications for theories of bias in social comparison. *Organizational Behavior and Human Decision Processes,* Vol. 102, N. 1, 42-58.
- Morris, M. W., & Keltner, D. (2000). How Emotions Work: The Social Functions Of Emotional Expression In Negotiations. *Research in Organizational Behaviour*, Vol. 22, 1-50.
- Morris, M. W., Leung, K., & Iyengar, S. S. (2004). Person Perception in the heat of conflict: Negative trait attributions affect procedural preferences and account for situational and cultural differences. *Asian Journal of Social Psychology*, Vol. 7, N. 2, 127-147.
- Nisbett, R. E. (2003). *The Geography of Thought.* New York, NY: The Free Press.
- Nisbett, R. E., & Norenzayan, A. (2002). *Culture and Cognition.* In H. Pashler (Ed.), *Stevens' Handbook of Experimental Psychology* (3rd ed.). Hoboken, NJ: John Wiley & Sons.
- Oettingen, G., & Zosuls, K. M. (2006). Culture and self-efficacy in adolescents. In F. Pajares, & T. Urdan (Eds.), *Self-efficacy in adolescents.* Greenwich, CT: Information Age Publishing.
- Oettingen, G., Sevincer, A. T., & Gollwitzer, P. M. (2008). Goal Pursuit in the Context of Culture. In R. Sorrentino, & S. Yamaguchi (Eds.), *Handbook of Motivation and Cognition Across Cultures.* San Diego: Academic Press.
- Pawlikova-Vilhanova, V. (1998). The African Personality or the Dilemma of the Other and Self in the Philosophy of Edward W. Blyden, 1832-1912. *Asian and African Studies*, Vol. 7, N. 2, 162-175.
- Peng, K., & Nisbett, R. E. (1999). Culture, Dialectics, And Reasoning About Contradiction. *American Psychologist*, Vol. 54, N. 9, 741-754.
- Schultheiss, O. C. (2008). Implicit motives. In O. P. John, R. W. Robins & L. A. Pervin (Eds.), *Handbook of personality: Theory and research* (3rd ed.). New York: Guilford Press.
- Sinha, J. B. P., & Kumar, R. (2004). Methodology for Understanding Indian Culture. *The Copenhagen Journal of Asian Studies*, 19, 89-104.

- Sorrentino, R. M., Szeto, A., Nezlek, J. B., Yasunaga, S., Kouhara, S., & Ohtsubo, Y. (2008). Uncertainty regulation: the master motive?. In R. Sorrentino, & S. Yamaguchi (Eds.), *Handbook of Motivation and Cognition Across Cultures*. San Diego: Academic Press.
- Soto, J. A., & Levenson, R. W. (2009). Emotion Recognition Across Cultures: The Influence of Ethnicity on Empathic Accuracy and Physiological Linkage. *American Psychological Association*, Vol. 9, N. 6, 874-884.
- Spina, R. R., Ji, L. J., Guo, T., Zhang, Z., Li, Y., & Fabrigar, L. (2010). Cultural Differences in the Representativeness Heuristic: Expecting a Correspondence in Magnitude Between Cause and Effect. *Personality and Social Psychology Bulletin*, Vol. 36, N. 5, 583-597.
- Tadmor, C. T., Galinsky, A. D., & Maddux, W. W. (2012). Getting the most out of living abroad: Biculturalism and integrative complexity as key drivers of creative and professional success. *Journal of Personality and Social Psychology*, Vol. 103, N. 3, 520-542.
- Triandis, H. C., Leung, K., Villareal, M. J., & Clack, F. I. (1985). Allocentric versus idiocentric tendencies: Convergent and discriminant validation. *Journal of Research in Personality*, Vol. 19, N. 4, 395-415.
- Uhlmann, E. L., Poehlman, A., & Bargh, J. A. (2008). Implicit Theism. In R. Sorrentino, & S. Yamaguchi (Eds.), *Handbook of Motivation and Cognition Across Cultures*. San Diego: Academic Press.
- Weber, E. U., & Hsee, C. K. (1998). Cross-cultural differences in risk perception, but cross-cultural similarities in attitude towards perceived risk. *Management Science*, 44, 1205-1217.
- Weber, E. U., & Morris, M. W. (2010). Culture and Judgment and Decision Making: The Constructivist Turn. *Perspectives on Psychological Science*, Vol. 5, N. 4, 410-419.
- Weber, E. U., Hsee, C. K., & Sokolowska, J. (1998). What folklore tells us about risk and risk taking: A cross-cultural comparison of American, German, and Chinese proverbs. *Organizational Behavior and Human Decision Processes*, 75, 170-186.
- Weiner, B. (1995). *Judgments of responsibility: A foundation for a theory of social conduct*. New York: Guilford.
- Weiner, B. (2008). An attribution theorist addresses the co-existence of theoretical generality and cultural specificity. In R. Sorrentino, & S. Yamaguchi (Eds.), *Handbook of Motivation and Cognition Across Cultures*. San Diego: Academic Press.
- Yates, J., Lee, J., & Shinotsuka, H. (1996). Beliefs about overconfidence, including its cross national variation. *Organizational Behavior and Human Decision Processes*, 65, 138-147.
- Zebian, S., & Denny, J. P. (2001). Integrative Cognitive Style in Middle Eastern and Western Groups: Multidimensional Classification and Major and Minor Property Sorting. *Journal of Cross-Cultural Psychology*, Vol. 32, N. 1, 58-75.
- Zou, X., Tam, K., Morris, M. W., Lee, S., Yee-Man Lau, I., & Chiu, C. (2009). Culture as Common Sense: Perceived Consensus Versus Personal Beliefs as

Mechanisms of Cultural Influence. *Journal of Personality and Social Psychology*, Vol. 97, N. 4, 579-597.

INTEGRATIVE THINKING – CREATIVITY

- Baron-Cohen, S. (2003). *The Essential Difference. Men, Women and the Extreme Male Brain*. London: The Penguin Press.
- Barrett, D. (1997). *The Paradox Process: Creative Business Solutions... Where You Least Expect to Find Them*. New York: Amacom.
- Birch, P., & Clegg, B. (2000). *Imagination Engineering: A Toolkit for Business Creativity*. London: Pearson Education.
- Brown, T. (2009). *Change by Design: How Design Thinking Transforms Organizations and Inspires Innovation*. New York: HarperCollins.
- Caronna, E. B., Milunsky J. M., & Tager-Flusberg, H. (2008). Autism spectrum disorders: clinical and research frontiers. *Archives of Disease in Childhood*, Vol. 93, N. 6, 518-523.
- Chua, R. Y. J. (2011). Innovating at the world's crossroads: how multicultural networks promote creativity. *HBS Working Papers 11-085*. Cambridge, MA: Harvard University Press.
- Csikszentmihalyi, M. (1996). *Creativity: Flow and the Psychology of Discovery and Invention*. New York: Harper Perennial.
- De Bono, E. (1973). *Lateral Thinking: Creativity Step by Step*. New York: Harper Colophon.
- Dyer, J., Gregersen, H., & Christensen, C. M. (2011). *The innovators's Dna, Mastering the Five Skills of Disruptive Innovators*. Boston: Harvard Business School Press.
- Fitzgerald, M. (2004). *Autism and Creativity: Is there a link between autism in men and exceptional ability?*. New York: Brunner Routledge.
- Franken, R. E. (1999). *Human Motivation* (3rd ed.). Pacific Grove, CA: Brooks/Cole.
- Gelb, M. J. (2000). *How to Think Like Leonardo da Vinci: Seven Steps to Genius Every Day*. New York: Bantham Dell.
- Kounios, J., Fleck, J. I., Green, D. L., Payne, L., Stevenson, J. L., Bowden, E. M., & Jung-Beeman, M. (2008). The origins of insight in resting-state brain activity. *Neuropsychologia*, Vol. 46, N. 1, 281-291.
- Martin, R. L. (2007). *The Opposable Mind: How Successful Leaders Win Through Integrative Thinking*. Boston: Harvard Business School Press.
- Michalko, M. (2001). *Cracking Creativity: The secrets of creative genius*. Berkeley, CA: Ten Speed Press.
- Perkins, D. (2000). *Archimedes' Bathtub: The Art and Logic of Breakthrough Thinking*. New York: W. W. Norton & Company.
- Robinson, K. (2011). *Out of our minds: learning to be creative*. Chichester, UK: Capstone Publishing.
- Rothenberg, A. (1971). The process of Janusian thinking in creativity. *Archives of General Psychiatry*, 24, 195-205.
- Snyder, A. (2004). Autistic Genius. *Nature*, Vol. 428, 470-471.

• Tadmor, C. T., Tetlock, P. E., & Peng, K. (2009). Acculturation Strategies and Integrative Complexity: The Cognitive Implications of Biculturalism. *Journal of Cross-Cultural Psychology*, 40, 105-139.

INTERNATIONAL NEGOTIATION

• Adachi, Y. (1997). Business Negotiations between the Americans and the Japanese. *Global Business Languages*, Vol. 2, 19-30.

• Adair, W. L., & Brett, J. M. (2004). Culture and Negotiation Processes. In M. J. Gelfand, & J. M. Brett (Eds.), *The Handbook of Negotiation and Culture*. Palo Alto, CA: Stanford University Press.

• Albin, C. (2001). *Justice and Fairness in International Negotiation*. Cambridge, UK: Cambridge University Press.

• Avruch, K. (2004). Culture as Context, Culture as Communication: Considerations for Humanitarian Negotiations. *Harvard Negotiation Law Review*, 9, 391-407.

• Bajoria, J., & Xu, B. (2013). *The Six Party Talks on North Korea's Nuclear Program*. New York: Council on Foreign Relations. Retrieved from http://www.cfr.org/proliferation/six-party-talks-north-koreas-nuclear-program/p13593.

• Barkai, J. (2008). Cultural Dimension Interests, the Dance of Negotiation, and Weather Forecasting: A Perspective on Cross-Cultural Negotiation and Dispute Resolution. *Pepperdine Dispute Resolution Law Journal:* Vol. 8, N. 3, Article 6. Available at: http://digitalcommons.pepperdine.edu/drlj/vol8/iss3/6.

• Barkai, J. (2008). Cultural Dimension Interests, the Dance of Negotiation, and Weather Forecasting: A Perspective on Cross-Cultural Negotiation and Dispute Resolution. *Pepperdine Dispute Resolution Law Journal*, Vol. 8, N. 3, 403-448.

• Benoliel, M. (2009). Negotiating Successfully in Asia. *Research Collection Lee Kong Chian School of Business.* Paper 1759. Available at http://ink.library.smu.edu.sg/lkcsb_research/1759.

• Benoliel, M. (2010). Master Negotiators: Intelligences and Competencies. *Research Collection Lee Kong Chian School Of Business*, Paper 3690. Available at: http://ink.library.smu.edu.sg/lkcsb_research/3690.

• Blaško, M., Netter, J. M., & Sinkey Jr., J. F. (2000). Value creation and challenges of an international transaction: The DaimlerChrysler merger. *International Review of Financial Analysis*, Vol. 9, N. 1, 77-102.

• Brett, J. M. (2001). *Negotiating Globally: How to Negotiate Deals, Resolve Disputes, and Make Decisions Across Cultural Boundaries*. San Francisco: Jossey-Bass.

• Brett, J. M., & Crotty, S. (2008). Culture and Negotiation. In P. B. Smith, M. F. Peterson, & D. C. Thomas (Eds.), *Handbook of Cross-Cultural Management Research*. Thousand Oaks, CA: Sage.

• Brewer, M. B., & Brown, R. J. (1998). Intergroup relations. In D. T. Gilbert, S. T. Fiske, & G. Lindzey (Eds.), *The Handbook of Social Psychology*. New York: Oxford University Press.

- Camuffo A., & Volpato G. (2002). Partnering in the global auto industry: the Fiat-GM strategic alliance. *International Journal of Automotive Technology and Management*, Vol. 2, N. 3, 335-352.
- Caputo, A. (2012). Integrative Agreements in Multilateral Negotiations: The Case of Fiat and Chrysler. *International Journal of Business and Social Science*, Vol. 3, N. 12, 167-180.
- Carnevale, P. J., & Choi, D-W. (2000). Culture in the Mediation of International Disputes. *International Journal of Psychology*, Vol. 35, N. 2, 105-110.
- Chang, L. C. (2003). An examination of cross-cultural negotiation: Using Hofstede framework. *Journal of American Academy of Business*, Vol. 2, N. 2, 567-570.
- Chen, D. (1999). Three-dimensional Chinese rationales in negotiation. In D. M. Kolb. (Ed.), *Negotiation Eclectics: Essays in Memory of Jeffrey Z. Rubin*. Cambridge, MA: PON Books.
- Clark, J. (2011). *Mondo Agnelli: Fiat, Chrysler, and the Power of a Dynasty*. Hoboken, NJ: John Wiley & Sons.
- Cohen, R. (1997). *Negotiating Across Cultures: International Communication in an Interdependent World*. Washington, DC: United States Institute of Peace.
- Cristal, M. (2012). The challenge of partnerism. In W. I. Zartman, M. Anstey, & P. Meerts (Eds.), *The Slippery Slope to Genocide: Reducing Identity Conflicts and Preventing Mass Murder*. Oxford, UK: Oxford University Press.
- De Dreu, C. K. W. (2004). Motivation in Negotiation: a social psychological analysis. In M. J. Gelfand, & J. M. Brett (Eds.), *The Handbook of Negotiation and Culture*. Palo Alto, CA: Stanford University Press.
- De Mente, B. L. (2004). *Japan's Cultural Code Words: 233 Key Terms That Explain Attitudes & Behavior of the Japanese*. North Clarendon, VT: Tuttle Publishing.
- Docherty, J. S. (2004). Culture And Negotiation: Symmetrical Anthropology For Negotiators. *Marquette Law Review*, Vol. 87, N. 4, 711-722.
- Dupont, C., & Faure, G. O. (2002). The Negotiation Process. In V. A. Kremenyuk (Ed.), *International Negotiation: analysis, approaches, issues* (2nd ed.). San Francisco: Jossey-Bass.
- Fang, T. (2006). The Chinese Negotiator. *Journal of Business and Industrial Marketing*, Vol. 21, N. 1, 50-60.
- Faure, G. O. (2012). *Unfinished Business: Why International Negotiations Fail*. Athens: the University of Georgia Press.
- Faure, G. O. (1998). Negotiation: The Chinese Concept. *Negotiation Journal*, 14, 137-148.
- Faure, G. O. (2000). *Negotiations to set up joint ventures in China*. International Negotiation, 5, 157-189.
- Finkelstein, S. (2002). The DaimlerChrysler Merger. *Tuck School of Business at Dartmouth*. Case Study n. 1-0071.
- Gelfand, M. J., & Cai, D. A. (2004). Cultural Structuring of the Social Context of Negotiation. In M. J. Gelfand, & J. M. Brett (Eds.), *The Handbook of Negotiation and Culture*. Palo Alto, CA: Stanford University Press.

- Gelfand, M. J., Raver, J. L., Nishii, L., Leslie, L. M., Lun, J., Lim, B. C. et al. (2011). Differences Between Tight and Loose Cultures: A 33-Nation Study. *Science*, Vol. 332, N. 6033, 1100-1104.

- Ghauri, P. N., & Usunier, J. C. (Eds.) (2003). *International Business Negotiations* (2nd ed.). London: Pergamon Press.

- Graham, J. L., & Lam, M. (2003). The Chinese Negotiation. *Harvard Business Review*, October, 82-91.

- Graham, J. L., Kim, D. K., Lin, C., & Robinson, M. (1988). Buyer-Seller Negotiations Around the Pacific Rim: Differences in fundamental Exchange Processes. *The Journal of Consumer Research*, Vol. 15, N. 1, 48-54.

- Graham, R. J. (1981). The role of perception of time in consumer research. *Journal of Consumer Research*, 7, 335-342.

- Gunia, B. C., Brett, J. M., & Nandkeolyar, A. (2014). Trust me, I'm a negotiator: Using cultural universals to negotiate effectively, globally. *Organizational Dynamics*, 43, 27-36.

- Gunia, B. C., Brett, J. M., Nandkeolyar, A., & Kamdar, D. (2011). Paying a price: Culture, trust, and negotiation consequences. *Journal of Applied Psychology*, Vol. 96, N. 4, 774-789.

- Hendon, D. W., & Ahmed, Z. U. (2002). Profile Of A Skillful International Business Negotiator. *Delhi Business Review*, Vol. 3, N. 2, 1-8.

- Ho-ying Fu, J., Morris, M. W., Lee, S., Chao, M., Chiu, C., & Hong, Y. (2007). Epistemic Motives and Cultural Conformity: Need for Closure, Culture, and Context as Determinants of Conflict Judgments. *Journal of Personality and Social Psychology*, Vol. 92, N. 2, 191-207.

- Hull, J. C. (2011). *Options, Futures and Other Derivatives* (8th ed.). Upper Saddle River, NJ: Prentice Hall.

- Janosik, R. (1991). Rethinking the Culture-Negotiation Link in Negotiation Theory and Practice. J. W. Breslin, & J. Z. Rubin (Eds.), *Negotiation Theory and practice*. Cambridge, MA: The Program on Negotiation at Harvard Law School.

- Jönsson, C. (2002). Cognitive Theory. In V. A. Kremenyuk (Ed.), *International Negotiation: analysis, approaches, issues* (2nd ed.). San Francisco: Jossey-Bass.

- Kim, H. S. (2002). We talk, therefore we think? A cultural analysis of the effect of talking on thinking. *Journal of Personality and Social Psychology*, 83, 828-842.

- Kissinger, H. A. (1994). *Diplomacy.* New York: Simon and Schuster.

- Koldau, C. (1996). Meanings of Cross-Cultural Differences in Establishing Relationships in Japanese-American Business Negotiations. *ISBM Report* 14.

- Kramer, R. M. (2004). The "Dark Side" of Social Context: the role of intergroup paranoia in intergroup negotiations. In M. J. Gelfand, & J. M. Brett (Eds.), *The Handbook of Negotiation and Culture.* Palo Alto, CA: Stanford University Press.

- Kumar, R. (2004). Brahmanical Idealism, Anarchical Individualism, and the Dynamics of Indian Negotiating Behavior. *International Journal of Cross Cultural Management*, 4, 39-58.

- Kumar, R. (2004). Culture and Emotions in Intercultural Negotiations: An Overview. In M. J. Gelfand, & J. M. Brett (Eds.), *The Handbook of Negotiation and Culture*. Palo Alto, CA: Stanford University Press.
- Kumar, R. (2005). Negotiating with complex, Imaginative Indians. *Ivey Business Journal*, March/April, 1-6.
- Lee, K., Yang, G., & Graham, J. L. (2006). Tension and trust in international business negotiations: American executives negotiating with Chinese executives. *Journal of International Business Studies*, 37, 623-641.
- Leung, K., & Tong, K. K. (2004). Justice across cultures: A three-stage model for intercultural negotiation. In M. J. Gelfand, & J. M. Brett (Eds.), *The Handbook of Negotiation and Culture*. Palo Alto, CA: Stanford University Press.
- Liu, L. A., Friedman, R. A., & Chi, S. (2005). 'Ren Qing' versus the 'Big Five': The Role of Culturally Sensitive Measures of Individual Difference in Distributive Negotiations. *Management and Organization Review*, Vol. 1, N. 2, 225-247.
- Liu, W. (2001). *International Business Negotiation*. Beijing: Higher Education Press.
- Luo, P. (2008). Analysis of Cultural Differences between West and East in International Business Negotiation. *International Journal of Business and Management*, Vol. 3, N. 11, 103-106.
- Magee, D. (2003). *Turnaround: How Carlos Ghosn Rescued Nissan*. New York: HarperCollins.
- March, R. M. (1990). *The Japanese negotiator: Subtleties and strategy beyond Western logic*. Tokyo, Japan: Kodansha International.
- Morris, M. W. (2005). *When Culture Counts - and When It Doesn't*. Harvard Business Publishing Newsletters, June, 3-5.
- Morris, M. W., & Gelfand, M. J. (2004). Cultural Differences and Cognitive Dynamics: expanding the cognitive perspective on negotiation. In M. J. Gelfand, & J. M. Brett (Eds.), *The Handbook of Negotiation and Culture*. Palo Alto, CA: Stanford University Press.
- Morris, M. W., Williams, K. Y., Leung, K, Larrick, R., Mendoza, T., Bhatnagar, D., Li, J., Kondo, M., Luo, J., & Hu, J. (1998). Conflict Management Style: Accounting for Cross-National Differences. *Journal of International Business Studies*, Vol. 29, N. 4, 729-748.
- Mortenson, G., & Relin, D. O. (2007). *Three Cups of Tea: One Man's Mission to Promote Peace One School at a Time*. London: Penguin Books.
- Narsness, Z. I., Bhappu, A. D. (2004). At the Crossroads of Culture and Technology social influence and information-sharing processes during negotiation. In M. J. Gelfand, & J. M. Brett (Eds.), *The Handbook of Negotiation and Culture*. Palo Alto, CA: Stanford University Press.
- Nueno, P., & Liu, G. (2012). How Geely won over Volvo. *CEIBS Case Center*.
- Oren, M. B. (2003). *Six Days of War: June 1967 and the Making of the Modern Middle East*. New York: Presidio Press.
- Palich, L. E., Carini, G. R., & Livingstone, L. P. (2002). Comparing American and Chinese negotiating styles: The influence of logic paradigms. *Thunderbird International Business Review*, Vol. 44, N. 6, 777-798.

- Pruitt, D. G. (2005). Escalation, readiness for negotiation, and third party functions. In I. W. Zartman, & G. O. Faure (Eds.), *Escalation and negotiation*. Cambridge, England: Cambridge University Press.
- Pruitt. D. G. (2002). Strategy in Negotiation. In V. A. Kremenyuk (Ed.), *International Negotiation: analysis, approaches, issues* (2nd ed.). San Francisco: Jossey-Bass.
- Requejo, W. H., & Graham, J. L. (2008). *Global Negotiation: The New Rules*. New York: Palgrave Macmillan.
- Reynolds, N, Simintiras, A., & Vlachou, E. (2003). International Business Negotiation: Present Knowledge and Direction for Future Research. *International Marketing Review*, Vol. 20, N. 3, 236-261.
- Roussanov, N. L., & Savor, P. G. (2013). Marriage and Manager's attitudes to risk. *AFA San Diego Meetings Paper*, December.
- Rubin, J. Z. (2002). Psychological Approach. In V. A. Kremenyuk (Ed.), *International Negotiation: analysis, approaches, issues* (2nd ed.). San Francisco: Jossey-Bass.
- Rubin, J. Z. (2002). The Actors in Negotiation. In V. A. Kremenyuk (Ed.), *International Negotiation: analysis, approaches, issues* (2nd ed.). San Francisco: Jossey-Bass.
- Rudd, J. E., & Lawsor, D. R. (2007). *Communicating in Global Business Negotiations: A Geocentric Approach*. Thousand Oaks: Sage Publications.
- Salacuse, J. W. (2003). *The Global Negotiator: Making, Managing, and Mending Deals Around the World in the Twenty-First Century*. New York: Palgrave Macmillan.
- Salacuse, J. W. (2010). Teaching International Business Negotiation: Reflections on Three Decades of Experience. *International Negotiation*, 15, 187-228.
- Sanchez-Burks, J., Neuman, E. J., Ybarra, O., Kopelman, S., Park, H., & Goh, K. (2008). Folk Wisdom About the Effects of Relationship Conflict. *Negotiation and Conflict Management Research*, Vol. 1, N. 1, 53-76.
- Sebenius, J. K. (2002). Caveats for Cross-Border Negotiators, *Negotiation Journal*, Vol. 18, N. 2, 121-133.
- Sebenius, J. K. (2002). International Negotiation Analysis. In V. A. Kremenyuk (Ed.), *International Negotiation: analysis, approaches, issues* (2nd ed.). San Francisco: Jossey-Bass.
- Sebenius, J. K. (2002). The Hidden Challenge of Cross-Border Negotiations. *Harvard Business Review*, Vol. 80, N. 3, 76-85.
- Shi, X., & Wright, P. C. (2000). Developing and validating an international business negotiator's profile: The China context. *Journal of Managerial Psychology*, Vol. 16, N. 5, 364-389.
- Shih, M. (2013). A Method to the Madness: North Korean Negotiating Strategy in the Six-Party Talks. WWS Case 3/09. New Jersey: Princeton University, Woodrow Wilson School of Public and International Affairs. In P. Kerr, & G. Wiseman (Eds.), *Diplomacy in a Globalizing World: Theories and Practices*. Oxford: Oxford University Press.

- Simintiras, A. C., & Thomas, A. H. (1998). Cross-cultural sales negotiations - A literature review and research propositions. *International Marketing Review*, Vol. 15 N. 1, 10-28.
- Stein, J. G. (1989). Prenegotiation in the Arab-Israeli conflict: The paradoxes of success and failure. In J. G. Stein (Ed.), *Getting to the table: the process of international negotiation.* Baltimore: Johns Hopkins University Press.
- Stein, K. W. (1999). *Heroic Diplomacy: Sadat, Kissinger, Carter, Begin and the Quest for Arab-Israeli Peace.* New York: Routledge.
- Tan, H. H., & Chee, D. (2005). Understanding interpersonal trust in a Confucian-influenced society. *International Journal of Cross Cultural Management.* Vol. 5, N. 2, 197-212.
- Ting-Toomey, S. (2005). The Matrix of Face: An Updated Face-Negotiation Theory. In W. B. Gudykunst (Ed.), *Theorizing About Intercultural Communication.* Thousand Oaks, CA: Sage Publications.
- Tinsley, C. H. (2001). How Negotiators get to yes: Predicting the constellation of conflict management strategies used across cultures. *Journal of Applied Psychology*, Vol. 86, N. 4, 583-593.
- Tinsley, C. H. (2004). Culture and Conflict enlarging our dispute resolution framework. In M. J. Gelfand, & J. M. Brett (Eds.), *The Handbook of Negotiation and Culture.* Palo Alto, CA: Stanford University Press.
- Torres, J. A. (2010). Understanding the Influence and Approaches to Effective Chinese Negotiations. *The Business Review*, Vol. 14, N. 2, 104-112.
- Tu, Y. T. (2012). A Comparison on Business Negotiation Styles with Education. *Information Management and Business Review*, Vol. 4, N. 6, 317-331.
- Ueda, K. (1974). Sixteen Ways to Avoid Saying No in Japan. In J. C. Condon, M. Saito, & K. K. Daikagu (Eds.), *Intercultural Encounters with Japan.* Perspectives from the International Conference on Communication Across Cultures, International Christian University, Tokyo.
- Verma, P. (2011). Inspirational Motivation. *International Journal of Modern Engineering Research*, Vol. 1, N. 6, 1-16.
- Vlasic, B. & Stertz, B. A. (2000). *Taken for a Ride: How Daimler-Benz drove off with Chrysler.* New York: HarperCollins Publishers.
- Von Senger, H. (1991). *The book of stratagems.* New York: Viking/Penguin.
- Weber, E. U., & Hsee, C. (1998). Cross-Cultural Differences in Risk Perception, but Cross-Cultural Similarities in Attitudes towards Perceived Risk. *Management Science,* Vol. 44, N. 9, 1205-1217.
- Weber, T. (2001). Gandhian Philosophy, Conflict Resolution Theory and Practical Approaches to Negotiation. *Journal of Peace Research*, Vol. 38, N. 4, 493-513.
- Weiss, S. (1999). Opening a Dialogue on Negotiation and Culture: A "Believer" Considers Skeptics' Views. In D. M. Kolb. (Ed.), *Negotiation Eclectics: Essays in Memory of Jeffrey Z. Rubin.* Cambridge, MA: PON Books.
- Weiss, S. E. (2003). Teaching The Cultural Aspects Of Negotiation: A Range Of Experiential Techniques. *Journal of Management Education*, Vol. 27, N. 1, 96-121.

- Weiss, S. E. (2011). Renault-Nissan Negotiation. In M. Benoliel (Ed.), *Negotiation and Persuasion*. Singapore: World Scientific Publishing.
- Winham, G. R. (2002). Simulation for teaching and analysis. In V. A. Kremenyuk (Ed.), *International Negotiation: analysis, approaches, issues* (2nd ed.). San Francisco: Jossey-Bass.
- Wu, L., Ray, F., & Ying-yi, H. (2009). Culture, Accountability, and Group Membership: A Dynamic Constructivist Approach to Cross-cultural Negotiation. *22nd Annual International Association of Conflict Management Conference*, Kyoto, Japan.
- Zartman, I. W. (2001). The Timing of Peace Initiatives: Hurting Stalemates and Ripe Moments. *The Global Review of Ethnopolitics*, Vol. 1, N. 1, 8-18.
- Zartman, W. I. (2002). Regional Conflict Resolution. In V. A. Kremenyuk (Ed.), *International Negotiation: analysis, approaches, issues* (2nd ed.). San Francisco: Jossey-Bass.
- Zartman, W. I. (2002). The Structure of Negotiation. In V. A. Kremenyuk (Ed.), *International Negotiation: analysis, approaches, issues* (2nd ed.). San Francisco: Jossey-Bass.
- Zhang, Z.-X. (2006). Chinese Conceptions of Justice and Reward Allocation. In U. Kim, K.-S. Yang, & K.-K. Hwang (Eds.), *Indigenous and Cultural Psychology, Understanding People in Context*. New York: Springer.
- Zhu, Y., McKenna, B., & Sun, Z. (2007). Negotiating with Chinese: success of initial meetings is the key. *Cross Cultural Management: An International Journal*, Vol. 14, N. 4, 354-364.

LEADERSHIP

- Adair, J. (2005). *How to grow leaders: the seven key principles of effective leadership management*. London: Kogan Page.
- Avolio, B. J. (2007). Promoting More Integrative Strategies for Leadership Theory-Building. *American Psychologist*, Vol. 62, N. 1, 25-33.
- Aycan, Z. (2006). Paternalism. In U. Kim, K.-S. Yang, & K.-K. Hwang (Eds.), *Indigenous and Cultural Psychology, Understanding People in Context*. New York: Springer.
- Ayman, R. (2003). Situational and contingency approaches to leadership. In J. A. Antonakis, A. T. Cianciolo, & R. J. Sternberg (Eds.), *The nature of leadership*. Thousand Oaks, CA: Sage.
- Barsh, J., & Lavoie, J. (2014). *Centered Leadership: Leading with Purpose, Clarity, and Impact*. New York: Crown Business.
- Barsh, J., Mogelof, J., & Webb, C. (2010). How centered leaders achieve extraordinary results. *The McKinsey Quarterly*, October.
- Barton, D., Grant, A., & Horn, M. (2012). Leading in the 21st Century. *The McKinsey Quarterly*, June.
- Bass, B. M., & Riggio, R. E. (2006). *Transformational Leadership* (2nd ed.). Mahwah, NJ: Lawrence Erlbaum Associates.
- Boaz, N., & Fox, E. A. (2014). Change leader, change thyself. *The McKinsey Quarterly*, March.

- Bower, M. (1997). Developing Leaders in a Business. *The McKinsey Quarterly*, N. 4, 4-17.
- Buckingham, M. (2006). *The one thing you need to know ... about great managing, great leading and sustained individual success.* London: Pocket Books.
- Chamorro-Premuzic, T. (2013). *Confidence: Overcoming Low Self-Esteem, Insecurity, and Self-Doubt.* New York: Hudson Street Press.
- Charan, R., Drotter, S., & Noel, J. (2001). *The leadership principle: how to build the leadership-powered company.* San Francisco: Jossey Bass Wiley.
- Coffee, R., & Jones, G. (2006). *Why should anyone be led by you?: what it takes to be an authentic leader.* Boston: Harvard Business School Press.
- Covey, S. R. (1992). *Principle-Centered Leadership.* London: Simon & Schuster.
- Dickson, M. W., Den Hartog, D. N., & Mitchelson, J. K. (2003). Research on leadership in a cross-cultural context: Making progress, and raising new questions. *The Leadership Quarterly*, 14, 729-768.
- Drucker, P. F. (1996). Your leadership is unique. *Christianity Today International Leadership Journal*, Vol. 17, N. 4, 54-55.
- Drucker, P. F. (2006). *The Effective Executive: the Definitive Guide to Getting the Right Things Done.* New York: Harper Business.
- Erben, G. S., & Güneşer A. B (2008). The Relationship Between Paternalistic Leadership and Organizational Commitment: Investigating the Role of Climate Regarding Ethics. *Journal of Business Ethics*, 82, 955-968.
- Ericsson, K. A., Krampe, R. T., & Tesch-Römer, C. T. (1993). The Role of Deliberate Practice in the Acquisition of Expert Performance. Psychological Review. Vol. 100, N. 3, 363-406.
- Ericsson, K. A., Prietula, M. J., & Cokely, E. T. (2007). The Making of an Expert. *Harvard Business Review*, July-August, 114-121.
- Ernst, C., & Chrobot-Mason, D. (2010). *Boundary Spanning Leadership: Six Practices for Solving Problems, Driving Innovation, and Transforming Organizations.* New York: McGraw-Hill Professional.
- Fiedler, F. E. (1967). *A Theory of Leadership Effectiveness.* New York: McGraw-Hill.
- French, J. R. P., & Raven, B. H. (1959). The bases of social power. In D. Cartwright (Ed.), *Studies in Social Power.* Ann Arbor, MI: Institute for Social Research.
- Fukuyama, F. (1995). *Trust: The Social Virtues and the Creation of Prosperity.* London: Penguin.
- Gardner, H. (1995). *Leading Minds: An Anatomy of Leadership.* New York: Basic Books.
- Gardner, J. W. (1990). *On leadership.* New York: Free Press.
- Goleman, D. (2000). Leadership that Gets Results. *Harvard Business Review*, March-April, 78-90.
- Goleman, D. (2004). What Makes a Leader?. Best of HBR on Emotionally Intelligent Leadership (2nd ed.). *Harvard Business Review*, January, 2-13.

- Goleman, D., Boyatzis, R., & McKee, A. (2001). Primal Leadership, The Hidden Driver of Great Performance. *Harvard Business Review*, December, 32-42.
- Grant, A. (2014). *Give and take: why helping others drives our success.* London: Penguin Books.
- Grint, K. (2005). *Leadership: Limits and possibilities.* Hong Kong, China: Palgrave Macmillan.
- Gupta, V., MacMillan, I. C., & Surie, G. (2004). *Entrepreneurial Leadership: Developing and Measuring a Cross-cultural Construct.* Journal of Business Venturing, Vol. 19, N. 2, 241-260.
- Hazy, J. K., Goldstein J. A., & Lichtenstein, B. B. (Eds.) (2007). *Complex Systems Leadership Theory: New Perspectives from Complexity Science on Social and Organizational Effectiveness,* A Volume in the *Exploring Organizational Complexity* Series: Volume 1. Mansfield, MA: ISCE Publishing.
- Hersey, P., & Blanchard, K. H. (1969*).* Life cycle theory of leadership. *Training and Development Journal*, Vol. 23, N. 5, 26-34.
- House, R. J., Hanges, P. J., Javidan, M., Dorfman, P. W., & Gupta, V. (Eds.) (2004). *Culture, leadership, and organizations: The GLOBE Study of 62 Societies.* Thousand Oaks, CA: Sage.
- House, R. J., Hanges, P., Javidan, M., Dorfman, P., & Gupta, V. (2002). Leadership and Cultures Around the World: Findings from GLOBE. *Journal of World Business*, Vol. 37, N. 1, 3-10.
- Hüther, G. (2008). The neurobiological preconditions for the development of curiosity and creativity. In H. von Seggern, J. Werner, & L. Grosse-Bächle (Eds.), *Creating Knowledge.* Berlin: Jovis Verlag.
- Javidan, M., Dorfman, P. W., Sully de Luque, M., & House, R. J. (2006). In the eye of the beholder: Cross Cultural lessons in leadership from project GLOBE. *Academy of Management Perspectives*, February, 67-90.
- Judge, T. A., Bono, J. E., Ilies, R., & Gerhardt, M. W. (2002). Personality and leadership: A qualitative and quantitative review. *Journal of Applied Psychology,* 87, 530-541.
- Kaplan, R. E., & Kaiser, R. B. (2006). *The versatile Leader: make the most of your strengths without overdoing it.* San Francisco: Pfeiffer.
- Kaplan, S. N., Klebanov, M. M., & Sorensen, M. (2012). Which CEO Characteristics and Abilities Matter?. *Journal of Finance*, Vol. 67, N. 3, 973-1007.
- Kashdan, T. B. (2010). *Curious?: Discover the Missing Ingredient to a Fulfilling Life.* New York: Harper Perennial.
- Kotter, J. P. (1990). *A Force For Change: How Leadership Differs From Management.* New York: Free Press.
- Kotter, J. P. (1999). *John P. Kotter on What Leaders Really Do.* Boston: Harvard Business School Press.
- Krames, J. (2005). *Jack Welch and the 4 E's of Leadership: How to Put GE's Leadership Formula to Work in Your Organization.* New York: McGraw-Hill.
- Linsky, M., & Heifetz, R. A. (2002). *Leadership on the Line: Staying Alive through the Dangers of Leading.* Boston: Harvard Business School Press.

- Loewenstein, G. (1994). The Psychology of Curiosity: A Review and Reinterpretation. *Psychological Bulletin*, Vol. 116, N. 1, 75-98.
- Neal, A., & Conway, K. (2013). *Leading from the edge*. Alexandria, VA: ASTD Press.
- Northouse, P. G. (2010). *Leadership: Theory and practice*. Thousand Oaks: Sage Publications.
- Ofman, D. (2004). *Core Qualities: a Gateway to Human Resources*. London: Cyan Communications.
- Palus, C. J., McGuire, J. B., & Ernst, C. (2012). *Developing Interdependent Leadership*. In S. Snook, N. Nohria, & R. Khurana (Eds.), *The Handbook Leadership, Knowing, Doing, and Being*. Thousand Oaks, CA: Sage Publications.
- Raven, B. H. (1965). Social influence and power. In I. D. Steiner, & M. Fishbein (Eds.), *Current studies in social psychology*. New York: Holt, Rinehart, Winston.
- Schein, E. H. (1985). *Organizational Culture and Leadership*. San Francisco, California: Jossey-Bass.
- Scouller, J. (2011). *The Three Levels of Leadership: How to Develop Your Leadership Presence, Knowhow and Skill*. Cirencester, UK: Management Books 2000.
- Simon, H. A., & Chase, W. G. (1973). Skill in chess. *American Scientist*, 61, 394-403.
- Warrell, M. (2013). *Stop Playing Safe: Rethink Risk. Unlock the Power of Courage. Achieve Outstanding Success*. Hoboken, NJ: John Wiley & Sons.

TRUST

- Arrow, K. J. (1974). *The Limits to Organizations*. New York: Norton.
- Atkinson, S., & Butcher, D. (2003). Trust in managerial relationships. *Journal of Managerial Psychology*, Vol. 18, N. 4, 282-304.
- Barney, J. B., & Hansen, M. H. (1994). Trustworthiness as a Source of Competitive Advantage. *Strategic Management Journal*, Vol. 15, Special Issue: Competitive Organizational Behavior, 175-190.
- Blomqvist K. (2008). Trust in a Knowledge-based organization. Presented at the *Conference for Organizational Knowledge, Competences and Learning*, April 30th- May 1st, Copenhagen, Denmark.
- Castelfranchi, C., & Falcone, R. (2001). Social Trust: A cognitive approach. In C. Castelfranchi, & Y.-H. Tan (Eds.), *Trust and Deception in virtual societies*. Norwell, MA: Kluwer Academic Publishers.
- Covey, S. R. (2006). *The Speed of Trust: The One Thing That Changes Everything*. New York: Free Press.
- D'Amico, L. C. (2003). Examining Determinants of Managerial Trust: Evidence from a Laboratory Experiment. Presented at *The 7th National Public Management Research Conference*, Oct. 10th, Washington, D.C.

- Engell, A. D., Haxby, J. V., & Todorov, A. (2007). Implicit Trustworthiness Decisions: Automatic Coding of Face Properties in the Human Amygdala. *Journal of Cognitive Neuroscience,* Vol. 19, N. 9, 1508-1519.
- Jarvenpaa, S. L., Leidner, D. E. (1999). Communication and Trust in Global Virtual Teams. *Organization Science,* Vol. 10, N. 6, 791-815.
- Kramer, R. M. (1999). Trust and distrust in Organizations: Emerging Perspectives, Enduring Questions. *Annual Review of Psychology,* 50, 569-598.
- Lewicki, R. J., & Bunker, B. B. (1996*).* Developing and Maintaining Trust in Work Relationships. In R. M. Kramer, & T. R. Tyler (Eds.), *Trust in Organizations, Frontiers of Theory and Research.* Thousand Oaks, CA: Sage.
- Lyman, A. (2012). *The Trust Worthy Leader: Leveraging the Power of Trust to Transform you Organization.* San Francisco: Jossey-Bass.
- Paliszkiewicz, J. O. (2011). Trust Management: Literature Review. *Management,* Vol. 6, N. 4, 315-331.
- Pirson, M., & Malhotra, D. (2007). What Matters to Whom? Managing Trust Across Multiple Stakeholder Groups. *Hauser Center Working Paper* N. 39.
- Schoorma, F. D., Mayer, R. C., & Davis, J. H. (2007). An Integrative Model Of Organizational Trust: Past, Present, And Future. *Academy of Management Review,* Vol. 32, N. 2, 344-354.
- Shockley-Zalabak, P., Ellis, K., & Winograd, G. (2000). Organizational trust: What it Means, Why it Matters. *Organizational Development Journal,* Vol. 18, N. 4, 35-48.
- Slovic, P. (1993). Perceived Risk, Trust, and Democracy. *Risk Analysis,* Vol. 13, N. 6, 675-682.
- Vuilleumier, P., & Sander, D. (2008). Trust and valence processing in the amygdala. *SCAN,* 3, 299-302.

SELF-CONTROL

- Baumeister, R. F. (2002). Yielding to Temptation: Self-Control Failure, Impulsive Purchasing, and Consumer Behavior. *The Journal of Consumer Research,* Vol. 28, N. 4, 670-676.
- Baumeister, R. F., Vohs, K. D., & Tice, D. M. (2006). The Strength Model of Self-Control. *Current Directions In Psychological Science,* Vol. 16, N. 6, 351-355.
- Casey, B. J., Somerville, L. H., Gotlib, I. H., Ayduk, O., Franklin, N., Askren, M. K., Jonides, J., Berman, M. G., Wilson, N. L., Teslovich, T., Glover, G., Zayas, V., Mischel, W., & Shoda, Y. (2011). Behavioral and neural correlates of delay of gratification 40 years later. *Proceedings of the National Academy of Sciences,* Vol. 108, N. 36, 14998-15003.
- Colcombe, S. J., Erickson, K. I., Scalf, P. E., Kim, J. S., Prakash, R., McAuley, E., Elavsky, S., Marquez, D. X., Hu, L., & Kramer, A. F. (2006). Aerobic exercise training increases brain volume in aging humans. *Journals of Gerentology,* Series A - Biological Sciences and Medical Sciences, 61, 1166-1170.
- Goleman, D. (2012). The Focused Leader. *Harvard Business Review,* December.

- Guenzi, P., & Ruta, D. (2013). *Leading Teams: Tools and Techniques for Successful Team Leadership from the Sports World.* San Francisco: Jossey-Bass.
- McConigal, K. (2011). *The Willpower Instinct: How Self-Control Works, Why it Matters and What you can Do to Get more of It.* New York: Avery Publishing.
- Mischel, W., Ayduk, O., Berman, M. G., Casey, B. J., Gotlib, I. H., Jonides, J., Kross, E., Teslovich, T., Wilson, N. L., & Shoda, Y. (2011). 'Willpower' over the life span: Decomposing self-regulation. *Social Cognitive and Affective Neuroscience*, Vol 6, N. 2, 252-256.
- Mischel, W., Ebbesen, E. B., & Zeiss, A. R. (1972). Cognitive and attentional mechanisms in delay of gratification. *Journal of Personality and Social Psychology*, Vol. 21, N. 2, 204-218.
- Mukhopadhyay, A., & Johar, G. V. (2005). Where There Is a Will, Is There a Way? Effects of Lay Theories of Self-Control on Setting and Keeping Resolutions. *Journal Of Consumer Research*, Vol. 31, N. 4, 779-786.
- Muraven, M., & Baumeister, R. (2000). Self-regulation and depletion of limited resources: Does self-control resemble a muscle?. *Psychological Bulletin*, Vol. 126, N. 2, 247-259.

PERSUASION & INFLUENCE – LATERAL LEADERSHIP

- Aristotle (1932). *The Rhetoric of Aristotle.* Translated by L. Cooper. New York: Appleton Century Crofts.
- Aristotle (2004). *Rethoric.* Translated by W. R. Roberts. Mineola, NY: Dover Publications.
- Bauer, J., & Levy, M. (2004). *How to Persuade People Who Don't Want to be Persuaded.* Hoboken, NJ: John Wiley & Sons..
- Bickman, L. (1974). The Social Power of a Uniform. *Journal of Applied Social Psychology,* Vol. 4, N. 1, 47-61.
- Binder, J. (2007). *Global Project Management: Communication, Collaboration and Management Across Borders.* Aldershot: Gower Publishing Limited.
- Carnegie, D. (1998). *How to win friends and influence people.* New York: Pocket Books.
- Cialdini, R. B. (1993). *Influence: The psychology of Persuasion.* New York: HarperCollins Publishers.
- Cohen, A. R., & Bradford, D. L. (2005). *Influence without authority* (2nd ed.). Hoboken, NJ: John Wiley & Sons.
- Conger, J. A. (1998). The Necessary Art of Persuasion. *Harvard Business Review,* May-June, 84-95.
- Darrow, C. (1996). *The Story Of My Life.* Boston: Da Capo Press.
- Diamond, S. (2010). *Getting More: how to negotiate to achieve your goals in the Real World.* New York: Crown Business.
- Duina, F., & Kurzer, P. (2004). Smoke in your eyes: The struggle over tobacco control in the European Union. *Journal of European Public Policy*, Vol. 11, N. 1, 57-77.

- Emerson, R. M. (1962). Power-Dependence Relations. *American Sociological Review*, Vol. 27, N. 1, 31-41.
- Ewington, N., & Hill, T. (2012). Push and Pull (The competencies required for working internationally). *Cultus Journal*, Training for a transcultural world.
- Fahnstock, J., & Secor, M. (2004). *A Rethoric of Argument* (3rd ed.). Boston: McGraw-Hill.
- Falk, E. B., Rameson, L., Berkman, E. T., Liao, B., Kang, Y., Inagaki, T. K., & Lieberman, M. D. (2010). The Neural Correlates of Persuasion: A Common Network across Cultures and Media. *Journal of Cognitive Neuroscience*, Vol. 22, N. 11, 2447-2459.
- Farmer, H., McKay, R., & Tsakiris, M. (2014). Trust in Me: Trustworthy Others Are Seen as More Physically Similar to the Self. *Psychological Science,* Vol. 25, N. 1, 290-292.
- Ferrazzi, K. (2005). *Never Eat Alone: And Other Secret to Success, One Relationship at a Time.* New York: Currency Doubleday.
- Fisher, R., & Sharp, A. (2004). *Lateral Leadership* (2nd ed.). London: Profile Books.
- Foroohar, R. (2014). We've All Got GM Problems. *Time Magazine*, June 23rd.
- Gardner, H. (2004). *Changing Minds.* Boston: Harvard Business School Press.
- Ghemawat, P. (2007). *Redefining Global Strategy: Crossing Borders in a World Where Differences Still Matter.* Cambridge, MA: Harvard Business Review Press.
- Ghemawat, P., & Mallick, R. (2003). The Industry-Level Structure of International Trade Networks: A Gravity Based Approach. *Harvard Business School*, working paper, February.
- Gouldner, A. W. (1960). The Norm of Reciprocity: A Preliminary Statement. *American Sociological Review*, 25, 161-178.
- Greenwald, A. G., Carnot, C. G., Beach, R., & Young, B. (1987). Increasing Voting Behavior by Asking People if They Expect to Vote. *Journal of Applied Psychology*, Vol. 72, N. 2, 315-318.
- Grenny, J., Maxfield, D., & Shimberg, A. (2008). Hoe to Have Influence. *MIT Sloan Management Review,* Vol. 50, N. 1, 47-53.
- Gulati, R. (2007). Silo Busting: How to Execute on the Promise of Customer Focus. *Harvard Business Review*, Vol. 85, N. 5, 98-108.
- Hamermesh, D. S. (2013). *Beauty pays: Why Attractive People Are More Successful.* Princeton: Princeton University Press.
- Heath, C., & Heath, D. (2008). *Made to Stick.* London: Arrow Books.
- Klaff, O. (2011). *Pitch Anything: an innovative method for presenting, persuading, and winning the deal.* New York: McGraw-Hill.
- Kuhl, S., Schnelle, T., & Tillmann, F.-J. (2005). Lateral Leadership: An Organizational Approach to Change. *Journal of Change Management*, Vol. 5, N. 2, 177-189.
- Lakhani, D. (2005). *Persuasion: the art of getting what you want.* Hoboken, NJ: John Wiley & Sons.

- Langer, E. J. (1989). Minding matters: The consequence of mindlessness-mindfulness. In L. Berkowitz (Ed.), *Advances in experimental social psychology,* Vol. 22, 137-174. San Diego: Academic Press.
- Malhotra, D., & Bazerman, M. H. (2008). Psychological Influence in Negotiation: An Introduction Long Overdue. *Journal of Management, Vol.* 34, N. 3, 509-531.
- McClelland, D. C. (1975). *Power: the Inner Experience.* New York: Irvington Publishers.
- Michael, U. (2001). *Leading Up: How to Lead Your Boss so You Both Win.* New York: Crown Business.
- Mintzberg, H. (2009). *Managing.* San Francisco: Berrett-Koehler Publishers.
- Orren, G. (2000). Gore vs. Bush: Why It's All Greek to Me. *Kennedy School Bulletin,* Autumn, 36-39.
- Peters, T. (1997). The Brand Called You. *Fast Company,* August 31st.
- Rahim, M. A. (2002). Toward A Theory Of Managing Organizational Conflict. *The International Journal of Conflict Management,* Vol. 13, N. 3, 206-235.
- Raven, B. H. (1992). A power/interaction model of interpersonal influence: French and Raven 30 years later. *Journal of Social Behavior and Personality,* 7, 217-244.
- Rosenberg, M. B. (2003). *Nonviolent Communication: A Language of Life.* Encinitas, CA: Puddledancer Press.
- Schwabel, D. (2013). *Promote Yourself: The New Rules For Career Success.* New York: St. Martin's Press.
- Shell, G. R., & Moussa, M. (2007). *The Art of Woo: Using Strategic Persuasion to sell your ideas.* New York: Penguin Group.
- Shell, R. G. (2001). Bargaining Styles and Negotiation: The Thomas-Kilmann Conflict Mode Instrument in Negotiation Training. *Negotiation Journal,* Vol. 17, N. 2, 155-174.
- Slater, R., Martin, R., Augustine, N., O'Neill, B. Goldman, P., Widnall, S., & Good, M. (2011). *A Road Forward: The Report of the Toyota North American Quality Advisory Panel.* Retrieved from http://www.changinggears.info/wp-content/uploads/2011/05/EMBARGOED_COPY_Toyota_Quality_Advisory_Panel_Report.pdf on June 7th 2014.
- Thompson, G. J. (2004). *Verbal Judo: The Gentle Art Of Persuasion.* New York: William Morrow Paperbacks.
- Trump, D. (1987). *The Art of the Deal.* New York: Random House.
- Uchil, A. (2007). *Relationship Selling: The Fine Art of Consultative Sales.* Parker, CO: Outskirts Press.
- Valukas, A. R. (2014). *Report to the Board of Directors of General Motors Company regarding Ignition Switch recalls.* Retrieved from http://www.nytimes.com/interactive/2014/06/05/business/06gm-report-doc.html?_r=0 on the 16th June 2014.
- Van Shendelen, R. (2007). *Macchiavelli in Brussels. The Art of Lobbying the EU.* (2nd ed.). Amsterdam, Netherlands: Amsterdam University Press.

- Zetter, L. (2008). *Lobbying: The Art of Political Persuasion.* Petersfield, UK: Harriman House Ltd.
- Zhu Yunxia, Z., & Hildebrandt, H. W. (2003). Greek and Chinese classical rhetoric: the root of cultural differences in business and marketing communication. *Asia Pacific Journal of Marketing and Logistics,* Vol. 15, N. 1, 89-114.

Social Network Theory

- Atkinson, R., Flint, J. (2001). Accessing hidden and hard-to-reach populations: Snowball research strategies. *University of Surrey, Department of Sociology,* Social Research Update, N. 33.
- Bernard, H. R., & Killworth, P. (1997). The Search for Social Physics. *Connections,* Vol. 20, N. 1, 16-34.
- Bourdieu, P., & Wacquant, L. J. D. (1992). *An Invitation to Reflexive Sociology.* Chicago: University of Chicago Press.
- Burt, R. S. (1992). *Structural holes: the Social Structure of Competition.* Cambridge, MA: Harvard University Press.
- Christakis, N. A., & Fowler, J. H. (2007). The Spread of Obesity in a Large Social Network over 32 Years. *The New England Journal of Medicine,* Vol. 357, N. 4, 370-379.
- Cross, R. L., Parise, S., & Weiss, L. M. (2007). *The role of networks in organizational change.* The McKinsey Quarterly, April.
- Cross, R., & Parker, A. (2004). *The Hidden Power of Social Networks, Understanding How Work Really Gets Done in Organizations.* Cambridge, MA: Harvard Business School Press.
- Cullen, K. L., Palus, C. J., & Appaneal, C. (2013). Developing Network Perspective: Understanding the Basics of Social Networks and their Role in Leadership. *Centre for Creative Leadership,* White Paper, March.
- Davenport, T. H., & Prusak L. (2000). *Working Knowledge: How Organizations Manage What they Know* (2nd ed.). Cambridge, MA: Harvard Business Review Press.
- de Sola Pool, I., & Kochen, M. (1978). Contacts and influence. *Social Networks,* Vol. 1, N. 1, 5-51.
- Duan, L., Sheeren, E., & Weiss, L. M. (2014). Tapping the power of hidden influencers. *The McKinsey Quarterly,* March.
- Dunbar, R. (1995). Neocortex size and group size in primates: a test of the hypothesis. *Journal of Human Evolution,* 28, 287-296.
- Easley, D., & Kleinberg, J. (2010). *Networks, Crowds, and Markets: Reasoning about a Highly Connected World.* Cambridge, UK: Cambridge University Press.
- Gibbs, T., Heywood, S., & Weiss, L. M. (2012). Organizing for an emerging world. *The McKinsey Quarterly,* June.
- Goyal, S., & Vega-Redondo, F. (2007). Structural holes in social networks. *Journal of Economic Theory,* 137, 460-492.
- Granovetter, M. (1995). *Getting a Job: A Study of Contacts and Careers* (2nd ed.). Chicago: University of Chicago Press.

- Herrero, L. (2008). *Viral Change* (2nd ed.). Bucks, UK: Meetingminds.
- Homans, G. C. (1958). Social Behavior as Exchange. *American Journal of Sociology*, Vol. 63, N. 6, 597-606.
- Ibarra, H., & Hunter, M. (2007). How Leaders Create and Use Networks. *Harvard Business Review*, Vol. 85, N. 1, 40-47.
- Kadushin, C. (2011). *Understanding Social Networks: An Introduction to Social Network Concepts, Theories and Findings*. Oxford, UK: Oxford University Press.
- Katz, N., Lazer, D., Arrow, H., & Contractor, N. (2004). Network Theory And Small Groups. *Small Group Research*, Vol. 35, N. 3, 307-332.
- Marin, A., & Wellman, B. (2011). *Social Network Analysis: An Introduction*, In J. Scott, & P. J. Carrington (Eds.), *The SAGE Handbook of Social Network Analysis*. London: SAGE Publications.
- Milgram, S. (1967). The Small World Problem. *Psychology Today*, Vol. 1, N. 1, 61-67.
- Rosen, E. (2009). *The Anatomy of Buzz Revisited. Real-life Lessons in Word-of-mouth Marketing*. New York: Doubleday.
- Stephenson, K. (2006). Trusted Connections. *World Business*, October, 56-59.
- Wasserman, S., & Faust, K. (1994). *Social Network Analysis: Methods and Applications*. Cambridge, UK: Cambridge University Press.
- Watts, D. (2003). *Six Degrees: The Science of a Connected Age*. New York: W. W. Norton.
- Willburn, P., & Cullen, K. L. (2013). A Leader's Network: How to Help Your Talent Invest in the Right Relationships at the Right Time. *Centre for Creative Leadership*, White Paper, October.

Printed in Great Britain
by Amazon

18687224R00271